ONE WEEK LOAN

Film Copyright in the European Union

Intellectual property issues in the film industry are often highly complex and in today's world are evolving rapidly. In the first book on this subject, Pascal Kamina unravels the complexities of film protection in the fifteen Member States of the European Union, giving special emphasis to the United Kingdom and France. As well as addressing key aspects of film copyright, Pascal Kamina also deals with the protection of film works within the European Union in the context of European harmonisation of copyright laws. He details the main features of the domestic legislations of EU Member States, and identifies the difficulties awaiting a further harmonisation of copyright and neighbouring rights in this field. This book will interest practitioners, academics and students. The developments on contracts and moral rights will be of particular interest to lawyers outside continental Europe.

PASCAL KAMINA, Dr. Jur. (France), L.L.M., Ph.D. (Cantab), is Assistant Professor at the University of Poitiers, as well as an Attorney at Law of the Paris Bar. He has published several articles on British film copyright in the *European Intellectual Property Review* and the *Entertainment Law Review*, and the contributes regularly to various law journals, both in France and abroad.

Cambridge Studies in Intellectual Property Rights

As its economic potential has rapidly expanded, intellectual property has become a subject of front-rank legal importance. *Cambridge Studies in Intellectual Property Rights* is a series of monograph studies of major current issues in intellectual property. Each volume will contain a mix of international, European, comparative and national law, making this a highly significant series for practitioners, judges and academic researchers in many countries.

Series editor
Professor William R. Cornish, University of Cambridge

Advisory editors
Professor François Dessemontet, University of Lausanne
Professor Paul Goldstein, Stanford University
The Hon. Mr Justice Robin Jacob, The High Court, England and Wales

Film Copyright in the European Union

Pascal Kamina

PUBLISHED BY THE PRESS SYNDICATE OF THE UNIVERSITY OF CAMBRIDGE
The Pitt Building, Trumpington Street, Cambridge, United Kingdom

CAMBRIDGE UNIVERSITY PRESS
The Edinburgh Building, Cambridge CB2 2RU, UK
40 West 20th Street, New York, NY 10011-4211, USA
477 Williamstown Road, Port Melbourne, VIC 3207, Australia
Ruiz de Alarcón 13, 28014 Madrid, Spain
Dock House, The Waterfront, Cape Town 8001, South Africa

http://www.cambridge.org

First published 2002

Printed in the United Kingdom at the University Press, Cambridge

Typeface Plantin 10/12 pt   *System* LATEX 2$_\varepsilon$ [TB]

A catalogue record for this book is available from the British Library

Library of Congress Cataloguing in Publication data

Kamina, Pascal.
Film copyright in the European Union / Pascal Kamina.
    p.   cm. – (Cambridge studies in intellectual property rights)
Includes bibliographical references and index.
ISBN 0 521 77053 X (hardback)
1. Copyright – Motion pictures – European Union countries.   2. Copyright –
Motion pictures – Great Britain.   3. Copyright – Motion pictures – France.
I. Title.   II. Series.
KJE2690 .K36   2002
341.7'582'094 – dc21   2001052880

ISBN 0 521 77053 X hardback

Contents

Foreword   *page* xxi
Preface   xxiii
Acknowledgments   xxv
List of abbreviations   xxvi

1   Introduction   1
    1. The audiovisual industry and film protection in the
        information age   1
    2. International tensions over film copyright   3
    3. European harmonisation of copyright   4
    4. The impact of new technologies   5
    5. The structure of this book   7

2   The history of film protection in Europe   9
    6. The birth of an industry   9

    SECTION I
    EARLY STAGES OF COPYRIGHT PROTECTION (1896–1908)

    7. Questions raised by 'photo-plays' and 'cinematograph films'   10

    PART I
    NATIONAL LEGISLATION BEFORE THE BERLIN CONFERENCE

    8. Films as series of photographs or dramatic works   11
    9. Early protection in the UK   11
    10. Early protection in France and countries influenced
        by French law   14
    11. Germany and countries influenced by German law   17
    12. Scandinavian countries   18

    PART II
    THE BERLIN CONFERENCE OF THE BERNE CONVENTION

    13. The Berne Convention   18

SECTION II

THE MODERN PERIOD: SEPARATION BETWEEN COPYRIGHT
AND AUTHORS´ RIGHTS COUNTRIES (1908–1992)

14. The separation of copyright and authors' rights approaches   21

PART I

THE EVOLUTION OF FILM PROTECTION
IN COPYRIGHT SYSTEMS

15. Film protection under the UK 1911 Act: indirect protection as
     a series of photographs and as dramatic work   22
16. Articulation of the two protections   23
17. The subject-matter of protection under the heading of dramatic
     work: the distinction between script and final audiovisual work   24
18. The difficult question of film authorship under the 1911 Act   26
19. The influence of new technologies   29
20. Infringement of films under the 1911 Act   31
21. Influence of the 1911 Act   31
22. The 1956 Act: a specific subject-matter for film protection   32
23. Infringement of films under the 1956 Act   35
24. The 1988 Act: continuation or departure from the 1956 Act?   35
25. A protection of audiovisual works as dramatic works under
     the 1988 Act   36
26. The situation in Ireland   37

PART II

THE EVOLUTION OF FILM IN AUTHORS´ RIGHTS SYSTEMS

27. Overview   38
28. The evolution of film protection in France   39
29. The French Law of 11 March 1957   42
30. The French Act of 3 July 1985 and the new Intellectual
     Property Code   44
31. Legislation influenced by French law   45
32. The specifics of Italian copyright   45
33. The Italian Act of 22 April 1941   46
34. The evolution of German film copyright   47
35. The German Act of 9 September 1965   49
36. Austria   49
37. The Netherlands   50
38. Scandinavian countries   51
39. Other European countries   52

SECTION III

TOWARDS EUROPEAN HARMONISATION (1992 TO
THE PRESENT)

40. The European harmonisation of copyright   53
41. The Rental Directive of 19 November 1992   54

Contents   ix

42. The Satellite and Cable Directive of 27 September 1993   55
43. The Term Directive of 29 October 1993   55
44. The Directive on Copyright and Related Rights in the
       Information Society of 22 May 2001   55
45. National implementations of the EC copyright directives   56
46. Further harmonisation   57

3 Subsistence of copyright   59
47. Introduction   59

SECTION I
THE SUBJECT-MATTER FOR PROTECTION

48. The determination of the subject-matter for film protection   60
49. Definition of the subject-matter for protection at the
       international and regional levels   61
50. The requirement of a double protection under the EC
       copyright directives   63
51. Structure   65

PART I
THE AUDIOVISUAL OR CINEMATOGRAPHIC WORK

52. Direct versus indirect protection   65

THE SITUATION IN THE UNITED KINGDOM AND IRELAND

53. The law in the UK: a protection through the audiovisual
       recording (the 'film')   66
54. An additional protection as dramatic work   67
55. Films as dramatic works: the question before *Norowzian*   67
56. The *Norowzian* case   69
57. What films are protected as dramatic works?   71
58. The requirement of fixation   74
59. The situation in Ireland   74

THE AUDIOVISUAL WORK IN AUTHORS' RIGHTS COUNTRIES

60. The main subject-matter for film protection   75
61. National definitions   75
62. The originality criterion   77
63. The absence of a requirement of fixation   78

AUDIOVISUAL WORKS AND BORDERLINE WORKS

64. Introduction   79
65. Multimedia works and videogames   79
66. Altered or remastered films   80
67. The protection of television formats   81
68. Copyright protection of formats   81
69. Misappropriation of formats and unfair competition   83

PART II

THE AUDIOVISUAL RECORDING

70.	Presentation	84
71.	The problem raised by the double protection of audiovisual works	85
72.	The neighbouring right of film producers in the EC copyright directives	87
73.	The videogram in domestic laws	88

THE 'FILM' UNDER UK COPYRIGHT

74.	The definition of the 'film' under the 1988 Act	88
75.	Range of works covered by the definition	89
76.	Multimedia works	92
77.	The protection of film frames	92
78.	The difficult question of film soundtracks	94
79.	The absence of the originality criterion	96
80.	Originality and the question of derivative films	97
81.	The 'film' under the Irish Copyright and Related Rights Act 2000	99

THE VIDEOGRAM IN AUTHORS' RIGHTS COUNTRIES

82.	Introduction	100
83.	National definitions of the right of the film producer	100

PART III

THE PROTECTION OF CONTRIBUTORY WORKS

84.	Main underlying works in film production	102
85.	Characters	103
86.	Titles	105

PART IV

BROADCASTS AND CABLE PROGRAMMES

87.	Introduction	107
88.	The Rome Convention of 1961	107
89.	The TRIPS Agreement	108
90.	The Brussels Convention of 1974	109
91.	Council of Europe	109
92.	Protection of broadcasts and cable programmes in the EC copyright directives	110
93.	Protection at the national level	112
94.	Protection in the UK	112
95.	New technologies and services	114
96.	The protection in Ireland	116
97.	Protection in authors' rights countries	117

PART V
PROTECTION AS A DATABASE?

98. The EC Directive of 11 March 1996 and films   118

SECTION II
THE TERM OF COPYRIGHT PROTECTION

 99. The extended duration for audiovisual works   120
100. Implementation in the UK   122
101. Other national implementations   124
102. The problem of war extensions   124
103. Revived and extended rights   125
104. Ownership of revived copyright   125
105. Use during the time the work was in the public domain 126
106. Ownership and exercise of extended rights   128

4   Authorship and initial ownership   130
107. Authorship, ownership and authorial rights   130
108. Authorship of films in the Berne Convention   131
109. The dichotomy between copyright and authors' rights systems 132
110. Determination of film co-authors   134
111. The EC copyright directives   135
112. Domestic laws   137

SECTION I
AUTHORSHIP OF AUDIOVISUAL WORKS IN THE
UNITED KINGDOM AND IRELAND

113. The specifics of UK copyright   137

PART I
THE AUTHOR OF THE `FILM´

114. Entrepreneurial authorship of films under the UK 1956 Act 138
115. The author of a film made before 1 July 1994   138
116. The definition of the film producer   139
117. Who is author in the absence of a producer?   140
118. The author of the film made on or after 1 July 1994   140
119. The author of the film in Ireland   141

PART II
THE AUTHOR OF THE AUDIOVISUAL DRAMATIC WORK

120. Cases of creative authorship of films under UK copyright law 141
121. Authorship and initial ownership: the relevance of
      authorship entitlement   142
122. The determination of authorship and ownership under the
      relevant copyright rules   143

123. Evaluation of potential claims to co-authorship in
       audiovisual works   144
124. The producer as creative author?   144
125. The director as author   146
126. Screenwriters as joint authors   146
127. The musical composer   148
128. The editor   149
129. The director of photography   149
130. The art director and related contributors   150
131. The main performers   151
132. Technicians   152
133. Conclusion: the co-authors of dramatic audiovisual works
       under joint authorship rules   152
134. The regime of joint works under UK copyright law   153

SECTION II
AUTHORSHIP OF AUDIOVISUAL WORKS IN AUTHORS'
RIGHTS COUNTRIES

135. Historical development: the difficult road to
       creative authorship   153
136. The rise of the film director   155
137. Countries without a statutory list of co-authors   156
138. Countries with a statutory list of co-authors   158
139. The case of Luxembourg: the film producer as 'author'   160

SECTION II
INITIAL OWNERSHIP

140. Introduction   161

PART I
OWNERSHIP OF RIGHTS IN AUDIOVISUAL WORKS

141. International agreements and EC directives   162
142. The law in the UK and Ireland   164
143. The law in authors' rights countries   165

PART II
OWNERSHIP OF UNDERLYING RIGHTS

144. Should the film producers be the initial owners of
       underlying rights?   166
145. International agreements and EC directives   168
146. The law in the UK and Ireland   170
147. The law in authors' rights countries   170

5   Copyright transfers and authorial rights   173
148. Introduction   173

SECTION I
COPYRIGHT TRANSFERS

149. Scope of the study   174
150. A limited European harmonisation   175
151. The existence of specific regimes for copyright and film
        production agreements   175
152. The transmissibility of copyright: assignments and licences   176
153. Transferability of copyright interest to a third party   178
154. Divisibility of copyright   179
155. Limitation in time   179
156. Writing requirements   180
157. Registration/priority of transfers   181
158. Statutory presumptions of grant/deemed assignments   182
159. Statutory presumptions of grant in the UK and Ireland   182
160. The presumption in France and Belgium   183
161. The presumption in other authors' rights countries   185
162. Construction of grants   187
163. Agreements relating to future works   189
164. Uses not contemplated at the time of the agreement   190
165. Duty to produce/distribute the film   191
166. Other obligations of the film producer   192
167. Termination of licence/reversionary rights   193
168. Applicable law   193

SECTION II
AUTHORIAL RIGHTS (EQUITABLE REMUNERATION)

169. The question of 'authorial rights'   195
170. Equitable remuneration at the international and regional levels   195
171. Equitable remuneration in domestic laws   197
172. Equitable remuneration in the UK and Ireland   199
173. The law and practice in France   200
174. Authorial rights in other authors' rights countries   204
175. Collective licensing of film rights in Europe   206

6 Exclusive rights   208
176. Introduction   208
177. The definition of exclusive rights under national laws   209
178. Structure   212

SECTION I
THE REPRODUCTION RIGHT

179. The reproduction right at the international level   212
180. The reproduction right at the Community level   214
181. Reproduction of film works in the UK and Ireland   215
182. The right of reproduction in authors' rights countries   216

SECTION II
THE ADAPTATION RIGHT

183. The adaptation right at international and Community levels   217
184. Adaptation of 'films' in the UK and in Ireland   219
185. Adaptation of audiovisual dramatic works in the UK
     and Ireland   220
186. Adaptation of film works in authors' rights countries   223

SECTION III
THE RIGHT OF COMMUNICATION TO THE PUBLIC

187. Introduction   226
188. Provisions of international agreements   227
189. The right of communication to the public at the European level   229
190. The right of communication to the public in the UK   233
191. Dissemination over telecommunications networks   234
192. The right of communication to the public in Ireland   237
193. The right of communication to the public in authors' rights Acts   238

SECTION IV
THE DISTRIBUTION RIGHT

194. International protection   240
195. European harmonisation   241
196. The distribution of film works in the UK and Ireland   243
197. The distribution of film works in authors' rights countries   245
198. Public lending of films   247

SECTION V
PROTECTION OF TECHNOLOGICAL MEASURES AND
RIGHTS-MANAGEMENT INFORMATION

199. Introduction   248
200. Protection of technological measures and rights-management
     information in the international agreements   248
201. European harmonisation   249
202. Technological measures   249
203. Rights-management information   251
204. The Conditional Access Directive of 1998   251

SECTION VI
THE LIABILITY OF INTERMEDIARIES

205. Introduction   252
206. The WIPO Copyright Treaty of 1996   253
207. The EC Directive on Electronic Commerce of 8 June 2000   253

7 Exemptions and permitted acts   256
208. Introduction   256

209. Copyright exemptions and limitations at the international level   256
210. European harmonisation before the Directive on Copyright and
     Related Rights in the Information Society   258
211. The Directive on Copyright and Related Rights in the
     Information Society of 22 May 2001   259
212. External limitations on copyright   263
213. Exhaustion of rights   263
214. Competition law   264
215. Free speech   266
216. Other doctrines   268
217. Structure   269

SECTION I
THE MAIN EXEMPTIONS APPLICABLE TO FILM WORKS

218. Introduction   269
219. Private copy   270
220. Performance in restricted circles   272
221. Information purpose, criticism, review and news reporting   275
222. Parodies   276
223. Incidental inclusion of copyright material   278
224. Educational use   279
225. Libraries and archives   279

SECTION II
COMPENSATION FOR PRIVATE COPYING

226. General view   280
227. Example of national laws   281
228. The treatment of foreign authors   282

8 Moral rights in films   284
229. Introduction   284
230. Understanding the moral right doctrine   284
231. International and EC law aspects   286
232. Compatibility with copyright doctrine   288
233. Basic problems of moral rights protection in relation to films   291
234. Structure   292

SECTION I
MORAL RIGHTS AND FILMS IN THE UNITED KINGDOM
AND IRELAND

235. Introduction   293

PART I
ENTITLEMENT TO MORAL RIGHTS IN FILMS

236. The situation in the UK   293
237. The film director   294

238. The co-directors   294
239. Absence of moral rights for the film producer   295
240. Authors of underlying literary, dramatic, musical and
     artistic works   295
241. Absence of moral rights in broadcasts and cable programmes   296
242. Entitlement to moral rights in films in Ireland   296
243. Foreign authors   296

PART II
SCOPE AND REGIME OF MORAL RIGHTS

244. The piecemeal approach to moral rights   296

THE 'RIGHT OF INTEGRITY' IN FILM WORKS

245. The right of integrity in the UK: definition   297
246. The objectionable treatments   297
247. The test of derogatory treatment   298
248. Exceptions and qualifications: certain works and reporting
     of current events   299
249. Exceptions and qualifications: employees' works/films   300
250. Application to treatments of films   300
251. Artistic and creative requirements   300
252. Censorship   301
253. Change in the story, action or characterisation   301
254. Changes to the soundtrack   302
255. Colourisation   303
256. Destruction of the work   303
257. Dubbing   303
258. Inappropriate or derogatory context   304
259. Insertion of advertisements, the broadcaster's logo or other
     information into the film   304
260. Modification of duration   305
261. Non-production, non-release or under-exploitation of the film   305
262. Panning and scanning   305
263. Parody   306
264. Product placements   306
265. The right of integrity in Ireland   306

THE RIGHT AGAINST FALSE ATTRIBUTION

266. The right against false attribution in the UK   307
267. The right against false attribution as a ground to object to
     mutilations of film works?   307
268. The right against false attribution in Ireland   308

THE RIGHT TO BE IDENTIFIED AS AUTHOR OR DIRECTOR

269. The right to be identified as author or director in the UK:
     definition and entitlement   308
270. Form taken by the identification   309

271. Exceptions and qualifications: employees' works, fair dealing,
     specific works, etc   310
272. The requirement that the right be asserted   311
273. The right to be identified as author in Ireland   311

GENERAL AND TRANSITIONAL PROVISIONS

274. Consent and waiver of moral rights   311
275. Form of the waiver/consent   312
276. Inequality of bargaining power and the invalidation of waivers   313
277. Duration of moral rights   313
278. Remedies and offences for infringement of moral rights   313
279. Transitional provisions: moral rights in old films   314
280. The preservation of other causes of action   316

SECTION II
MORAL RIGHTS AND FILMS IN CONTINENTAL EUROPE

281. Introduction   316

PART I
ENTITLEMENT TO MORAL RIGHT IN FILMS

282. General rules   317
283. Film authors: moral rights and multi-authorship   318
284. Authors of underlying works   319
285. Conflict of moral rights between authors   319
286. Moral rights for film producers   320
287. Foreign authors   321

PART II
THE SCOPE AND REGIME OF MORAL RIGHTS IN FILMS

288. Introduction: wide statutory principles and limited exceptions   321

THE RIGHT OF INTEGRITY

289. Definitions   321
290. Statutory adaptations to film productions   322
291. Absence of further exemptions similar to copyright exemptions   324
292. General limitations   324
293. Case law on the right of integrity   325
294. Colourisation   325
295. Directions and artistic control   325
296. Editing and modifications of the film   326
297. Advertising breaks   327
298. Derogatory association   327
299. Display of a broadcaster's logo during a telecast   327
300. Parody   328
301. Use of musical works   328
302. Excerpts   329

303. Non-exploitation of the work   329
304. Re-exploitation of the film   330

THE RIGHT OF PATERNITY

305. The right of paternity   330
306. Limitations on the right of paternity   331
307. Case law on the right of paternity   331

OTHER MORAL RIGHTS

308. The rights of divulgation and of reconsideration   332
309. Case law on the right of divulgation   334
310. Other prerogatives   334

COMMON QUESTIONS

311. Waivers and consents   335
312. Transfer and exercise of moral rights   336
313. The duration of moral rights in films   336
314. Remedies and offences for infringement of moral rights   337
315. Preservation of other causes of action   337

9   Performers' rights   338
316. Introduction   338
317. The situation in the European Union before harmonisation   338
318. European harmonisation   340
319. The Rental Directive and the extension of the related right
      of performers   341
320. The special regime of film production contracts and the right
      of equitable remuneration   342
321. The Satellite and Cable Directive   342
322. The Term Directive   343
323. The Directive on Copyright and Related Rights in the
      Information Society   343
324. Other international instruments   344
325. The Rome Convention of 1961   344
326. The TRIPS Agreement of 1994   345
327. The WIPO Performances and Phonograms Treaty of 1996   345
328. A new instrument on audiovisual performances?   347
329. Implementation of the EC directives   347
330. Structure   348

SECTION I
PERFORMERS' ECONOMIC RIGHTS

331. Introduction   348
332. The protected performances   349
333. Exclusive rights   351
334. Limitations and exemptions   354
335. Duration   355

336. Ownership and transfers of exclusive rights   355
337. Recording rights and other forms of protection   359

SECTION II
PERFORMERS' MORAL RIGHTS

338. Introduction   360
339. Performers' moral rights in Ireland   361
340. Performers' moral rights in continental Europe   362
341. Conflicts between moral rights of performers and moral rights
      of authors   363

10   Protection of foreign film works   365

342. Introduction   365
343. Multilateral conventions in the field of copyright   366
344. National treatment under the Berne Convention and
      TRIPS Agreement   367
345. Difficulties in relation to film works   369
346. The law applicable to the definition of 'author'   369
347. The law applicable to the definition of the owner of copyright   371
348. The definition of 'publication' under the Berne Convention 373
349. General rules applicable to related rights (national treatment)   374
350. National treatment under the EC Treaty   376
351. Most-favoured-nation treatment under the TRIPS Agreement   376
352. The protection of foreign film works in domestic laws   377
353. The protection of foreign film works in the UK   377
354. The law in droit d'auteur countries   378
355. The rule of shorter term   384

Appendices

Appendix 1   A basic guide to the European Union   386
Appendix 2   Principal national copyright legislation   391
Appendix 3   EC copyright directives   393
Appendix 4   Status of the adherence of EU Member States to
             international copyright conventions   394
Appendix 5   US copyright relations with EU Member States   400

Index   403

Foreword

In the realm of copyright, films and other audiovisual productions have become the archetypal complex work. The range of creative participants in the production of a film is often extensive, the risk to investors is considerable. Yet the prospects for the lucky few who succeed in scoring a hit with viewers are celestial: a powerful flow of revenues from the film itself, at the box-office and on television, a parallel stream from the sale of merchandise, and ultimately the chance of making sequels and other follow-ons. The legal organisation behind these exploitations turns at root on copyright protection and in economic detail upon contractual relationships. In future, technological controls over the exploitation of digital material will become increasingly crucial. The governing law has developed in different countries in response to pressures from national film-makers and also from powerful outsiders, led by the Leviathan that is Hollywood. On the film scene in Europe, Americanophobia is never far from the surface – as the negotiators of the GATT–WTO accord discovered as it was ripening for signature in 1994.

Beside these festering jealousies, there are differences of basic attitude: is film a grubby little form of mass entertainment, a tinsel make-believe which ordinary people need and will pay for in large numbers? Or is it the great new art of the twentieth century, through which directors illuminate our human condition in comparable degree with the greatest masters of language and music and the plastic arts? In the European Union, these differences of perception left their stamp upon national copyright legislation. As a result, the European Commission determined that there were major distortions across the Single Market. Since 1992, it has set about eliminating them by directive.

Dr Kamina's book analyses the process of 'approximation' that the intervention of EC legislation has induced in the national systems. A Frenchman, whose formation as an intellectual property lawyer has been divided between Poitiers and Cambridge, and who now practises and teaches in his own country, he is well equipped for the task. There will be many who seek his careful guidance through the legal quagmire that is the European law (or laws) of film copyright.

WILLIAM R. CORNISH
Series editor

Preface

This book deals with the protection of film works within the European Union. It is designed to help students, academics and practitioners discover and understand the richness and complexity of the matter, in the context of the European harmonisation of copyright laws. It attempts to describe in detail the main features of the domestic legislation of EU Member States, and to identify the difficulties awaiting a further harmonisation of copyright and neighbouring rights in this field.

Of course, the result falls short of my initial, ideal objectives. This book is not a reference book on film copyright. Rather, it aims to give students and academics alike an introduction to the subject, leading to further research. The book also aims to be of some help to professionals in the film industry.

It was impossible for me to give an account of the legislation of the fifteen EU Member States with the same level of detail. As a result, I have focused primarily on the laws of the United Kingdom and France. There is no need to justify the choice of UK copyright law, given the importance of the UK film industry in Europe and the role played by the Copyright Acts of 1956 and 1988 as legislative models in several copyright countries. Continental and American readers may be surprised to see how different UK solutions are from those of the US. The choice of the French system may also be justified for similar reasons. However, I should stress that, in several respects, French *droit d'auteur* is very different from other continental authors' rights laws. This is especially true not only as regards the laws of countries of the Germanic tradition, but also as regards Italian, Dutch and Scandinavian laws. I hope this book will help in understanding these differences. A Frenchman who speaks on behalf of authors' rights countries in general is not entirely to be trusted.

Although I have tried to balance the developments of UK copyright, on the one hand, and those of *droit d'auteur*, on the other hand, several parts of this book are much more detailed when it comes to UK law. This is mainly due to the casuistic approach adopted in the UK copyright Acts (the CDPA 1988 is more than 300 sections long, while the corresponding authors' rights Acts usually contain around 100 articles, drafted in a much more general and synthetic way), and to the complexity of certain choices made by UK law in this field (see, for example, the developments concerning the subject-matter for protection, moral rights and performer's rights).

Finally, the reader should be aware that several interesting questions, which are not specific to films, are left out of this study (for example, the question of the enforcement of rights).

Acknowledgments

I would like to thank the law firm Bersay & Associés in Paris, for its support, Joel Villasenor, for reading part of my manuscript, and Finola O'Sullivan and Jennie Rubio of Cambridge University Press, for their help.

I am also greatly indebted to Bill Cornish, for his support over the years. I would also like to thank the fellows of Trinity Hall and Trinity College, Cambridge, and the trustees of the Knox Scholarship, Trinity College. This book is dedicated to Sir John and Danielle Lyons, to John Collier of Trinity Hall, and to my parents, Pierre and Annie Kamina.

Finally, I would like to thank my wife, Marie-Aurore, for her continued support and encouragement in writing.

I apologise in advance for any possible errors of omission and commission in respect of certain domestic legislation. Needless to say, any errors that remain are entirely my own. I welcome any comments and suggestions for improvements, perhaps to appear in a future edition. The law is stated as of 1 January 2001.

Abbreviations

AC	*Appeal Cases*
AIR	*All India Reports*
ALAI	Association Littéraire et Artistique Internationale
All ER	*All England Law Reports*
BGH	Bundesgerichtshof (Federal Court of Justice)
CA	Court of Appeal
CDPA	Copyright, Designs and Patents Act 1988
CPR	*Canadian Patent Reporter*
DLR	*Dominion Law Reports*
EIPR	*European Intellectual Property Review*
EMLR	*Entertainment and Media Law Reports*
FSR	*Fleet Street Reports*
FTLR	*Financial Times Law Reports*
GRUR	*Gewerblicher Rechtsschutz und Urheberrecht*
GRUR Int.	*Gewerblicher Rechtsschutz und Urheberrecht, Internationaler Teil*
HL	House of Lords
IIC	*International Review of Industrial Property and Copyright Law*
KB	King's Bench
MCC	*MacGillivray Copyright Cases*
NZLR	*New Zealand Law Reports*
p.m.a.	*post mortem auctoris*
QB	Queen's Bench
QBD	Queen's Bench Division
RGZ	*Entscheidungen des Reichsgerichtes in Zivilsachen*
RIDA	*Revue Internationale du Droit d'Auteur*
RPC	*Reports of Patent, Design and Trade Mark Cases*
SABAM	Société des Auteurs Belges-Belgische Auteurs Maatschappij
SACD	Société des Auteurs et Compositeurs Dramatiques
SACEM	Société des Auteurs Compositeurs Editeurs de Musique

SCAM	Société Civile des Auteurs Multimédia
SDRM	Société pour l'Administration du Droit de Reproduction Mécanique des Auteurs, Compositeurs et Editeurs
SGAE	Sociedad General de Autores y Editores
SI	statutory instrument (UK)
SLT	*Scots Law Times*
TLR	*Times Law Reports*
TRIPs	Trade-Related Aspects of Intellectual Property Rights
UCC	Uniform Commercial Code
USC	United States Code
USPA	Union Syndicale de la Production Audiovisuelle
WIPO	World Intellectual Property Organization
WLR	*Weekly Law Reports*
WTO	World Trade Organization
ZUM	*Zeitschrift für Urheber- und Medienrecht*

1 Introduction

1) The audiovisual industry and film protection in the information age

It would be no exaggeration to say that the prospects of the audiovisual sector in Europe have never been so good. The European market for audiovisual works has expanded greatly over the past decade and will continue to do so in the near future.[1] Due to deregulation in national audiovisual industries, the growth of cable and satellite television has been spectacular.[2] The video market, both rental and sell-through, has become very significant.[3] Once threatened by these developments, the traditional cinema business is reshaping itself, and new multiplex cinemas are flourishing in the UK and throughout continental Europe.[4] The European film industry has produced its largest number of films in twenty years, and investment in this sector is increasing.[5] Moreover, the convergence

---

[1] According to a study carried out for the European Commission, the European audiovisual market is the fastest growing in the world (Nordcontel Ltd, 'Economic Implications of New Communication Technologies on the Audio Visual Markets', Final Report, 15 April 1997). The report estimates that the industry's overall revenue is likely to grow by 69 per cent over the period 1995–2000. See also 'Audiovisual Services', Background Note by the Secretariat of the WTO, 15 June 1998, S/C/W/40.

[2] There were 188,000 subscribers to cable services in the UK in 1986, 535,000 in 1991, 908,000 in 1994 and 2.7 million in 1998 (source: BFI/Screen Digest). The number of households equipped with a satellite dish rose from nil in 1986 to 2,040,000 in 1991; there were 4,100,000 satellite TV subscribers in 1998 (source: BFI).

[3] In the UK, the combined value of retail sales and rental of videotapes exceeds £1.3 billion per year (£940 million for retail transactions and £437 for rental transactions in 1998). In France, this value reached FFr3.7 billion in 1998.

[4] In the UK, the number of multiplex cinemas (five screens or more) rose from 29 in 1989 (285 screens) to 63 in 1992 (556 screens). The total number of screens was 1,550 in 1989, 1,848 in 1992 and 2,564 in 1998 (source: Screen Digest/CAA/BFI, *BFI Film and Television Handbook*, 2000). There were 4,762 active screens in France in 1998 (source: National Centre of Cinematography). Cinema admissions continue to grow: 702.4 million cinema tickets were sold in European cinemas in 1996, an 18 per cent increase compared to 1990 (see 'European Audiovisual Policy in the Digital Age', Report of the High Level Group on Audiovisual Policy, 26 October 1998).

[5] In the UK, 116 films were produced in 1997 for a total production cost of £562.8 million, compared with 67 films and £224 million in 1993 and 47 films and £185 million in 1992

1

of new technologies has opened new markets at the crossroads of the audiovisual and software industries for multimedia works and computer games, which will account for an ever-growing share of the entertainment industry. Finally, the development of high-speed, high-capacity, digital telecommunications networks will allow the expansion of new modes of distribution for audiovisual works, such as video-on-demand or on-line delivery of films, which will probably meet with success in the coming years. Although the US industry is dominant in most of these markets and is likely to remain so,[6] these developments create new prospects for the European audiovisual industries.

In this context, copyright protection has become a key question. The legal activity in this domain has been, and still is, exceptional. At the national level, most developed nations introduced changes in their copyright laws in order to protect more specifically new audiovisual actors and operators.[7] On a regional level, the European Union produced many reports which ended in several directives in that field.[8] On an international level, the need for a swift and efficient harmonisation of the level of protection for audiovisual works was one of the factors which caused the move from the WIPO in favour of a treatment of copyright through the GATT;[9] such protection at the international level was further reinforced by the WIPO Treaties of 1996, and a new instrument on the protection of audiovisual performance was discussed in December 2000.[10]

(see *BFI Film and Television Handbook*, 2000, p. 19); 183 films were produced in France in 1998 (against 136 in 1989), 119 in Germany and 92 in Italy. A total of 688 films were produced in Europe in 1998, for a total investment of US$2.523 billion (*BFI Film and Television Handbook*, 2000, p. 23).

[6] J. Wasko, *Hollywood in the Information Age*, Polity Press, 1994, pp. 219 *et seq.*; see also D. H. Horowitz and P. Davey, 'Financing American Films at Home and Abroad', paper prepared for the Paris Convention of the ALAI on the Centenary of Film, September 1995, especially p. 15. The US film and television industry is largely dominant in terms of works produced, but US companies also have the largest portfolios of intellectual property rights in information technologies.

[7] Mainly performers, broadcasters and cable operators.

[8] See, in particular, Council Directive 92/100/EEC of 19 November 1992 on rental right and lending right and on certain rights related to copyright in the field of intellectual property (hereinafter the 'Rental Directive'); Council Directive 93/83/EEC of 27 September 1993 on the coordination of certain rules concerning copyright and rights related to copyright applicable to satellite broadcasting and cable retransmission (hereinafter the 'Satellite and Cable Directive'); Council Directive 93/98/EC of 29 October 1993 harmonising the term of protection of copyright and certain related rights (hereinafter the 'Term Directive'); European Parliament and Council Directive 2001/29/EC of 22 May 2001 on the harmonisation of certain aspects of copyright and related rights in the information society (hereinafter the 'Directive on Copyright and Related Rights in the Information Society'); see paras. 40 *et seq.*

[9] See V. Porter, *Beyond the Berne Convention*, John Libbey, 1991, pp. 79–85.

[10] This Treaty, however, could not be concluded. See para. 328.

2.   International tensions over film copyright

However, more than eighty years after films[11] became protected under the Berne Convention, important differences continue to exist among signatory States on fundamental questions covering the whole spectrum of copyright protection. This divergence is unique in copyright law and generates important international tensions. These tensions, reinforced and nurtured by the suspicion that some of these differences are used as 'non-tariff trade barriers'[12] or unduly benefit national productions, came to a head during the negotiations of the Uruguay Round leading to the adoption of the TRIPs Agreement.

The first difference, at the very heart of copyright protection, concerns the *subject-matter of protection* for audiovisual works. Some countries, notably the US, protect audiovisual works as original works of expression, distinct from their recordings or other manifestations. In contrast, under present UK copyright law, the protected subject-matter is the visual recording,[13] irrespective of any condition of originality; in addition, broadcasts and cable programmes are protected as specific classes of copyright works. In some countries of the authors' rights tradition, both the audiovisual work and its recording are protected, but under two separate intellectual property rights, a *droit d'auteur* (copyright) on the one hand, and a *neighbouring right* on the other; in addition, specific neighbouring rights sometimes protect broadcasts and cable programmes. As a result of various qualification provisions, or of the characterisation of the right as copyright or neighbouring right, foreign producers or broadcasters can be excluded from protection under a given heading or from the flow of fees collected on a given national territory.[14]

Closely associated with this problem is the question of the determination of the rights granted to audiovisual actors and operators. In this regard, the scope of copyright protection can vary a great deal among copyright laws, thus creating uncertainties or tensions between users and producers, both in domestic markets and abroad. Differences exist on questions such as the definition of exclusive rights, private copy and

---

[11] Below, unless otherwise stated, the term 'film' will be used as a synonym for 'audiovisual work'. Although both elements are sometimes referred to using the same expression, one should be careful to avoid confusions between the work (the audiovisual work) and its embodiment (the recording, the negative, the film strip).

[12] In the same way as quotas and taxes on foreign productions.

[13] The 'film' under s. 5 of the CDPA 1988.

[14] Consider, for example, the difficulties for US film producers in obtaining a share of the fees collected in Europe in relation to the neighbouring right of 'videogram producers' (e.g. in relation to private copy). See para. 228.

copyright exemptions or the duration of protection. The financial interests at stake are enormous, and, although European harmonisation is on its way, these questions are very difficult to solve at the international level.

Another problem, more publicised, is the question of film 'authorship'. In this respect, modern copyright systems are often classified under two categories, which are thought to correspond to copyright and authors' rights systems. On the one hand, 'one approach, championed by the *droit d'auteur* systems of law, is to recognise the creativity involved in film production and equate it to other copyright works';[15] authorship is therefore granted to the 'creative' authors of the film. On the other hand, countries of the copyright tradition prefer to vest the copyright in the film producer. In the US, the producer is granted authorship through the 'work-made-for-hire' doctrine.[16] Under modern UK copyright and most UK-influenced copyright laws, the producer is the author of the 'film' as a specific subject-matter.[17] Although this opposition must be qualified in the light of practice and corrective provisions in most jurisdictions, it may affect the attribution of economic rights and the distribution of revenues from the exploitation of film works.

Finally, audiovisual works are now at the centre of the debate on moral rights, as evidenced by the legal and public interest over issues like film colourisation and advertising cuts.[18] The TRIPs negotiations proved that this question pits copyright systems against authors' rights systems in a way that is not always propitious for a uniform solution to the above-mentioned problems.

In practice, strong economic and cultural interests, opposing legal traditions and, it must be said, the unqualified assumption by lawyers that their legal protection scheme for films is the best for the needs of the film industry, make the field of film protection highly contentious.

3. European harmonisation of copyright

This question of film protection was central to the process of European harmonisation of copyright law initiated in the late 1980s. The disruptions

---

[15] G. Dworkin, 'Authorship of Films and the European Commission Proposals for Harmonising the Term of Copyright, Opinion' (1993) 15 EIPR 151 at 152.

[16] Section 62 of the 1909 Act (codified at 17 USC s. 26). Now ss. 201(b) and 101 of the Copyright Act 1976.

[17] Section 13 of the 1956 Act and s. 9 of the 1988 Act. Note, however, that, since the Copyright and Related Rights Regulations 1996 (SI 1996 No. 2967), the film producer now shares its copyright in the 'film' with the principal director, considered as co-author of the film (s. 18); see para. 118.

[18] See paras. 229 *et seq.*

in the functioning of the internal market created by disparities between domestic legislation prompted the adoption of several directives which required a modification of the system of film protection in several Member States. Although the directives can be seen as compromises between different legal traditions, their provisions were mostly influenced by the solutions adopted in authors' rights countries, which are in a majority in the European Union. As a result, the UK and Irish schemes for film protection were adapted and now depart from the solution adopted in other copyright systems.

The Rental Directive of 19 November 1992 instituted a high level of protection for performers, sound and film producers and broadcasting organisations. In the field of copyright, the Directive required the introduction of a rental right in film works and set up a system of 'equitable remuneration' for rental in favour of film authors (including film directors).[19] The Satellite and Cable Directive of 27 September 1993 provided for an exclusive right of film authors and performers to authorise satellite broadcasting of their works and regulates the exercise of cable retransmission rights.[20] The Term Directive of 29 October 1993 not only required an extension of the term of protection for films, but also brought about a radical change in the existing law on film authorship, by pointing to the film director as one of the authors of the film.

4.   The impact of new technologies

However, the convergence of new technologies is creating new, perhaps more serious, difficulties for film protection. The process of filmmaking has changed a great deal since the invention of the cinematograph. Cameras and recording media have evolved, and, from the combination of these devices, new types of 'films', sometimes involving new methods of film-making, have emerged. Until recently, most technological changes at this stage have had little effect on the copyright status of films.[21] In the last twenty years, however, new technological elements have appeared, which can in some circumstances have important consequences on film protection. In particular, the extent to which films now rely on computer

---

[19] The film director being the author or one of the authors of the film for the purposes of the Directive.

[20] *Ibid.*

[21] An exception was the introduction of sound films in the late 1920s, which obliged several jurisdictions to adapt their definition of the protected subject-matter, so as to take soundtracks or soundtrack elements into consideration.

imagery can create difficulties or inadequacies in their protection[22] or create novel copyright[23] or moral rights problems.[24]

Not only do technologies affect the film-making process, they also change the way films are exploited, and thus oblige us to assess the rights granted to film-makers. In this regard, broadcasting was a first major technological development, followed by videotechnology. The new challenge is digitisation. Digitisation, which can be defined as the act of converting copyright works into binary representations, has been the subject of important legal scrutiny. Its impact on the exploitation of copyrighted works, and especially audiovisual works, is tremendous. New compression techniques allow motion pictures to be distributed on-line over the Internet or through dedicated networks with a quality comparable to television or video. This relieves end-users from the interposition of a hard copy, and makes it more difficult (considering the complexity of electronic networks) to trace the actual uses of published works. At both ends of this process, high-density recording media like DVD-ROMs allow end-users to copy and store vast quantities of works in the privacy of their home; these copies are cheap and easy to produce, and virtually identical to their original. As a result, our perception of exclusive rights is challenged, and several fundamental concepts of copyright law (like fixation, distribution, public performance, private copying, etc.) have to be re-examined. This is undoubtedly the biggest concern of the industry, in Europe and abroad.[25] At the international level, it prompted the adoption of specific provisions in the WIPO Treaties of 1996. At Community level, following the European Commission's Green Paper of 19 July 1995, a new Directive on Copyright and Related Rights in the Information Society was adopted, which specifically addresses these questions.[26]

Needless to say, the new uses for audiovisual works will certainly create industrial conflicts which could oblige us to reconsider the flow of fees or even of rights between workers and operators in this field.[27] Also, a significant result of the multiplicity of uses and of growing markets for audiovisual and related works is the development of collecting and licensing

---

[22] E.g. most of these effects are created by outside contractors, which could in some instances 'short-circuit' straightforward systems of entrepreneurial authorship.

[23] E.g. there is little doubt that the foreseeable inclusion of 'virtual' actors in film productions will force a reconsideration of the rights in the underlying 'virtual' characters or even performances.

[24] Consider the numerous treatments of films allowed by the use of computer, such as colourisation.

[25] See T. Cohen (MPAA), 'Protecting Films On-Line: Implementing the WIPO Treaties', paper given at the International Conference on Electronic Commerce and Intellectual Property, Geneva, 14–16 September 1999.

[26] See para. 44.

[27] J. Wasko, *Hollywood in the Information Age*, Polity Press, 1994, pp. 36–7.

bodies.[28] The development of such bodies (and their justification) is intimately associated with the difficulties of tracing the protected uses of copyright works. Their role is traditionally important in countries of the authors' rights tradition. Although collective administration or licensing of films rights is limited in copyright countries like the UK, there is little doubt that these bodies are going to play a more important role in the future within the European Union.[29]

Finally, digitisation goes beyond a mere change in the way works are exploited: it creates new types of works at the border of audiovisual works, such as multimedia works. These can be close to audiovisual works, and the temptation to apply both the definition and the regime of existing works to some of them is great.[30] However, their legal status needs to be clarified and the consequences of protection as audiovisual works carefully evaluated.

5. The structure of this book

In what follows, there is an attempt to draw a picture of the scheme of film protection in Europe, at Community and national levels. After an historical introduction (Chapter 2), this study is divided into eight chapters covering the main aspects of film protection: the definition of the subject-matter of protection (Chapter 3); the question of authorship and initial ownership (Chapter 4); the regime of copyright transfers (Chapter 5); the exclusive rights granted to film authors (Chapter 6); the limitations of and exemptions from these rights (Chapter 7); the question of moral rights (Chapter 8); the regime of performers' rights (Chapter 9); and the protection of foreign film works (Chapter 10). Appendix 1 is a basic guide to the European Union, intended for readers unaware of the institutional

---

[28] See A. Kerever, 'Gestion collective des oeuvres audiovisuelles et nouvelles technologies', in *ALAI Congress for the Centenary of Films*, Paris, 1995.

[29] The Satellite and Cable Directive provides for a mandatory exercise of the cable retransmission right through collecting societies (art. 9(1)). The role of collecting societies has also been acknowledged in the Rental Directive, which provides that Member States can provide for the administration of the right to equitable remuneration through collecting societies (art. 4(3) and (4)).

[30] Broad definitions in copyright Acts sometimes accommodate such an assimilation: e.g. under UK copyright, see paras. 75 and 76. For a similar position under US copyright, see 'Intellectual Property and the National Information Infrastructure', Report of the Working Group on Intellectual Property Rights, USA, Information Infrastructure Task Force, September 1995, p. 45. In a Memorandum of January 1994, the International Bureau of the WIPO stated that multimedia works could be considered as audiovisual works within the meaning of the Treaty on the International Registration of Audiovisual Works of 20 April 1989. In addition to certain similarities in the creation process and the advantages presented by the authorship scheme, characterisation as an audiovisual work is sometimes used to attract public subsidies for film production.

system of the European Union and of Community law. Appendix 2 lists the principal national copyright legislation of the EU Member States discussed in this book. Appendix 3 lists the EC copyright directives. Appendix 4 details the status of the adherence of the EU Member States to international copyright conventions. Finally, Appendix 5 details US copyright relations with the EU Member States.

6.   The birth of an industry

Credit for the discovery of animated photography cannot be given to any one person.[1] Following a long line of inventions in the fields of optics and photography,[2] the first motion picture item, i.e. the first sequence of photographs taken on a film strip in order to give the impression of movement, was probably made in 1888,[3] and several patents on camera and viewing apparatuses were granted in the following years.[4] Edison applied for patents on the photographic camera called the Kineograph and on a viewing apparatus called the Kinetoscope in April 1891.[5] The first Kinetoscope parlour opened in New York on 16 April 1894.[6] However, the Kinetoscope could only be viewed by one person at a time,[7] and the Kinetograph was itself a rather heavy and clumsy device.[8] Shortly after their release, the French inventors Louis and Auguste Lumière built a handier apparatus which was a combined camera, processor and projector, patented as the *Cinématographe* in March 1895. The invention was

---

[1] A reference book on the matter is H. Hecht, *Pre-Cinema History, An Encyclopedia and Annotated Bibliography of the Moving Image Before 1896*, BFI/Bowker Saur, 1993. See also F. A. A. Talbot, *Moving Pictures, How They Are Made and Worked*, London, 1912.

[2] In optics, the illusion of movement had long been shown to public audiences by stroboscopic toys or devices which had been combined with magic lanterns. In photography, scientific interest had developed in the analysis of motion, in the US with the works of Edward Muybridge, and in France with Etienne-Jules Marey.

[3] In Edison's laboratory, and maybe earlier by Etienne-Jules Marey. See also the work of W. E. Friese Greene in the UK.

[4] E.g. in the US, Louis Aimé Augustin Le Prince obtained a patent for a combination of camera and projector in 1888. In the UK, in 1889, W. E. Friese Greene applied for a patent on a camera which could not be used as a projector.

[5] The Kinetograph was invented in the autumn of 1890.

[6] Edison did not market his invention himself but instead licensed it. On early film distribution practices, see S. M. Donahue, *American Film Distribution*, UMI Research Press, 1987. A Kinetoscope parlour opened in London in the autumn of 1894.

[7] Apparently, Edison refused to project motion pictures to a public audience, as he thought the effect would be lost.

[8] Although it produced sound films.

shown to an audience on 22 March 1895 and the first 'theatre' opened on 28 December 1895 in the basement of the Grand Café in Paris, on the Boulevard des Capucines.[9] Lumière's representatives gave the first public demonstration of the *Cinématographe* in London a few weeks later, on 20 February 1896, at the Marlborough Hall of the Royal Polytechnic Institute on Regent Street. The invention spread rapidly throughout Europe, and met with immediate success. Public screening developed rapidly,[10] especially when theatre owners replaced short sketches or documentaries with more elaborate dramas.[11]

SECTION I

Early stages of copyright protection (1896–1908)

7.   Questions raised by 'photo-plays' and 'cinematograph films'

The new works, soon to be called photo-plays, cinematograph works or cinematograph films,[12] were universally perceived not as a form of art, but, rather, as a form of entertainment or scientific curiosity. But the importance of the industry and the extent of piracy called for a clarification of their legal status. In terms of copyright protection, they raised two series of questions. The first concerned the protection of films against infringement by competitors and unlicensed theatre owners. The second concerned the possibility of infringing pre-existing works, mainly novels or dramas, through cinematography.

Due to a tradition of piecemeal or restrictively drafted legislation, in these early days most copyright laws in Europe were ill-adapted to the new medium (discussed in Part I below). This resulted in very diverse schemes for protection, if any, and created difficulties for the protection of films abroad, at a time when these silent works had a universal and immediate appeal. These difficulties were to be partly solved by the Berlin conference of the Berne Convention in 1908 (discussed in Part II below).

---

[9] Among the short films shown was 'La sortie des usines Lumières' ('Workers Leaving the Lumière Factory').

[10] E.g. there were around fifty Nickelodeons (theatres dedicated to motion pictures) in New York in 1900, more than 400 by 1908 and 6,000 in 1909 (S. M. Donahue, *American Film Distribution*, UMI Research Press, 1987, p. 8).

[11] Like Georges Méliès' 'A Trip to the Moon' in 1902, or E. D. Porter's 'The Great Train Robbery' in 1903. Méliès himself produced more than 400 films between 1895 and 1914.

[12] Hence creating a long-lasting confusion between the work and its physical recording.

PART I

National legislation before the Berlin Conference

8.   Films as series of photographs or dramatic works

Faced with the first claims for protection by the fast-growing industry, lawyers hesitated in their approach to the new works. A first reaction was to consider cinematograph films as mere mechanical apparatuses, not unlike phonogram cylinders, and to exclude them from copyright protection. More satisfactory was the analogy to photographs. The problem was that the copyright status of photographs was still being debated in most copyright countries. In this respect, European countries could be classified into three categories. In several countries, photographs were given the same protection as other copyright works, i.e. were protected under a 'full' copyright. This was the case in France and in countries influenced by French law. In other countries, the protection granted to photographs was more limited (at least in duration) than the protection granted to other subject-matter. This was the case in Germany, in countries influenced by German law and, to a lesser extent, in the UK. In the remaining countries, the protection of photographs was uncertain and subject to discussion.[13]

As films evolved from mere pantomimes to more elaborate dramas, more satisfactory analogies were developed to other copyright works, especially dramatic works, which in most countries was to result in protection as literary and artistic works.

These hesitations between protection as a series of photographs or as 'dramatic works' had consequences which remain visible in some aspects of modern copyright protection for film.[14]

9.   Early protection in the UK

In the UK, before 1911, the major copyright textbooks are silent on the subject of cinematographic works, and legal literature on the subject is scarce.[15] Before 1911, it was widely acknowledged that, since photographs were protected under the Fine Arts Copyright Act 1862,[16]

---

[13] At the international level, the copyright protection of photographs will be instituted in 1908 with the Berlin text of the Berne Convention.

[14] E.g. it can explain the adoption of a specific neighbouring right close to the photographic copyright in favour of the film producer in Germany, or the protection of non-dramatic films as series of photographs in Italy. See para. 61.

[15] See, however, a short study from W. Carlyle Croasdell, *The Law of Copyright in Relation to Cinematography*, London, Ganes, 1911.

[16] 25 & 26 Vict., c. 68.

cinematograph films could be protected as a series of photographs.[17] The main problem with this indirect protection was that, under the Fine Arts Copyright Act 1862, in case of transfer of the negative, the copyright was lost unless it was either expressly reserved to the vendor or conveyed to the assignee in a writing signed by them.[18] Also, no action was sustainable, nor any penalty recoverable, in respect of anything done before registration at Stationers' Hall.[19] The 1862 Act provided for a registration of each photograph taken from a different negative, but at that time photo-plays were registered only as reels of films. In consequence, some authors doubted that a registration of reels would be sufficient to trigger the protection of the 1862 Act.[20] Finally, there was no performing right or 'right of exhibition' in relation to photographs. Due to transitional arrangements, copyright subsisting in pre-1911 film frames as photographs has now expired.[21]

Protection under the heading of dramatic works was thought even more uncertain, due to the ruling in *Tate* v. *Fullbrook*,[22] in which the Court of Appeal decided that what was protected under the Dramatic Copyright Act 1833 and the Copyright Act 1842 had to be 'capable of being printed and published'.[23] However, it is clear that this condition could have been met by the written script. It has been submitted that the ruling did not prevent the final cinematographic work, distinct from the script and fixed in film form only, from being protected under the 1833 Act to the extent it was capable of being so printed and published.[24] But as far as the 1842 Act is concerned, the author of a dramatic work had the copyright in it only if it took the form of a 'book', which excludes fixations in film form only.[25] Therefore, copyright protection was limited to the written script,

[17] *Barker Motion Co.* v. *Hulton* (1912) 28 TLR 496. In the US, photographs and negatives were protected under an Act of 3 March 1865 (c. 126, 13 Stat. 540); accordingly, in *Edison* v. *Lublin*, 122 Fed. 240 (CCA 3d 1903), it was held that films were copyrightable as series of photographs under s. 5(j) of Title 17 USC.

[18] 1862 Act, s. 1.   [19] Section 4.

[20] W. Carlyle Croasdell, *The Law of Copyright in Relation to Cinematography*, London, Ganes, 1911, p. 12.

[21] 1956 Act, Sched. 7, para. 2; 1988 Act, Sched. 1, para. 5(1).

[22] [1908] 1 KB 821; 98 LT 706; 77 LJKB 577; 24 TLR 347; 52 SJ 276.

[23] See para. 17 below.

[24] H. Laddie, P. Prescott and M. Vitoria, *The Modern Law of Copyright*, Butterworths, 1995, para. 5.8: 'there would appear to have been no reason why a sequence of incidents, possessing enough dramatic unity to satisfy the above-quoted test, might not have been protected although fixated in cinematograph form only.' Sterling and Carpenter have also submitted that the celluloid strip might be regarded as a 'print' under *Tate* v. *Fullbrook*: J. A. L. Sterling and M. C. L. Carpenter, *Copyright Law in the United Kingdom*, Legal Books, London, 1986, para. 283, p. 112.

[25] See H. Laddie, P. Prescott and M. Vitoria, *The Modern Law of Copyright*, Butterworths, 1995, para. 4.111 (but compare with *ibid.*, para. 5.8, quoted in n. 24 above).

and the production of such a script was a prerequisite for protection. Under the old law, the author of the dramatic work was the initial owner of the rights subsisting in the works.[26]

The provisions as to commencement and duration of the statutory copyright and 'play-right' in dramatic works are complex and their construction uncertain.[27] In addition to this statutory protection, a perpetual common law copyright, perhaps including a performing right,[28] could subsist in film works neither published nor performed. This common law right did not require any fixation, in print or otherwise.[29]

What was the protection afforded to authors of adapted or filmed works? Under the then applicable law, copyright, which was 'the sole and exclusive liberty of printing or otherwise multiplying copies', did not include performing rights. These were granted only in relation to dramatic and musical works. Thus the author of a novel, who had only a copyright under the Copyright Act 1842,[30] could not prevent a public performance of his work. The dramatisation of his novel, once reduced to writing, could infringe its copyright, but only to the extent the dialogue employed in the novel was copied.[31] Moreover, a mere fixation on cinematograph film was probably not a 'copy' of the adapted novel under the 1842 Act.[32] Therefore the making and the exhibition of a film was not infringement of the copyright in a pre-existing novel,[33] unless a script was written down, using the actual words of the novel.

---

[26] This was true even if the work was commissioned, and there was no special provision regarding the dramatic works of employees; see *Shepherd* v. *Conquest* (1856) 17 CB 427 (compare with s. 18 of 1842 Act and s. 1 of the 1862 Act). Films published or performed before the 1911 Act are likely to be protected only through their script; in that case the author was the scriptwriter (and maybe the individual producer). On the determination of the author of the film as a dramatic work, see paras. 120 *et seq.*

[27] See H. Laddie, P. Prescott and M. Vitoria, *The Modern Law of Copyright*, Butterworths, 1995, para. 4.113 and para. 2.8, n. 3.

[28] See *ibid.*, para. 4.109.   [29] *Ibid.*, para. 4.107.   [30] 5 & 6 Vict., c. 45.

[31] *Reade* v. *Conquest* (1861) 9 CBNS 755; 3 LTNS 888; 30 LJCP 209; 7 Jur. NS 265; 9 WR 434; 127 RR 869; *Tinsley* v. *Lacy* (1863) 32 LJ Ch 535; 1 H&M 747; 2 NR 438; 11 WR 876; and *Warne & Co.* v. *Seebohm* (1888) 39 ChD 73; 58 LT 928; 57 LJ Ch 689; 36 WR 686. This was changed by s. 1(2)(c) of the 1911 Act (see e.g. *Corelli* v. *Gray* (1913) 29 TLR 570; 30 TLR 116).

[32] Under the Act, infringement was not limited to copies produced by print; copies produced by lithograph or photography were considered copies within the meaning of the Act (*Novello* v. *Sudlow* (1852) 12 CB 177; *Boosey* v. *Whight* [1900] 1 Ch 122). However, literary works, as well as dramatic and musical works, were protected if they took the form of a 'book', i.e. printed matter. In *Boosey* v. *Whight*, it was held that copyright in a musical work was not infringed by perforated scrolls for use in mechanical instruments, on the grounds that the 'copy' produced was not a reasonable substitute for the music in printed form. See also *Newmark* v. *National Phonograph Co.* (1907) 23 TLR 439; *Mabe* v. *Connor* [1909] 1 KB 515; *Monkton* v. *Gramophone Co.* [1905–10] MCC 304. By analogy, a film strip could not be a copy of a 'book'.

[33] See *Copinger on Copyright*, 1915, p. 248.

Although authors of dramatic works were granted a 'play-right' (i.e. a performing right) under the Dramatic Copyright Act 1833,[34] it was difficult to say whether or not the exhibition of a film could be considered as a 'performance in a place of dramatic entertainment' within the meaning of this Act.[35] Concerning the copyright, there was also a doubt as to whether a dramatic work could be infringed without the use of its actual words,[36] and presumably copies in film form only were not 'copies' of the underlying dramatic work within the meaning of the 1842 Act.[37]

Under section 24(1) of the 1911 Act, the common law copyright, the statutory copyright and the 'play-right' subsisting in film works as at the date of commencement of the Act were replaced by the corresponding new copyright.[38] Most dramatic copyrights in pre-1911 film works have now expired, but some of them have been revived by the operation of the Duration of Copyright and Rights in Performances Regulations 1995.[39]

10. Early protection in France and countries influenced by French law

The French film industry dominated the pre-war period in Europe, and the protection of both film producers and authors of adapted works became a great concern in France. The first reported decision on film

---

[34] 3 & 4 Will. 4, c. 15.

[35] *Copinger and Skone James on Copyright*, 1915, p. 248; J. S. Dubin, *Motion Picture Rights, US and International*, 1954, pp. 10–11; In *Karno* v. *Pathé Frères* (1909) 99 LT 114; 100 LT 260; 25 TLR 242; [1905–10] MCC 145, Jelf J considered that a cinematograph reproduction of a dramatic work could be a 'representation' within the meaning of the Dramatic Copyright Act 1833; he held, however, that a manufacturer who sells films to persons who, to his knowledge, intend to exhibit them in public does not represent or cause the work to be represented under the Act; the point was raised but not decided in *Glenville* v. *Selig Polyscope* (1911) 27 TLR 554; [1911–16] MCC 18; see also *London Theatre of Varieties* v. *Evans* (1914) 30 TLR 258 (public exhibition of a film held to be a 'representation' of the underlying performance expressly prohibited by contract). Compare with *Newmark* v. *National Phonograph Co.* (1907) 23 TLR 439 (held that sounds produced mechanically did not come within the Copyright Act).

[36] Contra *Planché* v. *Braham* (1838) 4 Bing. NC 17; and *Schlotz* v. *Amasis Ltd & Fenn* [1905–10] MCC 216; Pro, *Chatterton* v. *Cave* (1878) 3 App Cas 483; and *Nethersole* v. *Bell* [1901–4] MCC 64. For post-1911 case law, see paras. 17 and 185.

[37] Under the 1842 Act, dramatic works were also protected in the form of books.

[38] And the substituted rights subsisted for the term provided in the new Act, calculated from the date of the making of the work. Note that, if no 'play-right' subsisted before commencement, no performing, broadcasting and cable-casting right can subsist under present law. Conversely, if only a 'play-right' subsisted, present protection does not extend beyond the right to perform, broadcast or include the work in a cable programme service (1911 Act, Sched. 1; CDPA 1988, Sched. 1, para. 17).

[39] SI 1995 No. 3297. See paras. 99 and 100.

protection was handed down in 1904, and, from that date, case law and legal literature on the subject developed rapidly.[40]

The law of copyright in France consisted of two revolutionary Acts of 13–19 January 1791 and 19–24 July 1793. The Act of 1791 provided for a performing right for dramatic works, whereas the Act of 1793 provided for a copy-right (reproduction right) for authors of all 'writings', musical composers, painters and draughtsmen. These short Acts, which contained only a few articles, remained almost untouched during the nineteenth century.[41] Case law had to construe the list of protected works so as to protect other classes of works. In particular, after some hesitation, the French Supreme Court protected photographs by analogy to engravings and drawings.[42]

In the very first cases on cinematography, French courts refused to consider cinematographic works as copyright works, on the basis that they were only a mechanical device not entitled to copyright protection.[43] The first case protecting films is *Doyen v. Parnaland*, in 1905.[44] A surgeon, Dr Doyen, had the idea of having some of his surgical operations filmed, for teaching and scientific purposes, with the help of two camera operators. Without the authorisation of Dr Doyen, one of the operators, Mr Parnaland, kept negatives in order to print positives of the films and sold them (the films were later exhibited in fairs). The Tribunal of First Instance of Seine considered that cinematograph films consisted of a series of photographs, and held that Dr Doyen, who gave strict detailed instructions as to the filming, was the author of the film, and thus entitled to the reproduction right under the Law of 1793. The infringing films were seized and damages were awarded to Dr Doyen.

The fact that photographs were protected under the generally applicable regime of copyright, and that the list of copyright works was not exhaustive under French copyright law certainly facilitated the treatment of films as a specific subject-matter for protection, and avoided the technical

---

[40] See e.g. Izouard, 'Le cinématographe et le droit d'auteur', in *Annales de la Propriété Industrielle, Artistique et Littéraire*, 1908, p. 155; Maugras et Guégan, *Le cinématographe et le droit*, 1908; Potu, *La protection internationale des oeuvres cinématographiques d'après la Convention de Berne révisée à Berlin en 1908*, Dalloz, 1912; Taillefer, in *Revue Dalloz Sirey*, 1910, II, p. 257; Théry, note in *Annales des la Propriété Industrielle, Artistique et Littéraire*, 1910, I, p. 118.

[41] The duration of copyright, however, was progressively extended to fifty years p.m.a. for all copyright works.

[42] Court of Cassation, Crim., 15 January 1864, *Revue Dalloz*, 1865, I, p. 317.

[43] Tribunal of First Instance of Lourdes, 28 July 1904; Pau Court of Appeal, 18 November 1904, *Annales de la Propriété Industrielle*, 1906, p. 101, *Revue Dalloz*, 1910, II, p. 91.

[44] Tribunal of First Instance of Seine, 10 February 1905, *Doyen v. Parnaland, Revue Dalloz Périodique*, 1905, II, p. 389; Paris Court of Appeal, 10 November 1909, three cases, *Annales de la Propriété Industrielle*, 1910, 1, p. 118.

discussions on 'categorisation' as photographs or dramatic works that arose in the UK and Germany. In addition, the standard of originality appeared to be comprehensive enough to accommodate most films, including documentaries and newsreels. ⫰

In the absence of specific rules regarding photographs, the duration of protection afforded to films was the then standard duration of fifty years p.m.a., one of the longest available at that time.

At first, the question of film authorship did not raise major difficulties under French law. The reason is probably that, in those early days of the film industry, film producers usually wrote and directed their own films (although they were not camera operators). In addition, the question of authorship is associated with claims of artistic nature which were not yet raised concerning films.

Concerning the status of included or adapted works, case law admitted early on that public exhibition of a film was a performance under the Law of 1791.[45] Courts also held that reproduction or adaptation of a work of literature or of a play on film could be copyright infringement. The first decisions, however, set a standard of infringement which was very liberal for filmmakers.[46]

A specific difficulty of early French law was the then existing general requirement of deposit of copyright works. Until 1925, under French copyright law, copyright owners could not sue for infringement if copies of their work were not deposited at the national library (but the deposit was not in itself a prerequisite for copyright protection). The formalities applied to photographs, and were ill-adapted to cinematographic works. This created difficulties for the protection of foreign films in France, which were partly solved with the adoption and ratification in France of the Berlin text of the Berne Convention.

[45] The first decisions on the question refused such characterisation on the grounds that the performance was merely a mechanical movement (Tribunal of First Instance of Lourdes 28 July 1904; Pau Court of Appeal, 18 November 1904, *Annales de la Propriété Industrielle*, 1906, pp. 10 and 101, *Revue Dalloz Périodique*, 1910, II, p. 81, note Claro). However, the trend changed with Tribunal of First Instance of Seine, 17 March 1905, *Revue Dalloz*, 1905, II, p. 389; Tribunal of First Instance of Seine, 7 July 1908, cited; Paris Court of Appeal, 10 November 1909, *Revue Dalloz*, 1910, II, p. 81, note Claro; Court of Cassation, Req., 27 June 1910, *Revue Dalloz*, 1910, I, p. 296; Tribunal of First Instance of Seine, 18 December 1911; Paris Court of Appeal, 17 May 1912, *Annales de la Propriété Industrielle*, 1913, I, p. 165, *Revue Dalloz Sirey*, 1913, II, p. 141.

[46] Tribunal of First Instance of Seine, 7 July 1908, *Revue Dalloz Périodique*, 1910, II, p. 83, *Revue Dalloz Sirey*, 1910, II, p. 259 (infringement of a play by a film); reversed by Paris Court of Appeal, 12 May 1909, *Revue Dalloz Périodique*, 1910, II, p. 81, *Revue Dalloz Sirey*, 1910, II, p. 257; Court of Cassation, Req., 27 June 1910, *Revue Dalloz*, 1910, I, p. 206. The trend changed with Paris Court of Appeal, 10 November 1909, *Annales de la Propriété Industrielle*, 1910, I, p. 127, *Revue Dalloz Sirey*, 1910, II, p. 259 (infringement of 'Faust' by Barbier Carré and Gounod by means of a film adaptation).

In Italy, photographs were protected by the Act of 19 September 1882 under the full copyright afforded to other classes of works. As in France, legal commentators considered cinematographic works to be protected as a series of photographs under this Act.[47] A difference from French law lay in the requirement of deposit for copyright works, which was more stringent: copyright in a photographic or cinematographic work would lapse if the deposit was not made or not properly carried out.

In Belgium, the Law of 22 March 1882 did not contain any provisions relating to photographs, but photographs were protected by case law when cinematography appeared. The protection granted to films was similar to that granted under French law.

In Spain, photographs were protected as artistic works under the Act on Intellectual Property of 10 January 1879.[48] Although the question is not documented, films were probably protectable as series of photographs. The term of copyright protection available was the longest in Europe, with a term of eighty years p.m.a. This duration should be taken into consideration when determining which pre-First World War films or underlying works have their copyright revived in application of the provisions of the EC Term Directive of 29 October 1993.[49]

11.   Germany and countries influenced by German law

In Germany, the Act of 1901 on literary copyright did not contain any provisions on the protection of cinematograph films, or on infringement of copyright works through cinematography. Legal commentators admitted early on that literary or dramatic works could be infringed by being adapted or reproduced on cinematograph film.[50] However, a majority of such commentators were of the opinion that films themselves could not be protected under the Law of 1901.[51]

Accordingly, the only protection available was the protection granted to photographic works. The problem was that the German Act of 1876

---

[47] Cairola, *La tutela giuridica nell' opera cinematographica*, 1912, pp. 13 *et seq.*; Dina, *Le cinématographe et le gramophone dans la législation italienne et les législations étrangères*, Turin, A. Panizza, 1912, pp. 4 *et seq.*; C. Palombella, 'I cinematographi e il diritto d'autore' (1908) 31 *Rivista di giurisprudenza* 720–4; M. Turletti, 'I cinematographi e il diritto d'autore' (1907) 59 *Giurisprudenza italiana* No. 4, 250. For case law, see Praetor of Macerata, 22 December 1910, in *I Diritti D'autore*, March 1911, and the cases quoted in the April–May issue.

[48] Decree of 3 September 1880.   [49] See para. 99.

[50] J. Kohler, *Urheberrecht an Schriftwerken und Verlagsrecht*, 1906–7, pp. 173, 175 and 184; G. Cohn, *Kinematographenrecht*, 1909, pp. 22 *et seq.*

[51] See e.g. J. Kohler, *Urheberrecht an Schriftwerken und Verlagsrecht*, 1906–7, p. 173, and pp. 175 and 184, nn.; *Kunstwerkrecht*, 1908, pp. 26 and 54; G. Cohn, *Kinematographenrecht*, 1909, pp. 27 *et seq.*; and Riezler, *Urheberrecht und Erfinderrecht*, 1909, vol. 1, p. 429.

established a very limited protection for photographs. These were protected only against mechanical reproductions, and protection was granted
for five years post-publication (or after the occurrence of one of the facts
enumerated in the Act in the absence of publication). In addition, the
protection was subject to the performance of cumbersome registration
formalities. In particular, copyright would lapse if specific information
was not written on each registered picture. The Law of 1907 on artistic copyright abolished these formalities and extended protection to ten
years post-publication (or p.m.a. for unpublished photographs), without
retroactive effect. In contrast, the then applicable term of protection for
literary and dramatic works was thirty years p.m.a.

In Austria, photographs were granted express legislative protection in
the Law of 26 December 1895. As in Germany, this protection was more
limited than for other classes of works. The same is true for Switzerland
under the Law of 7 July 1883: duration of copyright in pictures did not
exceed five years, while protection for classic subject-matter was granted
for the author's lifetime plus thirty years after the author's death.[52]

12.   Scandinavian countries

In these countries, the early copyright Acts contained no provisions on
cinematographic works.[53] The protection afforded to photographs (and
possibly to cinematographic films) was only granted for a limited period
of time.[54]

PART II

The Berlin Conference of the Berne Convention

13.   The Berne Convention

The Berne Convention was the first legal instrument to tackle the new invention. Cinematographic works were included in the text of the Convention after a proposal by France at the Berlin Conference in 1908.[55] This

---

[52] F. Dessemontet, in M. B. Nimmer and D. Geller (eds.), *International Copyright Law and
Practice*, Matthew Bender, looseleaf, para. 1[2].
[53] Denmark, Law of 24 March 1865; Sweden, Law of 28 May 1897.
[54] E.g. in Norway, the Law of 11 May 1909 extended the duration of copyright in photographs to fifteen years p.m.a. Protection under the previous Law of 12 May 1877 was
even shorter.
[55] *Actes de la Conférence de Berlin 1908*, International Office, Berne, 1909, p. 190. The Paris
Act of 1896 and its preparatory works were silent on the subject.

proposal was not inspired by cinematographers, but by dramatists who complained against uses of their works through cinematography. It consisted in the inclusion of a new text in the Convention prohibiting infringement of literary and artistic works through reproduction on cinematographic films and cinematographic exhibition. The Conference decided to address the question of the protection of cinematograph films as well.

The system set up by the Convention is rather complex. Cinematographic works were not included in the list of protected works in article 2 of the Convention, but protection was granted through references made in its text.

The Convention first provided for the protection of photographic works in its article 3:

this convention shall apply to photographic works and to works produced by a process analogous to photography. The contracting countries shall be bound to make provisions for their protection.

In doing so, article 3 contained an indirect reference to cinematographic works, as 'works produced by a process analogous to photography'. However, a direct reference to the new works is to be found in article 14 of the Convention. This article extended the rights of authors of literary and artistic works to the right to authorise the reproduction and public performance of their works by cinematography, and instituted the protection of cinematographic works under the Convention:

Authors of literary, scientific or artistic works shall have the exclusive right of authorising the reproduction and public performance of their works by cinematography.

Cinematographic productions shall be protected as literary or artistic works, if, by the arrangement of the acting form or the combinations of the incidents represented, the author has given the work a personal and original character.

Without prejudice to the copyright in the original work the reproduction by cinematography of a literary, scientific or artistic work shall be protected as an original work.

The preceding provisions apply to reproduction or production effected by any other process analogous to cinematography.

The Convention thus suggested a dual system of protection for films: as series of photographs, and, for those having a 'personal and original character', as dramatic works distinct from their script. This distinction is made clear in the final report of the Conference:

We have just seen the cinematograph being used for purposes of reproduction or adaptation. It can also serve to give form to a creation. The person who takes the cinematographic shots and develops the negatives will also be the person who has imagined the subject, arranged the scenes and directed the moves of the actors . . . [W]e have here a dramatic work of a particular genre which it must not be possible to appropriate with impunity . . . It is not the question of monopolising an idea or a subject but of protecting the form given the idea or the development of the subject. Judges will assess the matter in the same way as for ordinary literary and artistic works.[56]

In addition, paragraph 3 of article 14 provides for the protection of cinematographic adaptations (reproductions of literary works) as original works of authorship.

Of course, concerning original cinematographic productions (non-adapted films), the criteria of originality set by the second paragraph was to create problems in several jurisdictions where this text was faithfully implemented, as the lack of 'personal and original character' would trigger the limited copyright protection sometimes granted to photographs. This created disparities and uncertainties as to the protection of documentary films and newsreels.[57]

Also, the text did not address the question of the protection of cinematographic works against adaptation, which for a while raised questions as to this possibility.[58]

The convention extended the minimum duration of protection for copyright works to fifty years p.m.a., but article 7 provided that until such unification in the terms of protection was made, the protection could not be longer than the duration in the country of origin.

Finally, another important aspect of the Berlin text, already mentioned, are the provisions regarding formalities. Without formally abolishing formalities of deposit and registration in internal laws, the Act provides that such formalities were not necessary for the protection sought under the Convention in signatory countries.[59] This resulted in situations in which a foreigner could sue in a country having a registration system for a work which was not registered there, where a national of that country could

---

[56] Report by Louis Renault. The Berne Convention includes dramatic works in the larger category of literary and artistic works. On the history of film protection under the Convention, see S. Ricketson, *The Berne Convention on the Protection of Literary and Artistic Works*, Kluwer, 1987, Chapter 10, pp. 549–89; W. Nordemann, K. Vinck and P. W. Hertin, *International Copyright and Neighbouring Rights Law* (trans. G. Meyer), VCH, 1990, pp. 141 *et seq.*

[57] Art. 14(2) of the Berne Convention, as amended in 1948, prevented the exclusion of documentary films and newsreels from protection as literary and artistic works.

[58] See M. Dungs, *Die Berner Uebereinkunft über internationales Urheberrechet*, 1910, pp. 55–6, discussed by the French author E. Potu in his note under Bâle, 2 July 1909 and 28 June 1910, *Revue Dalloz*, 1912, II, pp. 393 at 396.

[59] Art. 4(2).

not. This disadvantage to national productions led to the disappearance of formalities in most European countries.[60]

The modern period: separation between copyright and authors' rights countries (1908–1992)

14. The separation of copyright and authors' rights approaches

From 1908 onwards, copyright systems on the one hand, and authors' rights systems on the other hand, took different approaches to the protection of films and ancillary works. It is difficult to give a single explanation for this separation. However, the main factor appears to be the growing perception of films, on the continent, as a true form of art. The specific features of authors' rights legislation (creative authorship schemes, moral rights, protection of the author, considered as the weaker party in copyright dealings, etc.) are closely associated with the perception of copyright works as an expression of the author's personality (the so-called 'romantic vision of the author'). These aspects were already developed in relation to classic subject-matter, but could not be applied to film works as long as they were perceived as a scientific curiosity or as a simple form of entertainment (hence the tendency in pre-war *droit d'auteur* to consider the film producer as the author of the film).[61] This shift in the perception of cinematography prompted the application to film works of the protective rules developed for other classes of 'artistic' works.[62] In this respect, the questions of film authorship and moral rights became the focus of a growing opposition between UK copyright and continental authors' rights systems. This opposition came to a head during the discussion which led to the adoption of the EC Rental and Term Directives.[63] Major differences still subsist in relation to other aspects of copyright protection, such as the regulation of copyright transfers, the rules regarding the remuneration of authors and the treatment of 'related rights'.

---

[60] Germany in 1910, the UK in 1911, France in 1925.   [61] See paras. 28 and 135.

[62] But other factors have had an influence on the separation of the systems. On the technical side, one may consider, for example, the specific style of legislative drafting in the UK, which created very detailed schemes of copyright protection unequalled on the continent.

[63] See para. 111.

PART I

The evolution of film protection in copyright systems

15.   Film protection under the UK 1911 Act: indirect protection as a series of photographs and as dramatic work

In the UK, the Gorell Committee of 1909, which prepared the new law and the implementation of the Berlin Act provisions, did not concentrate on the protection of films or cinematographic productions as such; rather, it tended to focus on films as a way of infringing other copyrighted works.[64] However, in order to comply formally with the Berne Convention, cinematographic works were given express protection in the 1911 Act.

Under the new Act, copyright included both the right to produce and reproduce the work in any material form and the right to perform the work in public.[65] Moreover, no specified physical form of production was required for the protection of literary, dramatic, musical and artistic works. The Act contained an express reference to cinematographic copies or versions in section 1(2)(d), which stated that copyright in the case of a literary, dramatic or musical work included the right to make any 'cinematograph film by means of which the work may be mechanically performed or delivered'.[66] Also, under section 1(2)(c), authors of novels or other non-dramatic works or of artistic works were given the right to prevent their works from being converted into dramatic works 'by way of performance in public *or otherwise*'.

The protection of films was dealt with in section 35(1), which defined 'dramatic work' as including 'any cinematograph production where the arrangement or acting form or the combination of incidents represented give the work an original character'.[67]

This inclusion of cinematograph works in the definition of section 35(1) is interesting because it shows that, as far as dramatic copyright is concerned, the subject-matter for protection is not the film strip, the recording, but the dramatic work ('cinematograph production') produced for

---

[64] Report of the Committee on the Law of Copyright, Cd 4976, HMSO, 1909.
[65] Section 1(2).
[66] Artistic works were not expressly included in this provision, and it is not clear whether they could be infringed by cinematograph films, which would be contrary to art. 14 of the Berlin Act of 1908. Consider, however, the generality of s. 1(2) *in limine* (right to 'produce or reproduce . . . in any material form whatsoever') and the possibility to claim infringement by photography.
[67] Which echoes art. 14 of the Berne Convention. This definition of dramatic works in the 1911 Act did not raise special comments during the parliamentary debates. Section 35(1) further defined 'cinematograph' as including 'any work produced by a process analogous to cinematography'.

and expressed through cinematography. Conceptually, this work could be both the script and the final cinematic work recorded in film form only. However, the idea of protection of the visual recording constituted by the film strip as a specific subject-matter, by analogy to sound recordings, was expressed in the Gorell Committee Report, and comparison between the two 'recordings' was made.[68] The protection by the 1911 Act of the 'cinematic' dramatic work rather than its recording is a faithful implementation of article 14 of the Berne Convention.[69]

In addition to this protection as a dramatic work, the definition of photographs in section 35 of the 1911 Act included a 'photo-lithograph and any work produced by any process analogous to photography', which clearly encompassed the technology inaugurated by the Kinetograph. Thus cinematograph films (or, more exactly, cinematograph film frames) could be protected as photographs.[70]

16.   Articulation of the two protections

The two headings of protection were cumulative, and it was held that a film which could not meet the requirement of originality for a dramatic work could still be protected as a series of photographs.[71] However, one should not come to the conclusion that the originality criterion was different in the case of dramatic works, or that no such requirement existed in relation to photographs. Originality was a prerequisite for protection under both headings, and it appears that the emphasis put by section 35 on the originality of cinematograph productions did not set a more stringent test than for other types of works.[72] However, under such a scheme it was easier for a film to be protected as a series of photographs. For example, the mere filming of a live play, without re-editing or special work on camera movement or focus, would not create a new original dramatic work distinct from the play, but the level of originality required for photographs was likely to be met by each frame. Moreover, while all films

---

[68] The UK Government proposed the protection of gramophone discs, piano rolls and the like at the Berlin Conference of 1908 and later at the 1928 Rome Conference (S. Ricketson, *The Berne Convention on the Protection of Literary and Artistic Works*, Kluwer, 1987, para. 6.78, p. 309).

[69] Article judged reasonable by the Gorell Committee, Report of the Committee on the Law of Copyright, Cd 4976, HMSO, 1909, p. 27.

[70] *Nordisk Films Co. Ltd* v. *Onda* [1919–24] MCC 337; also, under a similar definition, the Canadian case of *Canadian Admiral Corp. Ltd* v. *Rediffusion Inc.* (1954) 20 CPR 75; 14 Fox Pat. C. 114.

[71] *Nordisk Films Co. Ltd* v. *Onda* [1919–24] MCC 337.

[72] S. Ricketson, *The Berne Convention on the Protection of Literary and Artistic Works*, Kluwer, 1987, para. 10.3, pp. 550–1; H. Laddie, P. Prescott and M. Vitoria, *The Modern Law of Copyright*, Butterworths, 1995, para. 5.13.

were made of photographs, they did not all comprise dramatic works, original or not. In that case, the question is less a question of originality than a question of characterisation as a dramatic work. For example, a film which consists of the continuous record of a real life scene would in most cases be the result of enough skill, labour and judgment to attract copyright protection (as a series of photographs or otherwise), but might not constitute a dramatic work, a *drama*.

This leads us to the problem of the definition of dramatic works. This question will be studied further in what follows,[73] but it presents a special difficulty under the 1911 Act because of the express inclusion of 'cinematograph productions' in the definition of dramatic works. Did it mean that cinematograph productions which could be likened to *dramas* were protected under the dramatic copyright, or that all cinematograph productions were to be considered as dramatic works? In the first scenario, works like newsreels or television shows would not be considered as dramatic works (even under a broad definition of 'dramas'), and could only be protected as series of photographs; in the second, all cinematograph productions would be protected as dramatic works, provided that they met the minimum level of originality. It is submitted that the first construction is reasonable, but the question is open to debate.[74]

The characterisation of a given film as a dramatic or a non-dramatic film (the latter being protected under the sole heading of photographs) is important. Dramatic films received protection for a longer period, i.e. author's life plus fifty years,[75] as against fifty years from their making for non-dramatic films.[76] Also, dramatic films could be reproduced by anyone, subject to payment of a royalty, twenty-five years after the author's death,[77] whereas this royalty did not apply to photographs.[78] Another important difference between the two types of protection is constituted by the definition of the exclusive rights, in particular in relation to acts of adaptation.[79]

17. **The subject-matter of protection under the heading of dramatic work: the distinction between script and final audiovisual work**

Protection as a dramatic work raised another problem. The term 'cinematograph production' in the 1911 Act could be applied to several film

---

[73] Paras. 54 *et seq.*   [74] *Ibid.*   [75] 1911 Act, s. 3.   [76] Section 21.
[77] Section 3. But this did not give a right of public performance.
[78] *Copinger and Skone James on Copyright*, 1915, p. 251.   [79] See para. 20.

works: to the script, in its various forms (from the initial treatment to the shooting script[80] which was sometimes written by the director), but also to the final audiovisual work derived from the script and fixed in film form only. Conceptually, both works could be considered as distinct dramatic works under the definition of section 35 (at least if the final audiovisual work adds, by the work of the director or the director of photography, something original to the written script). In *Milligan* v. *Broadway Cinema Production*,[81] the Scottish Court of Session held that there may be separate and independent copyrights in (a) a music-hall sketch, (b) a film scenario adapted from such sketch, and (c) a film produced from such a scenario. Accordingly, the copyright in the final cinematograph work is distinct from the copyright in the script,[82] and protection could be granted at both stages under the heading of dramatic work.

However, in *Tate* v. *Fullbrook*, the Court of Appeal decided that dramatic works within the meaning of the 1833 and 1842 Copyright Acts had to be 'capable of being printed and published'.[83] This construction was adopted under the 1911 Act by *Tate* v. *Thomas*.[84] This appears to suggest that the final audiovisual work could only be granted protection if the element added to the script could be printed and published.

It is respectfully submitted, however, that the authority of *Tate* v. *Fullbrook* on this point is limited to the 1833 and 1842 Acts.[85] Section 1 of the Dramatic Copyright Act 1833, while not requiring a fixation in print as a prerequisite for the granting of performing rights, suggested that dramatic works had to be *capable* of being printed and published, for

---

[80] The detailed plan which breaks down the film shot by shot.

[81] 1923 SLT 35; [1922–3] MCC 343, Court of Session.

[82] See e.g. *Copinger and Skone James on Copyright*, 1927, quoted below; G. Alchin, *Manual of Law for the Cinema Trade*, Pitman, London, 1934, p. 5. and H. Laddie, P. Prescott and M. Vitoria, *The Modern Law of Copyright*, Butterworths, 1995, para. 5.12; see also, in Canadian law under a similar scheme, H. G. Fox, *The Canadian Law of Copyright and Industrial Design*, 2nd edn, Carswell, Toronto, 1967, p. 175.

[83] [1908] 1 KB 821. See also *Karno* v. *Pathé Frères*, 99 LT 114; 100 LT 260; 25 TLR 242; [1905–10] MCC 145.

[84] [1921] 1 Ch 503; 90 LJ Ch 318; 124 LT 722; 65 SJ 327; [1917–23] MCC 246. Rejecting the claim that the scenic effects for a play were the constitutive elements of the dramatic work, Eve J stated: 'in *Tate* v. *Fullbrook* it was pointed out that the Act creates a statutory monopoly, and that there must be certainty in the monopoly so created in order that injustice may be avoided. To bring about this result there must be matter capable of being printed and published.'

[85] *Copinger and Skone James on Copyright*, 13th edn, 1991, para. 2–14. Also suggested by J. A. L. Sterling and M. C. L. Carpenter, *Copyright Law in the United Kingdom*, Legal Books, London, 1986, p. 72, n. For the opinion that *Tate* v. *Fullbrook* would have been decided differently under the new definition of dramatic works in the 1911 Act, see H. Hurrel, *Copyright Law and the Copyright Act*, Waterlow & Sons, London, 1911, p. 35; S. P. Kerr, *The Copyright Act 1911*, London, 1912, p. 27; and G. S. Robertson, *The Law of Copyright*, Clarendon Press, Oxford, 1912, p. 124.

printing and publication conditioned the statutory term of protection.[86] Moreover, under the Copyright Act 1842, dramatic works attracted copyright only if they were reproduced in the specified form of a 'book', i.e. in print.

In contrast, under section 35 of the 1911 Act, dramatic works included 'entertainments in dumb show, the scenic arrangement or acting form of which is fixed in writing *or otherwise*'. As a result, dramatic works and their constituting elements did not have to be reduced to book form or even be *capable* of being so printed. A mere fixation on film sufficed to grant protection.

In this regard, Eve J in *Tate* v. *Thomas* was misguided (and unnecessarily so) in following the language of *Tate* v. *Fullbrook*. Since in *Thomas* neither the parties nor the court referred to the new definition of dramatic work in section 35 of the 1911 Act, the authority of the case on this point could be questioned.[87] In any case, arguably the meaning of 'print' under the 1911 Act was wider and could encompass 'photographic prints' and fixations on celluloid.

18.   The difficult question of film authorship under the 1911 Act

Under the 1911 Act, the author of a work was the person who created it.[88] However, the author was not necessarily the first owner of the copyright. A distinction must be made between the film as a series of photographs and the film as a dramatic work:

When the film was protected as a series of photographs, the first owner of the negative was deemed the author.[89] Moreover, the copyright in a photograph vested in the person who ordered and paid for the original

---

[86] It reads: 'The Author of any Tragedy, Comedy, Play, Opera, Farce, or any other Dramatic Piece or Entertainment, composed, and not *printed or published* by the Author thereof or his assignee, or the assignee of such Author, shall have as his own Property the sole liberty of representing . . . any such production as aforesaid, not *printed and published* by the Author thereof or his Assignee, and shall be deemed and taken to be the Proprietor thereof; and the Author of such Production, *printed and published* within ten years before the passing of this act by the Author thereof or his Assignee, or which shall hereinafter be so *printed and published*, or the assignee of such Author, shall, from the time of passing this act, or from the time of such publication respectively, until the End of Twenty-eight years from the day of such first publication of the same . . . have as his own Property the sole liberty of representing, or causing to be represented, the same at any such Place of Dramatic Entertainment as aforesaid, and shall be deemed and taken to be the Proprietor thereof.' Emphasis added.

[87] On that question, see e.g. T. Prime, *The Law of Copyright*, Fourmat Publishing, 1992, p. 28.

[88] Section 5.   [89] Section 21.

negative.[90] In both cases, the text pointed to the producer (or rather to the production company, since this owner could be a legal person).[91] As first owner of the negative, and then deemed author, he was the first owner of the copyright; as the one who ordered and paid for the negative, he was also first owner, even if the contract with the contributor was not a contract of service. Accordingly, in relation to films protected only as series of photographs, the determination of authorship or co-authorship does not really create problems.[92]

However, when the film was protected as a dramatic work, the author of the work was the first owner of the copyright, except if he was in employment under a contract of service or apprenticeship, in which case the employer was the first owner.[93] The problem is that contracts between film producers and the main contributors to films were often contracts for services: the major contributors, at least in the post-war UK film industry, worked on a commission basis.[94] It is then more important to determine whether the 'creator-author' was what we call now the 'creative artist' or was the film producer. If the author was, say, the film director, and if he was commissioned, the producer needed to be assigned or licensed the rights in the audiovisual dramatic work, either expressly or impliedly.[95]

At this point, it is important to note that it is doubtful that a legal person could qualify as author of a dramatic work under the 1911 Act.[96] If corporate authorship was impossible, the hesitation should be in deciding between the 'creative artist' and the individual producer, and the production company could only become owner by virtue of a contract of employment or an assignment.

This question will be studied in detail in what follows,[97] but what can be said at this stage is that most authors were of the opinion that the

---

[90] Section 5(1)(a).   [91] Section 21.

[92] Especially since the term of copyright protection for photographs started from their making, and did not take into account the life of the author or co-authors (1911 Act, s. 21).

[93] Section 5(1)(b).

[94] See F. E. Skone James, 'Great Britain', in H. L. Pinner (ed.), *World Copyright*, A. W. Sijthoff, Leyden, 1953, vol. I, *Verbo Cinematographic Works*, p. 737: 'the authors and composers of dialogue and music are unlikely to be working under contracts of service . . . and consequently the copyright in these works will not so vest without express assignment.'

[95] *Ibid.* On implied licences or assignments, see paras. 121 and 156 below.

[96] Corporate authorship was expressly acknowledged in relation to photographs (s. 21) and sound recordings (s. 19), but the specific designation of the 'owner' of the negative or of the first recording as author could limit this solution to these two descriptions of works. Moreover, the absence of special provisions concerning duration for other classes of work suggests strongly that the author whose life and death were taken into consideration was the physical person who created the work. Finally, s. 5(1)(b) of the Act granted initial ownership, not authorship, to the employer.

[97] See paras. 120 *et seq.*

director was an author of the film.[98] This idea also appears confirmed by the only pre-1957 UK case on film authorship, *Milligan* v. *Broadway Cinema Ltd.*[99] It is also endorsed by modern authors.[100]

However, were directors the sole authors of pre-1957 dramatic films? As Laddie, Prescott and Vitoria justly remark, 'in many cases the combination of incidents portrayed and a good deal of the "character" of the film may also be supplied by the script or scenario writer who would also therefore be an author'.[101] Accordingly, provided the requirement of collaboration was met, pre-1957 dramatic audiovisual works could be of joint authorship.[102] However, the list might not be limited to the director and the scriptwriter(s); depending on the production, other contributors, including the individual producer, could claim co-authorship.[103]

What were the practical consequences of such a 'creative authorship' scheme? They were limited in terms of *copyright ownership*. In practice, there is little doubt that the rights of commissioned contributors were assigned to the production company.[104] Also, the provisions of the 1911 Act concerning reversionary rights were not applicable to audiovisual works.[105] In fact, a difficulty as to ownership would only arise if

---

[98] J. M. Easton, in *Copinger and Skone James on Copyright*, 1915, p. 252, refers to the scriptwriter: 'The "author" of a dramatic film is, of course, not the photographer who takes the picture, nor the actor, if any, who plays in front of the camera, but the person who invents the plot or arranges the incidents.' But see G. Alchin, *Manual of Law for the Cinema Trade*, Pitman, London, 1934, p. 5 (referring to the film director). From the sixth edition of *Copinger and Skone James on Copyright*, F. E. Skone James refers to 'the producer, who arranges the scenes to be filmed'; this would not be the film producer in the modern sense, but rather the film director. The film director was often called 'producer', under the terminology used for theatre.

[99] 1923 SLT 35 (despite the ambiguity of the term 'producer', as used by the court).

[100] See H. Laddie, P. Prescott and M. Vitoria, *The Modern Law of Copyright*, Butterworths, 1995, para. 5.14: 'Since a director is almost always responsible for the manner in which a film is shot, it is he who would supply the film with its original character and therefore be the author of the dramatic work.'

[101] *Ibid.*

[102] *Ibid.* Note that, under joint authorship rules, if there is no collaboration between the director and the screenwriter (the first starting where the second stopped), the director is likely to be the sole author of the final dramatic work derived from the script. See para. 122.

[103] On that question, see paras. 120 *et seq.*

[104] In absence of an express assignment, an implied licence or even assignment could be found by the courts. See paras. 121 and 156.

[105] Under the 1911 Act, an author (provided he was the first owner of copyright) could not assign or license part or the whole of his copyright for longer than twenty-five years after his death (s. 5(2)). The provision was repealed by the 1956 Act, but, due to transitional provisions (1956 Act, Sched. 8; 1988 Act, Sched. 1, para. 27.), it is still applicable to assignments and licences made before 1 June 1957. However, it does not apply to 'assignment of the copyright in a collective work or a licence to publish a work or part of a work as part of a collective work'. Since a 'collective work' was defined under s. 35 as 'any work written in distinct parts by different authors, or in which works or parts

assignments were deemed not to include modes of exploitation not developed at the time of the production, which then might have been retained by the author(s).[106] Note that the right vested in the producer in relation to the photographs would not allow him to exploit the dramatic work conveyed by the succession of these photographs if the owner of the right in the dramatic work was different.

The major problem with this scheme concerns the calculation of the *duration of copyright*, which requires the determination and the tracing of film co-authors. On that point, however, it is ironic to observe that the situation would have been more complex if production companies were regarded as authors, since no special rules as to duration in that case were provided for in the 1911 Act.[107] Also, individual producers or employers might not be easier to identify and trace than authors.

In contrast with the UK solution, in the US, the work-made-for-hire doctrine codified in the 1909 Act solved the problems of ownership and authorship by giving authorship in any case to the employer.[108]

Under present law in the UK, the determination of the author and the first owner of the copyright in pre-1957 films is made according to the provisions of the 1911 Act.[109]

19.   The influence of new technologies

Major technological evolutions of the film industry took place while the 1911 Act was in force. The introduction of *sound films* in the late 1920s[110]

---

of works of different authors are incorporated', audiovisual works were not affected by reversionary rights. See *Copinger and Skone James on Copyright*, 13th edn, 1991, para. 5–31, p. 116.

[106] Here, an analogy could be drawn from the cases concerning the question of whether the grant of film rights included the right to make a sound film, if these were not developed at the date of the contract. In *Pathé Pictures Ltd* v. *Bancroft* [1928–35] MCC 403, it was held that a licence to make a version of the work 'in moving picture films' does not authorise the production of a sound film, but that a licence of 'cinematographic rights' would allow this. In *Hospital for Sick Children* v. *Walt Disney Productions Inc.* [1968] Ch 52, it was held that the grant, in 1919, of a licence to adapt a work 'in cinematographic or moving picture films' did not grant the right to produce sound films (see *Copinger and Skone James on Copyright*, 13th edn, 1991, paras. 5–51 *et seq.*). Accordingly, the consent of the co-authors of pre-1957 films, provided they were not under a contract of service for their production, would be needed for the release of these films on videotape or laserdisc, or for the production of derivative works such as computer games (at least when the assignment was of listed rights and not of the whole copyright).

[107] Production companies might be difficult to trace, and their 'death' might be difficult to ascertain.

[108] See para. 109.

[109] CDPA 1988, Sched. 1, para. 11. However, for moral rights, authorship is determined according to the provisions of the 1988 Act (Sched. 1, para. 10); see para. 279.

[110] 'The Jazz Singer' (1927): a few scenes had sound added to them by phonograms; the first optical soundtrack was released with the film 'Hallelujah' (MGM, King Vidor) in

did not create problems in terms of protection; the soundtrack (the optical recording of sounds on the film strip) could be protected as a 'contrivance by means of which sounds may be mechanically reproduced' under section 19(1) of the 1911 Act, i.e. as a sound recording.[111]

There was some hesitation, however, about whether *broadcasting* was encompassed in the definition of 'performance' in section 35 of the Act[112] and could be considered as a 'public' performance of the underlying works (especially if the programme was only received in the privacy of homes).[113] In any case, a fixation was necessary to trigger copyright protection, and television pictures were held not to be protected when no previous recording took place.[114]

Moreover, with the development of *video technology* in the 1950s, it could be asked whether a film recorded on video only was produced by 'a process analogous to photography' and could trigger protection as a series of photographs under the 1911 Act. On the one hand, as Laddie, Prescott and Vitoria point out, both processes are analogous because they 'use the action of light to produce a permanent record of an image'; on the other hand, they are different, the first process being chemical, the second electronic.[115]

1929; the automatic synchronisation of sounds and projection cameras was developed at the beginning of the century.

[111] In contrast, protection of the film soundtrack became a long-standing problem under US copyright. See e.g. E. F. Brylawski, 'Motion Picture Soundtrack Music: A Gap or Gaff in Copyright Protection?' (1993) 40 *Journal of the Copyright Society of the USA* 333–48.

[112] ' "Performance" means any acoustic presentation of a work and any visual representation of any dramatic action in a work, including such a representation made by means of any mechanical instruments.'

[113] For such an assimilation, see *Messager* v. *British Broadcasting Co. Ltd* [1927] 2 KB 543; 138 LT 572; *Chappell & Co. Ltd* v. *Associated Radio Co. of Australia Ltd* [1925] VLR 350; and in the US, *Remick & Co.* v. *American Auto-Accessories Co.* [1923–8] MCC 173; but in *Mellor* v. *Australian Broadcasting Commission* [1940] AC 491, the Privy Council held that 'a broadcast *per se* is not an acoustic representation of the work' and that 'if the broadcast is picked up only by listeners in private it might be difficult to establish that there is a public performance'. The Privy Council, however, ruled that, whether the performance of a work in the studio was public or private, the broadcaster had facilitated its public performance by any listener who uses a loudspeaker to perform the programme in public. In *Performing Right Society Ltd* v. *Hammond's Bradford Brewery Co. Ltd* [1934] Ch 121, the defendants, hotel owners, made songs audible to their visitors through a loudspeaker; these were broadcast by the BBC under a licence which authorised only 'audition and reception by means of broadcasting for domestic and private use'; the court held that the defendants engaged in unauthorised public performance. See also *Performing Right Society Ltd* v. *Gillette Industries Ltd* [1943] Ch 167 and the Canadian case of *Canadian Admiral Corp. Ltd* v. *Rediffusion Inc.* (1954) 20 CPR 75; 14 Fox'Pat. C. 114.

[114] *Canadian Admiral Corp. Ltd* v. *Rediffusion Inc.* (1954) 20 CPR 75; 14 Fox Pat. C. 114(retransmission of sport broadcasts).

[115] H. Laddie, P. Prescott and M. Vitoria, *The Modern Law of Copyright*, Butterworths, 1995, para. 5.11. Note, however, that video recording was sufficient a fixation in relation to the dramatic audiovisual work conveyed. In any case, VCRs were invented in 1956, and it appears that televisual productions came to be recorded on videotape by broadcasters only after commencement of the 1956 Act.

These combined elements created uncertainties for broadcasters eager to stop unauthorised copying or rebroadcasting of their recorded or 'live' programmes.

20.   Infringement of films under the 1911 Act

In contrast with the old law, the 1911 Act granted film-makers a broad protection against unauthorised *copying* and theatrical *performance* of their works.[116] Concerning *adaptations*, a distinction must be made between the two bases for protection of film works. With the 1911 Act, it became clear that a dramatic work could be infringed by the sole borrowing of its plot and incidents, even if its actual words and phrases were not used or imitated.[117] Accordingly, adaptations from a film made without actual lifting of its frames or images could infringe the right in the dramatic work conveyed. Concerning the sequences of frames protected as photographs, infringement was not strictly limited to the actual lifting of images; in some circumstances, the shooting of similar scenes could infringe the copyright in the photographs.[118] However, this was confined to close imitations of original features of the photograph and would not prevent adaptations, sequels and even remakes of the film.

Of course, the lifting of a single image from the film would infringe the copyright in the frame as a photograph but was probably not substantial enough to infringe the copyright in the dramatic work.[119]

21.   Influence of the 1911 Act

The system set up by the 1911 Act was adopted under Australian,[120] Canadian,[121] Indian,[122] Irish,[123] New Zealand[124] and other UK-influenced

---

[116] See *Fenning Film Service* v. *Wolverhampton & Cinemas* [1914] 3 KB 1171; *Falcon* v. *Famous Players Film Co.* [1926] 2 KB 474 (unauthorised exhibition of film).

[117] *Rees* v. *Melville* [1911–16] MCC 96; *Sutton Vane* v. *Famous Players Film Co. Ltd* [1928–35] MCC 6; *Dagnall* v. *British and the Dominion Film Corp. Ltd* [1928–35] MCC 391; *Bolton* v. *British International Pictures Ltd* [1936–45] MCC 20; and *Wilmer* v. *Hutchinson & Co. etc. Ltd* [1936–45] MCC 13; for the same concerning infringement of literary works, see *Corelli* v. *Gray* (1913) 29 TLR 570; 30 TLR 116; *Kelly* v. *Cinema Houses Ltd* [1928–35] MCC 362; *De Manduit* v. *Gaumont British Picture Corp. Ltd* [1936–45] MCC 292; *Holland* v. *Vivian Van Damm Productions Ltd* [1936–45] MCC 69; and *Harman Pictures NV* v. *Osborne* [1967] 1 WLR 723. For the component elements protected under the dramatic copyright, see para. 185.

[118] *Copinger and Skone James on Copyright*, 13th edn, 1991, para. 8–62; H. Laddie, P. Prescott and M. Vitoria, *The Modern Law of Copyright*, Butterworths, 1995, para. 3.58; see *Baumann* v. *Fussell* [1978] RPC 485, CA; and *Krisarts SA* v. *Briarfine Ltd* [1977] FSR 557. Compare with the present law: see para. 181.

[119] Note, however, that all dramatic films were constituted by photographs, where a great deal of films protected as photographs did not attract protection as a dramatic work.

[120] Copyright Act 1912.   [121] Copyright Act 1913.   [122] Copyright Act 1914.

[123] Copyright Act 1927.   [124] Copyright Act 1913.

copyright laws.[125] It is still relevant under current UK copyright for pre-1957 films,[126] for pre-1969 films in Australia,[127] for pre-1958 films in India[128] and for pre-1963 films in New Zealand.[129] Interestingly, this system is still in force for all films under Canadian law,[130] but the question of authorship of dramatic films is still debated.[131]

22.   The 1956 Act: a specific subject-matter for film protection

The 1956 Act, which in many aspects was a modern Copyright Act, introduced in relation to audiovisual works a radical departure from the previous law, and from both authors' rights systems and US copyright.

The Act expressly excluded cinematographic works from the definition of photographs and dramatic works.[132] Instead, it introduced new subject-matter applicable to film works under the form of 'Part II' copyrights, i.e. 'entrepreneurial' copyrights which did not require originality as a condition for protection. The specific subject-matter for film protection was the 'cinematograph film', but broadcasts were equally protected under a distinct Part II copyright. The Cable and Broadcasting Act 1984 later introduced a copyright in cable programmes.

According to section 13(10) of the Act, the author of the 'cinematograph film' was 'the person by whom the arrangements necessary for the making of the film were undertaken', i.e. the producer.[133] The Gregory Committee Report shows that the rationale behind this new subject-matter was both to avoid multiple claims for authorship in what are, in essence, composite works, while complying formally with the provisions

---

[125] E.g. in South Africa with the Copyright Act 1916.
[126] 1956 Act, Sched. 7, paras. 14–17; 1988 Act, Sched. 1, para. 7. See also 1988 Act, Sched. 1, paras. 10 and 11.
[127] Copyright Act 1968, s. 222.   [128] Copyright Act 1957, s. 79.
[129] Copyright Act 1994, Sched. 1, para. 12.
[130] Under RSC 1985, c. C-42, s. 2; SC 1993, c. 44, s. 53(2). Note, however, that, following the North American Free Trade Implementation Act of 1993, the requirement of originality has been removed for 'cinematograph' productions. It is remarkable that these are still protectable as a sub-category of dramatic and photographic works, which remain original descriptions. See W. L. Hayhurst, 'Audiovisual Productions: Some Copyright Aspects' (1994) *Intellectual Property Journal* 319.
[131] See D. Létourneau, *Le droit d'auteur de l'audiovisuel: une culture et un droit en évolution, Etude comparative*, Yvon Blais, 1995.
[132] Section 48. '"photograph" means any product of photography or of any process akin to photography, other than part of a cinematograph film'. '"dramatic work" includes a choreographic work or entertainment in dumb show if reduced to writing in the form in which the work or entertainment is to be presented, but does not include a cinematograph film, as distinct from a scenario or script for a cinematograph film'.
[133] See paras. 114 *et seq.*

of the Berne Convention,[134] and to avoid the problems of the determination of originality.[135]

The idea of a protection of broadcasts as *sui generis* works was already widespread in 1956,[136] but had never been translated in copyright terms. The reasons behind a separate protection of broadcasts are dealt with very rapidly in the Gregory Report:

the position of the BBC, as we see it, is not, in principle, very different from that of a gramophone company or a film company. It assembles its own programmes and transmits them at considerable cost and skill. When using copyright material it pays the copyright owner and it seems to us nothing more than natural justice that it should be given the power to control any subsequent copying of these programmes by any means.[137]

This justification may appear less than adequate, especially considering the rejection by the same report of the idea of 'copyrights' in sporting events and performances.[138] At least broadcasting organisations were now guaranteed a stronger title in infringement actions, without the need to rely on underlying copyrights.[139]

The specific subject-matter for films, the 'cinematograph film', was defined in section 13(10) as:

any sequence of visual images recorded on material of any description (whether translucent or not) so as to be capable, by the use of that material,
(a) of being shown as a moving picture, or
(b) of being recorded on other material (whether translucent or not), by the use of which it can be so shown.

[134] Gregory Committee Report, Cmd 8662, 1952, Parliamentary Papers, 1951–2, vol. 9, para. 99: 'Nor, in view of the large number of persons now involved in the making of a modern film...can we regard it as practicable to treat a film as a work of "joint authorship", with all the complexity of claims that would result.'

[135] 'The difficulty of deciding what constitutes originality must be manifest; on any definition, some types of film, e.g. newsreels, would appear to be deprived of copyright protection, though there appears to be no equitable reason why they should be' (para. 100). 'We recommend therefore that a film, together with its soundtrack if it has one, should be regarded as a distinct type of work in which a distinct copyright may subsist.'

[136] France had proposed the protection of radio broadcasts at the 1928 Rome Conference of the Berne Convention. See WIPO Guide to the Rome Convention and to the Phonogram Convention, chapter XIX, p. 11.

[137] Gregory Committee Report, Cmd 8662, 1952, p. 117. This corresponds to the rationale exposed in the various drafts leading to the Rome Convention. See WIPO Guide to the Rome Convention and to the Phonogram Convention.

[138] Gregory Committee Report, Cmd 8662, 1952, p. 121.

[139] And without the problems raised by originality. The protection of broadcasts or cable programmes is thus advantageous in order to protect live programmes which do not convey protected underlying works (e.g. sport games).

This definition shows that, contrary to the general assumption[140] and the use of the term 'film', the copyright was not in the visual recording, as it is under the present Act, but in the (recorded) underlying visual work ('sequences of images...recorded').[141] As a consequence, from 1956 onwards, there may be separate and independent copyrights in (a) (say) a sketch (as dramatic work), (b) a film scenario adapted from such sketch (as dramatic work) and (c) the recorded final audiovisual work produced from such scenario (as cinematograph film); but this final audiovisual work could not be protected under the dramatic copyright or as a series of photographs.[142]

Film soundtracks were excluded from protection as sound recordings and became protected as part of the cinematograph film with which they were associated.[143]

Finally, under the 1956 Act, cinematograph films were protected without limit in time until first published (or registered for certain films) and the copyright expired fifty years after such publication (or registration).[144]

---

[140] Including my own in 'Authorship of Films and Implementation of the Term Directive' (1994) 16 EIPR 319 at 320.

[141] In contrast, in s. 1(2)(d) of the 1911 Act, the same expression, 'cinematograph film', designated a 'contrivance by which the work may be represented or delivered' (distinct from the 'cinematograph production' embodied therein, which is protected as a dramatic work). Note also the definition of cinematograph film in the Dramatic and Musical Performers' Protection Act 1925, as amended by the 1956 Act (Sched. 6): 'The expression "cinematograph film" means any print, negative, tape or other article on which a performance of a dramatic or musical work or part thereof is recorded for the purpose of visual reproduction...' This continuing hesitation in terminology is confusing. In *Netage Pty Ltd* v. *Cantley* (1985) 6 IPR 200 (NSW SC), a text similar to s. 13(10) in the Australian Act 1968 was held to 'include videotapes'. See also, in *EMI Ltd* v. *Sharif*, unreported, 2 February 1981, Chancery Division, *per* Whitford J: 'Video cassettes are, as I have indicated, in essence cinematograph films.' Compare with *Foo Loke Ying* v. *Television Broadcasts Ltd* [1987] FSR 57 (Malaysia SC), on a different definition. More precisely, the definition of s. 13(10) includes sequences of images, etc. recorded on videotape.

[142] The new scheme did not apply to films made before the commencement of s. 13, which remained protected as photographic and/or dramatic works, as the case may be (1956 Act, Sched. 7, paras. 14–16). *Prima facie*, commencement was 1 June 1957, but the 1956 Act had different commencement dates for foreign films. See H. Laddie, P. Prescott and M. Vitoria, *The Modern Law of Copyright*, Butterworths, 1995, para. 5.30. Laddie, Prescott and Vitoria highlight problems raised by these confusing transitional provisions (*ibid.*, para. 5.58). This does not, however, appear to create a cumulation of protection for the films concerned, but rather delays the implementation of the 1956 scheme. Para. 7 of Sched. 1 to the 1988 Act might also have substituted a uniform commencement date for the 1956 scheme (cf. H. Laddie, P. Prescott and M. Vitoria, *The Modern Law of Copyright*, Butterworths, 1995, para. 5.51).

[143] Sections 12(9) and 13(9).   [144] Section 13.

23.   Infringement of films under the 1956 Act

The 1956 Act solved the uncertainties associated with broadcasting under the previous Act by treating broadcasting and later inclusion in a cable programme service as a separate category of infringing acts. In general, the scope of rights granted to film-makers remained similar, but, under the 1956 Act, the copyright in the cinematograph film granted a narrower protection against adaptations or imitations than the dramatic copyright under the previous Act.[145]

24.   The 1988 Act: continuation or departure
from the 1956 Act?

The scheme inaugurated by the 1956 Act was said not to have been modified by the 1988 Act.[146] This is true to a certain extent only. The new Act does not repeat the previous distinction between Part I (original copyright works) and Part II (other subject-matter) copyrights, but continues to treat audiovisual works, broadcasts and cable programmes as specific descriptions of work which do not have to satisfy any requirement of originality. In that respect, the main difference from the previous law is that, under the new Act, the specific subject-matter for audiovisual works, the 'film', is defined in section 5(1) as the visual recording itself, and not as the underlying sequence of images. Then it can be said *prima facie* that cinematograph and audiovisual works are not given protection as such, but only through their recording.[147]

As before, according to section 9(2) (as enacted) the author of the 'film' is the 'person by whom the arrangements necessary for the making of the film are undertaken', i.e. the producer.[148] As a consequence, the director and the authors of the component elements (script, music, decor, etc.) are deprived of any copyright interest in the 'film', and also in the final cinematograph or audiovisual work fixed in film form only.

Contributory works continue to be treated as before, but performers are now granted a right akin to copyright which presents some peculiarities.[149]

---

[145] Compare with the situation under the 1988 Act: see para. 184 below.

[146] See R. Durie, 'Copyright, Designs and Patent Act 1988: The Key Changes for the Film Industry' (1989) 11 EIPR 197; and most law books on the subject. The Whitford Committee, Cmnd 6732, 1977, did not recommend significant changes in the way films were treated under the 1956 Act.

[147] Other differences include the treatment of film soundtracks (see para. 78) and the duration of protection.

[148] See paras. 22 and 25.

[149] Rights not generally assignable or transmissible, scope limited to recording, live broadcasting of the performance and dealings with illicit recordings, etc.

Curiously, the film director, who is refused authorship in the final work, is granted moral rights in the film.[150]

25.   A protection of audiovisual works as dramatic works under the 1988 Act

That being said, there appears to be a major difficulty with the scheme apparently continued by the 1988 Act. In the new Act, although audio-visual works are still expressly excluded from protection as a series of photographs,[151] the exclusion has been removed from the definition of dramatic works.[152] Moreover, it is now clear that the fixation of a dramatic work can take the form of a recording on film.[153] One must then admit, as several authors have suggested, that a door has been opened for the courts to consider claims for protection of audiovisual works, as distinct from their recording, under the heading of dramatic works.[154] This theory was recently confirmed by the Court of Appeal in *Norowzian* v. *Arks Ltd.*[155]

As a result of the decision in *Norowzian*, the protection scheme for 'dramatic' audiovisual works under the 1988 Act is now close to the scheme adopted in relation to musical or sound works. For example, in a theatrical film, there may be a copyright in the script(s), as dramatic work(s), but also in the final audiovisual work derived from the script. This copyright would be distinct from the copyright in the recording (the 'film'), in the same way as it is distinguished in the case of a musical phonogram between the copyrights in the musical work(s) and in the sound recording.

The theory acknowledged in *Norowzian* has many consequences in relation to immediate post-1988 'dramatic' audiovisual works. First, it gives a copyright in the dramatic audiovisual work to the director and

---

[150] See paras. 237 and 269. Accordingly, the right to be identified as author becomes the 'right to be identified as director'.

[151] Section 4(2).

[152] Section 3(1). There is no precise explanation for this removal in the parliamentary debates. See HL Debs, vol. 490, p. 837. See also New Zealand Copyright Act 1994, s. 1.

[153] Sections 3 and 178.

[154] Question raised by D. Lester and P. Mitchell, *Joynson-Hicks on UK Copyright Law*, Sweet & Maxwell, 1989, p. 5. See P. Kamina, 'Authorship of Films and Implementation of the Term Directive' (1994) 16 EIPR 319; see also H. Laddie, P. Prescott and M. Vitoria, *The Modern Law of Copyright*, Butterworths, 1995, para. 5.26, and at paras. 5.21 and 5.44; J. Holyoak and P. Torremans, *Intellectual Property Law*, Butterworths, 1995, pp. 153–4 and 162. Also suggested in W. R. Cornish, *Intellectual Property*, 3rd edn, Sweet & Maxwell, 1996, p. 342, n. 98 and p. 410, n. 63. The general provisions as to construction in s. 172 are not of any help, since this modification does not amount to a mere 'change of expression' without legal consequences.

[155] *Norowzian* v. *Arks Ltd (No. 2)* [2000] EMLR 67; [2000] FSR 363, CA. See para. 56.

maybe to other contributors as joint authors, provided they do not work under a contract of service.[156] Of course, in practice creative personnel in film productions always assign to film producers the copyright they might contribute in the course of their employment.[157] However, this situation could strengthen the bargaining power of the main contributors and redirect to them part of the returns from the exploitation of the work; it could even enable the constitution of licensing bodies in relation to these dramatic works.[158] Secondly, these authors are granted a moral right in their dramatic work.[159] Thirdly, the copyright in the dramatic work now guarantees assignee-producers greater protection against infringement by adaptation.[160]

Until the entry into force of the Duration of Copyright and Rights in Performances Regulations 1995, another consequence was the extension of the duration of protection for audiovisual works. The film producer, as assignee of the underlying dramatic audiovisual work, benefited from protection lasting fifty years p.m.a., as against a shorter period for the 'film' (fifty years post making or publication). However, on that point, the Duration of Copyright and Rights in Performances Regulations 1995[161] extended the duration for the 'film' to the standard of dramatic works.[162]

Finally, this theory brings UK copyright closer to authors' rights systems which implemented a dual protection of audiovisual works, which could facilitate the international flow of fees from the exploitation of 'neighbouring rights' in film recordings.

26.   The situation in Ireland

The scheme for film protection under the Irish Copyright Act of 1963 was similar to the one in the UK Copyright Act 1956, and remained so until the Copyright and Related Rights Act 2000. Audiovisual works were protected under a specific (non-original) description of work, the 'cinematographic film', under the same regime as described for the UK 1956 Act.[163] This film was also excluded from protection as a dramatic work or as a series of photographs.[164] The copyright in the film vested in its 'maker', defined as the person by whom arrangements necessary for the making of the film are undertaken, or, in the absence of an agreement to the contrary, in the person who commissioned the making of the film

---

[156] See paras. 120 *et seq.*
[157] And producers can benefit from implied licences or even assignments. See paras. 121 and 156.
[158] Compare with the situation in continental Europe described at paras. 173 and 174.
[159] See para. 240.   [160] See paras. 184 and 185.   [161] SI 1995 No. 3297.
[162] Thus incorrectly implementing the Directive. See para. 100.
[163] Copyright Act 1963, s. 18.   [164] Section 2(1).

and paid or agreed to pay for it in money or money's worth.[165] Copyright subsisting in a cinematographic film was to continue to subsist until the end of the period of fifty years from the end of the year in which the film was first published.[166]

The Copyright and Related Rights Act 2000 follows the scheme of its UK counterpart, as amended by the Copyright Regulations of 1995 and 1996. It retains the same list of copyright material associated with film works, and adopts the same rules as to authorship and initial ownership. In particular, the film producer and the film director are co-authors of the film and joint owners of the corresponding copyright. The provisions on exclusive rights, duration, limitations, transfers and moral rights are similar to the UK provisions, subject to minor differences. A notable difference, however, is the introduction of moral rights in favour of performers[167] and film producers.[168]

PART II

The evolution of film in authors' rights systems

27.   Overview

Authors' rights legislation acquired its characteristic features with regard to film protection after the First World War. The best known of these features is the regime of moral rights granted to film authors and to authors of adapted works. In most *droit d'auteur* countries, the protection developed in relation to other classes of works was applied with very few qualifications to film works.

Another major characteristic is the treatment of the question of film authorship. In authors' rights countries, as a matter of principle the author of a copyright work cannot be a legal person. In addition, authorship traditionally carries moral rights entitlement but also initial entitlement to copyright. In the first part of the past century, there was a tendency for case law throughout Europe to vest the rights in the cinematographic film in the film producer, using various legal doctrines.[169] However, this view did not prevail, and in modern authors' rights systems film producers are denied authorship in the film. The position of the creative artist is also reinforced in certain countries by the fact that employment rules do

---

[165] Section 18(3).
[166] Section 18(2). The duration provisions of the Term Directive were implemented by the European Communities (Term of Protection of Copyright) Regulations 1995 (SI No. 158 of 1995).
[167] See para. 339.   [168] See para. 242.   [169] See paras. 28 and 135.

not generally convey the copyright in the cinematographic works to the producer-employer (or commissioner).[170]

The third feature of film protection on the continent, which is probably the most important for practitioners, is the development of what authors' representatives call 'authorial rights', that is, economic rights or interests retained by film authors, usually in the form of a right to proportional or equitable remuneration.[171]

Finally, another specific feature of these systems is the dichotomy between authors' rights on the one hand, and neighbouring rights on the other. The category of 'neighbouring right' was created in continental Europe to accommodate those rights in works which are not the result of the creative activity of an 'author'. This, in fact, is the only common element between the various neighbouring rights, which are indeed rather diverse: they include performers' rights, rights in sound recordings, in audiovisual recordings and rights in broadcasts and cable programmes. In contrast, under UK copyright, most of these rights have been included in the realm of copyright.[172] Another common element of neighbouring rights is the absence of any requirement of 'originality' as a prerequisite for protection. This distinction between copyright and neighbouring rights is viewed in continental Europe as a way of preserving the orthodoxy of authors' rights. This separation made possible the definition of rights more adapted to commercial exploitation: except for performers, moral rights are not granted to neighbouring rights owners, transfers of rights are facilitated, etc.

Each of the above characteristics will be studied in detail in this book. What follows is a brief description of the evolution of authors' rights systems since 1908. Emphasis is placed on the definition of protected subject-matter and on authorship rules, as these elements are fundamental in order to determine the current status of old European films.[173]

28. The evolution of film protection in France

In France, the matter of film protection remained regulated until 1957 by the revolutionary laws of 1791 and 1793, which were left almost

---

[170] In addition, where implemented, statutory presumptions of assignment to the film producer are limited in scope.

[171] See paras. 148 and 169.

[172] This is true for the sound recording copyright since 1911, and for broadcasts since 1957. Performers' rights, however, are not copyright.

[173] Transitional provisions regarding duration and war extensions are described in paras. 102 *et seq.*

untouched.[174] As a result, copyright law was developed by case law and legal authors.[175]

Cinematographic works were protected as original works of authorship. The distinction suggested in the Berne Convention between 'dramatic' films protected as literary works and 'non-dramatic' films protected as series of photographs was not really discussed by legal commentators and was not instituted by case law. In a system in which photographs were protected as original works under a full copyright,[176] the protection of documentary films and newsreels did not raise difficulties.[177] Also, the absence of a requirement of fixation as a prerequisite for copyright protection facilitated the protection of television works and live television shows. As for other classes of works, protection was granted for fifty years p.m.a.

The main difficulties arose in relation to authorship. There was a tendency in the pre-Second World War French *droit d'auteur* to consider the film producer as the sole author of the cinematographic work. The idea was rejected by a majority of legal commentators, but had a few spokesmen in the 1930s, and was at one point favoured by case law. Some cases conferred authorship on a film producer by virtue of the contract of employment entered into with the director and other contributors.[178] Others presumed authorship without the help of any legal concept.[179] In the *Mascarade* case,[180] the Paris Court of Appeal considered that the

[174] With the notable exception of duration provisions.
[175] For the law before the 1957 Act, see e.g. Chartier, *Les droits du musicien sur son oeuvre*, 1923; Devillez, *L'Oeuvre cinématographique et la propriété artistique*, 1932; Marchais, *La cinématographie dans ses rapports avec le droit d'auteur*, 1912; Marotte, *De l'application des droits d'auteurs et d'artistes aux oeuvres cinématographiques*, 1930; and Meignen, *Le Code du Cinéma*, 1919.
[176] Leading to a situation in which almost all photographs could be protected. See e.g. Toulouse Court of Appeal, 17 July 1911, *Revue Dalloz Périodique*, 1912, II, p. 161; Tribunal of First Instance of Seine, 24 April 1953, *Gazette du Palais*, 1953, II, p. 192, for press photos.
[177] In any case, art. 14(2) of the Berne Convention, as modified in 1948, prevented the exclusion of documentary films and newsreels from protection as literary and artistic works. In addition, the originality criterion does not appear to have raised problems for photographs. 'News photographs' were protected as original works under French law. See e.g. Tribunal of First Instance of Seine, 24 April 1953, *Gazette du Palais*, 1953, II, p. 192.
[178] Paris Court of Appeal, 10 February 1936, *Guerlais v. Roubaud*, *Gazette du Palais*, 1936, I, p. 691; Tribunal of First Instance of Seine, 24 May 1938, *Gazette du Palais*, 1938, II, p. 508.
[179] Dijon Court of Appeal, 8 January 1936, *Gazette du Palais*, 1936, 1, p. 339, *Revue Dalloz Hebdomadaire*, 1936, p. 137.
[180] Tribunal of First Instance of Seine, interlocutory, 19 March 1935, *Gazette du Palais*, 1935, II, p. 62, *Revue Dalloz Sirey*, 1935, II, p. 101; and Paris Court of Appeal, 16 March 1939, *Gazette du Palais*, 1939, II, p. 210; *Revue Dalloz Sirey*, 1940, II, p. 35.

producer was the *only* author of the film, and that this author could be a legal person. The court used the concept of 'collective works' (*oeuvres collectives*) in order to vest authorship in the producer. This special category of works under French law was developed in cases involving dictionaries and is conceived as a variety of composite works made by several authors and published by an entrepreneur under his name, in which it is impossible to identify the part contributed by each author. In that case, the publisher could be considered as author of the work (even if it is a legal person, which was a remarkable exception to the general rule that an author can only be a natural person).[181] In the following years, French courts gave several judgments in favour of the producer. The appellate court decision in *Mascarade* was eventually overturned eight years later by the Supreme Court,[182] which did not directly consider the question of authorship, but clearly refused *as a general principle* to consider films as 'collective works'. Later cases rejected the concept of the producer as the sole author of the film.

The film director, the writer of the scenario and of the dialogue, and the musical composer were generally considered as the co-authors of the cinematographic work. Some legal commentators included in the list authors of adapted works. Authors of pre-existing works were protected without difficulties against reproduction of their works in cinematographic films[183] and against performance of their works through exhibition in theatres or broadcasting.[184] The regime of moral rights developed by

---

[181] The Law of 1957 does not characterise the publisher of a collective work as 'author', but instead specifies that the author's rights are 'vested in it' (art. L.113–5 of the French Intellectual Property Code).

[182] Court of Cassation, Civil Chamber, 10 November 1947, *Revue Dalloz*, 1947, p. 328; *La Semaine Juridique*, 1948, II, No. 4166, note Plaisant; *Revue Dalloz Sirey*, 1948, I, p. 157, note Reynaud.

[183] The first decision to admit infringement by cinematography was Tribunal of First Instance of Seine, 10 February 1905, *Doyen v. Parnaland*, *Revue Dalloz Périodique*, 1905, II, p. 389; see also Court of Cassation, 27 February 1918, *Annales de la Propriété Industrielle*, 1919, p. 53, *Revue Dalloz Sirey*, 1918, I, p. 96 ('infringement of a dramatic work can result from the production of the cinematographic works based on the same elements as this work'); and Paris Court of Appeal, 4 January 1934, *Droit d'auteur*, 1934, p. 79 (infringement by unauthorised reproduction of a song in a film soundtrack).

[184] Bordeaux Court of Appeal, 11 February 1930, *Gazette du Palais*, 18 April 1930. The possibility of an infringement by public performance of a pre-existing work was first rejected by the courts (e.g. Lourdes Court of Appeal, 28 July 1905; and Pau Court of Appeal, 18 November 1904), but this trend changed with Tribunal of First Instance of Seine, 7 July 1908, *Revue Dalloz*, 1910, II, p. 83. See also Tribunal of First Instance of Seine, 18 December 1911, Paris Court of Appeal, 17 May 1912, *Annales de la Propriété Industrielle*, 1913, I, p. 65, *Revue Dalloz Sirey*, 1913, II, p. 141 (adaptation of Dumas' *The Three Musketeers*), Paris Court of Appeal, 19 December 1913, *Annales de la Propriété Industrielle*, 1914, I, p. 212 (infringement of the novel *Michel Strogoff*); and Paris Court of Appeal, 4 January 1933, *Gazette du Palais*, 1934, I, p. 164.

case law was applied early and without qualification to the exploitation of cinematographic films.[185]

In the absence of statutory provisions on copyright agreements, case law progressively constructed the bulk of rules on copyright transfers and authorial rights. Contracts were construed restrictively.[186] For example, French courts held that the grant of film rights did not encompass the right to make sound films;[187] but a contract could validly cover through a specific clause any means of exploitation unknown at the time of the agreement. Also, case law developed the concept that authorisation must be granted each time the work is communicated to a new audience (e.g. in case of distribution of television programmes in hotel rooms).

There was no requirement that authors be remunerated in the form of royalties or other form of 'equitable remuneration'. Authors of adapted works and film authors were usually paid a lump sum for the assignment of their copyright. Agreements concluded before the entry into force of the 1957 Act remain valid in this respect.

Finally, although the question was debated, the general agreement was that there was no copyright for performers.

29.   The French Law of 11 March 1957

The Law of 11 March 1957 on Literary and Artistic Property codified these solutions and clarified several aspects of copyright protection for films. The new law included 'cinematographic works and works produced by a process analogous to cinematography' in the (open) list of protected works.[188]

Concerning film authorship, article 14 of the Act provided that, save proof to the contrary, the following persons are presumed to be co-authors of a cinematographic work made in collaboration:

1. the author of the scenario;
2. the author of the adaptation;
3. the author of the dialogue;

---

[185] Paris Court of Appeal, 21 March 1939 (*Zigomar* case): the author of a novel granted film rights and later considered that the film adaptation mutilated his work; the contract was rescinded, and the film prohibited; he was also awarded damages (*Droit d'auteur*, 1920, p. 32).

[186] Paris Court of Appeal, 28 February 1902, *Revue Dalloz*, 1904, II, p. 11; Court of Cassation, Req., 10 November 1930, *Gazette du Palais*, 1930, II, p. 771; Tribunal of First Instance of Seine, 9 March 1932, *Droit d'auteur*, 1932, p. 68; and Tribunal of First Instance of Seine, 16 March 1934.

[187] Tribunal of First Instance of Seine, 28 November 1934, *Revue Dalloz*, 1936, II, p. 97, note Sallé de la Marnière.

[188] Art. 3.

4. the author of the musical compositions with or without words, specially composed for the work; and

5. the director.

The Act immediately adds, without further specification, that 'when an audiovisual work is adapted from a pre-existing work or script which is still protected, the authors of the original work shall be considered as authors of the new work'. This extension of the list of co-authors to authors of adapted works is a specific feature of French and Belgian copyright laws.[189]

The new Act codified the protection of moral rights in its present form, but introduced qualifications in relation to films. Article 15 of the Act provides that, when an author refuses to complete or cannot complete his contribution by reason of *force majeure*, he cannot object to the use, for the completion of the audiovisual work, of the part of his contribution which is already made.[190] Article 16 draws a distinction between the exercise of moral rights before and after completion of the audiovisual work. It provides that moral rights can only be exercised once the work is completed.[191] However, once the film is completed, the normal scheme applies and moral rights can still be exercised by each co-author.

The Law of 1957 also codified the general principle of the narrow construction of copyright transfers. Its article 30 provides that a transfer of the performing right does not imply the transfer of the reproduction right, and, conversely, specifies that, in case of a total transfer of copyright, the effect of that transfer is limited to the means of exploitation provided in the contracts. In addition, article 31 establishes an obligation to detail the scope of the transfer in the agreement (as to its scope, purpose, place and duration), and article 33 prohibits total transfers of economic rights in future works. Transfers of copyright for unforeseeable means of exploitation are allowed, provided the clause is drafted in specific terms and the author is granted a share of the profits derived from this exploitation.[192]

More importantly for our purpose, the Law of 11 March 1957 introduced a mandatory system of proportional remuneration in the form of royalties, which is applicable to film authors and authors of adapted works.[193]

It further defined in detail the regime applicable to publishing and performing contracts.

---

[189] See para. 137.
[190] He will nevertheless keep his full status of author with regard to this contribution.
[191] See para. 290.   [192] Art. 38.
[193] Art. 5, subject to limited exemptions. See para. 173.

30.   The French Act of 3 July 1985 and the new Intellectual Property Code

The new Act of 3 July 1985 amended the 1957 Act with regard to new technological developments and means of exploitation. It addresses questions such as satellite and cable distribution, private copying, etc.

The amendment Act includes the category of cinematographic works in the wider category of 'audiovisual works', defined as 'works consisting of moving sequences of images, with or without sound'.[194]

In addition, it regulates film production contracts for the first time.[195] The amended 1957 Act provides *inter alia* that, subject to agreement to the contrary, the contract between the film producer and the co-authors of an audiovisual work conveys to the producer the exclusive exploitation rights in the film.[196] The musical composers are excluded from this presumption of assignment. The Code further provides that the remuneration of the authors is due for each mode of exploitation of their work and that, when the public pays a price to receive communication of an audiovisual work, such remuneration must be proportional to such price, subject to any decreasing tariffs granted by the distributor to the operator (subject to limited exemptions allowing lump sum payments).[197] It also adapts the basic rules on publishing contracts (e.g. accounting reports, duty for producer to exploit the work in accordance with the usages of the profession, specific rights of the authors in case of bankruptcy or reorganisation of the publisher) to film production contracts.

The 1985 amendment Act introduced the protection of neighbouring rights into French law:[198] economic rights akin to copyright were granted to film producers in relation to fixations of their audiovisual works, to sound recording producers and to broadcasters. Performers enjoyed both economic rights and statutory moral rights of integrity and paternity.

Finally, the Act introduced a remuneration for private copying of phonograms and videograms[199] and renovated the status of authors' collecting societies.[200]

The provisions of the various intellectual property Acts and decrees, including the Act of 1957, as amended, were consolidated in the Intellectual Property Code in 1992.

---

[194] This definition was wide enough to encompass video technology and was held wide enough to cover videogames (Court of Cassation, 7 May 1986, RIDA, 1986, No. 129, *Revue Dalloz*, 1986, p. 405, note Edelman).
[195] Arts. 63–1 to 63–7.   [196] Art. 63–1 (with the exception of graphic and stage rights).
[197] Art. 63–2. See para. 173.   [198] Arts. 17–30.   [199] Arts. 31–37.
[200] Arts. 38–44.

31.   Legislation influenced by French law

In Belgium, the Law of 1886 was of course silent in the matter of cinematography. Legal doctrine and case law adopted the French solutions at the beginning of the century,[201] and showed the same hesitation concerning film authorship.[202] The Copyright Act of 30 June 1994 repeats the principles of the French Intellectual Property Code.

In Spain, films were protected by case law under the 1879 Copyright Act (supplemented by a Cinematographic Act of 31 May 1966), under a scheme similar to French law. The main difference in the regime consisted in the duration of protection, which was eighty years p.m.a. The new Act of 11 November 1987 introduced provisions close to the French 1957 and 1985 Acts. The duration of protection for films was reduced to sixty years p.m.a., but it is worth noting that this reduction does not affect pre-1987 films. The 1987 Act was amended by a series of Acts,[203] which were codified in one single Act in 1996.

In Portugal, films were protected under the Law of 3 June 1927. It included specific rules regarding film authorship: films reproducing (or adapting) original works were to be treated like original works, and were the exclusive property of the 'reproducer'. This 'reproducer' was thought not to be the film producer, but the point was subject to discussion. In contrast, films 'which do not constitute the reproduction or transformation of another work' were expressly considered as the property of the film producer. The Law of 17 September 1985 put Portuguese copyright into line with most solutions under Spanish and French law. Films, however, were only protected for fifty years post-publication or making. Portuguese copyright law is now codified in the Code of Copyright and Related Rights.

32.   The specifics of Italian copyright

In Italy, the Copyright Act of 1925 adopted an original scheme for film protection.[204] It mentioned in its article 2 cinematographic works as a specific subject-matter, distinct from dramatic works and photographs,

---

[201] See Becquet, *Droit des auteurs en matière de cinema*, 1947.
[202] E.g. Tribunal of First Instance of Brussels, 21 January 1939, *Droit d'auteur*, 1939, p. 93.
[203] E.g. Acts of 7 July 1992 (*droit de suite*, remuneration for private copying, protection of sound recordings, etc.), 23 December 1993 (software), 30 December 1994 (rental and lending), 11 October 1995 (term of protection) and 11 October 1995 (cable and satellite).
[204] See E. Piola Caselli, in H. L. Pinner (ed.), *World Copyright*, A. W. Sijthoff, Leyden, 1953, vol. I, *Verbo Cinematographic Works*.

and protected these works independently of any requirement of originality. Therefore, all films, whether original or not, be they dramatic or scientific films or simple newsreels, were protected under the Act.

Concerning authorship and ownership, article 20 provided that, save provision to the contrary in individual contracts, the copyright in the cinematographic work belonged equally to the author of the scenario and to the author of the film. It further added that, in the case of music specially commissioned for inclusion in the film, the copyright vested in equal parts in the author of the scenario, in the composer of the music and in the author of the film. The 'author of the film' was not identified in the Act. Legal commentators suggested that several creative contributors to the film could be considered as 'author'. The possibility of treating the film as a 'collective work' owned by the film producer was not excluded. In addition, article 21 of the Act provided that, unless otherwise provided, the 'author' of the film had the right to exhibit it, without the permission of the writer of the scenario and, if any, of the musical composer. These films were protected under the standard duration for copyright works, which was fifty years p.m.a.

It is also important to note that in Italy before the Law of 1941, formalities of deposit and registration were a condition for copyright protection (as copyright would lapse if they were not carried out).

33.   The Italian Act of 22 April 1941

The Law of 22 April 1941 reinforced the originality of Italian law.[205] As to the subject-matter for protection, article 2(6) referred to 'works of cinematographic art, whether in silent or sound form, provided they are not mere documentaries'. As a consequence, documentary films and newsreels were protected not under the cinematographic copyright, but only as series of photographs under a specific neighbouring right for non-original photographs.[206] This neighbouring right endured for twenty years from the making of the negatives,[207] compared with thirty years after making or public exhibition for cinematographic films.[208]

The Act sets out a list of the presumptive co-authors of cinematographic works, which consists of the author of the subject-matter or treatment, the author of the scenario, the composer of the music and the film director.[209] The cinematographic work thus produced is therefore

[205] See Giannini, in *Rivista Trimestrale di Diritto et Procedura Civile*, June 1953, p. 496; *Rivista di Diritto Commerciale*, July 1953.
[206] Part II, Chapter V, 'Rights relating to photographs'.
[207] Copyright Act, art. 92.   [208] *Ibid.*, art. 32.   [209] *Ibid.*, art. 44.

a work of joint authorship. However, the exploitation rights in the film are exercised by the film producer, as statutory 'assignee' of the authors, with the exception of dubbing rights and other adaptation rights relating to the film, which remain with film authors (unless otherwise provided). Concerning adapted works, this 'presumption' is limited to the reproduction right.[210] Each co-author was granted a moral right in the film (of paternity and integrity), but article 22 provides that this moral right cannot be exercised once the author has been informed of the modification of the film and has accepted it. Rules on contracts resemble the French rules of the 1957 Act, but are provided for publishing contracts only.

The rights in the non-original photographs belong to the photographer, but provisions as to photographs in Chapter V granted copyright to the employer or commissioner (subject to equitable remuneration in case of commission).[211] Performers were granted a neighbouring right in the form of a right to equitable remuneration for use or reproduction of their performance,[212] but also moral rights of integrity and paternity.[213]

A Decree of 8 January 1979 included photographs with creative character in the list of copyright works. These are distinct from non-original photographs, which are still protected under a neighbouring right. It also extended the duration of copyright in a film to fifty years after making or public exhibition.

34.   The evolution of German film copyright

In Germany, the Literary Copyright Act of 1901 and the Artistic Copyright Act of 1907 did not contain provisions regarding films, but legal commentators considered that films could be protected as series of photographs under the Law of 1907. This situation was modified with two amendment Acts of 22 May 1910, which were to remain in force until the reform of 1965.[214] The first amendment Act concerned literary and musical works, and the second artistic works and photographs.

As a result of these amendments, cinematographic films were protected under several headings, and could be classified in two categories. Cinematographic works as such (i.e. dramatic theatrical cinematographic films) were protected by a full copyright (both as an artistic work and

---

[210] *Ibid.*, art. 46.   [211] *Ibid.*, arts. 88 and 89.
[212] *Ibid.*, art. 80.   [213] *Ibid.*, arts. 81 and 83.
[214] For a detailed bibliography on pre-1965 German law, see F. Caro and G. Benkard, in H. L. Pinner (ed.), *World Copyright*, A. W. Sijthoff, Leyden, 1953, vol. I, *Verbo Cinematographic Works*.

as a work of literature). However, a cinematographic work could also be protected as a series of photographs. Documentary films and newsreels, which could not be considered as artistic or literary works, were only afforded the limited protection granted to photographs.

Films protected under full copyright were protected for fifty years p.m.a. if they were published. A film was considered published when negatives were offered for distribution or the film was exhibited in public. If the film was not published, it enjoyed perpetual protection. In contrast, films protected as photographs were only protected for twenty-five years after publication.[215]

In the absence of a specific provision in the Act, the determination of who was the author of a film protected under full copyright depended on the generally applicable rules on joint authorship. Under German copyright law, a joint work is a work in which contributions are not separate, in the sense that they cannot be exploited separately.[216] As a result, for most legal commentators, musical composers and authors of dialogue could not be considered as joint authors of the film. Thus, in most cases, the author of the film was the film director, possibly with the editor or the cinematographer as joint authors. Note, however, that, prior to the 1965 Act, some early case law considered the producer as first owner of the copyright in the film, on the ground that the film was the result of an organised collective activity, and that copyright must vest in the natural or legal person who organised it.[217] Other cases confined this quality to the creative contributors.[218] A German draft statute of 1954 granted the producer the copyright title to the film work.[219] This view did not eventually prevail.

Copyright transfers were restrictively construed. A grant of copyright without express or implied inclusion of film adaptation rights could not convey these rights.[220] Contracts were also often construed as exclusive or non-exclusive licences rather than assignments. Assignment of future works were prohibited.

For some legal commentators, performers were protected as authors of a 'derivative' work, constituted by their performance.

[215] Under an Act of 12 May 1940.   [216] See para. 137.

[217] *Reichsgericht* (Supreme Court in civil matters) 158, September 1938, pp. 321 *et seq.* at p. 324; *Kammergericht*, in MuW, 1923, p. 13; and MuW, 1926, p. 229; *Reichsarbeitsgericht* (Supreme Court in labour law), in *Ufita*, IV, p. 405.

[218] *Kammergericht*, in *Ufita*, XI, p. 55; see also RGZ 107, 16 June 1923, p. 65.

[219] According to its art. 93, the owner of the company producing the cinematographic work would have been 'considered as the author'. A moral right would have been granted to the director.

[220] Literary Copyright Act, art. 14(5).

35.   The German Act of 9 September 1965

The Act of 1965 profoundly modified German copyright law. In the new Act, the definition of films includes 'cinematographic works, including works produced by processes similar to cinematography', thus encompassing documentary films and newsreels.[221] In order to avoid difficulties with borderline works, article 95 of the Act specifies that the regime of cinematographic works (with the exception of presumptions of assignments) is applicable *mutatis mutandis* to 'sequences of images and to sequences of images of images and sound which are not protected as cinematographic works'. Protection was granted for seventy years p.m.a. Like the previous law, the 1965 Act does not include a list of the co-authors of the film.[222]

The new Act established a presumption of grant of copyright to the film producer. It provides that any person who participates in the production of a film is deemed to have granted to the producer of the film the exclusive exploitation rights in the film (without prejudice to their rights in the underlying elements).[223] Several provisions reinforce this grant.

In addition, the moral right of integrity of film authors and of contributors to film productions is limited to the right to object to 'gross distortions or other gross mutilations of their works or of their contribution'.[224] Film producers were granted a neighbouring right in the 'fixations of their films', which includes a specific moral right of integrity.[225] Finally, the German Act was the first Act to implement a scheme of remuneration for private copy.[226]

36.   Austria

In Austria, the regime of film works was detailed in a Law of 9 April 1936. Like the German Act, the Austrian Act clearly distinguished 'cinematographic works' as such, protected by a full author's right,[227] and 'cinematographic productions' (documentaries), which were not protected by author's right, but under a 'neighbouring right', as photographs.[228]

The Act organised a specific regime for authorship and initial entitlement to copyright in films. Film creators retained their moral rights, but the economic rights (with the exception of adaptation rights) were initially vested in the film producer.[229] In addition, the film producer was

---

[221] Copyright Act, art. 2.   [222] On this list, see para. 290.
[223] Copyright Act, art. 89.   [224] *Ibid.*, art. 93. See para. 290.
[225] *Ibid.*, art. 93. See para. 239.   [226] See para. 286.   [227] Copyright Act, art. 4.
[228] *Ibid.*, art. 73(2).   [229] *Ibid.*, art. 38(1). See para. 161.

granted a distinct moral right to object to derogatory treatment of the film.[230] The rights in the 'cinematographic production' were granted to the film producer.[231]

'Cinematographic works' were protected for thirty years after making or first public exhibition, as the case may be.[232] For 'cinematographic productions' protected as photographs, the protection expired twenty years after taking or public exhibition.[233]

Performers were also granted neighbouring rights in the form of economic and moral rights akin to authors' rights.[234]

37.   The Netherlands

In the Netherlands, the Act of 23 September 1912 repeated the language of article 14, para. 12 of the Berne Convention and protected 'photographic and cinematographic works or works made by similar methods'. A distinction was made between original cinematographic works and cinematographic works lacking originality. The main consequence of this distinction was the duration of copyright protection, which was fifty years p.m.a. for the former and fifty years post-publication for the latter. The Act did not provide for specific rules concerning films.

Film producers were considered by early case law as authors of the cinematographic works. The solution was mainly based on article 5 of the 1912 Act, which, in case of a compilation of separate works created by two or more persons (a 'collective work'), considered as author the person under whose direction or supervision the whole work was accomplished. Employment rules also led to the same conclusion.

The Act of 30 May 1985 modernised this system. Authorship in films was granted to the creative contributors, but the Act contains no statutory list of co-authors. Under article 45b of the Act, all film co-authors (except the musical composer) are deemed to have assigned their copyright in the film to the film producer, unless otherwise provided. This presumption does not include adaptation rights, with the exception of subtitling and synchronisation rights. In addition, it does not prejudice the rights of each author in his or her underlying production. Employment rules and rules concerning 'collective works' were held not to apply to film producers.

Concerning moral rights, article 45f of the Act provides that, excepting a provision to the contrary, contributors are deemed to have waived their right to object to modifications to the film made by the producer or on his behalf.

---

[230] *Ibid.*, art. 38(2). See para. 286.   [231] *Ibid.*, art. 74(1).   [232] *Ibid.*, art. 62.
[233] *Ibid.*, art. 74(4).   [234] *Ibid.*, arts. 66 *et seq.*

38.   Scandinavian countries

The Danish Copyright Act of 1902 was silent on the protection of cinematography, but it appears that films, including scientific films and newsreels, could be protected by copyright. Double protection as a series of
photographs and as a dramatic work was also afforded under the Act of
13 May 1911 on Copyright in Photographic Works and under the Act
of 26 April 1933 on Copyright and Artistic Rights.[235] Concerning film
authorship, there does not appear to be case law on this point, but various
provisions of the applicable copyright Acts appeared to point to the film
producer (at least as initial owner). Copyright in a dramatic film endured
until fifty years p.m.a., or fifty years from the year of publication if the
author was a legal person. Moral rights protection applied to films without limitation, but a peculiarity of Danish law was that the *droit moral* was
vested in the Ministry of Education after the death of an author. On this
ground, one author reports an old case in which the Ministry opposed
the publication of an advertising film based on one of Hans Christian
Andersen's fairy tales.[236]

In Finland, the matter was regulated by the copyright Law of 15 March
1880, the Copyright Act of 3 June 1927 and the Photographic Copyright
Act of 3 June 1927.[237] Cinematographic works were protected both as
literary works under the Copyright Act of 3 June 1927 and as photographic works under the Photographic Copyright Act. Dramatic films
were protected under both Acts, and scientific films, advertising films
and newsreels could be protected under the Copyright Act provided sufficient originality was found. Concerning authorship, in a decision of 28
October 1936,[238] the Finnish Supreme Court held that a sound film was
a 'collective work', which had the effect of vesting the initial copyright
in the film (as distinct from the copyright in the contributions) in the
film producer. Concerning moral rights, the prohibition of mutilations
extended to works in the public domain. A Law of 8 July 1961 succeeded
the 1927 Acts.

In Sweden, films gained copyright protection in the 1919 Act on copyright in literary and musical works as a specific subject-matter for protection. By application of the general copyright rules, films were works
of joint authorship between the author of the screenplay, the author of
the adaptation and the musical composer. However, the producer and

---

[235] Cited by Torben Lund, 'Denmark', in H. L. Pinner (ed.), *World Copyright*, A. W. Sijthoff,
Leyden, 1953, vol. I, *Verbo Cinematographic Works*.
[236] *Ibid.*
[237] T. M. Kivimäki, 'Finland', in H. L. Pinner (ed.), *World Copyright*, A. W. Sijthoff, Leyden,
1953, vol. I, *Verbo Cinematographic Works*.
[238] KKO 1936 No. 476; summary in *Inter-Auteurs*, May 1937, VIII, p. 450.

the film director were apparently denied authorship in the film. The relations between film producers and authors were extensively dealt with in a standard agreement established in 1944 by the Society of Swedish Film Producers, the Society of Swedish Authors and the Society of Film Authors in Sweden. Copyright law was restated in 1960 in a law on copyright and in a specific law on photographic copyright, which were subject to many amendments.

39.   Other European countries

In Luxembourg, until recently, the protection of cinematographic works was dealt with in the Law of 29 March 1972, which replaced a Copyright Law of 10 May 1898. The Act contained very few provisions on 'cinematographic works'. However, a notable feature was the fact that copyright in a cinematographic work is vested in the 'maker' of the cinematographic work, i.e. the film producer.[239] The Act also instituted a presumption of assignment of the film rights in the underlying work to the film producer.[240] The protection expired fifty years after the cinematographic work has been lawfully made available to the public. The 1972 Act is now replaced by the Law of 18 April 2001 on Copyright, Neighbouring Rights and Databases. This new Act implements the EC copyright directives and the various international obligations of Luxembourg in this field. As in the UK and Ireland, the film producer and the main director are now co-authors of the film.[241]

In Greece, a Law of 1920[242] constituted the basic law on copyright until the law No. 2121 of 1993 was adopted. The provisions relating to films in the new Act are similar to the provisions in the French 1957 Act, as amended. However, under the Greek Copyright Act the film director is considered as the sole author of the film. Also, authors may waive their moral rights under certain conditions.[243]

In Switzerland, the Copyright Act of 1922 protected pictures for the same term as other works (thirty years p.m.a.). The duration of copyright protection was extended to fifty years p.m.a. by a copyright amendment Act of 1955. The Copyright Act of 1992 includes no provisions on film authorship, but provides for a specific duration of seventy years after the death of the sole director. Switzerland is not a European Union or EEA Member State; and this results in some peculiarities of its *droit d'auteur* system as compared to European Union countries.

[239] Art. 27.   [240] Art. 28.   [241] Art. 21.   [242] No. 2387.   [243] See para. 311.

SECTION III

Towards European harmonisation (1992 to the present)

40.   The European harmonisation of copyright

European copyright laws have undergone important changes in the process of European harmonisation of copyright law.[244] The origin of this
process was the resolution of the European Parliament of 13 May 1974
requesting the EC Commission to harmonise copyright and neighbouring
rights legislation in the context of general measures concerning cultural
policy. However, it was not until 1988 that the Commission proposed
a programme for harmonisation, in its Green Paper entitled 'Copyright
and the Technological Challenge'.[245] At that time, the provisions of the
EC Treaty on freedom of movement of goods had proved their limitations as an instrument to prevent diverging national laws from impeding
the functioning of the internal market.[246] The working programme of
the Commission was detailed in the Follow-up to the Green Paper of
1990.[247] Directives were felt to be an adequate vehicle for such a harmonisation, being more respectful of different national traditions and
legal techniques.[248]

[244] See G. Schricker, 'Harmonisation of Copyright in the European Economic Community'
(1989) 20 IIC 462; H. Cohen Jehoram, 'Harmonising Intellectual Property Law Within
the European Community' (1992) 23 IIC 622.
[245] Copyright and the Challenge of Technology – Copyright Issue Requiring Immediate
Action, COM (88) 172 final.
[246] See e.g. Case 341/87, *EMI Electrola GmbH* v. *Patricia Im- und Export Verwaltungsgesellschaft mbH* [1989] ECR 79; [1989] 2 CMLR 413; [1989] 1 FSR 544, ECJ: 'Insofar
as the disparity between national laws relating to the protection of literary and artistic
property may give rise to restrictions on intra-Community trade in sound recordings,
such restrictions are justified under Article 36 of the Treaty if they are the result of
differences between the rules governing the period of protection and this is inseparably
linked to the very existence of the exclusive rights. No such justification would exist if
the restrictions on trade imposed or accepted by the national legislation were of such
a nature as to constitute a means of arbitrary discrimination or a disguised measure to
restrict trade.' See also Case 158/86, *Warner Brothers Inc.* v. *Christiansen* [1988] ECR
2605; [1990] 3 CMLR 684; [1991] FSR 161, ECJ: 'The fact that an author has put
video-cassettes into circulation in a Member State which does not provide specific protection for the right to hire them out should not, therefore, have repercussions on the
right conferred on that same author by the legislation of another Member State to
restrain, in that State, the hiring-out of those video-cassettes.'
[247] 'Follow-Up to the Green Paper: Working Programme of the Commission in the Field
of Copyright and Neighbouring Rights', COM (90) 584 final.
[248] It should be recalled that, under the EC Treaty, a directive is binding on Member States
as to the result to be achieved, but that it leaves each Member State the choice as to the
form or method of its implementation. See Appendix 1 below.

In relation to film protection, the most important directives adopted are the Rental and Lending Directive of 19 November 1992, the Satellite and Cable Directive of 27 September 1993, the Term Directive of 29 October 1993 and the Directive on Copyright and Related Rights in the Information Society of 22 May 2001. These directives also apply to Member States of the European Economic Area, which, in addition to the fifteen EU Member States, includes Iceland, Liechtenstein and Norway.

41.   The Rental Directive of 19 November 1992

The Council Directive of 19 November 1992, on 'Rental Right and Lending Right and on Certain Rights Related to Copyright in the Field of Intellectual Property' contain several provisions affecting film protection. According to article 2(1) of the Directive, authors must be granted an exclusive right to authorise or prohibit the rental and lending of the original and copies of their work. These rights must also be granted to performers in respect of fixations of their performance, and to film producers in respect of the original and copies of their films. In addition, for the purposes of the Directive, the principal director of the film is to be considered as author or one of the authors of the film, Member States being free to provide for other co-authors.[249] These authorship provisions had to be implemented before 1 July 1994.[250]

The Directive allows Member States to provide for a presumption of transfer of the rental right to the film producer with the film production contract.[251] However, in that case or when the rental right has been transferred to the film producer, authors and performers shall retain an unwaivable right to equitable remuneration for the rental, the administration of which may be entrusted to collecting societies.[252] Member States have the possibility not to implement the lending right, but, in relation to films, shall introduce, at least for authors, a 'remuneration', without further specification.[253] This right had to be effective before 1 July 1997.[254]

In addition, Chapter II of the Directive provides for the introduction of related rights for performers, sound recording producers, film producers and broadcasting organisations (including fixation, reproduction, broadcasting and communication to the public[255] and distribution rights) before 1 July 1994.

---

[249] Art. 2(2).   [250] Art. 13.
[251] Subject to a clause to the contrary for authors (art. 2(6)), but not necessarily for performers (art. 2(5) and (7)).
[252] Art. 4.   [253] Art. 5.   [254] Art. 13.
[255] For performers and broadcasting organisations only. The Directive also provides for a compulsory licence for communication to the public of a phonogram published for commercial purposes.

42.   The Satellite and Cable Directive of 27 September 1993

The Directive of 27 September 1993 'on the Coordination of Certain Rules Concerning Copyright and Rights Related to Copyright Applicable to Satellite Broadcasting and Cable Retransmission' sets up an 'ownership' and 'equitable remuneration' scheme in relation to the satellite broadcasting and cable retransmission rights similar to that of the rental right in the Rental Directive.[256] It also defines the law applicable to satellite broadcasts.[257]

43.   The Term Directive of 29 October 1993

The Directive of 29 October 1993 'Harmonising the Term of Protection of Copyright and Certain Related Rights' sets the duration of copyright and related rights at the highest existing level in any Member State: life of the author plus seventy years for most copyright works, and fifty years from execution, fixation or publication for performers' and producers' rights. It contains special provisions regarding films in its articles 2 and 3.

Article 2, entitled 'cinematographic or audiovisual works', specifies that the principal director of such work is to be regarded as its author or one of its authors, Member States being free to designate other co-authors.[258] The protection of cinematographic and audiovisual works will expire seventy years after the death of the last of the following persons to survive, whether or not these persons are designated as co-authors: the principal director, the author of the screenplay, the author of the dialogue and the composer of music specifically created for use in the cinematographic or audiovisual work.[259]

Article 3(3) provides that the rights of the producer of the first fixation of a film shall expire fifty years after fixation or fifty years after the earlier date of either its communication to the public or its publication, if any. Implementation of these provisions was due by 1 July 1995.[260]

44.   The Directive on Copyright and Related Rights in the Information Society of 22 May 2001

The Follow-up to the Green Paper on copyright and related rights in the information society of 1996[261] called for a further harmonisation of copyright and related rights in order to respond to the new challenges of technology. This harmonisation is a prerequisite for the ratification of

---

[256] With, however, some differences. See para. 170 for details.
[257] See para. 189.   [258] Art. 2(1).   [259] Art. 2(2).   [260] Art. 13.
[261] Brussels, 20 November 1996, COM (96) 586 final.

the WIPO Treaties of 1996, to which all EU and EEA Member States as well as the European Community are signatories. It took the form of a new Parliament and EC Commission Directive 'on the Harmonisation of Certain Aspects of Copyright and Related Rights in the Information Society'. The aim of the Directive is to ensure an 'internal market' in copyright and related rights with particular emphasis on products and services (both on-line and on physical carriers) in the 'information society'. The Directive addresses the following issues:

1. the definition of the right of reproduction;[262]
2. the scope of the right of communication to the public;[263]
3. the right of distribution;[264]
4. exemptions from these rights (including a mandatory exemption for technical copies on electronic networks and an exhaustive, optional list of copyright exemptions);[265] and
5. technological measures and rights-management information.[266]

It is the result of more than three years of fierce discussions between the Council, the Commission and the Parliament and of unprecedented lobbying, notably on the difficult question of copyright exemptions. Implementation of its provisions is due by 22 December 2002.

45.   National implementations of the EC copyright directives

To date, the provisions of the Rental, Term and Satellite and Cable Directives have been implemented by all fifteen Member States. In the UK, implementation took the form of the Duration of Copyright and Rights in Performances Regulations 1995[267] and of the long-awaited Copyright and Related Rights Regulations 1996.[268] Among the numerous changes involved in this implementation, the principal film director is now co-author with the film producer of the 'film' under the 1988 Act.[269] Also, a rental right has been granted to film authors and to contributors to film productions,[270] and the right to equitable remuneration contemplated by the Rental Directive is now regulated under a complex scheme.[271] Finally, performers have been granted new 'property rights' in addition to the existing 'non-property rights', as well as rights to equitable remuneration.[272] The Irish Copyright and Related Rights Act 2000 includes similar provisions.[273]

---

[262] See para. 180.   [263] See para. 189.   [264] See para. 195.   [265] See para. 211.
[266] See para. 201.   [267] SI 1995 No. 3297. See para. 100.   [268] SI 1996 No. 2967.
[269] New s. 9(2). See para. 118.   [270] New ss. 16 and 18A. See paras. 142 and 146.
[271] New ss. 93A and 93B. See para. 172.   [272] New ss. 191A *et seq.* See para. 333.
[273] See also the European Communities (Term of Protection of Copyright) Regulations 1995 (SI No. 158 of 1995), implementing the Term Directive.

In several Member States of the authors' rights tradition, the implementation of the EC copyright directives was made through an almost *verbatim* transposition of their provisions in the various copyright Acts.[274] But this implementation is often a minimal implementation. For example, *droit d'auteur* countries modified their provisions on copyright duration in order to comply with article 2 of the Term Directive without changing their rules on film authorship, which often leads to the strange situation in which the life of persons who are denied authorship in a film is taken into consideration in the calculation of the duration of its copyright. The same could be said on the implementation of the lending right[275] and on the rights to equitable remuneration[276] provided in the Rental and Satellite Directives.

46.   Further harmonisation

Despite this tremendous effort, there remains plenty of room for further harmonisation of copyright law in the European Union. Even if we ignore the gaps in the existing directives and the unavoidable problems and disparities in their implementation, there still exist barriers to the internal market caused by other disparities in domestic copyright laws and practices. These concern mainly the status and operation of collecting societies or licensing bodies, the enforcement of copyright, collective bargaining agreements and copyright contracts.[277]

Hearings on collective management of copyright and related rights were held before the Commission in November 2000. The Commission appears to consider that a certain degree of control is appropriate for collective management, and might initiate legislative action in this field in 2002.

Also, the Commission adopted on 30 November 2000 a Communication announcing a series of practical measures 'intended to improve and step up the fight against counterfeiting and piracy in the Single Market'. These include the presentation, in 2002, of a draft directive on

---

[274] Austria: Act No. 151/1996 of 29 March 1996; Belgium: Act of 30 June 1994, as amended by the Act of 9 May 1995; Denmark: Act No. 395 of 14 June 1995; Finland: Act No. 1654 of 1995; France: Act No. 97–283 of 27 March 1997; Germany: Act of 23 June 1995 (rental and lending, duration); Greece: Act No. 2121/1993 amended by Act No. 2435 of 2 August 1996; Italy: Act No. 77 of 26 February 1996 and Act No. 154 of 26 May 1997; Luxembourg: Act of 8 December 1997; the Netherlands: Acts of 18 March 1993 and 21 December 1995; Portugal: pending; Sweden: Acts No. 447, 1273 and 1274 of 7 December 1995; Spain: Acts of 30 December 1994 (on rental and lending), of 11 October 1995 (duration) and of 11 October 1995 (satellite and cable).
[275] See para. 198.   [276] See paras. 173 *et seq.*
[277] See e.g. KPMG, 'Single Market Review Series, Subseries II – Impact on Services; Audiovisual Services and Production'; European Commission Document, December 1996.

the enforcement of intellectual property rights.[278] This Directive will harmonise the legislation of the Member States with respect to the measures and procedures for search, seizure and proof, the criteria for calculating damages and the right to information. The proposal will also establish a general framework for administrative cooperation among Member States and between Member States and the Commission. The Commission also announced its intention to examine the need to present proposals for harmonising the minimum thresholds for sanctions and criminal proceedings in this field. These measures would complement those taken by customs authorities on the basis of the Council Regulation of 22 December 1994 'laying down measures to prohibit the release for free circulation, export, re-export or entry for a suspensive procedure of counterfeit and pirated goods'.[279]

The question of moral rights was listed in the Commission's work programme for 1991.[280] A hearing of interested parties was held in November and December 1992, which (not surprisingly) showed a great divergence of opinions on that subject. The Commission, however, noted that moral rights were rarely invoked in order to prevent the exploitation of a work, and concluded that moral rights did not pose any real problems as far as the internal market was concerned. The Commission raised again the question in its Green Paper on Copyright and Related Rights in the Information Society of 1995,[281] in the context of the advent of digital technology. In its Follow-up to the Green Paper,[282] it pointed out that differences in the level of moral rights protection in the Community were gaining Single Market relevance in the information society. However, the Commission proposed to study further the impact of moral rights before any harmonisation initiative was discussed. At present, moral rights are not an immediate concern for the Commission.

---

[278] Which follows a Green Paper on Combating Counterfeiting and Piracy in the Single Market of 1998.
[279] Council Regulation No. 3295/94, OJ 1994 No. L341, 30 December 1994.
[280] On that question, see also para. 231.
[281] COM (95) 382 final.   [282] COM (96) 586 final.

3   Subsistence of copyright

47.   Introduction

This chapter addresses two fundamental aspects of copyright protection for audiovisual works: the determination of the *subject-matter for protection* and the duration of copyright protection. As pointed out, European countries adopted different approaches in the definition of the subject-matter of protection for audiovisual works. Countries of the authors' rights tradition protect audiovisual works as original works of expression, distinct from the recordings or other manifestations thereof. In contrast to this traditional view, under current UK and Irish copyright law the main subject-matter for film protection is the visual recording,[1] irrespective of any condition of originality. In authors' rights jurisdictions, this recording attracts protection under a specific neighbouring right, distinct from the copyright in the recorded audiovisual work. As a result, in these countries both the audiovisual work and its recording are protected, but under two separate intellectual property rights, a *droit d'auteur* on the one hand, and a *neighbouring right* on the other. In addition, different solutions were adopted concerning the protection of broadcasts and cable programmes.

Until recently important disparities existed also with regard to the *duration of copyright protection*. At the time of the adoption of the Term Directive, some continental countries applied the general copyright term to audiovisual works. This term was fifty years p.m.a., except in Germany and Spain, where it was respectively seventy and sixty years p.m.a. Moreover, the list of co-authors to be taken into consideration for this calculation varied. In other countries, including the UK and Ireland, films were protected by copyright for fifty years from production, publication or public presentation.[2] Where implemented on the continent, the neighbouring right of film producers conferred a 25- to 50-year protection

---

[1] The 'film' under s. 5 of the CDPA 1988 and ss. 2 and 17 of the Irish Copyright and Related Rights Act 2000.
[2] Also in Italy, Luxembourg and Portugal.

from the publication or making of the first fixation of the audiovisual work.[3]

Both aspects were covered in the process of European harmonisation of copyright laws, to the extent and with the effects described below.

SECTION I

The subject-matter for protection

48. The determination of the subject-matter for film protection

In each legal system, the determination of the subject-matter for film protection depends on basic choices regarding the list of protected works and on the importance of 'creative authorship' in the rationale for copyright protection.

Historically, the first approach to film protection was to protect films in the same manner as other categories of works. Such an approach can generate problems, especially in legislation which provides for a closed list of protected works. This is the case in the UK, where, as a legacy from a tradition of piecemeal legislation, the determination of the heading for protection is a prerequisite for copyright protection. Accordingly, protection for films works had first to be sought through an assimilation to existing classes of protected works, such as photographic and dramatic works, which created difficulties in terms of definitions and boundaries for certain types of audiovisual works.[4] In contrast, under US copyright law and most authors' rights systems, the list of protected works is only illustrative. As soon as a 'work of authorship' is original (and, in some countries, fixated in tangible form), copyright protection is in principle granted. Accordingly, the definition of the subject-matter does not have the same importance. However, in both systems the assimilation to or analogy with other classes of works can be inconvenient, as the imported regime may not be well adapted to some features of the new works (a constant claim of new industries – to be carefully weighed). Most authors' rights countries reacted by creating a sub-regime for audiovisual works, with specific features in terms of authorship, initial ownership and sometimes moral rights.[5] Such an adaptation, however, is not always

---

[3] Fifty years in Austria, France, Norway, Portugal and Sweden, forty years in Spain and twenty-five years in Germany.

[4] See e.g. para. 17.

[5] This is true also in the US, which implemented a specific work-made-for-hire regime for motion pictures in the 1976 Act.

satisfactory, as unwelcome aspects of the general scheme can always come out of the gaps in specific regulations.

This explains why some legislation adopted a more radical solution and devised a specific subject-matter for films. This technique allows more certainty in the definition of the protected works, and more freedom in the tailoring of a specific regime adapted to the needs of the industry. This was the choice of the UK, which introduced in the Copyright Act 1956 a specific subject-matter for audiovisual works. It was followed in Ireland in the Copyright Act 1963.

The fear of introducing germs of entrepreneurial copyright into the realm of *droit d'auteur* explains why this trend was not followed in authors' rights countries and why the regime of film protection in these countries remains, to this day, a mere adaptation of the general scheme of copyright protection. As a consequence, the protection of film works retains classic features of *droit d'auteur*, notably the requirement of originality and a system of 'creative authorship'. This may also explain the introduction, in addition to the *droit d'auteur* in the audiovisual work, of a separate neighbouring right of the film producer in the visual recording.

In this respect, the provisions of the EC copyright directives have been strongly influenced by the continental scheme of protection.[6]

49. Definition of the subject-matter for protection at the international and regional levels

The main international copyright agreements contain no real definitions of the terms 'cinematographic' or 'audiovisual works'. In its article 2(1), the Berne Convention uses the term 'cinematographic works, to which are assimilated works expressed by a process analogous to cinematography'; but the Convention gives no definition of that term. The same is true under the Universal Copyright Convention,[7] the TRIPs Agreement[8] and the WIPO Copyright Treaty of 1996.[9]

In contrast, the term 'audiovisual works' is used in the WIPO Draft Model Provisions[10] and in the Treaty on the International Registration of Audiovisual Works of 20 April 1989. In the WIPO Draft Model Provisions, audiovisual works are defined as works consisting of a series of related images and accompanying sounds, if any, which are intended to be shown by appropriate devices.[11] The definition in the Treaty appears to be more restrictive: an audiovisual work is defined as:

---

[6] See para. 50.
[7] Which also uses the term 'cinematographic works' (art. 1), without further specification.
[8] Art. 11. Cinematographic works, without further definition.
[9] Art. 7(1)(ii) and (2)(ii).   [10] Section 3(1)(vi).   [11] Art. 21(1).

any work that consists of a series of fixed related images, with or without accompanying sound, susceptible of being made visible and, where accompanied by sound, susceptible of being made audible.[12]

Possibly the broadest definition at the supranational level is given by the EC copyright directives. The Rental Directive uses the term 'film', but its article 2 specifies that:

for the purposes of this Directive, the term 'film' shall designate a cinematographic or audiovisual work or moving images, whether or not accompanied by sound.

The same definition is used in the other copyright directives.[13] Neither cinematographic nor audiovisual works are defined further in these directives, but the reference to 'moving images' is broad. We note, however, that the definition of audiovisual works is not directly within the scope of harmonisation. In this respect, Member States may probably retain a slightly different definition of the subject-matter, as long as the main objectives of the harmonisation are met. One should also observe that these various definitions at the international level do not indicate whether soundtrack elements should be treated as part of the film or not.

On these grounds, the definition of the subject-matter for protection raises a series of questions which are particularly relevant in the European context.

First, do these legal instruments require the introduction of a specific subject-matter for audiovisual work, or would a copyright Act indirectly protecting audiovisual works under other subject-matter (e.g. as dramatic works or as series of photographs) comply with their provisions?

It is submitted that nothing in the international copyright treaties or in the relevant EC copyright directives prevents the protection of films through another subject-matter. However, the creation of at least a sub-category is required in order to implement elements of the specific regime set by the EC directives in terms of duration,[14] authorship[15] and exclusive rights.[16] Problems of definition are thus unavoidable.

Secondly, would a scheme that protects only audiovisual recordings, without providing a specific protection for the underlying (recorded) audiovisual work, be acceptable? Although this is not stated expressly in the

---

[12] Art. 2.

[13] The Cable and Satellite Directive uses only the term 'cinematographic or audiovisual work'. However, its provisions refer to the protection under the Rental Directive, and therefore the above definition should extend to 'moving images' as well. The Term Directive uses the same language as the Rental Directive. Art. 2 of the Term Directive is headed 'Cinematographic or audiovisual works', but the Directive also uses the term 'film' to define the right of the 'producer of the first fixation of a film'. It further specifies in art. 3(3) that 'the term "film" shall designate a cinematographic or audiovisual work or moving images, whether or not accompanied by sound'. The Directive on Copyright and Related Rights in the Information Society uses the term 'film', without further definition.

[14] See para. 99.   [15] See para. 111.   [16] See Chapters 5 and 6.

Berne Convention, it seems to derive from the description of the cinematographic work as an original work of authorship and from preparatory
works to the Convention that the definition refers to the recorded work,
not to the recording itself.[17] However, it is submitted that such a system would meet the requirements of the Berne Convention: a protection
through the recording has no effect on the minimum protection guaranteed by the Convention which, in any case, allows the requirement of
a fixation as a prerequisite for copyright protection.[18] In contrast, it is
unlikely that such a system would comply with the requirements of the
EC copyright directives.[19]

Thirdly, is originality a necessary requirement for film protection? The
answer to this question appears negative, as long as under the definition of the subject-matter all 'original' films are protected. According to
article 14*bis* of the Berne Convention, 'a cinematographic work shall be
protected as an original work', and 'the owner of copyright in a cinematographic work shall enjoy the same rights as the author of an original work'. The absence of a requirement of originality for 'films' under
UK copyright does not appear to contravene these provisions, since all
'original' films are in any case protected.[20] However, the protection under the Convention might not extend to those cinematographic works
which are not 'original' according to the criterion used in each national
law. As a consequence, a limited number of 'films' protected under UK
law could lie outside the scope of the Convention.[21]

50.   The requirement of a double protection under
the EC copyright directives

A specific feature of film protection at the European level is the requirement of a double system of protection for films, inspired by the model

---

[17] See the General Report of the Berlin Conference, quoted on that point at para. 13.
Final reports are thought to present an 'authentic' or 'authoritative' interpretation of
the Convention (S. Ricketson, *The Berne Convention on the Protection of Literary and
Artistic Works*, Kluwer, 1987, p. 137, para. 4.12). See also art. 2 of the Convention:
'works . . . expressed by a process analogous to cinematography'; by analogy the work
'expressed by photography' is not the negative, but the underlying work of the photographer. See also Ricketson, *The Berne Convention*, p. 555, n. 3.

[18] However, would a country which does not protect musical works but only sound recordings comply with the Berne Convention?

[19] See the next paragraph.

[20] See Ricketson, *The Berne Convention*, para. 10.10, p. 557. Consider also the protection
as an original dramatic work as a result of the decision in *Norowzian* v. *Arks Ltd (No. 2)*
[2000] EMLR 67; [2000] FSR 363, CA; see paras. 54 *et seq*.

[21] E.g. footage produced by security cameras. A more stringent concept of originality in
a given signatory State could also exclude from the benefit of the Convention other
categories of films which would otherwise be considered as 'original' under UK copyright
(newsreels, for example).

adopted by most EU Member States: When it comes to the protection of audiovisual works, the main directives in the field of copyright, the Rental and Term Directives, clearly target *two different sets of rights*, which have *different terms and 'authors'*: the right of the author or authors of the film on the one hand, and the related right of the producer of the first fixation of the film, on the other hand.[22]

In article 2(1), the Rental Directive provides that the rental and lending right shall belong:

(a) to the author in respect of the original and copies of his work,
(b) to the performer in respect of fixations of his performance,
(c) to the phonogram producer in respect of his phonograms, and
(d) to the producer of the first fixation of a film in respect of the original and copies of his film.

The Directive thus makes a distinction between rights of authors, rights of performers and rights of phonogram and film producers. Article 2(2), further specifies that, for the purpose of this Directive, 'the principal director of a cinematographic or audiovisual work shall be considered as its author or one of its authors'. Accordingly, by this reference to the 'author', the right of the film director falls within the first category. In contrast, the right of the producer of the first fixation of a film is addressed in Chapter II of the Directive, dedicated to 'rights related to copyrights'.

The Term Directive adopts this distinction between authors' rights and related rights.[23] As a general rule, recital 11 and article 1 state that the duration of the 'author's right' is extended to seventy years after the death of the author. Article 2, titled 'Cinematographic or audiovisual works', provides that the principal director of a film shall be considered as its author or one of its authors, and adapts the 70-year duration to films. In contrast, article 3, titled 'Duration of related rights', specifies that the 'rights of producers of the first fixation of a film' shall expire fifty years after the fixation, publication or communication to the public, as the case may be. Therefore, by setting different terms for protection, the Term Directive leaves no doubt that the right of the author of the film and the right of the film producer are distinct.

Even if no proper definition of these elements is given, the directives clearly equate the 'film' and its synonym, the 'cinematographic or audiovisual work', with the underlying audiovisual work, and not with the visual recording.[24]

---

[22] The same distinction is found in the Directive on Copyright and Related Rights in the Information Society of 22 May 2001.

[23] In its title, recitals and in arts. 1 and 3. Related rights are also referred to as neighbouring rights in recital 10.

[24] The Directive talks about the 'first fixation of a film'. How can one fixate a recording?

In contrast, nothing requires formally that the right of the producer *of* the first fixation of the film be a right *on* this fixation; it could well be a perfectly overlapping right on the underlying audiovisual work (without the requirement of originality). However, the absence of a *fixation right* for film producers in the Rental Directive would appear to indicate that the right is on the recording itself, rather than on the underlying sequence of images. In addition, this right corresponds to the right of the 'videogram' producer, which is defined in the relevant Member States as the right on the *audiovisual recording.*

51.   Structure

From this, it appears that audiovisual works are protected in Europe under two main descriptions of works: the audiovisual work itself, as distinct from its recording (the 'motion picture' under US law) (discussed in Part I below), and the recording of this audiovisual work (protected by copyright or under a specific neighbouring right, as the case may be) (discussed in Part II below). These descriptions do not affect the status of underlying works in film production (discussed in Part III below). In addition, the law protects broadcasts and cable programmes under specific headings (discussed in Part IV below). Finally, we will address the question of a possible indirect protection of films as 'databases', following the extension of copyright protection to this class of works (discussed in Part V below).

PART I

The audiovisual or cinematographic work

52.   Direct versus indirect protection

The subject-matter for copyright protection in continental Europe is the audiovisual or cinematographic work, as distinct from its recording (film negative, videotape) and from underlying works (script, musical work, etc.). In contrast, the main subject-matter for film protection in the UK and in Ireland is the visual recording itself. However, in the UK audiovisual works can also, under certain conditions, attract indirect protection as 'dramatic works'.

Given this fundamental difference in approaches, we will first describe the law in the UK and Ireland before the law in Member States of the authors' rights tradition.

The situation in the United Kingdom and Ireland

53.   The law in the UK: a protection through the audiovisual recording (the 'film')

The choice made in the UK Copyright Act 1956 in relation to film works was to adopt a new and specific subject-matter under a Part II (entrepreneurial) copyright.[25] This specific subject-matter for films, the 'cinematograph film', was defined in section 13(10) as:

any sequence of visual images recorded on material of any description (whether translucent or not) so as to be capable, by the use of that material,
(a) of being shown as a moving picture, or
(b) of being recorded on other material (whether translucent or not), by the use of which it can be so shown.

This definition shows that, contrary to the general assumption[26] and the use of the term 'film', the copyright was not in the visual recording, as in the present Act, but in the (recorded) underlying visual work ('sequences of images . . . recorded'). This definition required two elements: a sequence of visual images; and a sequence recorded so as to be capable of producing, by the use of the recording, the illusion of motion. This is, in truth, a very accurate definition of televisual and cinematographic audiovisual works.[27]

This final audiovisual work could not be protected under another heading, as the 1956 Act expressly excluded 'cinematographic works' from the definition of photographic and dramatic works.[28]

The 1988 Act continues to treat audiovisual works as specific descriptions of works which do not have to satisfy any requirement of originality. In that respect, the main difference from the previous law is that, under the new Act, the specific subject-matter for audiovisual works, the 'film', is defined in section 5 as the visual recording itself, and not as the underlying sequence of images:

'film' means a recording on any medium from which a moving image may by any means be produced.[29]

Thus it can be said *prima facie* that cinematographic and audiovisual works are not given protection as such, but only through their recordings.[30]

[25] See para. 22.
[26] Including my own in 'Authorship of Films and Implementation of the Term Directive' (1994) 16 EIPR 319 at 320.
[27] For an application to recordings on videotapes, see th discussion of *EMI Ltd* v. *Sharif* in para. 22, n. 141, above.
[28] In s. 48.   [29] Originally s. 5(1), now s. 5B(1) of the Act.
[30] Other differences include the treatment of film soundtracks (see para. 78) and the duration of protection.

Accordingly, the right in the 'film' will be discussed below, in Part II on the 'audiovisual recording'.

54.   An additional protection as dramatic work

The 1988 Act also differs from the 1956 Act in that it reopened the possibility of additional or residual protection of audiovisual works as dramatic works. In contrast with the previous Act, in the 1988 Act, audiovisual works are no longer excluded from the definition of dramatic works. In addition, the specific subject-matter for film protection, the 'film', is the visual recording, and is thus distinct from this underlying work. Moreover, it is now clear that a dramatic work can attract protection when it is fixated in film form only.[31]

Accordingly, certain commentators suggested that audiovisual works could be protected both as films, through their recording, and as (recorded) dramatic works.[32] This theory was confirmed by the Court of Appeal in *Norowzian* v. *Arks Ltd*,[33] with important consequences for the scheme of copyright protection for films.

55.   Films as dramatic works: the question before *Norowzian*

There is little doubt that the various scripts which prepare the final audiovisual work are dramatic works.[34] However, could audiovisual works themselves be considered as dramatic works?

We saw that the text of the 1988 Act does not exclude this possibility. However, there would be a prerequisite to such protection. Under the 1911 Act, audiovisual works were expressly likened to dramatic works.[35] This is not the case under the 1988 Act. Therefore, the question comes down to this: in the absence of express assimilation in the Act, can audiovisual works meet the definition of dramas?

There is no comprehensive definition of a dramatic work in the 1988 Act or in the previous Acts.[36] Nor is there any modern UK authority

---

[31] CDPA 1988, ss. 3 and 178.   [32] See para. 25.

[33] *Norowzian* v. *Arks Ltd (No. 2)* [2000] EMLR 67; [2000] FSR 363, CA.

[34] E.g. *Telmak Teleproducts Australia Pty Ltd* v. *Bond International Pty Ltd* (1985) 5 IPR 203 (Australia); (1986) 6 IPR 97; 65 ALR 319, and most law books on the subject. See also the definition of dramatic work in the 1956 Act, below. The same is probably true for story-boards, without prejudice to a protection of each drawing as an artistic work. Note, however, that there might be 'scripts' limited to mere descriptions of plot or not developed enough to be 'performed' or 'acted', and which would not therefore qualify as dramatic works. Accordingly, early 'scripts' like the initial 'treatment' or a rough outline of the plot might be literary works.

[35] See paras. 15 *et seq.*

[36] The new text only states that 'dramatic work includes a work of dance or mime' (s. 3(1)). Previous texts operated by giving an exhaustive or non-exhaustive list of dramatic works (Dramatic Copyright Act 1833, s. 1; Literary Copyright Act 1842, s. 2; Copyright Act 1911, s. 35(1); Copyright Act 1956, s. 48(1)).

on the scope of such works. In *Tate* v. *Fullbrook*,[37] Farwell J specified the subject-matter of protection under the dramatic copyright, with special regard to scenic effects. He stated that what was protected under the Copyright Acts 1833 and 1842 must be 'capable of being printed and published',[38] but was not primarily concerned with giving a real definition of dramatic works (since everything which is capable of being printed and published is not a dramatic work).[39] Farwell J never went further than stating that:

> there must be something of a dramatic entertainment, for a mere spectacle stand-ing alone is no more within the [Dramatic Copyright] Act than a singer who sings in character costume is within it.

'Dramatic entertainment', however, is not defined.

Lord Bridge in the *Green* case[40] appeared to follow the general opinion in defining drama as a work capable of being performed:

> a dramatic work must have sufficient unity to be capable of performance.

The term 'performance' is of course not to be taken as meaning something as broad as 'any mode of visual or acoustic presentation' in the sense of section 19(2)(b) of the 1988 Act. This would be illogical, since virtually all copyright works are capable of being 'performed' in that way. Some commentators are more specific and suggest that a dramatic work is a work to be performed by acting or dancing:

> Where it is necessary to distinguish a dramatic work from a literary one (which it rarely is), the essence of the distinction would seem to be that a dramatic work is something to be performed by acting or dancing whereas a literary work is merely something to be read or recited (and a musical work something to be played or sung).[41]

---

[37] [1908] 1 KB 821; 98 LT 706; 77 LJKB 577; 24 TLR 347; 52 SJ 276.

[38] 'It follows, therefore, that scenic effects, taken by themselves, and apart from the words and incidents of the piece, are not the subject of copyright, because they cannot be the subject of printing and publication. I am far, however, from saying that, in dealing with the question of infringement of copyright in the case of two pieces, the words of which are more or less alike, similarity of scenic effects and the make-up of the actors, and such like matters, may not be regarded, though not by themselves subject of protection under the Act, as being evidence of the *animus furandi* on the part of the defendant ... Nor do I say that scenic effects may not be protected as part and parcel of the drama: scenes do of course form parts of drama, and it is the dramatic piece as a whole that is protected by the Act.'

[39] In addition, we saw that this requirement (and the authority of *Tate* v. *Fullbrook* on that point) is limited to the 1833 and 1842 Acts (see para. 17 above).

[40] *Green* v. *Broadcasting Corporation of New Zealand* [1989] 2 All ER 1056; [1989] RPC 700. See para. 68.

[41] G. Dworkin and R. Taylor, *Blackstone's Guide to the Copyright, Designs & Patent Act 1988*, Blackstone, 1989, p. 24; See also T. Prime, *The Law of Copyright*, Fourmat Publishing, 1992, p. 27: 'a dramatic work is one which is essentially created to be performed, usually

It is submitted that this view, which fits plays and works of dance or mime perfectly well, is too restrictive with regard to long-acknowledged dramatic works such as film scripts. If the film script is a dramatic work, how could its nature change if it is written for an animated picture, a picture featuring animals in which real actors, if any, play only a small part, featuring 3D or image-by-image animated puppets, or mixing all the possibilities? Acting is not the key word. The key words are *action* and *movement*. It is submitted that, as a more accurate definition, a dramatic work is a work created in order to be communicated in motion, i.e. through a sequence of actions or movements, irrespective of the technique by which this movement is retrieved or expressed, this communication in movement being the 'performance'.[42]

This view was adopted in the series of US cases which, given the silence of the 1909 Copyright Act on the subject, held that cinematographic works should be considered as dramatic works,[43] and corresponds to the definitions of dramatic works by US courts.[44]

56.   The *Norowzian* case

Mr Norowzian was the author of 'Joy', a short film without dialogue featuring one man dancing to music against a very simple background. In this film, Mr Norowzian used a specific editing technique known as

by a number of players'; H. Laddie, P. Prescott and M. Vitoria, *The Modern Law of Copyright*, Butterworths, 1995, para. 2.44: a dramatic work 'requires acting or dancing for its proper representation'. See also *WIPO Glossary of Terms of the Law of Copyright and Neighbouring Rights*, Geneva, 1980, where dramatic work is defined as 'a compilation of connected actors and discourses of one or usually more persons, to be performed *on stage* and reflecting reality through play' (emphasis added).

[42] Compare J. Phillips, R. Durie and I. Karet, *Whale on Copyright*, 4th edn, Sweet & Maxwell, 1993, p. 27. See J. Holyoak and P. Torremans, *Intellectual Property Law*, Butterworths, 1995, p. 154; see also C. Thorne, 'Copyright and Multimedia Products: Fitting a Round Peg in a Square Hole?' (1995) 49 *Copyright World* 18 at 19; contra H. Laddie, P. Prescott and M. Vitoria, *The Modern Law of Copyright*, Butterworths, 1995, para. 5.26, who contend that this definition would overlap with film as such. But, according to our definition, the 'film' under s. 5 of the Act is only the technique, the recording by which this movement is retrieved or expressed, and does not overlap with the dramatic work. In the same way, musical works are made to be heard, and sound recordings allow musical works to be heard.

[43] Particularly *Kalem Co. v. Harper Bros*, 222 US 55, 32 S.Ct 20 (1911) : the Supreme Court held that there was a copyright in a movie of 'Ben Hur' as a 'dramatic reproduction of the story': 'drama may be achieved by action as well as by speech. Action can tell a story, display the most vivid relations between men, and depict every kind of human emotion, without the aid of a word'; *Tiffany Productions Inc. v. Dewing*, 50 F. 2d 911, para. 3: 'It is no longer open to question that a moving picture presentation of an author's copyright work is a dramatization of such work.' See also *Photo-Drama Motion Picture Co. Inc. v. Social Uplift Film Corp.*, 220 F. 448 (CCA); *Klein v. Beach*, 239 F. 108 (CCA); *US v. Motion Picture Patents Co.*, 225 F. 800 (DC); *Atlas Mfg Co. v. Street & Smith*, 204 F. 398 (CCA).

[44] E.g. see *Seltzer v. Sunbrock*, 22 F. Supp. 621 (DC Cal. 1938) at 628–9 *per* Jenney J.

'jump cutting' in such a way that, in the final film, the actor would appear to perform movements or changes in position that could not have been performed in reality. Arks Ltd made an advertisement for Guinness called 'Anticipation'. The film portrayed a man who, having been served a Guinness, performs a strange dance while waiting for the beer to settle in his glass. Arks used the same technique in the filming and editing of the dance, with a similar 'surreal' result. Mr Norowzian claimed that Arks Ltd and Guinness, in their film 'Anticipation', copied a substantial part of 'Joy'.

In its judgment delivered on 17 July 1998,[45] Rattee J dismissed Norowzian's action for breach of copyright. In particular, he expressed the opinion that a film *per se* could not be a dramatic work within the meaning of the 1988 Act. This opinion was partly based on the separate categorisation of these works in the 1988 Act and on the mutual exclusion of these categories in the 1956 Act. Therefore, infringement had to be considered in relation to the 'film'. Since, under UK copyright, the copyright in the 'film' protects only against the lifting of actual images, infringement could not be constituted by the mere borrowing of the style and editing technique of 'Joy'.[46]

On appeal,[47] Nourse LJ disagreed with Rattee J and expressed the opinion that films could indeed be protected as dramatic works. He restated the definition of dramatic works in the following terms:

> In my judgment a film can be a dramatic work for the purpose of the 1988 Act. The definition of that expression being at large, it must be given its natural and ordinary meaning. We were referred to several dictionary and textbook definitions. My own, substantially a distilled synthesis of those which have gone before, would be this: a dramatic work is a work of action, with or without words or music, which is capable of being performed before an audience. A film will often, though not always, be a work of action and it is capable of being performed before an audience. It can therefore fall within the expression 'dramatic work' in section 1(1)(a) and I disagree with the judge's reasons for excluding it.

He pointed out that no mutual exclusivity between films and dramatic works is expressed in the 1988 Act, and noted that the absence of a requirement of originality for films is sufficient ground for none to be implied. He further stated that Parliament's failure to repeat the exclusion of films from the definition of dramatic works points rather towards their inclusion, and that the provisions of the 1988 Act must be construed as they stand:

---

[45] *Norowzian v. Arks Ltd (No. 2)* [2000] EMLR 67; [2000] FSR 363, CA.
[46] See para. 181.
[47] *Norowzian v. Arks Ltd (No. 2)* [2000] EMLR 67; [2000] FSR 363, CA.

Where a film is both a recording of a dramatic work and a dramatic work in itself [these provisions] do not exclude an overlap. In other cases there will be no overlap. Sometimes, a film will simply be a recording of something which is not a dramatic work. At other times it will not be a recording of a dramatic work but a dramatic work in itself.

However, the Court of Appeal dismissed Mr Norowzian's claims. The court held that, since no copyright subsists in mere style or technique, and the subject-matter of the two films was different, the similarities between the two films were insufficient to give Mr Norowzian a cause of action against the defendant.

As a result of this decision, it is now clear that audiovisual works can be protected in the UK as dramatic works. Therefore, the scheme for film protection would be close to that in relation to musical recordings, with two copyrights, one in the recording (sound recording/'film'), and one in the work embodied in this recording (musical work/audiovisual work). The consequences of this decision in terms of authorship and ownership are very important.[48]

It remains to be seen, however, which films could benefit from such additional protection.

57.   What films are protected as dramatic works?

Under the definition of Nourse LJ, fictional cinematic works are certainly dramatic works. The work of their creators, like the work of the author of the written play or a dance or mime or the script, is a work such as is capable of being performed before an audience. This final audiovisual work cannot be reduced to the dramatic contributory work constituted by the script, since it is obvious that new elements have been added which are included in the larger dramatic work.[49] In that case, the final cinematic work is not the mere performance of the script, but its visual translation and interpretation, i.e. a new derivative work.

What about 'non-fictional' audiovisual works, like newsreel or television shows? Here, we must separate the question of originality from the categorisation as dramatic work.

As far as originality is concerned, there is little doubt that works like *newsreels and television shows* require enough skill, labour and judgment

---

[48] See paras. 120 *et seq.*
[49] See *Milligan* v. *Broadway Cinema Production*, 1923 SLT 35; [1922–3] MCC 343, Court of Session. Suggested by Farwell J in *Tate* v. *Fullbrook*, quoted at para. 55 above. Compare also the case of a ballet, protected as a composite dramatic work, constituted by the music, the story, the choreography, the scenery and the costumes (*Massine* v. *De Basil* [1936–45] MCC 223).

in their production to be considered as original works.[50] But can they be considered as dramatic works?

In the Canadian case of *Hutton* v. *Canadian Broadcasting Corporation*,[51] a television show on pop music consisting of chart information and presentations of rock videos was held capable of being an original dramatic work.[52] Also, audio and video sales training programmes have been held to be dramatic works.[53] However, under present Canadian law, audiovisual works are expressly included in the definition of dramatic works,[54] which is not the case under the UK Act. This inclusion could be construed as allowing the protection of audiovisual works which are not dramas in the usual sense.[55] Also, Canadian copyright does not protect audiovisual recordings like UK law, which could explain the judicial 'stretching' of the definition of dramatic works. More definitely, by stating that a dramatic work 'must have sufficient unity to be capable of performance', Lord Bridge in *Green* appeared to point in the direction of the ordinary use of language. This would restrict protection as a dramatic work to those audiovisual works which convey a story in the usual meaning.

However, under this reasoning, non-fictional works such as *documentaries* could still be protected as dramatic works:

For example, in the case of a natural history documentary great skill and care will normally go into selecting the subject-matter and the manner in which the film is shot and then into editing the final product. The resulting film will be more than just a record of naturally occurring phenomena but will have its own 'story' and frequently will be designed so as to provoke sympathy or awe in the mind of the viewer.[56]

---

[50] And thus to attract protection under a specific subject-matter for audiovisual works, if any, or as an original work of authorship if the list of protected works is only illustrative.

[51] (1989) 29 CPR (3d) 398 (Alberta Queens Bench).

[52] Which is a step towards the protection of 'formats' as dramatic works, a solution rejected in the *Green* case (see para. 38 above). MacCallum J, after quoting *Seltzer* v. *Sunbrock*, 22 F. Supp. 621 (DC Cal. 1938), and reviewing the concept of the show, stated: 'I find the concept of "Music Central", with the female assistants busily gathering information for host Mulligan by means of computer, and the introduction of performances on three different star stages, lent enough dramatic incidents and seminal storyline to qualify it as a "dramatic work" ((1989) 29 CPR (3d) 398 at 443–4). The plaintiff claimed infringement of his programme by a subsequent show. It was held that the programmes were different.

[53] *Tom Hopkins International Inc.* v. *Wall & Redekop Realty Ltd* (1984) 1 CPR (3d) 348; (1985) 6 CPR (3d) 475, British Columbia Court of Appeal. The videotapes were entitled 'How to Master the Art of Listing and Selling Real Estate'. Trainor J remarked: 'In the course of the proceedings, I did have the opportunity to view a portion of one of the videotapes and, in my view, it does qualify as "dramatic work"', without developing the point further.

[54] As in the UK under the 1911 Act. See para. 21, n. 130, above.   [55] *Ibid.*

[56] H. Laddie, P. Prescott and M. Vitoria, *The Modern Law of Copyright*, Butterworths, 1980, pp. 7–9.

What about televisual productions of stage or other live dramatic works? In the case of a film made of a live play, the recording in film is undoubtedly a fixation of the dramatic work constituted by the live play. However, the larger audiovisual work made from the contribution of the director, the cameraman and the editor is not a derivative dramatic work. Even if it differs from the underlying play by its choice of shots, the introduction of close-ups, the cutting of some parts of the play or inserts of views of the audience, this audiovisual work, however 'original', does not give a new and original *expression* to the play.[57] It is a copy of the play, not a new (derivative) dramatic work. Conversely, Kenneth Branagh's film 'Much Ado About Nothing' is not a mere presentation, performance or copy of the play or of the film script derived from it, but a larger original dramatic work (a new *expression* of Shakespeare's work).

Concerning sporting events, a distinction must be made between the event or game as such and the production of the event. It is submitted that sporting events *as such* could not qualify as dramatic works. First, although games are ideally performances of pre-existing tactics and movements (the originality of which can be questioned), in practice the sequence of events is not the result of the performance of a pre-existing work of authorship.[58] Secondly, the resulting work (for example, fixed on film and later broadcast or edited), however original, does not meet the definition of a dramatic work. Although its outcome or development can create emotions, in the eyes of the public, it does not tell a *story* and lacks the unity characteristic of a dramatic work.[59]

Television productions of sports matches, as distinct from the matches themselves, with various shots, close-ups, commentary, etc., have been

---

[57] *Copinger and Skone James on Copyright*, 8th edn, 1948, p. 221. See also the reasoning below.

[58] As Lindey J stated in the Canadian case of *Joint Sports Claimants* v. *Canada (Copyright Board)* [1992] 1 FC 487; 81 DLR (4th) 412; 36 CPR (3d) 483, Federal Court of Appeal: 'Even though sports teams may seek to follow the plays as planned by their coaches, as actors follow a script, the other teams are dedicated to preventing that from occurring and often succeed. As well, the opposing team tries to follow its own game plan, which, in turn, the other team tries to thwart. In the end, what transpires on the field is usually not what is planned, but something which is totally unpredictable ... This is not the same as a ballet, where, barring an unforeseen accident, what is performed is exactly what is planned.' The court rejected the US cases in this field (e.g. *Baltimore Orioles* v. *Major League Baseball Players Association*, 805 F. 2d 663 (7th Cir. 1986), cert denied 480 US 941, 107 S.Ct 1593, 94 L.Ed. 2d 782 (1987)) because of different statutory provisions and case law.

[59] See *Joint Sports Claimants* v. *Canada (Copyright Board)* [1992] 1 FC 487; 81 DLR (4th) 412; 36 CPR (3d) 483, Federal Court of Appeal; and *Green* v. *Broadcasting Corporation of New Zealand* [1989] 2 All ER 1056; [1989] RPC 700. See also *Tate* v. *Fullbrook* (a 'mere spectacle standing alone' cannot be copyrighted). Moreover, it lacks the creative intent which is the threshold of any copyrighted work.

considered as dramatic works under Canadian copyright.[60] However, this solution relies on different statutory provisions and could be rejected under UK law on the same grounds as set out above in relation to newsreels and television shows. Under UK copyright law, in the absence of an express provision in the copyright Act, protection as a dramatic work would be restricted to works which convey a 'story' in the usual meaning.

58.   The requirement of fixation

The requirement of fixation applies to dramatic audiovisual works as it does for other classes of copyright works. Under the 1988 Act, any form of recording will be sufficient to meet this requirement.[61] In addition, section 3(3) provides that 'it is immaterial whether the work is recorded by or with the permission of the author'. Accordingly, the mere recording on film of a play, otherwise not reduced to writing, will suffice to trigger copyright protection.

59.   The situation in Ireland

The provisions of the Irish Copyright and Related Rights Act 2000 present striking similarities with the UK Act. The main subject-matter for film protection, the 'film', is defined in section 2 of the Act as the visual recording.[62] Films are expressly excluded from the definition of photographs,[63] but the exclusion is not repeated in the definition of dramatic works.[64] In addition, a dramatic work can attract protection when it is fixated in film form only.[65] Accordingly, nothing in the new Act appears to prevent an audiovisual work attracting separate protection as a dramatic work, and the regime of such works would be similar to the one described above.

---

[60] In *Canadian Admiral Corp. Ltd* v. *Rediffusion Inc.* (1954) 20 CPR 75; 14 Fox Pat. C. 114, Cameron J held that the televisual production of a football game using alternating shots by three cameramen lacked the originality required for a dramatic work. In *Joint Sports Claimants* v. *Canada (Copyright Board)* [1992] 1 FC 487; 81 DLR (4th) 412; 36 CPR (3d) 483, the Federal Court of Appeal appeared to follow a decision of the Copyright Board likening a television production of a game to a dramatic work, but refused protection to a compilation of sport programmes made by the broadcaster (the 'broadcast day') on the ground that 'there is no editing or creative input added to the shows themselves'.

[61] Section 3(2).   [62] See para. 81.   [63] Copyright and Related Rights Act 2000, s. 2.

[64] *Ibid.*   [65] *Ibid.*, s. 18(1) and (2).

The audiovisual work in authors' rights countries

60.   The main subject-matter for film protection

In all authors' rights systems, the protection of audiovisual works is mainly secured though an original description of copyright works. Several countries, such as France, adopted a broad definition of such works, capable of covering documentaries or newsreels, as long as they meet the required level of originality. Other countries, such as Germany and Italy, introduced additional descriptions for documentaries or newsreels of lesser artistic quality.

In all authors' rights countries, the importance of a characterisation as an 'audiovisual work' lies in the specific regime associated with this class of works in terms of authorship, ownership, contracts and the duration of protection.

61.   National definitions

In France, article L.112-2 of the Intellectual Property Code defines audiovisual works as 'cinematographic works and other works consisting of animated sequences of images [*séquences animées d'images*], with or without sound'. Accordingly, 'cinematographic works' are treated as a sub-category of 'audiovisual works'. The distinction between 'cinematographic' and 'audiovisual' works has no consequences in terms of copyright protection. However, transfers of rights in cinematographic works are subject to registration requirements, which is not the case for audiovisual works.[66] The characterisation also has consequences on the administrative regime of production and broadcasting and on the applicable VAT rate. Although 'cinematographic works' are not further defined in the Act, the notion corresponds to audiovisual works intended for theatrical exhibition.

In this French definition of audiovisual works, emphasis is placed on the animated sequences of images. This language is broad, and carries no exclusion for documentaries, newsreels or other types of film works. We will see that it may also cover certain videogames and multimedia works.[67] It is not clear whether it encompasses the sound part of the work or not (a positive answer would be consistent with the designation of the musical composer as co-author of the film).

[66] See para. 157.
[67] There might be problems, however, for a work or film which consists mainly in fixed sequences of non-animated scenes. Provided they are original, they would be protected by copyright but not under the specific regime of audiovisual works.

In Spain, the Copyright Act points to 'cinematographic works and any other audiovisual works' defined as:

creations expressed by means of a series of associated images, with or without incorporated sound, that are intended essentially to be shown by means of projection apparatus or any other means of communication to the public of the images and of the sound, regardless of the nature of the physical media in which the said works are embodied.[68]

Similarly broad definitions are found in the Netherlands[69] and Austria.[70] In Luxembourg, the audiovisual work is defined as a work 'consisting *mainly* in sequences of animated pictures, either with or without sound'.[71] In contrast, the 'audiovisual work' is not defined in the Belgian Copyright Act. However, its preparatory works define such work as 'a mixture of sounds and moving images, which once completed is destined to be shown in public'.[72] Although this definition appears to require sound, it is generally admitted that an audiovisual work can be silent. There is no definition of audiovisual works in the copyright Acts of Portugal,[73] Greece[74] and the Scandinavian Member States.[75]

As mentioned above, the scheme for protection is slightly different in Germany and in Italy. In Germany, the Copyright Act of 9 September 1965, as amended, refers to 'cinematographic works [*Filmwerke*], including works produced by processes similar to cinematography',[76] which is the language of article 2(1) of the Berne Convention. There is no further definition of these works. However, article 95 of the German Act introduces an additional subject-matter for audiovisual works, under the heading 'moving pictures' (*Bildfolgen*). It provides that most aspects of the regime of cinematographic works shall apply *mutatis mutandis* to 'sequences of images and to sequences of images and sounds which are not protected as cinematographic works'.[77] What audiovisual works could be considered only as *Bildfolgen* and not as *Filmwerke* is unclear.

---

[68] Art. 86 (WIPO translation).   [69] Copyright Act, art. 45a.

[70] Copyright Act, art. 4.

[71] Copyright Act (2001), art. 20. There was no definition of the audiovisual work in the 1972 Act.

[72] Report prepared by A. Strowel for the ALAI Congress of 1995, cited in J. Lahore, 'The Notion of an Audiovisual Work: International and Comparative Law', paper prepared for the Paris Convention of the ALAI on the Centenary of Film, September 1995.

[73] Art. 2 of the Code lists 'cinematographic, television, phonographic, video and radiophonic works', without further definition.

[74] The Copyright Act uses the term 'audiovisual work'.

[75] The Danish, Finnish and Swedish copyright Acts use the term 'cinematographic work' (art. 1).

[76] Art. 2(6).

[77] With the exclusion of the presumptions of assignment of arts. 89 (authors) and 92 (performers) of the Act. See paras. 161 and 336.

The neighbouring right in the audiovisual recording of article 94 also extends to recordings of *Bildfolgen*.[78]

The situation is also specifically dealt with in Italy. Article 2(6) of the 1941 Act, as amended, refers to:

> works of cinematographic art, whether in silent or sound form, provided they are not mere documentaries protected in accordance with the provisions of Chapter V of Part II [articles 87–92].

Accordingly, this definition excludes documentaries or newsreels lacking originality, which may be protected as series of photographs under a specific neighbouring right in photographs under articles 87 *et seq.* of the Act.[79] Article 87 provides that:

> Pictures of persons, or of aspects, elements or features of natural or social life, obtained by photographic or analogous processes, including reproductions of works of graphic art and stills of cinematographic film, shall be considered to be photographs for the purposes of the application of the provisions of this Chapter.[80]

Under this definition, it would appear that this neighbouring right is also applicable to (non-original and possibly original) stills of original cinematographic films. This exclusive right in photographs subsists for twenty years from their making.[81]

Original television works and documentaries may, however, be protected as works of cinematographic art.

62.   The originality criterion

In continental Europe, the originality criterion (sometimes, as in Germany, referred to as the requirement of a 'personal intellectual creation') applies to all descriptions of copyright works (as opposed to related or neighbouring rights descriptions), including cinematographic or audiovisual works. The definition of originality may vary from one Member State to another, but these variations would appear to have a limited effect on the range of film works attracting copyright protection.

The French definition of originality as the 'imprint of the author's personality' is often referred to, but is not very helpful in the definition of what constitutes an original film. It can be said, however, that it is a comprehensive concept, though probably not as much as the definition used in the UK and in other common law countries. It has been applied to a wide range of 'low-originality works', including photographs of products

---

[78] See para. 83.
[79] See M. Fabiani, in M. B. Nimmer and D. Geller (eds.), *International Copyright Law and Practice*, Matthew Bender, looseleaf, para. 2[3].
[80] WIPO translation.   [81] Art. 92.

for catalogues or software. Even newsreels or documentaries consisting of rough coverage with minimum or no editing may attract protection, as long as some originality can be found in the framing of the picture or in the choice of the position for filming, lights, etc. Amateur videos would probably be considered as copyright works, as amateur photos are. It is unlikely, however, that security camera videos would be considered original.

In contrast, the threshold of originality is usually said to be higher under German law, which had to set a specific (lower) definition of originality in the case of computer programs in order to comply with the requirements of the EC Software Directive.[82] This, however, would not appear to restrict the protection significantly further than under French law.[83]

Therefore, it is relatively safe to say that most documentaries or advertising films would meet the originality criterion in Member States of the authors' rights tradition. There is also little doubt that 'works' such as security camera videos would not satisfy this requirement. Between these extremes, there is doubt over the characterisation of newsreels.

Unless a difference in the definition of originality is held to hinder the free movement of goods or services within the European Union, disparities between Member States are likely to remain in this respect.

However, it is important to note that recent developments in EC law could suggest a possible evolution towards a harmonised definition of originality for all classes of copyright works. This trend was initiated by the Software Directive of 1991, which required only a low level of originality for software. Under article 3 of the Directive, a computer program must be protected if it is original, originality for this purpose being defined as the 'author's own intellectual creation'. This definition, which institutes a lower level of originality than that applied in several *droit d'auteur* jurisdictions, was extended to photographs in article 6 of the Term Directive, and was repeated in relation to databases in the Database Directive of 1996.[84] Therefore, a further harmonisation in this respect should not be entirely ruled out.

63.   The absence of a requirement of fixation

Fixation is not a requirement for copyright protection in authors' rights systems. It is difficult to imagine, however, an audiovisual work which

---

[82] Copyright Act, s. 69(a). See A. Dietz, in M. B. Nimmer and D. Geller (eds.), *International Copyright Law and Practice*, Matthew Bender, looseleaf, para. 2[1][b].

[83] See G. Schricker, 'Copyright Protection of Advertising Ideas, Concepts and Campaigns Under German Law' (1997) 28 IIC 477.

[84] Recital 16 and art. 3. See para. 98.

can be performed to the public without first having been recorded in some material form. This could conceivably happen in live television coverage of an event. But, in such a case, the requirement of originality may be difficult to meet. In any case, the work would be protected as a broadcast.[85]

Audiovisual works and borderline works

64.   Introduction

The definition of the audiovisual work can be applied to borderline works, such as multimedia works and videogames. It also raises interesting questions concerning altered or remastered films and formats.

65.   Multimedia works and videogames

In the UK, it is submitted that a multimedia work on CD-ROM could convey a dramatic audiovisual work, the existence of which would be determined in accordance with the criteria used in relation to, say, documentaries. However, this implies that the multimedia work is not only a mere compilation, such as an encyclopaedia, but carries a scenario or a story (even if this scenario can be modified to a certain extent by the input of the user). The audiovisual dramatic work would be distinct from the underlying script (itself a dramatic work), since new elements have been added (sound effects, images, animations, etc.) and original choices have been made by the persons in charge of the project.

Scripts and stories for videogames could also attract protection as dramatic works. When these are interactive, i.e. when the player can change the development of the plot, the story thus revealed would be protected to the extent it has been created, foreseen and recorded as a possible development by the author of the script. If the 'adventure' is created by the player from mere situations without any pre-programmed link between them, the resulting dramatic work, if any, is unlikely to be the creation of the author of the game. It could be a creation of the player himself, provided he has the amount of freedom in his choices (and probably the creative intent) compatible with the requirement of authorship.[86]

Under French law, screen displays of videogames can enjoy separate protection as audiovisual works.[87] However, in *Vincent v. Cuc Software*,

---

[85] See para. 94.   [86] And provided it is fixed in some material form.
[87] In France, Court of Cassation, 7 March 1986 (two cases, *Atari* and *Williams Electronics*), *La Semaine Juridique*, 1986, II, No. 20631, note J. M. Mousseron, B. Teyssié and M. Vivant; RIDA, 1986, 129, p. 132 and 134, note A. Lucas.

the Court of Appeal of Versailles held that a videogame on CD-ROM could not be considered as an audiovisual work because of its interactive nature, as opposed to the sequential and linear presentation of images in audiovisual works, and the accessory nature of audiovisual parts.[88] This emphasis on 'interactivity' appears to add to the definition in the French Act, and contradicts the solutions adopted by the French Supreme Court in relation to screen displays of videogames. The criterion of the accessory nature of the audiovisual work is more convincing.

But this exclusion does not mean that no videogames or multimedia works could be considered as audiovisual works. They could meet the definition if, for example, their 'audiovisual part' is not considered accessory to the rest of the work. Also, in any case, their audiovisual component will attract protection as a pre-existing audiovisual work.

It must be noted that the main advantage of distinguishing multimedia works from audiovisual works under French law is to avoid the application of some unwelcome or unadapted aspects of the regime of film protection. For example, in *Vincent* v. *Cuc Software*, the disqualification resulted in the application of the French doctrine of 'collective work', which grants a legal person the initial copyright in the works created by its employee (this doctrine being expressly excluded in the case of audiovisual works).[89] This certainly accounts for the solution adopted by the court.

66.   Altered or remastered films

In the UK, it seems fairly clear that a mere *technical enhancement* of the quality of the image or sound, or a *change in the format* of the 'dramatic' film (e.g. for release on video) would not create a new original derivative dramatic work. The same is true of *colourisation*, unless it can be said that colour enhances the dramatic impact of the story. In that case, the modification, no matter how original, is unlikely to be substantial enough to create a new derivative dramatic work. It might, however, create a derivative 'film'.[90]

In contrast to mere technical enhancements, a 'director's cut' made after theatrical release could well create a new dramatic work, itself derived from the dramatic work resulting from the 'producer's cut'. This could

---

[88] Tribunal of First Instance of Nanterre, 26 November 1997, *Gazette du Palais*, 19–21 April 1998, p. 220, note Demnard Tellier; RIPIA, 1998, p. 418. Versailles Court of Appeal, 18 November 1999, *Communication Commerce Electronique*, February 2000, No. 2, p. 13.

[89] See paras. 135 and 138.

[90] See para. 80. Note that colourisation does not create any separately protected artistic work, since colourised film frames are, as film frames, expressly excluded from protection under artistic copyright (1988 Act, s. 4(2); see para. 77).

well be the case, for example, if the ending and other elements of the plot are changed in this process.

In France, in the famous *Huston* case, the Court of Appeal of Paris indicated, *obiter dicta*, that a colourised movie could constitute an (original) adaptation of the underlying black-and-white movie.[91]

67.   The protection of television formats

Television formats, especially game show formats, have become a very valuable property. A format can be defined as resulting from 'fixed and repeated elements (for example, the planned sequence of particular types of events, catchphrases, scenery and music) which form the dramatic structure of a programme, and cause the dramatic movement through that structure'.[92] The opportunity of direct copyright protection for such elements has been, and is still being, debated.[93] Although copyright may provide some form of protection for the most developed formats, these works are mainly protected by contract and through unfair competition or more specific doctrines of misappropriation.

68.   Copyright protection of formats

In the UK, the closest available heading for the protection of formats is dramatic work. However, the protection of a television format as a dramatic work was expressly denied in the *Green* case,[94] because the features

---

[91] Paris Court of Appeal, 6 July 1989, *La Semaine Juridique*, 1990, II, No. 21410, note A. Françon; *Cahiers du Droit d'Auteur*, July 1989, p. 8. Decision overturned on other grounds by the Court of Cassation, 28 May 1991, RIDA, July 1991, pp. 197 and 161, obs. Kerever; *La Semaine Juridique*, 1991, II, No. 21731, note A. Françon.

[92] S. Lane and R. McD. Bridge, 'The Protection of Formats Under English Law, Part 1' (1990) 3 *Entertainment Law Review* 96; and S. Lane and R. McD. Bridge, 'The Protection of Formats Under English Law, Part 2' (1990) 4 *Entertainment Law Review* 131. The use of the term 'dramatic' appears superfluous in this definition.

[93] E.g. contra: T. Martino and C. Miskin, 'Format Rights: The Price Is Not Right' (1991) 2 *Entertainment Law Review* 31; pro: P. Smith, 'Format Rights: Opportunity Knocks' (1991) 3 *Entertainment Law Review* 63. See also D. Rose, 'Format Rights: A Never Ending Drama (or Not)' (1999) 6 *Entertainment Law Review* 170; and T. Steffenson, 'Rights to TV Formats: From a Copyright and a Marketing Law Perspective' (2000) 5 *Entertainment Law Review* 85. On continental law, see E. Ancel, 'La Protection Juridique des Formats et Emissions de Télévision', DESS thesis, University of Poitiers, September 2000 (France); A. Gagliari, 'Programme Format Protection in the French and Italian Systems' (1998) 5 *Entertainment Law Review* 200; and H. von Have and F. Eickmeier, 'Statutory Protection of Television Show Formats' (1998) 1 *Entertainment Law Review* 9 (Germany).

[94] *Green* v. *Broadcasting Corporation of New Zealand* [1989] 2 All ER 1056; [1989] RPC 700. Compare with the Canadian case of *Hutton* v. *Canadian Broadcasting Corporation* (1989) 29 CPR (3d) 398 (Alberta Queens Bench) (see para. 35 above). In *Wilson* v. *Broadcasting*

claimed as constituting the format, mere accessories used in the presentation of other dramatic or musical performances, lacked sufficient unity to be capable of performance.[95] In a reaction to this, in 1994 the Department of Trade and Industry announced that it was considering whether copyright protection should be extended to programme formats and issued consultation papers on the subject.[96] The document did not propose the introduction of a new *sui generis* right, but instead proposed extending the definition of 'copying' so as to include borrowings of 'format' elements.[97] It was not followed by any legislative action.

In authors' rights jurisdictions, formats for television programmes or game shows are not included in the statutory lists of protected works. But, since these lists are open, formats could be protected as long as they meet the requirements of expression and originality. This, of course, will depend on the complexity and degree of expression of the format. Formats in the form of complex documents including descriptions of characters, plot or dramatic events would certainly attract some form of copyright protection. Mere concepts and ideas would not. Between these extremes, the solutions may diverge. In France, for example, courts have had the occasion to refuse copyright protection for a concept of a television show aimed at a female audience supported by a basic structure:

The project of a programme for a female audience . . . only brought Ms Gautier to propose a mere idea in the form of a canvas, the content and expression of which (the list of debated themes, and the technical process of the interview or roundtable) does not constitute an intellectual creation and is not original since, before 1970, it was commonly used, in the press and at the radio or television.[98]

    Corp. of New Zealand (1988) 12 TPR 173; [1990] 2 NZLR 575, High Court, Wellington, a programme which used the concept of a projected television series was held to infringe the copyright in the 'format' developed by the plaintiff. But the court pointed out that the 'format' was developed at great length in a 'feasibility study' of fifty-seven pages, including the original concept and about twenty pages of detailed storylines.

[95] For the general opinion that such formats are not protected under US copyright, see R. I. Freedman and R. C. Harris, 'Game Show Rights Contracts: Winners and Losers' (1990) *Entertainment Law Review* 209 at 211. Also, under French law, see Paris Court of Appeal, 14 October 1975, RIDA, 1976, p. 136 (cited in E. Logeais, 'Record Fine for Plagiarism of a Reality Show: Is It Safer Under French Law to Sue for Unfair Competition Rather than for Copyright Infringement' (1993) 4 *Entertainment Law Review* 116). See also *Hutton v. Canadian Broadcasting Corporation* (1989) 29 CPR (3d) 398 (Alberta Queens Bench) (see para. 57 above).

[96] A *sui generis* protection akin to copyright was also proposed in an amendment introduced by the House of Lords during the passage of the Broadcasting Bill 1990.

[97] See (1996) 5 *Entertainment Law Review* 212. For example, the CDPA 1988 would have provided *inter alia* that 'copying in relation to a copyright work or series of copyright works recording a sufficiently elaborated scheme or plan for a series of programmes includes making a programme to that scheme or plan' (subject to various qualifications and definitions).

[98] Paris Court of Appeal, 14 October 1975, RIDA, 1976, p. 136.

Protection was also refused for the idea of a game show based on the use of identikits,[99] or for the idea of a programme in which the live performance of young talents is judged by professionals and a television audience.[100]

However, more elaborate formats could be copyright works. In a recent case, the Court of Appeal of Paris considered that a project for a game show, which consisted in an original compilation of well-known elements, was protectable by copyright. However, the infringement action brought by the author of the project against the producers of a subsequent programme based on the same idea was rejected on the basis that the elements borrowed were not original in themselves, and that the resemblance between the projects 'came from features common to all television game shows that could not be protected', and thus 'excluded even partial infringement'.[101]

In the French practice, authors of 'bibles' for television series are treated as authors and are accepted as members of the audiovisual rights societies.[102]

69. Misappropriation of formats and unfair competition

A lack of copyright protection does not prejudice the possibility of suing in tort for unfair competition or misappropriation. However, the protection offered by EU Member States is very different.

In the UK, protection through 'passing off' may prove illusory since the copying of a format is unlikely to give rise to misrepresentation and confusion.[103] In contrast, in several authors' rights countries, broader doctrines of unfair competition would protect against the most obvious cases of misappropriation. Although, as a general rule, works that are not protected by copyright can be freely copied, the circumstances in which the work is copied can give rise to liability under unfair competition rules.

This would be the case, for example in France under the general principle of civil liability in article 1382 of the Civil Code, which provides that any action that causes damage to someone else obliges the party who caused the damage by his fault to repair it. This article forms the basis for the French law on unfair competition. In this respect, an important case was decided in France in 1993 for 'slavish copying' of a format, which

---

[99] Amiens Court of Appeal, 9 July 1984, *Juris-Classeur Propriété Littéraire et Artistique*, fasc. 1140.

[100] Paris Court of Appeal, 12 February 1992, *Légipresse*, No. 76, 1990, III, p. 98.

[101] Paris Court of Appeal, 27 March 1998, *Revue Dalloz*, 1999, No. 28, p. 417.

[102] But these bibles are well developed: they either include a synopsis of the episodes (literary bibles) or graphic presentations of characters for animated series (graphic bibles).

[103] S. Lane and R. McD. Bridge, 'The Protection of Formats Under English Law, Part 1' (1990) 3 *Entertainment Law Review* 96 at 97–9.

ended in the largest fine awarded by a French court in this field.[104] A public broadcaster, Antenne 2, acquired from CBS the rights to the format for the programme 'Rescue 911', and broadcast a French version of this programme named 'La nuit des héros' ('Heroes' Night'). Some time later, a private broadcaster, TF1, produced a similar show, called 'Les marches de la gloire' ('Marches of Glory'), hosted by the same person who in the meantime had changed employer. The two programmes were based on the same concept of ordinary people involved in events in which they showed courage, re-enacted in short sequences. TF1 was held liable for unfair competition.[105]

But French courts have also developed from the same article of the Civil Code a broader doctrine of 'economic parasitism', which prevents competitors but also non-competitors from making profits from the investments of other persons, even if they do not cause confusion in the public as to the origin of the product. This form of unfair competition is perfectly adapted to misappropriation and the slavish imitation of formats.

In Italy and the Netherlands, general doctrines of misappropriation have been developed from provisions of the Civil Code. In other countries, specific Acts on unfair competition could provide adequate remedies in obvious cases of misappropriation, especially if they involve competitors. This appears to be the case in Austria,[106] Belgium,[107] Spain,[108] Germany[109] and Sweden.[110]

PART II

The audiovisual recording

70.   Presentation

As described, there are two ways of protecting the business of producing works of expression under copyright law. The common method is to grant a 'full' or classic copyright in the work; a more modern and often cumulative approach, is to grant an 'entrepreneurial copyright'[111] or

---

[104] Versailles Court of Appeal, 11 March 1993; E. Logeais, 'Record Fine for Plagiarism of a Reality Show: Is It Safer Under French Law to Sue for Unfair Competition Rather than for Copyright Infringement' (1993) 4 *Entertainment Law Review* 116.

[105] And ordered at first instance to pay FFr25 million; the damages were increased to FFr55 million on appeal.

[106] Unfair Competition Act 1980.   [107] Under a Law of 1991.

[108] Under a Law of 1989.   [109] *Gesetz gegen den Unlauteren Wettbewerb*, UWG.

[110] Marketing Act of 1975.

[111] W. R. Cornish, *Intellectual Property*, 2nd edn, Sweet & Maxwell, 1989, para. 10-016; and W. R. Cornish, *Intellectual Property*, 3rd edn, Sweet & Maxwell, 1996, paras. 1-6 and 1-11.

'neighbouring right' to the producer, which usually protects not the work itself, but rather its embodiment or manifestation. The classic example of this is the distinction between the copyright in the musical work and the copyright (or neighbouring right) in the sound recording, inaugurated by the UK Copyright Act of 1911. This duality is now almost universally accepted and, considering the long debates over various extensions of copyright protection, met with surprisingly little criticism. The copyright or neighbouring right in the recording is distinct from the copyright in the work embodied, and is in fact independent of the existence of any underlying copyright. Moreover, the right is exempt from the requirement of originality.[112] Such rights have two advantages: they avoid long discussions on originality, and they give to the producer a stronger title against infringers, especially for works involving numerous (licensed) underlying works. Therefore they can prove particularly useful to producers in relation to highly collective and derivative works like films.

The idea of a right in an audiovisual recording (or in a television broadcast) was proposed relatively late.[113] The UK 1956 Act was the first copyright Act to implement this idea, and introduced *inter alia* entrepreneurial copyrights in cinematographic films,[114] broadcasts and later in cable programmes. In Germany, the Copyright Act 1965 introduced neighbouring rights in film recordings in favour of film producers.[115] The German example was followed by several Member States in the context of the copyright reforms of the 1980s, and notably in France in the Copyright Amendment Act of 1985.[116] The resulting disparity in the scheme of film protection was thought to create a distortion in the internal market. The question was introduced in the harmonisation programme of the Commission which led to the institution of the related right of the film producer at Community level in the EC Rental Directive.

71.   The problem raised by the double protection of audiovisual works

Therefore, under present copyright law in the European Union, two copyrights may subsist in works which are very closely associated: the audiovisual work on the one hand, and its recording on the other. Moreover, these rights will, in most cases, be owned by the same person, as film producers will be granted or will otherwise acquire from film authors

---

[112] Note, however, that under US copyright, sound recordings are original works of authorship, and there is no special rule concerning authorship of sound recordings.
[113] But see para. 15.
[114] Although under the 1956 Act the 'cinematograph film' is not technically the recording but the 'sequence of images' recorded on film. See para. 22.
[115] See para. 35.   [116] See para. 30.

the copyright in the film. What are the consequences of such double protection?

The cumulation of copyright is commonplace in relation to audiovisual works; the pre-existing works, the various scripts and the final audiovisual works can attract separate protection as derivative works. In that situation, the derivative work is a work of original authorship, which often involves different contributors. Economists justify such a protection by the need to encourage the production of works based on other works, which sometimes requires considerable investment or effort.[117] This seems consistent with the incentive rationale behind copyright protection. However, here we are faced with a second type of cumulation, which involves the same work or works which cannot be separated on originality grounds. For an audiovisual dramatic work, the 'film', the visual recording, is nothing but a copy.

Where implemented, this double protection for films is always justified in economic terms (usually without any serious empirical analysis) and by analogy to the protection of sound recordings.[118] The problem is that the analogy to sound recordings is in truth an incomplete one.[119] In contrast to sound recording producers, in most cases film producers obtain the copyright in the audiovisual and contributory works embodied in the recording, and thus do not need another copyright title to protect their investments in infringement actions. Another difference is the possibility of likening sound recordings to original works of authorship,[120] or at least considering that there is a specific and distinct investment in the production of such recordings. In contrast, the work involved in the recording of an audiovisual work is difficult to separate from the work involved in the creation of the audiovisual work itself. It can therefore be questioned whether such double copyright protection is needed to encourage film producers to produce films.

Moreover, this scheme not only appears pointless in terms of incentives, it can have negative economic consequences. Where it operates, the cumulation has no effect if the producer has control of both rights. However, if a copyright interest is retained by the creative authors, or if the

---

[117] W. M. Landes and R. Posner, 'An Economic Analysis of Copyright Law' (1989) Journal of Legal Studies 325 at 354–5; see also J. Ginsburg, 'Creation and Commercial Value: Copyright Protection of Works of Information' (1990) 90 *Columbia Law Review* 1865 at 1910, who suggests that another reason for the protection of derivative works is to provide incentives to produce the initial work, since a potential exploitation of derivative works is often considered as part of the decision to create the initial work.

[118] See e.g. on the question of broadcasts, the extract from the Gregory Committee Report, Cmd 8662, 1952, quoted at chapter 2, n. 134 above.

[119] Except maybe in relation to film soundtracks involving substantial studio recording work (thus justifying their protection as sound recordings).

[120] This is the case under US copyright.

rights are granted to separate licensing bodies,[121] users (including further authors and producers) will bear higher costs in order to exploit audiovisual works. In some instances, they will have to obtain, and bargain for, two authorisations instead of one. In that situation there is no doubt that the cumulation increases the cost of using these works. Multimedia producers on the continent already experience such difficulties.[122]

Incidentally, it is important to recall that this scheme is designed to remedy two problems that are specific to continental systems of protection. In several *droit d'auteur* countries, authors of audiovisual works retain certain rights in their works or assign them to collecting societies, which weakens the title of film producers in infringement proceedings.[123] Also, higher standards in relation to 'originality' might leave valuable works unprotected. These problems either are unknown or cause fewer difficulties in copyright systems.

72. The neighbouring right of film producers in the EC copyright directives

The EC Rental Directive instituted at the European level the protection of the right of the 'producer of the first fixation of the film'. This right is addressed in Chapter II of the Directive, dedicated to 'Rights related to copyrights', regarding the rights of phonogram producers, performers and broadcasting organisations.

Under the Rental Directive, film producers were granted a reproduction right and a distribution right in their audiovisual recordings, but no performing right (or right of communication to the public). The reproduction right of film producers is defined as the exclusive right to authorise or prohibit the direct or indirect reproduction of the original and copies of their films.[124] The distribution right is defined as the exclusive right to make available the original and copies of the film to the public, by sale or otherwise.[125] This distribution right is subject to Community exhaustion (first sale doctrine).[126] Film producers also benefit from lending and rental rights in the conditions described for authors, which are excepted from Community exhaustion.[127]

---

[121] Compare with the situation regarding sound recordings. In the UK, sound recording performing rights are granted to the collecting society PPL, and musical performing rights to another collecting society, PRS. In continental Europe, where implemented, authors' rights and neighbouring rights in films are administered by separate licensing bodies.

[122] As the inclusion of film footage in multimedia works often involves clearance of both the copyright and the neighbouring rights in the film, and thus negotiation and payment of two fees.

[123] See e.g. at para. 160.   [124] Art. 7.   [125] Art. 9.   [126] Art. 9(2).   [127] Art. 2.

The Directive specifies that the distribution, rental and lending rights may be transferred or assigned or be subject to the granting of contractual licences.[128]

Article 10 provides that Member States may provide for limitations on these rights in respect of (a) private use (without prejudice to any existing or future legislation on remuneration for reproduction for private use); (b) use of short excerpts in connection with the reporting of current events; (c) ephemeral fixation by a broadcasting organisation by means of its own facilities and for its own broadcasts; and (d) use solely for the purposes of teaching or scientific research. More generally, Member States may provide for the same kinds of limitations as they provide for in connection with the protection of copyright in literary and artistic works.

The exclusive rights of film producers have been reinforced by the Directive on Copyright and Related Rights in the Information Society. In particular, the Directive provides for the introduction of a right of communication to the public for this class of works.[129]

Article 3 of the Term Directive specifies that the rights of producers of the first fixation of a film shall expire fifty years after the fixation, publication or communication to the public, as the case may be.[130]

73.   The videogram in domestic laws

In authors' rights countries, the protection granted to videogram producers is considered as an ancillary form of protection. As a consequence, the regime of this neighbouring right is usually neither detailed nor studied as extensively as the *droit d'auteur* in the audiovisual work. In contrast, in the UK and Ireland the copyright in the 'film' (the visual recording) is the main form of protection of audiovisual works. This raises complex problems of boundaries, and technical difficulties relating to the protection of film frames or soundtracks. Both approaches must be studied separately.

The 'film' under UK copyright

74.   The definition of the 'film' under the 1988 Act

Under section 13(10) of the 1956 Act, the specific subject-matter for audiovisual works, the 'cinematograph film', was defined as:

---

[128] Arts. 2(4) and 9(4).

[129] See para. 189. But see also paras. 180 (right of reproduction) and 211 (exemptions).

[130] Under art. 8 of the Directive, this term is calculated from 1 January of the year following this event.

any sequence of visual images recorded on material of any description (whether translucent or not) so as to be capable, by the use of that material:

(a) of being shown as a moving picture, or

(b) of being recorded on other material (whether translucent or not), by the use of which it can be so shown

In section 5B(1) of the 1988 Act, a 'film' is now defined as:

a recording on any medium from which a moving image may by any means be produced.[131]

As mentioned above, this change in the wording brought a shift in the subject-matter, from the recorded work to the recording. What this new definition refers to is no longer the (recorded) sequence of images but the recording itself,[132] and this recording must be capable of producing moving images.[133]

We saw that such a system, however unconventional, meets the requirements of the Berne Convention. Although the cinematographic works in the Convention are not the audiovisual recordings but the underlying audiovisual works,[134] protection through the recording has no effect on the minimum protection guaranteed by the Convention, which, in any case, allows the requirement of a fixation as a prerequisite for copyright protection.[135]

75.   Range of works covered by the definition

This definition in section 5 has important consequences on the range of works covered. In particular, in the present definition there is no longer a requirement that a moving image be produced by a *sequence* of recorded

---

[131] Art. 5(1) in the original 1988 text. The Duration of Copyright and Rights in Performances Regulations 1995 (SI 1995 No. 3297) added two new paragraphs (s. 5B(2) and (3)) concerning film soundtracks.

[132] See paras. 53 and 74.

[133] This idea of 'motion' is found in the US definition of 'motion pictures' in s. 101 of the 1976 Copyright Act, but movement is not required under US law for the larger category of 'audiovisual works'. In the same way, continental countries, while adopting definitions of audiovisual work close to that of the UK, have sometimes introduced neighbouring rights on audiovisual recordings which do not require movement, but only a sequence of related images.

[134] See the General Report of the Berlin Conference, quoted on that point at para. 13 above. Final reports are thought to present an 'authentic' or 'authoritative' interpretation of the Convention (S. Ricketson, *The Berne Convention on the Protection of Literary and Artistic Works*, Kluwer, 1987, p. 137, para. 4.12). See also art. 2 of the Convention: 'works . . . expressed by a process analogous to cinematography'; by analogy the work 'expressed by photography' is not the negative, but the underlying work of the photographer.

[135] See para. 49.

images. A moving image, or the impression of motion, can be produced from a single image, for example when distorted or manipulated according to a predetermined pattern by a computer program.[136] The illusion of motion can even be created without the recording of any image: a sequence of data or instructions can direct a computer to draw successive patterns giving the illusion of movement. The recording of these elements would constitute a 'film' under the 1988 Act, where there would have been no recorded sequences of images to attract protection as a 'cinematograph film' under the previous Act. This certainly extends the protection to recordings of videogames.[137]

But what about recordings of software? From the digital recording of most software, a moving image can be produced. On the computer screen menus scroll, blocks are moved, etc. It is submitted that these 'movements' do not produce a 'moving image' according to section 5B(1), at least not within the meaning Parliament intended for this word. It is submitted that there must be something in the nature of a pictorial work, and that the mere scrolling of a text, or incidental and limited motions on parts of the screen, would not suffice to create a 'film' in its own right.[138] In fact, the Duration of Copyright and Rights in Performances Regulations 1995,[139] by setting out a list of contributors including the director, the screenwriter, etc., for the purpose of calculating the term of copyright in the film, suggest that the works considered for protection do not extend beyond computer games or multimedia works. However, the point is not free of doubt, and there could be border cases of non-'game' or 'multimedia' software attracting protection both as literary work[140] and, through its digital recording, as 'films'.[141]

In contrast, the previous definition was more restrictive, and would probably only give protection to computer games or multimedia works

---

[136] This is the case of a single 'sprite' in a computer game programme.

[137] This question has never been brought before the UK courts, but it has been submitted by one author that the definition of 'films' applies; see J. A. L. Sterling, *Intellectual Property Rights in Sound Recordings, Films and Video*, Sweet & Maxwell, 1992, para. 4A.17.

[138] Compare with the US case of *WGN Continental Broadcasting Co. v. United Video Inc.*, 693 F. 2d 622 at 628 (7th Cir. 1982), where it was held that teletext information superimposed on a news broadcast is part of the protected audiovisual work.

[139] SI 1995 No. 3297.

[140] According to s. 3(1) of the 1988 Act. And irrespective of protection of the underlying artistic elements.

[141] See also J. A. L. Sterling, *Intellectual Property Rights in Sound Recordings, Films and Video*, Sweet & Maxwell, 1992, para. 4A.23, in relation to semiconductor topographies: 'Where a semiconductor topography embodies a series of patterns which, in conjunction with electronic processes, enables sounds to be heard or moving images to be seen, it may be that the article in question incorporates on the one hand a topography and on the other a recording of sounds and moving images.'

which are truly constituted by *sequences* of digitised and recorded images.[142]

It seems fairly clear that the term 'moving image' in the 1988 Act does not refer to the movement between given images in a sequence, but rather to the movement of a represented scene or item. Hence, film footage consisting only of still shots of still pictures (a 'slide-show on film'), even if accompanied by music or comments, might not be a film under the 1988 Act. Also, it has been pointed out that the definition requires a moving image, not a changing one.[143] But we can see no reason why footage consisting of a single fixed shot of, say, a landscape, slowly changing under the effect of the wind, would not be protected as a 'film'.[144] The same is true of a moving shot of a fixed picture.[145]

Finally, no reference is made in this definition to any particular technology, which is confirmed by the legislative history.[146] Hence, the recording can be made on optical (film), magnetic (videotape), electronic (semiconductor) or printed (paper) media, and the impression of motion can be created by mechanical (projection camera), electronic (computer, VCR) or even manual means. However, it is submitted that the use of the singular in the first part of the definition ('*a* recording') is of significance: the movement should be perceived from the use of *one* recording. If that is the case, slide sets, a series of separate photographs (as, for example, in a zoetrope), even if they are presented so as to give the impression of motion, could not be considered as a 'film'.[147] However, a close sequence of photographs of a moving scene taken through a motorised photographic device might attract protection as a 'film', if the related images have been fixed originally on a single recording (the roll of photographic film).[148]

---

[142] It is submitted that s. 172(2) of the Act, which states that a provision 'which corresponds to a provision of the previous law shall not be construed as departing from the previous law merely because of a change of expression', is of no help. The 'film' is a different subject-matter from the 'cinematograph film', since it refers to the visual recording itself, and not to the 'sequences of images recorded', i.e. the recorded work. This is not a mere change of expression.

[143] J. Phillips, R. Durie and I. Karet, *Whale on Copyright*, 4th edn, Sweet & Maxwell, 1993, p. 32.

[144] As would security camera footage of an empty corridor if from time to time a person walks in it (but then the protection might be limited to the 'moving' part of the footage; see the next paragraph).

[145] E.g. camera-on-shoulder footage of sculptures.

[146] See H. Laddie, P. Prescott and M. Vitoria, *The Modern Law of Copyright*, Butterworths, 1995, para. 5.35.

[147] However, under the same reasoning, filming the window of a zoetrope in motion, or including each slide in a film strip (for example, as in the case of cartoons) would result in a film. A flip book might be considered as a single 'recording' (the term is not defined in the CDPA 1988).

[148] See H. Laddie, P. Prescott and M. Vitoria, *The Modern Law of Copyright*, Butterworths, 1995, paras. 5.35 and 5.39. But can a moving image be perceived from this photographic film?

76.   Multimedia works

The definition of 'films' might be broad enough to allow the protection of recordings of most multimedia works, for example on CD-ROMs[149] However, in relation to multimedia works, the main difficulty of the definition is the requirement that a moving image be produced from the recording. Accordingly, when a work is constituted by still images shown sequentially, its recording may not attract protection as a 'film'.

It may be observed that multimedia works on CD-ROMs often involve film footage or animation. When that is the case, the recording of these 'moving images' may well qualify as a film under the 1988 Act. But here we come back to the question of knowing what constitutes such 'moving images'. Film footage certainly does, but, as stated above, it is not clear whether the movement of a single frame or the scrolling of a text on the screen would constitute such a moving image. This point is important, since protection as a film might be limited to the recording from which a moving image can be produced, and might not extend to the recording of non-moving elements. In other words, recordings of multimedia works might be protected as films to a certain extent only. Against this, one could consider the use of the singular in the definition of film ('*a* recording') and admit that a recording might be protected as a film, even if only a limited part of this recording conveys a moving image. If that is the case, however, then arguably this part must be of some significance.

Of course, concerning *interactive* works, the fact that pre-programmed animation is started by an action of the user does not change the characterisation as a film for the relevant part of the multimedia recording.

77.   The protection of film frames

Individual film frames can be a very valuable property, particularly in relation to merchandising and related activities, which have developed greatly over the last twenty years. Pictures taken from films play an important part in this business; they are used on toys, clothes, books, etc. The digitisation of films and the computer processing of images has made the unauthorised lifting of individual film frames easier than in the past. One can now easily, and at low cost, produce high-quality and exploitable shots, either from retail copies or from high-quality digital broadcasts of films. Adequate protection of film frames is, therefore, more than ever of major importance for the film industry.

We saw in the previous chapter that film frames were protected as photographs under the 1911 Act, but that the 1956 Act excluded photographs

[149] For the protection of the underlying multimedia work, see para. 65.

forming part of a film from this definition. Under the present 1988 Act, film frames are still excluded from protection as photographs.[150] Thus in the absence of any underlying work constituting another artistic or literary work,[151] the only subject-matter available for protection of film frames is the 'film' itself. Although each individual frame or image does not constitute a film, they are part of a film. But would the lifting of a single frame infringe the copyright in the film?

This problem was raised under the 1956 Act in the *Spelling Goldberg* case.[152] The defendants used photographs of scenes from the television series 'Starsky and Hutch' in two publications without the authorisation of the plaintiffs, owners of the copyright in the series. The plaintiffs claimed that the copying infringed their copyright in the cinematographic film. Under section 13 of the 1956 Act, the term 'copy' in relation to a cinematographic film was defined as meaning 'any print, negative, tape or other article in which the film or part of it is recorded'. In the High Court, Mervyn Davies QC considered that this 'part of the film' must have the same characteristic as the film itself ('sequence of visual images', 'recorded on material' and 'capable of . . . being shown as a moving picture'). Accordingly, he held that a copy of a single frame could not be considered as a copy of a substantial part of a film, lacking the characteristic impression of motion of a film. The Court of Appeal overturned the decision and held that a single frame was 'part of' the film under section 13.[153]

The 1988 Act reinforces this solution by defining copying in relation to a film as including the act of 'making a photograph of the whole or of any substantial part of any image forming part of the film'.[154] As a consequence, the lifting of any frame from the film infringes its copyright, irrespective of its importance in the footage but also irrespective of its originality, which extends the protection of film frames

---

[150] Section 4(2): '"photograph" means a recording of light or other radiation on any medium on which an image is produced or from which an image may by any means be produced, and which is not part of a film.' Had this exclusion been omitted in the 1988 Act (as in the definition of dramatic work), under the present definition of photographs, any film frame could be considered as a photograph, even if the film was recorded only on videotape or another electronic medium. Under the present rules on authorship for photographs, the author of the photograph would be the person who created it, i.e. arguably the film director or the director of photography.

[151] E.g. in relation to cartoons, each drawing is protected as an artistic work. In the same way, a pre-existing photograph 'filmed' in a film is still an artistic work.

[152] *Spelling Goldberg Productions Inc.* v. *BPC Publishing Ltd* [1981] RPC 283, CA; [1979] FSR 494. See K. J. Schulman, 'Starsky and Hutch – Copyright in Film Frames?' (1979) 1 EIPR 143; L. Stevenson, 'Starsky and Hutch – The Spelling Goldberg Decision – Copyright in Film Frames Rediscovered' (1980) 2 EIPR 370.

[153] Which is a generous construction of the text.

[154] Section 17(4). The same is true in relation to broadcasts and cable programmes.

beyond the standard set up for photographs.[155] This disparity is difficult to justify.

78.   The difficult question of film soundtracks

The copyright protection of film soundtracks is a troublesome question. The relationship between the soundtrack, the visual part of the film and the underlying works (mainly musical works) is difficult to analyse. In relation to the underlying works, the problem is to know whether or not the soundtrack should be treated like a normal derivative work. Under UK copyright law, the answer to this question is affirmative,[156] and this situation does not seem to create special problems.[157] In relation to the actual recording of sounds in the film strip, the question is whether the film soundtrack should be treated separately from the visual part of the film. In this regard, the solution has changed with each Copyright Act, and again recently with the Duration Regulations 1995, with unwelcome results.

Under the 1911 Act, film soundtracks were protected as 'records, perforated rolls and other contrivances by means of which sounds may be mechanically reproduced, in like manner as if such contrivances were musical works', in short as sound recordings.[158] As a result, the compulsory licence to reproduce a musical work[159] mechanically could be invoked for synchronisation in films but also for the synchronisation of a film

---

[155] Accordingly, the lifting of a frame which is a mere copy of a pre-existing drawing or photograph would infringe the copyright in the film as well as the copyright in the underlying work.

[156] Consider, however, s. 13(7) of the 1956 Act, which provided: 'Where by virtue of this section copyright has subsisted in a cinematograph film, a person who, after that copyright has expired, causes the film to be seen, or to be seen and heard, in public does not thereby infringe any copyright subsisting by virtue of Part I of this Act in any literary, dramatic, musical and artistic work.' The Performing Right Society would not have been able to collect fees in relation to these public domain films shown in cinemas or public places. Consider also the effect on music videos. This provision, which was contrary to the Berne Convention (Brussels Act, art. 14(2); Paris Act, art. 14bis(1)), was not re-enacted. Since s. 13 of the 1956 Act did not apply to cinematograph films made under the 1911 Act, no copyright in films made under the 1956 Act could expire before the adoption the 1988 Act.

[157] This is not the case in the US, due to various requirements of publication and registration. See E. F. Brylawski, 'Motion Picture Soundtrack Music: A Gap or Gaff in Copyright Protection?' (1993) 40 *Journal of the Copyright Society of the USA* 333–48; L. S. Sobel, 'The Legal and Business Aspects of Motion Picture and Television Soundtrack Music' (1988) *Loyola Entertainment Law Journal* 231–58.

[158] Section 19(1). For an application to videotapes, see *Tom Hopkins International Inc.* v. *Wall & Redekop Realty Ltd* (1984) 1 CPR (3d) 348; (1985) 6 CPR (3d) 475, British Columbia Court of Appeal (based on similar drafting in the Canadian Copyright Act).

[159] Section 19(2).

soundtrack music in a record.[160] The copyright in the soundtrack had the same duration as the copyright in the film as a series of photographs,[161] but expired before the copyright in the film as a dramatic work.[162]

The 1956 Act excluded film soundtracks from the definition of sound recordings,[163] and protected them under the new 'cinematograph film' copyright.[164] The main effect of this was to harmonise the regime of the visual and sound components of films.

This scheme was changed again by section 5 of the 1988 Act in its original form: in the new Act 'sound recording' simply means 'a recording of sounds, from which the sounds may be reproduced', whether the 'film' was defined as 'a recording on any medium from which a moving image may be by any means produced', without further specification. As a generally accepted consequence, two mutually exclusive copyrights had to be considered: the copyright in the film (or, rather, in the film less the soundtrack, i.e. the visual recording), and the copyright in the soundtrack as a sound recording. This change in the law had no real consequence: the two copyrights had the same regime with regard to authorship,[165] duration[166] and primary and secondary infringement.[167]

Finally, the protection for film soundtracks changed with the Duration Regulations 1995, which reverted to the situation of the 1956 Act. The Regulations extended the duration of the copyright in the film to seventy years after the death of one of the contributors listed in the new section 13B(2). In order to harmonise the duration of the copyright in the visual and sound parts of films, it was felt necessary to reunite them under the same copyright. As a consequence, under the new section 5B the definition of films expressly includes the soundtrack. The definition of sound recordings in section 5A remains unchanged. Needless to say, these reforms have created complex transitional provisions.[168]

---

[160] *Copinger and Skone James on Copyright*, 8th edn, 1948, p. 229.

[161] Copyright in the 'sound recording' subsisted fifty years from the making of the original plate from which the contrivance was directly or indirectly derived, against fifty years from the making of the original negative for photographs.

[162] Which expired fifty years p.m.a.   [163] Section 12(9).

[164] Section 13(9): 'For the purposes of this Act a cinematograph film shall be taken to include the sounds embodied in any soundtrack associated with the film, and references to a copy of a cinematographic work shall be construed accordingly.' See *Sharif*, unreported, 2 February 1981, Chancery Division, para. 22 above.

[165] Section 9(2).   [166] Section 13.   [167] Sections 16–20 and 22–26.

[168] Under reg. 26(1) of the Duration of Copyright and Rights in Performances Regulations 1995 (SI 1995 No. 3297), the new regime of film soundtracks applies to existing soundtracks as from commencement (1 January 1996). In addition, 'the owner of any copyright in a film has as from commencement corresponding rights as copyright owner in any existing soundtrack treated as part of the film' (reg. 26(2)). This is stated 'without prejudice to any rights of the owner of the copyright in the soundtrack as a sound recording'. Reg. 26(3) states that 'anything done before commencement under or in

Compared with the situation under the 1956 Act, the new scheme presents a major difficulty in relation to *soundtrack music*. The duration of the copyrights in sound recordings and films is now different.[169] This could create problems of articulation between the sound recording and the film copyrights not contemplated during the drafting of the Regulations.[170]

79.   The absence of the originality criterion

In the absence of any requirement of originality, the threshold of protection for recordings is probably, to paraphrase J. A. L. Sterling, the requirement of a 'causative intent'.[171] Once arrangements have been made for the making of a film, the resulting film is protected. Newsreels, and also security camera and amateur films certainly meet this minimum requirement. In fact, under such a reasoning, only fortuitous recordings might not attract protection as 'films'.

How does it compare with the application of the originality criterion? What can be said is that the sole criterion of originality would not necessarily exclude a wide range of audiovisual works from protection. In fact, provided audiovisual works are protected under a *specific subject-matter*, the current test of originality, as stated by Lord Devlin in the *Ladbroke* case,[172] which led to the protection of, among other works, examination papers, betting tickets, etc., would probably allow the protection of newsreels.

The same would be true if audiovisual works (or, more exactly, film frames) were protected as *photographic works*. Originality has always been required under UK copyright law for photographs, and under the 1911

relation to the copyright in the sound recording continues to have effect and shall have effect, so far as concerns the soundtrack, in relation to the film as in relation to the sound recording'. Finally, under reg. 26(4), 'it is not an infringement of the copyright in the film (or of any moral right in the film) to do anything after commencement in pursuance of arrangements for the exploitation of the sound recording made before commencement'.

[169] Fifty years post making or release for sound recordings (s. 13A(1)), and seventy years after the death of one of the contributors listed in s. 13B(2) for films.

[170] On these problems, see Kamina, 'The Protection of Film Soundtracks under UK Copyright After the Copyright Regulations 1995 and 1996' (1998) 9 *Entertainment Law Review* 153; H. Laddie, P. Prescott and M. Vitoria, *The Modern Law of Copyright*, Butterworths, 2000, para. 7.17; and *Copinger and Skone James on Copyright*, 14th edn, 1999, para. 4-64.

[171] See para. 80.

[172] *Ladbroke (Football) Ltd* v. *William Hill (Football) Ltd* [1964] 1 WLR 273; [1964] 1 All ER 465, HL: 'The product must originate from the author in the sense that it is the result of a substantial degree of skill, industry or experience employed by him' ([1964] 1 WLR 273 at 293). See also *University of London Press Ltd* v. *University Tutorial Press Ltd* [1916] 2 Ch 601 at 608–9 *per* Peterson J.

Act there was no doubt as to the protection of newsreels under this heading.

In fact, the major problem of the application of the originality criterion would seem to arise when audiovisual works are protected as *dramatic works*. However, we saw that the question is less a question of originality than a problem of characterisation as 'drama': however original, the audiovisual work must be a dramatic work, and, whatever definition is adopted, it appears difficult to consider works such as newsreels as 'dramas'.[173]

Under the present system, the only 'films' which would not otherwise attract protection, should originality be required, are probably recordings of security cameras and fortuitous films.[174] Thus it can be said that the absence of the criterion in relation to films does not unreasonably extend the range of works protected.

Note that the absence of originality may reinforce the protection of the copyright owner against infringement. Under an original description of work, difficulties may arise when the alleged infringer borrows non-original parts or components of the original work. This can influence the test of 'substantiality', i.e. the determination of the amount of copying or use necessary to constitute infringement. It is thought that the reproduction of a part which is not in itself original will not normally be a reproduction of a 'substantial part', and therefore will not be an infringement of copyright.[175] Arguably, this element cannot be taken into consideration in relation to a non-original descriptions of works such as 'films' or 'sound recordings'.[176]

This being said, the absence of originality raises a technical problem concerning the determination of what constitutes a derivative or new 'film'.

80.   Originality and the question of derivative films

An interesting question arises in relation to altered or new versions of pre-existing films.[177] According to section 5B(4) of the Act:

Copyright does not subsist in a film which is, or to the extent that it is, a copy taken from a previous film

---

[173] See para. 57.

[174] Under the criterion used for a photograph, a film composed of a single shot of a live scene could be original.

[175] See *Ladbroke (Football) Ltd* v. *William Hill (Football) Ltd* [1964] 1 WLR 273; [1964] 1 All ER 465, HL; and *Warwick Film Productions Ltd* v. *Eisinger* [1969] 1 Ch 508.

[176] See also para. 77 *in fine*.

[177] See H. Laddie, P. Prescott and M. Vitoria, *The Modern Law of Copyright*, Butterworths, 1995, para. 5.41.

This text draws the line between what is a mere copy and what is a new film, but does not reject the possibility of a film *derived* from a previous film. However, it does not indicate the test to apply in order to distinguish between the two. Under copyright law, the standard test for the existence and the copyrightability of a derivative work is the test of originality.[178] In the absence of such a requirement, what is the test to apply? For example, does a colourised version of a film, or a new cut (e.g. a director's cut), or a digitally enhanced or restored print, or even a release under another screen format (e.g. on videotape) constitute a mere copy of the film, or does it create a new derivative 'film', and thus a new film copyright? The question could be asked for sound recordings, concerning for example digitally enhanced tracks.

A solution to this problem is suggested by J. A. L. Sterling. The author points out that under UK copyright law, in the absence of a require-ment of originality, the criterion for copyright protection of recordings is reduced to the requirement of a 'causative contribution'.[179] Causative contributions are defined as 'contributions which bring the recording into being, without necessarily involving creative contributions'.[180] According to Sterling, these may be:

(a) organisational: i.e. related to the planning of the production, contracts with artists, provision of necessary equipment, etc., and (b) substantive: i.e. related to the making or processing of the recording itself.

Logically, one should use this criterion to distinguish between a mere copy which would not attract copyright protection and a derivative film. This would be consistent with the idea of a strict parallelism in copyright law between the conditions for protection of new works (originality for original works; causative contribution for non-original works) and the conditions for protection of derivative works (respectively, added origi-nality and added causative contribution).

Under such a reasoning, an alteration of the first recording would cre-ate a new film only if the modification has been intended and if some arrangement for its making has been made (and, of course, if it is not too

---

[178] See *Interlego AG* v. *Tyco Industries Inc.* [1989] AC 27; [1988] 3 WLR 678; [1988] 3 All ER 949; [1988] RPC 343, affirming [1987] FSR 409, HK CA.

[179] 'Under the UK 1988 Act, some arrangements for the making of the recording or the film must have been undertaken, otherwise there will be no right owner, for section 9(2)(a) provides that in the case of a sound recording or film, the right owner (author) is the person by whom the arrangements necessary for the making of the film are undertaken. Such arrangements provide the "causative element".' J. A. L. Sterling, *Intellectual Property Rights in Sound Recordings, Films and Video*, Sweet & Maxwell, 1992, para. 6.09.

[180] *Ibid.* The latter is defined as 'contributions affecting the form of the recording components'.

insignificant).[181] However, this criterion could be too comprehensive. In practice, only fortuitous modifications would not create a new derivative film, and any modification of some significance might give rise to a new copyright. Section 5B(4) appears to limit this possibility by requiring that a new film *add some new material* to the previous recording ('no copyright . . . *to the extent* that it is a copy'). Accordingly, a mere change in the format of a film would not create a separate copyright in the new recording, since no new elements have been added to the pre-existing work.

In any case, whatever the criterion is for the creation of derivative film or sound recording, one must admit the possibility of several copyrights in successive recordings. In particular, digital enhancements of pictures could well create a distinct copyright.

Against this solution, one may observe that the Rental and Term Directives describe the right of the film producer as the right in the 'first fixation' of the film.[182] Such wording might exclude the possibility of a new right arising in relation to a second fixation, even after substantial processing or modification. The point, however, is not free of doubt, and it appears that the question has not been raised in foreign systems with a similar definition.

In conclusion, it emerges that a right in audiovisual recordings creates specific technical problems which are sometimes difficult to solve. In particular, special attention should be given to the protection of soundtracks and film frames, and to the question of derivative films. We will see that a cumulation with underlying audiovisual works creates additional problems.

81.   The 'film' under the Irish Copyright and Related Rights Act 2000

The definition of 'film' in section 2 of the Irish Copyright and Related Rights Act 2000 is slightly different from the definition in the UK Act. In the Irish Act, a film is defined as 'a fixation on any medium from which a moving image may, by any means, be produced, *perceived or communicated through a device*'.[183] This language should, however, have no effect on the range of works covered.

The treatment of film frames is similar to the UK Act: in particular, frames are excluded from protection as photographs;[184] as in the UK,

---

[181] See H. Laddie, P. Prescott and M. Vitoria, *The Modern Law of Copyright*, Butterworths, 1995, para. 5.41, n. 3.
[182] Which is the language used in several continental Acts (e.g. the French Intellectual Property Code, art. L.215-1, neighbouring right of videogram producers).
[183] Emphasis added.   [184] Section 2 (definition of 'photograph').

copying in relation to a film includes the making of a photograph of the whole or a substantial part of any image forming part of the film.[185]

In contrast to the current solution adopted in the UK, under the Irish Act the sound part of the film (the soundtrack) is protected as a sound recording, and not as part of the film.[186] This avoids some of the difficulties of the UK solution described above.[187]

The videogram in authors' rights countries

82.   Introduction

A double system of protection for film works through a copyright in the audiovisual work and a neighbouring right in the visual recording was a common feature of continental laws at the time of the adoption of the EU Rental Directive, with the notable exception of Italy, Belgium and the Netherlands. The neighbouring right in the videogram was and is still viewed as an additional form of protection, allowing producers of newsreels to claim protection for their works and giving to all producers a stronger title in infringement proceedings. The industry appears to consider, however, that such a right has a limited interest.

As a consequence, this right has not been the subject of much legal scrutiny, and its regime is usually defined in a few sentences in the domestic copyright Act. However, in the gaps left by these provisions, a limited analogy with the regime of *droit d'auteur* could be possible.

83.   National definitions of the right of the film producer[188]

The provisions of the Rental and Term Directives on the related right of the film producer have been faithfully implemented in almost all Member States of the authors' rights tradition.[189] Differences remain, however, with respect to questions left out of the harmonisation (such as the right of communication to the public), but should disappear in the process of implementation of the Directive on Copyright and Related Rights in the Information Society of 22 May 2001.

In France, the regime of this right is contained in four articles of the Intellectual Property Code. The related right of the film producer is a

---

[185] Section 39(1)(c).   [186] See the definitions of 'film' and 'sound recording' under s. 2.
[187] See para. 78.
[188] For an international survey, see J. A. L. Sterling, *Intellectual Property Rights in Sound Recordings, Films and Video*, Sweet & Maxwell, 1992, Chapter 7.
[189] With the exception of Portugal (for some provisions).

right in the 'videogram', defined as 'the initial fixation of a sequence of images, whether accompanied by sounds or not'.[190] Thus defined, the 'videogram' encompasses all recordings of images, on any medium (film, videotapes, CD-ROMs, etc.). The term 'sequences of images' may be ill-adapted to videotechnology and to those films which consist in one shot only. It was not, however, the intent of the French legislator to exclude such films from this protection.

The film producer is further defined as 'the natural or legal person who takes the initiative and the responsibility' for this fixation.[191] Case law specified that a mere investor in film production could not be considered as a 'producer' under this wording if he does not have a role of 'impulse, direction and coordination'.[192]

The film producer is granted the exclusive rights to authorise 'any re-production, any making available to the public by means of sale, exchange or rental, or any communication to the public of his videogram'.[193]

The French Code contains an original provision as to transfers of the rights of the videogram producers. Article L.215-1 of the Code provides that the exclusive rights of the producers in the videogram may not be separately assigned from the authors' rights and the performers' rights he owns in respect of the work fixed on the videogram. The rationale behind this provision was to avoid complex clearance schemes. It is not clear, however, what the sanction for a separate assignment of both rights would be.[194]

The term of protection is the one provided for in the Term Directive: fifty years from the first day of the year following the first fixation or, if the film is lawfully communicated to the public during this period, fifty years from the first day of the year following this first communication to the public.[195]

The Belgian Copyright Act provides for a similar scheme, but there is no provision preventing a separate assignment of the neighbouring right from the corresponding authors' or performers' rights.[196] The protec-tion is similar in scope in Germany, Luxembourg, the Netherlands and Sweden.

In Portugal and in Spain, film producers are granted a right of com-munication to the public but in case of broadcasting this right is reduced

---

[190] Art. L.215-1.   [191] *Ibid.*
[192] 'D'impulsion, de direction et de coordination', Paris Court of Appeal, 22 July 1981, *Homsy delafosse* v. *Belier, Revue Dalloz*, 1982, Informations Rapides (under art. 17 of the Law of 1957).
[193] *Ibid.*
[194] Nullity of both assignments? Of the separate assignment of rights in the videogram only? Automatic transfer of the neighbouring right to the assignee of the copyright?
[195] Art. L.211-4.   [196] Copyright Act, art. 33.

to a mere right to equitable remuneration.[197] Film producers have no exclusive right of communication to the public of their videograms in Denmark, Greece and Italy.

A specific feature of the German Copyright Act is that videogram producers are granted a limited moral right 'to prohibit any distortion or abridgement of the video or audio recording which may prejudice their legitimate interests'.[198] A similar right is granted to film producers in Austria.[199] Also, a peculiarity of Portuguese law is that it requires the identification of phonograms and videograms by a specific notice of neighbouring right.[200]

As mentioned above, in several countries the protection scheme of videogram producers will be reinforced in the process of implementation of the Directive on Copyright and Related Rights in the Information Society of 22 May 2001.[201]

PART III

The protection of contributory works

84.   Main underlying works in film production

The protection of the main underlying works does not raise similar problems to those arising for final audiovisual works. In particular, the characterisation problems encountered for films in some systems do not exist in relation to their *underlying contributory works*. For example, in the UK, most film scripts, in their various forms, are protected as dramatic works,[202] and not as literary works.[203] The decor for a film is an artistic work; costumes and other elements may also be protected as artistic works.[204] Drawings forming part of a

---

[197] Portuguese Code, art. 184; Spanish Intellectual Property Law, art. 122.

[198] Art. 94(1) of the Copyright Act.   [199] Art. 38(2) of the Austrian Act.

[200] Art. 185 of the Copyright Act provides that protection granted to producers of phonograms and videograms is subject to the display of the letter 'P' surrounded by a circle on all authorised copies and their packaging, accompanied by an indication of the date of the original publication.

[201] See paras. 180 (right of reproduction), 189 (right of communication to the public) and 211 (exemptions).

[202] See para. 55.

[203] CDPA 1988, s. 3(1): 'literary work' means 'any work . . . other than a dramatic or musical work . . .'. On the possibility of 'non-dramatic' scripts, see para. 55, n. 34 above.

[204] See *Shelley Films Ltd* v. *Rex Features Ltd* [1994] EMLR 134. A photographer, without obtaining consent, took a picture of an actor wearing a costume on a set designed for the film 'Mary Shelley's Frankenstein'. The plaintiff claimed that the photograph infringed the copyright in the costume and the set (as works of artistic craftsmanship) and sought

cartoon or a story-board are artistic works.[205] The music is a musical work.[206]

There are, however, two important aspects in which differences may subsist between Member States. They concern the protection of characters and the protection of film titles.

85.   Characters

In the UK, the copyright protection afforded to fictional characters is very limited.[207] By exception, however, cartoon characters can attract protection as drawings. This was decided for example in cases involving Popeye[208] and the Teenage Mutant Ninja Turtles.[209] Passing off can offer

an injunction restraining the publication of similar photographs, with special reference to latex prostheses designed for the 'creature' (not reproduced in the photograph in question). The plaintiff claimed that the prostheses were copyrighted as sculptures or works of artistic craftsmanship. The defendant contended: (a) that the costumes lacked originality; (b) that copying the prostheses would not be an infringement since they were 'design documents' under s. 51 of the Act (under s. 51(1) it is not an infringement to copy a design document for a non-artistic work, unless it can be assimilated to a surface decoration); and (c) that the set was a building under s. 62 of the Act (in which case photographs do not infringe). The court held that there was a serious question to be tried as to the subsistence of copyright in the costumes. The court could not conclude that the prostheses were not surface decorations and that a photograph of the 'creature' would not be an infringement. The court held that it is plainly arguable that copyright can exist in a film set (*Merlet* v. *Mothercare plc* [1984] FSR 358 was distinguished on this point). The question of whether the set was a building under s. 62 was held arguable both ways. An injunction was therefore granted. See also *Merchandising Corp. of America* v. *Harpbond* [1983] FSR 32 (pop star Adam Ant's facial make-up held not permanent enough to attract copyright).

[205] In addition, the story-board conveys a dramatic work similar to or derived from the script.

[206] Music accompanying a dramatic work (dramatico-musical work) is protected as a musical work, but this does not seem to prevent a dramatico-musical work from attracting protection as a whole under the heading of dramatic work. See s. 3(1) of the 1988 Act (in contrast to the definition of literary work) and *Copinger and Skone James on Copyright*, 13th edn, 1991, paras. 2-12 and 2-19. But this finding has to be reconciled with the rules on joint authorship and the requirement of non-separability of the contributions (see para. 127).

[207] *Kelly* v. *Cinema Houses Ltd* [1928–35] MCC 362 (fictional characters such as Falstaff or Sherlock Holmes would probably not attract copyright protection). *O'Neill* v. *Paramount Pictures Corp.* [1983] CAT 235 (see the *dicta* of May LJ: 'while I agree that there is presently no copyright in fictional characters in books, films or plays, I am by no means satisfied that an author of such works, particularly when consisting of a series of books about the same character, who has become widely known, has no form of proprietary interest in that character'). Compare with the more favourable solutions of US courts; see in particular *Nichols* v. *Universal Pictures*, 45 F. 2d 119 at 121 (2nd Cir. 1930), cert denied, 282 US 1902 (1931) (by Judge Hand); L. A. Kurtz, 'The Rocky Road to Character Protection' (1990) 2 *Entertainment Law Review* 62.

[208] *King Features Syndicate Inc.* v. *O and M Kleeman Ltd* [1941] AC 417, HL.

[209] *Mirage Studios* v. *Counter-Feat Clothing Co. Ltd* [1991] FSR 145.

some kind of protection, but proving passing off is notoriously difficult, as evidenced in the UK cases on character merchandising.[210]

In contrast, copyright protection appears to be afforded to characters on a wider basis in authors' rights countries. In France, for example, there is no doubt that characters from an audiovisual work can be protected by copyright, independently from the copyright in the audiovisual work. This is true, of course, if the character is a cartoon character or is otherwise drawn;[211] but it may still be the case even if it is from a novel or a script.[212] Characters' names can also be protected.[213] The protection regime for cartoon characters and characters from audiovisual works appears similar in other continental countries,[214] but is less clear concerning literary characters which are not otherwise materialised or impersonated.[215] In any case, tort or unfair competition law would appear to provide adequate remedies in the most obvious cases of misappropriation.[216]

[210] See W. R. Cornish, *Intellectual Property*, 4th edn, Sweet & Maxwell, 1999, paras. 16-44 to 16-47. Cornish states, at *ibid.*, para. 16-44: 'Arguments that the relevant goodwill arises from the public's belief that originators do grant licences and that this acts as a guarantee of quality have been dismissed in cases concerned with the merchandising of a name alone, whether the name is of an entirely fictional character (such as the Wombles), a television character associated with a particular actor (such as Kojak) or a pop group (such as Abba).' See generally Adams, *Merchandising Intellectual Property*, 1987.

[211] Paris Court of Appeal, 9 January 1986, *Juris-Data*, No. 020012 (Maya the Bee). Also held for Donald Duck, the Pink Panther, ET, Felix the Cat, etc.

[212] E.g. Tarzan, as described physically and psychologically, but also certain secondary characters, such as Jane and Cheetah the monkey (Tribunal of First Instance of Paris, 21 January 1977 and 22 March 1978, *Revue Dalloz*, 1979, p. 99, note Desbois). It was held, however, that the creator cannot obtain a separate protection for the different elements which compose the character and that are in the public domain (Paris Court of Appeal, 13 September 1988, *Cahiers du Droit d'Auteur*, January 1989, p. 15).

[213] E.g. 'Tarzan', 'Chéri-Bibi' or 'Poil de carotte'. See the next paragraph below for the rules on 'Titles'.

[214] In Belgium, see e.g. Tribunal of First Instance of Brussels, 15 February 1996, *Auteurs et Media*, 1996, p. 319 (comic book and cartoon character 'Tintin'); Tribunal of First Instance of Brussels, 17 October 1996 (comic book characters Blake and Mortimer); Brussels Court of Appeal, 24 March 1994, *Auteurs et Media*, 1996, p. 318 (comic book character 'Lucky Luke'). In Germany, see BGH, 11 March 1993, in (1994) 25 IIC 605 and 610 (comic book characters 'Asterix' and 'Alcolix'): 'the Federal Court of Justice clarified that, not only can the concrete graphic configurations of a character be protected, but so can its comic-book personality that arises by virtue of a combination of outer elements as well as of features, abilities, specific attitudes and manners'; A. Dietz, in M. B. Nimmer and D. Geller (eds.), *International Copyright Law and Practice*, Matthew Bender, looseleaf, para. 2[4][b]. In Italy, see the cases on cartoon characters reported by M. Fabiani, in M. B. Nimmer and D. Geller (eds.), *International Copyright Law and Practice*, Matthew Bender, looseleaf, para. 2[4][b], footnotes.

[215] But see, in Italy, Court of Cassation, 22 June 1933, *Diritto di Autore*, 1933, p. 307 (Pinocchio case), in M. Fabiani, in M. B. Nimmer and D. Geller (eds.), *International Copyright Law and Practice*, Matthew Bender, looseleaf, para. 2[4][b].

[216] See e.g. para. 69.

86.   Titles

The extent to which copyright protection is afforded to titles of films or other copyright works varies among EU Member States. Under UK law, as a general rule, titles of copyright works do not attract copyright protection, on the ground that they lack enough originality or substantiality.[217] As a corollary, in most cases the borrowing of the title for a book, a film or a play will not be considered substantial enough to constitute infringement.

Copyright protection for original titles is sometimes expressly acknowledged in authors' rights countries, as in France or Spain.[218] Article L.112-4 of the French Intellectual Property Code provides that the title of a work is protected as the work itself if it is original. The same article provides for residual protection akin to unfair competition: the title of a work may not be used, even if the work is no longer protected, to distinguish a work of the same kind if such use is likely to create confusion.[219]

On this basis, French case law is sometimes difficult to follow and appears to borrow from trademark law. The following titles have been considered originals by courts: 'A l'école de la route' ('Road School'), 'La cage aux folles' (the English title for the remake of this film was 'The Birdcage'), 'Clochemerle' (fictional name for a village without a specific meaning), 'L'affreux Jojo' (a common French expression meaning 'naughty boy'), 'Le Père Noël est une ordure' ('Santa Claus is Trash'), 'Des poissons et des hommes' ('Of Fishes and Men'), 'Montmartre en délire' ('Crazy Montmartre'), 'Les hauts de Hurlevent' (a clever but imprecise translation of 'Wuthering Heights') and 'Paris Pas Cher' ('Cheap Paris'). In contrast, protection was refused to 'Le beau Danube bleu' ('The Beautiful Blue Danube') or 'Bourreaux d'enfants' ('Child Abusers', being an expression in common usage), 'Jeu de massacre' ('Slaughter Game'), 'La bande à Bonnot' ('The Bonnot Gang', being the name of a real gang operating in the 1910s), 'Le 6ème continent' ('The 6th

---

[217] See e.g. *Francis Day and Hunter Ltd* v. *Twentieth Century Fox Corp. Ltd* [1940] AC 112 at 123; [1939] 4 All ER 192 at 198; *Ladbroke (Football) Ltd* v. *William Hill (Football) Ltd* [1964] 1 WLR 273; [1964] 1 All ER 465, HL; *Dicks* v. *Yates* (1881) 18 ChD 76; *Exxon Corp.* v. *Exxon Insurance Consultants International Ltd* [1982] Ch 119; [1981] 3 All ER 241, CA; *Rose* v. *Information Services Ltd* [1987] FSR 254; *Noah* v. *Shuba* [1991] FSR 14 at 33. and H. Laddie, P. Prescott and M. Vitoria, *The Modern Law of Copyright*, Butterworths, 1995, para. 2.61. See also R. Stone, 'Copyright in Titles, Character Names and Catch-Phrases in the Film and Television Industry' (1996) 5 *Entertainment Law Review* 178.

[218] Art. L.112-4 of the French Intellectual Property Code; art. 10(2) of the Spanish Intellectual Property Law.

[219] See C. Colombet, 'L'évolution de la jurisprudence sur la protection des titres d'oeuvres de l'esprit par la loi du 11 mars 1957', in *Mélanges Chavanne*, Litec, 1990, p. 213; Plaisant, 'La protection des titres', RIDA, May 1964, p. 89; Sarraute, 'La Défense du Titre Banal', *Gazette du Palais*, 1971, 1, Doctr. 183.

Continent'), 'Tueurs de flics' ('Cop Killers'), 'Soif d'aventures' ('Taste for Adventure') and 'Hôtel de charmes' ('Charms Hotel'). Generic or descriptive expressions such as 'Karaté', 'Plan de Lyon' ('Map of Lyon') or 'La Bible de Jérusalem' ('The Bible of Jerusalem') were also held not to be protected by copyright.

Note, however, that under unfair competition law the title does not have to be original and protected as such under copyright law. For example, 'Le petit missel de Jérusalem' ('The Little Missal of Jerusalem') was held to compete unfairly with 'La Bible de Jérusalem' ('The Bible of Jerusalem'), although the latter is not copyright.[220]

Under article 32 of the French Code of Cinematography, the provisional or final title of a film intended for theatrical exhibition in France must be registered at the public registry by the film producer or his proxy. However, the deposit does not grant priority over previous uses.[221]

In Germany, in the absence of specific provisions to that effect in the Copyright Act of 1965, copyright protection of titles is said to be difficult because of the more stringent requirement of originality applicable in that country.[222] However, titles of works are protected as 'commercial designations' under sections 5 and 15 of the Trademark Act of 1994. Section 5 of this Act defines titles of works as 'the names or special designations of printed publications, cinematographic works, musical works, dramatic works and other comparable works'. The exclusive rights of the proprietor of a commercial designation are defined under section 15, which prohibits third parties from using the designation or a similar one in the course of trade, without authorisation, in a manner capable of causing confusion with the protected designation.

In Italy, titles of copyright works are not protected under copyright, but under a specific neighbouring right. Article 100 of the Copyright Act provides that the title of a work, 'when it uniquely identifies the work', may not be used for any other work without the consent of the author. However, this prohibition does not apply in the absence of a likelihood of confusion between the works. Article 102 provides for an additional protection for titles and related elements on the grounds of unfair competition.[223]

---

[220] Paris Court of Appeal, 8 July 1986, *Revue Dalloz*, 1987, Sommaire, p. 152, note Colombet.

[221] Paris Court of Appeal, 4 January 1972, *La Semaine Juridique*, 1972, II, No. 17103, note De Grisenoy.

[222] See A. Dietz, in M. B. Nimmer and D. Geller (eds.), *International Copyright Law and Practice*, Matthew Bender, looseleaf, para. 2[4][a].

[223] 'The reproduction or imitation of other works of a similar nature of headings, emblems, ornamentations, arrangements of printing signs or characters, or any other particularity of form or color in the external appearance of an intellectual property work, where such reproduction or imitation is capable of creating confusion between works or authors, shall be prohibited as an act of unfair competition' (WIPO translation).

In Sweden, titles are protected by copyright under a specific provision which borrows from unfair competition law. Article 50 of the Copyright Act provides that a literary or artistic work may not be made available to the public under a title if that title may be easily confused with a previously published work.

PART IV

Broadcasts and cable programmes

87.   Introduction

The history and rationale for the protection of broadcasts and cable programmes has been discussed in the previous chapter. France had proposed the protection of radio broadcasts at the 1928 Rome Conference of the Berne Convention. As mentioned above, the UK was the first country to translate this idea into copyright terms.[224] This class of works is now covered by several international agreements, but harmonisation at the international level has not yet been achieved. A more complete regional harmonisation was accomplished at the European level.

88.   The Rome Convention of 1961

The Rome Convention of 1961 was the first international agreement to provide for protection of audiovisual broadcasts. Sixty-eight States, with the notable exception of the United States, are bound by this Convention, including all EU and EEA Member States. The Convention provides for a rule of national treatment, subject to the protection specifically guaranteed, and the limitations specifically provided for in its text.[225] The definition of 'broadcasts' in the Convention is restricted to wireless hertzian broadcasts and does not cover cable programmes.[226]

Under article 13 of the Convention, the minimum protection of broadcasters includes the rights to authorise or prohibit:

(a) the rebroadcasting of their broadcasts;
(b) the fixation of their broadcasts;
(c) the reproduction:
   (i) of fixations, made without their consent, of their broadcasts;
   (ii) of fixations, made in accordance with the provisions of article 15 [on permitted exceptions and limitations], of their broadcasts, if the reproduction is made for purposes different from those referred to in those provisions;

---

[224] See para. 22.   [225] On national treatment under the Convention, see para. 349.
[226] Art. 3(f).

(d) the communication to the public of their television broadcasts if such communication is made in places accessible to the public against payment of an
entrance fee.

Article 13(d) further adds that it shall be a matter for the domestic
law of the State where protection of this right is claimed to determine
the conditions under which it may be exercised. Also, a contracting
State can give notice that it will not apply the provisions of this article, in which case the other contracting States are not obliged to grant
this right to broadcasting organisations whose headquarters are in that
State.[227]

The protection for broadcasts shall last at least until the end of a period
of twenty years from the end of the year in which the broadcast took
place.[228]

89.   The TRIPs Agreement

The Agreement provides for a principle of national treatment of broadcasters with respect to their broadcasts, subject to the exceptions already
provided in the Rome Convention.[229] In addition, article 4 provides for a
most-favoured-nation treatment, applicable to broadcasters, but subject
to exemptions.[230]

The minimum rights are defined under article 14(3), which grants
broadcasting organisations the right to prohibit the unauthorised fixation, the reproduction of fixations, and the rebroadcasting by wireless
means of their broadcasts, as well as communication to the public of television broadcasts of the same. It further states that members which do
not grant such rights to broadcasting organisations shall provide owners
of copyright in the subject-matter of the broadcasts with the possibility of preventing the above acts, subject to the provisions of the Berne
Convention (1971 text).[231]

The Agreement provides that contracting States may provide for conditions, limitations, exceptions and reservations to the above rights to
the extent permitted by the Rome Convention.[232] The term of protection granted to broadcasting organisations shall last for at least twenty
years from the end of the calendar year in which the broadcast took
place.[233]

---

[227] Art. 16(1)(b).   [228] Art. 14.   [229] Art. 3(1). See para. 349.   [230] See para. 351.
[231] See 'Implications of the TRIPs Agreement on Treaties Administered by WIPO', WIPO
Publication No. 464(E), 1996, para. 67.
[232] Art. 14(6).   [233] Art. 14(5).

90.   The Brussels Convention of 1974

The 1974 Brussels Convention Relating to the Distribution of Programme-Carrying Signals Transmitted by Satellite does create a property right but obliges contracting States to take adequate measures to prevent the unauthorised distribution on or from its territory of any programme-carrying signal transmitted by satellite. The distribution is unauthorised if it has not been authorised by the originating (broadcasting) organisation. The obligation applies when the originating organisation is a national of another contracting State and where the signal distributed is a derived signal.[234] The Convention does not cover signals that are intended for direct reception by the general public.[235] This Convention has only twenty-four signatory States. Within the European Union, the Convention was ratified by Austria, Germany, Greece, Italy and Portugal. Switzerland and the US are among the other signatory States.

91.   Council of Europe

Several treaties in the area of broadcasting have been elaborated within the framework of the Council of Europe. The main agreement is the European Agreement on the Protection of Television Broadcasts of 1960, as amended by one protocol and two additional protocols.[236] A third additional protocol to this Agreement is not yet in force.[237] The Agreement is binding on the following EU Member States: Belgium, Denmark, France, Germany, Spain, Sweden and the UK.

The minimum protection exceeds the protection of the Rome Convention but is inferior to the level of protection under the EC directives. It grants to broadcasting organisations constituted in the territory and under the laws of a contracting party or transmitting from such territory, in the territory of all parties to the agreement, the right to authorise or prohibit: (a) the rebroadcasting of such broadcasts; (b) the diffusion of such broadcasts to the public by wire; (c) the communication of such broadcasts to the public by means of any instrument for the transmission of signs, sounds or images; (d) any fixation of such broadcasts or still photographs thereof, and any reproduction of such a fixation; and (e) rebroadcasting, wire diffusion or public performance with the aid of the fixations or reproductions referred to in paragraph (d), except where

---

[234] Art. 2.   [235] Art. 3.
[236] Protocol of 22 January 1965 and the Additional Protocols of 14 January 1974 and of 21 March 1983.
[237] Additional Protocol of 20 April 1989.

the organisation in which the right vests has authorised the sale of the said fixations or reproductions to the public.[238] The parties may, under certain conditions, withhold protection granted in relation to (b), (c), (d) and (e).[239] It is also open to the parties, in respect of their own territory, to provide exceptions to the protection of television broadcasts for the purpose of reporting current events or the making of ephemeral fixations.

The Agreement further adds that broadcasting organisations constituted in the territory and under the laws of a party to the Agreement or transmitting from such territory shall enjoy, in respect of all their television broadcasts in the territory of any other party to this Agreement, the same protection as that other party may extend to organisations constituted in its territory and under its laws or transmitting from its territory, where such protection is greater than that provided for in the Agreement.

The protection is granted for a period of not less than twenty years from the end of the year in which the broadcast took place.

Another treaty established within the Council of Europe, the European Convention Relating to Questions on Copyright Law and Neighbouring Rights in the Framework of Transfrontier Broadcasting by Satellite of 11 May 1994, has not yet entered into force.[240]

92.   Protection of broadcasts and cable programmes in the EC copyright directives

Broadcasts have been included in the process of European harmonisation of copyright and neighbouring rights. This subject-matter is dealt with in the Rental Directive of 19 November 1992, the Satellite and Cable Retransmission Directive of 27 September 1993, the Term Directive of 29 October 1993 and the Directive on Copyright and Related Rights in the Information Society of 22 May 2001. Under these directives, the term 'broadcast' has a broad meaning and covers broadcasts transmitted by wire or over the air, including by cable or satellite.[241] Accordingly, the term 'broadcast' covers both broadcasts, *stricto sensu*, and cable programmes.

Note that the protection of broadcasts is not conditioned by a type of programme or its content. Accordingly, a broadcast may not necessarily

---

[238] Art. 1.   [239] Art. 3.

[240] Its art. 5 provides that, as far as transfrontier broadcasting by satellite is concerned, performers, producers of phonograms and broadcasting organisations from signatory parties shall be protected, at a minimum, in accordance with the provisions of the Rome Convention.

[241] See e.g. Rental Directive, arts. 6(2) (fixation right) and 7(1) (reproduction right).

consist in a television programme, or in the transmission of a copyright work or performance. Accordingly, the protection could well extend to transmissions over digital networks or to interactive services.

This appears to be confirmed by the Directive on Copyright and Related Rights in the Information Society of 22 May 2001, which clearly encompasses such services under its definition of 'communication to the public'.[242] If that is the case, broadcasts may well have become a major subject-matter in the digital environment.[243]

Under the Rental Directive, Member States shall provide for broadcasting organisations to have exclusive rights in their broadcasts, consisting in a fixation and reproduction right,[244] a right of communication to the public[245] and a distribution right.[246] Optional limitations on the exclusive rights are detailed in article 10 and concern: (a) private use; (b) use of short excerpts in connection with the reporting of current events; (c) ephemeral fixation by a broadcasting organisation by means of its own facilities and for its own broadcasts; and (d) use solely for the purposes of teaching or scientific research. More generally, any Member State may provide for the same kinds of limitations with regard to broadcasting organisations as it provides for in connection with the protection of copyright in literary and artistic works. However, compulsory licences may be provided for only to the extent they are compatible with the Rome Convention.

The Satellite and Cable Directive first clears the legal uncertainty over the law applicable to broadcast in its article 1 on definitions.[247] It then provides that, for the purposes of communication to the public by satellite, the rights of broadcasting organisations shall be protected in accordance with the provisions of articles 6, 7, 8 and 10 of the Rental Directive.[248] It further deals with the cable retransmission right.[249] It provides that Member States shall ensure that, when programmes from other Member States are retransmitted by cable in their territory, the applicable copyright and related rights are observed and that such retransmission takes place on the basis of individual or collective contractual agreements

---

[242] See recital 25: 'It should be made clear that all rightholders recognised by this Directive should have an exclusive right to make available to the public copyright works or any other subject-matter by way of interactive on-demand transmissions. Such interactive on-demand transmissions are characterised by the fact that members of the public may access them from a place and at a time individually chosen by them.' See para. 189.

[243] For an illustration, see the case of *Shetland Times Ltd* v. *Wills*, 1997 SC 316; 1997 SLT 669; [1997] EMLR 277; [1997] FSR 604, Court of Session, Outer House, discussed at para. 95.

[244] Arts. 6(2) and 7(1).   [245] Art. 8(3).   [246] Art. 9(1).   [247] See para. 189.

[248] Art. 4. For this purpose, 'broadcasting by wireless means' in the Rental Directive shall be understood as including communication to the public by satellite.

[249] Art. 8.

between copyright owners, holders of related rights and cable operators. Article 9, on the exercise of cable retransmission rights, provides that Member States shall ensure that the right of copyright owners and holders of related rights to grant or refuse authorisation to a cable operator for a cable retransmission may be exercised only through a collecting society. However, article 10 adds that article 9 does not apply to the rights exercised by a broadcasting organisation in respect of its own transmission, irrespective of whether the rights concerned are its own or have been transferred to it by other copyright owners and/or holders of related rights.

Article 3 of the Term Directive provides that the rights of broadcasting organisations shall expire fifty years after the first transmission of a broadcast, whether this broadcast is transmitted by wire or over the air, including cable or satellite.[250]

Finally, as for other classes of related rights, the protection scheme for broadcasting organisations has been reinforced by the Directive on Copyright and Related Rights in the Information Society of 22 May 2001.[251]

93.   Protection at the national level

Provisions of the Rental and Lending, Satellite and Cable and Term Directives relating to broadcasts and cable programmes have now been implemented in all Member States. Differences may subsist at the national level, for example in the definition of the subject-matter (particularly with regard to new technologies) and in the list of applicable exemptions. Several of these differences should disappear with the implementation of the Directive on Copyright and Related Rights in the Information Society.

94.   Protection in the UK

UK law defines broadcast and cable programmes as two distinct subject-matters for copyright protection. A 'broadcast' is defined in section 6 of the 1988 Act as a transmission 'by wireless telegraphy' of visual images, sounds or other information which is capable of being lawfully received by members of the public, or which is transmitted for presentation to the public.[252] 'Wireless telegraphy' is defined in section 178 as meaning 'the

---

[250] This term is calculated from 1 January of the year following this transmission (art. 8).
[251] See paras. 180 (right of reproduction), 189 (right of communication to the public) and 211 (exemptions).
[252] The definition was different under the 1956 Act, and was amended by the Cable and Broadcasting Act 1984. The language of these Acts still governs the broadcasts made when they were in force (on these pre-1988 broadcasts, see H. Laddie, P. Prescott and M. Vitoria, *The Modern Law of Copyright*, Butterworths, 1995, paras. 7.7 and 7.8). Broadcasts made before 1 June 1957 are not protected (1988 Act, Sched. 1, para. 9). On previous definitions, see Laddie, Prescott and Vitoria, paras. 7.6 to 7.9.

sending of electromagnetic energy over paths not provided by a material substance constructed or arranged for that purpose'. The Copyright and Related Rights Regulations 1996 exclude 'transmission of microwave energy between terrestrial fixed points' (which covers so-called MMDS (Multipoint Microwave Distribution System) services) from this definition of 'wireless telegraphy'. Accordingly, such services would fall under the definition of cable programme services.

An encrypted transmission is to be regarded as capable of being lawfully received by members of the public only if decoding equipment has been made available to members of the public by or with the authority of the person making the transmission or the person providing the content of the transmission.[253]

Copyright does not subsist in a broadcast which infringes, or to the extent that it infringes, the copyright in another broadcast or in a cable programme.[254]

The provisions of the Satellite Directive on the determination of the law applicable in relation to broadcasts were implemented in the Act by the Copyright and Related Rights Regulations 1996.[255]

The definition of cable programmes is more complex. According to section 7(1), any item included in a cable programme service is a 'cable programme'.[256] 'Cable programme service' is further defined as meaning:

a service which consists wholly or mainly in sending visual images, sounds or other information by means of a telecommunications system, otherwise than by wireless telegraphy, for reception
(a) at two or more places (whether for simultaneous reception or at different times in response to requests by different users), or
(b) for presentation to members of the public,

and which is not excepted under the Act. The first exceptions concern two-way, internal and domestic services.[257] In addition, the Secretary of State may by order add or remove exceptions.[258] Finally, copyright does not subsist in a cable programme if it is included in a cable programme service by reception and immediate retransmission of a broadcast, or if it infringes, or to the extent that it infringes, the copyright in another cable programme or in a broadcast.[259]

---

[253] Section 6(2).   [254] Section 6(6).
[255] Section 6(4) provides that the place from which the broadcast is made is the place where, under the control and responsibility of the person making the broadcast, the programme-carrying signals are introduced into an uninterrupted chain of communication (including, in the case of a satellite transmission, the chain leading to the satellite and down towards the earth). The new s. 6A provides for safeguards in case of certain satellite broadcasts, in accordance with art. 1 of the Satellite and Cable Directive.
[256] Cable programmes included in a cable programme service before 1 January 1985 are not copyrighted (1988 Act, Sched. 1, para. 9).
[257] Section 7(2).   [258] Section 7(3) and (4). This power has not been used yet.
[259] Section 7(6).

95.   New technologies and services

These definitions raise interesting questions in relation to new technolog-ical developments such as digital broadcasting, on-demand broadcasting or interactive wireless services.

Digital broadcasting

As mentioned above, 'wireless telegraphy' is defined in section 178 as meaning 'the sending of electromagnetic energy over paths not provided by a material substance constructed or arranged for that purpose', to the exclusion of transmission of microwave energy between terrestrial fixed points. Digital broadcasting is a different way of coding the information transmitted, but the mode of communication is still wireless telegraphy according to section 178. Accordingly, digital broadcasts are protected broadcasts.

Wireless video-on-demand

Does the definition of broadcasts cover wireless point-to-point services, such as wireless video-on-demand, as well as point-to-multipoint ones? According to section 6 of the Act, the element conveyed must be 'capable of being received by members of the public' or 'transmitted for presenta-tion to members of the public'. The second condition covers broadcasts received at one point but presented to several members of the public. However, video-on-demand is typically a service provided for reception at one point only and for presentation to one person only. It appears difficult to consider that a transmission directed at one person only can be likened to a transmission to 'members of the public'.[260] Accordingly, wireless video-on-demand services would not give rise to protected broadcasts. In contrast, the same services available by cable will become protected cable programmes.[261]

Wireless two-ways and interactive systems

There is no requirement in section 6 that the service be one-way. There-fore, systems like pay-per-view or encrypted programmes are covered by the definition. The programme is sent for reception by members of the public, and the separate communication set up beforehand or simultaneously in order to pay or decrypt the programme does not change

---

[260] Once down this track, wireless 'telephone' communications would be protected as broadcasts.
[261] See below.

this fact. However, a fully interactive system (e.g. allowing remote playing of videogames) could amount to a one-to-one transmission probably excluded from the definition of broadcasts.

Video-on-demand and on-line delivery of films

Under the definition in section 7(1), could the on-line transmission of films, under a pay-per-view or video-on-demand cable service, or even through electronic bulletin boards or other Internet-connected servers, give rise to a cable programme? These transmissions will be cable programmes if, and only if, the 'provider' can be considered as a cable programme service. In the Act, the definition of 'cable programme service' clearly covers point-to-point and one-to-one transmissions.[262] However, a difficulty is represented by section 7(2)(a), which excepts 'interactive' or 'two-way' services. The excluded service is defined as:

a service or part of a service of which it is an essential feature that while visual images, sounds and information are being conveyed by the person providing the service there will or may be sent from each place of reception, by means of the same system or (as the case may be) the same part of it, information (other than signals sent for the operation or control of the service) for reception by the person providing the service or other persons receiving it.

This covers telephone, videophone, electronic mail and other two-way text services. But what about pay-per-view, video-on-demand and on-line delivery services?

Under a pay-per-view cable system, the 'payment' information given by the user can be given through the same telecommunications system, but this mere element does not except the service from the definition of a cable programme service. The signal sent by the user is typically 'sent for the operation or control of the service' under section 7(2)(a).

Video-on-demand services do not transmit programmes to the public continuously or at regularly intervals, but only when requested by the user at the time of his or her choosing. The user connects to a 'video library' and selects a film from a database; he can then watch the film, as he would do on a VCR (the subscriber can even use such functions as pause, rewind or fast forward). Then the main difference from a pay-per-view system is that the signal sent by the user is more complex. But this signal is still 'sent for the operation or control of the service', and in this respect video-on-demand services provide cable programmes to their clients.

---

[262] According to s. 7(1)(a), the reception can take place 'at two or more places, whether for simultaneous reception or at different times in response to requests by different users'.

What about services providing on-line *delivery* of films in electronic form? These are different from video-on-demand services because they do not have as their purpose the showing of films simultaneously with their reception. Rather, they deliver a copy, or more exactly they allow the making of a copy at the point of reception. However, nothing in the first part of section 7 requires a simultaneous showing of the element conveyed as a condition for protection. The text mentions 'reception' (as opposed to 'presentation' in point (b)), and the film is undoubtedly received at the point of recording. Thus, transmissions made under such a system might be protected as cable programmes.

Transmissions over digital networks

The applicability of the definition of cable programmes and cable programme services to Internet services such as websites, as suggested by legal commentators,[263] was confirmed in *Shetland Times* v. *Wills*.[264] The plaintiff established a website to make available on the Internet items appearing in the printed editions of its newspaper, the *Shetland Times*. The *Shetland News*, a rival newspaper, created its own website and included on this website headlines taken from the plaintiff's website, which were hyperlinked to the plaintiff's website. Such access allowed visitors to bypass the front page of the plaintiff's website, and accordingly they would not be confronted with the advertising on this page. The plaintiff sought an interlocutory injunction against the defendants on the grounds that their actions constituted an infringement of their copyright. They argued *inter alia* that the headlines on their own website were cable 'programmes' within the meaning of section 7 of the 1988 Act, that their service to users was a cable programme service within the meaning of section 7, and that the inclusion of those items in that service constitutes an infringement of copyright under section 20 of the Act. Lord Hamilton held that there was a sufficient case for liability under section 20 of the Act and granted an interim injunction against the *Shetland News*.

96.   The protection in Ireland

The definition of broadcasts in the Irish Copyright and Related Rights Act 2000 is close to the one in the UK Act. It also expressly excludes MMDS (Multipoint Microwave Distribution System) services, which

---

[263] See H. Laddie, P. Prescott and M. Vitoria, *The Modern Law of Copyright*, Butterworths, 1995, para. 7.18.
[264] 1997 SC 316; 1997 SLT 669; [1997] EMLR 277; [1997] FSR 604, Court of Session, Outer House.

are protected as cable programme services.[265] The provisions on cable programmes are equally complex. 'Cable programme' is defined as any item included in a cable programme service. The definition of cable programme services is similar in scope to the UK definition.[266]

97.   Protection in authors' rights countries

The protection of broadcasts is similar in most authors' rights countries. This protection is afforded under a neighbouring right, and not under a copyright (*droit d'auteur*). As a general rule, the copyright Acts make no distinction between broadcasts and cable programmes, which are usually protected under the same heading as 'broadcasts'. The regime of this right is usually similar to that of the neighbouring right of videogram producers. As with all neighbouring rights, provisions are usually not set out in much detail.

There are, however, differences in the definitions of either the protected broadcast or the broadcasting organisation, which may affect the scope of the subject-matter in the digital environment.

In France, article L.216-1 of the Intellectual Property Code defines the rights of the 'audiovisual communication enterprise' in its 'programmes'. The term 'programme' is not defined, but audiovisual communication enterprises are referred to as bodies which exploit an audiovisual communication service within the meaning of the Law of 30 September 1986 on the Freedom of Communication. Accordingly, the definition of 'programmes' covers broadcasts, cable programmes, but also probably websites or web services, which are otherwise subject to the Law of 1986 as 'audiovisual communication enterprises'.

The definitions of 'broadcasting organisation' and 'broadcast programmes' in the Portuguese Code also seem broad enough to cover Internet, on-demand or interactive services.[267] In contrast, the statutory definition of the broadcaster and/or of broadcasts may seem to be more restrictive in other countries. For example, in Italy, article 79 of the Copyright Act refers to those persons carrying out broadcasting activities 'by radio or television'. Also, the WIPO translation of the Greek Act refers to 'radio or television organisations'.[268] In a similar way, in the Dutch Act on neighbouring rights, the definition of 'programme' refers to 'radio or television programmes' only.[269]

Other countries (for example, Spain and Germany) do not provide a statutory definition of the broadcasting organisation in their copyright

---

[265] Section 2.   [266] Section 2.   [267] Art. 176(9).   [268] Copyright Act, art. 48.
[269] Law of 1993 on neighbouring rights, art. 1(i).

Acts. Most Acts are also silent on the definition of the protected broad-casts or programmes.

In any case, one should observe that a wide construction of the term 'broadcast'[270] has now been instituted by the provisions of the Rental Directive.[271] The Directive on Copyright and Related Rights in the Information Society may well have extended this protection to the net-worked and interactive environments.[272]

In all Member States the rights granted to broadcasters comply for-mally with the provisions of the Rental, Satellite and Term Directives, or would be construed accordingly. For example, article L.216-1 of the French Code provides laconically that the authorisation of the audio-visual communication enterprise is required for any reproduction of its programmes, for making them available to the public by sale, rental or exchange, and for any telediffusion and communication to the public in a place to which the latter has access in exchange for the payment of an entry fee. The provisions of the Satellite and Cable Directive have also been implemented almost *verbatim*. The exemptions from the exclusive rights are similar to those applicable to audiovisual works,[273] and there are no additional specific exemptions from these rights. The duration provisions implement the provisions of the Term Directive.

The protection of 'broadcasting organisations' is afforded under a similarly laconic language in Germany,[274] Italy[275] and Spain.[276] Other countries set out more detailed provisions but with a similar effect as to the scope of protection. This is the case in Belgium,[277] Denmark,[278] Greece,[279] the Netherlands[280] and Sweden.[281]

PART V

Protection as a database?

98.   The EC Directive of 11 March 1996 and films

The EC Directive on the Legal Protection of Databases of 11 March 1996[282] provides for a protection of database structures, in whatever

---

[270] And arguably of the terms 'broadcasting organisation'.
[271] See para. 92.   [272] *Ibid.*
[273] Art. L.211-3 (performances in family circle, private copy, short quotations, press re-views, news reports and parody). See Chapter 7 below.
[274] Copyright Act, art. 87.   [275] Copyright Act, art. 79.
[276] Copyright Act, arts. 126 *et seq.*   [277] Copyright Act, arts. 44 *et seq.*
[278] Copyright Act, art. 69.   [279] Copyright Act, arts. 48 and 52.
[280] Law on neighbouring rights of 1993, art. 8.   [281] Copyright Act, art. 48.
[282] Directive 96/9/EC, OJ 1996 No. L77, 27 March 1996, p. 20.

form. In particular, the protected databases can be on-line but also off-line. The protected subject-matter is defined in the Directive as 'a collection of independent works, data or other materials arranged in a systematic or methodical way and individually accessible by electronic or other means'.[283] This protection must be granted through copyright, but the Directive also requires the creation of a *sui generis* right for database protection.

Recital 17 of the Directive makes clear that the definition of databases does not apply to a single cinematographic work:

Whereas the term 'database' should be understood to include literary, artistic, musical or other collections of works or collections of other material such as texts, sound, images, numbers, facts, and data; whereas it should cover collections of independent works, data or other materials which are systematically or methodically arranged and can be individually accessed; whereas this means that a recording or an audiovisual, cinematographic, literary or musical work as such does not fall within the scope of this Directive . . .

However, this does not prevent 'multimedia works' from being protected as databases. Moreover, recital 17 expressly admits that a 'collection' of films could constitute a protected database. But, in that case, account must be taken of recital 19, which states:

Whereas, as a rule, the compilation of several recordings of musical performances on a CD does not come within the scope of this Directive, both because, as a compilation, it does not meet the conditions for copyright protection and because it does not represent a substantial enough investment to be eligible under the *sui generis* right . . .

This suggests, by analogy, that a mere compilation of several films on a single medium (e.g. DVD) could not be protected as a database. However, a DVD containing an important number of short films or film footage, selected in order to reflect a certain theme or subject, and which can be individually accessed by the user according to complex queries, will certainly constitute a protected database.

In sum, it can be said that, apart for some descriptions of 'multimedia works', the protection described in the Directive does not appear to overlap with the protection of 'films' under the various copyright Acts of Member States.[284] The provisions of the Databases Directive have now been implemented in most Member States.[285]

[283] Art. 1(2).
[284] On the protection of multimedia recordings as films, see para. 76.
[285] E.g. the UK, Copyright and Rights in Databases Regulations 1997, SI 1997 No. 3032; Ireland, Copyright and Related Rights Act 2000; France, Law of 1 June 1998; Spain, Act of 6 March 1998; and Germany, Act of 22 July 1997. In July 1999, the Commission

SECTION II

The term of copyright protection

99.   The extended duration for audiovisual works

The duration of copyright in film works in Europe was modified in the process of European harmonisation of copyright law, following the adoption of the Term Directive.[286] It should be recalled that the minimum requirement of the Paris Act of the Berne Convention in relation to cinematographic works is fifty years after the publication or the making of the work,[287] which is shorter than the standard copyright term.

As a result, the terms of copyright protection for audiovisual works were different within the European Community. At the time of the Term Directive, some continental countries applied the general copyright term. This term was fifty years p.m.a. except in Germany and Spain, with respectively seventy and sixty years p.m.a.[288] Moreover, the list of co-authors to be taken into consideration for this calculation varied. In other countries, including the UK and Ireland, 'films' were protected by copyright for fifty years from production, publication or public presentation.[289] Where implemented on the continent, the neighbouring right of film producers conferred a twenty-five to 50-year protection from the publication or making of the first fixation of the audiovisual work.[290]

The need for a harmonisation of the term of copyright was felt following the decision of the European Court of Justice in *EMI* v. *Patricia*,[291] which involved differences in the duration of sound recording (neighbouring) rights in Germany and Denmark. All classes of copyright works have been drawn into this process. The European Commission chose to harmonise

---

undertook an action against Greece, Luxembourg and Portugal for their failure to implement the Directive. Luxembourg implemented the Directive in its new Copyright Act of 2001.

[286] See paras. 40 *et seq.* G. Dworkin, 'The EC Directive of the Term of Protection of Copyright and Related Rights', in H. Cohen Jehoram, P. Keuchenius and J. Seignette (eds.), *Audiovisual Media and Copyright in Europe*, Kluwer, 1994, p. 27.

[287] Art. 7(2), introduced in the Stockholm Act. Compare with the provisions of the previous Acts (Brussels, art. 7(3), Berlin and Rome, art. 7(1) and (2)); see S. Ricketson, *The Berne Convention on the Protection of Literary and Artistic Works*, Kluwer, 1987, paras. 10.20 to 10.22, pp. 566–8.

[288] Outside the EU, the term was also seventy years in Norway and Switzerland (after the death of the last co-author in Norway and of the film director in Switzerland).

[289] Also in Italy, Luxembourg and Portugal.

[290] Fifty years in Austria, France, Norway, Portugal and Sweden; forty years in Spain; and twenty-five years in Germany and Iceland.

[291] Case 341/87, *EMI Electrola GmbH* v. *Patricia Im- und Export Verwaltungsgesellschaft mbH* [1989] ECR 79; [1989] 2 CMLR 413; [1989] 1 FSR 544, ECJ.

the various terms of protection upwards, to the longest existing duration in the Union.

Accordingly, the Term Directive of 29 October 1993 provides in its article 1 that the rights of an author of a literary or artistic work within the meaning of article 2 of the Berne Convention shall run for the life of the author and for seventy years after his death, irrespective of the date when the work is lawfully made available to the public.[292] Under article 3 of the Convention, related rights are protected for fifty years from performance, making or communication to the public, as the case may be.

The Term Directive, however, contains special provisions regarding audiovisual works. The disparity of national solutions on film authorship had effects on the term of protection. A solution for harmonising the term of protection was to harmonise the law on this question, but UK representatives were strongly opposed to a modification of the existing scheme for film authorship. After fierce debate inside the Commission and in the European Parliament,[293] a compromise was reached, which took the form of article 2 of the Directive, entitled 'Cinematographic or audiovisual works'.

Article 2(1) specifies that the principal director of such work is to be regarded as its author or one of its authors, Member States being free to designate other co-authors. Article 2(2) sets out a special list of contributors, for the sole purpose of measuring the duration of the copyright in the 'cinematographic or audiovisual works': these are the principal director, the author of the screenplay, the author of the dialogue and the composer of any specially commissioned music.

One of the main aspect of the Term Directive is that the new term shall apply to all works which are still protected in a Member State on 1 July 1995.[294] As a consequence, the copyright in many films was revived throughout the Community.

As Professor Dworkin pointed out, 'there has been remarkably little detailed examination of the policy considerations applicable to the determination of appropriate periods of protection either for copyright or for related rights'.[295] Recital 5 of the Directive states that the term was no

---

[292] Subject to adaptations for works of joint authorship, anonymous, pseudonymous, collective works and other categories of works.

[293] See G. Dworkin, 'The EC Directive of the Term of Protection of Copyright and Related Rights', in H. Cohen Jehoram, P. Keuchenius and J. Seignette (eds.), *Audiovisual Media and Copyright in Europe*, Kluwer, 1994, pp. 33–5. See also (1993) 7 *WIPO Report* 6–7.

[294] Art. 10(2).

[295] 'The EC Directive on the Term of Protection of Copyright and Related Rights', in H. Cohen Jehoram, P. Keuchenius and J. Seignette (eds.), *Audiovisual Media and Copyright*

longer sufficient to cover two generations, which is simply wrong.[296] In fact, because it was more difficult to deprive German copyright owners of twenty valuable years of protection than to grant an additional protection to copyright industries, harmonisation was made to the highest standard and according to the dominant scheme.

Note also that the Term Directive requires Member States to implement the rule of the shorter term.[297] Dictated by the desire not to lose twenty years of valuable protection in Europe, the US extended the term of copyright protection by an additional twenty years in every category.[298]

100.   Implementation in the UK

The Duration of Copyright and Rights in Performances Regulations 1995,[299] which came into force on 1 January 1996, partially implemented the provisions of the Directive concerning film works. The new section 13B(2) of the 1988 Act, which follows article 2(2) of the Directive, now reads:

Copyright expires at the end of the period of seventy years from the end of the calendar year in which the death occurs of the last to die of the following persons –
(a) the principal director,
(b) the author of the screenplay,
(c) the author of the dialogue, or
(d) the composer of music specially created for and used in the film.[300]

In addition, in order to harmonise their duration, the 1988 Act now protects film soundtracks as part of the film, and no longer as sound recordings, thus reverting to the solution of the 1956 Act.[301]

---

in Europe, Kluwer, 1994, p. 27. On that question, see S. Ricketson, 'The Copyright Term' (1992) 6 IIC 753; K. Puri, 'The Term of Copyright Protection – Is It Too Long in the Wake of the New Technologies' (1990) 12 EIPR 12; and P. Parrinder, 'The Dead Hand of European Copyright' (1993) 15 EIPR 391.

[296] With an average lifespan of seventy years, a 50-year p.m.a. duration covers two generations. If one author has his or her child at the age of forty and dies at seventy, the child will be eighty at the end of the 50-year period.

[297] Art. 7. See the new ss. 13B(7) and (8) and 15A of the CDPA 1988. On the consequences of this rule for the protection of foreign films in the UK, see R. Stone, 'Problems of International Film Distribution' (1996) 2 *Entertainment Law Review* 62.

[298] Sonny Bono Copyright Term Extension Act, signed into law on 27 October 1998. In relation to motion pictures made-for-hire, the copyright subsists for ninety-five years from the year of its first publication, or for 120 years from the year of its creation, whichever term expires first. Subsisting copyrights in works created but not published before January 1978 are extended accordingly.

[299] SI 1995 No. 3297.

[300] Subject to special provisions when the identity of one or more of these persons is not known, or when there is no such person.

[301] With unwelcome results. See para. 78.

In conformity with article 10(2) of the Term Directive, the Duration of Copyright and Rights in Performances Regulations 1995[302] provide that the new provisions relating to the duration of copyright apply to existing works in which copyright expired before 31 December 1995 but which were on 1 July 1995 protected in another EEA State under legislation relating to copyright or related rights.[303]

There is, however, a technical problem in the UK implementation. We saw that the Term Directive sets a double system of protection of audiovisual works, with an 'author's right' in the 'cinematograph or audiovisual work'[304] and a 'related right',[305] which must have different terms.[306] The related right, which can be copyright,[307] is defined in article 3(3) of the Directive as the right of producers of 'first fixations of films', or 'first fixations of cinematograph or audiovisual works'.[308] These 'fixations' are clearly the visual recordings.

The problem is that the Regulations extended the right in the 'film', which is the right in the recording, to seventy years after the death of the last contributor listed for this purpose, which went further than the term provided for this class of work in the Directive, which must be fifty years from making or publication. This extension would have had no consequence in the absence of protection for the underlying audiovisual work. However, we saw that some of these works are likely to be protected as dramatic works. And, according to the Directive, the duration of the dramatic copyright has been extended to seventy years p.m.a.[309] Thus it can be said that UK producers will sometimes obtain two rights lasting for seventy years p.m.a. (or p.m. contributors for the 'film') whereas their continental counterparts benefit only from a 50-year neighbouring right in the film recording in addition to the seventy years p.m.a. copyright in the audiovisual work. The fact that in practice film producers hold both these rights certainly limits the consequences of such an over-extension, but there could easily well be litigation on that subject.

---

[302] SI 1995 No. 3297.   [303] Section 16.   [304] Art. 1.
[305] Art. 3(3). Also arts. 2, 7, 9, 10 and 12 of the Rental Directive.
[306] Arts. 2(2) and 3(3).
[307] The Directive does not make the distinction between copyrights and neighbouring rights but operates a categorisation based on initial ownership (author's right in art. 1, producer's right in art. 3).
[308] In art. 3(3), the term 'film' is defined to mean the 'cinematograph or audiovisual work', thus creating a confusion with the 'film' under the UK Act. But obviously it is not the same element which is referred to.
[309] Which is not a correct implementation of the Directive either. For example, under UK copyright law, the composer of the specially commissioned music cannot be co-author of the dramatic work including his musical work (see para. 127). However, according to the Directive, his or her life must be taken into account for the calculation of the duration of the copyright in the underlying audiovisual work (which, arguably, is the dramatic copyright under present UK law).

The provision of article 2(1) of the Term Directive was implemented in the UK by the Copyright and Related Rights Regulations 1996.[310]

101.   Other national implementations[311]

The provisions of the Term Directive relating to film works have been implemented in all Member States, in most case faithfully.[312]

102.   The problem of war extensions

An interesting problem in relation to the extension of duration for film works in some authors' rights countries is constituted by the fate of extension for war periods. For example, in France, the Intellectual Property Code provides for three kinds of extensions of the standard copyright term, all of which are applicable to film works. Article L.123-8 is concerned with First World War extensions. It provides that the copyright shall be extended for a period equal to that which elapsed between 2 August 1914 and the end of the year following the day of signature of the peace treaty, for all works published before the latter date and which had not fallen into the public domain on 3 February 1919. French courts have expressed different opinions as to what constitutes the 'end of the year following the day of signature of the peace treaty'. At least two decisions fixed the date at 31 December 1920,[313] while other decisions fixed it at 24 October 1920.[314] Accordingly, the extension is six years and either 152 or 83 days, as the case may be. Article L.123-10 contains a similar provision relating to the Second World War, amounting to an extension of around eight years and 120 days. Finally, article L.123-10 grants a further 30-year extension for authors who 'died for France'. These extensions are cumulative. War extensions are also applicable in Belgium[315] and Italy.[316]

---

[310] See para. 118.

[311] See G. Lea, 'The Term Directive and Its Implementation' (1999) *Yearbook of Copyright and Media Law* 177.

[312] Austria, Copyright Amendment Law of 1996; Belgium, Copyright Act 1994; Denmark, Law of 14 June 1995; Spain, Law of 11 October 1995; Finland, Law of 22 December 1995; France, Law of 27 March 1997; Germany, Law of 23 June 1995; Ireland, EC (Term of Protection) Regulations of 1995; Italy, Legislative Decree of 26 May 1997; the Netherlands, Act of 1995.

[313] Tribunal of First Instance of Seine, 31 May 1939, *Gazette du Palais*, 1939, II, p. 208; Paris Court of Appeal, 5 December 1956, *La Semaine Juridique*, 1957, II, No. 9728.

[314] E.g. Versailles Court of Appeal, 5 March 1984, D. 1986, IR, p. 187.

[315] A Law of 25 June 1921 extends for ten years the duration of protection for works published before 4 August 1924, which were not in the public domain on 25 June 1921.

[316] Legislative Decree No. 440 of 20 July 1945 apparently extends for six years the duration of protection for works published before 17 August 1945. See M. Fabiani, in

The question then becomes to determine whether these extensions comply with the provisions of the Term Directive. In Italy, the Law of 6 February 1996 implementing the Term Directive abrogated the wartime extension provisions.[317] The French and Belgian implementing instruments are silent on that point. The case was not decided by the European Court of Justice or by national courts and is open to debate. On the one hand, the subsistence of longer terms would appear to contradict the objectives of the Directive. On the other hand, article 10(1) of the Directive expressly provides that, where a term of protection, which is longer than the corresponding term provided for by the Directive, is already running in a Member State on 1 July 1995, the Directive shall not have the effect of shortening that term of protection in that Member State.

103. Revived and extended rights

Although the provisions of the Term Directive have now been implemented in all Member States, disparities remain between them in relation to revived and extended rights. Article 10(3) of the Term Directive provides that the provisions of the Directive shall be without prejudice to any acts of exploitation performed before 1 July 1995. It further provides that Member States shall adopt the necessary provisions to protect in particular acquired rights of third parties. It does not, however, specify further the regime of revived and extended rights, in particular in terms of ownership. Accordingly, the implementation made in this respect differs between Member States. Three situation must be distinguished: the ownership of revived copyright; the fate of uses made during the time the work was in the public domain; and the ownership and exercise of extended rights.

104. Ownership of revived copyright

In the UK, under the Duration of Copyright and Rights in Performances Regulations 1995,[318] as a matter of principle the person who was the owner of the copyright in a work immediately before it expired is as from 1 January 1996 the owner of any revived copyright in the work.[319] However, if that person died or ceased to exist before that date, the revived copyright shall vest:

M. B. Nimmer and D. Geller (eds.), *International Copyright Law and Practice*, Matthew Bender, looseleaf, para. 3[2][b], footnote.

[317] *Ibid.*   [318] SI 1995 No. 3297.

[319] Section 19(1). See also the provisions for prospective ownership of revived copyright, Duration of Copyright and Rights in Performances Regulations 1995 (SI 1995 No. 3297), reg. 20.

1. in the case of a film, in the principal director of the film or his personal representatives; or
2. in any other case, in the author of the work or his personal representatives.[320]

Where the revived copyright so vests in personal representatives, it must be held by them for the benefit of the person who would have been entitled to it had it been vested in the principal director or author immediately before his death and had devolved as part of his estate.[321]

Revived copyright is subject to compulsory licence under section 24 of the Regulations. In relation to revived copyright, any acts restricted by the copyright must be treated as licensed by the copyright owner, subject only to the payment of such reasonable royalty or other remuneration as may be agreed or determined, or, failing such agreement, by the Copyright Tribunal.[322] A person intending to avail himself of the right conferred by the Regulations must give reasonable notice of his intention to the copyright owner, stating when he intends to begin to do the acts; otherwise, his acts shall not be treated as licensed.[323] If he does give such notice, his acts shall be treated as licensed, and a reasonable royalty or other remuneration shall be payable in respect of such acts despite the fact that the amount of such royalty or remuneration is not agreed or determined until later.[324] This licence does not apply if or to the extent that a licence to do the acts could be granted by a licensing body, whether or not under a licensing scheme.[325]

In France, Germany and Belgium, the revived right would belong to the heirs of the author.[326] In Italy, the last owner of the revived copyright before it fell into the public domain is deemed to be the owner of the revived rights.[327]

105.   Use during the time the work was in the public domain

As mentioned above, under article 10(3) of the Term Directive the provisions of the Directive shall be without prejudice to any acts of exploitation performed before 1 July 1995, and Member States shall adopt the necessary provisions to protect in particular the acquired rights of third parties. This provision was implemented in different ways by Member States.

In the UK, section 23(1) of the Duration Regulation provides that no act done before 1 January 1996 shall be regarded as infringing revived

[320] Section 19(2).   [321] Section 19(3).   [322] Section 24(1).
[323] Section 24(2) and (3).   [324] Section 24(4).   [325] Section 24(4).
[326] In Germany, art. 137f(3) of the Copyright Act, as amended.
[327] Law of 23 December 1996, art. 57.

copyright in a work. In addition, it is not an infringement of revived copyright:

1. to do anything after 1 January 1996 pursuant to arrangements made before 1 January 1995 at a time when copyright did not subsist in the work;
2. to issue to the public after 1 January 1996 copies of the work made before 1 July 1995 at a time when copyright did not subsist in the work;
3. to do anything after 1 January 1996 in relation to a literary, dramatic, musical or artistic work or a film made before that date, or made pursuant to arrangements made before that date, which contains a copy of that work or is an adaptation of that work if the copy or adaptation was made before 1 July 1995 at a time when copyright did not subsist in the work in which revived copyright subsists, or if the copy or adaptation was made pursuant to arrangements made before 1 July 1995 at a time when copyright did not subsist in the work in which revived copyright subsists; or
4. to do after 1 January 1996 anything which is a restricted act in relation to the work if the act is done at a time when, or is done pursuant to arrangements made at a time when, the name and address of a person entitled to authorise the act cannot by reasonable inquiry be ascertained.

In France, the Law of 27 March 1997 provides that owners of revived rights cannot invoke these rights against acts of exploitation lawfully carried out before 1 July 1995. In addition, these owners cannot:

1. object, during one year as from 1 July 1995, to a further exploitation of the work;
2. object, during one year as from 1 July 1995, to a further exploitation of a work created before that date derived from their work; after that period, an equitable remuneration must be paid; or
3. object to the making of an audiovisual work which is the object of an audiovisual adaptation contract prior to 1 July 1995, registered with the public registry of cinematography. An equitable remuneration must also be paid in that case.[328]

The Belgian Copyright Act provides that the revival of rights may not be invoked against persons who have undertaken in good faith the exploitation of works in the public domain before 1 July 1995, provided they continue the same modes of exploitation.[329]

In Germany, an exploitation started before 1 July 1995 can be continued in the same conditions. However, from 1 July 1995, an equitable remuneration must be paid.[330]

[328] Art. 16.   [329] Art. 88(2).   [330] Copyright Act, art. 137f(3).

In Italy, under article 17(4) of Law No. 52/96, as amended, the revived copyright does not prejudice instruments and contracts entered into before 1 July 1995. In particular, the following are not affected:

1. the distribution and reproduction of works, within the limits of the graphic composition and editorial presentation in which the publication has taken place, by the persons who have undertaken the distribution and reproduction of the works before that date; further updates required by the nature of the works may also be distributed and reproduced without payment; and

2. the distribution, for three months following the date of entry into force of Law No. 52/96, of phonograph records and analogous media in respect of which rights of use have expired under the previous legislation, by the persons who have reproduced and marketed the said media before that date.

This last limitation of the Italian law was held compatible with the provisions of article 10(3) of the Term Directive by the European Court of Justice.[331]

106.   Ownership and exercise of extended rights

In the UK, regulation 18 of the Duration of Copyright and Rights in Performances Regulations 1995[332] grants ownership of extended copyright to the person who was the owner of the copyright work immediately before 1 January 1996.[333]

In France, the Law of 27 March 1997 provides that the extension of copyright in a work that is the object of a publishing contract does not extend the duration of this contract if its duration is fixed by reference to the legal duration of copyright.[334] However, in such a case, the publisher has a right of preference on the extended copyright. Nothing is said on other types of copyright contracts, including film production contracts.

The Belgian Act is silent on the subject. However, its article 88(3) provides that the Act shall not affect rights acquired by operation of law or through the effect of a legal instrument before its entry into force,

---

[331] Case C-60/98, *Butterfly Music Srl* v. *Carosello Edizioni Musicali e Discografiche Srl* [1999] ECR I-3939; [2000] 1 CMLR 587; [1999] EMLR 847, ECJ.

[332] SI 1995 No. 3297.

[333] However, if he is entitled to copyright for a period less than the whole of the copyright period under the 1988 provisions, any extended copyright is part of the reversionary interest expectant on the termination of that period (s. 18(2)). See also the provisions for prospective ownership of extended copyright, in the Duration of Copyright and Rights in Performances Regulations 1995 (SI 1995 No. 3297), reg. 20.

[334] Art. 16.

which appears to suggest that extended copyright belongs to the person who was the owner of the copyright at the time of extension.

The German Copyright Act provides that in case of doubt the assignment or licence made before 1 July 1995 extends to the extended period, subject to an equitable remuneration.[335]

In Italy, it was necessary for the last owner to proceed with a registration before 23 April 1996; otherwise, rights reverted to the author. In any case, equitable remuneration must be paid to the co-authors (and performers) of the film the copyright of which was extended.

---

[335] Art. 137f(4).

4   Authorship and initial ownership

107.   Authorship, ownership and authorial rights

Among the problems raised by audiovisual works, the question of copyright entitlement has proved to be one of the most complex and controversial in copyright law, at both the national and international levels. These difficulties are closely connected to the way commercial theatrical films are generally produced.[1] Problems arise not so much from the fact that they involve a number of contributors rarely equalled in other areas of copyright law. Rather, they are caused by the nature of the numerous contributions to the final work, which cannot be reduced to a single model for copyright purposes: products of highly specialised professionals, these contributions can be artistic or simply technical, and, when artistic, can cover the whole spectrum of copyright subject-matter (literary, artistic, dramatic and musical works) or amount to *sui generis* elements which are not separately protectable (*mise-en-scène*, editing); some can and some cannot be protected and exploited independently from the film; some exist before the film and some can be made at any stage of the production process; moreover, each production appears to involve different degrees in terms of creative responsibility and autonomy of contributors. This 'atomisation' of creative inputs makes the determination of the creator(s) difficult and the regime of exploitation of the final work particularly complex.

In contrast, the whole production process is generally under the responsibility of a well-defined entity which initiates and finances the project, controls and directs the work of the contributors, and undertakes the commercial release and exploitation of the work.

As a consequence, when it comes to copyright entitlement, cinematographic works can be seen both as a form of intellectual creation in search

---

[1] Note that most studies on film copyright start from the model of theatrical film productions, which is sometimes too narrow, given the importance of televisual works, and the fact that televisual works involve different standards in terms of production.

of its authors, and as a form of commodity production closely associated with the production company.

All copyright and authors' rights systems have been torn between the need to protect the individual activity of the creator and the need to grant effective protection to film producers. Where some jurisdictions decided not to depart from their traditional line of vesting rights in the intellectual creators of the work, other jurisdictions took the option of redefining the title in cinematographic works in terms of capital investment. But here the legal technique used varies greatly. One approach is to grant *ownership* to the producer through presumptions of assignment or employment rules. Another, more categorical, approach is to consider the producer as the sole *author* of the film for copyright purposes. This last solution, which had advocates in almost every legal system, avoids the problems associated with the determination of the intellectual creators of the work; it can also vest in the producer rights which are usually retained by authors and are either not assignable or difficult to convey by contract (such as moral rights, copyright renewal or termination rights).[2]

108. Authorship of films in the Berne Convention

In this regard, the Berne Convention appears to leave a total freedom to signatory States. There is no definition of the term 'author' in the Convention, and its usual meaning is still the subject of controversy.[3] In addition, when it comes to cinematographic works, the Convention clearly avoids the questions of authorship and original entitlement to copyright, and

---

[2] Note, however, that copyright countries which have implemented moral rights in films are reluctant to grant these rights to film producers, even when they are considered to be the 'author' of the film in the copyright Acts. This is the case in the UK, where moral rights have been granted to the film director, and not to the producer-author. This is also the case in New Zealand, in the 1994 Act, and in Australia, with the Copyright Amendment (Moral Rights) Act 2000.

[3] For the opinion that 'author' means only the physical person who created the work, see S. Ricketson, *The Berne Convention on the Protection of Literary and Artistic Works*, Kluwer, 1987, para. 5.2, p. 159; W. Nordemann, K. Vinck and P. W. Hertin, *International Copyright and Neighbouring Rights Law* (trans. G. Meyer), VCH, 1990, p. 48; A. Dietz, 'The Concept of Author Under the Berne Convention', RIDA, January 1993, para. 155; See also H. Desbois, A. Françon and A. Kerever, *Les Conventions Internationales du Droit d'Auteur et des Droits Voisins*, Dalloz, Paris, 1976. Contra: the 'Guide to the Berne Convention (Paris Act, 1971)', WIPO, Geneva, 1978 (though this guide does not represent an authoritative interpretation of the Convention); Chapter XIV of the 'Final Report of the Ad Hoc Working Group on US Adherence to the Berne Convention' (1986) 10 *Columbia-VLA Journal of Law and the Arts* 513; J. Ginsburg, 'Colors in Conflicts: Moral Rights and the Foreign Exploitation of Colorised US Motion Pictures' (1988) 36 *Journal of the Copyright Society of the USA* 80.

tackles film protection in terms of ownership.[4] This compromise indicates that a conventional concept of the author as the 'natural person who has made the work'[5] could be departed from in relation to cinematographic works, and that the producer, individual or body corporate, employer or commissioner, could be granted authorship by signatory States.[6]

109.   The dichotomy between copyright and authors' rights systems

As a result, modern copyright systems are often classified under two categories, which, it is generally assumed, correspond to copyright and authors' rights systems. Where *droit d'auteur* countries grant authorship and vest copyright in the creative authors, countries with a copyright tradition prefer to vest the rights in the film producer, considering him as the 'author' of the film. In the US, the producer is granted authorship in the motion picture, but also in the commissioned contributory works, through the 'work-made-for-hire' doctrine.[7] Under UK copyright from the 1956 Act until the entry into force of the Copyright and Related Rights Regulations 1996, the producer was the sole author of the specific subject-matter for audiovisual works, i.e. the 'cinematograph film' under the 1956 Act and the 'film' under the CDPA 1988. Similar schemes have been adopted in Australia,[8] India,[9] Ireland,[10] New Zealand[11] and by some other jurisdictions influenced by UK law.[12]

However, this opposition between authors' rights and copyright jurisdictions must be qualified. Historically, most major legal systems have experienced both situations,[13] and it is still possible to find copyright laws

---

[4] Art. 14*bis* reads: '(1) . . . The owner of copyright in a cinematographic work shall enjoy the same rights as the author of an original work, including the rights referred to in the preceding article. (2) (a) Ownership of copyright in a cinematographic work shall be a matter for legislation in the country where protection is claimed . . .'

[5] S. Ricketson, *The Berne Convention on the Protection of Literary and Artistic Works*, Kluwer, 1987, para. 5.2.

[6] This is reinforced by examination of the works of the Stockholm conference (quoted in Dietz, 'The Concept of Author Under the Berne Convention', RIDA, January 1993, p. 31 and n. 18). See also Ricketson, *The Berne Convention*, para. 5.2, p. 159 and para. 10.10, p. 557; and W. Nordemann, K. Vinck and P. W. Hertin, *International Copyright and Neighbouring Rights Law* (trans. G. Meyer), VCH, 1990, pp. 142–4.

[7] Section 62 of the 1909 Act (codified at 17 USC s. 26). Now ss. 201(b) and 101 of the Copyright Act 1976.

[8] Copyright Act 1968.   [9] Copyright Act 1957.

[10] Copyright Act 1963.   [11] Copyright Act 1962.

[12] But note that Canadian copyright law retains the scheme set up by the 1911 Act.

[13] We saw that under the 1911 Act authorship in the film as a dramatic work vested in the intellectual creator (see para. 18). More surprisingly, early in the twentieth century,

in which rights in the film are vested initially in the creator as author,[14] and to find *droit d'auteur* countries which grant authorship and initial ownership to film producers.[15] Moreover, most authors' rights jurisdictions have established a system which can be seen as a compromise: creative artists are considered as the authors of the film, but in some countries economic rights (or some of them) are initially vested in the production company, while moral rights vest in the creator;[16] in other countries, the economic rights are initially vested in the co-authors but granted to the producer through presumptions of assignment (either rebuttable or not).[17]

In fact, in terms of economic rights, the real difference between copyright and authors' rights systems lies in the fact that film authors in *droit d'auteur* jurisdictions often retain a statutory interest in the exploitation of their work, even when exploitation rights have been assigned or otherwise transferred to the producer. The *droit d'auteur* philosophy considers that it is up to the legislature to protect the author, regarded as the weaker party in the contracts he enters, by providing for protective measures of some sort.[18] For example, the presumption of assignment, where implemented, is often limited in its scope, and does not encompass 'residual rights' which are retained by authors.[19] Also, several systems provide for

several continental jurisdictions departed from the classic view of authors' rights, and vested the rights in cinematographic films in the producer. See para. 135.

[14] E.g. Canada and some Commonwealth countries; but also in the UK, due to transitional provisions, for films under the 1911 Act (see para. 18), and, under the present Act, for films protected as dramatic works (see paras. 120 *et seq.*).

[15] E.g. Luxembourg art. 27 of the Act of 29 March 1972. Art. 21 of the new Copyright Act of 18 April 2001 (the producer is the co-author of the film with the principal director).

[16] This is the case in Austria and Italy. See para. 161.

[17] See para. 161. French law provides for a broad presumption of assignment of economic rights subject to agreement to the contrary (but this presumption excludes the musical composer). A similar presumption is found in Germany (ss. 88 and 89 of Law of 9 September 1965), Denmark (construed from s. 42 of the Law of 31 May 1961), the Netherlands (1912 Act, as amended by the Law of 30 May 1985), Portugal (Law of 17 September 1985), Spain (Law of 11 November 1987; limited to some specific rights) and Sweden (Law of 30 December 1960, arts. 39 and 40). On the presumption set by art. 14*bis*(2) and (3) of the Berne Convention in favour of film producers, see W. Nordemann, K. Vinck and P. W. Hertin, *International Copyright and Neighbouring Rights Law* (trans. G. Meyer), VCH, 1990, pp. 147–50, and S. Ricketson, *The Berne Convention on the Protection of Literary and Artistic Works*, Kluwer, 1987, paras. 10.26 *et seq.*

[18] See P. Katzenberger, 'Protection of the Author as the Weaker Party to a Contract Under International Copyright Contract Law' (1988) IIC.

[19] E.g. where implemented in relation to the final work, the presumption sometimes reserves to authors 'remake' or adaptation rights (which means that they can still bargain for these rights, which in most cases remain assignable). When implemented for protected contributions as well, the presumption does not generally apply to specially commissioned music. See para. 161.

an equitable remuneration to be paid to film authors or contributors; for example, under French law, in spite of a broad presumption of assignment to the producer, film co-authors retain a statutory right to proportional remuneration, and to remuneration for each mode of exploitation of the film.[20] In other countries, the author has the right to demand additional remuneration if the agreed fee is grossly out of proportion to the profits derived from a successful exploitation of the work.[21] In addition to these specific rules, one should also take into consideration the provisions which, in some authors' rights systems, limit the possibility of an assignment of future works, prevent implied assignments or licences, impose a duty of exploitation for the producer, impose special construction rules in favour of the author and limit the duration of copyright contracts.[22]

Again, the Berne Convention allows signatory States to impose any kind of compromise in relation to films.[23]

110.   Determination of film co-authors

Another difficulty of film protection lies in the determination of the list of co-authors of the film. The problem with audiovisual works is that there are very different requirements among jurisdictions concerning the nature of the contributions to a joint work, which results in disparities in the list of potential co-authors. In this respect, most systems can be roughly separated into two categories:

In some systems, those who collaborated in creating a work, provided a minimum standard of creativity is met, are considered co-authors, irrespective of the fact that their contribution can be separated: for example, songs, dramatico-musical works and motion pictures are considered as joint works in all their elements.[24] This comprehensive view is adopted under US copyright, provided that the separable contributions are interdependent,[25] and in authors' rights jurisdictions such as France[26] and Belgium.[27]

---

[20] See paras. 173 *et seq.*   [21] *Ibid.*
[22] These provisions, or at least one of them, can be found in almost all authors' rights Acts. See Chapter 5 below.
[23] Art. 14*bis*(2)(b) and (c) and (3).
[24] US Congress, House Committee on the Judiciary, 'Copyright Law Revision', House Report 94-1476 on S. 22, 94th Cong., 2nd Sess., 1976, gives examples of inseparable and interdependent joint works. Novels or paintings are 'inseparable' works (*ibid.*, p. 120), and examples of interdependent works include a motion picture, an opera and a song.
[25] Section 101 of the Copyright Act 1976 reads: 'A "joint work" is a work prepared by two or more authors with the intention that their contributions be merged into inseparable or interdependent parts of a unitary whole.'
[26] Arts. L.113-2 and L.113-3 of the Intellectual Property Code.
[27] Arts. 5, 6 and 18 of the Law of 22 March 1886.

In other systems, contributions giving rise to joint authorship must not be 'distinct', 'separate' or 'separable'. Under such a doctrine, typically a song is not a joint work comprising words and music but a mere composite work,[28] and a motion picture might only be partly joint, music in particular being considered as a composite element. This is the solution adopted under UK copyright, and in countries of the authors' rights tradition such as Germany.[29]

Beyond this distinction, the determination of joint authors in cinematographic and audiovisual works involves several questions in each legal system, for example on the requirements of intent, actual collaboration, contemporaneity of contributions, separate copyrightability, etc.

Some jurisdictions solved the problem by setting out a list of presumptive co-authors. For example, under French law, the author of the script, the author of the adaptation, the dialogist, the author of any music specially composed for inclusion in the audiovisual work and the director are presumed to be co-authors of the final audiovisual work, subject to proof to the contrary; in addition, the author of the adapted work is in any case considered co-author.[30] This list is open and other participants, including the (individual) producer,[31] can be co-authors, provided they meet the requirements of collaboration and creativity. In Italy, the list of co-authors is a closed list and includes the author of the subject-matter, the scriptwriter, the musical composer and the director.[32]

111.   The EC copyright directives

The determination of the author of the audiovisual work was one of the most contentious questions debated during the discussions of the Rental and Term Directives. It resulted in the designation of the director as the author or one of the authors of the audiovisual work. This choice was not based on an analysis of the rules on co-authorship or on an assessment of the weight of the various creative contributions to film production. More pragmatically, the Commission chose to propose a minimum compromise, by choosing the only contributor considered as author or co-author

[28] For a song not being a joint work under UK law, see *Redwood Music Ltd* v. *B. Feldman & Co.* [1979] RPC 1, on appeal [1979] RPC 385, CA, affirmed sub nom *Chappel & Co. Ltd* v. *Redwood Music Ltd* [1980] 2 All ER 817; [1981] RPC 337, HL.

[29] Art. 8 of the Law of 1965. See para. 137.

[30] Art. L.113-7 of the Intellectual Property Code (also in Belgium). This is, indeed, a very odd assumption.

[31] I.e. a natural person.

[32] Art. 44 of the Law of 22 April 1941. In Spain and Portugal, the list is similar and includes the director, the authors of the script, of the adaptation and of the dialogue, and the authors of any musical composition created specifically for the work. See para. 138 below.

in all Member States of the authors' rights tradition. In this process, the solution adopted in these countries, which are a majority in the Union, prevailed over the views expressed by UK and Irish representatives. This harmonisation involved two stages.

Article 2 of the Rental Directive conferred on the author or co-authors of the film the exclusive right to authorise or prohibit its rental and lending. Article 2(2) further defined the author as the film director but, as the result of the strong resistance of UK representatives, limited this designation to the sole purpose of directive:

> For the purposes of this Directive the principal director of a cinematographic or audiovisual work shall be considered as its author or one of its authors. Member States may provide for others to be considered as its co-authors.

Accordingly, this designation does not necessarily involve a formal designation of the film director as author of the film, as long as he is granted the rental right like other film authors.

The conflict culminated during the elaboration of the Proposal for the Term Directive. The Commission Proposal provided that the authors of a cinematographic or audiovisual work referred to the natural persons who were the intellectual creators of the work, and considered the director as one of those authors.[33] This view was strongly opposed by the UK representatives in the European Parliament.[34] The Proposal went to the Council, which decided that it would not address this question. After much discussion, an agreement was reached in the form of a compromise. Article 2(1) of the Term Directive sets out a more general rules than the Rental Directive by requiring that, in all cases, the principal director is considered as author of the cinematographic work:[35]

> The principal director of a cinematographic or audiovisual work shall be considered as its author or one of its authors. Member States shall be free to designate other co-authors.

The recitals of the Rental Directive make clear that this is a rebuttable presumption.[36] Member States are free to extend the list of film authors

---

[33] See G. Dworkin, 'Authorship of Films and the European Commission Proposals for Harmonising the Term of Copyright, Opinion' (1993) 15 EIPR 151 at 152.

[34] See (1993) 7 *WIPO Report* 6–7. Despite this opposition, the amendment adopted by the Assembly in 19 November 1993 defined the author as 'the natural person(s) responsible for the creation of the work. In the absence of evidence to the contrary, the following shall be presumed to be authors: the director, script-writer, dialogue-writer, adaptor and the composer of music with or without words which has been specially written for that work.'

[35] Art. 2(1).

[36] See recital 13: 'the question of authorship in the whole or in part of a work is a question of fact which the national courts may have to decide.'

to include other contributors, even non-artistic contributors such as the film producer, whether a natural or a legal person.

112.   Domestic laws

Given the very different traditions and statutory provisions of Member States of common law and authors' rights traditions on this subject, we will study separately the law of the UK and Ireland, on the one hand, and the law of continental authors' rights countries, on the other.

SECTION I

Authorship of audiovisual works in the United Kingdom and Ireland

113.   The specifics of UK copyright

When it comes to film authorship, the peculiarities of UK law are re-inforced by the very peculiar way in which the authorship provisions of the copyright directives have been implemented in the UK. As described in the previous chapter, audiovisual works are protected mainly under a specific copyright in their recordings, the 'film', which corresponds to the neighbouring right of the film producers in authors' rights countries. Before the decision of the Court of Appeal in *Norowzian*,[37] it was assumed by a majority that this form of protection was the only one available to film works. As a consequence, the provisions of the Term Directive, which required, at the minimum, that the principal director be considered author or one of the authors of the audiovisual works, were implemented in relation to this specific subject-matter: the principal film director and the producer are now considered co-authors of the 'film' (discussed in Part I below).

However, the decision of the Court of Appeal in the *Norowzian* case confirmed that audiovisual works may be protected as dramatic works under the CDPA 1988, thus creating an additional protection for films. The problem is that, in the absence of specific rules on authorship for this class of works in the Act, the generally applicable rules on author-ship must apply. UK copyright is then faced with the very difficulties of joint authorship it tended to avoid by implementing a specific form of protection (discussed in Part II below).

---

[37] See para. 56.

PART I

The author of the 'film'

114.   Entrepreneurial authorship of films under the UK 1956 Act[38]

We saw that the rationale behind the introduction of a system of entrepreneurial authorship in the 1956 Act was to avoid multiple claims for authorship in audiovisual works and the difficulties in tracing film authors.[39] As a consequence, section 13(10) of the 1956 Act granted the copyright in the 'cinematograph film' to 'the person by whom the arrangements necessary for the making of the film were undertaken'.[40] It is interesting to observe that the 1956 Act did not formally designate this 'maker' as 'author' of the cinematographic film, but only as initial owner of the copyright.[41] Then in strict terms, and according to transitional provisions in the 1988 Act,[42] it can be said that a cinematograph film made under the 1956 Act has no 'author' as such.[43] The definition of the 'maker' has not been modified in section 9(c) of the 1988 Act in relation to the 'film', but the maker is now expressly designated as 'author' of the film.[44]

115.   The author of a film made before 1 July 1994

Under section 9 of the 1988 Act, as enacted, 'author', in relation to a work, means the person who creates it. According to section 9(2)(b), in the case of a film, that person shall be taken to be 'the person by whom

[38] See J. Phillips, 'The Concept of "Author" in Copyright Law – Some Reflections on the Basis of Copyright Law in the United Kingdom', *Copyright*, January 1990, p. 26.

[39] See para. 22.

[40] This definition was borrowed from the Cinematograph Films Acts 1938 and 1948.

[41] Section 13(14): 'The maker of a cinematographic film shall be entitled to any copyright subsisting in the film by virtue of this section.'

[42] According to Sched. 1, para. 10, the question who was the author is to be determined in accordance with the law in force at the time the work was made (except for moral rights purposes).

[43] J. Phillips, 'The Concept of "Author" in Copyright Law – Some Reflections on the Basis of Copyright Law in the United Kingdom', *Copyright*, January 1990, p. 29. As the author points out, under the 1956 Act, 'the term author was used of the human agency by which an author's work was generated, while other terminology was used for copyright subject-matter other than authors' work' (*ibid.*, p. 27). However, this does not appear to have consequences on the protection granted to film producers, in the UK and abroad.

[44] Phillips remarks that with the 1988 Act the word 'author' has been given its widest application ever under UK law (*ibid.*). Note that, although there may be some doubt concerning pre-1957 works (see para. 12), under the 1956 and the 1988 Act the author can be a legal person (1956 Act, s. 1(5); 1988 Act, s. 154(1)(c)).

the arrangements necessary for the making of the film were undertaken'. This language still applies for films made before 1 July 1994.

This definition is drafted in broad terms, and does not expressly mention the film producer.[45] It certainly excludes purely creative contributors, including the film director,[46] but various financial contributors or organisers in film productions could claim to be 'makers' under such a wording. In fact, this text must be read in the light of the Gregory Committee report, which pointed more clearly to the film producer:

> This may be either a company or an individual; in either case what we have in mind is the entrepreneur (if the word is not too old-fashioned) under whose care the labours of the many contributors are brought to a successful issue.[47]

116.   The definition of the film producer

Case law provides some additional guidance on the definition of the 'author' of the film. In *Century Communications* v. *Mayfair Entertainment UK Ltd*,[48] a conflict as to authorship in a film shot in China arose between a company from Hong Kong, which initiated and was to finance the project, and a Chinese corporation, responsible for obtaining shooting permissions and for assisting the actual filming on location. It was held that the first company was the sole 'author' of the film under section 9(c). In *Beggars Banquet Records* v. *Carlton Television*,[49] a record company commissioned a film production company to make a video about a dance party. After a dispute with the production company, the commissioner sought an interlocutory order for delivery up and interlocutory injunctions claiming authorship in the film. In support of its claim, the record company contended that it financed the making of the footage, that it had arranged access to the site for the film-makers, and that it had chosen the production company. The court held that these elements do not necessarily make the commissioner 'author' of the film under section 9(c).[50]

---

[45] For corresponding definition in foreign Acts, see J. A. L. Sterling, *Intellectual Property Rights in Sound Recordings, Films and Video*, Sweet & Maxwell, 1992, para. 5.21.

[46] *Adventure Film Productions Ltd* v. *Tolley*, *The Times*, 14 October 1982; [1993] EMLR 376; see also *A&M Records Ltd* v. *Video Collection International Ltd* [1995] EMLR 25.

[47] At para. 102. See also, in the parliamentary debates of 1988, HL Debs, vol. 490, p. 887, *per* Lord Lloyd: 'the Bill follows the pattern of the 1956 Act by giving ownership, in the first instance, to the producer as the man who has brought the whole thing together, and directly or through distributors or other finance has been able to organise the film.'

[48] [1993] EMLR 335.   [49] [1993] EMLR 349.

[50] The record company also claimed co-authorship, but Warner J doubted that this submission was bound to succeed. *Re FG (Films) Ltd* [1953] 1 WLR 483 (a shadow production company was held not to be the 'maker' of the film under the Cinematographic Film Act 1938) was distinguished.

Guidance can also be found in cases dealing with authorship in sound recordings.[51]

117.   Who is author in the absence of a producer?

Although the system inaugurated by the 1956 Act and continued under the present Act is based on the assumption that films are made under the control of an entrepreneur, in practice an important number of protected films, such as 'home' or 'amateur' movies, do not have such 'producers'. For example, a group of friends gather and decide to make a film; they find finance without giving up control over the project, make their film and afterwards sell it to a production company or a television channel. The production company and the television channel are not authors, but assignees or licensees. Who is author of the 'film'? Another example is where a person films a wedding ceremony with the camera of one of his friends, on a tape given to him by another, after being asked to do so by a third person. Who is the author of the 'film'? In both cases, one hesitates between the person who initiates the filming, the one who finances the film, the one who provides the technical equipment and the one who undertakes the filming. To be the author, they need the kind of control over the production required by the definition of section 13(10). Sometimes, several people will have some degree of control. In that case, will they be co-authors? And, if so, under which criterion?

Here the difficulties are not unlike the ones created by the determination of co-authorship under a 'creative authorship scheme', even though they are focused on other factors.[52]

118.   The author of the film made on or after 1 July 1994

In implementing the authorship provisions of the copyright directives, the Copyright and Related Rights Regulations 1996 substituted a new section 9(2)(ab) in the 1988 Act, which designates the 'producer' and the 'principal director' as co-authors of the film. Accordingly, the film is

---

[51] *A&M Records Ltd* v. *Video Collection International Ltd* [1995] EMLR 25 appears to be more favourable to commissioners; a company commissioned a conductor to produce a sound recording. The conductor commissioned and paid for the arrangements, booked and paid for recording sessions, paid the musicians and various expenses incurred by the recording. The court held that the conductor 'made the recording', but that its commissioner 'undertook the arrangements necessary for that making', under s. 9(2). See also *Mad Hat Music Ltd* v. *Pulse 8 Records Ltd* [1993] EMLR 172. Compare with s. 12(4) of the 1956 Act, which granted to commissioners of sound recordings the initial copyright in the work. See *Presentaciones Musicales SA* v. *Secunda* [1995] EMLR 118.

[52] See paras. 122 *et seq.*

now to be treated as a work of joint authorship.[53] This new provision is applicable to films made on or after 1 July 1994.

There may be difficulties as to who may qualify as the principal director of the film. What can be said is that this provision does not appear to exclude the possibility of two 'principal' directors, in case, for example, of co-direction of a film.

Although the term 'producer' is now used expressly in section 9, the existing definition is left unchanged: the amended section 178 provides that 'producer' in relation to a sound recording or film means 'the person by whom the arrangements necessary for the making of the sound recording or film are undertaken'.

119.   The author of the film in Ireland

In Ireland, the initial owner of the copyright in a 'cinematograph film' made under the Copyright Act 1963 was the person by whom the arrangements necessary for the making of the film were undertaken, i.e. the producer.[54] Like the UK 1956 Act, the Irish 1963 Act did not formally designate the producer as 'author' of the 'cinematograph film', but only as initial owner of the copyright.[55]

The producer and the principal director of the film are now co-authors of the film under section 21 of the Irish Copyright and Related Rights Act 2000.

PART II

The author of the audiovisual dramatic work

120.   Cases of creative authorship of films
under UK copyright law

Under UK law the problem of the determination of the 'creative' author of a film may arise in two situations. First, in relation to films protected as dramatic works under the 1911 Act:[56] under transitional arrangements these films are still protected under this heading,[57] and the person who was the author of the work under the 1911 Act shall be taken to be author

---

[53] On the regime of such works, see para. 134.

[54] 1963 Act, s. 18; and Copyright and Related Rights Act 2000, Sched. 1, para. 8.

[55] Section 13(14): 'the maker of a cinematographic film shall be entitled to any copyright subsisting in the film by virtue of this section.'

[56] See para. 18.

[57] Sched. 7, paras. 15 and 16 of the 1956 Act; and Sched. 1, para. 7 of the 1988 Act.

under the new Act.[58] A great many of these films are still in their copyright term.[59]

Secondly, in relation to final audiovisual works recorded in film form only under the present Act, provided they can be characterised as dramatic works:[60] the *Norowzian* case made clear that these dramatic audiovisual works would attract protection separate from the 'film', i.e. the visual recording. As under the 1911 Act, authorship would be granted to their 'creative' authors.[61]

121.   Authorship and initial ownership: the relevance of authorship entitlement

In relation to these dramatic works, the exact determination of authorship is fundamental for the calculation of the *duration* of copyright protection.[62] It is also important in relation to *ownership*, but only in those cases where the contributors are not under a contract of service or apprenticeship.[63] In this respect, it may be observed that, if film directors in the UK film industry are likely to work under contracts of service, creative contributors such as screenwriters (and possibly other creative contributors) would in most cases work under contracts for services.[64]

In any case, it must be remembered that, even if the author is commissioned and has not expressly granted the rights in his work to the producer, a term to that effect can be implied.[65] It has been suggested,

---

[58] Sched. 1, para. 10 of the 1988 Act.

[59] Sched. 7, para. 15 of the 1956 Act; and Sched. 1, para. 12 of the 1988 Act. The term of copyright of many dramatic films made before 1956 has been extended by the Duration of Copyright and Rights in Performances Regulations 1995 (SI 1995 No. 3297). See paras. 9 and 103 *et seq.*

[60] See paras. 56 *et seq.*

[61] Under s. 9 of the CDPA 1988, the author of the dramatic work is its creator.

[62] As the term of protection for a dramatic work is calculated from the death of its author or the last surviving co-author.

[63] In which case, the employer is the first owner. CDPA 1988, ss. 11 and 178.

[64] See para. 142.

[65] Following *Massine* v. *De Basil* [1936–45] MCC 223; on equitable ownership for commissioners, see also *A&M Records Ltd* v. *Video Collection International Ltd* [1995] EMLR 25 at 33 *per* Mervyn Davies J: 'When A makes or creates a work for B and A becomes at law the owner of the copyright in the work, B will sometimes be regarded as the equitable owner of the copyright and entitled to have an assignment made in his favour by A. B will be so regarded when it is a necessary implication from the facts of the case that copyright should belong to B.' *Merchant Adventurers Ltd* v. *M Grew & Co. Ltd* [1972] Ch 242; [1971] 3 WLR 791; [1971] 2 All ER 657; *Leisure Data* v. *Bell* [1988] FSR 367, CA. See also the recent computer cases: *John Richardson Computers Ltd* v. *Flanders* [1993] FSR 497; and *Ibcos Computers Ltd* v. *Barclays Mercantile Highland Finance Ltd* [1994] FSR 275, and the general review of case law in G. Lea, 'Expropriation or Business Necessity?' (1994) 16 EIPR 452. Finally, consider the doctrine of non-derogation

however, that these implied terms should extend 'no further than to that which is necessary to give business efficacy to the contract'.[66]

Finally, authorship entitlement is important in relation to moral rights, as moral rights in dramatic works are granted to their authors.

122.   The determination of authorship and ownership under the relevant copyright rules

The determination of the authors of pre-1957 and post-1988 dramatic audiovisual works depends on the rules applicable to works of joint authorship. Under UK law, joint authorship generally requires both a special degree of collaboration and certain conditions concerning the nature of the contributions. Under section 10 of the 1988 Act a 'work of joint authorship' is defined as:

> a work produced by the collaboration of two or more authors in which the contribution of each author is not distinct from the contribution of the other author or authors.[67]

To be jointly owned, a copyright work must satisfy three requirements, relating to the nature of the contributions, the collaboration of contributors, and the non-separability of the contributions. First, the work of the co-author must be *original*, i.e. in UK terms, it must be the product of sufficient skill, labour and judgment. This originality accounts for part of the originality of the work contributed to. Although the elements contributed do not have to be equal, a contribution must be substantial enough to give rise to co-authorship.[68] But, provided it is substantial and contributes to the originality of the work, a contribution can give rise to joint authorship even if it is not separately copyrightable.

---

from the grant (*British Leyland Motor Corp. Ltd* v. *Armstrong Patents Co. Ltd* [1986] AC 577; [1986] 2 WLR 400; [1986] 1 All ER 850; [1986] RPC 279; [1986] FSR 221).

[66] '[A]nd thus to allow use of the work for the purposes which were in contemplation of both parties at the time the contract was made, but not further' *Copinger and Skone James on Copyright*, 13th edn, 1991, para. 8-147. D. Lester and P. Mitchell, *Joynson-Hicks on UK Copyright Law*, Sweet & Maxwell, 1989, para. 9.28, p. 251.

[67] Under s. 11(3) of the 1956 Act, a work of joint authorship was 'a work produced by the collaboration of two or more authors in which the contribution of each author is not separate from the contribution of the other author or authors'. See also s. 16(3) of the 1911 Act: 'For the purposes of this Act, "a work of a joint authorship" means a work produced by the collaboration of two or more authors in which the contribution of one author is not distinct from the contribution of the other author or authors'. The requirement of a 'non-distinct' contribution was introduced in the 1911 Act.

[68] *Samuelson* v. *Producers Distribution Co. Ltd* [1932] 1 Ch 201; *Levy* v. *Rutley* (1871) LR 6 CP 523; *Tate* v. *Thomas* [1921] 1 Ch 503; 90 LJ Ch 318; 124 LT 722; 65 SJ 327; [1917–23] MCC 246.

Secondly, co-authors must *collaborate*, which means at least that the contributors must influence each other in their work.[69]

Thirdly, even if the above two conditions are fulfilled, there is no joint work when the contributions are *distinct* or *separate*.[70] In that case, copyright subsists only in each contribution. As noted,[71] 'separate' must not be construed as relating to the *efforts* of the contributors, which are always separate, but to the parts contributed by them. Moreover, these *parts* must not be separate in the *final* work.

123.   Evaluation of potential claims to co-authorship in audiovisual works

Under such rules, who would be author or co-author of a dramatic audiovisual work?[72] In order to answer this question, we must assess the role and function of the main contributors in the film-making process.

124.   The producer as creative author?

The 'creative' role of the various 'producers' in film productions can be summarised as follows. In the motion picture industry, the *production company* usually takes the initiative for the film, finances or gathers the necessary financing for the project and delegates responsibility for the project to an *executive producer* (or *production supervisor*). This individual has responsibility for the whole production, and is usually an independent contractor hired by the production company. He does not always initiate the film, but chooses the different contributors and has the final word concerning all creative aspects of the film. Although he controls and to a certain extent directs the work of the main contributors, he usually does not undertake himself the rewritings of the scripts, and is not directly involved in the shooting and cutting of the film.

---

[69] In the US case of *Maurel* v. *Smith* [1915] MCC 283, 220 Fed. R 195, Judge Hand expressed this idea by insisting on the requirement of a 'common and pre-concerted design' (220 Fed. R 195 at 199, quoting Keating J and Montague Smith J in *Levy* v. *Rutley* (1871) LR 6 CP 523 at 529 and 530). Note that 'collaboration' here does not necessarily require that the authors work at the same time on the common project. Accordingly, a work made of successive contributions could in some circumstances be considered as a joint work. See para. 126.

[70] The change from the term 'separate' in the 1956 Act to the term 'distinct' in the 1988 Act does not seem to effect any change in the law (see s. 172(2)). See *Copinger and Skone James on Copyright*, 13th edn, 1991, para. 7-1.

[71] G. Dworkin and R. Taylor, *Blackstone's Guide to the Copyright, Designs & Patent Act 1988*, Blackstone, 1989, p. 48.

[72] Or of an audiovisual work as specific subject-matter under the standard authorship scheme.

In the television industry, the television *channel* finances or co-finances the programme[73] and/or decides to broadcast it. The *individual producer*, in addition to the tasks of the executive producer for theatrical motion pictures, is responsible for the format of the show and often himself undertakes changes in the expression of the audiovisual work, by rewriting the script or being involved in the editing.

From this, it appears clear that the creative input, if any, is to be found at the level of the individual producers. The role of the production company appears too remote in the creative process. The mere fact of initiating the project, of requiring that some changes be made after preview or after discussions with the executive producer and of deciding whether the final product is satisfactory or not, does not account for a substantial part of the 'expression' of the work. In fact, the only way for the company to be considered as a co-author would be for it to show a creative activity distinct from that of the individual producer. It can then be said that in most cases the production company cannot be the author (as opposed to the initial owner) of the dramatic audiovisual work under present joint authorship rules.

What about individual producers? The *television producer*, if he undertakes substantial rewriting of the script and directs the editing, might be considered a co-author under UK copyright. But this level of involvement in the creative process is unique to the television industry, and is probably limited to television series. Other producers, including the *executive producer* in the theatrical film industry, only perform a task of control and supervision, without contributing to the expression of the work. In logic they should be denied authorship in the dramatic audiovisual work.

Under US copyright, it was proposed that actual control and supervision be considered a sufficient contribution in cases involving commissioned works to give rise to co-authorship.[74] Under UK copyright, a contrary view is strongly suggested by case law.[75]

---

[73] Alone or with a production company.

[74] E.g. J. Katzman, 'Commissioned Works as Works of Joint Authorship' (1989) *Columbia Law Review* 867.

[75] See *Tate* v. *Thomas* [1921] 1 Ch 503; 90 LJ Ch 318; 124 LT 722; 65 SJ 327; [1917–23] MCC 246, where a producer of musical revues was denied co-authorship in the play he produced. The producer had conceived the idea of a war sketch. He thought of a name for the play and drew up a rough outline, describing the scenes, characters and key lines in the dialogue. His contribution was held not substantial enough to give rise to joint authorship. *Tate* v. *Thomas* was followed on similar facts by *Wiseman* v. *George Weidenfeld & Nicolson Ltd and Donaldson* [1985] FSR 525 (a joint authorship claim of a stage producer was rejected; the author conceded that some lines or even an essential idea might have come from the producer); see also *Ashmore* v. *Douglas-Home* [1987] FSR 553 (the stage producer explained what he wanted to the author, but did not undertake the writing himself). See also the US case of *Geshwind* v. *Garrick*, 734 F. Supp. 644

As a consequence, it is very unlikely that the individual producer who limits himself to actual supervision, control and direction, without undertaking substantial rewriting, editing or stage direction, will be considered a co-author under present joint authorship rules.

125.   The director as author

We saw that there is very little doubt that the director of a dramatic audiovisual work is in most cases the author, if not the only author, of the work.[76] However, one should not come to the conclusion that the director will always be author of a given dramatic audiovisual work. In some productions his contribution will not be substantial or original enough, as could be the case for example regarding soap operas, or some television commercials in which the creative power of the director is diverted to other contributors (the producer, the scriptwriter or even the client). In that respect, it is important to recall that the Term Directive only sets a *rebuttable* presumption of authorship for film directors.[77]

126.   Screenwriters as joint authors

When it comes to joint authorship, two questions arise in relation to the work of the scriptwriter. The first question concerns the 'separate' or 'distinct' character of the script as a work. In a work of joint authorship contributions must not be separate.[78] We saw that 'separate' does not mean separately exploitable, but separate in the *final* work.[79] It does not matter if the script is separately protected and separately exploitable; what matters is that the work is merged in the film in such a way that no one can distinguish the elements contributed by the scriptwriter from the elements contributed by the director. In terms of plot and visual appearance, the contribution of the scriptwriter *in the final work* is not separate. But what about dialogues? Under UK copyright, a typical example of a composite work is a song, where music and text have separate copyrights. The same could be true concerning films: music, spoken words and the visual part of the audiovisual work are separate. As a consequence, it may well be that the author of the dialogue could not be co-author of the

---

(SDNY 1990). Compare with *Kenrick & Co.* v. *Lawrence & Co.* (1890) 25 QBD 99 (held that a person who had the idea of a sketch, directed the artist what to draw and suggested alterations might be joint author).

[76] See para. 18.

[77] Recital 13: 'the question of authorship in the whole or a part of the work is a question of fact which the national courts may have to decide.'

[78] CDPA 1988, s. 10. See para. 122.   [79] *Ibid.*

audiovisual dramatic work, but only author of his pre-existing dialogue (as dramatic work). It is not clear whether a substantial borrowing of the sole dialogue will infringe only his copyright or both his copyright and the copyright in the larger dramatic work.[80]

Film scripts create a second, more delicate, problem. We saw that the term 'script' covers different works elaborated over a period of time, sometimes by successive writers who may or may not collaborate together. Logically, it would be possible to consider the script, at least at some remote point, as a pre-existing work. If that is the case, the audiovisual work becomes a mere derivative work, a dramatic adaptation, a translation of the script. If we follow the traditional copyright thought, the author of the pre-existing work cannot be considered as author of the work derived from it. Thus the author of the pre-existing script cannot be co-author of the film.

But what is a pre-existing script? The question is complicated by the fact that the final audiovisual work is elaborated over a long period of time:

Although there seems to be no case on the point, it must be a question of fact and degree as to whether the skill, labour and judgment expended on a work by one party was rendered so long after another party's contribution that it is no longer factually true to say that there was collaboration. In such circumstances, the revised work may be the subject of a separate copyright, and the second contributor the author of that copyright in so far as it consists of the skill, labour and judgment which he applied to the work.[81]

In any case, based on the above, it seems reasonable to consider that the writing of a script can give rise to co-authorship only when it was *commissioned* for the making of a film: joint authorship requires collaboration, and there cannot be collaboration in handing an unsolicited script to a producer.

---

[80] The dialogue is undoubtedly part of the dramatic work, and arguably the rules on joint authorship ought not to be confused with the definition of the protected subject-matter.

[81] D. Lester and P. Mitchell, *Joynson-Hicks on UK Copyright Law*, Sweet & Maxwell, 1989, para. 3.21, p. 61. In *Evans* v. *Hulton & Co. Ltd* (1924) 131 LT 534; [1924] All ER 24; 40 TLR 489, it was held that the interviewee whose reminiscences were later put in narrative form by a journalist was not a co-author of the final text; followed in *Donoghue* v. *Allied Newspapers Ltd* [1938] Ch 106 (a person who provided ideas for stories which were later used by a journalist was held not to be an author or joint author of the resulting articles); in *Bagge* v. *Millar* [1917–23] MCC 179, the court held that a person who provides a plot idea is not a joint author of a play based on it; but in *Kenrick & Co.* v. *Lawrence & Co.* (1890) 25 QBD 99, it was held that a person who had the idea of a sketch, who directed the artist as to what to draw and suggested alterations might be a joint author; also, in the US case of *Maurel* v. *Smith* [1915] MCC 283, 220 Fed. R 195, the court held that the author of a scenario for an opera becomes a joint author in the opera based thereon, even though he contributed nothing further.

127.   The musical composer

Under UK copyright, *prima facie* the work of the composer cannot give rise to co-authorship in the dramatic audiovisual work. His contribution is separate from the contributions forming the visual part, just as music is separate from the words in the composite work constituted by a song. However, in the new Act, while the copyrights in musical and literary works are exclusive,[82] thus justifying that a song be treated as a 'composite work', this does not appear to be the case between dramatic and musical works.[83] Accordingly, a dramatico-musical work might be protected as a whole as a dramatic work, irrespective of the protection of the underlying music as a musical work.[84] In that case, if one person alone creates such a dramatico-musical work, he could well benefit from two (partly overlapping) copyrights: one in the music (as musical work), and one in the dramatico-musical work as a whole (as dramatic work).

What happens now when several persons are involved in the making of such work? According to UK rules on joint authorship, they would be co-authors, and thus reinforce the unity of the work, only if their contributions are not 'separable'. But, if one writes the music and the other the plot and the dialogue, they will not be co-authors of the dramatico-musical work, which will then be composite (music on the one hand, dramatic work on the other).

Note that the situation could be more complex. For example, a musical composer could gain co-authorship in the dramatic part of this composite work while remaining the sole author of his music.[85] In the same way, a film director could compose the music with the composer: in that case, they would be co-authors of the music, but the director would remain sole author of the dramatic work.

On the opportunity of granting co-authorship to musical composers, one may observe that composers are guaranteed a fair share from the exploitation of the film (or, more precisely, from the exploitation of their music through the film) by virtue of their membership in performing right societies. Granting additional authorship in the final audiovisual work could give rise to a double remuneration, as author of the music and as co-author of the film. In that respect, it is interesting to note that in France composers of specially commissioned music are not members

---

[82] CDPA 1988, s. 3(1): 'literary work means any work, other than a dramatic or musical work...'

[83] *Ibid.*

[84] *Copinger and Skone James on Copyright*, 13th edn, 1991, paras. 2-12 and 2-19.

[85] In exceptional cases in film production, the music is written during production and the film is edited accordingly. Provided there is collaboration on this point, the musical composer could claim to have contributed to the development of the visual part of the dramatic audiovisual work.

of SACD (the society of audiovisual authors), although they are listed as co-authors of the film in the Copyright Act; their equitable remuneration is only paid by musical right societies.

128.   The editor[86]

There is little doubt that editing can be part of the creative process which gives the dramatic work its original character.[87] This creative role is more evident in the case of theatrical films. But, in terms of copyright, co-authorship by the editor presupposes that he is given sufficient autonomy by the director, and it is questionable whether this contribution could be substantial enough to give rise to co-authorship. It is submitted that the editor could qualify as co-author of the dramatic work only in limited circumstances.

129.   The director of photography

The director of photography is also called a cinematographer, a lighting cameraman or simply a cameraman. The word 'cameraman' is unfortunate, since it conveys far too technical a meaning.[88] The director

[86] 'The role of the film editor is a mystery to most people who are not directly involved in film production. Indeed, it is seldom fully understood by those other film production departments who are directly involved. They often think that the editor puts his scissors through the film just as the director shouts "cut!" at the end of a shot and there are some who think that a film is photographed in short pieces, just as it appears in the final print. All this, of course, is very untrue . . . The work performed by the film editor and his assistants is basically divided into two functions, the artistic assembly of film and the physical problem of handling it. One is impossible without the other.' E. Walter, *The Technique of the Film Cutting Room*, Focal Press, 2nd edn, 1973, p. 15.

[87] The playwright, screenwriter and director David Mamet explains: 'The main questions a director must answer are: "where do I put the camera?" and "what do I tell the actors?"; and subsequent question, "what's the scene about?" There are two ways to approach this. Most US directors approach it by saying, "let's follow the actors around", as if the film were a record of what the protagonist did . . . That's the way most US films are made, as a supposed record of what real people really did. There's another way to make a movie, which is the way that Eisenstein suggested a movie should be made. This method has nothing to do with following the protagonist around but rather is a succession of images juxtaposed so that the contrast between these images moves the story forward in the mind of the audience. This is a fairly succinct rendition of Eisenstein's theory of montage; it is also the first thing I know about film directing, virtually the only thing I know about film directing.' See David Mamet, *A Whore's Profession*, Faber & Faber, 1994, p. 347.

[88] 'Apart from the director, he is the most important creative member of a film unit. He works in very close collaboration with the director who, before the film starts, will have discussed in broad outlines as well as in detail the photographic style he has in mind . . . Director and cameraman will then go through the script together, they will consult on the choice of the locations and, with the art director, on the style, architecture and decorative scheme of the sets.' W. Rilla, *A–Z of Movie Making*, Studio Vista, London,

of photography is not responsible for the narrative of the film, like the scriptwriter, the director and the editor, but for its aesthetic appeal. Both are essential aspects of the dramatic audiovisual work. If we take the example of theatrical films, even if the artistic value of the photography is not obvious to the eyes of the average filmgoer, it cannot be denied that a considerable amount of labour, skill and judgment was required in the photography which, considering the necessary adaptation to camera and actors' movements, is often more important than for still photography.[89] Therefore it appears difficult to deny to a cinematographer *as a matter of principle* the designation of co-author. In fact, the contribution of the director of photography may seem substantial enough to give rise to co-authorship in the case of certain *theatrical feature films*. However, for *documentaries* made from real life, his creative role is often reduced to the strict minimum, and in that case he should be denied authorship, either for lack of originality, or because of the insubstantiality of his contribution. *Television shows* rarely involve directors of photography but only camera operators and a lighting team who follow the instructions of the director strictly.

130.   The art director and related contributors

The art director, or production designer, is in charge of the construction or design of the decor. In contrast to the director of photography, he cannot, under UK copyright, be considered as co-author of the final audiovisual work, because his contribution, even if original, is separate in the final work: in fact, his contribution contributes to the originality of the audiovisual work in the same way that an original building contributes to the originality of a documentary on architecture. But the art director is author of his own creations, which can be separately protected as artistic works.

The contributions of the authors of special effects, costumes and make-up do not appear either original or substantial enough to give rise to co-authorship. In any case, they are distinct in the final work. Their contributions can sometimes be protected separately as artistic work,[90] or as audiovisual work,[91] as the case may be.

1970, p. 19. The director of photography can also handle the camera physically, but usually that task is assigned to a technician, the camera operator.

[89] If films were still protected as series of photographs, the director of photography would certainly contribute to their originality. See para. 77, n. 150; and para. 120 (the possibility of claiming moral rights in pre-1957 non-dramatic films).

[90] See para. 84.

[91] E.g. when special effects are constituted by computer animated sequences.

131. The main performers

The fact that actors are granted performers' rights does not appear to prevent the granting of a copyright in the work to which they contribute. However, if the only contribution of the actor is his performance, one would be tempted to reject any co-authorship claim on the ground that *he only performs a pre-existing work, and does not create a work in itself.*[92]

Against this idea, one could argue that there is a fundamental difference between the work of actors in theatre and their work in motion pictures: while actors in theatre mainly perform a pre-existing work, actors in a film are involved in the making of the final dramatic work. They do not act after the film is completed, but contribute to its completion. Also, the contribution of film actors cannot be considered as ephemeral. Moreover, we saw that a contribution does not have to be separately copyrightable to give rise to joint authorship.[93]

It is submitted, however, that these differences are not sufficient to consider the main actors as co-authors of the dramatic audiovisual work. What cinema actors do and say is clearly directed by the director and the script. Hence, an actor can contribute to the originality of a film in only three ways:

1. By his look and appearance. But this element exists before the film, or is the work of the make-up artist. Also, in most cases, this element is not substantial enough to give rise to co-authorship.

2. By the 'way' he performs the text or the tasks he is assigned in the script. But the task of the film director is precisely to direct the actors. As a consequence, whatever part the actor may play in determining how he is to perform his role, it is neither original nor substantial enough to give rise to authorship in the dramatic audiovisual work. The solution would be different if the director allowed the actor great freedom in his performance, and if this performance is the main object of the film, or covers most of the work.[94]

3. By adding lines or changing the development of a scene (improvisation, etc.). In that case, the actor may create an original work which accounts for part of the originality of the final work, but his contribution is

---

[92] 'The performance of a work by an actor . . . is merely an ephemeral and insubstantial execution of the idea of another, and thus does not merit copyright protection.' J. Phillips and A. Firth, *Introduction to Intellectual Property Law*, 2nd edn, Butterworths, 1990, para. 17.1, p. 197.

[93] See para. 122.

[94] To some extent, the development of new technologies such as 'video assist' in the film-making process can increase the 'creative role' of the main actors by diverting the creative control from the director to the actors. Video assist units are cameras which shoot both on film strip and on video, allowing an immediate review of the scene shot on video monitor.

unlikely ever to be substantial enough having regard to the length of the film and the other contributions.[95]

132.   Technicians

Under present copyright law, sound technicians, camera operators, chief electricians, the electrical crew and other technicians involved in the film-making process cannot be considered as co-authors, their contribution to the film being neither original (they strictly follow the instructions of the director, the director of photography or of another major contributor) nor substantial enough for that purpose.

133.   Conclusion: the co-authors of dramatic audiovisual works under joint authorship rules

From these developments, we have now a clearer idea of the potential creative co-authors of dramatic audiovisual works under the 1911 and 1988 Acts. For a theatrical feature film, it is submitted that the film director and the author(s) of the non-pre-existing script(s) will always qualify as co-authors of the final work. Depending of their role in a given production the editor and the director of photography could also claim co-authorship.[96]

For television productions, the solution depends on the type of work considered. Concerning television series, the individual producer could share authorship with the director and the author(s) of the non-pre-existing script(s).[97] The list should be the same for documentaries, sometimes with the exception of the individual producer, whose contribution may not be substantial enough. Provided talk shows and other programmes are original and can be considered as dramatic works,[98] the director should be their sole author, or be co-author with the individual producer.

It is important, however, to insist on the complexity of the determination of this list of co-authors and on the difficulties associated with the

---

[95] See *Tate* v. *Thomas* [1921] 1 Ch 503; 90 LJ Ch 318; 124 LT 722; 65 SJ 327; [1917–23] MCC 246.

[96] However, the share in the joint work of the editor and the director of photography is likely, in some cases, to be less important than that of the other contributors (but the reasoning should in that case be based on substantiality or originality, not on artistic merit).

[97] Very rarely with the editor or the director of photography, if their task is not undertaken by the producer or the director, and if they are given enough freedom, account being taken of 'format' rules (television series).

[98] See para. 57.

copyright status of dramatico-musical works. In this regard the remarks of the Gregory Committee may have been justified.[99]

134.   The regime of joint works under UK copyright law

Under UK copyright, joint owners (be they joint authors or not) are tenants in common and not joint tenants. The consent of all joint owners is required for the exploitation of the work, by one joint owner[100] or by a third party.[101] One joint owner by himself may, however, take proceedings for infringement.[102]

SECTION II

Authorship of audiovisual works in authors' rights countries

135.   Historical development: the difficult road to creative authorship

As a general rule, and with the notable exception of Luxembourg,[103] under all continental authors' rights systems the author of the film is the individual who created it. In France, this position is enshrined in article L.113-7 of the Intellectual Property Code, which states that 'authorship of an audiovisual work shall belong to the natural person or persons who have carried out the intellectual creation of the work'. However, and contrary to the general assumption, *droit d'auteur* systems did not always favour such a rule in relation to films.

As mentioned above, there was a tendency in the pre-Second World War French *droit d'auteur* to consider the film producer (an individual or legal person) as the sole author of the cinematographic work. This idea was rejected by a majority of legal commentators, but had a few advocates in the 1930s, and was at one point favoured by case law: some cases conferred authorship on the film producer by virtue of the contract of employment entered into with the director and other contributors.[104]

---

[99] See para. 22. Note, however, the near absence of reported litigation on this question under the 1911 Act.

[100] *Cescinsky* v. *George Routledge & Sons Ltd* [1916] 2 KB 325.

[101] *Powell* v. *Head* (1879) 12 ChD 686.

[102] *Lauri* v. *Renad* [1892] 3 Ch 402, CA; *Cate* v. *Devon and Exeter Constitutional Newspaper Co.* (1889) 40 ChD 500.

[103] See para. 139.

[104] Paris Court of Appeal, 10 February 1936, *Guerlais* v. *Roubaud*, *Gazette du Palais*, 1936, I, p. 691; Tribunal of First Instance of Seine, 24 May 1938, *Gazette du Palais*, 1938, II, p. 508.

Others granted authorship without the help of any legal concept.[105] In the *Mascarade* case,[106] the Court of Appeal of Paris considered that the producer was the only author of the film, and that this author could be a legal person. The court used the notion of 'collective works' (*oeuvres collectives*) in order to vest authorship in the film producer; this category of complex works under French law (along with composite works and works of joint authorship) was developed by the courts in cases involving dictionaries, and is conceived as a variety of composite works published by an entrepreneur under his name, in which it is impossible to identify the part contributed by each author: in that case the publisher is considered the author of the work.[107] In subsequent years, the French courts gave several judgments in favour of the producer. The appellate decision in *Mascarade* was eventually overturned eight years later by the Supreme Court,[108] which did not address directly the question of authorship, but clearly refused to consider that films were necessarily 'collective works'. Later cases rejected the concept of the producer as the sole author of the film and the application of the concept of 'collective works'.

The new Law of 1957 confirmed this view by providing in its article 14 (now article L.113-7 of the Intellectual Property Code) that films were works of joint authorship (thus excluding characterisation as collective works) and by setting a list of presumptive co-authors.[109] The principle that the author can only be a natural person was also reinforced in the Act.[110]

In Germany, prior to the 1965 Act, some early case law considered the film producer as first owner of the copyright in the film, on the ground that the film was the result of an organised collective activity, and that copyright must vest in the natural or legal person who organised it.[111] Other cases confined this quality to the creative contributors.[112] A draft German statute of 1954 proposed to grant the production company the copyright title to the film work (according to its article 93, the owner of the company

---

[105] Dijon Court of Appeal, 8 January 1936, *Gazette du Palais*, 1936, I, p. 339, *Revue Dalloz Hebdomadaire*, 1936, p. 137.

[106] Tribunal of First Instance of Seine, 19 March 1935, *Gazette du Palais*, 1935, II, p. 62, *Revue Dalloz Sirey*, 1935, II, p. 101; and Paris Court of Appeal, 16 March 1939, *Gazette du Palais*, 1939, II, p. 210; *Revue Dalloz Sirey*, 1940, II, p. 35.

[107] The Law of 1957 codified the theory but does not characterise the publisher as 'author'. Instead, it specifies that authors' rights are 'vested in it' (art. L.113-5).

[108] Court of Cassation, 10 November 1947, *Revue Dalloz*, 1947, p. 328; *La Semaine Juridique*, 1948, II, No. 4166, note Plaisant; *Revue Dalloz Sirey*, 1948, I, p. 157, note Reynaud.

[109] See para. 29.

[110] See e.g. the new regime of 'collective works', n. 107 above.

[111] *Reichsgericht* (Supreme Court in civil matters) 158, September 1938, pp. 321 *et seq.*, at p. 324; *Kammergericht*, in MuW, 1923, p. 13 and 1926, p. 229; *Reichsarbeitsgericht* (Supreme Court in labour law) in *Ufita*, IV p. 405.

[112] *Kammergericht*, in *Ufita*, XI, p. 55; cf also RGZ 107, 16 June 1923, p. 65.

producing the cinematographic work would have been 'considered as the author'; a moral right would have been granted to the director).

In the Netherlands, before the Law of 30 May 1985 expressly granted authorship in films to its creative contributors, producers were considered by early case law as authors of the cinematographic work. This solution was mainly based on article 5 of the Act of 23 September 1912, which, in case of a compilation of separate works created by two or more persons, considered as author the person under whose direction or supervision the whole work was accomplished (a doctrine close to the French doctrine of *oeuvre collective*). On similar grounds, the producer was found to be author of the film in Denmark and Finland before their current copyright Acts.

Other countries, without formally granting authorship, decided to vest economic rights or some of them in the film producer: this has been the case in Austria, since 1936,[113] and in Italy since 1941.[114]

136.   The rise of the film director

Almost all authors' rights systems have now reverted to a system of creative authorship for films, which will be described in detail below. Although the list of film co-authors varies, the film director is the only contributor who is always recognised as the author or one of the authors of the film. It is important to note, however, that this pre-eminence of the film director over other contributors is a recent phenomenon. It can be seen as a consequence of the ideas on film authorship developed in the 1950s in France.

Following the success of sound movies, in the 1930s and the 1940s, the director as creator became secondary to the writer.[115] This conception of the director as a mere technician was clearly adopted in Europe in pre-war case law[116] and legal literature. In this respect, it is interesting

---

[113] Art. 38(1) of the Law of 9 April 1936.   [114] Law of 22 April 1941.

[115] The novelist, scriptwriter and movie-maker Gore Vidal gave an interesting account of the rise of the director in the film-making process in 'Who Makes the Movies', *New York Review of Books*, 25 November 1976, p. 35, though this is not to say that directors were not previously valued by film critics. 'Established criticism valued as artists a small number of directors, predominantly European, who produced work which had a certain highly variable quality of "greatness" (which was typically either a moral quality or a social penetration) and a certain "seriousness" (which involved the apparent commitment of the artist to his theme)', thus showing a complete disinterest for the 'commercial' pictures, especially those produced by Hollywood (see J. Caughie, *Theories of Authorship, A Reader*. Routledge & Kegan Paul, 1981).

[116] See para. 135. In particular, Paris Court of Appeal, 10 February 1936, *Guerlais* v. *Roubaud*, *Gazette du Palais*, 1936, I, p. 691: 'The hiring of the *metteur en scène* must, according to the contract, be considered as a employment contract; the *metteur en scène* is not an author but a director; he is in essence replaceable without the nature of the work being modified.'

to observe that, under the list of co-authors set by the Italian Act of 1941 and the French Act of 1957, the director comes last, the first author mentioned being the scriptwriter. Then came the so-called *auteur* theory, initiated by French film critics.[117] The theory created a distinction between real *auteurs* (or *cinéastes*), 'consistently expressing their own unique obsessions', and *metteurs en scène*, mere technicians 'lacking the consistency which betrayed the profound involvement of a personality'.[118] The 'director-author' transforms the material given to him into an expression of his own personality through the *mise en scène*. This imprint of personality can be traced 'in a thematic and/or stylistic consistency in all (or almost all) the director's films'.[119] To a large extent, the theory itself appears to be a late application to film studies of the concept of romantic authorship. But if by attention to the *mise en scene* and the inclusion of Hollywood cinema the theory was beneficial to film studies, the rise in importance of the director was detrimental to other contributors, especially scriptwriters.[120] The director was to emerge as a leading figure in the eyes of film critics and remains so for the public today, despite attacks of later film studies theories. Clearly, a film is now defined by the name of its director, whereas before the 1950s it was defined by the name of the scriptwriter, the acting star or the producer.[121]

137.   Countries without a statutory list of co-authors

In several authors' rights countries, the copyright Act does not provide a list of co-authors of audiovisual works. Within the European Union, this is the case in Denmark, Finland, Germany, the Netherlands and Sweden.

---

[117] An article by French author, Alexandre Astruc, 'The Birth of a New Avant-Garde: The Camera-Pen', dated from 1948 (*Ecran Français*, para. 143), has strongly influenced the tenets of the new movement (in Peter Graham (ed.), *The New Wave*, Secker & Warburg, London, 1968, pp. 17–23).

[118] *Ibid.*, p. 10.

[119] *Ibid.*, p. 9. Thus a larger number of directors could be considered as authors. This explains in particular the promotion of Hollywood cinema, which outraged established film critics: despite the lack of creative freedom and the practice of the industry in which US directors worked, one could show recurrent themes and style over several films, which evidenced the imprint of the director. Variants of the *auteur* theory were introduced in the UK and in the US.

[120] This attitude can be seen in Astruc's essay (see n. 117 above): 'between the pure cinema of the 1920s and filmed theatre, there is plenty of room for a different and individual kind of film-making. This of course implies that the scriptwriter directs his own scripts; or rather, that the scriptwriter ceases to exist, for in this kind of film-making the distinction between author and director loses all meaning. Direction is no longer a means of illustrating or presenting a scene, but a true act of writing' Cited in G. Vidal, 'Who Makes the Movies', *New York Review of Books*, 25 November 1976, p. 35.

[121] The name of the director is undoubtedly an important element in the choice of keen cinema-goers. In addition, screen credits are often given to him under the form 'a film by ...' (possessory credit).

As a consequence, the determination of the authors of audiovisual works depends on the application of the standard rules on joint authorship (as long as the works are created by more than one person, which is usually the case). This may give rise to some uncertainties.

Under German law, these rules are specified in articles 7 and 8 of the Copyright Act. Article 7 states, in a general way, that the author of a work is the person who creates it. Article 8(1) further provides that, if several persons have created a work jointly, and if their respective contributions cannot be *separately exploited*, they shall be deemed joint authors of the work.

The criteria of separability of the contribution, which also exists under UK copyright, is a peculiarity of German and German-influenced authors' rights laws, and is generally not applied in other *droit d'auteur* systems. In Germany, the condition is particularly strict, since 'separate' does not refer to a physical 'separability' in the final work, but to the possibility of a separate exploitation of the contribution. As a consequence, in relation to films, not only are musical works separate, but also scripts and other literary elements, which reduces the scope of the joint work and the list of co-authors to its bare minimum; under such a rule, only the director, the director of photography and possibly the editor could claim co-authorship in the film.[122] This list of co-authors is reflected in the membership of the German collecting societies dealing with audiovisual works.

The regime applicable to works of joint authorship is detailed in article 8 of the 1965 Act. The right of publication and exploitation belongs jointly to the joint authors, and cannot be exercised by one author without the consent of all the others. Alterations to the work are permissible only with the consent of the joint authors. The Act provides, however, that a joint author may not unreasonably refuse his consent to the publication, exploitation or alteration of the work. Finally, each author may sue for infringement of moral or economic rights without the consent of the others.

In Denmark, Sweden and Finland, a work is of joint authorship if (and to the extent) it is not made of 'independent works'.[123] This language would appear to exclude the scriptwriter and the musical composer from the list of eligible film co-authors. However, legal commentators consider that these contributors could be considered as joint authors with the film director (and possibly other contributors).[124]

[122] See e.g. A. Dietz, in M. B. Nimmer and D. Geller (eds.), *International Copyright Law and Practice*, Matthew Bender, looseleaf, para. 4[1][a].
[123] Danish Copyright Act, art. 6; Swedish Copyright Act, art. 6.
[124] See G. Karnell, in M. B. Nimmer and D. Geller (eds.), *International Copyright Law and Practice*, Matthew Bender, looseleaf, para. 4[1][a]; and M. Salokannel, *Ownership of Rights in Audiovisual Productions: A Comparative Study*, Kluwer, 1997, pp. 146 *et seq.* (the author relies on the preparatory works of the Nordic copyright Acts).

Under modern Dutch copyright law, a joint work may result from separable contributions.[125] Accordingly, in most cases, the author of the scenario and the musical composer should be considered co-authors with the film director.

138.   Countries with a statutory list of co-authors

Under French law, article L.113-7 provides that, unless proved otherwise, the following contributors are presumed to be co-authors of an audiovisual work, considered as a joint work: (1) the author of the script; (2) the author of the adaptation; (3) the author of the dialogue; (4) the author of the musical compositions with or without words, specially composed for the work; and (5) the director. In addition, this article includes a remarkable provision, which extends film authorship to the author of pre-existing adapted works in protection at the time of the making of the film:

If an audiovisual work is adapted from a pre-existing work or script which is still protected, the authors of the original work shall be assimilated to the authors of the new work.

As mentioned above, an important aspect of article L.113-7 is that it expressly characterises audiovisual works as works of 'joint authorship'. This characterisation (which may be considered as an irrebuttable presumption) applies even if the conditions of creation of the work do not correspond to those of a joint work.[126] The main effect of this provision is to prevent the application of the concept of 'collective works' to audiovisual works. We saw that this special doctrine allows, under certain conditions, a legal person to be the initial owner of the copyright in works created at its initiative by its employees or by freelance workers under its supervision.[127] For French courts, the language of article 14 of the 1957 Act, reproduced in article L.113-7, prevents the application of this concept to audiovisual works.[128]

The list in article L.113-7 has two main features. First, inclusion in the list is a rebuttable presumption, which means that, in some cases, it is possible to prove that the creative input of one of the persons mentioned was not sufficient to give rise to authorship. This was held in case of

---

[125] Cohen Jehoram, in M. B. Nimmer and D. Geller (eds.), *International Copyright Law and Practice*, Matthew Bender, looseleaf, para. 4[1][a][ii].

[126] E.g. in case of successive input of authors without collaboration.

[127] See paras. 135 and 147.

[128] See e.g. Paris Court of Appeal, 22 November 1990, *Juris-Data*, No. 25856; Court of Cassation, 16 May 1994, *La Semaine Juridique*, 1991, II, No. 22375, note Linant de Bellefonds.

mere technical services rendered by directors.[129] Note, however, that the presumption is not rebuttable in relation to the author of the adapted pre-existing work (as it is, in any case, a pure fiction).

Secondly, and perhaps more importantly, the list is an open list, and other contributors (including the individual producer) may claim co-authorship in the film, if their contribution meets the criteria of joint authorship.[130]

Traditionally, French courts have proved reluctant to extend the list of co-authors. It was held, for example, that authorship for a director of photography can only result from the accomplishments of acts that are distinct from its traditional activities.[131]

An example of the judicial stretching of the list of film co-authors is found in a recent decision by the Court of Appeal of Paris, which held that a chef who performed a recipe in front of the camera was co-author of the resulting audiovisual work.[132]

As to the regime of works of joint authorship, article L.113-3 of the Intellectual Property Code provides that the audiovisual work is the common property of the co-authors independently of the importance and artistic merit of their respective contribution.[133] Acts of exploitation require the agreement of all co-authors.[134] This means, *inter alia*, that all co-authors must consent to the rescission of a publishing contract,[135] and that the co-author who brings a suit for the defence of his economic rights must join the other co-authors in the suit.[136] The Code further adds in the same article that, where the contribution of each of the co-authors is of a different kind, each may, unless otherwise agreed, separately exploit his

---

[129] Paris Court of Appeal, 4 March 1987, RIDA, April 1987, p. 71; *Revue Dalloz*, 1988, Sommaire, p. 204, note Colombet; Court of Cassation, 29 March 1989, RIDA, July 1989, p. 262; Poitiers Court of Appeal, 7 December 1999 (*Charlenu et Atlas* v. *Chaye*), *La Semaine Juridique* (E), 2000, p. 1375, note Brochard (unreported).

[130] In this respect, French authors' rights rules do not exclude co-authorship because of the separability of the contribution.

[131] Paris Court of Appeal, 2 November 1981, *Revue Dalloz*, 1983, Informations Rapides, p. 91, note Colombet; Tribunal of First Instance of Paris, 19 November 1979, *Revue Dalloz*, 1981, Informations Rapides, p. 81, note Colombet. For the rejection of claims by a camera operator, see Paris Court of Appeal, 17 June 1988, *Revue Dalloz*, 1988, Informations Rapides, p. 306; Paris Court of Appeal, 2 November 1981, *Revue Dalloz*, 1983, Informations Rapides, p. 91, note Colombet.

[132] Paris Court of Appeal, 17 March 1999, *Communication Commerce Electronique*, October 1999, No. 1, note Caron; RIDA, October 1999, No. 182, p. 202; *Revue Trimestrielle de Droit Commercial*, 2000, p. 94, note Françon; *La Semaine Juridique* (E), 7 September 2000, p. 1376, note Bougerol.

[133] Court of Cassation, 2 April 1996, RIDA, 1996, No. 987.

[134] Court of Cassation, 19 December 1983, RIDA, July 1989, p. 251.

[135] E.g. Paris Court of Appeal, 16 December 1932, *Gazette du Palais*, 1933, I, p. 368.

[136] Court of Cassation, 10 May 1995, RIDA, October 1995, pp. 285 and 247.

own personal contribution. In doing so, he must not, however, prejudice the exploitation of the common work. This provision applies to film productions. In practice, however, film production contracts include provisions which limit or remove this possibility.

Article 14 of the Belgian Act sets out a list similar to the French one, but is somewhat more specific as the list includes 'the graphical author in the case of animated works or of animated sequences in audiovisual works where they represent a significant part of such work'. The author of the adapted work is also 'assimilated' to a co-author of the film, 'if his contribution is used in the film'. The presumption is rebuttable (except for the film director, and presumably for the author of the adapted work), and the list is also non-exhaustive.

In contrast to the French and Belgian Acts, the Spanish, Portuguese and Italian Acts include shorter lists of presumptive co-authors. The Spanish Act refers to the film director, the authors of the script and the adaptation and the authors of any musical compositions, with or without words, created specially for the work.[137] But the author of the adapted work is not included in the list, and should not be considered a co-author by the application of joint authorship rules. Legal commentators appear to be divided as to whether the list is exhaustive or not. The list in the Portuguese Act is similar to the Spanish one.[138]

In Italy, article 44 of the 1941 Act refers to the author of the subject-matter, the author of the scenario, the composer of the music and the artistic director. Legal commentators consider that the list is non-exhaustive. Finally, under the Greek Copyright Act, the principal director is the sole author of an audiovisual work.[139]

139.   The case of Luxembourg: the film producer as 'author'

Luxembourg provides the exception to the tradition expressed in the other authors' rights Acts. Its Copyright Act of 1972 already included authorship provisions that resembled those of the UK 1956 Act. Article 27 of the Act provided that the copyright in a cinematographic work shall originate with the 'maker' thereof. There was no definition of the 'maker' in the Act, but the general opinion is that this term referred to the film producer (natural or legal person). However, like the UK 1956 Act, the Luxembourg Act did not use the term 'author'; accordingly, it could be said that the film has no author at all, or alternatively that

---

[137] Intellectual Property Law, art. 87.   [138] Copyright Code, art. 22.
[139] Copyright Act, art. 9.

the author is another person, entitled to moral rights only. The new Act of 2001 continues this trend and adopts the current UK solution on film authorship: article 21 of the Act provides that the authors of the audiovisual work are the producer and the main director.

SECTION II

Initial ownership

140.   Introduction[140]

As mentioned above, most copyright and authors' rights systems enshrined the idea that copyright, or at least the part necessary for the exploitation of the film, should be vested in the film producer.[141] But this idea was implemented in different ways. One approach is to grant *ownership* of these rights to the producer through presumptions of assignment or employment rules. Another approach is to consider the producer as the sole *author* of the film (and sometimes of contributory works) for copyright purposes. This latter solution avoids the problems associated with the determination of the intellectual creators of the work and the limitations of a presumption scheme. However, it is difficult to implement in authors' rights countries for two reasons. First, it would create a breach in the doctrine of creative authorship. One should recall that this principle is almost universal in these countries, and explains the creation of specific neighbouring rights in favour of entrepreneurs (for which the term 'author' is not used). Secondly, it would entail the very objectives of protection of moral rights, which are closely associated with the status of author. This is why the second solution was implemented only in copyright countries, while the first was generally adopted in *droit d'auteur* systems.

An analysis of the relevant provisions of the domestic laws of the European Union Member States shows that the question of initial ownership of film copyright in reality covers two distinct problems. The first problem concerns initial ownership of the copyright in the audiovisual work (discussed in Part I below). The second problem concerns initial ownership of the copyright in the underlying works (discussed in Part II below).

---

[140] See M. Salokannel, *Ownership of Rights in Audiovisual Productions: A Comparative Study*, Kluwer, 1997.
[141] See para. 109.

PART I

Ownership of rights in audiovisual works

141.   International agreements and EC directives

As a matter of principle, protection under the Berne Convention is granted to authors. Under article 1 of the Convention Union members constitute a Union for the protection of the rights of 'authors' in their literary and artistic works. Article 2(6) further provides that protection under the Convention is to operate 'for the benefit of the author and his successors in title'. This indicates that copyright in a work must vest initially in its author. Accordingly, one can doubt whether a Union member fulfils its obligations under the Berne Convention if it accords initial ownership of a work to the employer, to the commissioner or to any other person who is not considered the author of the work under local law.[142]

However, since the Stockholm Act, the Convention provides for a presumption of assignment of rights in cinematographic works to the film producer in its article 14*bis*(2), which constitutes one of the most complex and obscure provision of the Convention.[143]

This presumption applies where the film producer is not the author or the first owner of copyright in the film under the national provisions.[144] As a consequence, it does not apply to copyright systems in which the producer is the author of the film (such as the US and the UK), nor to those *droit d'auteur* systems which implemented *cessio legis* (legal assignment) systems under which the film producer is the first owner of the copyright in the film (such as Italy and Austria).[145] Although it is drafted as an obligation for other Union members, its exceptions make it optional in practice.

Article 14*bis*(2)(b) allows Union members to include, in their legislation, among the *owners* of copyright in a cinematographic work 'authors who have brought contributions to the making of the work'. However, in such a case, they must provide for a presumption of assignment of rights in the film to the film producer, subject to a contrary or special

---

[142] See e.g. Australian Copyright Law Review Committee, *Report on Journalists' Copyright*, 1994, paras. 6-08 to 6-14, quoting the British Whitford Committee, Cmnd 6732, 1977. On the distinct question as to whether this author could be a legal person (e.g. the employer or commissioner expressly designated as 'author'), see para. 108.

[143] On the history of this provision, see S. Ricketson, *The Berne Convention on the Protection of Literary and Artistic Works*, Kluwer, 1987, paras. 10.26 *et seq.*

[144] *Ibid.*

[145] See paras. 143 and 161. Such a system was also in force in the Netherlands at the time of the Stockholm conference. See S. Ricketson, *The Berne Convention on the Protection of Literary and Artistic Works*, Kluwer, 1987, paras. 10.32 and 10.35.

stipulation. This presumption is limited in scope, as it concerns only the rights of 'reproduction, distribution, public performance, communication to the public by wire, broadcasting or any other communication to the public, or to the subtitling or dubbing of texts, of the work'.[146] In addition, under article 14*bis*(3), unless otherwise provided by national legislation, the presumption is not applicable to the authors of scenarios, dialogue and musical works created for the cinematographic work, and to the principal director. A Union member must notify the Director-General of WIPO if it does not apply the presumption to the principal director. These provisions are incorporated in the TRIPs Agreement[147] and the WIPO Copyright Treaty of 1996.[148]

What is the situation at Community level? The exclusive rights in copyright works harmonised by the EC directives are granted to authors,[149] which indicates that the author should be the initial owner of these rights. This principle permits no exception for films. Accordingly, film authors, including film directors,[150] must be first owners of the copyright in the film (at least as far as the harmonised rights are concerned).

But the directives do not appear to prevent the implementation of either a presumption of assignment or a *cessio legis* (legal assignment) to the employer, to the commissioner or to the investor in film productions. There are three reasons for this. First, recital 10 of the Rental Directive provides that the legislation of the Member States should be approximated in such a way as not to conflict with the applicable international conventions in the field of copyright and related rights. Secondly, recital 4 of the Term Directive provides that its provisions do not affect the application by the Member States of the provisions of article 14*bis*(2)(b), (c) and (d) and (3) of the Berne Convention. Thirdly, article 2(6) of the Rental Directive allows Member States to provide for a presumption of assignment to the film producer of the rental right of authors (subject to contractual clauses to the contrary).

In conclusion, it could be said that the implementation of a *cessio legis* (legal assignment) or another form of *irrebuttable* presumption of transfer

---

[146] Accordingly, it does not include the right of adaptation. Thus, rights to produce remakes, sequels and spin-offs would be excluded from the presumption.

[147] Art. 9.   [148] Art. 1(4).

[149] Under art. 2(1) of the Rental Directive of 19 November 1992, the exclusive right to authorize or prohibit rental and lending shall belong 'to the author in respect of the original and copies of his work'. Under art. 2 of the Satellite and Cable Directive of 27 September 1993, Member States shall provide an exclusive right for the author to authorise the communication to the public by satellite of copyright works. In the Directive on Copyright and Related Rights in the Information Society of 22 May 2001, the reproduction right, the right of communication to the public and the distribution right are granted to authors (arts. 2–4).

[150] Term Directive, art. 2(1).

of economic rights in the film to the employer, the commissioner or an-other person who is not the author of the work would not comply with the international obligations derived from the Berne Convention and from Community law if implemented in a country in which film contributors are considered as initial owners of the copyright in a work under article 14*bis*(2). But in those countries a presumption of assignment, subject to agreement to the contrary, is always admissible.

142.   The law in the UK and Ireland

In the UK and Ireland, a distinction must be made between the copyright in the 'film' (the visual recording) and the copyright in the underlying audiovisual dramatic work, if any.[151] In the UK, under the 1988 Act, in relation to 'films', and as a result of the amendments made by the Copyright and Related Rights Regulations 1996 to authorship provisions, a further distinction must be made between films made before 1 July 1994 and films made on or after this date.

The copyright in a film made before 1 July 1994 vests in its author, the film producer.[152] For films made on or after that date, the copyright vests jointly in the film producer and in the principal film director, considered as co-authors of the film.[153] However, if the principal director is employed and the film is made in the course of his employment, then, subject to an agreement to the contrary, copyright vests in his employer (arguably, the film producer).[154] Under section 178 of the 1988 Act, 'employment' means a contract of service or apprenticeship.

There is no precise test as to what constitutes a contract of service. To complicate the matter, so-called 'freelance' workers or independent contractors in the film industry do sometimes work under a contract of service. In determining whether an author is employed under a contract of service (in which case copyright vests in the employer) or is a true in-dependent contractor (i.e. works under a contract for services, in which case copyright vests in the author), a court will consider a number of factors including the existence of a direct control by the 'employer', the degree of independence of the author, the place in which the services are performed, the nature of the work and its integration into the final work, etc.[155]

---

[151] We will not address here the status of films made under the previous UK and Irish copyright Acts. See paras. 10, 18, 22 and 26.

[152] Defined as 'the person by whom the arrangements necessary for the making of the film were undertaken'. See para. 115.

[153] See para. 118.

[154] Section 11(2) (as amended by the Copyright and Related Rights Regulations 1996 (SI 1996 No. 2967), reg. 18).

[155] See *Copinger and Skone James on Copyright*, 14th edn, 1999, para. 5-11.

Accordingly, depending on the actual conditions of production, film directors in the UK could be considered as employees or as independent contractors. It seems, however, that in practice in most cases they work as employees, due to the conditions under which their technical services are rendered.[156] As a result, their share of copyright in the joint work would initially vest in the producer-employer.[157]

In any case, under section 93A(1), of the 1988 Act, as amended by the Copyright and Related Rights Regulations 1996, an agreement concerning film production concluded between the principal film director (whether an employee or an independent contractor) and the film producer, is deemed, subject to an agreement to the contrary, to transfer to the film producer the rental right in relation to the film.[158]

The ownership provisions of the Irish Copyright and Related Rights Act 2000 are similar.[159]

Concerning the copyright in the underlying audiovisual dramatic work, in the UK, in the absence of specific rules for this class of works the film producer will obtain initial *ownership* of the copyright in this work if its authors are employees and if the work is made in the course of their employment, subject to an agreement to the contrary.[160]

If the co-authors of this dramatic audiovisual work are independent contractors (which should be the case of the scriptwriter),[161] they will be the first owners of the copyright in it.[162] As a consequence, in such a situation the film producer needs to be assigned or licensed the necessary rights in order to exploit the dramatic audiovisual work.[163] An exception to this rule is now made for the rental right, which is presumed to be transferred to the film producer as a result of the implementation of the Rental Directive by the Copyright and Related Rights Regulations 1996.[164]

The solution would appear to be similar in Ireland under the Copyright and Related Rights Act 2000.[165]

143.   The law in authors' rights countries

As in the UK and Ireland, in authors' rights countries the copyright in a work usually vests in its author. Subject to limited exemptions, which are

---

[156] This is in contrast to the situation of other contributors, such as scriptwriters. See *Hexagon Pty* v. *Australian Broadcasting Commission* [1976] RPC 628 (n. 161 below). See also para. 146.

[157] Section 11(2).   [158] See para. 159.   [159] Section 23.   [160] Section 11(2).

[161] See *Hexagon Pty* v. *Australian Broadcasting Commission* [1976] RPC 628 (scriptwriter hired to write a sequel to a film held independent contractor). Compare with *Hall (Inspector of Taxes)* v. *Lorimer* [1992] 1 WLR 939 (freelance 'vision mixer').

[162] Section 11(1).

[163] Subject to rules on implied licences or equitable assignments. See paras. 121 and 156.

[164] See para. 159.   [165] Section 23.

either not applicable or ill-adapted to audiovisual works,[166] the author is the physical persons who created the work. Accordingly, under this general rule the copyright in the audiovisual work will vest jointly in its co-authors, as identified in the Copyright Act or determined by the application of the relevant joint authorship rules.[167]

However, the situation of authors as regards initial entitlement to copyright is reinforced in *droit d'auteur* countries in two ways. First, in most authors' rights countries employment contracts do not convey the copyright in the works created by employees to the employer.[168] Secondly, contractual rules may render voluntary transfers more difficult or limited in scope.[169]

As a result, in order to ensure that producers will obtain the necessary rights to exploit the film, all Member States of the authors' rights tradition have established a system of presumption of assignment or of legal assignment of economic rights in films in favour of the film producer.[170]

Such presumptions of assignment have been implemented in Belgium,[171] Denmark,[172] Finland,[173] France,[174] Germany,[175] Greece,[176] the Netherlands,[177] Portugal,[178] Spain[179] and Sweden.[180] A system of *cessio legis* (legal assignment) was implemented in Austria,[181] Italy[182] and Luxembourg.[183] The scope and regime of these presumptions will be studied in detail in Chapter 5 below.[184]

PART II

Ownership of underlying rights

144.   Should the film producers be the initial owners of underlying rights?

Film productions may involve the creation or the use of the following protected works:

---

[166] Such as the doctrine of 'collective works'. See e.g. para. 147.
[167] See paras. 137 and 138.   [168] See para. 147.
[169] In particular, restrictive construction rules. See Chapter 5 below.
[170] See Chapter 2 above for an historical account.
[171] Art. 18 of the Copyright Act.   [172] Art. 58.   [173] Art. 39.   [174] Art. L.132-24.
[175] Art. 89(1).   [176] Art. 34.   [177] Art. 45d.
[178] Arts. 124 *et seq.*, but their scope is narrow.
[179] Arts. 88 and 89 of the Copyright Act.   [180] Section 39.
[181] Arts. 38-40.   [182] Art. 45.
[183] 1972 Act, art. 27. But the new Act of 2001 implements a presumption of assignment (art. 24).
[184] See paras. 160 and 161.

Literary works	• pre-existing novel
Dramatic works	• script(s)
Musical works	• pre-existing musicv
	• commissioned music
Artistic works	• decor, costumes[185]
Performances	• actors' performances
	• musical performances (in pre-existing music)
	• musical performances (in commissioned music)
Sound recordings	• of pre-existing music
Films	• e.g. special effect footage

If we endorse the necessity to vest in the film producer the necessary rights to exploit the film, it could be useful to provide for a presumption which allows the transfer to the film producer of at least the underlying rights necessary for its exploitation. The solution of granting *authorship* in contributory works is generally rejected, even in copyright systems such as the UK system. The reason is that it would be practically impossible and ethically difficult to deprive authors such as screenwriters and musical composers of authorship in their works. Moreover, in relation to musical works, a strict application of this mechanism would conflict with the collective organisation through authors' societies, which is highly integrated at the international level.

A more acceptable solution would be to leave authorship to the natural authors and to adopt a system of initial *ownership* of rights in contributory works through a presumption of assignment in favour of the producer. For the practical reasons noted above, such a presumption appears difficult to implement in relation to musical composers; but the presumption could prove useful in relation to script works (when the scriptwriter is not a co-author of the film) and to performances. However, it must be proved that film producers have a better case than other commissioners (or employers, as the case may be) to benefit from such a presumption. In fact, in practice, under the present rights clearance system, film producers appear to be guaranteed the necessary rights for the exploitation of their film through collective agreements,[186] and screenwriters and performers seem

---

[185] See *Shelley Films Ltd* v. *Rex Features Ltd* [1994] EMLR 134 (see para. 84 above).

[186] E.g. in the UK, in the agreement between the Writers' Guild of Great Britain and independent television and film producers (PACT), effective 3 February 1992, which covers feature films, television films and series, the rights granted to the producer are set out in wide terms: 'Full copyright in the work for which the Writer is engaged shall vest in and be the sole property of the Associate for all media' (section 25). The writer retains only a limited interest in the publishing and merchandising of his work (sections 25 and 26), which take the form of a right to negotiate the terms of such use.

to obtain a fair remuneration from the exploitation of their work.[187] Considering the bargaining power of film producers and the relative weakness of trade unions in the European film industry, it would be unfair (and maybe dangerous) to deprive these contributors of their main bargaining tool. There is no doubt, for example, that the favourable situation of screenwriters and musical composers compared to film directors in the UK in terms of 'authorial rights'[188] is due to the fact that they have a copyright to bargain for, which, until recently, was not the case of film directors.[189] The introduction of an automatic assignment scheme could deprive commissioned authors of an important part of the royalties or residual payments obtained through collective bargaining or collective licensing of their copyright.

In order to avoid this difficulty, some continental European countries have implemented limited presumptions of assignment of underlying rights in films to the film producer, subject to mandatory rights to equitable remuneration.

145.   International agreements and EC directives

The provisions of article 14*bis*(2) of the Berne Convention are not applicable to the works of those contributors who are not considered owners of the copyright in the cinematographic work.[190] Accordingly, for our purpose, a distinction should be made between those authors of underlying works who are considered co-authors of the cinematographic work, and those who are denied authorship in the film. Only the latter are excluded from the scope of article 14*bis*(2). Depending on the legal system, contributors such as scriptwriters could fall into either category. But contributors such as authors of decor, who are generally denied authorship in the film, will fall in the second category.

In terms of ownership, the situation of authors excluded from article 14*bis*(2) appears more favourable than that of film authors. As mentioned above, under the Berne Convention, the author is to be the initial owner of the copyright in his work.[191] Accordingly, a Union member granting initial ownership of a work to the employer or to the commissioner (at least without allowing a clause to the contrary) may be in breach of the Convention's obligations.[192]

---

[187] Although this can (and maybe should) be improved.
[188] See para. 169.
[189] In this respect, it is not clear whether UK practice has followed the decision of the Court of Appeal in *Norowzian* v. *Arks Ltd (No. 2)* [2000] EMLR 67; [2000] FSR 363, CA; see paras. 120 and 125.
[190] See para. 141.   [191] *Ibid.*   [192] *Ibid.*

The same principles may apply under Community legislation.[193] The Rental Directive enshrined the technique of presumptions of assignment of underlying rights to the film producer. However, it is made compulsory only in relation to the rental right of performers. Article 2 of the Rental Directive sets out two presumptions in the case of film production agreements with a performer: article 2(5) provides for a presumption of transfer of the rental right of the performer, subject to a contractual clause to the contrary, and article 2(7) provides for an irrebuttable presumption of authorisation of rental, both presumptions being subject to the payment to the performer of an 'equitable remuneration'.[194] The relationship between these two provisions is not clear but it appears that the presumption of article 2(5) is mandatory for Member States if they do not choose the system of article 2(7).[195]

The Directive allows Member States to extend the presumption of article 2(7) to all related rights under the Directive. Accordingly, Member States may introduce a presumption encompassing all performers' economic rights. The Directive also allows Member States to introduce the presumption of article 2(5) with respect to the rental right of authors,[196] subject to an equitable remuneration. This could concern the authors of audiovisual works, but also authors of underlying works.

More generally, nothing in the Directive prevents a Member State from extending the presumption to exploitation rights which are not harmonised under the Directive. But it is submitted that the presumptions established by Member States should in any case be subject to agreement to the contrary.

The Directive on Copyright and Related Rights in the Information Society may reinforce this solution. The enshrining by this Directive of rights of reproduction, of communication to the public and of distribution in favour of authors does not appear to prevent the implementation of a presumption of assignment of these rights to the employer or commissioner, subject to agreement to the contrary (as this would probably go beyond the scope of harmonisation). However, it certainly prevents the implementation of a *cessio legis* (legal assignment) of these rights.

---

[193] *Ibid.*
[194] The non-rebuttable character of the presumption in art. 2(7) is not an exception to the principle described in relation to authors. See e.g. art. 2(6).
[195] J. Reinbothe, 'The EC Directive on Rental and Lending Rights and Rights Related to Copyright', in H. Cohen Jehoram, P. Keuchenius and J. Seignette (eds.), *Audiovisual Media and Copyright in Europe*, Kluwer, 1994, pp. 44–5; and J. Reinbothe and S. von Lewinski, *The EC Directive on Rental and Lending Rights and on Piracy*, Sweet & Maxwell, 1993, pp. 60–1.
[196] Art. 2(6).

146.   The law in the UK and Ireland

UK copyright law grants to film producers authorship (now co-authorship) in the audiovisual recording constituted by the 'film', but, until the enactment of the Copyright and Related Rights Regulations 1996, did not address specifically the question of ownership of underlying rights in film productions. Under the CDPA 1988, as a general rule, the author of a literary, dramatic, musical or artistic work is the first owner of the copyright in it,[197] unless he is an employee and his work is made in the course of his employment, in which case the copyright vests in his employer (subject to an agreement to the contrary).[198]

By way of exception, the Copyright and Related Rights Regulations 1996 implemented a presumption of transfer of the rental right of authors of literary, dramatic, musical or artistic work to the film producer;[199] however, this presumption does not apply to the author of the screenplay or the dialogue nor to the author of any music 'specifically created for and used in the film'.[200] A similar presumption was introduced for the rental right of performers.[201]

Note that certain authors of contributory works in film productions work as independent contractors.[202] As a consequence, and subject to the exception concerning rental rights, the film producer will need to be assigned or licensed the necessary rights in order to exploit his derivative 'film'.[203]

The Irish Act contains similar provisions.[204]

147.   The law in authors' rights countries

In Member States of the authors' rights tradition, the solutions regarding ownership of underlying rights are more complex and diverse than usually assumed by common law practitioners. They are also in strong contrast to the rules regarding ownership of rights in audiovisual works.

As a first rule, in countries where the film producer is denied authorship in the audiovisual works, entrepreneurial *authorship* of contributory works is *a fortiori* rejected. However, in the Netherlands, article 7 of the Copyright Act includes a provision which is close to the US doctrine of work-made-for-hire:

---

[197] Section 11(1).   [198] See para. 142.   [199] Section 12 (new s. 93A). See para. 159.
[200] *Ibid.* (new s. 93A(3)).   [201] Section 21 (new s. 191F). See para. 336.
[202] See *Hexagon Pty v. Australian Broadcasting Commission* [1976] RPC 628 (scriptwriter hired to write a sequel to a film held to be an independent contractor).
[203] Subject to rules on implied licences or equitable assignments. See paras. 121 and 156.
[204] Copyright and Related Rights Act 2000, s. 23 (first ownership of copyright) and s. 124 (presumption of transfer of rental right in case of film production agreement).

Where work performed in the service of another person consists in the production of certain literary, scientific or artistic works, the person in whose service they were produced shall be deemed to be the author thereof, unless otherwise agreed between the parties.[205]

This provision would not only vest in the employer the economic rights in works made in the course of employment, but also the corresponding moral rights.[206] This could well be applicable to some underlying works in film productions. This provision does not appear to be repeated in other Member States. In those States, the closest regime would be that of 'collective works', which is found in several continental copyright Acts.[207] However, in the case of a 'collective works', the 'publisher' is usually not considered the 'author' of a work, but the initial owner of the copyright in it. In addition, the concept of 'collective work' would rarely apply in relation to underlying works in film productions.

This leads us to the question of initial *ownership*. Some Member States provide for a rebuttable presumption of assignment to the film producer of those underlying rights necessary to exploit the final audiovisual work, which complements the presumption of assignment of rights in the audiovisual work. This is the case in Germany, Luxembourg and Spain.[208] Typically, these rights do not include adaptation or remake rights. Other Member States apply their standard ownership rules. As mentioned above, in this respect the basic rule is that the author of a work is the first owner of the copyright in it.

A limited exception could be provided for in some systems by employment rules. For example, the Spanish Copyright Act provides, in the absence of a written agreement with the employer, for a presumption of transfer to the employer of the exploitation rights, which is restricted to the extent necessary for the exercise of the employer's customary activity.[209] A similar rule applies under Greek law.[210]

But such provisions are exceptional. In most Member States of the authors' rights tradition, an employment agreement does not convey to the

---

[205] WIPO translation.
[206] Cohen Jehoram, in M. B. Nimmer and D. Geller (eds.), *International Copyright Law and Practice*, Matthew Bender, looseleaf, para. 4[1][b][ii].
[207] See e.g. art. L.113-5 of the French Intellectual Property Code; art. 8 of the Spanish Intellectual Property Law; art. 19 of the Portuguese Code; and art. 6 of the Luxembourg Act of 2001 ('directed work'). The definition of collective works varies, but these works are usually a variety of composite works published by an entrepreneur under his name.
[208] German Act, art. 88; Luxembourg Act of 1972, art. 28; Luxembourg Act of 2001, art. 24 (the new presumption, which covers 'the authors *and other creators* of the audiovisual works', may not apply to all contributors); and the Spanish Intellectual Property Law, art. s. 89(1). See para. 161.
[209] Art. 51.
[210] G. Koumantos, in M. B. Nimmer and D. Geller (eds.), *International Copyright Law and Practice*, Matthew Bender, looseleaf, para. 4[1][b].

employer the copyright in the work created by the employee in the course of his employment.[211] This principle is strictly enforced by the courts in France, where article L.111-1 of the Intellectual Property Code provides that the existence or conclusion of a contract for hire or of service by the author of a work 'shall not derogate from the enjoyment of the copyright' afforded to the author. In the absence of a contractual transfer clause in the employment agreement, the employer would not even benefit from an implied exclusive or non-exclusive licence to use the work.[212] An employment contract would not in principle convey copyright to the employer in Portugal, Sweden[213] and other Scandinavian countries. In Belgium, the Copyright Act requires that the assignment to the employer be explicitly laid down.[214] In Italy, the transfer must be agreed, at least impliedly.[215] The same rule applies in Germany.[216]

In any case, authors of underlying works in film productions are often independent contractors (this is almost always true for the musical composer and the scriptwriter), and in practice employment rules will have little relevance for certain classes of works.

Finally, in all Member States of the authors' rights tradition, under the general regime applicable to commissioned works, the copyright in the commissioned work vests in its author and is not transferred to the commissioner.[217]

---

[211] Subject to limited exceptions regarding, e.g. journalists.
[212] Case law provides for limited exceptions to this rule in the field of applied arts.
[213] G. Karnell, in M. B. Nimmer and D. Geller (eds.), *International Copyright Law and Practice*, Matthew Bender, looseleaf, para. 4[1][b].
[214] Art. 3(3).
[215] M. Fabiani, in M. B. Nimmer and D. Geller (eds.), *International Copyright Law and Practice*, Matthew Bender, looseleaf, para. 4[1][b][iv].
[216] A. Dietz, in M. B. Nimmer and D. Geller (eds.), *International Copyright Law and Practice*, Matthew Bender, looseleaf, para. 4[1][a].
[217] Subject, in some countries, to the possibility of implied (limited) assignments, and to the doctrine of 'collective work'.

5   Copyright transfers and authorial rights

148.   Introduction

The regime of copyright contracts is one of enormous tensions between the interests of authors and producers in Europe, as evidenced by the discussions surrounding the introduction in the EC Rental Directive of a 'right to equitable remuneration' in favour of authors and performers for the rental of films and sound recordings. The interests at stake are enormous and may affect the exploitation of film works far more than the more publicised, but less litigated, question of moral rights. In this respect, EU Member States have adopted very different approaches and solutions, which are sometime presented as irreconcilable. These differences can be explained by philosophical and historical preferences, by the weight given in each legal system to the principle of freedom of contract or to other, conflicting principles, but also by the successful lobbying by pressure groups (representing authors or rights owners, as the case may be). The relative absence of provisions on copyright transfers in the relevant international agreements does nothing to harmonise national solutions.[1]

Here too, the line should be drawn between the copyright systems of the UK and Ireland, on the one hand, and continental legislation, on the other hand (although authors' rights systems are more diverse in this respect than is usually assumed by copyright lawyers). In copyright countries the matter of copyright contracts is left to a large extent to the operation of standard contract law rules. The matter is further simplified by the fact that the film producer is in most cases the initial owner of the copyright in the film.

The law is more complex in authors' rights countries. It evidences two main concerns. The first concern is to grant to the film producer the

---

[1] See, however, the provisions of art. 14*bis* of the Berne Convention, which provides for a presumption of assignment of rights in films to the producer (art. 14*bis*(2); see para. 141) and for conditions of form for the corresponding film production agreement (art. 14*bis*(3)).

necessary rights to exploit the film. In most domestic laws it is addressed by the implementation of a presumption of assignment of the copyright in the film to the film producer, more rarely of a *cessio legis* (legal assignment) or of initial entitlement to copyright through employment rules. However, the scope of this transfer varies and is often qualified in several ways.

The second concern is to ensure an adequate protection for the weak party to the contract, which is assumed to be the author (although authors' societies may in practice shift the bargaining power in their favour). This protection is assured by restrictive rules regarding transfers (reservation of rights, restrictive construction provisions) and by rights of equitable remuneration or similar provisions ensuring that the author will share in the benefits from the exploitation of the work.

Therefore, when it comes to copyright contracts in the European Union, it is useful to distinguish two series of rules: first, the rules applicable to copyright transfers in film works, in each legal system (discussed in Section I below); and, secondly, the rules concerning what we will call 'authorial rights' (discussed in Section II below). By authorial rights, we mean those monetary interests, apart from the salary, which are paid to authors in compensation for the exploitation of the work, that is, rights to equitable remuneration, royalty rights or rights to review the remuneration in case of gross distortion or unexpected success of the film. Strong authorial rights for film authors are one peculiarity of the law in the European Union, at least as compared to US copyright law and to copyright systems outside the UK and Ireland; authorial rights have also been the subject of a limited harmonisation at Community level.

SECTION I

Copyright transfers

149.   Scope of the study

The matter of copyright transfers in films is complex. It involves, in each legal system, a knowledge of general contract law, of the general rules applicable to all copyright contracts and, in some legal systems, of rules applicable to specific types of copyright agreements, such as publishing contracts or film production contracts. In addition, the rules applicable to film production contracts in the narrow meaning (contracts between film authors and producers) may not be applicable to other types of contracts involved in film productions, such as music publishing agreements, literary rights contracts (including literary options), talent agreements, etc.

Accordingly, it would be unrealistic to attempt in this book to draw a complete picture of the matter. In this section we will restrict ourselves to general indications, with a focus on the legal systems of the main film industries within the EU. Some questions will also be left out: the regime of employees' and commissioned works (which were discussed in the previous chapter[2]); the rules regarding transfers *mortis causa*; the use of copyright as a security; questions such as capacity, the effect of marital community on copyright entitlement or other questions involving standard contract law. Performers' agreements will be addressed in the chapter dedicated to performers' rights.[3]

150.   A limited European harmonisation

As mentioned above, due to the relative absence of provisions in applicable international agreements, domestic laws in the European Union show a great diversity as to the regime of film production contracts. A partial harmonisation was attempted by the EC Rental and Satellite and Cable Directives, but the scope of such harmonisation is limited. The Rental Directive allows Member States to provide for a presumption of transfer of the rental right to the film producer with the film production contract, subject to agreement to the contrary.[4] In addition, the Directive requires the introduction of a *statutory right to compensation* in case of transfer of the rental right in the form of an unwaivable right to 'equitable remuneration',[5] the administration of which may be entrusted to collecting societies.[6] The main problem, within the scope of the harmonisation, is that this concept of 'equitable remuneration' is not defined in the Directive. We will see that Member States have had different approaches as to what constitutes an equitable remuneration for rental.

The Satellite and Cable Directive provides that the satellite broadcasting right can only be acquired by agreement, which excludes presumptions of assignment.[7]

Subject to these limited provisions, a significant number of questions have been left unanswered by the EC copyright directives, as we will see below.

151.   The existence of specific regimes for copyright and film production agreements

A first difference between national systems lies in the existence and importance of specific regimes for film production contracts. In this respect,

---

[2] See paras. 146 and 147.   [3] See Chapter 9 below.   [4] Art. 2(6).
[5] Art. 4.   [6] Art. 4(3).
[7] Art. 3(1). Also, that the cable retransmission rights must be exercised only through collecting societies (art. 9(1)).

it is possible to divide EU Member States in two groups. The first group of countries provides for some general rules on copyright contracts, and for a few specific rules on film production agreements, mainly resulting from the implementation of the EC Rental Directive. This is the case in the UK, where the main feature of film production contracts is now the presumption of assignment of the rental right to the film producer. But film production contracts are otherwise subject to the standard rules applicable to all copyright contracts. The situation is similar in Ireland. Other countries in this group implement broader presumptions of assignment of rights to the film producer, but without regulating in detail film production contracts. This is the case in the Netherlands, Sweden, Belgium, Spain and most other authors' rights jurisdictions.

A second group of countries sets out in more detail the regime for the main types of copyright contracts, including film production contracts. This is the case in France and in Portugal. The French 1957 Act was the first Act to provide detailed provisions applicable to copyright contracts.[8] The French Intellectual Property Code details provisions applicable to all copyright contracts[9] and the specific regime applicable to four main types of contracts: publishing contracts (which are not restricted to printed matter but include all agreements granting the right to produce and distribute copies of a work, in any form),[10] performance contracts,[11] and, from the 1985 Copyright Amendment Act, audiovisual production contracts[12] and commission contracts for advertising.[13] The regime of publishing contracts is the most detailed, and some of the provisions included in the section dedicated to these contracts have been extended *mutatis mutandis* to other types of contract by French courts. The regime of audiovisual production contracts is inspired from the statutory regime of publishing contracts. Most of these provisions are mandatory.

152.   The transmissibility of copyright: assignments and licences

In most Member States, copyright (in the sense of economic rights for *droit d'auteur*) is considered as a moveable property transferable by assignment, licences (the term 'authorisations' being sometimes preferred)

---

[8] See D. Lypszyc, *Copyright and Neighbouring Rights*, UNESCO, 1993, p. 260.
[9] Arts. L.131-1 to L.131-8.   [10] Arts. L.132-1 to L.132-17.
[11] Arts. L.132-18 to L.132-22.
[12] Arts. L.132-22 to L.132-20. Defined as the contract entered into between the producer and the author, irrespective of its nature (employment contract or commissioned work).
[13] Arts. L.132-31 to L.132-33.

or other types of contracts. This transmissibility of copyright is expressly acknowledged by the law in the UK,[14] Belgium,[15] Denmark,[16] Finland,[17] France,[18] Greece,[19] Italy,[20] Ireland,[21] Luxembourg,[22] the Netherlands,[23] Portugal,[24] Spain[25] and Sweden.[26]

The solution is different in Germany, where article 29 of the copyright Act states that copyright may be transferred *mortis causa* but shall not otherwise be transferable. This peculiarity of German copyright law is due to the adoption of the so-called 'monistic' theory of copyright, as explained by Adolf Dietz:

The particular thrust of [German law governing copyright transfers] can only be understood against the background of the so-called 'monistic' theory of German copyright. According to this concept, copyright as a whole, that is, author's right, safeguards both the financial and the personal or intellectual interest of an author. Thus, the author's economic right of exploitation may serve his personal or intellectual interests as well, and his moral right may also serve his financial interests … As a consequence of this monistic concept, German author's right, even in the narrow sense of economic copyright, cannot be entirely alienated … German copyright law does not recognise the complete or even partial assignment of copyright, but rather the contractual granting of 'rights of use'.[27]

Accordingly, article 31(1) of the German Copyright Act provides that the author may grant a right to another to *use the work* in a particular manner or in any manner. This right to use (which is not an assignment) can be exclusive or non-exclusive. An exclusive exploitation right entitles the 'user' to use the work, to the exclusion of all other persons, including the author, and to grant non-exclusive exploitation rights within the scope of his grant.[28] The exclusive user also has standing to sue in copyright infringement.[29] Austrian law appears to adopt the same theory and language. It remains to be seen whether this elaborate but cumbersome terminology is followed by contractual practice. It is interesting to note that this approach was abandoned in Switzerland, otherwise influenced by German copyright law: there, copyright is freely transferable under the

---

[14] Section 90.   [15] Art. 3(1).   [16] Section 53.   [17] Art. 27.   [18] Art. L.122-7.
[19] Arts. 12 and 13.   [20] Art. 107.   [21] Section 120.
[22] Art. 3 of the 1972 Act; art. 12 of the 2001 Act.
[23] Art. 2.   [24] Art. 40.   [25] Art. 43.   [26] Art. 27.
[27] A. Dietz, in M. B. Nimmer and D. Geller (eds.), *International Copyright Law and Practice*, Matthew Bender, looseleaf, para. 4[2]. On these theories and their consequences, see P. Kamina, 'Author's Right as Property: Old and New Theories' (2001) 48 *Journal of the Copyright Society* 383.
[28] Art. 31(3).
[29] A. Dietz, in M. B. Nimmer and D. Geller (eds.), *International Copyright Law and Practice*, Matthew Bender, looseleaf, para. 4[2]. See the *Alf* decision, involving a transfer subject to US contract law, BGH, 17 June 1992, noted in English in (1993) 24 IIC 539.

1992 Copyright Act and can be freely assigned or licensed, exclusively or not.[30]

153.   Transferability of copyright interest to a third party

In most European countries copyright, once assigned, can be freely re-assigned (or licensed) by the copyright owner to a third party. In some countries, however, save convention to the contrary, an assignment of *droit d'auteur* does not convey the right to reassign the copyright to a third party. This is the case in Greece[31] and Sweden.[32] In Denmark, an exception to this rule is provided if 'the reassignment is usual or obviously presumed'.[33] In other countries, this rule is restricted to publishing contracts.[34] This is the case in France, where article L.132-16 of the Intellectual Property Code contains a provision to that effect:

> The publisher may not transmit the benefits of the publishing contract to a third party, for or without payment, or as a contribution to the assets of a partnership, independently of the business, without first having obtained the authorisation of the author.
>
> In the event of transfer of the business in such a way as to seriously compromise the material and moral interests of the author, the latter shall be entitled to obtain reparation even by means of termination of the contract . . . [35]

This provision is important since under French law publishing contracts have a wider scope than in other countries and encompass all contracts for the making and distribution of copies in any form of any work.[36] However, it is generally thought in France that a transfer of copyright *in a film* conveys the right to retransfer this copyright to a third party. In doubt, it is always possible (and advisable) to include a specific clause to that effect in the agreement.

In other countries, the assignee or more specifically the film producer may transfer rights deriving from the contract, in whole or in part, to

---

[30] Art. 16.   [31] Art. 13(6).

[32] Art. 28. Karnell, 'La liberté contractuelle dans le droit d'auteur suédois', ALAI Symposium on 'Contractual Freedom in the Field of Authors' Rights', 1–2 October 1975, Berlin.

[33] Section 56(2).   [34] E.g. in Italy, art. 132; in Spain, art. 68(d).

[35] WIPO translation.

[36] Under art. L.132-1 of the Code, a publishing contract is a contract by which the author of a work assigns to a person the right to manufacture or have manufactured a number of copies, in order for the latter to ensure publication and dissemination thereof. In contrast, the Italian Supreme Court in a decision of 23 June 1998, held that arts. 118 *et seq.* of the Italian Copyright Act on 'publishing contracts' apply only to publication in print in the form of printed books, and do not extend to music publishing contracts providing for the manufacture of copies on recording media.

a third party; but the assignee/film producer nevertheless sometimes remains liable towards the author for the strict performance of the contract. This is expressly stated in the copyright Acts of Denmark,[37] Germany,[38] Portugal[39] and Spain.[40]

Finally, several copyright Acts contain specific provisions to deal with the case of assignment of ongoing business or of the winding up of the right owner. Such provisions grant the author the right to rescind his contract or a right of preference for the reversion of his rights. French law adapts these rules to film production agreements in article L.132-30 of the Intellectual Property Code: in contrast to the solution adopted for publishing contracts, the winding up of the film producer does not terminate the audiovisual production contract. However, the author or joint authors have a right of pre-emption of the copyright in their work unless one of the co-producers notifies them of his intention to acquire it. Failing agreement, the purchase price is fixed by expert opinion. In addition, when the activities of the production company have ceased for more than three months or where liquidation is ordered, the author and the joint authors may require termination of the audiovisual production contract. Such provisions have very important practical effects in a country in which films are often produced by small companies, sometimes constituted for a single project.

154. Divisibility of copyright

As a general rule, in those countries where copyright is freely transferable, assignments and licences can be total (subject to mandatory rules described below and to the question of unknown uses and technologies) or partial. Also, grants can be divided along rights, territories, means of exploitation, or any combination of these. But such divisions may sometimes blur the distinction between assignments and licences.

155. Limitation in time

Most copyright Acts do not limit the duration of copyright assignments and licences. Therefore, assignments are often stipulated for the period for which the copyright is to subsist. However, the Spanish Copyright Act provides that a failure to specify the duration of the grant

---

[37] Art. 56(2).   [38] Art. 34(5).   [39] Art. 133.
[40] Art. 49. But the law here states that, in the case of publishing contracts, an author may terminate the contract where the publisher assigns his rights to a third party without permission (art. 68(d)).

limits the duration of the transfer to five years.[41] The same general rule and duration apply in Greece.[42] In Portuguese law, this period is extended to twenty-five years.[43] Some countries limit the duration of the grant in specific contracts, such as publishing contracts.[44]

Contractual practice sometimes tends to limit the duration of assignments. This is the case in France for contracts negotiated with certain talent agents, or when the author is represented by an authors' society. In such cases, a limitation of twenty or thirty years is usually sought. However, model agreements by producers' associations transfer the copyright in the film for the entire duration of the right.

156.   Writing requirements

In the UK, an assignment of copyright is not effective unless it is in writing and signed by or on behalf of the assignor.[45] This requirement does not apply to licences; therefore licences can be implied from conduct or contractual relations.[46] The Irish Copyright and Related Rights Act 2000 uses the same language as the UK Act.[47]

In addition, even when the film production contract does not expressly convey the copyright or part of it to the film producer, in some limited cases the producer could own the copyright in equity or benefit from an equitable licence to use the work.[48] This would be the case, for example, if there were an express or implied term that he should own the copyright in the work or otherwise exploit or use it.[49]

The French Intellectual Property Code provides that performance, publishing and audiovisual production contracts shall be in writing.[50] The writing is only required for proof as against the author; the requirements of proof as against the other party are less stringent. For other contracts, the Code refers to the provisions of the Civil Code as to the proof of obligations. However, the Code provides for a specific formality in relation to grants of audiovisual adaptation rights. Article L.131-3 of the Code provides that the grant of audiovisual adaptation rights in a written

---

[41] Art. 43(2).   [42] Art. 15(1).   [43] Art. 43.4.   [44] Italy, art. 122.

[45] Section 90(3).

[46] See the case law in para. 121. It has been suggested, however, that these implied terms should extend 'no further than to that which is necessary to give business efficacy to the contract', 'and thus to allow use of the work for the purposes which were in contemplation of both parties at the time the contract was made, but not further'. *Copinger and Skone James on Copyright*, 14th edn, 1999, para. 5-208. D. Lester and P. Mitchell, *Joynson-Hicks on UK Copyright Law*, Sweet & Maxwell, 1989, para. 9.28, p. 251.

[47] Section 120(3).

[48] *Copinger and Skone James on Copyright*, 14th edn, 1999, paras. 5-10 and 5-166 *et seq.*

[49] *Ibid.*   [50] Art. L.131-2.

or printed work must be made in a written agreement separate from the publishing agreement. The same requirements exist in Belgium.[51] In addition, in both countries, case law consistently denies the possibility of implied licences and assignments.

The Spanish Act provides that all copyright transfers shall be evidenced in writing,[52] and adds that if, after having been formally called upon to do so, the transferee fails to meet this requirement, the author may choose to terminate the contract. In addition, writing is required *ad validitatem* for publishing contracts. Also, using broader language than the French and Belgian Acts, article 57 of the Spanish Intellectual Property Law provides that, in the case of the licensing of rights for the production of audiovisual works, the licensing for each of the various modes of exploitation shall be evidenced in 'independent documents'.

In Italy, writing is required for transfers of exploitations rights, but only *ad probationem*.[53] In the Netherlands, writing is required *ad probationem* for assignments, but licences do not have to be set in writing.[54] Writing is required *ad validitatem* in Greece,[55] but nullity can be claimed by the author only.

In contrast, there are no specific formal requirements for copyright contracts in the German Copyright Act.[56] A limited possibility of implied assignments also appears to exist in Germany.[57] The same seems true in Sweden.[58]

157.   Registration/priority of transfers

In most European countries film production contracts, like copyright contracts in general, are not subject to registration. However, registration requirements exist in France in the field of theatrical audiovisual works. The French Code of Cinematography provides that contracts conveying rights in cinematographic works (i.e. theatrical films) must be registered

---

[51] Arts. 3(1) and (2) and 17.   [52] Art. 45.   [53] Art. 110.

[54] Art. 2(2) of the Act. See H. Cohen Jeroham, in M. B. Nimmer and D. Geller (eds.), *International Copyright Law and Practice*, Matthew Bender, looseleaf, para. 4[2][b].

[55] Art. 14. For all acts dealing with the transfer of economic rights, including assignment and licences.

[56] Subject to art. 40 of the Act, which provides that contracts relating to future works must be made in writing.

[57] A. Dietz, in M. B. Nimmer and D. Geller (eds.), *International Copyright Law and Practice*, Matthew Bender, looseleaf, para. 4[2][b].

[58] Section 28 of the Copyright Act. G. Karnell, 'La liberté contractuelle dans le droit d'auteur suédois', in ALAI Symposium on 'Contractual Freedom in the Field of Authors' Rights', 1–2 October 1975, Berlin. Also in M. B. Nimmer and D. Geller (eds.), *International Copyright Law and Practice*, Matthew Bender, looseleaf, para. 4[2][b].

with the National Centre of Cinematography.[59] The contracts subject to registration include assignments, licences, contracts for contributions to the capital of companies and partnerships (including co-production agreements), pledges on exploitation rights, assignments and grants of proceeds from the exploitation of a film and distribution agreements. This registration determines the priority of transfers and enables the enforcement of the contract as against third parties. An unregistered contract, however, remains valid and enforceable as between the parties. The registry of the National Centre of Cinematography is accessible to the public, and it is possible to obtain copies of registered agreements.

Registration is optional in Spain and in Italy, and does not affect the enforceability of the agreement.

158.   Statutory presumptions of grant/deemed assignments

As mentioned above, the Berne Convention provides for a presumption of assignment of rights in cinematographic works to the film producer in its article 14*bis*(2). Union members which have included as first owners of the copyright in the film authors of contributory works must provide for a presumption of assignment of the latter's rights in the film to the film producer, subject to agreement to the contrary.[60] However, this presumption is subject to so many exemptions that it has become almost optional.[61] These rules are repeated in the TRIPs Agreement[62] and the WIPO Copyright Treaty of 1996.[63]

Statutory presumptions of assignment or legal assignments (*cessio legis*) of copyright in film works to the film producer are a common feature of the law in *droit d'auteur* countries, where films are treated as works of joint authorship.[64] Until recently, they were of little use in the UK or Ireland.

159.   Statutory presumptions of grant in the UK and Ireland

In the UK, the only statutory presumption of assignment of copyright to the film producer concerns the transfer of the rental right in the film.

---

[59] Art. 33 of the Code of Cinematography.

[60] Limited to the rights of 'reproduction, distribution, public performance, communication to the public by wire, broadcasting or any other communication to the public, or to the subtitling or dubbing of texts, of the work'. See para. 141.

[61] Under art. 14*bis*(3), unless otherwise provided by the national legislation, the presumption is not applicable to the authors of scenarios, dialogue and musical works created for the making of the cinematographic work, and to the principal director. A Union member must notify the Director-General of WIPO if it does not apply the presumption to the principal director. *Ibid.*

[62] Art. 9.   [63] Art. 1(4).

[64] On the rationale for such presumptions, see paras. 144 and 147.

Section 93A(1) of the CDPA 1988, as amended by the Copyright and Related Rights Regulations 1996, provides that:

Where an agreement concerning film production is concluded between an author and a film producer, the author shall be presumed, unless the agreement provides to the contrary, to have transferred to the film producer any rental right in relation to the film arising by virtue of the inclusion of a copy of the author's work in the film.

However, this presumption does not apply to any rental right in relation to the film arising by virtue of the inclusion in the film of the screenplay, the dialogue or music specifically created for and used in the film.[65]

The same section of the CDPA 1988 takes into account the inter-mediation of agents or other persons between the author and the film producer and further specifies that reference to an 'agreement concluded between an author and a film producer' includes any agreement having effect between those persons, whether made by them directly or through intermediaries.[66]

Finally, the right to equitable remuneration on transfer of the rental right applies to transfers presumed under section 93A as in the case of voluntary transfers.[67]

Apart from this rental right, and if we set aside the employment rules described above,[68] there is no further presumption of assignment of film copyright to the film producer, and the latter needs to be assigned or licensed the necessary rights in order to exploit fully the film or the dramatic audiovisual work.

The Irish Copyright and Related Rights Act 2000 adopts the UK solution.[69]

160. The presumption in France and Belgium

In France, the heart of the statutory regime of the audiovisual production contract is the presumption of assignment of the exploitation rights in article L.132-24 of the Intellectual Property Code, which provides:

Contracts binding the producer and the authors of an audiovisual work, other than the author of a musical composition with or without words, shall imply, unless otherwise stipulated . . . assignment to the producer of the exclusive exploitation rights in the audiovisual work.

Audiovisual production contracts shall not imply assignment to the producer of the graphic rights and theatrical rights in the work . . .[70]

---

[65] Section 93A(3).   [66] Section 93A(5).   [67] Section 93A(6).   [68] See para. 146.
[69] Section 124.   [70] WIPO translation.

The scope of this presumption is limited in several ways. First, the presumption does not apply to the contract entered into with the musical composer, who will, in most cases, have assigned his reproduction and performing rights to the French musical performing rights society (SACEM).

This raises an important question with regard to other co-authors of the film, who may have also transferred their rights in future works to the French audiovisual licensing bodies, SACD (for theatrical film authors) or SCAM (for television programmes). If that is the case, a conflict arises between the presumption of assignment to the film producer and the transfer to these societies. French law does not provides any rule to settle such a conflict, and it is not clear whether some rights assigned to the film producer are not in fact held by these societies. In practice, licensing bodies continue to licence the performing and mechanical reproduction rights of film works by their members. Most contracts with film producers include a clause called a 'SACD/SCAM rights reservation', similar to the clause inserted in contracts with musical composers with regard to their performing rights societies.

Secondly, in the absence of a clause to the contrary, the presumption does not grant to the producer the 'graphic' and 'theatrical' rights over the work, which cover the right to publish an illustrated book version (which probably includes comic book adaptations) or a stage play version of the work.

Thirdly, another limitation comes from the exploitation right each co-author retains over his own contribution, again in the absence of a clause to the contrary.[71]

Fourthly, article L.132-24 only refers to the authors of audiovisual works. Accordingly, the presumption does not apply to authors of pre-existing works who do not qualify as authors of the film (e.g. authors of the decor or other pre-existing elements).

Subject to the above, the transfer is effective for all possible means of exploitation, for the duration of the right and for the whole world. The question as to whether, in the absence of a specific clause, this presumption confers the right to make a 'sequel' or a 'remake' of the film, together with 'merchandising rights', has still not been brought before the courts.[72]

A presumption similar to that in French law is found under Belgian law.[73]

---

[71] Art. L.132-29. See para. 138.
[72] Against such an extension, see e.g. P.-Y. Gautier, *Propriété Littéraire et Artistique*, Puf, 1991, para. 233, p. 393.
[73] Art. 18.

161.   The presumption in other authors' rights countries

Other countries organise either a system of presumption of assignment of copyright to the film producer, or a system which is closer to a *cessio legis* (legal assignment). German law provides for presumptions of 'grants' which relate both to the audiovisual work and to underlying works. The presumption relating to the copyright in the audiovisual work is defined in article 89 of the Copyright Act, which provides that any person who undertakes to participate in the production of a film and owns a copyright in it is deemed, in case of doubt, to have granted to the film producer an exclusive right to utilise the film and translations and other adaptations or transformations thereof in any known manner.[74] However, rights in underlying works such as novels, screenplays and film music remain unaffected.[75] Concerning pre-existing works, article 88 provides that, if an author permits another person to make a cinematographic adaptation of his work, he shall be deemed, in doubt, to have granted the following exploitation rights:

1. the right to use the work in its original form or as an adaptation or transformation for the purpose of producing a cinematographic work;
2. the right to reproduce and distribute the cinematographic work;
3. the right to publicly present the cinematographic work if it is a work intended for presentation;
4. the right to broadcast the cinematographic work if it is a work intended for broadcasting;
5. the right to exploit translations and other cinematographic adaptations or transformations of the cinematographic work to the same extent as the work itself.[76]

However, in case of doubt, the rights referred to in paragraph (1) do not include the right to produce a remake of the film.[77] In addition, in case of doubt, the author shall be deemed to have the right, after the expiration of ten years from the conclusion of the contract, to utilise his work otherwise than for cinematographic purposes.[78]

In Spain, a film production agreement is deemed to assign to the film producer the exclusive rights of reproduction, distribution and communication to the public, and also the rights of post-synchronisation or subtitling of the work. However, the Act provides that the consent of the authors is necessary for an exploitation by distribution to the public of copies in whatever mode or format for use within the family circle, or by means of communication to the public by broadcasting. In addition, unless otherwise provided, the co-authors may make use of their individual

---

[74] Art. 89(1).   [75] Art. 89(3).   [76] WIPO translation.   [77] Art. 88(2).   [78] *Ibid.*

contributions separately, provided that the normal exploitation of the audiovisual work is not thereby prejudiced.[79] The presumption of assignment is also extended to pre-existing works, but article 89(2) provides that, save provision to the contrary, the author of the pre-existing work shall retain graphic publication and stage performance rights in his work, and that, in any event, he may make use of the pre-existing work for any other audiovisual work during the fifteen years following the delivery of his contribution to the producer.

Presumptions of various scope are also found in Denmark,[80] Finland,[81] Greece,[82] Portugal,[83] Sweden[84] and the Netherlands.[85]

In contrast, the Italian and Austrian Acts implement a *cessio legis* (legal assignment) of copyright to the film producer. As a result, the initial copyright in the film, or at least part of it, is initially vested in the film producer.[86] In Italy, article 45 of the Copyright Act provides that the exercise of the exploitation rights in a cinematographic work shall belong to the person who has organised the production of the work. These rights are limited in article 46 to the 'cinematographic exploitation' of the work produced. The meaning of this term is not restricted to exploitation of the film in theatres, but also includes exploitation on television.[87] It might not, however, cover video distribution.[88] In the absence of an agreement to the contrary, the producer shall not make or show adaptations, transformations or translations of the produced work without the consent of the co-authors of the film. The Act further provides that the authors of the literary or musical parts of a cinematographic work may reproduce them or utilise them separately in any manner, provided no prejudice is caused to the exploitation rights of the producer.

In Austria, article 38 of the Copyright Act provides for a similar entitlement to the exploitation right of commercial films.[89]

---

[79] Art. 88(1) and (2).   [80] Section 58.   [81] Art. 39.   [82] Art. 34(1).

[83] Portuguese law does not provides for a straight presumption of assignment to the producer, but rather provides for presumptions deriving from the initial express or implicit authorisation of the film producer. For example, art. 125 of the Code provides that 'where the author has specifically or implicitly authorized the film's projection, the exercise of the rights of economic exploitation of the cinematographic work shall belong to the producer' (WIPO translation). See also art. 127. But this 'presumption' is limited in scope. In particular, art. 129 provides that translations, dubbing or any other transformations of the cinematographic work shall be subject to the written authorisation of the authors.

[84] Art. 39.   [85] Section 45d.

[86] On the compatibility of this scheme with art. 14*bis*(2), see para. 141.

[87] Rome Court of Appeal, 16 November 1989, *Germi* v. *Reteitalia and Rissoli Film*, RIDA, No. 144, p. 184.

[88] M. Fabiani, in M. B. Nimmer and D. Geller (eds.), *International Copyright Law and Practice*, Matthew Bender, looseleaf, para. 4[1][a].

[89] Arts. 38–40.

As mentioned above, in Luxembourg, article 27 of the 1972 Copyright Act provided that the copyright in a cinematographic work shall belong initially to the film producer.[90] But the Act also included a presumption of assignment of film rights in the underlying works.[91] The new Act of 2001 combines initial authorship with a rebuttable presumption of assignment for a similar effect. The film producer is now co-author of the film with the film director.[92] But, unless provided to the contrary, the authors *and the other creators* of the film (with the exception of the musical composer) are deemed to have assigned to the film producer the rights necessary for the exploitation of the film.[93]

162.   Construction of grants

The question of the construction of copyright grants is too complex to be studied in detail here, and will be addressed briefly. Under UK copyright, there are no statutory provisions governing how an ambiguous or broad transfer of copyright shall be construed.[94] In fact, it seems that a simple 'assignment of copyright' would, in most cases, be construed as transferring all the rights which are included in the copyright.[95] The position of the assignee or the licensee is strengthened by the possibility of implied licences.[96]

In contrast, most authors' rights systems apply a restrictive construction or a construction in favour of the author. However, such a construction, which is, in essence, aimed at protecting the author, may not apply to contracts between the assignee of copyright and third parties.

For example, under French law, the matter of interpretation of authors' rights transfers is dominated by a general principle of restrictive interpretation in favour of the author.[97] This principle is reinforced by the refusal by courts to admit the possibility of implied licences and by special interpretative provisions in the Intellectual Property Code. For

---

[90] See para. 143.
[91] Art. 28 of the Act provided that, in the absence of any provision to the contrary, the contract concluded by the film producer with the authors of the works used in the film, with the exception of musical works with or without words, implies a transfer to the film producer of the right to exploit the cinematographic work 'by all means and processes, including the subtitling or dubbing of the text, and to make whatever alterations may be essential to such exploitation', provided these alterations are not prejudicial to moral rights.
[92] Art. 21.   [93] Art. 24.
[94] The same is true under the 1911 and 1956 Acts.
[95] *Copinger and Skone James on Copyright*, 13th edn, 1991, para. 5-22; *Cumberland* v. *Planché* (1834) 1 A. & E. 580; *Ex parte Hutchins & Romer* (1879) 4 QBD 483.
[96] See paras. 121 and 156.
[97] The term author is deliberately used here, since the same principle does not apply to further transfers by the assignee (Court of Cassation, 13 October 1993, *Revue Dalloz*, 1994, p. 166).

example, article L.122-7 of the Code provides that an assignment of the performance right does not convey the reproduction right, and *vice versa*; it further specifies that, when a contract conveys in its entirety one of these rights, the scope of the assignment is limited to the exploitation mode provided for in the contract. On the basis of this article, it was held, for example, that the painting of portraits to be placed in the decor of a stage play and the authorisation to exhibit them for that purpose did not include an authorisation to reproduce them in the film of the play.[98] It has also been held that an authorisation to reproduce a cinemato-graphic film in 35mm and 16mm formats does not cover reproduction on magnetic tapes.[99] In a more stringent way, article L.131-3 of the Code states:

> The transfer of the rights of the author is subject to the condition that each of the assigned rights be the subject of a separate reference in the assignment contract and that the exploitation scope of the assigned rights be delimited as to its extent and its intended purpose, as to the territory and as to the duration.

This results in the typical drafting of copyright contracts to include in detail each mode of exploitation of the work.

Based on these provisions, courts usually refuse to give effect to blanket or broad assignments of copyright. This was held, for example, by the French Supreme Court in respect of an assignment clause which stated 'all rights included'.[100] Simply informing the author of each exploitation mode after signature is insufficient to comply with the provisions of article L.131-3.[101]

The French Code also includes specific rules for the construction of broadcasting agreements, with regard to cable retransmission, public communication of broadcasts and satellite transmission.[102]

Similar rules are found in other authors' rights systems. In particular, the principle of narrow construction of grants (or purpose-restricted

---

[98] Paris Court of Appeal, 23 September 1981, RIDA, July 1982, p. 159.

[99] Court of Cassation, 29 June 1982, Bull. Civ., I, No. 244; *Revue Dalloz*, 1983, p. 33, note B. Edelman; *Revue Dalloz*, 1983, Sommaire, p. 99, note Colombet; *Revue Trimestrielle de Droit Commercial*, 1983, p. 435, note Françon.

[100] Court of Cassation, 9 October 1991, *Revue Dalloz*, 1993, Sommaire, p. 91, note Colombet; RIDA, January 1992, p. 292; *La Semaine Juridique*, 1991, IV, p. 429. Held also, that an 'assignment of copyright' which does not include any provision as to the duration and scope of the rights granted is null and void. Court of Cassation, 23 January 2001, Bull. Civ., I, No. 13.

[101] Court of Cassation, 26 January 1994, Bull. Civ., I, No. 34; RIDA, July 1994, p. 309; *La Semaine Juridique*, 1994, IV, p. 846.

[102] Art. L.132-20 of the Intellectual Property Code.

transfers) is expressly included, in various forms, and with different exemptions, in almost all national Acts.[103]

163. Agreements relating to future works

EU Member States have very different standards concerning agreements relating to future works. In the UK and in Ireland such agreements are possible.[104] In contrast, the French Intellectual Property Code provides that 'total transfers' of future works are null and void.[105] The only specific exception to this rule relates to the assignment of performing rights made to authors' societies.[106] However, the prohibition on the assignment of future works is not applied strictly, and some assignments of future works have been upheld, provided they are limited in some manner. It was held, for example, that the prohibition does not apply when it is possible to separate and identify the works in question, as in a series involving the same characters.[107] An option or right of preference should also be admissible, at least when done in compliance with the conditions set down by the Code for publishing contracts (i.e. limited to five new works of a clearly specified kind).[108]

Transfer of rights over future works are also prohibited in Spain,[109] and are limited to ten years in Portugal[110] and in Italy.[111] In Belgium, such assignments can be valid if they are limited in time and if the types of work to which the assignment applies are specified. Similar conditions apply under Greek law.[112]

In Germany, agreements as to future works which are not specified or only referred to by type are valid, but must be in writing.[113] They may be

---

[103] E.g. in Belgium, art. 3 of the Copyright Act (subject to exemptions for works made in the course of employment or on commission in a non-cultural field or in advertising); Spain, art. 43 of the Copyright Act; Portugal, arts. 41 and 43 of the Code; Germany, arts. 31(5) and 37 of the Copyright Act; Austria, art. 33 *et seq.* of the Copyright Act; Switzerland, art. 16(2) of the Copyright Act ('assignment of one right comprised in copyright shall only comprise the assignment of other partial rights when such is agreed'); Italy, e.g. art. 19 of the Copyright Act; Denmark, art. 53 of the Copyright Act; Luxembourg, art. 12 of the Act, Sweden, art. 28 of the Copyright Act; and Greece, art. 15 of the Copyright Act.

[104] Section 91 of the UK 1988 Act; s. 121 of the Irish Copyright and Related Rights Act 2000.

[105] Art. L.131-1.   [106] Art. L.132-18.

[107] Court of Cassation, 6 November 1979, *Revue Dalloz*, 1980, Informations Rapides, p. 207.

[108] Art. L.132-4.   [109] Copyright Act, art. 43.

[110] Copyright Act, art. 48.   [111] Copyright Act, art. 120.

[112] Copyright Act, art. 13(5).   [113] Copyright Act, art. 40.

terminated by either party after a period of five years from the conclusion of the agreement, upon prior notice of six months, if no shorter notice period has been agreed.[114] Such agreements also appear admissible in the Netherlands and in Sweden.

164.   Uses not contemplated at the time of the agreement

Another difference relates to the treatment of uses not contemplated at the time of the agreement. Some Member States grant such uses to the film producer under common law or contractual construction rules. Other Member States have introduced specific provisions in their copyright Acts to exclude such extensions.

In the UK, in the absence of specific provisions in the successive copyright Acts, the question was dealt with by the courts. Most decisions arose on the question as to whether the grant of rights to adapt a work into a film included the right to produce a sound film, even where this technology was not available at the date of the contract. In *Pathé Pictures Ltd* v. *Bancroft*,[115] it was held that a licence to make a version of the work 'in moving picture films' did not authorise the production of a sound film, but that a licence of 'cinematographic rights' would include a sound film. In *Hospital for Sick Children* v. *Walt Disney Productions Inc.*,[116] it was held that the grant, in 1919, of a licence to turn works into 'cinematographic or moving picture films' did not grant the right to produce sound films.[117]

Most authors' rights Acts contain specific provisions on the question, but their content varies. For example, in France, a grant of right to exploit the work under a mode which was unknown at the time of the contract is valid, but the contract must be in writing.[118] In contrast, in Belgium, such assignments are null and void, except for works made in the course of employment or on commission in a non-cultural field or in advertising.[119] They are also null and void in Germany.[120] In Spain, the Copyright Act provides that the transfer of exploitation rights shall not apply to methods of use or means of dissemination that do not exist or are unknown at the time of the transfer.[121] It is not clear whether a clause to

---

[114] *Ibid.*   [115] (1928–35) Mac. CC 403.
[116] [1966] 1 WLR 1055; [1966] 2 All ER 321.
[117] This position was criticised as too narrow in a limited appeal. See *Copinger and Skone James on Copyright*, 14th edn, 1999, paras. 5-52 *et seq.*
[118] Art. L.131-6.   [119] Copyright Act, art. 3.
[120] Copyright Act, art. 31(4). See A. Dietz, in M. B. Nimmer and D. Geller (eds.), *International Copyright Law and Practice*, Matthew Bender, looseleaf, para. 4[2][a], which gives examples from case law.
[121] Copyright Act, art. 43(5).

that effect is admissible. The Italian and Dutch Acts are silent on the question.[122]

165.   Duty to produce/distribute the film

An important aspect of copyright laws in Europe in relation to film is the existence of statutory requirements of actual production or exploitation of the film. No such duty exists under UK and Irish copyright laws. But individual contracts or collective agreements sometimes contain provisions to that effect, which provide either for a reversion of copyright, or for a possibility for the author to buy back his rights, should the film not be produced or released within a set period of time

The situation is different on the continent. Several copyright Acts contain a provision imposing on film producers a duty to produce the film within a certain set time, or according to the practice of the film industry. Thus, a film producer who failed to produce the film would be in breach of his contract with the author; the contract can be rescinded and the rights would revert to the author, with various effects on the chain of rights.

For example, under French law, as a general rule, a transfer of copyright (either in the form of a licence or an assignment) implies for the transferee a duty to exploit the work in accordance with the usual practice of the profession.[123] This general rule for audiovisual contracts is found in article L.132-27 which provides that the producer 'shall ensure for the work an exploitation according to the practice of the profession'. Accordingly, in certain circumstances, a film producer can be held liable, and his contract rescinded, if he does not produce or exploit the work.

French case law provides some applications of this rule. In a case in the Paris Court of Appeal, a television channel acquired the broadcasting rights of a theatre play. On the agreed day for recording, the actors went on strike. The broadcaster refused to record the play at the end of the strike. The court held that the strike did not justify the refusal by the broadcaster unless the latter could provide evidence that it was impossible to record the play in the following days.[124]

The enforceability of a clause to the contrary is doubtful,[125] but such a clause was validated in at least one decision. In a case decided by the

---

[122] For an analysis under Italian law with examples from case law, see M. Fabiani, in M. B. Nimmer and D. Geller (eds.), *International Copyright Law and Practice*, Matthew Bender, looseleaf, para. 4[3][d].
[123] Art. L.131-3(4).
[124] Paris Court of Appeal, 14 May 1990, *Revue Dalloz*, 1990, Sommaire, p. 358, obs. Hassler; also Court of Cassation, 1st Civil Chamber, 3 April 1974, RIDA, July 1974, p. 124.
[125] There are strong legal arguments against such a possibility. Cf. P.-Y. Gautier, *Propriété Littéraire et Artistique*, Puf, 1991, para. 233, p. 390.

Court of Appeal of Versailles, a contract was entered into between a producer and authors for scenarios which included the following clause: 'The producer is, *vis-à-vis* the author, under no obligation to make the film, or to communicate it to the public.'[126] The film was in the event not produced. The court held that there was no breach of contract, as the object of the contract was not the making of a film.[127] In this case, it appears that the fact that the work was still in a preparatory stage allowed the producer, 'according to the practice of the profession', to stop the venture if he was not satisfied with the work or if he could not find the necessary funding. But after completion of the production stage, he is obliged to exploit the work 'according to the practice of the profession'.

Note, however, that the liability of the film producer for non-exploitation (non-release) is not automatic, and that this liability is likely to be different for each exploitation mode. For example, the duty is probably greater for a primary exploitation in cinemas than for a secondary exploitation through video release. Also, the 'practice of the profession' will be considered in the assessment of this liability. Wording similar to the French Act is used in the Belgian[128] and Spanish[129] Acts.

Other countries set more specific time limits for the production or exploitation of the film. In Portugal, the producer must complete production of the film within three years of the date of delivery of the script and of the musical score and must release the finished film within three years of completion. If he fails to meet these deadlines, the author or co-authors have the right to cancel the contract.[130] In Denmark, Finland and Sweden, the author may cancel the agreement if the assignee has not exploited the work within a reasonable time or at the latest five years after the date when the agreement was performed by the author.[131] It is not clear whether a clause to the contrary is enforceable in these countries.

Other countries implement this obligation indirectly by granting to the author a moral right of revocation of his grant.[132]

166.   Other obligations of the film producer

In addition to the above, film producers may also have specific obligations under several authors' rights Acts. This is the case in France, where the

---

[126] 'Le producteur ne prend, vis-à-vis de l'auteur, aucun engagement concernant la réalisation du film, ni sa diffusion.'

[127] Versailles Court of Appeal, 27 January 1988, *Revue Dalloz*, 1988, Sommaire, p. 223, note Hassler.

[128] Copyright Act, arts. 3(1) and (5) and 17.

[129] Copyright Act, art. 48(2).   [130] Copyright Act, art. 136.

[131] Danish Act, art. 54; Finnish Act, art. 40; Swedish Act, art. 40.

[132] But this right is subject to conditions, including prior indemnification of the assignee, which are a strong deterrent against its exercise. See para. 308.

Intellectual Property Code imposes on the film producer an obligation to preserve the elements of the film. The Code also obliges the film producer to provide accounts to the authors.[133] The producer shall produce to the authors, at least once a year, a statement of the receipts for each exploitation mode of the work. Moreover, he shall, at the author's request, provide him with all information necessary to audit these documents, including contracts with third parties.[134] Similar provisions are found in other authors' rights Acts.

167.   Termination of licence/reversionary rights

Notwithstanding the rights of revocation and other rules described above, in all EU Member States the author has the right to rescind an assignment or a licence of copyright if the producer does not fulfil his obligations. This usually results in the reversion of the assigned copyright to the author. But this may also affect the entire chain of title (i.e. subsequent assignments made by the film producer).

168.   Applicable law

The question of the law applicable to copyright contracts is highly complex, and it is not possible here to enter into the details of the private international laws of the EU Member States. We can, however, provide general information which may serve as a starting point for further research.

A first difficulty concerns the scope or reach of the elected or applicable contract law (*lex contractus*). It is usually said that the *lex contractus* governs the obligations of the parties, and not the regime of protection of the work. However, it should be recalled that this distinction is not always clear, and that national courts may have different views on the characterisation of certain rules or questions.[135]

Subject to this, the matter is regulated at the European level by the Rome Convention of 19 June 1980 on the law applicable to contractual obligations, signed by the Member States of the European Community and ratified by new members, which came into force on 1 April 1991. This Convention is designed to eliminate differences between national conflict rules in relation to contractual obligations which impede the free movement of persons, goods, services and capital. Its scope covers copyright contracts.

---

[133] Arts. L.132-24 and L.132-28.   [134] Art. L.132-28.
[135] This could be the case, for example, regarding the question of transferability of copyright.

Article 3 of the Convention enshrines the principle of party autonomy. Article 3(1) provides:

A contract shall be governed by the law chosen by the parties. The choice must be express or demonstrated with reasonable certainty by the terms of the contract or the circumstances of the case. By their choice the parties can select the law applicable to the whole or a part only of the contract.

It is important to note that the chosen law can be the law of a non-EU Member State. It is relatively safe to assume that such a choice would be validated in most EU countries, provided that the contract presents an international element related to the chosen law, and subject to the application of mandatory rules, as described below.

In the absence of a choice of law clause, article 4(1) of the Convention provides that the contract shall be governed by the law of the country 'with which it possesses the closest links'. Article 4(2) further presumes that 'the contract possesses the closest links with the country where the party that is to furnish the characteristic service had his habitual place of residence or, in the case of a firm, association, legal person, his central administration at the time of conclusion of the contract'. However, this presumption may be set aside 'where the overall circumstances show that the contract possesses closest links with another country'.[136]

The application of this concept of 'characteristic service' to copyright contracts and, more specifically, to film production contracts has raised controversies in Europe, with commentators divided between the user or the copyright holder as the person providing such services.[137]

In addition, account must be taken of the 'mandatory rules' referred to in article 3(3) of the Rome Convention, which provides:

The fact that the parties have chosen a foreign law, whether or not accompanied by the choice of a foreign tribunal, shall not, where all the other elements relevant to the situation at the time of the choice are connected with one country only, prejudice the application of rules of the law of that country which cannot be derogated from by contract, hereinafter called 'mandatory rules'.

The problem is that Member States may have different views as to the content of this notion, applied to copyright. In most countries of the authors' rights tradition, rules on moral rights would be considered as mandatory rules under the Convention. As a consequence, domestic judges may refuse to enforce waivers of moral rights insofar as they are prohibited under domestic law. This is certainly true in France, and is probably also

[136] Art. 4(5).
[137] See e.g. André Lucas, in 'Private International Law Aspects of the Protection of Works and Objects of Related Rights Transmitter Through Digital Networks', WIPO Report (GCPIC/1), 25 November 1998.

true in those Member States in which moral rights are unwaivable.[138] But some rules on copyright transfers or on equitable remuneration may well also be considered in certain Member States as 'mandatory rules'.

SECTION II

Authorial rights (equitable remuneration)

169.   The question of 'authorial rights'

As mentioned above, when it comes to economic rights, a major difference between copyright and *droit d'auteur* systems lies in the *statutory reallocation of some of the benefits from the exploitation of the work to the artistic creators.* In *droit d'auteur* countries, the entitlement of the film producer is often qualified in several ways, the most common qualification being the express reservation to the authors of a statutory right to obtain an additional remuneration, under the form of a 'statutory royalty right' (France, Belgium, Spain and Greece), a 'bestseller clause' (Germany), or some type of 'equitable' remuneration (Netherlands, Italy and Austria). These elements correspond to what representatives of authors sometimes call 'authorial rights' or 'rights to equitable remuneration', i.e. those *monetary interests, apart from the salary or the initial remuneration, which are paid to authors in compensation for the exploitation of the copyrighted work.*[139]

170.   Equitable remuneration at the international and regional levels

The international agreements in the field of copyright do not provide for mandatory rights to equitable remuneration for film authors. One exception is the right to 'equitable remuneration' provided in the Berne Convention when the non-voluntary licences for broadcasting permitted under article 11*bis*(2) are implemented.[140]

In contrast, several equitable remuneration schemes have been established at Community level. If we limit our discussion to those applicable

---

[138] See para. 311.
[139] Note that for union representatives the recognition of 'authorial rights' does not necessarily imply copyright entitlement. Authorial rights can be granted through industry agreements or through a statutory right to 'equitable remuneration', independently of the initial entitlement to copyright to the producer. They remain, however, closely associated with the status of 'author'.
[140] But the Convention does not define the term 'equitable remuneration'.

to film works,[141] the most important are established by the Rental and Lending Directive and the Satellite and Cable Retransmission Directive. The Rental and Lending Directive of 19 November 1992 requires the introduction of an unwaivable right to 'equitable remuneration' for authors and performers in case of transfer of their rental right,[142] the administration of which may be entrusted to collecting societies.[143] In the view of the Commission, 'equitable remuneration' does not necessarily imply a royalty interest, remuneration in the form of residuals or a supplementary payment where the work is successful. This view is reinforced by recital 16, which states that 'equitable remuneration may be paid on the basis of one or several payments at any time on or after the conclusion of the contracts'. A flat fee could therefore constitute such equitable remuneration. However, in their commentary on the Directive, Reinbothe and von Lewinski state that:

the amount . . . must always meet the requirement . . . that the remuneration itself has to be 'equitable' in any event. In addition, the flat-rate payment must relate to rental only and may not include non-specific payments for other kinds of exploitation. Accordingly, one payment on conclusion of the contract or a reasonable time after its conclusion, or several payments the first of which is made on conclusion of the contract or a reasonable time thereafter, may possibly, but will not necessarily, fulfil the criterion of 'equitable remuneration'.[144]

Recital 17 provides that the equitable remuneration must take account of the importance of the contribution to the film by the authors and performers concerned. In addition, if the exclusive public lending right is not implemented by Member States, they must at least introduce a 'remuneration', without further specification, for film authors.[145] This remuneration could take the form of a lump sum.

The Satellite and Cable Retransmission Directive of 27 September 1993 does not specifically provide for a right to equitable remuneration. However, its article 9 provides that Member States shall ensure that the right of copyright owners and holders of related rights to grant or refuse

---

[141] And thus exclude equitable remuneration for broadcasting or communication to the public of phonograms (Rental Directive, art. 8).

[142] Art. 4.   [143] Art. 4(3).

[144] Reinbothe and von Lewinski, *The EC Directive on Rental and Lending Rights and on Piracy*, Sweet & Maxwell, 1993, pp. 70–1. In Spain, the Law of 30 December 1994 implementing the Directive defines equitable remuneration as 'part of the income obtained from the rental of the work', and states that the remuneration must be administered through collecting societies. See J. J. Garcia and C. Pina, 'Rental Rights and Lending Rights in Spain' (1995) 6 *Entertainment Law Review* 292. A similar scheme was set up in Germany by the Act of 23 June 1995: see S. von Lewinski, 'The Implementation of the EC Rental and Duration Directives in Germany' (1995) 55 *Copyright World* 30.

[145] Art. 5(2).

authorisation to a cable operator for a cable retransmission may be exercised only through a collecting society.[146] In doing so, it secures some form of equitable remuneration scheme to authors and rightholders for cable retransmission of film works.

The Directive on Copyright and Related Rights in the Information Society of 22 May 2001 allows Member States to implement exceptions or limitations on the reproduction right, but in relation to several exemptions this implementation is subject to the payment of 'fair compensation' to the rightholders.[147] Although some indication as to what constitutes fair compensation is given in recital 35 of the Directive,[148] important differences with respect to private copy schemes are likely to remain between Member States of the European Union.

171. Equitable remuneration in domestic laws

It is difficult to present a catalogue of the various rights to 'equitable remuneration' granted to authors and rightholders within the European Union, as a result of statutory or collective management schemes. The main forms of equitable remuneration offered by one or more Member States could be classified under the following categories.

1. Theatrical exhibition. In general, there is no specific right to equitable remuneration for the theatrical exhibition of film works. However, broadly defined statutory rights to equitable remuneration, when implemented, would cover this form of exploitation. This equitable remuneration could be paid by the film producer, or through collecting societies. However, very few collecting societies license the theatrical exhibition of films. In France, for example, only musical composers would benefit from the collection made by the performing rights society, SACEM, from theatres. The collecting societies for authors of cinematographic films, SACD, does not license theatres. Accordingly, the equitable remuneration of authors for this form of exploitation is provided for in the film production agreement and is paid by the

---

[146] See para. 189.   [147] See paras. 211 and 226.

[148] 'In certain cases of exceptions or limitations, rightholders should receive fair compensation to compensate them adequately for the use made of their protected works or other subject-matter. When determining the form, detailed arrangements and possible level of such fair compensation, account should be taken of the particular circumstances of each case. When evaluating these circumstances, a valuable criterion would be the possible harm to the rightholders resulting from the act in question. In cases where rightholders have already received payment in some other form, for instance as part of a licence fee, no specific or separate payment may be due. The level of fair compensation should take full account of the degree of use of technological protection measures referred to in this Directive. In certain situations where the prejudice to the rightholder would be minimal, no obligation for payment may arise.'

film producer.[149] This scheme is repeated in several Member States implementing a general right to equitable remuneration.

2. Video reproduction. In several Member States, a remuneration for video reproduction is paid to authors and rightholders by collecting societies handling their mechanical reproduction rights.[150]

3. Video rental. The equitable remuneration for rental has been enshrined at the European level by the Rental Directive. However, due to the lack of precision of the Directive, it was implemented in different ways by the Member States. In most cases, however, the remuneration is handled by collecting societies.

4. Video lending. Films are usually excluded from the public lending schemes (and from lending altogether). They may, however, be covered by the lending schemes established in some countries.[151]

5. Video sales. This form of remuneration is usually not handled by collecting societies. It may be provided for in individual contracts, especially when a broadly defined statutory right of remuneration applies.[152]

6. Television broadcasting. In several Member States, this form of remuneration is paid by collecting societies operating in a similar way to performing rights societies.[153]

7. Cable retransmission. This remuneration is handled by collecting societies as a result of the Satellite and Cable Retransmission Directive. It is paid by cable operators for the cable retransmission of terrestrial broadcasts.

8. Public performance. Some collecting societies license the public performance of broadcasts or videotapes in business premises and other institutions.

9. Private copying. The mechanism of the private copy levy implemented in several Member States is described in Chapter 7 below.[154] It is conceived as a specific right, either in the form of an exclusive right, or resulting from a levy or tax imposed on the manufacturer or importer of blank videotapes. In the European Union, this levy is collected by collecting societies, usually specifically created for this purpose.

10. Educational use. So far, only a few countries have established specific schemes for such uses. They are imposed on universities, schools and other educational establishments for the copying of broadcasts and audiovisual works, and are managed by collecting societies.[155]

---

[149] See para. 173.

[150] E.g. the French SDRM, which administers mechanical rights due for reproductions of works in the repertoires of SACEM (musical works), SACD (dramatic and cinematographic works) and SCAM (multimedia and television).

[151] See para. 198.   [152] See para. 173 (French practice).   [153] *Ibid.*

[154] See paras. 226 *et seq.*   [155] E.g. Avu-kopier in Denmark.

11. Digital rights. Certain collecting societies have extended their licensing schemes to digital and on-line exploitation of works or have created specific licensing bodies or 'one-stop clearance shops' for this purpose.[156]

The following discussion is limited to a description of the statutory rights to equitable remuneration applicable to film works which may be claimed by film authors or authors of pre-existing works. The regime of film soundtracks and musical works, and the question of remuneration for lending or private copying, will not be discussed here, but are instead studied in Chapters 6 and 7 below.[157] Also, it would be impossible to detail here the operation of licensing bodies in the field of film copyright within the Union. However, a brief description of the main collecting societies in the area of film copyright will be given.[158]

172.   Equitable remuneration in the UK and Ireland

In the process of implementation of the Rental and Term Directives, directors' and screenwriters' representatives in the UK lobbied for a recognition of authorial rights in the form of a more general right to equitable remuneration. However, the 'authorial rights provisions' of the directives were strongly opposed by UK film producers, who feared that giving a copyright interest to directors or other artistic personnel would lead to the siphoning off of the revenues before net profits are reached, and discourage investment in the European film industry.[159]

As a result, the UK, followed by Ireland, implemented only the minimum level of authorial rights required under the copyright directives, i.e. the right of remuneration for the rental of the film. Remuneration is otherwise left for the parties to decide and the courts have no power to re-evaluate or lower the agreed remuneration (subject to generally applicable contractual doctrines).

In the UK, the right to equitable remuneration for the rental of the film was introduced by the Copyright and Related Rights Regulations 1996 in the new section 93B of the 1988 Act. Under the scheme, the right to equitable remuneration belongs to the author of a literary, dramatic,

---

[156] For example the French SESAM, which administers in this respect the use of repertoires managed by ADAGP (artistic works), SACD (dramatic and cinematographic works), SACEM (musical works) and SCAM (multimedia and television).

[157] See paras. 196 et seq. and 226 et seq.   [158] See para. 175.

[159] See J. Reinbothe and S. von Lewinski, *The EC Directive on Rental and Lending Rights and on Piracy*, Sweet & Maxwell, 1993, p. 18. See also R. Snoddy, 'Copyright Plans Alarm Film World', *Financial Times*, 12 May 1992 (on equitable remuneration); R. Snoddy, 'Copyright Plan Sparks Concern', *Financial Times*, 7 November 1992; and the 'Memorandum Submitted by Polygram to the National Heritage Committee', in 'The British Film Industry', House of Commons, National Heritage Committee, Session 1994–5, HC 57-I; 57-II; 57-III; 57-i to ix; and 653-i and ii, HMSO, London, p. 158.

musical or artistic work, and to the principal director of a film, and applies whenever the latter have transferred their rental right concerning a film to the film producer.[160] The right may not be assigned except to a collecting society for the purpose of enabling the society to enforce the right on his behalf. The right is, however, transmissible by testamentary disposition or by operation of law as personal or moveable property; and it may be assigned or further transmitted by any person into whose hands it passes.[161] An agreement is of no effect in so far as it purports to exclude or restrict the right to equitable remuneration for rental.[162]

The equitable remuneration is payable by the person for the time being entitled to the rental right, that is, the person to whom the right was transferred or any successor in title.[163] The amount of this equitable remuneration is agreed by or on behalf of the persons by and to whom it is payable.[164] It may be fixed or varied by the Copyright Tribunal upon application by the person to or by whom the remuneration is payable.[165] However, except with the special leave of the Tribunal, no application to vary the amount may be made within twelve months from the date of a previous determination. Agreements purporting to prevent a challenge to the amount of equitable remuneration or to restrict the powers of the Copyright Tribunal are of no effect.[166]

The Act further provides that, on such an application, the Tribunal shall consider the matter and make such order as to the method of calculating and paying the equitable remuneration as it may determine to be reasonable in the circumstances, taking into account the importance of the contribution of the author to the film.[167] More importantly, section 93B(4) provides that the remuneration shall not be considered inequitable merely because it was paid by way of a single payment or at the time of the transfer of the rental right.

The right of equitable remuneration for rental is subject to similar provisions in Ireland.[168]

173.   The law and practice in France

French law is probably one of the regimes which grant film authors the most complete and favourable set of statutory authorial rights. These rights are strictly enforced by the courts, and any attempts by the

---

[160] Section 93B(1). Under s. 93B(6), references in s. 93B to the transfer of rental right by one person to another include any arrangement having that effect, whether made by them directly or through intermediaries.
[161] Section 93B(2).   [162] Section 93B(5).   [163] Section 93B(3).
[164] Section 93B(4).   [165] Section 93C(1) and (2).   [166] Section 93C(5).
[167] Section 93C(3).   [168] Sections 125 and 126.

producers to reduce the author's rights to remuneration may result in the rescission of the production agreement. The heart of the system is a statutory royalty right. A statutory royalty right is first granted to all authors under article L.131-3 in relation to adaptations of their works. Article L.131-3 provides:

> The assignee shall undertake by such contract to endeavour to exploit the assigned right in accordance with trade practice and to pay to the author, in the event of adaptation, a remuneration that is proportional to the revenue obtained.

But this right is extended to all assignments under article L.131-4:

> Assignment by the author of the rights in his work may be total or partial. Assignment shall comprise a proportional participation by the author in the revenue from sale or exploitation of the work.

It is also specified in the case of audiovisual production contracts under article L.132-25:

> where the public pays a price to receive communication of a given, individually identifiable audiovisual work, remuneration shall be proportional to such price, subject to any decreasing tariffs afforded by the distributor to the operator; the remuneration shall be paid to the authors by the producer.[169]

Case law consistently holds that the proportional remuneration of the author must be calculated on the price paid by the public ex-VAT, and regardless of any intermediation of further assignees or licensees.[170] This applies, in the case of audiovisual works, to the price paid on videotapes.[171] Non-compliance with these conditions may lead to rescission of the entire agreement.[172] In one case,[173] a theatrical film production agreement was rescinded because the remuneration of the author for exploitation in theatres was stipulated as follows:

> remuneration of the authors will consist in a percentage of 0.5% of the receipts made from entries, less VAT and less the contribution paid to the National Centre of Cinematography.

For the Tribunal of Paris, the mere deduction of the contribution to the National Centre of Cinematography, which is payable by the film producer, sufficed to justify the annulment of the clause and, by way of consequence, rescission of the contract.

---

[169] WIPO translation.
[170] Court of Cassation, 9 October 1984, Bull. Civ., No. 252, *Revue Dalloz*, 1985, Informations Rapides, p. 316, obs. Colombet; RIDA, July 1985, p. 144.
[171] Court of Cassation, 16 July 1998, *Revue Dalloz Affaires*, 1998, p. 1911.
[172] Paris Court of Appeal, 9 October 1995, RIDA, 1996, p. 311.
[173] Tribunal of First Instance of Paris, *Le Friant* v. *MKD/Renn*, 9 February 1999, unreported.

Article L.131-4 of the French Code provides for exemptions to the right to proportional remuneration, allowing the author's remuneration to be calculated as a lump sum. Some exemptions are general, and may be applicable to various contracts entered into in the context of film production. The author may be paid a lump sum:

1. when the basis for calculating the proportional participation cannot be practically determined; this is the case for example when the communication to the public is free, as in the case of a free distribution of advertising brochures,[174] or for 'collective works';[175]
2. when the means of supervising the uses in question are lacking;
3. when the cost of the calculation and supervising operations would be out of proportion to the expected results; and
4. when the nature or conditions of exploitation make application of the rule of proportional remuneration impossible, either because the author's contribution does not constitute one of the essential elements of the intellectual creation of the work or because the use of the work is only of an accessory nature in relation to the subject-matter exploited. The decor of a film would be considered accessory under this provision.

In addition, under article L.132-6 of the Code, a lump sum remuneration may also be paid for the assignment of rights by or to a person or enterprise established abroad. The parties to a contract providing for royalties may also convert, at the author's request, the royalties into a lump sum payable annually.[176]

However, some protection is also granted to authors falling within one of these exceptions. Article L.131-5 of the Code provides that, where the work has been lawfully assigned for a lump sum remuneration, the author may ask for a review of the agreed price if he suffers a loss of more than seven-twelfths of the remuneration as a result of a burdensome contract or of an insufficient advance estimate of the proceeds of the work. The burdensome contract must be assessed taking into account the overall exploitation by the assignee.

Note that under French law the remuneration of the author may consist solely of the statutory royalty right. The law does not fix the percentages due to the author, which can be freely decided by the parties. The percentage should not, however, be fixed at such a low level that it has no practical significance (for example, 0.1 per cent might be too low to be acceptable for one of the main authors). In practice, film authors are paid a

---

[174] Tribunal of First Instance of Paris, 16 December 1980, RIDA, July 1981, p. 223.
[175] Tribunal of First Instance of Paris, 4 January 1971, RIDA, October 1971, p. 146, note Desbois. On the concept of collective works, see paras. 137 and 147.
[176] Art. L.131-4.

fixed remuneration in advance of their proportional remuneration, which in most cases will constitute their only remuneration.

It is also important to observe that, in practice, the proportional remuneration for certain modes of exploitation of the work is paid through the film authors' societies, either SACD or SCAM as the case may be. This concerns mainly television broadcasting and mechanical reproduction. In addition, SACEM collects remuneration for musical composers directly from cinemas. As a consequence, the payment of the proportional remuneration is divided as follows in a typical film production contract entered into with a film author.

Theatrical commercial exploitation in France

The author is paid by the film producer a percentage on the ex-VAT price of the ticket paid by the public. For musical works, this remuneration is collected and paid directly by SACEM.

Theatrical commercial exploitation outside France

The above-described principle is difficult to apply in the context of international co-productions, especially in relation to countries which do not implement royalty rights for film authors. In such a case, SACD applies the following principles, which are often followed by producers:

First, if the co-production agreement carries the payment of fees by the foreign co-producers ('distribution territories'), the proportional remuneration is based on the exploitation in France and on the sums paid by the foreign producer to the French producer on the exploitation abroad.

Secondly, for co-productions in which the foreign co-producers hold 100 per cent of the rights in certain territories without any payment to the French producer ('home territories'), SACD tries to impose a clause integrating the investment of the foreign co-producer into the definition of net receipts. This clause is usually drafted as follows:

If the film is produced under international co-production, the amount of the participation of the foreign producer and all sums which would be paid in addition to the producer will be considered as Net Receipts for the countries in which the exploitation rights belong exclusively to the foreign co-producer. As a consequence, the receipts from exploitation in said territories and allocated to the foreign co-producer will not be accounted for the purpose of this agreement

If this clause is not accepted, SACD asks the French co-producer to pay a proportional remuneration based on information on the exploitation of the film abroad (for example, *Variety* figures).

This policy corresponds to the situation in which SACD negotiates the production contract on behalf of the film author.[177] The model contract from the USPA, a film producers' association, proposes a different clause, drafted as follows:[178]

If the work is produced in international co-production, with users that do not have agreements with authors' societies, in order to take account of the fact that no receipts will appear for the exploitation of the work in the countries reserved by the co-producer in the co-production agreement, the additional remuneration of the author will consist of a percentage applied to the average commercial value of an equivalent programme in each of the concerned countries.

Television

The contract provides that the author is paid his proportional remuneration through SACD/SCAM, as the case may be, in countries in which those societies can collect directly or in which they have entered into reciprocal arrangements with their counterparts. For other countries, the author is paid by the producer a percentage of the receipts from television distribution.

Video distribution

The author is paid by the film producer a percentage on the public price ex VAT. Very often, contracts provide for an alternative remuneration based on net receipts if remuneration based on the public price is not practicable. The author is also paid a share of the collection made by the society dealing with mechanical reproduction rights.

Merchandising

A percentage of gross receipts from this form of exploitation is paid by the producer.

174.   Authorial rights in other authors' rights countries

The provisions regarding the proportional remuneration and its exceptions in the Spanish Act are similar to those of the French Act.[179]

---

[177] Note that contracts which are not negotiated by SACD are controlled when the member author files the same with SACD in order to claim his or her right to remuneration, and can be rejected by the latter in the absence of the above-mentioned clauses.

[178] November 1996 edition.

[179] Copyright Act, art. 46. A. and G. Bercovitz, in M. B. Nimmer and D. Geller (eds.), *International Copyright Law and Practice*, Matthew Bender, looseleaf, para. 4[3][a] report

However, the right of review in the case of remuneration for a lump sum is drafted in broader terms.[180] The right to proportional remuneration is also granted on a broad basis in Greece.[181]

The Belgian Copyright Act appears less favourable to film authors that its French counterpart, as it includes broader possibilities to stipulate a lump sum remuneration. Under article 17 of the Act, the assignee of the right of audiovisual adaptation of an existing work shall pay to the author, unless otherwise provided, a remuneration proportional to the gross revenue from the exploitation of the work. Article 19 further states that, except for audiovisual works in the non-cultural field or in advertising, authors shall be entitled to a separate remuneration for each mode of exploitation which, unless otherwise provided, shall be proportional to the gross revenue obtained from the exploitation.

As mentioned above, in Germany, the Copyright Act does not grant to authors a statutory right to proportional remuneration for exploitation of the work. Instead, authors benefit from a 'bestseller clause' under which they can claim additional remuneration where the exploitation of their work was successful. Under article 36 of the Act, when the initial price paid becomes grossly insignificant to the income from the use of the work, the author's contractor shall be required, on the demand of the author, to modify the agreement in order to secure for the author a more equitable share of the income. Such a claim is unwaivable, but is subject to limitations in time.[182] A similar system exists in Portugal.[183]

In Italy, statutory authorial rights take the form of an unwaivable right to equitable remuneration payable for each mode of exploitation of the work. Apparently, this remuneration does not have to be a royalty right, and production agreements may provide for lump sum payments or residuals.[184]

Subject to the limited rights of remuneration derived from the EC directives, the Dutch, Swedish and Danish Acts do not include specific provisions on equitable remuneration, or any bestseller clause.

---

that the proportionate share is usually calculated on the public price of copies of a work or entrance tickets to a performance, after deducting VAT.

[180] Copyright Act, art. 47.

[181] Copyright Act, art. 32, with some exemptions similar to the French ones. G. Koumantos, in M. B. Nimmer and D. Geller (eds.), *International Copyright Law and Practice*, Matthew Bender, looseleaf, para. 4[3][a][ii] reports that audiovisual authors are to receive proportional remuneration for each mode of exploitation of the film.

[182] The author is barred from claiming the right two years after he has knowledge of the circumstances which justify the claim, or after ten years irrespective of such knowledge.

[183] Copyright Act, art. 49(1).

[184] See M. Fabiani, in M. B. Nimmer and D. Geller (eds.), *International Copyright Law and Practice*, Matthew Bender, looseleaf, para. 4[3][a][i].

175.   Collective licensing of film rights in Europe[185]

The collective management of rights is rapidly developing within the European Union, notably under the pressure of the European harmonisation of copyright law.[186] A specific feature of these societies in continental Europe is that their repertoire is not limited to musical works, as is traditionally the case in copyright countries. Authors of audiovisual works and of pre-existing works often have their own societies, which operate like performing rights societies.[187] Sometimes, their works are included in the repertoire of the main societies, which administer rights in all copyright works.[188] However, the status, structure, size and methods of licensing and distribution of these societies vary from one Member State to another.

Also, in contrast to the situation regarding musical works, the network of reciprocal arrangements is less developed for audiovisual authors.[189] This is mainly due to disparities in the lists of co-authors of audiovisual works, and to the existence of union agreements dealing with copyright and royalty issues in certain countries.

Community law has important consequences for the operation of these societies. For example, the judgment of the European Court of Justice of 20 October 1993 in the *Phil Collins* case[190] confirmed that the general principle of non-discrimination on the grounds of nationality derived from the EC Treaty[191] prohibits discrimination between EU nationals with regard to membership, thus opening the way to claims from foreign film authors in various countries.

But collecting societies are also subject to Community competition law rules, and especially to article 81 of the EC Treaty, which prohibits anti-competitive agreements and concerted practices, and to article 82 on abuse of a dominant position.[192] For example, the European

---

185 See e.g. 'La Gestion collective des droit d'auteur et des droits voisins', Report to the French Senate (Service des affaires européennes du Sénat, étude de législation comparée), November 1997.

186 See e.g. the examples of the UK and Ireland.

187 E.g. if we restrict ourselves to the societies for film authors (and to the exclusion of specific societies dedicated to private copy or other forms of specific remuneration, which are often affiliates of the main existing societies), in France: SACD (dramatic and cinematographic works) and SCAM (multimedia and television); in Germany: VFF, VGF, Bild-Kunst, GWFF and Güfa (the latter apparently specialising in erotic and pornographic movies).

188 E.g. SIAE in Italy or SGAE in Spain.

189 In this respect, composers of film music, whether they are considered as co-authors of the film or not, benefit from the highly integrated network of performing rights societies.

190 Joined Cases C-92/92 and C-326/92, *Collins* v. *Imtrat Handelsgesellschaft mbH* [1993] ECR I-5145; [1993] 3 CMLR 773; [1994] EMLR 108; [1994] FSR 166, ECJ.

191 Art. 12 (formerly art. 7). See para. 350.

192 See also para. 214.

Court of Justice, in a case involving the validity of a contract between two authors and the Belgian collecting society SABAM under article 82, stated that 'a compulsory assignment of all copyrights, both present and future, no distinction being drawn between the different generally accepted types of exploitation, may appear an unfair condition, especially if such assignment is required for an extended period after the member's withdrawal'.[193] Also, the European Court of Justice stated that concerted action by national copyright-management societies (notably through reciprocal arrangements) with the effect of systematically refusing to grant direct access to their repertoires to foreign users must be regarded as amounting to a restrictive concerted practice under article 81.[194] The question of the level of fees proposed by these societies was also examined by the Commission and the Court of Justice.

In its Follow-Up to the Green Paper on copyright and related rights in the information society of 1996,[195] the Commission concluded that there are already indications 'for the need to define, both under the Single Market and the competition rules of the EC Treaty, at Community level the rights and obligations of collecting societies in particular with respect to the methods of collection, to the calculation of tariffs, to the supervision mechanisms, and to the application of the rules on competition to collecting societies and collective management'.[196] Hearings on collective management of copyright and related rights were held before the Commission in November 2000. As mentioned above, the Commission appears to consider that a certain degree of control is appropriate for collective management, and might initiate legislative action in this field in 2002.

[193] Case 127/73, *BRT* v. *SABAM* [1974] ECR 51, ECJ.
[194] Case 395/87, *Ministère Public* v. *Tournier* [1989] ECR 2521; [1991] 4 CMLR 248; [1991] FSR 465, ECJ.
[195] Brussels, 20 November 1996, COM (96) 586 final.
[196] See also recital 17 of the Directive on Copyright and Related Rights in the Information Society: 'It is necessary, especially in the light of the requirements arising out of the digital environment, to ensure that collecting societies achieve a higher level of rationalisation and transparency with regard to compliance with competition rules.'

6 Exclusive rights

176. Introduction

Subject to limited exceptions, the scope of copyright protection granted to audiovisual works in European Union Member States always equated the standard of protection of the main classes of copyright works. However, films, like musical works, were particularly affected by major technological developments in the entertainment and communication industries, which forced adaptations of the existing set of rights and limitations. The development of broadcasting in the 1930s necessitated a reconsideration of the scope of the performing right (*droit de représentation*). This resulted either in a wide construction of this right encompassing broadcasting (under a new 'right of communication to the public') or in the introduction of a specific broadcasting right. The same process applied in relation to cable and satellite distribution, which prompted adjustments in the protection of film works. The diffusion of video technology in the 1970s generated an important debate concerning rental[1] and private copying[2] of films. As a result, several countries introduced a rental right for 'films' and reassessed the scope of their private copy exemptions (in particular, in relation to recording for time-shifting).

---

[1] The question was first raised in relation to sound recordings. See also, in the UK, *CBS Inc.* v. *Ames Records & Tapes Ltd* [1982] Ch 91; [1981] 2 WLR 973; [1981] 2 All ER 812; [1981] RPC 407 (the proprietor of a record lending library was held not to be 'authorising' any infringement of copyright by borrowers).

[2] See the much publicised US case of *Sony Corporation of America* v. *Universal City Studios Inc.*, 104 S.Ct 774 (1984), where, in an action brought by film producers to prevent Sony from selling videotape recorders, the Supreme Court decided that recording for time-shifting purpose was 'fair use' under the 1976 Act. See J. Wasko, *Hollywood in the Information Age*, Polity Press, 1994, pp. 126–9. It was echoed in the UK by *Amstrad Consumer Electronics plc* v. *BPI* [1986] FSR 159, CA, affirming [1986] ECC 531; *CBS Songs Ltd* v. *Amstrad Consumer Electronics plc* [1988] AC 1013; [1988] 2 WLR 1191; [1988] 2 All ER 484; [1988] 2 FTLR 168, HL, affirming [1987] 3 WLR 144, in which the Court of Appeal and the House of Lords held that Amstrad was not authorising infringement by the release of twin-deck tape recorders enabling users to make duplicate recordings. See Chapter 7 below.

With the advent of digital technology, there is now fear in the industry that the rights granted to film producers be not adapted to new modes of exploitation of films, like *video-on-demand* or *on-line distribution* of films.

Motion picture piracy has been on the rise since the advent of home videotape recorders in the early 1970s made copyright cheap and easy. Unfortunately, copyright piracy on the Internet threatens to cause far worse damage to the audiovisual industry. Currently, the audiovisual industry is protected by one simple factor – the amount of bytes needed for a full-length motion picture. With the increased availability of 'Broadband' Internet access allowing for faster downloads and the companion development of higher and better levels of compression, the motion picture industry is rapidly approaching the Internet piracy problem confronting the software, video game and music industries.[3]

Accordingly, the definition of the exclusive rights and their exceptions has become a key issue in the off-line and on-line digital environment. As a result of the long-awaited EC Directive on Copyright and Related Rights in the Information Society of 22 May 2001, the solutions of EU Member States in this respect will soon be harmonised to a high level of protection.

The discussion below evaluates the content of the exclusive rights granted to film-makers in the European Union with regard to the main modes of exploitation of films. First, however, some preliminary remarks should be made on the definition of the exclusive rights in domestic laws.

177.   The definition of exclusive rights under national laws

Below, the expression 'exclusive rights' is used to describe the principal rights of copyright owners. Some copyright Acts, however, do not use this terminology. In the UK and in Ireland, the property right of copyright owners is traditionally defined in the copyright Acts as the right to oppose certain 'infringing acts'. Accordingly, most copyright books address the various 'infringing acts' rather than the corresponding 'exclusive rights'. As outlined, this merely represents a different way of expressing the same idea.[4]

Beyond this question of terminology, the way exclusive rights are defined in the domestic copyright Acts varies to a large extent from one Member State to another. In this respect, a distinction can be made between those Member States which implemented a detailed, media-specific

---

[3] T. Cohen, 'Protecting Films On-Line', paper prepared for the MPAA and the IIPA International Conference on Electronic Commerce and Intellectual Property, Geneva, 14–16 September 1999, WIPO/EC/CONF/99/SPK/18-C.

[4] *Copinger and Skone James on Copyright*, 14th edn, 1999, para. 7-01.

list of rights, and those which opted for a brief list of rights, organised around two or three principal rights. This distinction does not correspond to the distinction between copyright and authors' rights systems.

Most Member States adopt a list of exclusive rights organised around four principal rights, i.e. a right of reproduction, a right of communication to the public (which may be broken down into a right of public performance and a broadcasting right), a right of distribution (the scope of which may vary, but generally includes at least a rental right for certain classes of works) and a right of adaptation. The list of exclusive rights may also be broken down to a higher level of detail, for example in Germany,[5] Greece[6] and Italy.[7]

Additional principal rights may also be granted to copyright owners, which are often restricted to specific classes of copyright works, such as the *droit de suite*, the right of public display of artistic works or the right of access to copies of the work; these are either not applicable or are of limited relevance to audiovisual works; rights of remuneration are also sometimes conceived as distinct economic rights.[8]

In this first group of countries, the UK shows some peculiarities in relation to films. Under the present law in the UK, and in relation to all descriptions of work, the copyright owner has the exclusive right: (a) to copy the work;[9] (b) to issue copies of the work to the public;[10] (c) to perform, show or play the work in public;[11] and (d) to broadcast or include the work in a cable programme service.[12] However, the making of an adaptation of the work[13] is an act restricted by the copyright in literary,

---

[5] In Germany, the 1965 Act distinguishes between the right to exploit the work in material form, and the right to communicate the work to the public in non-material form (right of communication to the public) (s. 15). However, the right to exploit the work in material form encompasses the right of reproduction (s. 16), the right of distribution (s. 17) and the right of exhibition (s. 18), which are separately defined. The right of communication to the public includes the right of recitation, performance and presentation (s. 19), the right of broadcasting (s. 20), the right of communication by means of video or audio recordings (s. 21) and the right of communication of broadcasts (s. 22).

[6] In Greece, art. 3 of the 1993 Copyright Act distinguishes the right to permit or prohibit: (a) the fixation and reproduction of the work by any means, such as mechanical, photochemical or electronic means; (b) the translation of the work; (c) the arrangement, adaptation or other alteration of the work; (d) the distribution of the original or copies of the work; (e) the communication of the work to the public; (f) the public performance of the work; (g) the broadcasting or rebroadcasting of the work to the public and (h) the import of copies of the work.

[7] In Italy, the copyright owner is granted exclusive rights of: (a) reproduction (s. 13); (b) transcription (s. 14); (c) public performance or recitation (s. 15); (d) diffusion (including broadcasting and cable distribution) (s. 16); (e) distribution (s. 17); (f) translation (s. 18); and (g) rental (s. 18*bis*).

[8] German copyright law treats some of these rights as distinct from the economic and moral rights. See Dietz, in M. B. Nimmer and D. Geller (eds.), *International Copyright Law and Practice*, Matthew Bender, looseleaf, para. 8[1][b][v].

[9] Section 17.   [10] Section 18.   [11] Section 19.   [12] Section 20.   [13] Section 21.

dramatic, musical and artistic works only.[14] In other words, there is no adaptation rights in 'films' (as distinct from their underlying works). The scheme is similar in Ireland, under the Copyright Act 1963 and the Copyright and Related Rights Act 2000.

In contrast to this first group of countries, the set of economic rights granted to copyright owners in France, Belgium and the Netherlands was traditionally defined around two principal rights: the right of reproduction and the right of communication to the public (or performing right), stated in broad terms.[15] This peculiarity was enshrined in article 26 of the French 1957 Act,[16] which provides that: 'The right of exploitation of the author comprises the right of performance and the right of reproduction.'

This dichotomy can be traced back to the origins of protection by *droit d'auteur*. Historically, the performing right was the first principal right granted to French authors, under the revolutionary Law of 13–19 January 1791. The right of reproduction (*publishing right*) was protected two years later under a subsequent Act of 19–24 July 1793. As these two Acts formed the basis of copyright protection in France for almost two centuries, the system of protection evolved on the basis of these two principal rights. This resulted in a wide construction of these rights, sometimes referred to as a 'synthetic definition'.[17] For example, the adaptation right was derived from the reproduction right.[18] More strikingly, in the absence of a specific text providing for a distribution right, such a right had to be inferred from the fundamental right of reproduction (under the so-called doctrine of *droit de destination*, described below).[19]

It is also interesting to observe that in several domestic Acts the list of rights granted is not *exhaustive*, but only *illustrative* of the general right of 'exploitation' of the work. This is the case for example in Germany, Spain, Portugal and, outside the European Union, in Switzerland. It is not clear, however, whether courts in these countries have had the opportunity to use this freedom of action to elaborate new rights outside the statutory list.[20]

In addition to these definitions of exclusive rights, all domestic laws contain secondary infringement provisions prohibiting various acts of

---

[14] See para. 184.
[15] The *droit de suite* (resale royalty right) would form, however, a separate and distinct economic right.
[16] Now art. L.122-1 of the French Intellectual Property Code.
[17] The expression is from Professor Strömholm.
[18] As specifically stated in s. 13 of the Dutch Act. See also art. L.122-4 of the French Intellectual Property Code.
[19] See para. 197.
[20] Which appears to be comprehensive enough, at least as far as the principal rights are concerned.

possessing and dealing with infringing copies or permitting infringement.[21] These will not be studied here.

178.   Structure

The protection of underlying works such as scripts or artistic works will not be discussed below; rather the discussion will concentrate on the protection of the final audiovisual work. However, when it comes to the definition of their exclusive rights, film authors and producers need to be aware of the possible disparities of protection between the copyright in the audiovisual work (or in the broadcast or cable programme) and the copyright in the underlying original works. Of course, when these elements co-exist (film and script for example), the film producer will in most case own the copyright in the audiovisual work as well as the copyright in the underlying commissioned works (although he may only be licensed certain underlying works). In some cases, however, the ground on which he will rest his claim for copyright infringement could have consequences for the success of his claim.

The text below will distinguish between three series of exclusive rights: the reproduction and adaptation rights (discussed in Section I below), the right of communication to the public (discussed in Section II below) and the distribution right (including the more reduced rental and lending rights) (discussed in Section III below). The text will also address related issues which are currently being harmonised within the European Union, and which are particularly relevant to film protection: the protection of technological measures and rights-management information (discussed in Section IV below), and the liability of intermediaries in the context of digital networks (discussed in Section V below). We will not address enforcement issues.[22]

SECTION I

The reproduction right

179.   The reproduction right at the international level

The principle of the protection of audiovisual works against copying is universal. The reproduction right of film authors and other contributors

---

[21] In the UK, these are: (a) importing an infringing copy (s. 22); (b) possessing or dealing with an infringing copy (s. 23); (c) providing the means for making infringing copies (s. 24); (d) permitting the use of premises for infringing performance (s. 25); and (e) providing apparatus for infringing performance, etc. (s. 26).
[22] On developments in EC law in this respect, see para. 46.

to film productions is secured in broad terms under article 9(1) of the Paris Act of the Berne Convention:

Authors of literary and artistic works protected by this Convention shall have the exclusive right of authorising the reproduction of these works, in any manner or form.[23]

Cinematographic works are encompassed in this definition by virtue of article 14*bis*. Article 9(3) of the Convention specifies that sound or visual recordings shall be considered as reproductions for the purposes of the Convention, and cinematographic reproductions are expressly mentioned in article 14(1).

The language of article 9(1) is thought to be broad enough to cover all means and methods of direct or indirect reproduction, including electronic or digital reproduction, as was expressly acknowledged during the negotiations which led to the adoption of the two new WIPO Treaties of 1996.[24] However, the applicability of this definition to transient or incidental reproduction proved to be more contentious during the negotiation of the Treaty, and was not decided.[25]

The definition of the Berne Convention was incorporated into article 9 of the TRIPs Agreement and into article 1(4) of the WIPO Copyright Treaty of 1996.[26] These agreements do not permit compulsory licence systems in relation to the reproduction right in non-musical works.

The WIPO Performances and Phonograms Treaty provides for a definition of the right of reproduction which is close to the definitions in articles 9(1) and 10 of the Berne and Rome Conventions.[27] Article 7 of

---

[23] The reproduction right was not *expressly* enshrined for all classes of works in the Brussels Act, although it could be implied from certain provisions of the Convention.

[24] See the Agreed Statement Concerning Article 1(4): 'The reproduction right, as set out in Article 9 of the Berne Convention, and the exceptions permitted thereunder, fully apply in the digital environment, in particular to the use of works in digital form. It is understood that the storage of a protected work in digital form in an electronic medium constitutes a reproduction within the meaning of Article 9 of the Berne Convention.'

[25] The proposed text of art. 7 on the scope of the right of reproduction stated that the right of reproduction in art. 9(1) includes both permanent and temporary reproductions. In addition, art. 7(2) allowed contracting parties to limit the right of reproduction 'in cases where a temporary reproduction has the sole purpose of making the work perceptible or where the reproduction is of a transient or incidental nature, provided that such reproduction takes place in the course of use of the work that is authorized by the author or permitted by law'. Both the Internet and the hardware industry resisted this text. As a result of both intensive lobbying and a shortage of time, the whole of art. 7 was eventually abandoned.

[26] And used in arts. 7 and 11 of the WIPO Performances and Phonograms Treaty (in a wording that is more specific than that used in the Rome Convention and the TRIPs Agreement).

[27] Art. 10 of the Rome Convention grants to phonogram producers the right to authorise the direct or indirect reproduction of their phonograms.

the Treaty grants performers the exclusive right of authorising the direct or indirect reproduction of their performances fixed in phonograms, *in any manner and form*. Producers of phonograms are granted a similar right in their phonograms in article 11. Again, the definition of 'phonograms' under the Treaty excludes incorporations of sounds in a cinematographic or audiovisual work.[28]

180.   The reproduction right at the Community level

At the time of the WIPO Copyright Treaty, the reproduction right had been harmonised in Europe in the field of neighbouring rights, and for copyright was only harmonised in relation to computer programs.[29]

Faced with the difficulties created by the digitisation of works, the European Commission in its Green Paper of 1995 advocated the solution adopted in the Computer Programs Directive, i.e. a concept of 'reproduction', including such acts as loading the work to the central memory of a computer.[30] The Follow-Up to the Green Paper on copyright and related rights in the information society of 1996[31] called for a further harmonisation of the definition and scope of the reproduction right, as well as for a harmonisation of its limitations and exceptions. This harmonisation is a prerequisite for the ratification of the 1996 WIPO Treaties, to which all EU and EEA Member States as well as the European Community are signatories. It took the form of the European Parliament and Council Directive on Copyright and Related Rights in the Information Society of 22 May 2001,[32] which adjusts and complements the existing EU framework on copyright and related rights in relation to the use of new technologies. Article 2 of the Directive, entitled 'Reproduction right', provides for a single definition of the reproduction right for authors and holders of related rights:

the exclusive right to authorise or prohibit direct or indirect, temporary or permanent reproduction by any means and in any form, in whole or in part:
(a) for authors, of their works;
(b) for performers, of fixations of their performances;
(c) for phonogram producers, of their phonograms;
(d) for the producers of the first fixations of films, in respect of the original and copies of their films;

---

[28] Art. 2(b).   [29] Art. 4(a) of the Computer Programs Directive of 1991.
[30] 'Copyright and Related Rights in the Information Society', COM (95) 382 final, 19 July 1995, pp. 51–2.
[31] Brussels, 20 November 1996, COM (96) 586 final.   [32] See para. 44.

(e) for broadcasting organisations, of fixations of their broadcasts, whether those broadcasts are transmitted by wire or over the air, including by cable or satellite.

The article thus makes clear that the reproduction right covers transient reproductions on digital networks. The Directive then sets out an exhaustive list of mandatory and optional exceptions to the right of reproduction, which exceptions are significantly fewer in the context of digital copying.[33]

181. Reproduction of film works in the UK and Ireland

In the UK, the copyright in the 'film' confers strong protection against the actual *copying* of the work. According to section 17(4) of the 1988 Act, 'copying', in relation to a film, a television broadcast or a cable programme, includes:

making a photograph of the whole or any substantial part of any image forming part of the film, broadcast or cable programme.

This language would for example prevent the lifting of images which are not separately protected as photograph and which would not be a substantial part of the underlying dramatic work.[34] However, in the absence of similar provisions to that effect, one must admit that the normal test of substantiality continues to apply in relation to other infringing acts.[35] Thus the mere showing of a film for a few seconds may not amount to the showing of a substantial part of the film, whereas the copy of a single frame would be infringing.[36]

The 1988 Act takes into consideration digital storage of literary, dramatic, musical and artistic works by specifying in section 17(2) that copying in relation to these works 'includes storing the work in any medium by electronic means'. This certainly covers digitisation and copy on a hard

---

[33] See para. 211.

[34] But, if the film is a cartoon, arguably the lifting of an image infringes the underlying drawing protected as an artistic work. See also *Shelley Films Ltd* v. *Rex Features Ltd* [1994] EMLR 134 (see para. 84 above) for photographs of costumes and film sets.

[35] H. Laddie, P. Prescott and M. Vitoria, *The Modern Law of Copyright*, Butterworths, 1995, para. 5.67, n. 2.

[36] In *British Broadcasting Corporation* v. *British Satellite Broadcasting Ltd* [1992] Ch 141; [1991] 3 WLR 174; [1991] 3 All ER 833, the defendants admitted that the use in their programmes of BBC coverage of football games, consisting of excerpts ranging from five to thirty-seven seconds, was *prima facie* infringement of copyright, but rested their defence on fair dealing. The court held that the use was fair dealing for the purpose of reporting current event under s. 30 of the 1988 Act.

disk or other computer-readable medium. This provision is not repeated for films, but since electronic copying is the normal way to copy a 'film' (i.e. a visual *recording*) there is no doubt that copies in relation to these works include electronic copies, whether in digitised form or not. Moreover, section 17(6) specifies that copying in relation to any description of works includes 'the making of copies which are transient or are incidental to some other uses of the work'; this encompasses temporary storage in a computer's dynamic memory (RAM).[37]

Thus, it can be said that the unauthorised storage, even if transient, of a substantial part of a film in a computer memory is infringement by copying. Note, however, that such storage limited to a *single frame* might not always result in an infringing copy: section 17(4) assimilates to copying the act of 'making a photograph of the whole or any substantial part of any image forming part of the film'; *prima facie* digital storing cannot be assimilated to a photograph, and the definition of photographs in section 4(2) might not be wide enough to encompass digital recording of visual elements.[38]

The Irish Act contains almost identical language,[39] and thus arguably the scope of the reproduction right is similar in Ireland.

182.   The right of reproduction in authors' rights countries

The right of reproduction is defined in a similar manner for all classes of works in all Member States of the authors' rights tradition. The right is usually defined in broad terms. For example, in France, reproduction is defined as 'the physical fixation of a work by any process permitting it to be communicated to the public in an indirect way', and expressly includes 'photography, mechanical, cinematographic or magnetic recording'.[40] In Germany, the right of reproduction is 'the right to make copies of the work irrespective of the method and the quantity', and also includes reproduction on video or audio recording media. Other definitions are similar.

These concepts of reproduction are generally considered broad enough to encompass digital copies on all media, including copies in computer

---

[37] H. Laddie, P. Prescott and M. Vitoria, *The Modern Law of Copyright*, Butterworths, 1995, para. 5.68; *Copinger and Skone James on Copyright*, 13th edn, 1991, para. 8-19. Under US law, for an assimilation of a copy in a computer's memory to a fixation, see *Advanced Computer Services of Michigan Inc.* v. *MAI Systems Corp.*, 845 F. Supp. 356 at 363 (ED Va 1994); and *Triad Systems Corp.* v. *Southeastern Express Co.*, 1994 US Dist., Lexis 5390 (ND Cal., 18 March 1994).

[38] 'Photograph' is defined as 'a recording of light or other radiation on any medium on which an image is produced or from which an image may by any means be produced'. If s. 17(4) was not applicable, the taking would have to be substantial.

[39] Section 39.   [40] Art. L.122-3 of the Intellectual Property Code.

memories. In France, courts have had, since 1996, the occasion to punish the reproduction on websites of digitised works.[41] The same would be true under the current definitions of the reproduction right in Belgium,[42] Spain,[43] Germany,[44] Sweden,[45] the Netherlands,[46] Greece[47] and Italy,[48] and probably in other Member States as well.

The status of temporary, transient or ephemeral reproductions, however, is less clear, and solutions may vary from one Member State to another. But it appears that the lack of specification in the relevant definitions would favour the copyright holder as against the copyright user.

The extent to which the reproduction right would cover the lifting of a single frame of the audiovisual work is uncertain. Most Acts do not address this question. Accordingly, the problem would be to determine whether the copying of a frame is substantial enough to constitute infringement of the film, or whether the image in question can be considered 'original' (which may amount to the same question). There does not appear to be case law on this point. But film frames may sometimes attract separate protection, and thus be protected as an independent work. This is apparently the case in Italy, where stills of cinematographic films appear to be protected under the neighbouring right granted to 'non-original photographs'.[49]

SECTION II

The adaptation right

183.   The adaptation right at international and Community levels

At the international level, both the translation and adaptation rights are secured for authors of original works under the Berne Convention, respectively in its articles 8 and 12. The cinematographic adaptation of literary or artistic works is mentioned in article 14(1) and this protection is extended to cinematographic works by virtue of article 14*bis*.

---

[41] 'The reproduction by digitization of musical works protected by author's right intended for access by persons connected to the Internet network must be expressly authorised by the authors or right owners.' Tribunal of First Instance of Paris, *Brel and Sardou*, interlocutory injunction, 14 August 1996, *Revue Droit de l'Informatique et des Télécoms*, 1996, No. 4, p. 31. See also Tribunal of First Instance of Paris, *Queneau*, 5 May 1997, *La Semaine Juridique*, 1997, II, No. 22906.

[42] Copyright Act, art. 1.   [43] Copyright Act, art. 18.   [44] Copyright Act, art. 16.

[45] Copyright Act, art. 2.   [46] Copyright Act, arts. 13 and 14.

[47] Copyright Act, art. 3.   [48] Copyright Act, art. 13.

[49] Copyright Act, art. 87; see para. 61.

Although the adaptation right is not harmonised within the European Union, all copyright owners in Member States benefit, directly or indirectly, from this right, defined as a distinct right or derived from the right of reproduction.

A special case should be made, however, for the UK and Ireland. As mentioned above, a peculiarity of UK and Irish copyright law is that no right of adaptation is granted in relation to the specific subject-matter for film protection, i.e. the 'film'. This protection is only afforded indirectly through the copyright in underlying elements such as the script.[50] This peculiar situation is justified by the fact that the 'film' corresponds to a recording description for which adaptation is either unnecessary or is of little relevance. In the same way, film producers on the continent are usually not granted adaptation rights in their 'videograms'. However, until recently, the conformity of this scheme with the obligations derived from the Berne Convention could be questioned, as audiovisual works were thought to be protected only through the copyright in the 'film'. Fortunately, the ruling of the UK Court of Appeal in the *Norowzian* case would appear to bring UK copyright into line with the obligations of the Convention, by enshrining the existence of an (underlying) audiovisual work distinct from its script and protected as a dramatic work, which therefore benefits from the adaptation right recognised for this class of works.[51]

Subject to this peculiarity of UK and Irish laws, the regime of protection of adaptations or derivative works, be they audiovisual adaptations of pre-existing works or adaptations of audiovisual works, is similar throughout Europe, and could be summarised in two (almost universal) rules.

First, the right to exploit a derivative work is subject to the copyright in the original work, and thus to the consent of the owner of the copyright in this pre-existing material. In practice, this authorisation is negotiated with the copyright owner (adaptation of literary work, filming of a script, synchronisation of music) or with a collecting society (inclusion of pre-existing images or artistic works). Note that, if the various presumptions of assignments of copyright to the film producer described in the preceding chapter[52] effectively grant him the right to adapt or reproduce the relevant work in the film, such presumptions may not cover a subsequent adaptation of the resulting film. Rights to remakes, sequels, prequels and spin-offs are usually a delicate point in negotiations with authors.

Of course, no consent is necessary when a derivative work is created through the free use of the original work. This free use is to be determined by application of the relevant copyright rules, and thus requires

---

[50] See s. 21.   [51] See para. 56.   [52] See paras. 158 *et seq.*

a knowledge both of the conditions for copyright protection (e.g. originality)[53] and of the applicable test for copyright infringement in each legal system.

The second rule concerning adaptations is that their protection does not prejudice or otherwise modify the rights in the adapted work. In other words, the creation of a derivative work does not affect or enlarge the scope, duration, ownership or subsistence of any copyright in the pre-existing material.

184.   Adaptation of 'films' in the UK and in Ireland

As mentioned above, under both the UK and Irish copyright Acts, the making of an adaptation of the work is not an act restricted by the copyright in the 'film' (the visual recording), but only by the copyright in the underlying literary, dramatic, musical or artistic works.[54]

In the UK (as in other countries), the distinction between an adaptation and a copy is not always clear. The 1988 Act provides that 'adaptation', in relation to a literary or dramatic work, means:

1. a translation of the work;
2. a version of a dramatic work in which it is converted into a non-dramatic work or, as the case may be, of a non-dramatic work in which it is converted into a dramatic work; and
3. a version of the work in which the story or action is conveyed wholly or mainly by means of pictures in a form suitable for reproduction in a book, or in a newspaper, magazine or similar periodical.[55]

However, the Act further provides that no inference is to be drawn from the provisions on adaptation as to what does or does not amount to copying a work,[56] which appears to indicate that infringement by reproduction and by adaptation can be closely related (in their assessment) and that in some cases one act could fall under both rights. The provisions of the Irish Act are similar.[57]

Concerning the 'film', it is also notable that infringement by copying in relation to a 'film' requires the lifting of its actual images (or sounds) and not a mere imitation.[58] In other words, the reshooting of similar

---

[53] As it is generally accepted that a 'taking' or borrowing is infringing only when it is the taking of an original part of the pre-existing material.

[54] UK Act, s. 21; Irish Act, s. 43.

[55] Section 21(3)(a). Adaptation is further defined in relation to musical works (as an 'arrangement or transcription of the work') and computer programs.

[56] Section 21(5).

[57] But the Irish Act does not contain a provision similar to s. 21(5) of the UK Act.

[58] See *Norowzian* v. *Arks Ltd (No. 1)* [1999] EMLR 57; [1998] FSR 394, Chancery Division; see also the Australian case of *Telmak Teleproducts Australia Pty Ltd* v. *Bond*

scenes would not infringe the copyright in a 'film'; *a fortiori* unauthorised remakes, sequels, or book or play versions would not be infringement of the 'film'. Accordingly, in the UK and Ireland, film producers must rely on the copyright in the underlying works (and notably in the script) to object to these forms of adaptation of their 'films'.

Note also that, in the UK, the existence of a dramatic copyright in the final audiovisual work distinct from the dramatic copyright in the script, as acknowledged in *Norowzian*, would further strengthen the protection against adaptations, since it conveys elements which are not described in the script: the unauthorised adaptation of a scene from a film could not be substantial or close enough to the script to infringe its copyright, but could infringe the copyright in the final audiovisual dramatic work.[59]

185.   Adaptation of audiovisual dramatic works in the UK and Ireland

But what is protected under the dramatic copyright in an audiovisual work? To answer this, it is first important to separate this question from the question of the definition of dramatic works. As J. A. L. Sterling and M. C. Carpenter pointed out:

> It is important . . . to distinguish between (a) a work in which copyright may subsist and (b) acts which infringe copyright in a work. Thus merely because performance of a work in public constitutes infringement of copyright in a work, this does not mean that there is copyright in the performance as such; and because reproduction of the dramatic incidents in a play constitute infringement of the copyright in the play, this does not mean that there is copyright in such dramatic incidents.[60]

International Pty Ltd (1985) 5 IPR 203 (Aus); (1986) 6 IPR 97; 65 ALR 319, which involved similar television adverts. Wilcox J relied on s. 10 of the Australian Act of 1968, which defines 'copy' in relation to a cinematograph film as 'any article or thing in which the visual images or sounds comprising the film are embodied' to deny that an advertisement reshot in the manner of the plaintiff's advert was a copy. Section 10 of Australian 1968 Act is close to s. 13(10) of the UK 1956 Act, and there is no doubt that this reasoning applies to cinematograph films under the latter Act: See H. Laddie, P. Prescott and M. Vitoria, *The Modern Law of Copyright*, Butterworths, 1995, para. 5.40, n. 2. This is confirmed by the legislative history (see the remarks of Lord Mancroft in the House of Lord on s. 13(10) of the Bill, that making a copy of the film meant 'making an actual copy or a negative or a tape recording of the film'; cited in W. J. Leaper, *Copyright and Performing Rights*, Stevens & Sons, London, 1957, p. 105). This solution is also suggested by analogy with a similar case concerning 'sound-alike' recordings, *CBS Records Australia Ltd* v. *Telmak Teleproducts (Aus) Pty Ltd* (1987) 9 IPR 440. See H. Laddie, P. Prescott and M. Vitoria, *The Modern Law of Copyright*, Butterworths, 1995, para. 5.68; and *Copinger and Skone James on Copyright*, 13th edn, 1991, para. 8-82.

[59] See below on the elements protected under the dramatic copyright.

[60] J. A. L. Sterling and M. C. L. Carpenter, *Copyright Law in the United Kingdom*, Legal Books, London, 1986, para. 237, pp. 71–2.

Farwell J in *Tate* v. *Fullbrook*, while rejecting the possibility that scenic effects may *per se* constitute a dramatic work, admitted that they were part of the dramatic work, and implied that in some cases their sole borrowing could infringe the copyright in the play[61] (provided, of course, that the borrowings are substantial enough, and the elements copied are original). But it appears that the part copied does not have to be separately copyrightable.[62]

This question must also be separated from the question of infringement of the underlying artistic and musical works. What we are concerned with here is the infringement of either the script or the larger dramatic audiovisual work, if any. The question is: what are the elements of a dramatic audiovisual work protected against substantial copying?

To answer this question, it is possible to draw an analogy with written and live stage plays. For Sterling and Carpenter:

> In accord with Scrutton LJ's dictum, it may be said that a dramatic work such as a play consists of the title, the *dramatis personae*, the text of the play, the recorded stage directions plus the dramatic incidents or action of the play resulting from the following of the text and directions of the dramatist.[63]

In *Massine* v. *de Basil*,[64] a ballet was protected as a composite dramatic work constituted by the music, the story, the choreography, the scenery and the costumes. What is the situation concerning dramatic films?

We saw that the copyright in dramatic works can be infringed merely by borrowing their *plot and dramatic incidents*, even if their actual language is not imitated or reproduced.[65] In this regard, the solutions developed by

---

[61] 'Nor do I say that scenic effects may not be protected as part and parcel of the drama: scenes do of course form parts of drama, and it is the dramatic piece as a whole that is protected by the Act.' Also in *Tate* v. *Thomas* [1921] 1 Ch 503; 90 LJ Ch 318; 124 LT 722; 65 SJ 327; [1917–23] MCC 246. See para. 17.

[62] By implication from *Tate* v. *Fullbrook* and the line of cases cited below.

[63] J. A. L. Sterling and M. C. L. Carpenter, *Copyright Law in the United Kingdom*, Legal Books, London, 1986. The authors refer to Scrutton LJ in *Sutton Vane* v. *Famous Players* [1928–35] MCC 6: 'the copyright protected is not the idea or motive of the play, but the words and dramatic incidents or action in which that idea is embodied.' They further give an interesting illustration: 'Thus, the dramatic work *Hamlet* by Shakespeare is constituted by (a) the title, *Hamlet, Prince of Denmark*, (b) the *dramatis personae* or a list of characters and their descriptions, (c) the text of the words of the play, allotted to the various characters by the dramatist, (d) the recorded stage directions (e.g. Elsinore – a platform before the Castle – Flourish – enter Ghost – Laertes falls – King dies), (e) the dramatic incidents or action thus described: Ancient Denmark, King murdered by his brother, who marries his widow. Ghost of King appears to soldiers on castle ramparts, then to King's son, etc. This element may contain a large number of separate incidents' (p. 72).

[64] [1936–45] MCC 223.

[65] See para. 20. *Rees* v. *Melville* [1911–16] MCC 96; *Sutton Vane* v. *Famous Players Film Co. Ltd* [1928–35] MCC 6; *Dagnall* v. *British and the Dominion Film Corp. Ltd* [1928–35] MCC 391; *Bolton* v. *British International Pictures Ltd* [1936–45] MCC 20; and *Wilmer* v. *Hutchinson & Co. etc. Ltd* [1936–45] MCC 13.

case law certainly apply to dramatic scripts and films, and film-makers are protected against remakes or adaptations of their dramatic films. But the incidents or facts borrowed must be original and substantial enough.[66] This idea is further developed under US copyright through the doctrine of *scènes-à-faire*, which covers common and standard scenes or scenes indispensable or inherent in a given situation.[67] The dramatic copyright would not protect against the borrowing of such scenes. A mere plot is not subject to copyright protection, and its sole borrowing (i.e. without dramatic incidents) would not constitute infringement.

Valuable elements such as *characters* are not protected as such,[68] but for example the making of 'spin-offs' (similar characters in a different story) might involve the borrowing of psychological, historical or other elements related to the character which, as a whole, might well contribute to a substantial extent to the originality of the first film.

Concerning *scenic effects* and the like, it is clear that these can be protected as part of the dramatic work constituted by the final audiovisual work, provided the latter is separately protected. But they are not part of the script, so far as it contains only dramatic incidents and dialogue. The extent to which these scenic effects are protected as part of the dramatic work will be a matter for the courts to decide. As pointed out, *Tate v. Fullbrook* and *Tate v. Thomas* do not state what scenic effects were being considered in those cases, and thus their value as precedents is limited.[69] Disputes will inevitably turn on the ground of 'substantiality' and 'originality' of the effects. Note that a single effect is unlikely to be original but that some combination of scenic effects might be. A mere borrowing of *filming and editing style or technique* would not constitute infringement, as stated by Nourse LJ in the *Norowzian* case.[70] Copies or imitations of *costumes, decors* or elements like *make-up* would probably not be considered substantial enough to infringe the copyright in the dramatic work as a whole. Costumes and decors may, however, attract protection as artistic works.[71] As a general rule there is no copyright in *titles*.[72]

Finally, as noted above,[73] in some limited circumstances, copying of the music could infringe both the copyright in the underlying musical work

[66] *MacGregor* v. *Powell* [1936–45] MCC 233; *De Manduit* v. *Gaumont British Picture Corp. Ltd* [1936–45] MCC 292; *Poznanski* v. *London Film Productions Ltd* [1936–45] MCC 107; *Harman Pictures NV* v. *Osborne* [1967] 1 WLR 723; [1967] 2 All ER 324; *Fernald* v. *Jay Lewis Productions Ltd* [1975] FSR 499; and *Ravenscroft* v. *Herbert* [1980] RPC 193.
[67] See L. A. Kurtz, 'Copyright: The Scenes à Faire Doctrine' (1989) 41 *Florida Law Review* 79. Compare with *De Manduit* v. *Gaumont British Picture Corp. Ltd* [1936–45] MCC 292.
[68] See para. 85.
[69] J. A. L. Sterling and M. C. L. Carpenter, *Copyright Law in the United Kingdom*, Legal Books, London, 1986, p. 72, n.
[70] See para. 56.   [71] See para. 84.   [72] See para. 86.   [73] At para. 127.

and the copyright in the dramatic (in fact dramatico-musical) audiovisual work.

186.   Adaptation of film works in authors' rights countries

The discussion here will concentrate on French law, which offers interesting case law relating to adaptations of films or scripts. Article L.122-4 of the French Code provides:

> Any complete or partial performance of reproduction made without the consent of the authors or of his successors or assigns is unlawful. The same shall apply to the translation, the adaptation or the transformation, arrangement or reproduction by any technique or process whatsoever.

Accordingly, in France, the right of adaptation is derived from the right of reproduction. In contrast, and as mentioned above, most authors' rights systems have introduced a separate and distinct right of adaptation in their copyright Acts.

In passing, it may be observed that this inclusion of the adaptation right in the wider reproduction right does not necessarily mean that an assignment of the reproduction right, without specification, conveys the adaptation rights. In France, in application of the principle of restrictive construction of copyright transfers, a blanket assignment of the reproduction right will in most case result in the reservation by the assignor of the adaptation right (at least if the assignor is the author of the work).[74]

Under French copyright law, an 'adaptation' is said to involve a change in the mode of expression: from literary to dramatic, from literary or dramatic to audiovisual. But the characterisation as an 'adaptation' rather than as a 'reproduction' has little relevance in terms of infringement, unless a separation of these rights has been operated by contract. This is mainly due to the test of infringement applicable under French law, which is that infringement is assessed by the resemblances, and not by the differences, between the original work and the alleged copy.[75] Under this test, dissimilarities between the works must be disregarded. Therefore, the test of infringement by adaptation is in principle the one used for infringement by reproduction: an infringement by adaptation involves the unauthorised borrowing (and thus the reproduction) of a protected expression (plot, language, storyline, etc.), and the amount of new material added to it is in principle irrelevant. Certain French courts, however, appear to resist that approach.

---

[74] On construction rules, see para. 162.
[75] Court of Cassation, 16 June 1955, *Revue Dalloz*, 1955, p. 554; Court of Cassation, 13 April 1988, RIDA, October 1988, p. 297.

French case law makes clear that there is reproduction or adaptation of a work each time the public is communicated original features of the work,[76] irrespective of the extent, form or duration of the borrowing, or of the media used. When it comes to literary and audiovisual works, infringement can occur when the composition, plot or dramatic developments are borrowed.[77] French case law offers several examples of the application of these rules to film works.

In the famous *Bicyclette Bleue* case, Margaret Mitchell's heirs brought in 1987 a suit against Régine Desforges, the French writer of a novel called *La Bicyclette Bleue*, for infringement of the copyright in the book *Gone with the Wind*. The Tribunal of First Instance of Paris held that the French book infringed the copyright in the US novel after an extensive and detailed comparison between the two books. The Court of Appeal of Paris[78] reversed the judgment after a short analysis of the French book, on the ground that, despite the fact that the two books had the same starting point, the idea was commonplace and the two works were written differently. This decision was overturned by the French Supreme Court[79] on the ground that, instead of making general statements, the Court of Appeal should have considered whether the composition or expression of the two books had such similarities that the scenes in the second novel were to be considered reproductions or adaptations of the scenes in the first one. The Supreme Court thus confirmed (a) that the composition of the theme of a novel is protected as an original element of this work, and (b) that an alleged infringement is evidenced by the similarities, not the dissimilarities, between two works.

This test of similarities implies a careful comparison of the resemblances between the two works, and takes no account of the differences. It appears, however, that dissimilarities play a certain role, at least in the evaluation of the 'substantiality' of the taking or in the assessment of the state of mind of the borrower (is it plagiarism, unconscious copying or independent creation?). This is illustrated by the judgment of the Court of Appeal of Versailles in the *Bicyclette Bleue* case which, following the decision of the Court of Cassation, held in favour of the French novelist.[80] The Court of Appeal first made a careful and detailed comparison of

---

[76] Court of Cassation, 16 July 1987, Bull. Civ., I, No. 225; *La Semaine Juridique*, 1987, IV, p. 311; RIDA, January 1988, p. 94.

[77] Court of Cassation, 27 June 1910, *Revue Dalloz Périodique*, 1910, I, p. 296; Tribunal of First Instance of Paris, 16 May 1973, RIDA, October 1974, p. 166.

[78] Paris Court of Appeal, 21 November 1990, *Revue Dalloz*, 1991, p. 85.

[79] Court of Cassation, Civ., 4 February 1992, *Revue Dalloz*, 1992, p. 182.

[80] Versailles Court of Appeal, 15 December 1993, *Revue Dalloz*, 1994, p. 132, note P.-Y. Gautier. See X. Daverat, 'Libres propos sur les critères de la contrefaçon des œuvres littéraires et artistiques', *La Semaine Juridique*, 1995, No. 3827.

the two works, as suggested by the Court of Cassation, which revealed striking similarities. The Court noted that the two works in question presented the same basic theme and plot development (transposed to France in the Second World War):

Against a background of war and defeat, a young woman – strongly attached to the family domain she will desperately try to save from war disaster – who passionately loves a man who loves her too but who voluntarily married another woman, seeks to conquer this man, who was her first failed love affair and who resists her, for reasons of principle and because of the love he feels for his wife. She is loved by a mature man she is attracted to but the complex personality of whom she does not understand; she does not see the deep love this mature man has for her, since she is blinded by her own passion, while he knows that her passion is just an illusion.

The Court also noted numerous similarities in terms of characterisation. In addition, there was no doubt that the French author had access to the novel. Margaret Mitchell was even acknowledged with other authors and public figures in the foreword of the book for her 'involuntary collaboration'. Despite these findings, the Court of Appeal held in favour of the French author by insisting on the differences in terms of expression, treatment and general tone between the two works. This decision was heavily criticised by legal commentators and might not have survived a new appeal to the Supreme Court. It is, however, representative of a certain attitude of the lower French courts.

Another example of this trend can be found in the *Boisset-Curtelin, UGC, DA* v. *Worldvision Enterprise* case,[81] Yves Boisset, a French director of a movie named 'Le prix du danger' ('The Price of Danger'), brought an action against the US producer of another movie, 'The Running Man', featuring Arnold Schwarzenegger. Both film had the same basic theme, the influence of television over the masses, and depicted a television game featuring a death race between a competitor and five armed killers. However, the US movie was more humorous and action-oriented and was directed at a wider public than the French film, and contained a happy ending, which was absent from the latter. In addition, the US movie was adapted from a novel by Stephen King, whereas the French movie was not. The Paris Court of Appeal held that there was no copyright infringement by the second film, since the general spirit, the plot and the attitudes of character in the second movie were different from those in the first. The Supreme Court overturned this decision on the ground that the Court of Appeal should have ascertained whether the expression of

---

[81] Court of Cassation, 25 May 1992, *Revue Dalloz*, 1993, II, p. 184; *La Semaine Juridique* (E), 1992, No. 25.

the television game was a main and original feature of the French movie, the reproduction or adaptation of which would amount to a copyright infringement.

More orthodox views were shown by the Tribunal of First Instance of Paris and the Court of Appeal of Paris in the *Universal City Studios v. UGC* case, which involved a claim by the owners of the copyright in the film 'Jaws' against a another film with similar features. Holding against the second film, the Court of Appeal stated:

> The comparison must concern the form of the expression of the theme common to the works, primarily the plot. In the two works, the story takes place in the US, in summer, which was not essential to the story. The main characters are the same in the two movies and some of them have quasi-identical personalities. Numerous similarities of scenes are retained in the two works. All of these elements were not at all necessary in order to treat the theme common to these works. Some of these elements show the imprint of the personality of the author of the literary work *Jaws* and one of the authors of the two cinematographic adaptations. In fact, the similarities noted in the cinematographic work in question demonstrate the absence of novelty of this work. The film *La mort au large* infringes the literary and cinematographic work *Jaws*.[82]

The same suit was brought in Belgium, with the same result.[83]

SECTION III

The right of communication to the public

187.   Introduction

Historically, there was little difficulty in adapting the performing right in musical, dramatic and literary works, initially designed for live performances, to acts of performance done through mechanical devices, including phonograms and films. Film works thus became equally protected against unauthorised public exhibition in cinemas.

However, the development of broadcasting raised new questions, which often proved the definition of the performing right to be poorly adapted to this form of exploitation. Depending on the actual statutory definition of the performing right, there remained difficulties regarding the possibility of treating radio and later television broadcasting as a mean of public performance, mainly due to the difficulty in considering that a broadcast received in the intimacy of a home was made 'to the public' or 'in

---

[82] Paris Court of Appeal, 10 December 1987, *Cahiers du Droit d'Auteur*, 1988, No. 2, p. 31.
[83] Tribunal of First Instance of Brussels, 22 January 1988, RIDA, 1989, No. 142, p. 363.

public'. Due to the pre-eminence of radio broadcasting, these questions were mainly raised by the phonographic industry, but were rapidly extended to other classes of copyright works. The questions found answers in most domestic laws in the 1920s, through case law or through specific provisions in copyright Acts.[84] In this respect, divergences between European Union Member States mainly concerned the treatment of specific situations such as the transmission of broadcasts into hotel rooms and buildings.

The questions raised by the development of satellite and cable distribution in Europe have been studied elsewhere.[85] Although there was little difficulty in Europe to consider that distribution by direct broadcasting satellites amounted to broadcasting under the applicable international agreements, there was hesitation concerning the broadcast quality of transmissions by point-to-point systems such as fixed satellite services. In addition, the determination of the law applicable to satellite broadcasts proved to be a controversial question, with a possible choice between the law of the country in which the signal is 'up-legged' to the satellite, and that of the country in which it is 'down-legged' to reception. This led to different national solutions within European Union Member States.

The development of cable television raised two series of difficulties, which are closely associated. The first series of difficulties were caused by national definitions of the act of broadcasting being limited to wireless broadcasting, which could not encompass cable distribution of programmes (either cable-originated or retransmitted from broadcasts). The second series of difficulties concerned copyright liability for cable retransmission of wireless broadcasts (also known as 'passive distribution') and the implementation of non-voluntary licences.

After much discussion, these issues were harmonised at Community level by the adoption of the Satellite and Cable Directive of 1993.[86] All these questions have also been reassessed in the context of the transmission of copyright works over digital networks such as the Internet.

188.   Provisions of international agreements

The right of communication to the public is regulated by the Berne Convention in a rather fragmented manner. Article 11(1)(ii) of the

---

[84] For case law assimilating broadcasting to public performance, see e.g., in the UK, *Messager v. British Broadcasting Co. Ltd* [1927] 2 KB 543; 138 LT 572; in France, Court of Cassation, 10 November 1930, *Gazette du Palais*, 1930, II, p. 771; in Germany, *Reichsgericht*, 12 May 1926, RGZ 113, p. 413, GRUR, 1926, p. 343.

[85] See e.g. M. H. Pilcher, *Copyright Problems of Satellite and Cable Television in Europe*, Martinus Nijhoff, 1987.

[86] Commission Proposal for a Council Directive Concerning Broadcasting Activities, COM (86) 146 final.

Convention provides that authors of dramatic, dramatico-musical and musical works shall enjoy the exclusive right of authorising 'any communication to the public of the performance of their work'. Article 11(2) extends this right to translations of their original works. Article 11*ter* contains similar provisions for recitations of literary works.

Article 11*bis* specifies the regime of broadcasting and 'related rights'. Article 11*bis*(1) grants to authors of all categories of literary and artistic works: (i) the right of broadcasting and of communication to the public by any other means of wireless diffusion of signs, sounds or images; (ii) the right of communication to the public by wire and the right of rebroadcasting of the broadcast of their work; and (iii) the right of communication to the public by loudspeaker or any other analogous instrument. Article 11*bis*(2) allows the establishment of non-voluntary licences in relation to these rights.

Article 14(1)(ii) grants to authors of literary or artistic works the exclusive right of authorising the communication to the public by wire of cinematographic adaptations and reproductions of their work. This protection is extended to owners of copyright in cinematographic works under article 14*bis*(1). The right of communication to the public under the Berne Convention does not extend to literary works (except in the case of recitations), photographic works, works of pictorial art and graphic works.

Several provisions of the Convention have been subject to divergent construction. These concern the status of cable transmission and satellite broadcasting and the conditions of implementation of non-voluntary licences under article 11*bis*(2). In addition, the applicability of the Convention to new technological developments has been questioned. This prompted a revision of the scope and definition of this right in article 8 of the WIPO Copyright Treaty of 1996, entitled 'Right of communication to the public', which is one of the most important provision of the Treaty:

Without prejudice to the provisions of Articles 11(1)(ii), 11*bis*(1)(i) and (ii), 11*ter*(1)(ii), 14(1)(ii) and 14*bis*(1) of the Berne Convention, authors of literary and artistic works shall enjoy the exclusive right of authorising any communication to the public of their works, by wire or wireless means, including the making available to the public of their works in such a way that members of the public may access these works from a place and at a time individually chosen by them.

This language has two consequences. First, it extends the right of communication to the public to all categories of works. Secondly, it makes clear that the right of communication to the public is applicable to interactive on-demand transmissions of protected works over digital networks.[87]

---

[87] During the Diplomatic Conference, telecommunications companies were anxious that they might be held liable for the provisions of conduits or other facilities for transmissions

The agreed statement concerning article 8 specifies that nothing in article 8 precludes a contracting party from applying the compulsory licences mentioned in article 11*bis*(2) of the Berne Convention.

189.   The right of communication to the public at the European level

Until recently, the right of communication to the public was only subject to a partial harmonisation in Europe. It was first harmonised in relation to related rights in article 8 of the Rental Directive of 19 November 1992.[88] Article 8(1) provides for an exclusive right of performers to authorise or prohibit the broadcasting by wireless means and the communication to the public of their performances, except where the performance is itself already a broadcast performance or is made from a fixation.

Article 8(2) provides for a compulsory licence for broadcasting by wireless means or for any communication to the public of phonograms published for commercial purposes, subject to a single equitable remuneration to be shared between the relevant performers and phonogram producers.

Article 8(3) provides for an exclusive right of broadcasting organisations to authorise or prohibit the rebroadcasting of their broadcasts by wireless means or the communication to the public of their broadcasts if such communication is made in places accessible to the public on payment of an entrance fee.

The Cable and Satellite Directive of 27 September 1993 further harmonises the legislation of Member States with regard to satellite broadcasting and cable retransmission.

The Directive first clears the legal uncertainty over the law applicable to such broadcasts in its article 1 on definitions. Article 1(2)(b) provides that the act of communication to the public by satellite occurs solely in the Member State where, under the control and responsibility of the broadcasting organisation, the programme-carrying signals are introduced into an uninterrupted chain of communication leading to the satellite and down towards the earth (the 'up-leg' country); accordingly, a licence is not necessary for the 'down-leg' country. Article 1 also states the rule for the determination of the applicable law in situations where an act of

---

of copyright works. Their concern is addressed in the Agreed Statement Concerning Article 8: 'The mere provision of physical facilities for enabling or making a communication does not in itself amount to communication within the meaning of this Treaty or the Berne Convention.' See also paras. 205 *et seq*.

[88] The right of communication to the public is also harmonised in relation to databases by art. 5 of the Database Directive.

communication to the public by satellite occurs in a non-EC State which does not provide the level of protection provided for under the Directive.

The Directive then sets out the definition and regime of the granted rights. Under article 2 of the Directive, Member States shall provide an exclusive right for the author to authorise the communication to the public by satellite of copyright works. Under article 3, this authorisation may be acquired only be agreement, which thus excludes non-voluntary schemes.[89]

However, a Member State may provide that a collective agreement between a collecting society and a broadcasting organisation concerning a given category of works may be extended to rightholders of the same category who are not represented by the collecting society under certain conditions.[90] But this provision does not apply to cinematographic works, including works created by a process analogous to cinematography.[91]

The rights of performers, phonogram producers and broadcasting organisations in article 8 of the Rental Directive are extended to communication to the public by satellite.[92] This also excludes statutory licensing systems.[93]

The scope of harmonisation is much narrower in relation to cable retransmission. The Directive does not require Member States to introduce a specific cable retransmission right and does not define the scope of such a right.[94] However, article 8 of the Directive provides that Member States shall ensure that when programmes from other Member States are retransmitted by cable in their territory the applicable copyright and related rights are observed and that such retransmission takes place on the basis of individual or collective contractual agreements between copyright owners, holders of related rights and cable operators. This provision thus prevents the establishment of statutory licences in respect of these intra-Community retransmission.[95]

The exercise of the cable retransmission right is further dealt with in article 9. It provides that Member States shall ensure that the right of

[89] See recital 21.

[90] Art. 3(2). Namely, that the communication to the public by satellite simulcasts a terrestrial broadcast by the same broadcaster, and that the unrepresented rightholder has, at any time, the possibility of excluding the extension of the collective agreement to his works and of exercising his rights either individually or collectively.

[91] Art. 3(3).

[92] Art. 4. The provisions of art. 2(7) of the Rental Directive, which allows a Member State to implement an irrebuttable presumption of assignment of performers' rights to the film producer, also extend to this right.

[93] Recital 21.   [94] See art. 8 and recital 27.

[95] However, it allowed Member State to retain until 31 December 1997 their statutory licence systems which were in operation or were expressly provided for by national law on 31 July 1991.

copyright owners and holders of related rights to grant or refuse authorisation to a cable operator for a cable retransmission may be exercised only through a collecting society. However, this article is not applicable to the rights of broadcasting organisations.[96] Accordingly, the Directive establishes a sort of 'non-voluntary licence' (a compulsory collective management scheme) limited to underlying works in broadcasts. The conditions of exercise of the right are further defined in the article.[97]

Nothing in the Directive prevents the establishment of non-voluntary licences for cable retransmissions of national programmes.

The European Court of Justice had occasion to decide a case concerning the construction of the provisions of the Satellite and Cable Directive.[98] A Spanish hotel, operated by a company named Hoasa, installed a system for the reception of television programmes broadcast terrestrially or by satellite and then distributed the programme to the guests occupying rooms at the hotel. The Spanish collecting society for audiovisual producers, Egeda, sued Hoasa for copyright infringement. Hoasa disputed that the hotel had made any 'communication to the public' or 'cable retransmission' within the meaning of article 1 of the Satellite Directive. The Tribunal of First Instance of Oviedo referred to the European Court of Justice for a preliminary ruling under article 177 of the EC Treaty (now article 234) a question on the interpretation of article 1 of the Satellite Directive in this respect. The European Court of Justice held that the question whether the reception by a hotel of satellite or terrestrial television signals and their distribution by cable to the rooms of that hotel is an 'act of communication to the public' or 'reception by the public' is not governed by the Satellite Directive, and must consequently be decided in accordance with national laws.

The new Directive on Copyright and Related Rights in the Information Society of 22 May 2001 complements the harmonisation for all classes of copyright works and related rights. In line with article 8 of the WIPO Copyright Treaty, article 3(1) of the Directive provides:

Member States shall provide authors with the exclusive right to authorise or prohibit any communication to the public of their works, by wire or wireless means, including the making available to the public of their works in such a way that members of the public may access them from a place and at a time individually chosen by them.[99]

---

[96] Art. 10.   [97] Art. 9(2) and (3).

[98] Case C-293/98, *Entidad de Gestion de Derechos de los Productores Audiovisuales (EGEDA)* v. *Hosteleria Asturiana SA (HOASA)* [2000] ECDR 231; [2000] EMLR 523, ECJ.

[99] Without prejudice to art. 2 of the Cable and Satellite Directive and to art. 5 of the Database Directive.

Recital 23 specifies that the right of communication to the public must be understood in a broad sense as covering all communication to the public not present at the place from where the communication originates, and that it covers transmission or retransmission of a work to the public by wire or wireless means, including broadcasting. Accordingly, the Directive would appear to enshrine the cable retransmission right. It does not, however, appear to prevent the implementation of non-voluntary licences for cable retransmissions of national programmes.[100]

The new right of communication to the public will clearly cover inter-active 'on-demand' transmissions. More generally, it is clear that an act of communication to the public will occur when the work is made available to the public on a publicly accessible site on the Internet.

The extension brought about by this definition is applied to holders of neighbouring rights in article 3(2) of the Directive.

Member States shall provide for the exclusive right to authorise or prohibit the making available to the public, by wire or wireless means, in such a way that members of the public may access them from a place and at a time individually chosen by them:
(a) for performers, of fixations of their performances;
(b) for phonogram producers, of their phonograms;
(c) for the producers of the first fixations of films, of the original and copies of their films;
(d) for broadcasting organisations, of fixations of their broadcasts, whether these broadcasts are transmitted by wire or over the air, including by cable or satellite.

In line with the *acquis communautaire* in that field, article 3(3) confirms that the doctrine of Community exhaustion is not applicable to the right of communication to the public.[101]

The question of the law applicable to cross-border transmissions is not solved in the Directive. The issue was examined during the consultations which followed the Green Paper on Copyright and Related Rights in the Information Society.[102] Most commentaries opposed harmonisation in that respect, and in particular opposed the application of the solution adopted in the Satellite Directive, which would result in the law of

---

[100] As it does not specify that the right may be only acquired by agreement (compare with art. 3 of the Rental Directive). Recital 30 provides that the rights referred to in the Directive may be transferred, assigned or be subject to the grant of contractual licences, but this is 'without prejudice to the relevant national legislation on copyright and related rights'.

[101] See Case 62/79, *Coditel* v. *Ciné-Vog Films* [1980] ECR 881; Case 262/81, *Coditel* v. *Ciné-Vog Films* [1982] ECR 3381; Case 156/86, and *Warner Brothers and Metronome Video* v. *Christiansen* [1988] ECR 2605.

[102] COM (95)382 final.

the country of origin of a transmission being the law applicable to this transmission. They contended mainly that the place where transmission originates is more difficult to establish in the digital environment, and outlined the risks of a lesser protection for rightholders in case of transmissions originating from outside the European Union. In its Follow-Up to the Green Paper,[103] the Commission concluded that the issue required further evaluation.[104]

190.   The right of communication to the public in the UK

Under section 16 of the 1988 Act, the owner of the copyright in a work has the exclusive right (a) to perform, show or play the work in public, and (b) to broadcast the work or include it in a cable programme service. These rights are further defined in sections 19 and 20 of the Act.

Section 19 makes a distinction between the copyright in original works and the copyright in sound recordings, films, broadcasts and cable programmes. As regards original descriptions, the performance of the work in public is an act restricted by the copyright in a literary, dramatic or musical work only. Performance is defined as including, in general, any mode of visual or acoustic presentation, including presentation by means of a sound recording, film, broadcast or cable programme of the work. Section 19 further states that the playing or showing of the work in public is an act restricted by the copyright in a sound recording, film, broadcast or cable programme.[105]

It is left to the courts to draw the line between performances in public and in private. The following performances have been considered public in the UK: a performance of dance music in a club where guests were admitted;[106] a performance in a private room audible to persons dining in a restaurant;[107] a performance to workers at a factory during working hours;[108] a performance at a club for football supporters;[109] and a

---

[103] COM (96) 586 final.
[104] On that question in a European context, see A. Lucas, 'Private International Law Aspects of the Protection of Works and of the Subject-Matter of Related Rights Transmitted over Digital Networks', Doc. WIPO/PIL/01/1 Prov.
[105] Section 19(3). Section 19(4) adds: 'Where copyright in a work is infringed by its being performed, played or shown in public by means of apparatus for receiving visual images or sounds conveyed by electronic means, the person by whom the visual images or sounds are sent, and in the case of a performance the performers, shall not be regarded as responsible for the infringement.'
[106] *Harms (Inc.) Ltd and Chappell & Co. Ltd* v. *Martans Club* [1927] 1 Ch 526 at 532 and 533, CA.
[107] *Performing Right Society Ltd* v. *Camelo* [1936] 3 All ER 557.
[108] *Ernest Turner Electrical Instruments Ltd* v. *Performing Right Society Ltd* [1943] Ch 167; [1943] 1 All ER 413, CA.
[109] *Performing Right Society Ltd* v. *Rangers Football Club Supporters Club*, 1974 SLT 151.

performance of phonograms in a record shop.[110] In the Australian case of *Rank Film Production Ltd* v. *Dodds*,[111] the Supreme Court of New South Wales held that the presentation of films in hotel bedrooms was public since the clients were guests and not individuals in their private homes. In fact, it appears that a performance will be considered private in the UK only if it is restricted to the domestic or quasi-domestic circle.

Section 20 of the Act provides that the broadcasting of the work or its inclusion in a cable programme service is an act restricted by the copyright in a literary, dramatic, musical or artistic work, a sound recording or film, or a broadcast or cable programme. The copyright in a sound recording is subject, however, to a statutory licence for broadcasting.[112]

Since the Cable and Broadcasting Act 1984, the definition of 'broadcasting' includes direct broadcasting by satellite (or direct-to-home broadcasting).[113] The provisions of the Satellite and Cable Directive of 27 September 1993 which were not already part of UK law were implemented by the Copyright and Related Rights Regulations 1996. The regulations determine the law applicable in relation to broadcasts in the European Economic Area in conformity with article 1 of the Directive in the new sections 6(4) and 6A of the 1988 Act. The provisions of the Directive on the collective exercise of the right of retransmission by cable are implemented in the new section 144A of the 1988 Act.

Concerning cable retransmission of broadcasts, in two limited cases cable operators do not have to obtain a separate consent from copyright owners. The rights in the broadcast and in included works are not infringed in the case of a 'must-carry' duty.[114] Also, these rights are not infringed if and to the extent that the broadcast is made for reception in the area in which the cable programme service is provided;[115] but in that case the authorisation of the broadcaster is necessary if the broadcast is a satellite or an encrypted transmission.[116]

191.   Dissemination over telecommunications networks

Under present UK law, the provisions applicable to digital transmission or dissemination over telecommunications networks are fragmented and their construction is sometimes uneasy, but there is little doubt that such

---

[110] *Performing Right Society Ltd* v. *Harlequin Record Shops Ltd* [1979] 2 All ER 828.
[111] [1983] 2 NSWLR 553; 2 IPR 113.   [112] Sections 135A–135G.
[113] Where a signal is sent to a satellite and distributed directly to users equipped with reception devices. On previous law and practice, see S. White, S. Bate and T. Johnson, *Satellite Communications in Europe: Law and Regulation*, Longman, London, 1994, para. 8.19, p. 325.
[114] E.g. of BBC and IBA programmes, s. 73(2)(a) and (3)(a).
[115] Section 73(2)(b) and (3)(b).   [116] Section 73(2)(b).

activities fall within the scope of the exclusive rights. First, most digital transmissions require a copy at both ends of the operation,[117] and thus might be covered indirectly under section 17 of the Act.[118] In addition, according to section 16(2), copyright is infringed by a person who 'authorises' another to do any of the acts restricted by copyright. Therefore, in the context of digital networks, bulletin board or server operators might be liable for authorising copying by their subscribers if they offer copyright works for download.[119]

The mere remote presentation of a film, for example under a video-on-demand system, cannot constitute an infringement by *issue of copies to the public* under section 18 in the absence of a copy at the point of reception.[120] Also, the prohibition of unauthorised rental, which applies to copies previously put into circulation, is difficult to extend to remote presentation or to transmissions for downloading, since the copy is either not delivered to the user, or not returned to the sender according to the definition of rental in section 178 of the Act.

However, the unauthorised transmission of a copyright work for downloading is clearly *secondary infringement* under section 24(2) of the Act, which provides:

---

[117] I.e. when the element is 'uploaded' to the server (a copy on the hard disk), and when it is 'downloaded' in the user's computer (a copy on the hard disk or in RAM).

[118] And especially s. 17(6) (transitory recording). Compare with the US case of *Sega Enterprises Ltd* v. *MAPHIA*, 857 F. Supp. 679 (ND Cal. 1994); and *Advanced Computer Services of Michigan Inc.* v. *MAI Systems Corp.*, 845 F. Supp. 356 (ED Va 1994).

[119] This is so even if they have no reason to believe that an unauthorised copying will take place, as the liability for primary infringement is a strict liability. See also G. J. H. Smith *et al.*, *Internet Law and Regulation*, FT Law & Tax, 1996, p. 19. See also *ibid.*, p. 20, on the inapplicability of copyright exemptions concerning libraries. But it will be necessary to take into account the provisions of the EC Directive on Electronic Commerce of 8 June 2000. See para. 207.

[120] There are three particular difficulties here. (1) Section 18 appears equally difficult to apply if the film is not shown, but downloaded to a computer's RAM or hard disk. Technically, downloading is not *transmitting* a copy, but rather the *making* of a copy at the point of reception. However, this did not prevent a US court from considering that the unauthorised downloading of copyrighted works infringed the distribution right of the copyright owner (*Playboy Enterprises Inc.* v. *Frena*, 839 F. Supp. 1552 (MD Fla. 1993)). 17 USC s. 106 grants the exclusive right to 'sell, give away, rent or lend' any material embodiment of a copyright work. (2) Another difficulty in applying s. 18 is that, under UK copyright law, the general right to authorise the issue of copies to the public is limited to copies not previously put into circulation within the EEA. If downloading amounted to issuing copies to the public, it is not clear whether the copy allegedly distributed and made from, say, a videotape previously commercially available, could be considered previously put into circulation or not. It is submitted that in this case exhaustion would not apply as long as no such copy (in electronic form) is put into circulation by the copyright owner: copies in electronic form are different from copies on videotapes and constitute a new mode of exploitation of films. Logically, there should be no exhaustion of the right. (3) Finally, under s. 18 the distribution must be made 'to the public'; the offer to download made on a bulletin board accessible to the public might be an offer 'to the public', but a downloading effected between two individuals would probably not infringe s. 18.

Copyright in a work is infringed by a person who without the licence of the copyright owner transmits the work by means of a telecommunications system, knowing or having reason to believe that infringing copies of the work will be made by means of the reception of the transmission in the UK or elsewhere.[121]

The owner of a server or bulletin board might be considered as the person who 'transmits' the work under this provision. In fact, what he does is to make available for use a machine which, following instruction by the user, will transmit a work.[122] But it is submitted that the circumstance that this transmission is automated is irrelevant under section 24(2).[123]

One could also think of applying section 19 of the Act (infringement by performance, showing or playing of the work in public) to on-line presentations of films (video-on-demand). According to section 19, in relation to literary, dramatic or musical work, performance includes 'any mode of visual or acoustic presentation', which covers digital transmission. For sound recordings, films, broadcasts and cable programmes, reference is made to 'playing or showing of the work', irrespective of the technical means used. However, the notion of 'performance' in section 19 would not cover the mere *downloading* of films, without simultaneous viewing. Moreover, it is difficult to see how point-to-point and one-to-one transmissions such as video-on-demand could be assimilated to performances 'in public'. Here, the analogy with the relay of television programmes or music in hotel bedrooms is incomplete:[124] under a video-on-demand service the signal is transmitted to private homes[125] and is only directed to one user at his or her request.

[121] Compare with the US case of *Sega Enterprises Ltd* v. *MAPHIA*, 857 F. Supp. 679 (ND Cal. 1994), where bulletin board activities were held to be direct and contributory infringements of the copyright in downloaded videogames. On the test to apply in order to determine if a person had 'reason to believe' that infringement will take place, see H. Laddie, P. Prescott and M. Vitoria, *The Modern Law of Copyright*, Butterworths, 1995, paras. 10.4 *et seq.*

[122] Compare with *CBS Inc.* v. *Ames Records & Tapes Ltd* [1982] Ch 91; [1981] 2 WLR 973; [1981] 2 All ER 812; [1981] RPC 407; and *CBS Songs Ltd* v. *Amstrad Consumer Electronics plc* [1988] AC 1013; [1988] 2 WLR 1191; [1988] 2 All ER 484; [1988] 2 FTLR 168, HL, affirming [1987] 3 WLR 144. In *Religious Technology Center* v. *Netcom Online Communications Services Inc.*, 907 F. Supp. 1361 (ND Cal. 1995), in a motion for a preliminary injunction the court refused to consider that automatic copying and transmission of works by Internet service providers is a direct infringement. The court held that the question of contributory infringement was to be decided at trial.

[123] In any case, operators of automatic relays are protected against infringement actions based on this provision by the requirement of a knowledge or reason to believe that an infringing copy will take place at the point of reception.

[124] This question is itself unsolved. In the Australian case of *Rank Film Production Ltd* v. *Dodds* [1983] 2 NSWLR 553, the Supreme Court of New South Wales held that the presentation of films in hotel bedrooms was public since the clients were guests and not individuals in their private homes.

[125] Compare with the case law cited at para. 13. See also, *a contrario*, *Rank Film Production Ltd* v. *Dodds* [1983] 2 NSWLR 553. But see the Indian case of *Garware Plastics and*

Another possibility is to apply section 20 (infringement by broadcasting or inclusion in a cable programme service). This requires that the service in question can be assimilated to a cable programme service. This is the case for pay-per-view and video-on-demand services,[126] but also, under the decision in *Shetland Times* v. *Wills*,[127] for services providing on-line delivery of films.

192. The right of communication to the public in Ireland

Under section 37 of the Irish Copyright and Related Rights Act 2000, the owner of the copyright in a work has the exclusive right to 'make available the work to the public'. This 'making available' right is particularly broad as it covers the following rights:[128]

(a) making available to the public . . . copies of the work, by wire or wireless means, in such a way that members of the public may access the work from a place and at a time chosen by them (including the making available of copies of works through the Internet);
(b) performing, showing or playing a copy of the work in public;
(c) broadcasting a copy of the work;
(d) including a copy of the work in a cable programme service;
(e) issuing copies of the work to the public;
(f) renting copies of the work; [and]
(g) lending copies of the work without the payment of remuneration to the owner of the copyright in the work.

Rights (b), (c) and (d) are defined in a similar manner as the corresponding rights in the UK Act. The definition of right (a) implements the provisions of the WIPO Copyright Treaty of 1996 and corresponds to those of the Directive on Copyright and Related Rights in the Information Society. The provisions of the Satellite Directive on the collective exercise of certain rights in relation to cable retransmission have been implemented in section 174 of the Act, and are similar to the UK provisions.

As under the UK Act, rights in broadcasts and in underlying works are not infringed in the case of a 'must-carry' duty[129] where the broadcast is made for reception in the area in which the cable programme

---

Polyester Ltd Bombay v. *Telelink*, 1989 AIR Bombay 331, High Court of Bombay, noted at (1990) 3 *Entertainment Law Review* E-41, in which the inclusion of videotaped films in pay cable services was held to be a communication 'in public' under s. 14 of the Indian Copyright Act 1957.
[126] See para. 95.
[127] *Shetland Times Ltd* v. *Wills*, 1997 SC 316; 1997 SLT 669; [1997] EMLR 277; [1997] FSR 604, Court of Session, Outer House. See para. 95.
[128] Section 40. [129] Section 103(2)(a) and (3)(a).

service is provided.[130] However, in this latter case, the authorisation of all rightholders is necessary if the broadcast is a satellite or an encrypted transmission.[131]

193.   The right of communication to the public in authors' rights Acts

Subject to minor differences in the definition of the 'public' and to the application of specific copyright exemptions which will be studied below,[132] the definition of the 'right of communication to the public' in other Member States has a similarly wide scope when it comes to 'standard' public performance, broadcasting and distribution by cable. For example, in France, article L.1222 of the Intellectual Property Code grants to authors the right to communicate their works to the public 'by any process whatsoever', and merely gives illustrations of this right, which covers public recitation, lyrical performance, dramatic performance, public presentation, public projection and transmission in a public place of a telediffused work, but also 'telediffusion', defined as 'distribution by any telecommunications process of sounds, images, documents, data and messages of any kind'.

In Spain, article 17 of the Copyright Act grants to authors a 'right of communication to the public'. Under article 20(1) 'communication to the public' is defined as 'act whereby two or more persons are afforded access to the work without the prior distribution of copies to each of them', with the exception of communications taking place in a strictly domestic environment. Article 20(2) gives numerous illustrations of this right, including distribution or access through telecommunications networks.

In Germany, article 15(2) of the Copyright Act grants to authors the exclusive right to communicate their work to the public in non-material form (right of communication to the public), which comprises 'in particular' a right of recitation, performance and presentation,[133] a right of broadcasting;[134] a right of communication by means of video or audio recordings;[135] and a right of communication of broadcasts.[136] The definition of the public in the German Act appears to be somewhat more restrictive than the definition found in other copyright Acts.[137]

---

[130] Section 103(2)(b) and (3)(b).   [131] Section 73(2)(b).   [132] See Chapter 7 below.
[133] Art. 19.   [134] Art. 20.   [135] Art. 21.   [136] Art. 22.
[137] Art. 15(3) provides that the communication of a work shall be deemed public if it is intended for a plurality of persons, 'unless such persons form a clearly defined group and are connected by personal relationship with each other or with the organiser'. For example, s. 22 was held not applicable to the reception of a television broadcast by two patients in a hospital room. BGH (Federal Court of Justice), 11 July 1996, GRUR,

In Italy, article 15 of the Copyright Act grants to authors a right of public performance or recitation. Article 16 grants an exclusive right of diffusion, constituted by 'the use of any means of diffusion at a distance, such as telegraphy, telephony, radio or television broadcasting, or other similar means'.

In the Netherlands, the right of communication to the public in article 12 of the Copyright Act covers public performance, but also broadcasting, cable distribution and communication to the public through telecommunications networks.[138]

It appears that in all Member States copyright owners have the right to control the secondary retransmission of broadcasts to individual rooms in hotels.[139] On-demand distribution systems would also be covered under most definitions, at least if the distribution is made outside the private circle and 'to the public'. Transmission over telecommunications networks is sometimes expressly included in the definition of the performing right. In addition, the provisions of the Satellite and Cable Directive have been implemented in all Member States,[140] sometimes almost verbatim.

Outside the scope of European harmonisation, the treatment of simultaneous and integral cable retransmissions in the area serviced by the retransmitted broadcast may differ from one Member State to another. It appears, however, that in most Member States of the *droit d'auteur* tradition the cable distribution of broadcasts within the service area is not an exception or a defence to copyright liability.[141]

1996, p. 875, quoted by A. Dreier, in M. B. Nimmer and D. Geller (eds.), *International Copyright Law and Practice*, Matthew Bender, looseleaf, para. 8[1][b][iv].

[138] See H. Cohen Jehoram, in M. B. Nimmer and D. Geller (eds.), *International Copyright Law and Practice*, Matthew Bender, looseleaf, para. 8[1][b][v]. According to Cohen Jehoram, 'the right applies whether or not the members of the public are grouped together in a single space, and whether or not they receive the work simultaneously or "on demand" (*ibid.*).

[139] E.g. in France, Court of Cassation, 6 April 1994, RIDA, July 1994, p. 367, note Kerever; *La Semaine Juridique*, 1994, II, No. 22273, note Galloux; *Revue Dalloz*, 1994, p. 450, note Gautier; see also, in Germany, A. Dreier, in M. B. Nimmer and D. Geller (eds.), *International Copyright Law and Practice*, Matthew Bender, looseleaf, para. 8[1][b][iv], quoting BGH, 8 July 1993, GRUR, 1994, p. 45 (retransmission to prison cells), and BGH, 9 June 1994, GRUR, 1994, p. 797 (retransmission to hospital rooms).

[140] With the notable exception of Portugal.

[141] Though there may be compromise arrangements. For example, under French law the matter is regulated in a section dedicated to performing contracts, and is presented as a contract construction rule. Art. L.132-20 of the Intellectual Property Code provides that, unless otherwise stipulated, the authorisation to broadcast a work by hertzian waves does not include the cable distribution of this broadcast, unless it is carried simultaneously and integrally by the body which benefits from this authorisation, and without extension of the contractually agreed geographical zone. However, in practice, collecting societies have reserved the contrary stipulation in their agreements with broadcasters, and thus license all cable retransmissions.

SECTION IV

The distribution right

194.   International protection

In spite of competition with other delivery systems such as cable tele-vision and pay-per-view, the video (and now the DVD) market is still a major source of revenues for the film industry, and control of this mode of exploitation is of primary importance for film producers. The Berne Convention does not implement a general right of distribution, either in the form of a limited right to put copies on the market for the first time or in the form of a full right to control the circulation of copies of copy-right works. However, the Convention enshrines this right in relation to cinematographic works, by granting in its article 14(1)(ii) to authors of literary or artistic works the exclusive right of authorising the distribution of the cinematographic reproductions or adaptations of their works, and by granting similar rights to the owners of copyright in cinematographic works in article 14*bis*(1). The Convention does not, however, contain any provision on the rental or lending of copies of literary and artistic works.

Article 11 of the TRIPs Agreement does not provide for a general right of distribution, but grants rental rights in respect of computer pro-grams and cinematographic works.[142] However, a contracting party is excepted from according the rental right in respect of cinematographic works unless such rental has led to the widespread copying of such works and is materially impairing the exclusive right of reproduction conferred on authors.[143] In addition, the TRIPs Agreement is careful to avoid the question of the exhaustion of rights in its article 6:

For the purposes of dispute settlement under this Agreement, subject to the provisions of articles 3 [national treatment] and 4 [most-favoured-nation] nothing in this agreement shall be used to address the issue of exhaustion of intellectual property rights.

General rights of distribution and rental have been introduced in the WIPO Treaties of 1996. In the WIPO Copyright Treaty the right of dis-tribution is dealt with in article 6, which provides that authors of literary and artistic works shall enjoy the exclusive right of authorising the making

---

[142] 'In respect of at least computer programs and cinematographic works, a Member shall provide authors and their successors in title the right to authorize or to prohibit the commercial rental to the public of originals or copies of their copyright works.'

[143] Article 11 of the TRIPs Agreement, *in fine*. 'In respect of computer programs, this obligation does not apply to rentals where the program itself is not the essential object of the rental.'

available to the public of the original and copies of their works (defined as tangible objects)[144] through the sale or other transfer of ownership. Therefore, the right of distribution under the Treaty does not cover rental or lending nor any other form of distribution which does not convey ownership in the physical media reproducing the work. Article 6 also leaves contracting parties free to determine the extent of the exhaustion of right, if any.[145]

The rental right is dealt with in article 7. This right is restricted to authors of computer programs, cinematographic works and those works embodied in phonograms as determined in the national law of the contracting parties. The right is defined as 'the exclusive right of authorising commercial rental to the public of the originals or copies of their works'. However, like the TRIPs Agreement, the Treaty provides that the rental right is not applicable: (i) in the case of computer programs, where the program itself is not the essential object of the rental; and (ii) in the case of cinematographic works, unless such commercial rental has led to the widespread copying of such works materially impairing the exclusive right of reproduction.

195.   European harmonisation

The harmonisation of the right of distribution (and its more reduced rental and lending rights) within the European Union involves two stages. A partial harmonisation was first made by the Rental Directive of 19 November 1992; the Directive harmonises the distribution right only in relation to neighbouring rights,[146] and limits its scope in the field of copyright to rental and public lending. It provides that a *rental right* must be granted to all authors in relation to the original and copies of their works, and to performers in respect of fixations of their performances.[147] 'Rental' is defined in article 1(2) as the act of 'making available for use, for a limited period of time and for direct or indirect economic or commercial

---

[144] In the Agreed Statement Concerning Articles 6 and 7.

[145] Art. 6(2): 'Nothing in this Treaty shall affect the freedom of Contracting Parties to determine the conditions, if any, under which the exhaustion of the right in paragraph (1) applies after the first sale or other transfer of ownership of the original or a copy of the work with the authorization of the author.'

[146] According to art. 9 of the Rental Directive, a *distribution right*, defined as the right to make available copies to the public by sale 'or otherwise', must be introduced for performers, in respect of fixations of their performances, for film producers, in respect of their audiovisual recordings, and for broadcasting organisations, in respect of fixations of their broadcasts. This distribution right is subject to Community exhaustion (art. 9(2)) (and, given the *acquis communautaire* in this field, should also prohibit international exhaustion).

[147] Art. 2.

advantage'. Recital 13 makes clear that this definition does not cover the rental of copies of films to exhibitors or broadcasters for public performance or broadcasting.

As a consequence, a rental right must be granted: (a) to film authors, the Directive requiring that the film director be considered the author or one of the authors of the film for its purpose; and (b) to authors of contributory literary, dramatic, artistic and musical works in film productions.

However, it is not clear whether the rental of 'copies' according to the Directive extends beyond copies of the actual work, to copies of derivative works or adaptations. In other words, it is not clear whether the Directive requires that the author of, say, a musical work released on a phonogram included in a film soundtrack be granted a rental right or a rental interest in the film, as opposed to a rental right in the phonogram. In any case, a limit must be drawn somewhere. If an extensive construction is adopted, a film producer might need to clear the rental right in underlying works such as novels or artistic works if he intends to proceed with the rental of videotapes of the film. Note, however, that in that case authors of underlying contributions might not have a right to equitable remuneration from the rental of copies of the film; according to article 4 of the Directive the right of equitable remuneration is retained 'when an author . . . has transferred or assigned his rental right concerning . . . an original or copy of a film'; arguably, the right transferred by contributors other than film authors is transferred in relation to the original and copies of their contribution, not in relation to the original or copies of the film made from it. In that case, only performers and film authors could claim the equitable remuneration.

The Directive also provides for a *public lending right* to be granted to authors, performers and producers of phonograms and videograms. However, this right is subject to limitations in article 5 of the Directive. First, Member States may derogate from the public lending right, provided that at least authors obtain a remuneration for such lending. Article 5(1) provides that Member States shall be free to determine this remuneration taking account of their cultural promotion objectives. Article 5(2) further adds that, when Member States do not apply this right as regards phonograms, films and computer programs, they shall introduce, at least for authors, a remuneration. Accordingly, some sort of remuneration should be implemented for film authors for the public lending of their films. Secondly, article 5(3) specifies that Member States may exempt certain categories of establishment from the payment of this remuneration, without further specification.

The second stage of harmonisation took the form of the Directive on Copyright and Related Rights in the Information Society of 22 May 2001.

This Directive harmonises the *distribution right* of authors of all categories of copyright works, including film works. Under article 4(1) of the Directive:

Member States shall provide for authors, in respect of the original of their works or of copies thereof, the exclusive right to authorise or prohibit any form of distribution to the public by sale or otherwise.

In line with the case law of the European Court of Justice in this field,[148] article 4(2) further subjects this right to Community exhaustion.[149] Recital 28 makes clear that this Community-wide exhaustion excludes international exhaustion.[150]

196.   The distribution of film works in the UK and Ireland

In the UK, the issue to the public of copies of the work is an act restricted in respect of every description of copyright work.[151] In its original form, the CDPA 1988 provided that references to the issue to the public of copies of a work were to the act of putting into circulation copies not previously put into circulation, in the UK or elsewhere, and not to any subsequent distribution, sale, hiring or loan of those copies, or importation of those copies into the UK.[152]

However, a rental right was granted in relation to sound recordings, films and computer programs.[153] Rental was further defined in section 178 as commercial rental, but paragraph 8 of Schedule 7 to the Act extended the provision concerning rental to lending in public libraries. Under section 66 of the Act, in the absence of a certified licensing scheme the Secretary of State may establish a compulsory licensing scheme in relation to rental.

There was no such rental right and no exclusive lending right in relation to literary, dramatic, musical and artistic works. The public lending right

---

[148] See e.g. Case C-61/97, *Foreningen af Danske Videogramdistributorer* v. *Laserdisken* [1999] All ER (EC) 366; [1998] ECR I-5171; [1999] 1 CMLR 1297; [1999] EMLR 681, ECJ.

[149] 'The distribution right shall not be exhausted within the Community in respect of the original or copies of the work, except where the first sale or other transfer of ownership in the Community of that object is made by the rightholder or with his consent.'

[150] See para. 213.

[151] On the complexity and uncertainties of the current law, see J. Phillips and L. Bently, 'Copyright Issues: The Mysteries of Section 18' (1999) 21 EIPR 133.

[152] The right was thus characterised as a 'right of divulgation', as opposed to a right of distribution (*ibid.*). However, we will avoid this wording, which may cause confusion with the moral right of divulgation described in Chapter 8 below.

[153] Section 18(2) (original text): 'in relation to sound recordings, films and computer programs, the restricted act of issuing copies to the public includes any rental of copies to the public.'

scheme established under the Public Lending Right Act 1979 is limited in its scope and does not apply to films. The right to issue copies of the work to the public in section 18(1) was subject to international, not Community, exhaustion.

The Copyright and Related Rights Regulations 1996 modified this scheme by implementing the provisions of the Rental Directive. The Regulations first modified the existing right to issue copies of a work to the public in section 18 by reducing the scope of the exhaustion of the right from an international exhaustion to an EEA-wide exhaustion, in line with the *acquis communautaire* in this field.[154] The Regulations then extended the rental and lending rights to all literary, musical and dramatic works, and to artistic works other than works of architecture in the form of a building (including their models) and works of applied art.[155] In the new section 18A, 'rental' is defined as:

the making of a copy of the work available for use, on terms that it will or may be returned, for direct or indirect economic or commercial advantage.

In contrast, 'lending' is:

the making of a copy of a work available for use, on terms that it will or may be returned, otherwise than for direct or indirect economic or commercial advantage, through an establishment which is accessible to the public.

Section 18A further states that these expressions do not include making available a copy for the purpose of: (a) public performance, broadcasting or inclusion in a cable programme service; (b) exhibition in public; or (c) on-the-spot reference use, and that 'lending' does not include making available between establishments which are accessible to the public. In addition, section 18 specifies that there is no direct or indirect economic or commercial advantage under the above definitions where lending by an establishment accessible to the public gives rise to a payment which does not go beyond what is necessary to cover its operating costs. The Copyright and Related Rights Regulations 1996 except from the lending right the lending by public libraries of works subject to the public lending right scheme and any lending by educational establishments and certain libraries and archives.[156] Under the new section 66 of the Act, the lending (as opposed to rental) of copies of literary, dramatic, musical or artistic works, sound recordings or films may be subject to a compulsory licence by order of the Secretary of State. The provisions regarding the

---

[154] New s. 18(2) to (4).   [155] New ss. 16(1)(ba) and 18A.
[156] Reg. 11, new ss. 36A and 40A.

presumption of transfer of the rental right of the film producer and the right to equitable remuneration for the transfer of the rental right have been described in Chapter 5.[157] The provisions of the Irish Copyright and Related Rights Act 2000 are similar.[158]

197. The distribution of film works in authors' rights countries

As mentioned above, a distinction must be drawn between those authors' rights countries which implement a specific distribution right and those in which such a right is deduced from the reproduction right. The majority of Member States belong to that first category. A specific distribution right exists in Spain,[159] Portugal,[160] Germany,[161] the Netherlands,[162] Sweden,[163] Denmark,[164] Italy,[165] and Greece.[166] Rental and lending rights are either a part of the distribution right, or are conceived as independent rights. All these countries have now implemented the rental and lending rights, and apply the principle of EEA-wide exhaustion of rights, with the exception of rental and lending. National exhaustion applies in several countries, such as Germany, Greece, Italy and the Netherlands, but does not affect the rental and lending rights.

French law is representative of the second group. Under French law, the rights of distribution, rental and lending are not defined as independent rights, but are deduced from the right of reproduction, and in particular from article L.131-3 of the Intellectual Property Code, which provides that:

Transfer of authors' rights shall be subject to each of the assigned rights being separately mentioned in the instrument of assignment and the field of exploitation of the assigned rights being defined as to its scope and purpose, as to place and as to duration.

---

[157] See paras. 159 and 172.   [158] Sections 41 and 42.   [159] Copyright Act, art. 19.
[160] Copyright Act, art. 68.
[161] Copyright Act, art. 17 In Germany, the 1965 Act in its original version provided for a right of remuneration in case of rental of copyright works, and such a remuneration has existed in respect of public lending since 1972. The Law of 23 June 1995 amending the Copyright Act, which implemented the Rental Directive, changed this right to remuneration for rental into an exclusive right, but kept the system in place for public lending. The remuneration for public lending was extended, however, to performers and to producers of phonograms and videograms.
[162] Copyright Act, art. 12.   [163] Copyright Act, art. 19.
[164] Copyright Act, art. 2. But the right is derived from the general 'right to make the work available to the public', which also includes the performing right. Compare with the Irish Act, above.
[165] Art. 17.   [166] Copyright Act, art. 3.

The reference to the 'purpose' (*destination*, in French) in article L.131-3 gave the name to a prerogative called *droit de destination*. This theory, acknowledged by the French Supreme Court, was invoked to justify the view of the French performing right society (SACEM) of an additional mechanical reproduction right for public use of commercially released phonograms. As labels on these phonograms indicate that they are distributed for private use only, their use for acts of broadcasting or communication to the public involves, in addition to the authorisation to broadcast and communicate to the public, an authorisation to *use* the phonogram for this purpose (the additional reproduction right). In other words, these labels are considered as an expression of the right of the author to limit uses of copies of his work (*droit de destination*), and justify SACEM's view of this double remuneration. The Supreme Court validated this (quite extraordinary) theory in a long line of cases in the 1980s between SACEM and discotheque operators.[167]

But the right of destination goes beyond the control of 'public uses' of copies. According to most legal commentators, it also allows the control of rental, lending or any other right of distribution. French courts have not so far had the occasion to validate such an extension of the right. However, based on this assumption, the French legislator thought that French law already complied with the provisions of the Rental Directive, and chose not to implement it formally.

It is notable, however, that the right of destination differs from a full right of distribution or rental, as it requires that the author determines in advance the modes of distribution of copies of his works, and then prohibits particular modes of distribution. In this respect, the theory would not appear to comply with EC law, as far as rental is concerned. In addition, the scope of this theory is unclear. For example, does this right pass to the subsequent copyright owners, or is it exercisable only by the author? There is also doubt regarding the moment at which the right must be exercised (before copies are put on the market or also after?) and the form of its exercise. Finally, it does not appear to be subject to internal exhaustion.

The theory of the *droit de destination* was applicable in Belgium before the 1994 copyright reform, but the new Belgian Act of 1994 now expressly includes rental and lending in the list of exclusive rights.[168] It appears,

---

[167] Court of Cassation, 1 March 1988, *La Semaine Juridique*, 1988, II, No. 21120, note Françon; 22 March 1988, Bull. Civ., I, No. 88, p. 56, RIDA, October 1988, p. 295; 19 April 1988, Bull. Civ., I, No. 112, p. 76, RIDA, April 1989, p. 212; F. Pollaud-Dullian, *Le droit de destination*, LGDJ, Paris, 1989.

[168] Copyright Act, art. 1(1).

however, that the theory could still be valid to justify a control over the resale of copies of copyright works or other acts of distribution not covered by the rental and lending rights.

198.   Public lending of films

Member States adopted very different solutions and attitudes on public lending. For example, in France, although the general opinion is that authors have an exclusive right to authorise the lending of their works (based on the doctrine of *droit de destination*), there exists no organised system of remuneration for lending, and this right is not yet enforced by rightholders against public libraries (except with regard to audiovisual works, phonograms and software, which are usually excluded from lending). Following a report commissioned by the government,[169] France is now considering legislative action in this field.

In Belgium, authors may not prohibit the lending of literary works, the scores of musical works, sound and audiovisual works when lending is carried out with an educational and cultural intention by approved institutions.[170] The same is applicable to performers.[171] In such a case, however, authors, performers and producers are granted a right to remuneration.[172] So far, this right has not been implemented. Public libraries are also excluded from the lending right in Spain and Italy.

In other Member States, the right of public lending is in most cases reduced to a right to equitable remuneration.[173] But this remuneration is implemented in very different manners. It seems that in Scandinavian countries the remuneration for lending is not a remuneration based on copyright.[174] Other countries have implemented the remuneration within their copyright laws. In certain countries, an important part of the remuneration can be reserved to social funds, as in Germany.[175] In general, the remuneration is paid to authors, but, in some countries (e.g. Germany, Austria and the Netherlands), the remuneration is shared with publishers. The scheme is generally not applicable to films. Reciprocal arrangements are currently being negotiated between authors' societies in Europe.

---

[169] J.-M. Borzeix, 'La question du droit de prêt dans les bibliothèques, rapport au Ministre de la culture et de la communication', July 1998.
[170] Copyright Act, art. 23.   [171] Copyright Act, art. 47.   [172] Copyright Act, art. 62.
[173] See below. Denmark implemented such a right in 1946.
[174] Apparently, the remuneration in those Member States is not based on an actual audit of the lendings; it is also only open to national authors (and to living ones), subject to EC rules on non-discrimination on the grounds of nationality.
[175] More than 50 per cent of the remuneration is allocated to the social security of authors.

SECTION V

Protection of technological measures and
rights-management information

199.   Introduction[176]

The protection regime for technological measures protecting copyright
works and for rights-management information will be harmonised within
the European Union as a result of the Directive on Copyright and Related
Rights in the Information Society, in line with the provisions of the WIPO
Treaties of 1996. A present, the treatment of these questions varies within
the Union.

200.   Protection of technological measures and rights-management information in the international agreements

Obligations concerning technological measures are dealt with in article
11 of the WIPO Copyright Treaty of 1996, which provides:

> Contracting Parties shall provide adequate legal protection and effective legal
> remedies against the circumvention of effective technological measures that are
> used by authors in connection with the exercise of their rights under this Treaty
> or the Berne Convention and that restrict acts, in respect of their works, which
> are not authorised by the authors concerned or permitted by law.

Article 12 is dedicated to 'rights-management information', defined as
information which identifies the work, its author, the owner of any right
in the work, the terms and conditions of use, and any numbers or codes
that represent such information, which is attached to a copy of a work
or which appears in connection with its communication to the public.[177]
Article 12(1) provides:

> Contracting Parties shall provide adequate and effective legal remedies against
> any person knowingly performing any of the following acts knowing, or with
> respect to civil remedies having reasonable grounds to know, that it will induce,
> enable, facilitate or conceal an infringement of any right covered by this Treaty
> or the Berne Convention:
> (i) to remove or alter any electronic rights-management information without
>   authority;

---

[176] See 'Protection of Technological Measures', Institute for Information Law, Amsterdam,
November 1998, available at www.imprimatur.alcs.co.uk.
[177] Art. 12(2).

(ii) to distribute, import for distribution, broadcast or communicate to the public, without authority, works or copies of works knowing that electronic rights-management information has been removed or altered without authority.

The agreed statement on article 12 specifies that the reference to 'infringement of any right covered by this Treaty or the Berne Convention' includes both exclusive rights and rights of remuneration.[178]

201. European harmonisation

The question of technological measures was first addressed at the European level in the Software Directive of 14 May 1991.[179] The Directive on Copyright and Related Rights in the Information Society contains detailed provisions aimed at preserving and protecting both technological measures and rights-management information for all classes of works in its articles 6 and 7 respectively. The laws, regulations and administrative provisions necessary to comply with these provision must be adopted by Member States before 22 December 2002.

202. Technological measures

The wording used in article 6 of the Directive is inspired by the corresponding provisions in the WIPO Treaties of 1996. Under article 6(1), Member States shall provide adequate legal protection against the circumvention of any effective 'technological measures', which the person concerned carries out in the knowledge, or with reasonable grounds for knowing that he or she pursues that objective. This protection is extended in article 6(2) in respect of any activities that promote, enable or facilitate this circumvention.[180]

---

[178] And adds: 'It is further understood that Contracting Parties will not rely on this Article to devise or implement rights-management systems that would have the effect of imposing formalities which are not permitted under the Berne Convention or this Treaty, prohibiting the free movement of goods or impeding the enjoyment of rights under this Treaty.'

[179] Council Directive 91/250/EEC of 14 May 1991 on the legal protection of computer programs, OJ 1991 No. L122, 17 May 1991. Art. 7(1) of the Directive provides that Member States shall provide, in accordance with their national legislation, appropriate remedies against a person committing any act of putting into circulation, or the possession for commercial purposes of, any means the sole intended purpose of which is to facilitate the unauthorised removal or circumvention of any technical device which may have been applied to protect a computer program.

[180] 'Member States shall provide adequate legal protection against the manufacture, import, distribution, sale, rental, advertisement for sale or rental, or possession for commercial purposes of devices, products or components or the provision of services which: (a) are promoted, advertised or marketed for the purpose of circumvention of, or (b) have only a limited commercially significant purpose or use other than to circumvent, or (c) are primarily designed, produced, adapted or performed for the purpose of enabling or facilitating the circumvention of, any effective technological measures.'

The term 'technological measures' is defined in article 6(3) as:

> any technology, device or component that, in the normal course of its operation, is designed to prevent or restrict acts, in respect of works or other subject-matter, which are not authorised by the rightholder of any copyright or any right related to copyright as provided for by law or the *sui generis* right provided for in Chapter III of Directive 96/9/EC [on database protection]. Technological measures shall be deemed 'effective' where the use of a protected work or other subject-matter is controlled by the rightholders through application of an access control or protection process, such as encryption, scrambling or other transformation of the work or other subject-matter or a copy control mechanism, which achieves the protection objective.

In order to qualify such a broad definition, the Council introduced in its Common Position a new paragraph 6(4), which aims at balancing the legitimate interests of all parties concerned. The first paragraph of article 6(4) provides that rightholders must provide the beneficiaries of several exceptions listed in paragraph 5 of the Directive with the means to benefit from these exceptions:

> Notwithstanding the legal protection provided for in paragraph 1, in the absence of voluntary measures taken by rightholders, including agreements between rightholders and other parties concerned, Member States shall take appropriate measures to ensure that rightholders make available to the beneficiary of an exception or limitation provided for in national law in accordance with Article 5(2)(a), (2)(c), (2)(d), (2)(e), (3)(a), (3)(b) or (3)(e) the means of benefiting from that exception or limitation, to the extent necessary to benefit from that exception or limitation and where that beneficiary has legal access to the protected work or subject-matter concerned.[181]

Paragraph 2 provides for an additional (optional) protection of users in case of private copy:

> A Member State may also take such measures in respect of a beneficiary of an exception or limitation provided for in accordance with Article 5(2)(b), unless reproduction for private use has already been made possible by rightholders to the extent necessary to benefit from the exception or limitation concerned and in accordance with the provisions of Article 5(2)(b) and (5), without preventing rightholders from adopting adequate measures regarding the number of reproductions in accordance with these provisions.[182]

These paragraphs are not applicable to the provision of interactive on-demand services (in such a way that members of the public may access works or other subject-matter from a place and at a time individually chosen by them), when such services are governed by contractual arrangements.

---

[181] See para. 211.   [182] See para. 211.

Article 6(4) further provides that the technological measures applied voluntarily by rightholders, including those applied in implementation of voluntary agreements, and technological measures applied in implementation of the measures taken by Member States, shall enjoy the legal protection provided for in paragraph 1.

Finally, article 6(4) applies *mutatis mutandis* when article 6 is applied in the context of the Rental and Databases Directives. The provisions of article 6 are accompanied by important interpretative recitals aiming at promoting voluntary measures taken by rightholder in this field.[183]

203. Rights-management information

Obligations concerning rights-management information are included in article 7 of the Directive. Member States shall provide for adequate legal protection against any person performing knowingly without authority the removal or alteration of any electronic rights-management information or the distribution, importation for distribution, broadcasting, communication or making available to the public, of works or other subject-matter protected under the Directive or under Chapter III of the Database Directive (*sui generis* right) from which electronic rights-management information has been removed or altered without authority, if such person knows, or has reasonable grounds to know, that by so doing he is inducing, enabling, facilitating or concealing an infringement of any copyright or any rights related to copyright as provided by law (or of the *sui generis* right over databases).

The expression 'rights-management information' is defined as meaning:

any information provided by rightholders which identifies the work or other subject-matter referred to in this Directive or covered by the *sui generis* right provided for in Chapter III of Directive 96/9/EC [on database protection], the author or any other rightholder, or information about the terms and conditions of use of the work or other subject-matter, and any numbers or codes that represent such information.

The first subparagraph shall apply when any of these items of information is associated with a copy of, or appears in connection with the communication to the public of, a work or other subject-matter referred to in this Directive or covered by the *sui generis* right provided for in Chapter III of Directive 96/9/EC [on database protection].

204. The Conditional Access Directive of 1998

Another important piece of European legislation in this field is the European Parliament and Council Directive of 20 November 1998 on the Legal Protection of Services Based on, or Consisting of, Conditional

---

[183] Recitals 51 and 52.

Access.[184] This Directive harmonises within the EU the legal protection of all those services whose remuneration depends on 'conditional access' techniques such as encryption and electronic locks. Its scope includes all services that are supplied on a conditional access basis, such as pay-TV, video-on-demand, electronic publishing and on-line services offered to the public on a subscription or usage-related basis. However, it does not cover off-line products.

The Directive is not directed at services providing content protected by intellectual property, but is certainly applicable to such services.[185] Accordingly, certain type of services could benefit from a double protection, under the provisions of the Copyright and Conditional Access Directives and their implementation texts. The Conditional Access Directive also provides protection for those service providing access to public domain works. Member States had to bring into force the laws, regulations and administrative provisions necessary to comply with this Directive by 28 May 2000.

SECTION VI

The liability of intermediaries

205.   Introduction[186]

We are concerned here with the question of the liability under copyright law of intermediaries playing a role in the distribution over digital networks of copyright material such as films. The term 'intermediaries' will be used here with a broad meaning encompassing access providers (i.e. a persons providing access to the digital network), service providers (i.e. persons providing services such as the hosting of computers in their premises or of websites on their servers) and all other intermediaries (such as the owners of nodes in digital networks).

It is reasonably safe to say that the copyright laws of European Union Member States are not, in their present state, very favourable to the activities of such intermediaries. We saw that the dissemination of works over digital networks is covered in most systems by the exclusive rights of copy or reproduction (at the origin and outset) and by the right of communication to the public, or at least by one of these rights.[187] In

---

[184] Directive 98/84/EC, OJ 1998 No. L320, 28 November 1998, pp. 54–7.
[185] Recital 21.
[186] See the report, 'Liability for On-Line Intermediaries', Institute for Information Law, Amsterdam, 1997, commissioned in the framework of the 'Imprimatur' project, www.imprimatur.net.
[187] See paras. 191 and 193.

almost all cases, secondary infringement provisions or general provisions on vicarious liability extend the liability (either under a strict or with-fault liability) to intermediaries.[188] In addition, the private copy exemptions are usually drafted in such a restrictive way that a third party enabling or providing the infrastructure for copying would not benefit from them.[189] The same is true for the exemptions applicable to communication to the public in restricted circles, when they are implemented.[190]

In Germany, the AOL case,[191] in which AOL was condemned for allowing subscribers to swap infringing music files on its service, put the onus on access providers to verify the infringing nature of the activities of its subscribers. Similar cases arose in France in relation to the right or privacy and publicity, and to defamatory/illegal content of websites.[192] This liability is now being limited in the process of implementation of the WIPO Copyright Treaty of 1996 and of the EC Directive on Electronic Commerce of 8 June 2000.

206.   The WIPO Copyright Treaty of 1996

As mentioned above, the question of the liability of on-line intermediaries was addressed during the negotiations of the WIPO Copyright Treaty. The Agreed Statement on article 8 provides:

> It is understood that the mere provision of physical facilities for enabling or making a communication does not in itself amount to communication within the meaning of the Treaty or the Berne Convention . . .

This Statement limits the liability of certain intermediaries, but its scope is unclear. In addition, the Statement is limited to the right of communication to the public and leaves open the question of the provision of physical facilities for the copying of works.

207.   The EC Directive on Electronic Commerce of 8 June 2000

Article 4 of the EC Directive on Electronic Commerce of 8 June 2000[193] harmonises the position of Member States in respect of electronic commerce. This article concerns dedicated to the liability of intermediary service providers. A service provider is defined as 'any natural or legal person

---

[188] See e.g. para. 191.   [189] See para. 219.   [190] See para. 220.
[191] Tribunal of First Instance of Munich, 30 March 2000.
[192] E.g. Tribunal of First Instance of Paris, *Lefebure* v. *Lacambre*, 6 September 1998 (Internet service provider held responsible for violation of the right of privacy/publicity for allowing a subscriber to publish photos of a nude celebrity on his website).
[193] OJ 2000 No. L178/1 of 17 July 2000.

providing an information society service',[194] which includes Internet-based services. Under the Directive, intermediary services providers will have no obligation to monitor the information which they transmit or store, nor a general obligation actively to uncover illegal activity in case of *mere conduit, caching* or *hosting,* provided some standards are met.[195] However, in all cases, the provider may still be required by a court or administrative authority to terminate or prevent an infringement.[196]

Mere conduit is defined in article 12(1) as the transmission in a communication network of information provided by the recipient of the service, or the provision of access to a communication network. Article 12(2) specifies that transmission and provision of access includes the automatic, intermediate and transient storage of the information transmitted in so far as this takes place for the sole purpose of carrying out the transmission in the communication network, and provided that the information is not stored for any period longer than is reasonably necessary for the transmission. For such activities, Member States shall ensure that the service provider is not be liable for the information transmitted, on condition that it:

1. does not initiate the transmission;
2. does not select the receiver of the transmission; and
3. does not select or modify the information contained in the transmission.

Caching is defined in article 13(1) as the automatic, intermediate and temporary storage of information performed for the sole purpose of making more efficient the transmission of information in a communication network. Member States shall ensure that the service provider is not liable for such activities, on condition that it

1. does not modify the information;
2. complies with conditions on access to the information;
3. complies with rules regarding the updating of the information, specified in a manner widely recognised and used by industry;
4. does not interfere with the lawful use of technology, widely recognised and used by industry, to obtain data on the use of the information; and

[194] Art. 2(b).
[195] '1. Member States shall not impose a general obligation on providers, when providing the services covered by Articles 12 to 14, to monitor the information which they transmit or store, nor a general obligation actively to seek facts or circumstances indicating illegal activity. 2. Member States may establish obligations for information society service providers promptly to inform the competent public authorities of alleged illegal activities undertaken or information provided by recipients of their service or obligations to communicate to the competent authorities, at their request, information enabling the identification of recipients of their service with whom they have storage agreements.'
[196] Arts. 12(3) (mere conduit), 13(2) (caching) and 14(3) (hosting). For hosting, the Directive adds that Member States may establish procedures governing the removal or disabling of access to information.

5. acts expeditiously to remove or to disable access to the information it has stored upon obtaining actual knowledge of the fact that the information at the initial source of the transmission has been removed from the network, or access to it has been disabled, or that a court or an administrative authority has ordered such removal or disablement.

Hosting is defined in article 14(1) as the storage of information provided by a recipient of the service. In such a case, Member States shall ensure that the service provider is not liable for the information stored at the request of a recipient of the service, on condition that the provider:

1. does not have actual knowledge of illegal activity or information and, as regards claims for damages, is not aware of facts or circumstances from which the illegal activity or information is apparent; or

2. upon obtaining such knowledge or awareness, acts expeditiously to remove or to disable access to the information.

This limitation does not apply when the recipient of the service is acting under the authority or the control of the provider.[197] Member States had to implement these provisions before 17 January 2002.

---

[197] Art. 14(2).

7   Exemptions and permitted acts

208.   Introduction

Exemptions and limitations to copyright are currently at the heart of the debate on copyright harmonisation in Europe. The delay in the adoption of the Directive on Copyright and Related Rights in the Information Society was mainly caused by the difficulties of Member States agreeing on the scope of copyright exemptions in the digital networked environment. One explanation is that exemptions are often the result of a delicate balance between conflicting interests and policy objectives, and for that reason are difficult to adapt or modify. Another explanation can be found in the intense lobbying of certain pressure groups.

In this respect, Member States' legislation is extremely diverse, not only in the list of exemptions, but also in the definition of the generally accepted exemptions. Within the European Union, some copyright Acts include a very limited list of exemptions, which are usually narrowly defined and restrictively construed by courts. This is the case, for example, in France and in Belgium. In contrast, the UK and Irish copyright Acts contain a very extensive and detailed list of exemptions. Some of these exemptions are very broad, such as the so-called 'library privileges'. Other Member States implement less detailed lists including a great variety of limitations. These can be strictly delimited in their scope or take the form of 'fair dealing' exemptions. However, in Europe, 'fair use' as such does not form a general defence to copyright infringement claims. The existing limitations can also be outright exemptions to copyright or take the form of compulsory licences or rights of remuneration.

209.   Copyright exemptions and limitations
at the international level

The Berne Convention provides for both compulsory and optional exemptions or limitations to copyright. Article 2(8) excludes from the protection of the Convention current news and more generally miscellaneous facts having the character of mere items of press information. Article 10(1) adds short quotations to that list.[1] Most of the limitations are, however, optional. Some may take the form of a compulsory licence, as in article 11*bis* for broadcasting and article 13 for the recording of music works. Others are designed as outright exceptions, and concern official texts,[2] certain speeches[3] or use for an educational purpose.[4] Three exemptions are of interest for our purpose. The first two concern articles and broadcasts on current events and the reporting of current events and are included in article 10*bis* of the Convention. But the most important, included in article 9(2), concerns the right of reproduction:

It shall be a matter for legislation in the countries of the Union to permit the reproduction of such works in certain special cases, provided that such reproduction does not conflict with a normal exploitation of the work and does not unreasonably prejudice the legitimate interests of the author.

It contains the so-called 'three steps' test, under which exceptions to the right of reproduction are possible (1) only in certain special cases, (2) if they do not conflict with the normal exploitation of the work and (3) if they do not unreasonably prejudice the legitimate interest of the author or copyright owner.

The language and test of article 9(2) of the Berne Convention were extended under article 13 of the TRIPs Agreement to all exemptions to the exclusive rights of copyright owners covered by the agreement:

Members shall confine limitations or exceptions to exclusive rights to certain special cases which do not conflict with a normal exploitation of the work and do not unreasonably prejudice the legitimate interests of the rightholder.

They were also adopted by article 10 of the WIPO Copyright Treaty in relation to the rights under the Treaty.

Concerning related or neighbouring rights, the Rome Convention contains in its article 15 several exemptions to the rights of performers and phonogram producers concerning 'private use', 'use of short excerpts in connection with the reporting of current events', 'ephemeral fixation by a broadcasting organisation' and use solely for teaching or scientific purposes. In addition, other limitations are allowed if they correspond to those applicable to copyright under domestic law. These provisions are incorporated in article 14(6) of the TRIPs Agreement:

---

[1] 'It shall be permissible to make quotations from a work which has already been lawfully made available to the public, provided that their making is compatible with fair practice, and their extent does not exceed that justified by the purpose, including quotations from newspaper articles and periodicals in the form of press summaries.'
[2] Art. 2(4).   [3] Art. 2*bis*.   [4] Art. 10(2).

Any Member may, in relation to the rights conferred under paragraphs 1, 2 and 3, provide for conditions, limitations, exceptions and reservations to the extent permitted by the Rome Convention. However, the provisions of Article 18 of the Berne Convention (1971 text) shall also apply, *mutatis mutandis*, to the rights of performers and producers of phonograms in phonograms.

However, neither Convention implements the three steps approach of article 9(2) of the Berne Convention in relation to neighbouring rights. This test was, however, reproduced in article 16 of the WIPO Performance and Phonogram Treaty.

210.   European harmonisation before the Directive on Copyright and Related Rights in the Information Society

At the time of the WIPO Treaties, copyright exemptions were only harmonised in Europe in relation to computer programs, neighbouring rights and databases. Article 5 of the Software Directive of 14 May 1991 excepts from the authorisation of the rightholder acts that are necessary for the use of the computer program by the lawful acquirer in accordance with its intended purpose, including for error correction, the making of a backup copy, and the observation, study and test of the program. Article 6 contains details of the regime of decompilation and subjects the exemption to the three steps test of article 9(2) of the Berne Convention.

Under article 10 of the Rental Directive, Member States may provide for limitations on the related rights of performers, producers of phonograms, broadcasting organisations and producers of videograms in respect of:

1. private use (without prejudice to any existing or future legislation on remuneration for private copy);
2. use of short excerpts in connection with the reporting of current events;
3. ephemeral fixation by a broadcasting organisation by means of its own facilities and for its own broadcasts;
4. use solely for the purposes of teaching or scientific research.

In addition, the Directive allows Member States to provide for the same kinds of limitations as implemented in relation to the copyright in literary and artistic works.[5]

Finally, the Directive provides for a compulsory licence for use of phonograms published for commercial purposes for broadcasting by wireless means or for any communication to the public.[6] Its wording,

---

[5] Art. 10(2). However, compulsory licences may be provided for only to the extent to which they are compatible with the Rome Convention.
[6] Art. 8(2).

however, clearly suggests that this licence is not applicable to film sound-tracks reproducing such phonograms.

The Database Directive of 11 March 1996 sets out various exceptions to the copyright in original databases and to the *sui generis* right over databases, in respectively its articles 6 and 9. The private copy exemption is restricted to non-electronic databases.

211. The Directive on Copyright and Related Rights in the Information Society of 22 May 2001

The Directive on Copyright and Related Rights in the Information Society has a much broader scope than the previous European instruments in relation to copyright exemptions. It provides for a detailed list of exemptions in its article 5 applicable to all classes of copyright and related rights works. The acts concerned are not limited to uses of works in electronic forms. This list is a closed list, which means that Member States will not be allowed to implement or keep other exceptions within the scope of the harmonisation.[7]

The difficulties in reaching an agreement over article 5 explain the delays in the adoption process of this Directive, subject to the co-decision procedure. Article 5(1) introduces an *obligatory* exception to the right of reproduction for certain *technical acts of reproduction* on individual computers or digital networks. The text reads:

Temporary acts of reproduction referred to in Article 2, which are transient or incidental, which are an integral and essential part of a technological process whose sole purpose is to enable:
(a) a transmission in a network between third parties by an intermediary or
(b) a lawful use
of a work or other subject-matter to be made, and which have no independent economic significance, shall be exempted from the reproduction right provided for in Article 2.

The purpose of this exemption is to exclude acts of reproduction dictated by technology (such as a transient copy on computer memory or caching) which have no separate economic significance. In its proposal, the Commission stressed the importance of such an exemption in the transnational environment:

Such an obligatory exception at Community level is vital as such short lived reproductions ancillary to the final use of a work will take place in most acts of exploitation of protected subject-matter, which will often be of a transnational nature. For

---

[7] Which may be difficult to determine precisely (see the discussion on the external limits to copyright, at paras. 212 *et seq.*).

instance, when transmitting a video on-demand from a database in Germany to a home computer in Portugal, this retrieval will imply a copy of the video, first of all, at the place of the database and afterwards, on average, up to at least a hundred often ephemeral acts of storage along the transmission to Portugal. A divergent situation in Member States with some requiring authorisation of such ancillary acts of storage would significantly risk impeding the free movement of works and services, and notably on-line services containing protected subject-matter.[8]

Corresponding exemptions to the liability of intermediaries in the on-line environment are found in the Directive on Electronic Commerce of 8 June 2000.[9]

With regard to the condition of lawful use in article 5(1)(b), recital 33 specifies that a use should be considered lawful where it is authorised by the rightholder or not restricted by law. The application of this exception is subject to the three steps test approach, reproduced in article 5(5).[10]

Article 5(2) allows Member States to implement *optional* exceptions to the reproduction right, relating to reprography, reproductions of audio and audiovisual material for private use, some establishments of public interest and ephemeral fixations by broadcasting organisations, some of which are subject to equitable remuneration. The text of the Directive reads:

Member States may provide for exceptions or limitations to the reproduction right provided for in Article 2 in the following cases:
(a) in respect of reproductions on paper or any similar medium, effected by the use of any kind of photographic technique or by some other process having similar effects, with the exception of sheet music, provided that the rightholders receive fair compensation;
(b) in respect of reproductions on any medium made by a natural person for private use and for ends that are neither directly nor indirectly commercial, on condition that the rightholders receive fair compensation which takes account of the application or non-application of technological measures referred to in Article 6 to the work or subject-matter concerned;
(c) in respect of specific acts of reproduction made by publicly accessible libraries, educational establishments or museums, or by archives, which are not for direct or indirect economic or commercial advantage;
(d) in respect of ephemeral recordings of works made by broadcasting organisations by means of their own facilities and for their own broadcasts; the preservation of these recordings in official archives may, on the ground of their exceptional documentary character, be permitted;

---

[8] COM (97) 628 final, OJ 1998 No. C108, 7 April 1998, p. 6 at p. 37.
[9] See para. 207. The Directive specifies that it is without prejudice to provisions relating to liability in the Directive on Electronic Commerce of 8 June 2000 (recital 16).
[10] 'The exceptions and limitations provided for in paragraphs 1, 2, 3 and 4 shall only be applied in certain special cases which do not conflict with a normal exploitation of the work or other subject-matter and do not unreasonably prejudice the legitimate interests of the rightholder.'

(e) in respect of reproductions of broadcasts made by social institutions pursuing non-commercial purposes, such as hospitals or prisons, on condition that the rightholders receive fair compensation.

The exception for private copying proved to be highly controversial. The original proposal made no distinction between analogue and digital technology in article 5(2)(b). It also left Member States with the possibility not to implement a remuneration for private copy. Upon first reading, the European Parliament proposed that analogue and digital private copying be made conditional upon fair compensation for rightholders. It proposed, however, that they be treated separately. This view was adopted in the Commission's amended proposal,[11] but the Council considered that no distinction should be made in article 5 between analogue and digital private copying. However, recitals 38 and 39 of the adopted text recognise that due account should be taken of the differences between analogue and digital private copying:

(38) Member States should be allowed to provide for an exception or limitation to the reproduction right for certain types of reproduction of audio, visual and audiovisual material for private use, accompanied by fair compensation. This may include the introduction or continuation of remuneration schemes to compensate for the prejudice to rightholders. Although differences between those remuneration schemes affect the functioning of the internal market, those differences, with respect to analogue private reproduction, should not have a significant impact on the development of the information society. Digital private copying is likely to be more widespread and have a greater economic impact. Due account should therefore be taken of the differences between digital and analogue private copying and a distinction should be made in certain respects between them.

(39) When applying the exception or limitation on private copying, Member States should take due account of technological and economic developments, in particular with respect to digital private copying and remuneration schemes, when effective technological protection measures are available. Such exceptions or limitations should not inhibit the use of technological measures or their enforcement against circumvention.

It is also interesting to observe that the limitation of private use in the amended proposal to 'strictly personal use' has been deleted by the Council, as it was considered too restrictive.

Some general guidance on the term 'fair compensation' can be found in recital 35 of the Directive, which provides:

(35) In certain cases of exceptions or limitations, rightholders should receive fair compensation to compensate them adequately for the use made of their protected works or other subject-matter. When determining the form, detailed

---

[11] Art. 5(b) and (b)*bis.*

arrangements and possible level of such fair compensation, account should be taken of the particular circumstances of each case.

When evaluating these circumstances, a valuable criterion would be the possible harm to the rightholders resulting from the act in question. In cases where rightholders have already received payment in some other form, for instance as part of a licence fee, no specific or separate payment may be due. The level of fair compensation should take full account of the degree of use of technological protection measures referred to in this Directive. In certain situations where the prejudice to the rightholder would be minimal, no obligation for payment may arise.

Recital 36 further specifies that Member States may provide such a fair compensation also when applying the optional provisions on exceptions or limitations which do not require such compensation. Finally, the exceptions under article 5(2) are subject to the three steps test under article 5(5).

Article 5(3) allows Member States to implement certain limitations on the right of reproduction and communication to the public, for example relating to illustration for teaching or scientific research purposes or for information purposes. The list of exemptions has been substantially extended by the Council in the Common Position. The article now reads:

Member States may provide for exceptions or limitations to the rights provided for in Articles 2 and 3 in the following cases:
  (a) use for the sole purpose of illustration for teaching or scientific research, as long as, whenever possible, the source, including the author's name, is indicated, unless this proves impossible, and to the extent justified by the non-commercial purpose to be achieved;
  (b) uses, for the benefit of people with a disability, which are directly related to the disability and of a non-commercial nature, to the extent required by the specific disability;
  (c) reproduction by the press, communication to the public or making available of published articles on current economic, political or religious topics or of broadcast works or other subject-matter of the same character, in cases where such use is not expressly reserved, and as long as the source, including the author's name, is indicated, or use of works or other subject-matter in connection with the reporting of current events, to the extent justified by the informatory purpose and as long as, whenever possible, the source, including the author's name, is indicated, unless this proves impossible;
  (d) quotations for purposes such as criticism or review, provided that they relate to a work or other subject-matter which has already been lawfully made available to the public, that, unless this proves impossible, the source, including the author's name, is indicated, and that their use is in accordance with fair practice, and to the extent required by the specific purpose;
  (e) use for the purposes of public security or to ensure the proper performance or reporting of administrative, parliamentary or judicial proceedings;
  (f) use of political speeches as well as extracts of public lectures or similar works or subject-matter to the extent justified by the informatory purpose and

provided that, whenever possible, the source, including the author's name, is indicated, except where this proves impossible;

(g) use during religious celebrations or official celebrations organised by a public authority;

(h) use of works, such as works of architecture or sculpture, made to be located permanently in public places;

(i) incidental inclusion of a work or other subject-matter in other material;

(j) use for the purpose of advertising the public exhibition or sale of artistic works, to the extent necessary to promote the event, excluding any other commercial use;

(k) use for the purpose of caricature, parody or pastiche;

(l) use in connection with the demonstration or repair of equipment;

(m) use of an artistic work in the form of a building or a drawing or plan of a building for the purposes of reconstructing the building;

(n) use by communication or making available, for the purpose of research or private study, to individual members of the public by dedicated terminals on the premises of establishments referred to in paragraph 2(c) of works and other subject-matter not subject to purchase or licensing terms which are contained in their collections;

(o) use in certain other cases of minor importance where exceptions or limitations already exist under national law, provided that they only concern analogue uses and do not affect the free circulation of goods and services within the Community, without prejudice to the other exceptions and limitations contained in this Article.

The three steps approach applies here too. Finally, article 5(4) allows the extension to the distribution right of exceptions to the reproduction rights:

Where the Member States may provide for an exception or limitation to the right of reproduction pursuant to paragraphs 2 and 3, they may provide similarly for an exception or limitation to the right of distribution as referred to in Article 4 to the extent justified by the purpose of the authorised act of reproduction.

212.   External limitations on copyright

In addition to these exceptions to copyright, we must take into consideration those limitations on the rights of copyright owners which in Europe result from the application of rules which are 'external' to copyright, such as the principle of free circulation of goods, the operation of competition law, the principle of free speech or specific doctrines such as 'abuse of right' or 'copyright misuse'.

213.   Exhaustion of rights

The principle of exhaustion of rights (or first sale doctrine) provides a major limitation to the right of distribution of protected goods. Based on the principle of freedom of movement of goods enshrined in the EC Treaty, the European Court of Justice (ECJ) developed the principle of Community exhaustion (now EEA-wide exhaustion), under which, once copies of a work protected by intellectual property right have been lawfully placed on the market in one Member State by the owner of the right or with his consent, the intellectual property right cannot be invoked to prevent copies from entering the territory of another Member State.[12] This principle was applied in the field of copyright and neighbouring rights.[13] It was held inapplicable, however, to the right of communication to the public and in the case of rental.[14] These principles were partly codified in the EC copyright directives, and are restated in article 4(2) of the Directive on Copyright and Related Rights in the Information Society:

> The distribution right shall not be exhausted within the Community in respect of the original of their works or of copies thereof, except where the first sale or other transfer of ownership in the Community of that object is made by the rightholder or with his consent.

Two remarks must be made, however, concerning this exhaustion principle. First, Community exhaustion does not necessarily involve *internal* (or national) exhaustion. Accordingly, some differences may subsist in the scope of the distribution right (rental and lending excepted) among Member States. Secondly, the ECJ in the now famous *Silhouette* trademark case[15] held that national rules providing for international exhaustion of trademark rights are contrary to Community legislation relating to trademarks. This rule applies to the distribution right harmonised under the copyright directives.[16]

214.   Competition law

Another external limit to the exploitation of intellectual property rights is constituted by competition law rules, both at domestic and Community level. At Community level, the main provisions are article 81 (formerly

---

[12] E.g. Case 16/74, *Centrafarm* v. *Winthrop* [1974] ECR 1183, ECJ; Case 119/75, *Terrapin Ltd* v. *Terranova Industrie* [1976] ECR 1039, ECJ; Case 58/80, *Dansk Supermarked* v. *Imerco* [1981] ECR 181, ECJ; and Case 144/81, *Keurkoop* v. *Nancy Kean Gifts* [1982] ECR 2853, ECJ.

[13] E.g. Joined Cases 55/80 and 57/80, *Musik-Vertrieb Membran* v. *GEMA* [1981] ECR 147, ECJ.

[14] Case 62/79, *Coditel* v. *Ciné Vog Films* [1980] ECR 881, ECJ; Case 158/86, *Warner Bros Inc.* v. *Christiansen* [1988] ECR 2605, ECJ; and Case C-61/97, *Foreningen af Danske Videogramdistributorer* v. *Laserdisken* [1998] ECR I-5171, ECJ.

[15] Case C-355/96, *Silhouette International* v. *Hartlauer* [1998] ECR I-4799, ECJ.

[16] See para. 195.

article 85) of the EC Treaty, which prohibits collusion between under-
takings which may affect trade between Member States and which have
the object or effect of restricting competition within the common market, and article 82 (formerly article 86) on the abuse of a dominant
position.

The prohibition of concerted practice certainly applies to agreements
in the field of copyright. The ECJ has repeatedly stated that some aspects
of the manner in which an intellectual property right is exercised may
prove to be incompatible with article 81, 'where they serve to give effect
to an agreement, decision or concerted practice which may have as its
object or effect the prevention, restriction or distortion of competition
within the common market'.[17]

But article 82, on the abuse of a dominant position, may also prove to
be a powerful tool against the behaviour of individual copyright owners.
In the landmark case *Magill* of 6 April 1995[18] the ECJ held that the refusal by a copyright owner to grant a licence could constitute, in certain
circumstances, an abuse of a dominant position. Three television stations in the UK and Ireland, which published their own weekly television
guide covering exclusively their own programmes, sued Magill TV guide
when the latter attempted to publish a guide of their programmes, for
infringement of the copyright in their listings. The Commission found
this behaviour abusive under article 82 and required each station to
grant a licence to Magill. The decision was upheld by the Court of First
Instance and by the ECJ. The ECJ confirmed that mere ownership of
an intellectual property right cannot *per se* confer a *dominant position* under article 82,[19] but considered that the stations occupied such a position, since they were the only source of the required information for
Magill:

However, the basic information as to the channel, day, time and title of programmes is the necessary result of programming by television stations, which
are thus the only source of such information for an undertaking, like Magill,
which wishes to publish it together with commentaries or pictures. By force of
circumstance, RTE and ITP, as the agent of ITV, enjoy, along with the BBC, a
de facto monopoly over the information used to compile listings for the television
programmes received in most households in Ireland and 30 per cent to 40 per
cent of households in Northern Ireland. The appellants are thus in a position
to prevent effective competition on the market in weekly television magazines.
The Court of First Instance was therefore right in confirming the Commission's
assessment that the appellants occupied a dominant position.

---

[17] Case 262/81, *Coditel/Ciné-Vog Films (Coditel II)* [1982] ECR 3381, ECJ, para. 14.
[18] Joined Cases C-241/91 P and C-242/91 P, *RTE and ITP* v. *Commission* [1995] ECR
I-743, ECJ.
[19] *Ibid.*, para. 46.

The Court stated that the exercise of an exclusive right such as copyright by the proprietor may, in exceptional circumstances, involve *abusive conduct*.[20] It then examined the circumstances taken into account by the Court of First Instance in concluding that the conduct in question was abusive (the absence of an actual or potential substitute for a weekly television guide offering information on the programmes for the week ahead; and the existence of a specific, constant and regular potential demand on the part of consumers) and considered with the Commission and the Court of First Instance that the stations' refusal to provide basic information on their programming prevented the appearance of a new product, a comprehensive weekly guide to television programmes, which they did not offer and for which there was a potential consumer demand. It also noted that the stations reserved to themselves the secondary market of weekly television guides by excluding all competition from that market. Such conduct was held to constitute an abuse under article 82.

There has been extensive discussions on the scope and implications of this decision. Several commentators thought, in particular, that the decision would in effect open the way to compulsory licensing on a large scale. Their fear, however, was exaggerated. The test of article 86 is a demanding one, and would be met only in exceptional cases of the refusal of a licence.[21] For example, in its judgment of June 1997 in the case of *Tiercé Ladbroke* v. *Commission*,[22] the Court of First Instance rejected a complaint under article 86 based on a refusal by French horse-racing companies to provide a Belgian betting house with its audiovisual coverage of horse races in France for the latter's betting outlets in Belgium. In its judgment the Court relied, *inter alia*, on the fact that the programmes were neither exploited nor licensed for the territory of Belgium (thus excluding any discrimination or restriction on competition in the relevant market) and on the fact that the non-transmission did not and still does not prevent Belgian bettors from continuing to bet on French races (and thus was not essential for the activity in question).

215.   Free speech

The 'right of the public to be informed' and other principles of free speech may also conflict with the exclusive right of the copyright owner

---

[20] *Ibid.*, para. 50.
[21] See W. R. Cornish, *Intellectual Property*, 4th edn, Sweet & Maxwell, 1999, para. 18-16.
[22] Case T-504/93, *Tiercé Ladbroke SA* v. *Commission of the European Communities* [1997] ECR II-923; [1997] 5 CMLR 309.

to license the communication to the public of his work. In the European context, the most relevant provision in this respect is article 10 ('Freedom of information') of the European Convention on Human Rights, which provides:

(1) Everyone has the right to freedom of expression. This right shall include freedom to hold opinions and to receive and impart information and ideas without interference by public authority and regardless of frontiers. This article shall not prevent States from requiring the licensing of broadcasting, television or cinema enterprises.

(2) The exercise of these freedoms, since it carries with it duties and responsibilities, may be subject to such formalities, conditions, restrictions or penalties as are prescribed by law and are necessary in a democratic society, in the interests of national security, territorial integrity or public safety, for the prevention of disorder or crime, for the protection of health or morals, for the protection of the reputation or rights of others, for preventing the disclosure of information received in confidence, or for maintaining the authority and impartiality of the judiciary.

The European Court of Human Rights has had no occasion to apply this provision to copyright.[23] It remains to be seen if, and to what extent, copyright can be subject to article 10(1), and to what extent the justification under 10(2) may apply.[24]

In this respect, national courts have had different attitudes. In the UK, in *Ashdown* v. *Telegraph Group Ltd*,[25] an infringement action was brought by a Member of Parliament and former leader of the Liberal Democrats party against a newspaper which published articles incorporating sections of the minute of a secret political meeting. The High Court acknowledged that intellectual property rights in general and copyright in particular constituted a restriction on the exercise of the right to freedom of expression. It held, however, that article 10 of the Convention could not be relied on to create defences to an alleged infringement of copyright over and above those provided for in the CDPA 1988, on the ground that the balance between the rights of the owner of the copyright and those of the public had been struck in the legislation itself, and that it did not follow that because article 10 is engaged the facts of each case have to be considered to determine whether the restriction imposed by the law of copyright went further than was necessary in a democratic society.

---

[23] See, however, Case 30261/96, *France 2* v. *France*, European Commission of Human Right, 15 January 1997.

[24] See P. Bernt Hugenholtz, 'Copyright and Freedom of Expression in Europe', in R. Cooper Dreyfuss, H. First and D. Leenheer Zimmerman (eds.), *Innovation Policy in an Information Age*, Oxford University Press, 2000.

[25] [2001] Ch 685; [2001] 2 WLR 967; [2001] 2 All ER 370.

On appeal to the Court of Appeal,[26] after a review of the existing case law of the European Court of Human Rights, the Court of Appeal reached the conclusion that rare circumstances can arise where the right of freedom of expression will come into conflict with the protection afforded by the copyright Act, notwithstanding the express exceptions to be found in the Act. For the Court of Appeal, in such circumstances, the court is bound to apply the Act in a manner that accommodates the right of freedom of expression. That makes it necessary for the court to look closely at the facts of individual cases. However, the Court of Appeal saw no reason in principle why, in such cases, the defendant should not indemnify the author for any loss caused to him or account to him for any profit made as a result of copying his work, as freedom of expression would not normally carry with it the right to make free use of another's work. This decision appears to exclude the application of article 10 in a case where copyright is exercised merely to obtain remuneration, as opposed to a case where it is exercised to prevent a discourse.[27] French courts have also had occasion to examine this question, and seem more reluctant to apply article 10 of the Convention.[28] These cases certainly open the way to a new type of litigation in this field.

216.   Other doctrines

Another external limit to copyright can be found in the general doctrine of abuse of right (*abus de droit*), applicable in some continental systems. Under this theory, the holder of a property right can be barred from exercising his right when this exercise is held abusive. This theory is applicable to the authors' rights, and is even enshrined in some provisions

---

[26] [2001] 4 All ER 666; [2001] EMLR 44, CA.

[27] See the conclusion of Hugenholtz, 'Copyright and Freedom of Expression'. This also seems to be suggested by *France 2* v. *France*, European Commission of Human Right, 15 January 1997.

[28] In the French case of *Fabris* v. *France 2* (Tribunal of First Instance of Paris, 23 February 1999, *Revue Dalloz*, 1999, p. 580, obs. Kamina), the legatee of the painter Maurice Utrillo, Mr Fabris, objected to the broadcasting of news coverage of an exhibition of Utrillo's paintings. The news coverage was two minutes long, and included a presentation of several paintings by Utrillo. In the absence of any applicable statutory exemption, the Tribunal of First Instance of Paris found that the television channel France 2 was justified by the right of the public to information, which constituted an exception to copyright (without applying the test of art. 10). This judgment was reversed by the Court of Appeal of Paris, on the ground that the *droit d'auteur* was justified as a proportionate limitation on the freedom of expression under art. 10 by the existence of the doctrine of abuse of *droit d'auteur*. See also the Dutch case of *Dior* v. *Evora*, *Hoge Raad* (Dutch Supreme Court), 20 October 1995 [1996] *Nederlandse Jurisprudentie* 682 (art. 10 may justify exemptions outside the statutory list of the Copyright Act).

of the French Copyright Act.[29] However, in several Member States, the
criteria of the abuse could be difficult to meet. Under French law, for example, an abuse of right would require in most cases proof of a malicious
intent on the part of the copyright owner (intent to harm the defendant).
The fact that there does not appear to be any significant case law on the
question may be an indication of the difficulties of applying this theory
in the field of copyright.[30]

217. Structure

Below we will concentrate on the main copyright exemptions in relation
to film works (discussed in Section I below) and on the regime of the
remuneration for private copying (discussed in Section II below)

SECTION I

The main exemptions applicable to film works

218. Introduction

We will address only the main exceptions to copyright, as stated in the
relevant domestic Acts, which are relevant in the context of film productions. For our purpose, these exceptions may be classified under the following categories: private copy exemptions, exceptions for performance
in restricted circles, information purpose, criticism, review and news reporting, parodies, incidental inclusion of copyright material, educational
use and libraries and archives.

At this stage it must be recalled that there exist no general defences
to infringement in the various national laws comparable to the US 'fair
use' defence, as codified in the US Copyright Act of 1976. Although this
concept was introduced in early UK copyright by courts, and still exists under the name of 'fair dealing', its scope is restricted in the 1988
Act to the statutory exceptions relating to research and private study[31]
and to criticism, review and news reporting.[32] The situation is similar in
Ireland.[33]

---

[29] Arts. L.121-3 and L.122-9 (abuse of the exercise or non-exercise of the right of
divulgation).
[30] See, however, in France, Court of Cassation, 14 May 1945, *La Semaine Juridique*, 1945,
II, No. 2835; Court of Cassation, 4 December 1956, *Gazette du Palais*, 1957, I, p. 56
(abuse of moral right); and Court of Cassation, 14 May 1991, *La Semaine Juridique*,
1991, II, No. 21760 (abuse of right of withdrawal).
[31] Section 29.   [32] Section 30.
[33] Sections 50 and 51 of the Copyright and Related Rights Act 2000.

219.   Private copy

No reminder is needed that home copying can become a major form of exploitation of copyright works, especially in the digital environment;[34] this led, at a time when digital networks were still in their infancy, to the banning of private copying in relation to computer programs.[35] The development of global networks make the problem more acute. We will address here only the exemptions applicable to films or broadcasts.

Under present law in the UK, there is no general exemption for private copying, apart from an exemption for research and private study which does not apply to films, broadcasts and cable programmes.[36] However, the acts of 'recording', 'digitising' or 'downloading' a film, a broadcast, a cable programme or an audiovisual work for private and domestic use could fall under two specific exemptions.

First, under the 1956 Act, recording broadcasts for private purpose was not an infringement of the right in the broadcast but infringed the copyright in the underlying works, thus making most VCR owners potential infringers. Section 70 of the 1988 Act corrects this anomaly by introducing a specific private use exemption for recording for time-shifting purposes:

The making for private and domestic use of a recording of a broadcast or cable programme solely for the purpose of enabling it to be viewed or listened to at a more convenient time does not infringe any copyright in the broadcast or cable programme or in any work included in it.

But the copy thus made must not be kept permanently,[37] which forbids the constitution of private video-libraries from television broadcasts.

Secondly, section 71 of the 1988 Act provides that:

The making for private and domestic use of a photograph of the whole or any part of an image forming part of a television programme or cable programme, or a copy of such photograph, does not infringe any copyright in the broadcast or cable programme or in any film included in it.

---

[34] See G. Davies and M. E. Hung, *Music and Video Private Copying: An International Survey of the Problem and the Law*, Sweet & Maxwell, 1993. See also Y. Smyth, *Audio and Video Recording in Information Technology: The Challenge to Copyright*, Sweet & Maxwell, 1984, p. 41.

[35] That is, in countries which implemented large private copying exemptions. There were no such exceptions under UK copyright at the time of the Computer Programs Directive.

[36] Note, however, that performers' rights are not infringed by a person who makes a recording of a performance for his private and domestic use (s. 182(1)(a)).

[37] See G. Dworkin and R. Taylor, *Blackstone's Guide to the Copyright, Designs & Patent Act 1988*, Blackstone, 1989, p. 163, who report that the UK Government had suggested that a recording should not be kept for more than twenty-eight day after the broadcast from which it was made. This condition was considered unworkable.

In contrast to the exemption for time-shifting in section 70, this exemptions does not extend to the underlying protected literary, dramatic, musical or artistic work. Within this limit, it certainly allows the constitution of permanent video libraries (for example, of live sport games).

Are these exceptions applicable in the digital environment? There is no doubt that the 'recording' in section 70 can be a recording in digitised form. However, it is not clear whether a digitisation on a hard disk or a CD-ROM would meet the definition of 'photograph' in section 71 of the Act.[38] Moreover, sections 70 and 71 are limited to recordings of broadcasts and cable programmes. We saw that cable pay-per-view and video-on-demand services are cable programmes services under section 7 of the 1988 Act,[39] and thus distribute 'cable programmes'. In that respect, private recording for time-shifting purposes could be fair dealing under the Act.[40] As a result of the decision in *Shetland Times* v. *Wills*, recording from a server in a computer network providing digitised films or digitised film footage on-line could fall under this exception.[41]

The Irish Copyright and Related Rights Act 2000 contains more detailed provisions on recording for time-shifting purposes.[42] It extends the exemption to the making of a copy by an 'establishment' specified by ministerial order. In addition, it provides that, where a fixation which would otherwise be an infringing copy is covered by the exemption and is subsequently sold, rented or (otherwise than to a person's family member or friend for private and domestic purposes) lent, offered or exposed for sale, rental or loan, or otherwise made available to the public, it is deemed to be an infringing copy for those purposes and for all subsequent purposes.[43] The provisions on the making of photographs of television broadcasts or cable programmes are similar to the corresponding provisions of the UK Act.[44]

In France, article L.122-5 of the Intellectual Property Code allows in general terms copies or reproductions of copyright works 'reserved strictly for the use of the copier and not intended for collective use', with the exceptions of identical copies of works of art and copies of software other than backup copies. French courts have applied this exception restrictively, but it remains broad enough to cover strictly private copies of all

---

[38] Under s. 4(2) of the Act, 'photograph' means 'a recording of light or other radiation on any medium on which an image is produced from which an image may by any means be produced, and which is not part of a film'.

[39] See para. 95.

[40] So is permanent recording under s. 71 if no underlying work distinct from the film is conveyed by the cable programme, provided it can be assimilated to a 'photograph'.

[41] See para. 95.   [42] Section 101.   [43] Section 101(4).   [44] Section 102.

works, on all media. A similar exemption applies to neighbouring rights.[45] Exceptions are drafted in a similar way in the Spanish,[46] Portuguese,[47] Greek[48] and Luxembourg[49] Acts, and have a similar scope in relation to films in Belgium.[50]

In Germany, article 53(1) of the Copyright Act allows the production of single copies of a work for private use. The article further specifies that a person may also cause such copies to be made by another person. However, this rule is applicable to the video or audio recordings media and to the reproduction of works of fine art only if no payment is received for the copy.

In Sweden, article 12 of the Copyright Act allows single copies made for private purpose, but provides that this provision does not confer the right to engage, for private purpose, another person to make copies of musical or cinematographic works. The scope of the exemption is similar in Denmark[51] and Finland.[52]

The scope of the private copy exemption is wider in the Netherlands. Article 16b of the Copyright Act allows reproduction of a limited number of copies of copyright works for the sole purpose of the personal practice, study or use of the copier. In addition, legal persons may also benefit from this exemption. In Italy, the language of the private copy exemptions does not appear to cover the reproduction of audiovisual works.[53]

220.   Performance in restricted circles

In all Member States, the right of performance or of communication of a work is restricted to its performance *in public* or to its communication *to the public*. Therefore, strictly private performance should fall outside the scope of copyright protection. The problem, however, is to delimit the line between the private and public spaces. This led to the adoption,

[45] Art. L.211-3.
[46] See Copyright Act, art. 31(2) for copyright, applicable to neighbouring rights under art. 132.
[47] Art. 81(b) of the Copyright Act, which reproduces the language of art. 9(2) of the Berne Convention.
[48] Copyright Act, art. 18(1).   [49] Copyright Act, art. 10(4).
[50] In Belgium, the Copyright Act contains several provisions relating to private copy applicable to different classes of works or modes of reproduction. Of interest for our purpose is art. 22(5) which allows, in broad terms, reproductions of sound and audiovisual works made within the family circle and exclusively intended for that circle. This provision is repeated for neighbouring rights in art. 46(4).
[51] Section 12.   [52] *Ibid.*
[53] Art. 68(1) provides that 'the reproduction of single works or of portions of works for the personal use of the reader, when made by hand or by a means of reproduction unsuitable for marketing or disseminating the work in public, shall be permitted' (WIPO translation).

in most copyright Acts, of specific exemptions in relation to performance in restricted circles.

The UK Copyright Act does not contain any exemption for the performance of films in restricted circles.[54] The only relevant exemption for our purpose is the exception for the performance, playing or showing of a work in the course of activities of educational establishment.[55] But the exemption can be deduced *a contrario* from the definition of 'public' in section 19 of the 1988 Act (infringement by performance, showing or playing a work in public). As mentioned above, the determination of whether a work is performed in private or in public is a question of fact and is left to the courts to decide. From the existing case law, it appears that a performance will be considered private in the UK only if it is restricted to the domestic or quasi-domestic circle.[56]

However, the 1988 Act contains a rather broad exemption for free public showing or playing of broadcast or cable programmes. Under section 72 of the Act, the showing or playing in public of a broadcast or cable programme to an audience which has not paid for admission to the place where the broadcast or programme is to be seen or heard does not infringe any copyright in the broadcast or cable programme, or any sound recording or film included in it.[57]

In Ireland, section 97 of the Copyright and Related Rights Act 2000 provides that it is not an infringement of the copyright in a sound recording, broadcast or cable programme to cause it to be heard or viewed when this is done (a) in part of the premises where sleeping accommodation is provided for the residents or inmates, and (b) as part of the amenities provided exclusively or mainly for residents or inmates, unless a discrete charge is made for admission by the premises.

In *droit d'auteur* Member States, the exemption is usually restricted to performances in the domestic or family circle. In France, the Intellectual Property Code provides that the author and neighbouring rights owners

---

[54] In contrast, s. 67 provides for an exemption for the playing of sound recordings as part of the activities of, or for the benefit of, certain non-profit or charitable clubs, societies or other organisations.

[55] See para. 224.   [56] See the case law in para. 190.

[57] Section 72(1). The audience is treated as having paid for admission to a place: (a) if it has paid for admission to a place of which that place forms part; or (b) if goods or services are supplied at that place (or a place of which it forms part) (i) at prices which are substantially attributable to the facilities afforded for seeing or hearing the broadcast or programme, or (ii) at prices exceeding those usually charged there and which are partly attributable to those facilities (s. 72(2)). Persons admitted as residents or inmates of the place and persons admitted as members of a club or society where the payment is only for membership of the club or society and the provision of facilities for seeing or hearing broadcasts or programmes is only incidental to the main purposes of the club or society are not to be regarded as having paid for admission to a place (s. 72(3)).

may not prohibit 'private and gratuitous performances carried out exclusively within the family circle'.[58] The notion of the family circle is much narrower than the notion of the private circle. It clearly excludes legal persons or associations from the benefit of this provisions. The family circle is a notion which must be construed restrictively, and includes only parents or close friends.[59] The exemption has a similar scope in Belgium,[60] the Netherlands[61] and Sweden.[62]

In Spain, the Copyright Act contains no specific exception for performance in family or restricted circles. But article 20(1) of the Act specifies that communication to the public means any act whereby two or more persons are afforded access to the work. It further specifies that a communication shall not be considered public 'where it takes place in a strictly domestic environment, that is not an integral part of or connected to a dissemination network of any kind'.

In some countries, however, the scope appears to extend beyond the limits of domesticity. This would appear to be the case in Germany, in the absence of a generally applicable exemption, as a result of the construction of the notion of public performance. According to Dietz:

a communication of a work is deemed public if it is intended for a number of persons, unless such persons form a clearly defined group and are interconnected personally by mutual relations or by a relationship to the organiser of the communication.[63]

In addition, under article 52 of the Copyright Act, the communication to the public of a published work is permissible if the communication serves no gainful purpose on the part of the organiser, if spectators are admitted free of charge and, in the case of recitation or performance of the work, if none of the performers receive special remuneration. However, in this case, an equitable remuneration must be paid. This exemption does not apply to public stage performances, broadcasts of a work and public presentations of cinematographic works.

In Italy, article 15 of the Copyright Act excepts from the exclusive right of public performance free performances within the normal circle of a family, community, school or retirement home.

[58] Arts. L.122-5 (authors' rights) and L.211-3 (neighbouring rights).
[59] See Tribunal of First Instance of Paris, 24 January 1984, *Gazette du Palais*, 1984, I, p. 240 (person who organised free showings of films at his home held to be an infringer).
[60] Copyright Act, art. 22(1) and (3).   [61] Copyright Act, art. 12(4).
[62] See G. Karnell, in M. B. Nimmer and D. Geller (eds.), *International Copyright Law and Practice*, Matthew Bender, looseleaf, para. 8[1][d].
[63] *Ibid.*, para. 8[1][b][iv].

221. Information purpose, criticism, review and news reporting

In the UK, fair dealing with a work for the purpose of criticism or review, of that or another work or of a performance of a work, does not infringe any copyright in the work provided that it is accompanied by a sufficient acknowledgment.[64] Fair dealing with a work, other than a photograph for the purpose of reporting current events, does not infringe any copyright in the work provided that it is accompanied by a sufficient acknowledgment.[65] However, no acknowledgment is required in connection with the reporting of current events by means of a sound recording, film, broadcast or cable programme.[66]

In Ireland, the exemptions are similarly drafted, but acknowledgment is required in all cases for uses of sound recordings, films, broadcasts or cable programmes.[67]

In France, the Intellectual Property Code provides for exceptions in case of reproductions for information or criticism in the same terms for author's rights[68] and neighbouring rights,[69] thus avoiding possible conflict between their owners. Under the condition of a sufficient indication of the source, 'short quotations' are allowed, 'when justified by the critical, polemic, pedagogic, scientific or informative aspect of the work in which they are included'. These conditions were applied strictly to audiovisual works by several court decisions.[70]

Article 50 of the German Copyright Act provides for an exception for visual and sound reporting on 'events of the day' by broadcast or film and in newspapers mainly devoted to current events. The exemption for quotations in article 51 of the German Act appears ill-adapted to quotations in the audiovisual environment.[71]

---

[64] Section 30(1).
[65] Section 30(2). ' "sufficient acknowledgment" means an acknowledgment identifying the work in question by its title or other description, and identifying the author unless (a) in the case of a published work, it is published anonymously; (b) in the case of an unpublished work, it is not possible for a person to ascertain the identity of the author by reasonable inquiry' (s. 178).
[66] Section 30(3).   [67] Section 51.   [68] Art. L.122-5. Art.   [69] Art. L.211-3.
[70] In particular, French courts consistently hold that the integral reproduction of an artistic work in a film cannot constitute a short quotation under art. L.122-5 of the Intellectual Property Code (e.g. Court of Cassation, 17 December 1991, Bull. Civ., 360, *Revue Dalloz*, 1993, p. 89 (copy of a photograph in a film); Court of Cassation, 4 July 1995, *La Semaine Juridique*, 1995, II, No. 22486, note Galloux (reproduction of wall ornamentations in a theatre by a television programme)).
[71] 'Reproduction, distribution and communication to the public shall be permitted, to the extent justified by the purpose, where 1. individual works are included after their publication in an independent scientific work to illustrate its contents; 2. passages from

Italian law permits the abridgement, quotation or reproduction of fragments or parts of a work for the purpose of criticism or discussion or for instructional purpose in a way similar to French law.[72] The same is true under the Spanish Act,[73] which contains a provision similar to article 50 of the German Act.[74] In addition to quotation exemptions, comprehensive exemptions for news reporting exist in the Netherlands[75] and in Sweden.[76]

222.   Parodies

In the UK, parody and satire are not included in the list of copyright exemptions, and there appears to be no specific test for infringement for such adaptations. Accordingly, the question will be to determine if the second work reproduces a substantial part of the parodied or satirised work:

> In assessing this flexible concept a court will consider whether or not such references have been made as are necessary to enable an audience to 'conjure up' the satirised work or whether the so-called satirist or parodist has used far more of the work and, indeed, has gone beyond what is necessary for satire in order to enable him commercially to exploit another's work.[77]

A parodist might, however, rely in some circumstances on the defence of fair dealing for the purposes of criticism or review.

The French Intellectual Property Code provides for an exception of parody and caricature in the same terms for authors' rights[78] and neighbouring rights.[79] The Code provides that the parody must be 'conforme aux lois du genre' (consistent with the rules of this style), which means that no possibility of confusion shall exist between the two works,[80] but

---

a work are quoted after its publication in an independent work of language; 3. individual passages from a published musical work are quoted in an independent musical work' (WIPO translation).
[72] Copyright Act, art. 70.   [73] Copyright Act, art. 32.
[74] Art. 34 on the use of works in news reports.
[75] Copyright Act, art. 15.   [76] Copyright Act, arts. 25 and 49a(4).
[77] G. Dworkin and R. Taylor, *Blackstone's Guide to the Copyright, Designs & Patent Act 1988*, Blackstone, 1989, p. 61. See *Joy Music Ltd* v. *Sunday Pictorial Newspaper* [1960] 2 QB 60; [1960] 1 All ER 703 (parody held non-infringing); *Williamson Music Ltd* v. *Pearson Partnership Ltd* [1987] FSR 97 (pre-existing musical tune used in a parodic advertisement; held to be a substantial taking and an infringement of the first work); *Schweppes Ltd* v. *Wellingtons Ltd* [1984] FSR 210 (infringement of the 'Schweppes' indian tonic water label by the use of a similar label 'Schlurppes').
[78] Art. L.122-5.   [79] Art. L.211-3.
[80] E.g. *Enoch* v. *Faizant et le Point*, Paris Court of Appeal, 11 May 1993, *Revue Trimestrielle de Droit Commercial*, 1993, No. 3, p. 510, note Françon.

does not appear to provide for very strict limits in terms of good taste or cruelty.[81] It appears that moral rights can only be exercised against a parody which would amount to a defamation.[82]

A parody is designed to make fun of the author, but in at least one decision (criticised by legal commentators) the exception of parody was recognised for a modification of a song as a *post mortem* homage in a journal.[83] It has also been held that a parody of a song can lawfully use the same music as the original without authorisation, the use of the original music being only a support of the parody.[84]

An interesting case of cinematographic parody was decided in the 'Tarzoon' case.[85] The cartoon 'Tarzoon' presented a character parody of Tarzan (wearing the same outfit but ridiculously slim), involved in a succession of burlesque adventures, aiming to give a caricature of the modern world. An action by the Burroughs heirs (owners of the copyright) was based on various grounds: copyright infringement, trademark infringement, unfair competition and moral rights. Regarding copyright infringement, the court held that 'the movie, which made fun of diverse aspects of the contemporary world, without slavishly copying the Tarzan cycle, presented a strong individuality, without likelihood of confusion', and therefore dismissed the claim. On the trademark ground, the court held that there was no infringement where the similarity is between two very different productions communicated to the public. The unfair competition claim was rejected because of the absence of likelihood of confusion and the difference between the two works (Tarzan films and the cartoon parody 'Tarzoon'). The moral rights claim was based on the numerous erotic or obscene scenes in the cartoon. The court rejected this claim, considering that the difference between the two works was such that there was no likelihood of assimilation of the two characters and themes.

---

[81] *Le Luron*, Court of Cassation, 12 January 1988, *Revue Dalloz*, 1989, p. 1; *Revue Dalloz*, 1988 Sommaire, p. 206, obs. Colombet, *Revue Trimestrielle de Droit Commercial*, 1988, p. 227, note Françon.

[82] *Ibid.*

[83] *Enoch v. Faizant et le Point*, Tribunal of First Instance of Paris, 7 October, *Revue Trimestrielle de Droit Commercial*, 1993, No. 1, p. 96, note Françon, which refused to consider the adaptation as a parody, reversed by Paris Court of Appeal, 11 May 1993, *Revue Trimestrielle de Droit Commercial*, 1993, No. 3, p. 510, note Françon.

[84] *Le Luron*, Court of Cassation, 12 January 1988, *Revue Dalloz*, 1989, p. 1; *Revue Dalloz*, 1988 Sommaire, p. 206, obs. Colombet, *Revue Trimestrielle de Droit Commercial*, 1988, p. 227, note Françon.

[85] Tribunal of First Instance of Paris, 3 January 1978, *Revue Dalloz*, 1979, p. 99, note Desbois. See Edelman, *Revue Dalloz*, 1980, Chron., p. 225.

A similar statutory exemption for parodies exists in Belgium,[86] Spain[87] and Switzerland.[88] In other countries, for example, Germany,[89] parodies are viewed with leniency by courts.

223.   Incidental inclusion of copyright material

In the UK, under section 17(6) of the CDPA 1988, and in relation to any description of work, the making of copies 'which are transient or are incidental to some other use of the work' is prohibited. The UK Act, however, contains specific exemptions for incidental inclusion of copyright material.[90] Under section 31 of the Act, copyright in a work is not infringed by its incidental inclusion in an artistic work, sound recording, film, broadcast or cable programme.[91] Nor is the copyright infringed by the issue to the public of copies, or the playing, showing, broadcasting or inclusion in a cable programme service, of anything whose making was, by virtue of this exemption, not an infringement of the copyright.[92] A musical work, words spoken or sung with music, or so much of a sound recording, broadcast or cable programme as includes a musical work or such words, shall not be regarded as incidentally included in another work if it is deliberately included.[93] Section 68 provides for an exemption for incidental recording for purposes of broadcast or cable programme under certain circumstances. The Irish Act contains similar provisions.[94]

In France, the Intellectual Property Code does not provide for exemptions for incidental inclusion of copyright works. It appears, however, that an incidental inclusion of a protected work in a film is possible if the display is fleeting.[95] In addition, the Code provides for such an exemption to performers rights. Under article L.212-10 of the Code, performers cannot prevent the reproduction and public communication of their performance if it is accessory to an event constituting the principal subject of a sequence in an audiovisual work.

In Germany, article 55 of the Copyright Act grants to broadcasting organisations the right to make ephemeral recordings, if they have already

---

[86] Copyright Act, art. 22.   [87] Copyright Act, art. 39.   [88] Copyright Act, art. 11(3).
[89] See A. Dietz, in M. B. Nimmer and D. Geller (eds.), *International Copyright Law and Practice*, Matthew Bender, looseleaf, para. 8[2], referring to the 'Alcolix' and 'Asterix' decisions, in (1994) 25 IIC 605 and 610.
[90] See also Copyright Act, Sched. 2, para. 16 (performances).
[91] Section 31(1).   [92] Section 31(2).   [93] Section 31(3).
[94] Copyright and Related Rights Act 2000, s. 52 (copyright works) and s. 222 (performances).
[95] See e.g. Paris Court of Appeal, 14 September 1999 (*ADAGP* v. *ADR*), *La Semaine Juridique*, 7 September 2000, No. 1376, note Magnant; *Juris-Data*, No. 024710 (representation of a wall painting in a film).

acquired the right to broadcast the work concerned. Article 57 of the Act allows the reproduction, distribution and public communication of works if they may be regarded as 'insignificant and incidental with regard to the actual subject of the reproduction, distribution or public communication'.

224. Educational use

The UK Act contains numerous exemptions for educational use which would be impossible to detail here. The exemptions applicable to film works concern things done for the purposes of instruction or examination,[96] or the performing, playing or showing of a work in the course of the activities of an educational establishment,[97] the recording by an educational establishment of broadcasts and cable programmes for the purposes of that establishment,[98] and the lending of copies of a work by an educational establishment.[99]

In contrast, no such exemption exists in France, nor does the exemption apply to film works in Germany.[100] Limited exemptions exist in the Netherlands, but such uses are subject to remuneration.[101]

225. Libraries and archives

Such exemptions are traditionally very developed in the UK and Ireland. A certain number are applicable to film works. In the UK Act, a they concern mainly:
1. the copying by libraries of articles in periodicals;[102]
2. the copying by libraries of parts of published works;[103]
3. the lending of copies by libraries or archives;[104]
4. the supply by libraries of copies of articles and works to other libraries;[105]
5. the supply by libraries and archives of replacement copies of works;[106]
6. the copying by libraries and archives or certain unpublished works;[107] and
7. copying a work required to be made as a condition of export.[108]

---

[96] Section 32.   [97] Section 34.   [98] Section 35.
[99] Section 36A, added by the Copyright and Related Rights Regulations 1996 (SI 1996 No. 2967).
[100] See, however, art. 47 of the Copyright Act, which grants a limited right to record 'school broadcasts' for educational purpose.
[101] Copyright Act, art. 16(1)(a).   [102] Section 38.   [103] Section 39.
[104] Section 40A.   [105] Section 41.   [106] Section 42.   [107] Section 43.
[108] Section 44.

Similar exemptions apply in Ireland.[109] In contrast, such exemptions are more limited on the continent. There are no such exemptions in France. Spanish law provides for exemptions for reproduction and lending in museums, libraries and archives.[110] Public lending of films by public libraries is often excluded from the existing lending schemes.[111]

SECTION II

Compensation for private copying

226.   General view

Within the European Union, a right of remuneration for private copying was first introduced in the German Act of 1965. This example was followed by Austria in 1980 and by several *droit d'auteur* countries in the 1980s. Currently such a remuneration exists in France, Belgium, the Netherlands, Italy, Spain, Portugal, Germany, Austria, Switzerland, Greece and Denmark. There is no system of levy or equitable remuneration for private copy in the UK, Ireland and Luxembourg.

Some countries, for example Finland, Iceland and Sweden, do not provide for a remuneration for private copy in their copyright Act, but organise a levy system which forms a *sui generis* system outside the field of copyright. The levy is due to the State, and is dedicated to cultural or other purposes; only part of the levy is distributed to authors, performers or producers. This 'tax' aspect would appear to justify, in the view of the government of these countries, the absence of national treatment under the TRIPs Agreement.[112]

When implemented, the remuneration for private copying generally takes the following form. The remuneration is usually payable by the manufacturer or the importer. It may be levied on blank audio and video-tapes but also on recording equipment. It consists of a percentage of the selling price of the recording equipment and of a lump sum for the recording media, which may vary according to type or recording capacity. The right to equitable remuneration is unwaivable and unassignable. It is collected and distributed by collecting societies, and divided among authors, performers and videogram producers. Part of the remuneration can also be reserved for public interest purposes.[113] The remuneration can be refunded under certain conditions to certain categories of users, such as

[109] Copyright and Related Rights Act 2000, ss. 59–70.
[110] Section 37.   [111] See para. 198 above.
[112] See the reply by the Finnish Government to a question asked by the United States before the WTO (Doc. IP/Q/FIN/1).
[113] Which can be high. For example, in Finland, this percentage is two-thirds of the remuneration.

producers of sound and audiovisual works, broadcasting organisations, or official institutions and educational establishments.

It should be remembered that the Directive on Copyright and Related Rights in the Information Society of 22 May 2001 allows Member States to implement optional private copying exemptions, which are subject to the condition that the rightholder receive 'fair compensation'.[114] Several Member States will have to introduce such a 'compensation' when they implement this Directive, unless they chose to abandon their private copy exemptions. Although the Directive sets no strict obligation as to the form of this compensation,[115] it might take the form of an extension or of an implementation of the already existing schemes for private copying.

227. Example of national laws

In France, a remuneration for private copy was introduced in the 1985 Act amending the 1957 Copyright Act. The system is now codified in articles L.311-1 *et seq.* of the Intellectual Property Code. This remuneration is granted to authors, performers and producers of phonograms and videograms. It is paid by the manufacturer, importer or intra-Community purchaser of the recording medium that may be used for private copy of works fixated on phonograms or videograms. The amount of remuneration, which consists of a lump sum, depends on the medium and on its recording capacity. The types of medium, the remuneration rates and the conditions of payment are determined by a Mixed Committee. The remuneration is collected by collecting societies. For videograms, it is allocated in equal parts to authors, performers and producers. Twenty-five per cent of the remuneration collected must be allocated by the relevant collecting societies to promoting new artists. In 1999, COPIE France, the society for the collection of remuneration for the private copy of audiovisual works, collected FFr457 million.

In Belgium, as of 1 August 1995, authors, performers and producers of phonograms and audiovisual works are entitled to remuneration for the private reproduction of their works, under articles 55 *et seq.* of the Copyright Act. This remuneration is paid by the manufacturer, importer or intra-Community purchaser of sound or audiovisual recording media or of appliances permitting such reproduction on entry into circulation on the national territory of such media and such appliances. Collection and distribution are carried out by collecting societies. The remuneration is fixed by Royal Decree and is based on the selling price for the recording equipment applied by the manufacturers and importers and, where appropriate, on the price of the media. In the absence of such a Decree,

[114] See para. 211.   [115] *Ibid.*

the Copyright Act fixes the remuneration at 3 per cent of the selling price of recording equipment, BFr2 per hour for analogue media and Bfr5 per hour for digital media. The remuneration is allocated in equal parts to authors, performers and producers of phonograms and audiovisual works. In addition, the State authorities may decide to allocate 30 per cent of the proceeds from this remuneration to promoting the creation of new works.

In Germany, authors, performers and producers of phonograms and audiovisual works are entitled to an equitable remuneration for private copy paid by manufacturers and importers of audio and video recording media and appliances. The equitable remuneration is subject to compulsory collective administration. The rates of remuneration are fixed in an annex to the Copyright Act. The remuneration for the private copy of audiovisual works is shared as follows: 21 per cent for GLV (the society for performers and producers of phonograms), 21 per cent for GEMA (the musical rights society), 8 per cent to VG WORT (the literary rights society) and 50 per cent to film authors and producers.

In Italy, the Law of 5 February 1992 grants to authors, performers and producers of phonograms and videograms a right to remuneration for private copy. The remuneration is owed to the SIAE (the collecting society) by manufacturers and importers of blank audio and video tapes and audio recording equipment. It consists of a percentage of the whole-sale price to dealers of these items.

228.   The treatment of foreign authors

Some European Union Member States take the view that their remuneration for private copying is not an intellectual property right, and therefore is not subject to national treatment (this seems to be the case of Finland, Greece and Denmark). In the other Member States, national treatment is in principle afforded on the basis of articles 3 and 9(1) of the TRIPs Agreement. This national treatment is sometimes expressly granted to foreign authors and producers in the copyright Acts.[116] There are, however, some limitations. For example, article L.311-2 of the French Intellectual Property Code restricts the remuneration for the private copy of phonograms and videograms to those phonograms and videograms fixated for the first time in France.[117] Also, in certain countries the

---

[116] For example in Austria.

[117] This provision is made 'subject to [existing] international agreements'. In its reply to a question on this subject asked by the United States before the WTO (WTO Doc. IP/Q/FRA/1, 22 October 1996), France stated that: 'levies for private copying for American authors of musical and audiovisual works are paid through collective management companies responsible under the law for collecting and distributing the levies', without further specification.

remuneration may be granted only to authors, and not to performers and phonogram producers from WTO members, as appears to be the case in Germany. In addition, in most cases the remuneration right is subject to compulsory collective administration. As a consequence, authors, performers and producers from WTO members must be represented by a collecting society in order to be able to claim their share in the distribution of the levy collected. This means that rightholders must become members of these societies or enter into an agreement with them, or that the relevant foreign rightholders' organisations must enter into a reciprocal agreement with the national societies.

8   Moral rights in films

229.   Introduction

Audiovisual works are at the very heart of the debate on moral rights. The general public was informed of these questions on the occasion of widely publicised controversies on film cuts and colourisation, and moral rights have been used as a line of defence by some *droit d'auteur* countries during the discussions on the audiovisual aspects of the GATT. Thus, an important part of the legal literature on moral rights in copyright countries is concerned with their application to audiovisual works.[1] However, due to their foreign origin, moral rights remain one of the areas of copyright law which is less familiar to the common law practitioner.

230.   Understanding the moral right doctrine

The so-called 'moral rights' (from the French *droit moral*) have their origin in the continental doctrine of authors' rights. The concept of *droit moral* was developed in continental Europe from the middle of the nineteenth century, by case law and legal commentators.[2] This form of protection is

---

[1] See e.g. R. Durie, 'Colorisation of Films' (1988) 10 EIPR 37; D. H. Horowitz, 'Film Creators and Producers vis-à-vis the New Media: Reflections on the State of Authors' Rights in Audio Visual Works' (1989) *Columbia-VLA Journal of Law and the Arts* 157; L. A. Beyer, 'Intentionalism, Art, and the Suppression of Innovation: Film Colorization and the Philosophy of Moral Rights' (1988) 82 *Northwestern University Law Review* 1011; J. C. Ginsburg, 'Colors in Conflicts: Moral Rights and the Foreign Exploitation of Colorized US Motion Pictures' (1988) 36 *Journal of the Copyright Society of the USA* 81; K. L. Gulick, 'Creative Control, Attribution, and the Need for Disclosure: A Study of Incentives in the Motion Picture Industry' (1994) *Connecticut Law Review* 53; D. A. Honicky, 'Film Labelling as a Cure for Colorization: A Band-Aid for a Hatchet Job' (1994) 12 *Cardozo Arts and Entertainment Law Journal* 409; W. H. Husband, 'Resurrecting Hollywood's Golden Age: Balancing the Rights of Film Owners, Artistic Authors and Consumers' (1993) 17 *Columbia-VLA Journal of Law and the Arts* 327; G. Karnell, 'The Broadcasting of Audiovisual Works and Moral Rights' (1993–4) 36 *Copyright World* 24; and J. M. Kernochan, 'Moral Rights in US Theatrical Productions: A Possible Paradigm' (1993) 17 *Columbia-VLA Journal of Law and the Arts* 385.

[2] The leading work on moral right is S. Strömholm, *Le droit moral de l'auteur*, Stockholm, 1967. Moral rights appeared in continental countries only after economic rights were

now enshrined in all *droit d'auteur* countries' copyright Acts. It acknowledges and protects the special relationship between the author and the product of his work, seen not only as a mere commodity, but also as an expression of his personality (a 'spiritual offspring of the author'). At its greatest, this protection includes the following rights:

1. the right of paternity, i.e. the right to be identified as the author of the work;[3]
2. the right of integrity, i.e. the right to object to derogatory treatments of the work;[4]
3. the right of divulgation or of dissemination, i.e. the right to decide when and how a work should be made public (including the right not to make it public);[5]
4. the right to revoke a grant of right or to withdraw a work from commerce, on the condition that the author indemnifies the transferee for any loss (sometimes called the 'right of reconsideration').[6]

The expression *droit moral* is normally used to refer to these rights only.[7] However, the expression sometimes refers to the whole *droit d'auteur* or even some economic rights, but it then has a philosophical, rather than a technical, meaning; in particular, moral rights ought not to be confused with those rights which protect economic interests, such as the resale royalty right (the French *droit de suite*), the compulsory royalty right and the rules intended to prevent assignments of future works or long-term contracts (which were discussed above[8]).

Technically, the nature of moral rights remains unclear.[9] In civil law countries, they are usually considered part of, or at least sharing strong

secured. The first cases were developed in France from 1814, but the expression *droit moral* itself was used for the first time in French legal doctrine in the 1870s, and was adopted by case law at the beginning of the twentieth century. The bundle of rights which *droit moral* now constitutes was not put together in French case law before the end of the nineteenth century.

[3] Art. 6 of the French 1957 Act; art. 13 of the German 1965 Act; art. 20 of the Italian 1941 Act; art. 14 of the Spanish 1987 Act.

[4] Art. 6 of the French 1957 Act; art. 14 of the German Act; art. 20 of the Italian Act, art. 14 of the Spanish Act.

[5] Art. 19 of the French Act; art. 12 of the German Act; art. 111 of the Italian Act; art. 14 of the Spanish Act.

[6] Art. 32 of the French Act; art. 42 of the German Act; arts. 142 and 143 of the Italian Act; art. 14 of the Spanish Act.

[7] Some legal commentators consider the author's 'right of access' to the copy of his work as a moral right. However, when implemented, this right is granted to allow the artist to exercise his economic rights as well as his moral right (of divulgation). Therefore it cannot really be considered as a moral right in the narrow sense.

[8] See Chapter 5 above.

[9] Especially, it is not clear whether they are separate from the economic rights, of a different nature, or whether they are just one aspect of the unitary *droit d'auteur*, considered either as a property right, a right of personality or a *sui generis* type of right. The characterisation, which has important legal consequences in civil law countries (the power to assign, seize,

similarities with, the category of 'personality rights' (*droits de la personnalité* in France, *Persönlichkeitsrechte* in Germany), which includes such rights as the right to privacy, the right to honour and the right to one's name, likeness, etc. Like most of these rights, moral rights are usually inalienable, unwaivable and imprescriptible. In several countries, the *droit moral* or some of its elements are considered to be perpetual.[10] Where transmissible on death, they are likely to follow a mode of transmission different from that of economic rights.

231.   International and EC law aspects

The continental doctrine of *droit moral* has been enshrined to a limited extent in the text of the Berne Convention since 1928 (Rome Act), which expressly provides for the protection of the moral rights of paternity and integrity in its article 6*bis*(1):

Independently of the author's economic rights, and even after the transfer of the said rights, the author shall have the right to claim authorship of the work and to object to any distortion, mutilation or other modification of, or other derogatory action in relation to, the said work, which would be prejudicial to his honour or reputation.

The proposal made by France that these rights be inalienable was rejected during the Brussels revision conference of 1948. Accordingly, national provisions allowing waivers of moral rights are not incompatible with the Convention. Also, the Convention does not specify any exemption or qualifying condition, or the form of remedies to be granted in case of infringement.[11]

Under article 6*bis* of the Convention these moral rights are to subsist, after the death of the author, at least until the expiry of the economic rights, and shall be exercisable by the persons or institutions authorised by the legislation of the country where protection is claimed.[12]

Moral rights are excluded from the scope of the TRIPs Agreement;[13] the WIPO Copyright Treaty is silent on the question, but its contracting

---

maintain in perpetuity, etc.), is less relevant when the regime of these rights is set out in detail in the Acts. See P. Kamina, 'Author's Right as Property: Old and New Theories' (2001) 48 *Journal of the Copyright Society* 383.

[10] See para. 313.

[11] Art. 6*bis*(3) provides that the means of redress for safeguarding the rights granted by this Article shall be governed by the legislation of the country where protection is claimed.

[12] However, those countries whose legislation, at the moment of their ratification of or accession to this Act, does not provide for protection after the death of the author of all the rights set out in the preceding paragraph may provide that some of these rights may expire on his death (art. 6*bis*(2) *in fine*).

[13] Under art. 9 of the Agreement, signatory States are obliged to comply with arts. 1–21 of the Berne Convention, with the express exception of art. 6*bis*.

parties must comply with articles 1–21 of the Berne Convention.[14] A less specific requirement than that of article 6*bis* of the Berne Convention is also included in the UN Universal Declaration on Human Rights.[15]

Outside the field of copyright, a significant extension of moral rights at the international level was made by article 5 of the WIPO Performance and Phonogram Treaty, which institutes moral rights for performers in the form of a right of paternity and a right of integrity. This provision is further studied in Chapter 9 below.[16]

Moral rights have not been the subject of any harmonisation at Community level. The EC Commission included moral rights within the scope of its working programme in 1990.[17] Hearings on moral rights were held in November and December 1992 with representatives of the film industry, who presented their (widely diverging) views regarding the need for harmonisation in this field. The Commission concluded that moral rights, at least at that time, did not pose any real problem as far as the Single Market was concerned. The Commission admitted, however, that this situation could change with the emergence of the digital environment. As a result, the question was introduced by the Commission in its Green Paper on Copyright and Related Rights in the Information Society of 1995.[18] In its Follow-Up to the Green Paper of 1996,[19] the Commission summarised the comments submitted in the consultation as follows:

An overwhelming number of interested parties stress the importance of moral rights in the digital environment. In view of the sensitive character of the issue, opinions as to the need for their harmonisation differ widely. With reference to the new risks for mutilations of works, a large number of parties, notably rightholders and end users, are in favour of strong and coherent moral rights protection across the EU. The need for consistent protection is also stressed by sections of industry, whereas other sections prefer to see only minimum rules, fearing that strong moral rights might impede efficient exploitation of multimedia creations. The visibly strong trend to tackle moral rights issues by contract is contested by rightholders. Frequently, subsidiarity reasons are invoked to oppose any harmonisation.

The Commission, however, considered that the time had not yet come for concrete legislative initiative in this domain.

In their present state, the EC Directives in the field of copyright do not affect moral rights. This is confirmed in article 9 of the Term Directive, which states that the Directive 'shall be without prejudice to the provisions of the Member States regulating moral rights'. Also, recital 19 of the

---

[14] Art. 1(4).
[15] Art. 27(2): 'Everyone has the right to the protection of the moral and material interests resulting from any scientific, literary or artistic production of which he is the author.'
[16] See para. 327.   [17] P (90) 97 of 5 December 1990.   [18] COM (95) 382 final.
[19] Brussels, 20 November 1996, COM (96) 586 final.

Directive on Copyright and Related Rights in the Information Society states that the moral rights of rightholders should be exercised according to the legislation of Member States and according to the provisions of the Berne Convention and the WIPO Treaties, but that such moral rights remain outside the scope of this Directive.

It is also important to note that, in its judgment in the *Phil Collins* case,[20] the European Court of Justice included the protection of moral rights within the fundamental scope of copyright protection:

> The specific subject-matter of those rights, as governed by national legislation, is to ensure the protection of the moral and economic rights of their holders. The protection of moral rights enables authors and performers, in particular, to object to any distortion, mutilation or other modification of a work which would be prejudicial to their honour or reputation.[21]

Accordingly, the objective of the protection of moral rights must be taken into account when dealing with single market issues under the EC Treaty (e.g. non-discrimination or justification of restrictions on imports or on the provision of services). But this position does not imply or require a harmonisation of moral rights within the European Union.

232.   Compatibility with copyright doctrine

A general doctrine of *droit moral* is mostly foreign to copyright systems. Of course, it is possible to find under US or UK copyright law rights which, if not moral rights in the narrow sense, are nevertheless conferred in order to protect authors by interfering with freedom of contract, for example termination or reversionary rights.[22] However, these rights remain embryonic, and until recently there was no bundle of rights equivalent to those offered in authors' rights countries for the sole protection of their moral interests.

Why is this so? The philosophical, historical or cultural explanations sometimes proposed (the social status of the artist, the public interest aspect at the basis of copyright, etc.) are not entirely convincing.[23]

---

[20] Joined Cases C-92/92 and C-326/92, *Collins* v. *Imtrat Handelsgesellschaft mbH* [1993] ECR I-5145; [1993] 3 CMLR 773; [1994] EMLR 108; [1994] FSR 166, ECJ. See para. 350.

[21] *Ibid.*, para. 20.

[22] In addition, under UK copyright law, a limited statutory right of integrity was conferred on the author of artistic works by s. 7(4) of the Fine Arts Copyright Act 1862, and later by s. 43(4) of the 1956 Act (now s. 84(6) of the 1988 Act).

[23] Jane Ginsburg outlined strong similarities between the ideology behind the introduction of copyright legislation in the US and a country such as France in the late eighteenth and early nineteenth centuries (see J. Ginsburg, 'A Tale of Two Copyrights: Literary Property in Revolutionary France and America' (1990) 64 *Tulane Law Review* 991; and

Certainly, it can be said that a judicial development or a statutory implementation of moral rights in copyright countries has been impaired by the importance of the freedom of contract and the more business-oriented aspect of the common law. This *laissez faire* approach explains how copyright has evolved more readily in favour of the person who exploits the work. For historical reasons, commercial law and practice never really influenced Continental civil law, which tended to develop its concepts with less regard to economic or market consequences.[24] There, freedom of contract was and is still viewed with more scepticism, and it is generally accepted that law should intervene to protect the weaker party to a contract.

Another aspect which explains the development of moral rights in continental Europe has been underestimated. In civil law systems, case law had the technical tools to expand the rights of authors, even before a formal implementation of moral rights in a copyright Act (which, in France, was made only in the 1957 Act); this could be done primarily through general principles of tortious liability in the civil codes. In this respect, there is here a notable similarity between the efforts of French case law in the nineteenth century based on article 1382 of the Civil Code (general principle of civil liability) and the efforts made by the US and UK judiciary the twentieth century in copyright or similar fields with their more limited tools.[25]

Finally, the need to theorise and to develop general principles and concepts, however vague and uncertain in their application, is a characteristic of civil law systems, and can certainly account for the reticence of the Anglo-American legal systems to accept a similar concept of *droit moral*.

However, over the last twenty years, there has been an increasing pressure on copyright systems to adopt moral rights legislation, not only in order to comply with the Berne Convention,[26] but also because of a growing public concern for this kind of protection, as evidenced by the debates on advertising cuts and film colourisation, which were widely discussed in the legal literature.

Although the UK was an original member of the Berne Convention and a signatory to the Rome Act, it never expressly incorporated article 6*bis*

---

in B. Sherman and A. Strowel (eds.), *Of Authors and Origins*, Clarendon Press, Oxford, 1994, pp. 131–58). Again, moral rights were developed rather late in continental case law and jurisprudence. And the fact that the *droit d'auteur* retains in continental Europe a natural law basis lost in copyright countries does not in itself imply the recognition of moral rights (on the continent, property has a natural law basis, but there is no equivalent to moral rights in relation to physical property).

[24] In continental systems, the *droit d'auteur* is traditionally a civil rather than a commercial law subject-matter.

[25] Defamation, passing off, unfair competition, etc.

[26] After all, the UK has been a signatory State of the Rome Act without explicitly providing for moral rights for sixty years. In the same way, the US did not find it necessary to implement the provisions of art. 6*bis* when it acceded to the Convention.

into its copyright law. The general assumption was that UK law complied with the Berne Convention by protecting *indirectly* the moral rights under article 6*bis* through common law torts (such as passing off, defamation and injurious falsehood), the law of contract and limited provisions in the 1956 and earlier copyright Acts.[27] However, in 1977 the Whitford Committee expressed the opinion that these indirect methods of protection were insufficient to comply with the Convention and recommended a formal implementation of article 6*bis*.[28] As a consequence, the Copyright, Designs and Patents Acts 1988 expressly introduced four types of moral rights into UK law:[29]

1. the right to be identified as the author or director ('right of paternity');[30]
2. the right to object to derogatory treatment of the work ('right of integrity');[31]
3. the right against false attribution of work;[32] and
4. the right to privacy of certain photographs and film.[33]

The notion of moral rights, as implemented in the UK, differs from the *droit d'auteur* orthodoxy. The right against false attribution and the limited right to privacy do not really correspond to the continental definition of *droit moral*, since they are not creators' rights in their works. Moreover, all these rights constitute a set of rights which is separate from copyright. This is evident from the fact that before the entry into force of the Copyright and Related Rights Regulations 1996 moral rights were granted to the film director under a system in which the producer was the sole author of the film. In practice, the only common element between these four rights is that: they give a person the possibility of controlling certain uses of a work which could be harmful to his or her honour, reputation or feeling, despite an assignment of copyright or property right.

---

[27] This view was expressed by the Gregory Committee Report, Cmd 8662, 1952, paras. 219–26. Contra, G. Dworkin, 'The Moral Right and English Copyright Law' (1981) 12 IIC 476. A similar position was held in most Commonwealth countries, with the exception of Canada and India, which implemented art. 6*bis* in respectively 1931 and 1957.

[28] Whitford Committee, Cmnd 6732, 1977, paras. 51–7.

[29] The governmental decision to implement statutory moral rights was taken in the 1980s (see 'Reform of the Law Relating to Copyright, Designs and Performers' Protection', Cmd 8302, 1981, and the White Paper on Intellectual Property and Innovation, Cmd 9712, 1986). See W. R. Cornish, 'Moral Rights Under the 1988 Act' (1989) 11 EIPR 449; and R. Durie, 'Moral Rights and the English Business Community' (1991) 2 *Entertainment Law Review* 40.

[30] Sections 77–79.   [31] Sections 80–83.

[32] Section 84, which is an extension of the similar right in s. 43 of the 1956 Act.

[33] Section 85.

This regime also presents peculiarities. Like their continental counterparts, UK moral rights are not assignable,[34] and are transmissible after death.[35] However, in contrast to the *droit d'auteur* approach, all moral rights under the 1988 Act can be waived, by formal[36] and informal waiver,[37] and the right of paternity must be asserted.[38] Finally, the rights of paternity, integrity and privacy expire with the copyright in the work they are related to.[39]

The possibility of waiving the right has been criticised by legal commentators[40] and is still strongly opposed by representatives of authors.[41] In allowing the contracting out of moral rights, the UK Government clearly indicated its preference for commercial practicalities over non-economic concerns.

Similar moral rights have been implemented in Ireland in the Copyright and Related Rights Act 2000.[42]

233. Basic problems of moral rights protection in relation to films

The doctrine of *droit moral* is expressed in general terms in continental *droit d'auteur* and is traditionally applicable to all categories of works protected by copyright. However, even in these countries, its application to audiovisual works raises specific problems which are difficult to solve.

The fundamental difficulty in dealing with moral rights in films lies in the very process of film production, and in the dilution of the classic concept of authorship. In the same way it caused authors' rights (and copyright) countries to question the applicability of the traditional rules on authorship to films, it also weakens the argument for a moral right protection equivalent to that offered to literary works or works of fine art.

The other problem is that audiovisual works are almost always derivative works, the production of which involves the use or adaptation of numerous pre-existing or underlying works (literary works, scripts, music,

---

[34] Section 94.   [35] Only to a limited extent: s. 97 (also ss. 90(2) and 95(2) and (3)).
[36] Section 87(2).   [37] See s. 87(4).   [38] Section 78.
[39] Section 86(1). The right against false attribution expires twenty years after the death of the alleged author.
[40] See e.g. W. R. Cornish, 'Moral Rights Under the 1988 Act' (1989) 11 EIPR 449 at 452.
[41] See e.g. P. Campbell, 'Moral Rights Legislation Puts the Writer at the Mercy of Entrepreneur', *The Writer's Newsletter* (the official periodical of the Writer's Guild of Great Britain), May 1990, p. 1: 'Almost before the copies of the Act had left the Stationery Office, television producers were demanding a waiver of moral right as a condition of signing a contract.'
[42] Sections 107 *et seq.*

etc.). As a consequence, moral rights problems arise not only between film contributors and producers or users, but also between film authors and authors of adapted or included works. This creates potential conflicts of interests (too often, film directors are ready to claim, as creators, rights they refuse to authors of adapted works). Of course, when the law acknowledges the collaborative nature of audiovisual works, such conflicts can also exist between the co-authors of the film. In practice, producers and users are faced with an unprecedented number of potential moral rights claims, and with the difficulty of identifying their origins.

Moreover, audiovisual works are exploited worldwide according to very complex contractual schemes and can be the object of a whole range of alterations or modifications, some dictated by technical requirements, some by commercial concerns, some in order to comply with censorship or administrative rules. These potential areas of conflicts are very wide by comparison with other descriptions of works: moral rights can be used to object not only to film colourisation, cuts or editing, but also to changes of format, dubbing, subtitles, parody, adaptations, marketing, merchandising, etc. This is a factor that creates uncertainty.

These elements could prove to be a serious impediment to the exploitation of films. As a consequence, some European countries have sought special solutions, reducing, organising or sometimes refusing certain aspects of moral rights protection in relation to films.

234.   Structure

It is in relation to moral rights that copyright and authors' rights systems present the most radical differences. This opposition is concerned not only with the existence and scope of moral rights, and with the philosophy underlying this form of protection, but also with the technique used by the legislator in implementing these rights. In authors' rights systems statutory protection of moral rights relies on a very small number of provisions in the copyright Acts (typically two or three articles), drafted in a similar way as article 6*bis* of the Berne Convention. As a consequence, the definition of the regime of moral rights is left to a large extent to the judiciary. In contrast, the UK and Ireland adopted a very different style of statutory draftsmanship and implemented detailed provisions dealing with all aspects of moral rights protection. This approach resulted in an entirely different set of rules, with complicated cross-references and exemptions.

For these reasons, we will study separately the law in the UK and Ireland on the one hand (discussed in Section I below), and the regime of moral rights in continental Europe, on the other hand (discussed in Section II below).

SECTION I

Moral rights and films in the United Kingdom and Ireland

235.   Introduction

The provisions of the UK 1988 Act concerning moral rights have been extensively studied elsewhere. Below we will concentrate on their application to film works. In doing so, we will focus on the main moral rights for our purposes, that is, the right to claim against derogatory treatments, the right against false attribution and the right to be identified as author or director. The term 'moral rights' in this section will refer to these rights only.

Under the CDPA 1988, moral rights in films are vested in the film director, and the film director alone, which provides a solution to the problem of multi-authorship described above.[43] But apart from this solution, there is no specific regime for moral rights in films; the general regime, including the general limitations on the exercise of moral rights (waiver, assertion, etc.) apply and in this regard film directors and authors are treated as poorly as any author. Remedies for moral rights infringement are potentially strong, but, given the numerous qualifications, exemptions and limitations on the application of the statutory scheme, the general level of moral rights protections can be considered as weak. Finally, transitional arrangements in the UK Act render it virtually impossible for film directors to claim moral rights in relation to pre-1989 films, which constitute a large field for moral rights claims.

In Ireland, the Copyright Act 1963 contained only limited provisions on false attribution of authorship. The Copyright and Related Rights Act 2000 introduced moral rights for authors similar in their scope and regime to those granted in the UK. There exists, however, some significant differences with UK law (mainly, moral rights for film producers – and performers – and no requirement that the right of paternity be asserted), which will be described below.

PART I

Entitlement to moral rights in films

236.   The situation in the UK

When it comes to moral rights in films works, it is important to distinguish moral rights in the 'film' under the CDPA 1988 (the audiovisual

---

[43] See para. 233.

recording), on the one hand, and moral rights in the underlying copyright works, on the other hand. The entitlement to moral rights in the 'film' is specific, as moral rights in this description of work are only granted to the film director, to the exclusion of other contributors or co-authors. The entitlement to moral rights in underlying literary, dramatic, artistic or musical works is not modified by their inclusion in a film or by their exploitation through the audiovisual media.

237.   The film director

Moral rights of paternity and integrity in the 'film' are granted to the film director, and not to the film producer.[44] The fact that producers were sole authors of the film before implementation of the Copyright and Related Rights Regulations 1996 and are now co-authors with film directors does not entitle them to moral rights in this class of works.

In addition to these moral rights in the film, nothing in the Act prevents the film director from being entitled to other moral rights in relations to underlying works, if he can be considered as their author or co-author. This may have practical importance when the director is involved in the writing or rewriting of the script or when he contributes to the creation of further dramatic or artistic material during production. As a consequence of the decision in the *Norowzian* case, the director of dramatic films (and probably at least the screen writer) would be entitled to additional moral rights in the underlying audiovisual dramatic work.[45]

238.   The co-directors

Following the Copyright and Related Rights Regulations 1996, the copyright in the 'film' is now jointly held by the film producer and the 'principal director'.[46] We saw that there could be doubt in specific cases as to who may be considered as the 'principal film director' under the new copyright provisions. However, in contrast to the provisions regarding copyright entitlement, moral rights provisions still refer to the 'director of the film', without further specification. Accordingly, it appears that two film directors could be joint owners of the moral rights in the film, even if one of them cannot be considered as the 'principal director' of the film.

Section 88 of the CDPA 1988 adapts the rules on moral right to joint works. The right to be identified as author or director is a right of each joint author to be identified as a joint author, and must be asserted by each joint author in relation to himself.[47] The right to object to derogatory

---

[44] Sections 77(1) and 80(1).   [45] See paras. 120 and 125.
[46] See para. 118.   [47] Section 88(1).

treatment of a work is a right of each joint author, and his right is satisfied if he consents to the treatment in question.[48] The Act further specifies that a waiver under section 87 of these rights by one joint author does not affect the rights of the other joint authors.[49]

239.   Absence of moral rights for the film producer

It seems that the opportunity of granting moral rights to film producers as authors or owners of the copyright in the film was not debated in the UK. The idea is not foreign to all *droit d'auteur* countries: for example, a right of integrity is granted to film producers in Germany in relation to their neighbouring right in the audiovisual recording.[50] One justification for such a protection is that films can be the subject of numerous mutilations or treatments by third parties which would not amount to copyright infringement or tortious liability. For example, in the US case of *Paramount Pictures Corp.* v. *VBS*,[51] Paramount failed to obtain a preliminary injunction against a company which placed advertisements on the blank section of videotapes of its films rented or sold by retailers. Interestingly, the plaintiff failed on two alternate grounds for the protection of moral rights in the US, namely, false representation under the Lanham Act (the federal trademark Act) and infringement of the right to make derivative works. In such a case, specific moral rights (of integrity and of identification) could prove useful to the film producer.

240.   Authors of underlying literary, dramatic, musical and artistic works

Authors of all pre-existing literary, dramatic, musical and artistic works are entitled to moral rights in relation to their copyright works. This would include the authors of pre-existing literary work (adapted novels), the authors of script works, the authors of pre-existing music, the authors of music specially written for and included in the film and the designers and authors of included artistic works. However, contributors such as the cinematographer (the director of photography or lightning cameraman) and the editor are not in principle entitled to moral rights, as they do not create a copyright work (unless they are considered as co-authors of an audiovisual dramatic work).[52]

As mentioned above, due to the decision in the *Norowzian* case, the director of a 'dramatic' film will be granted an additional moral right in

---

[48] Section 88(2).   [49] Section 88(3).   [50] See para. 286.
[51] 724 F. Supp. 808 (Kansas District Court 1989).   [52] See para. 128.

the underlying audiovisual dramatic work recorded in the film, if any.[53] This moral right would also be granted to the co-author(s) of such a dramatic film, if any.[54]

Nothing is provided in the UK Act for the settlement of conflicts of moral rights between authors or co-authors. In contrast, several continental copyright Acts provide for such rules in relation to films, in order to avoid untimely claims before completion of the audiovisual work.[55]

241.   Absence of moral rights in broadcasts and cable programmes

Authors of other classes of copyright works such as sound recordings, broadcasts and cable programmes are not entitled to moral rights in the UK.

242.   Entitlement to moral rights in films in Ireland

A peculiarity of the Irish Copyright and Related Rights Act 2000 is that the moral rights of integrity and paternity and on the false attribution of authorship are granted to 'authors' of literary, dramatic, musical or artistic work or films, without further specification. Accordingly, the film producer, who is co-author of the film with the principal director under section 21 of the Act, appears to benefit from moral rights.

243.   Foreign authors

The treatment of foreign authors is studied in Chapter 10 below.[56] What can be said at that stage is that the treatment of foreign authors as regards moral rights in the UK and in Ireland follows the rules on copyright. This is in contrast to the situation in several *droit d'auteur* countries, where moral rights protection is afforded to foreign authors on a wider basis than economic rights.

PART II

Scope and regime of moral rights

244.   The piecemeal approach to moral rights

As a result of the choice made in the UK and Irish Acts to detail the rules applicable to each moral right, their regimes present differences.

---

[53] See paras. 120 and 125.   [54] See paras. 120 *et seq.*
[55] See para. 285.   [56] See para. 353.

Therefore, below we will (i) distinguish the right of integrity; (ii) the right against false attribution; and (iii) the right of paternity. However, some rules, in particular those regarding waivers or remedies, are common to all moral rights, and will be addressed separately, together with the question of the applicability of these rights to old films.

The 'right of integrity' in film works

245.   The right of integrity in the UK: definition

Under section 80(1) of the 1988 Act, the author of a copyright literary, dramatic, musical or artistic work, and the director of a copyright film, have the right in the circumstances mentioned in this section not to have their work subjected to derogatory treatment. The UK Act further specifies the central concept of 'derogatory treatment'.

246.   The objectionable treatments

What constitutes objectionable treatment is carefully defined in section 80(2) of the Act. 'Treatment' of a work means 'any addition to, deletion from or alteration to or adaptation of the work, other than a translation of a literary or dramatic work, or an arrangement or transcription of a musical work involving no more than a change of key or register'. Such treatment is derogatory if it amounts to distortion or mutilation of the work or is otherwise prejudicial to the honour or reputation of the author or director.

The definition of 'treatment' appears narrower than the definition in article 6*bis* of the Berne Convention, which refers to treatments amounting to a 'distortion, mutilation or other modification' of the work, but also to 'other derogatory action'.[57] The use of the term 'otherwise' in the second paragraph of section 80(2) suggests that the condition 'prejudicial to the honour or reputation' governs all derogatory treatment, including distortions or mutilations.[58] More generally, there is no requirement that the work be presented as the work of the author and no need of a likelihood of deceiving the public, which is an improvement on the use of 'substitutes' for moral rights protection such as passing off.

For our purpose, it is notable that the 'translation of a literary or dramatic work' is excepted from the definition of 'treatment' in the Act.[59]

---

[57] H. Laddie, P. Prescott and M. Vitoria, *The Modern Law of Copyright*, Butterworths, 1995, para. 27.17.
[58] *Ibid.*   [59] Section 80(2)(a)(i).

Accordingly, screenwriters and dialogists may not object to a bad translation of their dialogue in a foreign version of their film, nor (probably) to dubbing or the use of subtitles.

Sections 80(3) to (6) define the acts amounting to primary infringement of the right of integrity. For our purpose, a distinction must be made between infringement of the right of integrity in the 'film' and infringement relating to the underlying copyright works. The right in the underlying literary, dramatic, musical or artistic work is infringed by a person who publishes commercially, performs in public, broadcasts, or includes in a cable programme a derogatory treatment of the work, or issues to the public copies of a film including a derogatory treatment of the work.[60] This appears to exclude the liability of the film director in the case of derogatory treatment of an underlying work made in the film. Section 80(6) adapts these provisions to 'films', but does not mention commercial publication.

Section 83 of the Act on secondary infringement provides that the right of integrity is infringed by a person who possesses in the course of a business, or sells or lets for hire, etc., an article which is, and which he knows or has reason to believe is, an article which has been subjected to derogatory treatment.

247.   The test of derogatory treatment

The Act does not specify the test to apply in determining whether or not a treatment is 'prejudicial to the honour or reputation of the author or director'. Legal commentators suggest an *objective* test:[61] the prejudicial character of the treatment is to be evaluated *in abstracto*, without reference either to the feelings, to the situation of the artist or the quality of the work.[62] Case law appears to confirm this view.[63]

---

[60] Section 80(3) and (4).

[61] See e.g. H. Laddie, P. Prescott and M. Vitoria, *The Modern Law of Copyright*, Butterworths, 1995, para. 27.18.

[62] In contrast, if the standard is subjective, these elements can be taken into consideration. This appears to be the view adopted by continental countries. But note that, under a subjective test, the element of subjectivity could refer either to the judgment of the court (artistic quality of the work, reputation of the artist) or to the judgment of the artist (the fact that he finds the treatment derogatory).

[63] In *Tidy v. Trustees of the Natural History Museum*, unreported, High Court, 29 March 1995, Rattee J, noted in (1996) 18 EIPR D-81 (application for summary judgment): the plaintiff claimed that a reduction in size of some of his drawings in books (from 420mm × 297mm to 67mm × 42mm) amounted to a distortion of his works or alternatively was prejudicial to his honour or reputation. The court held that it could not be satisfied by the plaintiff's submission without the benefit of evidence from the public as to how the reproduction affected his reputation in their minds. The application failed. In contrast, the Canadian case of *Snow v. Eaton Centre Ltd* (1982) 70 CPR (2d) 105, Ontario High

248. Exceptions and qualifications: certain works and reporting of current events

The UK Act contains several exceptions and qualifications to the infringement provisions.[64] Under section 81 the integrity right does not apply:

1. to a computer program or to any computer-generated work;
2. in relation to any work made for the purpose of reporting current events;
3. in relation to the publication in a newspaper, magazine or similar periodical, or an encyclopaedia, dictionary, yearbook or other collective work of reference, of a literary, dramatic, musical or artistic work made for the purposes of such publication or made available with the consent of the author for the purposes of such publication; nor does the right apply in relation to any subsequent exploitation elsewhere of such a work without any modification of the published version;
4. to an act permitted on assumptions as to expiry of copyright, etc., which would not infringe copyright;[65]
5. to anything done for the purpose of avoiding the commission of an offence, complying with a duty imposed by or under an enactment, or, in the case of the British Broadcasting Corporation, avoiding the inclusion in a programme broadcast by them of anything which offends against good taste or decency or which is likely to encourage or incite to crime or to lead to disorder or to be offensive to public feeling;[66] provided, however, where the author or director is identified at the time of the relevant act or has previously been identified in or on published copies of the work, that there is a sufficient disclaimer. A sufficient disclaimer is defined in section 178 as meaning a clear and reasonably prominent indication, given at the time of the act and, if the author or director is then identified, appearing along with the identification, that the work has been subjected to treatment to which the author or director has not consented.

Court, decided on s. 12(7) of the previous Canadian copyright Act, appeared to favour a more subjective test. Relying on his moral right, the plaintiff applied for an interlocutory injunction requiring the defendants to remove Christmas decorations (ribbons) added to his sculptures, which were suspended from the ceiling of a shopping centre. In granting the injunction, O'Brien J said that the words 'prejudicial to his honour or reputation' in s. 12(7) implied a 'certain subjective element or judgment on the part of the author so long as it is reasonably arrived at' (rejected in *Tidy* v. *Trustees of the Natural History Museum*). Compare with *Patsalas* v. *National Ballet of Canada* (1986) 13 CPR (3d) 522, Ontario High Court.

[64] Section 81. See also s. 80(5) concerning works of architecture.

[65] Sections 57 and 66A.

[66] This exception is not repeated for commercial television companies but their situation is similar under point 2, which covers the various duties imposed under s. 6 of the Broadcasting Act 1990.

249.   Exceptions and qualifications: employees' works/films

In addition, according to section 82 of the Act, the right of integrity does not apply to anything done in relation to:

1. works in which copyright originally vested in the author's employer by virtue of section 11(2) (works produced in the course of employment) or in the director's employer by virtue of section 9(2)(a) (person to be treated as author of the film);
2. works in which Crown copyright or Parliamentary copyright subsists; and
3. works in which copyright originally vested in an international organisation by virtue of section 168,

by or with the authority of the copyright owner, unless the author or director is identified at the time of the relevant act, or has previously been identified in or on published copies of the work. And where in such a case the right does apply, it is not infringed if there is a sufficient disclaimer.[67]

This provision sets a serious limitation on the moral right of integrity in film works. This is particularly true if we consider that the exclusion in section 82 is not limited to the right of the film director, but extends to the right of integrity of other contributors as well: on close reading this text provides that the right of integrity under section 80 does not apply to anything done *in relation to* a film (as a 'work in which copyright originally vested in the director's employer');[68] this would encompass acts done in relation to underlying works in film production.

However, in practice, film directors and authors of underlying works are generally given sufficient credit to ensure that the right of integrity will apply, unless a waiver is granted.

250.   Application to treatments of films

What would amount to actionable treatment can be tested in relation to potentially derogatory treatments of a film.

251.   Artistic and creative requirements

It is submitted that the fact that a film producer has given directions to the film director and/or the screenwriters before or during the making of the film, thus reducing the latter's artistic freedoms, would not *per se*

---

[67] As defined above.

[68] It could be contended, however, that the term 'employer', under s. 178 of the Act, refers to employment under a contract of service or apprenticeship. This would exclude from the scope of this provision films for which the director is not employed by the film producer, but rather works under a contract for services.

amount to a 'treatment' of the work under section 80(2). The reason
for this is mainly that, in such a situation, the work or the part of the
work attracting moral rights protection and therefore subject to potential
derogatory treatment has not yet been created.[69]

252.   Censorship

We saw that, in the case of the BBC, the right to object to derogatory
treatment is not infringed by any act done for the purpose of 'avoiding
the inclusion in a programme broadcast by them of anything which offends against good taste or decency or which is likely to encourage or
incite to crime or to lead to disorder or to be offensive to public feeling',
provided there is a sufficient disclaimer,[70] and that the same rule applies
to commercial television by virtue of section 6 of the Broadcasting Act
1990. Outside these cases, and if the act is not justified by the need to
avoid giving offence (for example, under the Obscene Publications Act
1959) or by the necessity to comply with a statutory duty, censorship
which amounts to a derogatory treatment is actionable.

253.   Change in the story, action or characterisation

It is difficult to foresee what the attitude of the courts will be and at what
point they will hold that a modification to the story, style, narrative or
characterisation of a work becomes prejudicial to the honour or reputation
of its author.[71] This will inevitably in some cases involve a certain measure
of artistic judgment. Apparently, *de minimis non curat praetor*,[72] but in
Frisby v. *BBC*[73] the deletion of one line in a television play was considered
by Goff J as a 'structural alteration' prohibited by a clause granting a
contractual right to artistic control.

An interesting case dealing with these matters is the Indian case of
Bhandari v. *Kala Vikas Pictures Pvt Ltd*,[74] based on section 57(1) of the
Indian copyright Act, which is drafted in terms similar to article 6*bis* of the
Berne Convention. This section was successfully relied on by a novelist
against an adaptation of her work in a film. The author objected to the
title of the film, to the characterisation of its main characters, to dialogue
she considered vulgar and to the different ending in the film. The court

---

[69] Compare with the French case discussed at para. 295 below.
[70] Section 81(6)(c).
[71] Unless they choose to consider that any departure from the original work is a potential
infringement of the moral right of integrity, which is unlikely.
[72] *Carlton Illustrators Ltd* v. *Coleman & Co. Ltd* [1911] 1 KB 771.
[73] [1967] Ch 932; [1967] 2 WLR 1204; [1967] 2 All ER 106.
[74] [1987] AIR De 13, Delhi High Court.

ordered a change to the title, the deletion of the passages which distorted the characters and the deletion of part of the ending of the film. On the vulgarity of the dialogue, Wad J remarked:

The Court does not sit as a sentinel of public morals or super-censor in exercise of its powers under the same section [section 57(1)]. It cannot impose its views (prudish or liberated) on sex or its depiction in the works of art. The concern of the Court is to examine how far the new 'avatar' is true and authentic and what changes are necessary due to constraints of a medium.[75]

The court considered that passages in the film distorted the characters and ordered their deletion.[76]

254.   Changes to the soundtrack

The soundtrack now being protected as part of the film, modifications affecting soundtracks could constitute a derogatory treatment of the film which could be objected to by the film director. One can think of the substitution of soundtrack music or of the modification sound elements in a soundtrack (music, comments or dialogue).[77]

Such treatments are also actionable by the music's composer if they amount to a treatment of his music, or by the screenwriter if they modify his dialogue.

---

[75] [1987] AIR De 13 at 22.

[76] See also the Canadian case of *Pollock* v. *CFCN Productions Ltd* (1983) 26 Alberta LR (2d) 93; 73 CPR (2d) 204; 43 AR 78, QB. The plaintiff, a playwright, entered into a contract with a producer. The playwright licensed and assigned all motion picture and television rights in her play, including the right to 'write film and television treatments, film and television scripts and other film and television dialogue versions of all kinds of the Property and at all times to add to, take from, use, alter, adapt, translate into any language and to change, adapt or alter the title, characters, plot, theme, dialogue and sequences thereof as it may think fit in the exercise of its rights or any of them'. Subsequently to the rewriting of her draft screenplay, Pollock sought an interim injunction restraining the defendants from televising the film based on her play, on the ground that her play and screenplay, as rewritten, had been seriously 'distorted, violated and mutilated to an extent that her reputation will be damaged if the film is shown', in violation of s. 12(7) of the copyright Act (drafted in a language similar to art. 6*bis* of the Berne Convention). Moore J found that there was a serious question of law to be determined by trial, and an interim injunction was granted.

[77] See also under 'dubbing' in para. 257 below. Compare with *Morison Leahy Music Ltd* v. *Lightbond Ltd* [1993] EMLR 144. The author and owner of the copyright in songs objected to the production of a sound recording of a 'medley' of his works, mixing words and music and adding fill-in music. The plaintiff sought an injunction on the ground of copyright and moral rights infringement. On the question of moral rights, the court held that the production of the sound recording amounted to a treatment, and that it was arguable whether it amounted to a distortion or mutilation within s. 80(2)(a) of the Act. An injunction was granted.

255.   Colourisation

This alteration is actionable if it amounts to a derogatory treatment. The decision in *Carlton Illustrators* that 'colouring in a black-and-white drawing would normally be considered an alteration'[78] concerns a case of false attribution of authorship under section 7(4) of the Fine Art Copyright Act 1862, and may not be applicable under section 80 of the 1988 Act. It is, however, applicable under section 84(6) of the 1988 Act, which re-enacts section 7(4) of the 1862 Act and section 43(4) of the 1956 Act. Transitional arrangements in the 1988 Act, however, make the exercise of these rights difficult to establish in relation to most black-and-white films.[79]

256.   Destruction of the work

The destruction by Lady Churchill of the portrait of Sir Winston by Graham Sutherland is a classic example in the UK of the destruction of a work of art. Since the destruction of a work is not listed in the definition of 'treatments' in section 80(2)(a), the film producer or another person can probably destroy the film without infringing the right of integrity of the director.[80] Nor does it appear possible to extend the phrase 'deletion from' to cover the deletion or destruction of the entire work. In addition, there is no duty on film producers to maintain the original of their films in good condition.

This solution is regrettable in relation to films in the absence of a system of public deposit.[81] In the UK, there is no obligation to deposit a master copy of the film in the National Film Archive, and film preservation operates on a purely voluntary basis.

257.   Dubbing

We saw that scriptwriters or authors of dialogue cannot object on moral right grounds to the translation of their works, and therefore possibly to their dubbing in a foreign language (or to the use of subtitles for that

---

[78] *Carlton Illustrators Ltd* v. *Coleman & Co. Ltd* [1911] 1 KB 771 at 780.
[79] See para. 279.
[80] See H. Laddie, P. Prescott and M. Vitoria, *The Modern Law of Copyright*, Butterworths, 1995, para. 27.17.
[81] On the continent, it has been said, for example, that 40 per cent of French pre-war films have disappeared or are unexploitable, because producers did not protect the original copies; similarly, 80 per cent of Charlie Chaplin films have disappeared, and the only remaining ones are those of which he was copyright owner (film director, Bertrand Tavernier, during the parliamentary debates on the French 1985 Act, report by Jolibois, para. 212, vol. 1, p. 117, cited in B. Edelman, *Droits d'auteur, droits voisins*, Dalloz, Paris, 1993, p. 58).

purpose).[82] They might, however, object to the choice of voices for dubbing if it proves derogatory to their work, as the treatment constituted by the vocal performance is independent of the translation. Of course, if dubbing is not merely a translation but is instead new dialogue, it can amount to a treatment actionable by the screenwriter.

In contrast to script works, the act of dubbing or inserting subtitles may constitute an actionable treatment of the 'film'. Therefore a film director might object on moral rights grounds to choices of voices or to the use of subtitles (for example, if they mask a large part of the screen).

258.   Inappropriate or derogatory context

The honour or reputation of a person can be damaged when his work is shown or used in a derogatory context, or when it is subject to unfair criticism. However, it is difficult to see how such acts could amount to 'treatment' under section 80(2)(a).[83] In fact, this might prove beneficial for film-makers. Gene Kelly is said not to have appreciated the use of the song 'Singing in the Rain' as the soundtrack in a choreographed murder scene in Stanley Kubric's film 'A Clockwork Orange'. If this inclusion was considered as a 'treatment' under section 80(2)(a), the author of the song could have a claim against the film producer.[84] In any case, the most damaging derogatory treatments of this kind may well be actionable under the law of defamation.

259.   Insertion of advertisements, the broadcaster's logo or other information into the film

These acts are either an alteration or an addition to the film. Whether they amount to a distortion or a mutilation must be answered by the courts. In the absence of a clause to that effect, it may be possible to consider that authors have impliedly consented to such alterations or additions with their grant of television rights, especially if it is the usual practice of the particular broadcaster to cut the films for advertising (but then, to a certain extent only).[85]

---

[82] See para. 246.

[83] See H. Laddie, P. Prescott and M. Vitoria, *The Modern Law of Copyright*, Butterworths, 1995, para. 27.17.

[84] But not against the director. See para. 246. See also the US case of *Shostakovich v. Twentieth Century Fox*, 80 NYS 2d 575 (1948), in which Russian composers objected to the use of their music in a film derogatory to the Soviet Union. They failed in the US but were succeeded in France.

[85] This was held in the US case of *Autry v. Republic Productions*, 213 F. 2d 667 (9th Cir. 1954), and is also suggested in *Preminger v. Columbia Pictures Corp.*, 49 Misc. 2d 363;

Article 11 of the Television Without Frontiers Directive of 3 October 1989[86] deals with interruptions of audiovisual programmes for advertising and allows limited insertions in some programmes.[87] In the UK, these rules are implemented and detailed by the ITC rules on advertising breaks. These provisions might influence the judicial appreciation of the prejudicial character of advertising cuts.

260.   Modification of duration

In order to be able to compensate for unexpected delays or overrunnings of programmes, broadcasters use computer-assisted devices capable of extending or reducing the duration of any theatrical film by 6 or 7 per cent, in a way which cannot be noticed by the viewer. This act could be considered as an 'alteration' of the work, but it is difficult to see how this alteration could be held derogatory if it is unnoticeable.

261.   Non-production, non-release or under-exploitation of the film

The refusal by the film producer to release the film, once completed, is not a 'treatment' within the meaning of section 80(2)(a) of the Act, and thus is not an infringement of moral right. The same is true for the commercial choices made by the producer in the exploitation of the film (e.g. the direct-to-video release of a theatrical film).

262.   Panning and scanning

'Pan and scan' techniques allow the size of the original pictures in a film be modified by 'zooming' in or moving during the telecast so that it can fit onto the television screen with maximum effect. This could well amount to an alteration, but it is difficult to imagine it being held derogatory if it is dictated by the television format itself. Indeed, the black bands at the top and the bottom of the screen which result in a substantial reduction in the size of the picture could equally be held to be derogatory. Yet the change of format which produces the bands is almost always necessary. Once one starts down this track, the mere act of telecasting could be held derogatory. Of course, the choice of a format which distorts the image

267 NYS 2d 594; affirmed 25 AD 2d 830; 269 NYS 2d 913; affirmed 18 NY 2d 659; 273 NYS 2d 80 (1966).
[86] Directive 89/552/EEC, OJ 1989 No. L298, as amended by Directive 97/36/EC of 30 June 1997.
[87] See also art. 14.1 of the Council of Europe Convention on Transfrontier Television of 1989.

for no good reason, or a grossly inaccurate pan-and-scan, could be held derogatory.[88]

263.   Parody

Although under UK law a parody is not a statutory exemption to copyright, it is nevertheless viewed with leniency by the courts.[89] Logically, there is no reason why parodies should be treated more leniently in relation to moral rights, since parodies are as prejudicial to economic interests (copyright) as they are to moral interests. Parodies are even given a favourable treatment in those continental countries where the protection of the moral right of integrity is at its greatest and where almost no exemptions are available in the copyright Act.

264.   Product placements

In extreme cases, product placement may well amount to a derogatory treatment of the work of the screenwriter. It is submitted that it would not, however, infringe the moral right of the director (for example, if the placement is imposed against his will by the film producer), since the treatment in question is made before the film itself is made.[90]

265.   The right of integrity in Ireland

Under section 109 of the Irish Copyright and Related Rights Act 2000, the author of a work has the right to object to any distortion, mutilation or other modification of, or other derogatory action in relation to, his or her work which would prejudice his or her reputation. This right also applies in relation to an adaptation of the work. The section further specifies that the right of integrity applies:

to any addition of, deletion from or alteration to or adaptation of parts of a work resulting from any previous addition to, deletion from or alteration to or adaptation of a work or parts of a work by a person other than the author, where those parts are attributed to, or are likely to be regarded as the work of, the author.

---

[88] By way of comparison, in *Preston v. Raphael Tuck & Sons Ltd* [1926] 1 Ch 667, under s. 7 of the Fine Arts Copyright Act 1862, Tomlin J considered that the act of removing the decorative border of a square picture, making it round, and blacking in the background would constitute an alteration of such character that it might affect the character or reputation of the artist (*ibid.*, p. 673); however, the altered work, which did not bear the name of the artist, was not considered published under his name under s. 7 of the 1862 Act.

[89] See para. 222.

[90] See above (artistic and creative requirements). Under Canadian copyright, the right of integrity is also infringed when the work is used 'in association with a product, service, cause or institution': s. 18.2(1).

The right of integrity is subject to exceptions and qualifications specified in sections 110 and 111, which are similar in their drafting and scope to those in sections 81 and 82 of the UK Act. The Irish Act does not repeat the complex provisions of the UK Act on primary infringement,[91] but section 112 includes similar provisions on secondary infringement.

The right against false attribution

266.   The right against false attribution in the UK

According to section 84 of the CDPA 1988, a person (which does not have to be the author or director for that purpose) has the right not to have a work falsely attributed to him as author, or as director in the case of a film. This attribution can be express or implied. Primary and secondary infringement correspond to what has been described in relation to the right of integrity.

267.   The right against false attribution as a ground to object to mutilations of film works?

UK and US courts hold that publishing in the name of an author a mutilated version of his work constitutes a misrepresentation which could, in some circumstances, give rise to contractual liability, passing off or libel.[92] Accordingly, in the same way section 84 could provide an interesting ground to object to a substantial mutilation of a film work when it is presented without disclaimer under the name of its creator, even when

---

[91] Sections 80(3) to (6); see para. 246.
[92] See e.g. *Joseph* v. *National Magazine Co. Ltd* [1959] Ch 14; [1958] 3 WLR 366; [1958] 3 All ER 52. The plaintiff entered into a contract to write an article for a journal, to be published under his name. A rewriter commissioned by the publisher changed the title and the conclusion of the article, and made considerable stylistic alterations and certain alterations of fact. The plaintiff refused to allow the revised article to appear under his name. Harman J held: 'The plaintiff was entitled to write his own article in his own style, expressing his own opinions, and was not bound to submit to have his name published as the author of a different article expressing other opinions in a different style.' That no mutilation should occur where there is a contractual right to credit is also strongly suggested by US case law. See e.g. *Granz* v. *Harris*, 198 F. 2d 585 (2nd Cir. 1952), and *Packard* v. *Fox Film Corp.*, 207 App. Div. 311; 202 NYS 164 (NY Sup. Ct 1923). In the same way, the misrepresentation of a mutilated work as the author's could amount to passing off. See the Canadian case of *Times/System International* v. *Custom Planner* (1986) 12 CPR (3d) 441 (introduction of a calendar made by the defendant in the time-planning system designed by plaintiff, presented under same name) and the US cases of *Prouty* v. *National Broadcasting Co.*, 26 F. Supp. 265 (D Mass. 1939) (use of the title of a book in connection with a series of low quality radio comedy sketches adapted from it) and *Granz* v. *Harris*, 198 F. 2d 585 (2nd Cir. 1952) (edited version of a recording).

it is outside the special case of mutilation provided by section 84(6).[93] There are two reasons for this: first, because the exceptions to the right of integrity are not repeated in relation to the right against false attribution; and, secondly, because this statutory right is not subject to the same conditions as passing off.

Note, however, that a disclaimer or a mere notice of the modification will cure the misrepresentation. Note also that the provisions concerning consents and waivers of moral rights apply.

268.   The right against false attribution in Ireland

In the Copyright and Related Rights Act 2000, the right against false attribution is defined in a similar way for all classes of copyright works. In particular, the right of the film director is a right not to have a work falsely attributed to him as 'author', and not as 'director'. Its regime is otherwise similar to that of the UK Act.

The right to be identified as author or director

269.   The right to be identified as author or director in the UK: definition and entitlement

Under section 77 of the UK Act, the author of a copyright literary, dramatic, musical or artistic work, and the director of a copyright film, has the right to be identified as the author or director of the work.[94]

The Act further defines the circumstances in which the right of paternity applies for each class of works. For authors of *literary works* (other than words intended to be sung or spoken with music) and *dramatic works*, the right applies whenever the work is published commercially, performed in public, broadcast or included in a cable programme service, or copies of a film or sound recording including the work are issued to the public. The right extends in relation to an adaptation of the work. The author must then be identified as the author of the work from which the adaptation was made.[95]

For authors of *musical works*, or of literary works intended to be sung or spoken with music, the right to be identified applies whenever the work is published commercially, copies of a sound recording of the work are

---

[93] Which particularly mentions the attribution of altered artistic works. Compare with *Carlton Illustrators Ltd* v. *Coleman & Co. Ltd* [1911] 1 KB 771; *Preston* v. *Raphael Tuck & Sons Ltd* [1926] 1 Ch 667; and *Noah* v. *Shuba* [1991] FSR 14.
[94] Section 77(1).   [95] Section 77(2).

issued to the public, or a film the soundtrack of which includes the work is shown in public or copies of such a film are issued to the public. The right similarly extends to adaptations of the work.[96]

For authors of *artistic works*, the right applies whenever the work is published commercially or exhibited in public, or a visual image of it is broadcast or included in a cable programme service, a film including a visual image of the work is shown in public or copies of such a film are issued to the public, or in the case of a work of architecture in the form of a building or a model for a building, a sculpture or a work of artistic craftsmanship, copies of a graphic work representing it, or of a photograph of it, are issued to the public.[97]

The director of a *film* has the right to be identified whenever the film is shown in public, broadcast or included in a cable programme service or copies of the film are issued to the public.[98]

In the Act, the right of the director is a right to be identified as the film director, and not as the author of the film. In other words, the statutory provisions do not appear to give to film directors a right to a 'possessory' credit ('a film by X'). This situation may have changed with the Copyright and Related Rights Regulations 1996, as film directors are now 'co-authors' of the film.[99] But it should be noted that the provisions on the right to be identified have not been modified accordingly, and that the Act continues to refer to the right to be identified as *director* in relation to the 'film'.

Note that the film producer, formerly sole 'author' and now co-author of the film, is not entitled to the right to be identified as such. It is unlikely that he could rely on common law torts such as passing off against an attribution of possessory credit to a film director. Nevertheless, he could rely on this action to oppose the film being presented as another producer's.

270.   Form taken by the identification

The form of identification is further specified in section 77(7) of the Act. In the case of commercial publication or of the issue to the public of a film or sound recording, the right of the author or director under this section is the right to be identified in or on each copy or, if that is

---

[96] Section 77(3).

[97] Section 77(4). The author of a work of architecture in the form of a building also has the right to be identified on the building, or, where more than one building is built to the same design, on the first to be so built (s. 77(5)).

[98] Section 77(6).

[99] Consider, also, authorship in the underlying audiovisual dramatic work, if any.

not appropriate, in some other manner likely to bring his identity to the notice of a person acquiring a copy.[100] In the case of identification on a building, the right is the right to be identified by appropriate means visible to persons entering or approaching the building.[101] In any other case, identification must be made in a manner likely to bring the identity of the author or director to the attention of a person seeing or hearing the performance, exhibition, showing, broadcast or cable programme in question.[102] In each case, the identification must be clear and reasonably prominent.[103]

If the author or director, in asserting his right to be identified, specifies a pseudonym, initials or some other particular form of identification, that form shall be used; otherwise, any reasonable form of identification may be used.[104] Collective agreements contain detailed provisions as to the size, position, etc. of the film credits on the screen and on the different copies and by-products of the work.

271.   Exceptions and qualifications: employees' works, fair dealing, specific works, etc

Like the right of integrity, the right of identification is subject to several exemptions. First, like the integrity right, the right does not apply in relation to certain works such as computer programs, the design of a typeface and any computer-generated work, or in relation to the publication in a newspaper, magazine or similar periodical, etc.[105] More importantly, it does not apply to anything done with or by the authority of the copyright owner where the copyright originally vested 'in the author's employer by virtue of section 11(2) (works produced in course of employment) or in the director's employer by virtue of section 9(2)(a)'.[106] Again, the question of screen credits is extensively dealt with in the various collective agreements applicable in the industry, and in practice screen credits are guaranteed to directors and other contributors.[107]

Also, under section 79(4) and (5) the right is not infringed by an act which does not constitute an infringement of copyright under most of the statutory copyright exemptions, for example the reporting of current events and the incidental inclusion of a work in an artistic work, sound recording, film, broadcast or cable programme.

---

[100] Section 77(7)(a).   [101] Section 77(7)(b).   [102] Section 77(7)(c).
[103] Section 77(7) *in fine*.   [104] Section 77(8).   [105] Sections 79(2), (6) and (7).
[106] Section 79(3). See the remarks at para. 249.
[107] At least by film producers. Credit provisions could prove difficult to enforce against third parties such as broadcasters.

272.   The requirement that the right be asserted

An important limit on the right of paternity is that this right must be asserted.[108] The right can first be asserted on an assignment of copyright in the work.[109] It can also be asserted by an 'instrument in writing signed by the author or the director'.[110] If the assertion is made on the assignment of copyright, it binds the assignee and anyone claiming through the assignee, whether or not that person has notice of the assertion.[111] However, if the assertion is made in an 'instrument in writing', it binds only the persons to whose notice the assertion was brought.[112] The requirement for an instrument signed by the author or the director could make collective assertion by unions more difficult.[113]

273.   The right to be identified as author in Ireland

The right of paternity in Ireland has a similar scope and is subject to similar exemptions as described for the right of integrity.[114] It is simply defined as the right of the author of a work to be identified as the author of the work, without further specification as to the circumstances and form of the identification, as in the UK.[115] But, more importantly, there is no requirement that the right be asserted.

General and transitional provisions

274.   Consent and waiver of moral rights

According to section 87(1) of the UK Act, 'it is not an infringement of any of the rights conferred by this Chapter [i.e. Chapter IV on moral rights] to do any act to which the person entitled to the right has consented.' Section 87(2) further specifies that moral rights can be waived. Consent is not defined, but would seem to include acquiescence. Nothing in section 87 prevents a consent being given in advance, which blurs the distinction with waivers.

The scope of the waiver (or consent) is left to the appreciation of the parties.[116] This permits unions to negotiate complex waiver conditions

---

[108] Section 78.   [109] Section 78.(2)(a).   [110] Section 78.(2)(b).
[111] Section 78(4)(a).   [112] Section 78(4)(b).
[113] See D. Lester and P. Mitchell, *Joynson-Hicks on UK Copyright Law*, Sweet & Maxwell, 1989, para. 11.15.
[114] Sections 107 and 108.   [115] Sections 107.
[116] According to s. 87, a waiver '(a) may relate to a specific work, to works of a specified description or to works generally, and may relate to existing or future works, and (b) may be conditional or unconditional and may be expressed to be subject to revocation; and if

identifying each potentially derogatory treatment and setting up conciliation or arbitration procedures, such conditions being incorporated in the individual contract signed by the writer or the director.

However, due to the state of the job market and to the relative weakness of unions in the film industry, film authors and contributors rarely have the bargaining power to refuse a waiver of moral rights. Such waivers have become almost a standard clause in film production contracts. The right to be identified is generally protected through contractual rights to credit, but the right of integrity is generally waived.

The Irish Act contains similar provisions on the waiver and consent of moral rights.[117]

275.   Form of the waiver/consent

In the UK and Ireland, the prescribed form of waiver is by an instrument in writing signed by the person giving up the right.[118] But this is not necessarily the only form of consent. Mere inaction might even amount to a consent.[119]

Waivers do not have to be included in a separate instrument. They can be incorporated in standard contracts, as long as such contracts are signed by the parties. The incorporation in individual contracts of the terms of a collective agreement including a waiver would probably meet this condition. No standards are set as to the construction of waivers, but in the UK it has been suggested that waivers should be construed restrictively in favour of the author.[120]

In addition, by way of exception to the prescribed form, section 87(4) of the UK Act and section 116(4) of the Irish Act allow the operation of informal waivers.[121] If this undoubtedly reinforces the position of film producers, it does not mean that in the absence of a written waiver a court will automatically find an implied waiver of moral rights. Moreover, the introduction of a concept of moral rights can be seen as an exception

made in favour of the owner or prospective owner of the copyright in the work or works to which it relates, it shall be presumed to extend to his licensees and successors in title unless a contrary intention is expressed'.

[117] Section 116.   [118] UK 1988 Act, s. 87(2); Irish 2000 Act, s. 116(2).

[119] On acquiescence and estoppel in passing off, see *Habib Bank* v. *Habib Bank AG Zurich* [1981] 1 WLR 1265; [1981] 2 All ER 650; [1982] RPC 1, CA.

[120] 'Since the right [to object to modifications] will in any case arise only in "quasi-defamatory" circumstances, it may well be that the waiver will be effective only if it is drafted in wholly unequivocal terms.' W. R. Cornish, 'Moral Rights Under the 1988 Act' (1989) 11 EIPR 449 at 452.

[121] Both provisions read: 'Nothing in the Chapter shall be construed as excluding the operation of the general law of contract or estoppel in relation to an informal waiver or other transaction in relation to any of the rights mentioned in subsection (1).'

to the pattern of reasoning founded on the practicality and efficiency of commercial relations; this might suggest that the intention of both parties is the only criterion in the finding of an implied waiver.

276. Inequality of bargaining power and the invalidation of waivers

In the UK, it has been submitted that the common law doctrine of restraint of trade and the equitable doctrine of undue influence might help to invalidate express waivers of moral right in some cases.[122] It has also been suggested that the provisions of the Unfair Contract Terms Act 1977 could also be applied in appropriate circumstances to restrictive clauses on moral rights.[123]

277. Duration of moral rights

In the UK and in Ireland, the rights to be identified and to object to derogatory treatment subsist for the same period of time as the copyright in the work.[124] The right against false attribution subsists for twenty years after the death of the person on whom it is conferred.[125]

278. Remedies and offences for infringement of moral rights

In the UK, under section 103 of the Act, an infringement of moral rights is actionable as a breach of statutory duty owed to the person entitled to the right. Despite the absence of a reference to section 96 of the Act, which deals with copyright remedies in general, it has been suggested that additional damages could be awarded for the infringement of moral rights.[126]

---

[122] E.g. W. R. Cornish, *Intellectual Property*, 2nd edn, Sweet & Maxwell, 1989, p. 452. But a comparison with the existing cases in the music industry suggests that this would only apply in exceptional circumstances involving long-term agreements (see W. R. Cornish, *Intellectual Property*, 4th edn, Sweet & Maxwell, 1999, paras. 12-20 to 12-33).

[123] D. Lester and P. Mitchell, *Joynson-Hicks on UK Copyright Law*, Sweet & Maxwell, 1989, para. 11.35, p. 392: 'The Unfair Contract Terms Act 1977 may possibly apply in appropriate circumstances, although that Act does contain some exceptions to contracts so far as they relate to the creation or transfer of a right in copyright or other intellectual property. Moral rights are not property rights, and could not be classed as intellectual property. This is borne out by paragraph 2 of Schedule 7 of the 1988 Act which amends the Unfair Contract Terms Act to include a reference to the new design right created by the 1988 Act. No similar amendment is made to incorporate moral rights.'

[124] UK 1988 Act, s. 86(1); Irish Act 2000, s. 115.

[125] UK 1988 Act, s. 95(5); Irish Act 2000, s. 115.

[126] G. Dworkin and R. Taylor, *Blackstone's Guide to the Copyright, Designs & Patent Act 1988*, Blackstone, 1989, p. 101.

Section 103 further specifies that, in proceedings for infringement of the right to object to derogatory treatment of the work, the court may, if it thinks it is an adequate remedy in the circumstances, grant an injunction on terms prohibiting the doing of any act unless a disclaimer is made, in such terms and in such manner as may be approved by the court, dissociating the author or the director from the treatment of the work. In addition, in relation to the right of paternity, under section 78(5) of the Act, a court must, in considering remedies, take into account any delay in asserting the right. Infringement of moral rights is not a criminal offence under UK copyright law. The provisions of the Irish Act are similar.[127]

279.   Transitional provisions: moral rights in old films

Old films constitute a potential field for moral rights disputes. However, transitional provisions in the current UK and Irish Acts make the enforcement of moral rights claims in relation to these films difficult. This is in strong contrast to the situation on the continent, where applicable transitional provisions or rules do not generally deprive old films of moral rights protection, especially in relation to acts done under the current Acts.

In the UK, as a first rule, nothing done before commencement of the 1988 Act is actionable by virtue of the rights of paternity and integrity.[128] In addition, these rights do not apply:
1. in relation to a literary, dramatic, musical and artistic work the author of which died before the commencement of the Act; or
2. in relation to a film made before the commencement of the Act.[129]
Note that under present law the 'film' in point 2 above is the recording of the audiovisual work, not the audiovisual work itself. However, it seems reasonable to consider that this reference applies also to the 'cinematographic film' under the 1956 Act.[130] But it is clear that this point does not apply to audiovisual works treated as dramatic or artistic works under the 1911 Act, which are dealt with in point 1 above.[131]

According to paragraph 10 of Schedule 1 to the Act, the question of who was the author of an existing work for the purpose of moral rights is to be determined in accordance with the new copyright provisions. The

---

[127] Section 137.   [128] Sched. 1, para. 22(1).
[129] Sched. 1, para. 23(2).   [130] See Sched. 1, para. 4(4).
[131] Sched. 1 to the Act specifies that 'where a film made before [1 June 1957] was an original dramatic work within the meaning of the 1911 Act, the new copyright provisions have effect in relation to the film as if it was an original dramatic work within the meaning of Part I' (s. 7(2)). Thus the references to 'films' in Sched. 1 must exclude pre-1957 dramatic films. Section 7(3) further specifies that 'the new copyright provisions have effect in relation to photographs forming part of a film made before June 1, 1957, as they have effect in relation to photographs not forming part of a film'.

author of a film protected as a dramatic work or as a series of photographs would then be the author of the dramatic or artistic work under present law. As a consequence, moral rights could apply in relation to an important number of cinematographic films made under the 1911 Act, and could possibly by owned by contributors other than the film director.[132]

However, authors or co-authors of pre-1957 films will have difficulty in claiming a *right of paternity*, which must be asserted by an instrument in writing signed by them. And it is unlikely that the screen credits would be considered as such an instrument.[133] In relation to pre-1957 films, claims based on the *rights of integrity and paternity* are further limited by paragraph 23(3)(a) of Schedule 1, which provides that the rights in relation to literary, dramatic, musical or artistic works do not apply:

1. where the copyright was first vested in the author, to anything which by virtue of an assignment of a copyright made or a licence granted before the commencement of the Act may be done without infringing copyright;
2. where the copyright was first vested in a person other than the author, to anything done by or with the licence of the copyright owner.

Therefore, such rights in pre-1957 dramatic films can only be claimed in relation to acts done after the commencement of the 1988 Act which also infringe the copyright. This reduces to almost nothing the scope of their application. Let us take three examples of potential derogatory treatment: colourisation; extensive cutting of the film with the addition of a new soundtrack; and the insertion of commercial advertisements. For the author(s) of the pre-1957 film to be able to object, these treatments must also infringe the copyright. For the 'colourised' and newly edited versions, this implies that the author retained at a minimum the right to adapt or to make another version of the film. This must have been extremely rare in practice.[134] Concerning breaks for advertising, it is difficult to see how these could infringe the right to adapt or to make a derivative work, if reserved.

These various limitations might reinforce the interest of relying on the false attribution of authorship to counter alterations of film works.[135] First, according to paragraph 22(2) of Schedule 1 to the 1988 Act, section 43 of the 1956 Act continues to apply in relation to acts done before the commencement of the 1988 Act. In addition, there is no requirement that the 'false attribution' infringe the copyright in the work as well.

[132] See Chapter 4 above.
[133] But an instrument to include credits would be. Assertion can be at any time, but remedies are affected by lateness.
[134] On the question of pre-1957 films and technologies unknown at the time of production, see para. 18, n. 106, above.
[135] See para. 267.

Secondly, the recourse to section 84 of 1988 new Act is not limited by paragraph 23(3)(a) of Schedule 1 thereto. Accordingly, the author of a pre-1957 film as 'artistic work' (i.e. the author of the film frames) could object to post-1988 attributions of altered copies of his work on this ground (and this includes the special right against alterations of artistic works in section 84(6)). However, the insertion of a notice of the modification will cure the false attribution.

The Irish Copyright and Related Rights Act 2000 contains similar transitional provisions.[136]

280.   The preservation of other causes of action

Section 171(4) of the UK 1988 Act provides that the Act does not affect 'any right of action or other remedy, whether civil or criminal', available otherwise than under the Act in respect of acts infringing statutory moral rights. Therefore, the moral interests of authors and creators can be protected through contract and tort law. Given the obvious limitations of moral rights provisions in the UK Act and the growing concern of the artistic community for a protection of the artistic integrity of film works, the recourse to common law actions could in some cases prove interesting to authors.[137]

SECTION II

Moral rights and films in continental Europe

281.   Introduction

The extent to which moral rights are protected in continental Europe is a source of concern for foreign film producers. Despite several adaptations of the statutory regime of moral rights in relation to films, the

[136] Copyright and Related Rights Act 2000, Sched. 1.
[137] See e.g. the cases discussed in para. 267. See also *Frisby* v. *BBC* [1967] Ch 932; [1967] 2 WLR 1204; [1967] 2 All ER 106, in which Goff J expressed the view that UK courts would readily imply a term limiting the right to make alterations in case of licences. The tort of passing off has been successfully relied upon in cases where a work was falsely attributed to an author: *Lord Byron* v. *Johnson* (1816) 2 Mer. 29 (passing off of works published as writings from Byron); *Wood* v. *Butterworths* [1905–10] MCC 16 (passing off writings under the name of a deceased author); and *Ridge* v. *English Illustrated Magazine Ltd* (1913) 29 TLR 592; [1911–16] MCC 91 (publication of a story in a magazine under the name of the plaintiff); see also *Landa* v. *Grinberg* (1908) 24 TLR 441, *Modern Fiction Ltd* v. *Fawcett* (1949) 66 RPC 230, *Forbes* v. *Kemsley Newspapers Ltd* [1951] 2 TLR 656, 68 RPC 189, and *Sykes* v. *John Fairfax & Sons Ltd* [1977] 1 NSWLR 415; [1978] FSR 312, which involve the use of journalists' pen-names for articles they did not write.

protection granted to film contributors and authors remains significant, and in most countries it is difficult, if not impossible, to restrict the exercise of these rights through contractual provisions. Moreover, the *Huston* case confirmed that foreign film authors could claim moral rights in certain Member States irrespective of the provisions of the contractual agreements entered into in the country of origin of the work.[138] As a result, for those works intended to be exploited in Europe, the risks of moral rights claims should be assessed with care.

The picture, however, may not be as dark for film producers and broadcasters as generally thought by US or UK film producers. Litigation from film authors on moral rights is scarce. Also, litigation is generally resolved by the allocation of damages or the insertion of a disclaimer, and rarely ends with injunctions against the showing of the film. In contrast, the consequences of the violation of some mandatory provisions such as the compulsory royalty right of authors, where implemented, can lead to a rescission of the production contract and to the destruction of the chain of copyright.[139]

However, the risk of having to withdraw and modify copies of the audiovisual works cannot be entirely excluded, and therefore foreign producers must be aware of the legislation on moral rights before production and distribution in each country. In this respect, the respective authors' rights Acts provide a regime which is very different from the regime implemented in the UK and Ireland.

PART I

Entitlement to moral right in films

282.   General rules

In the *droit d'auteur* tradition, moral rights are not distinct from copyright. Authors' rights are made of economic rights (which correspond to the Anglo-American copyright), on the one hand, and of moral rights, on the other hand. Therefore, the initial entitlement to moral rights follows the rules on initial entitlement to economic rights. In relation to films, this means that the rules on authorship and co-authorship apply equally to moral rights. As a consequence, the number of moral rights holders in film productions can be significant. Another general rule is that moral rights are usually granted to individuals only.[140]

---

[138] See paras. 168, 287, 346 and 354.   [139] See para. 167.
[140] One exception to this rule is constituted by the so-called category of 'collective works' under several continental Acts (see para. 147). However, we saw that audiovisual works

283.   Film authors: moral rights and multi-authorship

The rules on film authorship have been studied elsewhere in this book,[141] but their application to moral rights can be summarised as follows. In France and Belgium, the statutory list of co-authors of the audiovisual work, and therefore co-owners of a moral right in the work, includes the film director, the author of the script, the author of the adaptation, the dialogist, the author of any music specially commissioned for inclusion in the film and the author of the adapted work. In Portugal and Spain, the author of the adapted work is excluded from this list.

These lists are non-exhaustive[142] and in specific productions other contributors could share copyright and moral rights in the audiovisual work. Thus the director of photography, the editor or even the individual film producer, if he has a creative role in the film-making process could share copyright and moral rights in the audiovisual work.[143]

The co-authors of the film, to the extent they also create a protected work distinct from the final audiovisual work (the script, the adapted novel, the musical work), also benefit from a moral right in this 'underlying' work. Often, however, the distinction between the moral right in this contribution and the moral right in the resulting audiovisual work is not made: in practice these co-authors usually claim infringement of the moral right in their protected contribution, if any. But in theory nothing would prevent, for example, a musical composer objecting, as co-author of a film, to the colourisation of the film, even if his music is left untouched.

In Italy, the statutory list of co-authors, and therefore holders of moral rights in the film, includes the author of the subject-matter, the scriptwriter, the musical composer and the film director.[144] By application of the general rules on joint authorship, the list should be similar in the Netherlands and possibly in Sweden, Denmark and Finland.[145]

In Germany, due to more restrictive rules as to joint authorship, the list would be limited to the film director, the director of photography and possibly the editor.[146] The list would be similar under Austrian law. In Greece, the copyright Act designates only the principal director as the deemed author of the audiovisual work.[147] In Luxembourg, the film producer is now co-author of the audiovisual work with the film director.[148]

---

and underlying works in film productions cannot be characterised as 'collective works' in most countries (see paras. 143 and 147).

[141] See paras. 137–9.   [142] The point is discussed, however, for Spain.
[143] See para. 138.
[144] We saw that it is not clear whether this list is an exhaustive or a non-exhaustive list.
[145] See para. 137.   [146] See para. 137.   [147] See para. 138.   [148] See para. 139.

Nothing appears to prevent the film producer from holding moral rights in the film, even if he is a legal person.[149]

284.   Authors of underlying works

In *droit d'auteur* countries the list of authors of underlying works entitled to moral rights is roughly the same as described for the UK and Ireland.[150] However, in the absence of a closed list of copyright works and of a criteria of fixation as a condition for copyright protection, some underlying contributions which would not necessarily attract protection in copyright jurisdictions could be protected by authors' rights on the continent. This would be the case, for example, for the make-up works or the editing. In addition, characters and titles are sometimes given copyright protection on a broader basis.[151]

285.   Conflict of moral rights between authors

Conflicts of moral rights may arise between film authors, and also between film authors and authors of underlying works. For example, a claim by the film director against the editing of his film could prejudice the economic and moral interests of the other co-authors. In the same way, a claim raised by the author of the adapted work could prejudice the moral rights of the co-authors of the film derived from his work.

General rules on joint authorship may provide solutions in the case of conflict between co-authors of films. In general, these rules apply to moral rights without modification. This means that any joint holder of a moral right may object to a treatment of the work (he may, however, have to call his co-authors in the suit),[152] and that the consent of all co-authors is required. In particular, where this right is implemented, each author must consent to the 'divulgation' (i.e. publication or release) of the work.[153] This rule may cause difficulties in joint works such as films. However, most copyright Acts provide that, in case of conflict between co-authors, courts may authorise publication of the work. This is the case,

---

[149] In contrast, under the 1972 Act, it was not clear whether the film producer, who is the initial holder of the copyright in the film, could claim the status of author for moral rights purposes.

[150] See para. 240.   [151] See paras. 85 and 86.

[152] In France, it is not necessary for an author to join his co-authors in the suit for moral rights infringement. However, he must do so for economic rights.

[153] A divulgation made without the consent of one co-author is an infringement of his moral right; see e.g. in France, Court of Cassation, 19 May 1976, RIDA, January 1977, p. 104.

for example, in France,[154] Belgium[155] and Spain.[156] Also, the German Act provides that a joint author cannot unreasonably refuse his consent to publication, alteration or modification of the joint work.[157] The Italian Act contains a similar provision.[158]

In addition, in relation to films, the French Intellectual Property Code provides that, when an author refuses to complete or cannot complete his contribution to the audiovisual work, he cannot object to the use, for the completion of the audiovisual work, of that part of his contribution which is already made.[159] This is also the case in Belgium[160] and Spain[161] (but, in Spain, only in the case of non-completion by 'unjustified refusal' or *force majeure*).

In contrast, continental authors' rights acts are silent on the relationship between film authors and authors of underlying works. It is left to the courts to arbitrate this kind of conflict.[162]

286.   Moral rights for film producers

A concept of moral rights for film producers is foreign to most *droit d'auteur* systems. In these countries, as a matter of principle, corporate bodies cannot be considered as 'authors' of copyright work. Accordingly, production companies are not entitled to moral rights. In most cases, the film producer, where it is a legal person, will be able to protect its reputation or other 'moral interests' through tort law, although this type of protection could be narrower than that offered to authors.

However, a right of integrity is granted to film producers in Germany in relation to their neighbouring right in audiovisual recordings. Under section 94 of the German Copyright Act, the producer has the right 'to prevent any distortion or shortening of the visual and sound record which may prejudice his legitimate interest'. A similar provision is found in the Austrian Copyright Act.[163]

As mentioned above, in Luxembourg the film producer, considered as co-author of the film, might be granted the corresponding moral rights in the film.

---

[154] Art. L.113-3(3).   [155] Copyright Act, art. 4.   [156] Copyright Act, art. 7.
[157] Copyright Act, art. 8(2).   [158] Copyright Act, art. 10.
[159] Art. L.121-6. He will nevertheless keep his full status of author with regard to this contribution.
[160] Copyright Act, art. 15.   [161] Copyright Act, art. 91.
[162] See the case law at para. 341 (conflict between moral rights of authors and moral rights of performers).
[163] Copyright Act, art. 38(2).

287.   Foreign authors

The protection of foreign authors' moral rights will be studied in detail below when considering the protection of foreign works.[164] We will see that under several authors' rights Acts moral rights are granted to foreign authors regardless of their nationality and without any further pre-condition.

PART II

The scope and regime of moral rights in films

288.   Introduction: wide statutory principles and limited exceptions

Statutory moral rights are drafted in broad terms in all continental Acts, and their regime is usually contained in very few articles. In addition, there are no exceptions and qualifications to moral rights similar to those found in the UK and Irish Acts. However, some *droit d'auteur* Acts contain specific adaptations of the statutory scheme in relation to films. Described below are the scope and application of the right of integrity, of the right of paternity and of the other moral rights applicable to film works, as well as the rules common to all moral rights.

The right of integrity

289.   Definitions

Most authors' rights countries have introduced moral rights clauses in their copyright Acts drafted in terms similar to article 6*bis* of the Berne Convention. For example, the Belgian Copyright Act provides that the author enjoys 'the right to oppose any distortion, mutilation or other alteration of his work or any other prejudicial act to this work which may damage his honour or reputation'.[165] The wording is similar in Italy,[166] the Netherlands,[167] Portugal[168] and Sweden.[169]

The language is slightly different in Germany, where article 14 of the Copyright Act provides that the author can prevent any distortion or any other impairment of his work which would prejudice 'the legitimate

---

[164] See Chapter 10 below.   [165] Copyright Act, art. 1(2).   [166] Copyright Act, art. 20.
[167] Copyright Act, art. 25(1)(d).   [168] Copyright Act, art. 56.
[169] Copyright Act, art. 3.

intellectual or personal interest' he has in the work. The Spanish Act also refers to acts which could cause prejudice to the 'legitimate interests' or the reputation of the author.[170]

Other jurisdictions do not repeat the condition that the infringing act be prejudicial to the honour, reputation or legitimate interest of the author. For example, French law only states that the author 'enjoys a right to the respect of his name, of his status as author, and of his work', without further specification.[171] The language used is similarly broad in Greece.[172]

In practice, these differences in wording do not seem to affect the scope of protection under the right of integrity. In particular, in those countries which require that the treatment be prejudicial 'to the honour or reputation' of the author, the protection will not be refused to an author on the sole ground that he has no or very little reputation in the industry. In addition, in most cases the prejudice to the honour or reputation will not need to be actual.

290.   Statutory adaptations to film productions

Several authors' rights countries have adapted or limited the exercise of moral rights in relation to films. This is the case in Belgium, Finland, France, Germany, the Netherlands, Portugal and Spain. In France, articles L.121-5 and L.121-6 of the Intellectual Property Code, which codify articles 15 and 16 of the Copyright Act of 1957, contain several provisions adapting the regime of moral rights to film productions. Their main objective is to avoid the situation where a claim by one co-author prevents the exploitation of the entire film, to the prejudice of other co-authors. The provisions, however, remain very protective of the interests of film authors, in particular with regard to the final cut of the film.

Article L.121-5 provides that the moral rights of paternity and integrity of the co-authors of the film can only be exercised over the completed audiovisual work.[173] The article further provides that an audiovisual work is deemed completed when the final version has been established by agreement between the director and the producer or, possibly, between the joint authors and the producer. However, once the film is completed, the normal scheme applies and moral rights can still be exercised by each co-author.

The language of article L.121-5 is somewhat confusing. In fact, this restriction to the exercise of moral rights is rather limited. It obliges the

---

[170] Copyright Act, art. 14.   [171] Art. L.121-1 of the Intellectual Property Code.
[172] Copyright Act, art. 4.
[173] This also applies to authors of adapted works, since they are considered co-author of the audiovisual work in the Act.

co-author to wait until completion before exercising their moral rights. However, it appears that this does not prevent them refusing to agree the final version of the film because of acts done before completion. It has been held, for example, that a musical composer can object to cuts made at the editing stage.[174]

In any case, the film producer cannot complete the film (i.e. decide the final cut) without the agreement of at least the film director. This agreement to the final cut carries the exercise of the *droit de divulgation* (the right to decide upon first publication or release).[175] The destruction of the master copy of such a final cut is prohibited. In addition, article L.121-5 provides that any change made to that cut by addition, deletion or modification of an element thereof requires the agreement of the film director or, alternatively, of the co-authors of the film (which anyway includes the film director).

Finally, the article provides that any transfer of an audiovisual work to another type of medium for a different mode of exploitation requires prior *consultation* with the director. This includes, for example, exploitation on videotape. This consultation can be the occasion for the film director to discover treatments made to his film.

A more serious limitation on the exercise of moral rights is included in article L.121-6, which provides that a co-author who refuses to complete his contribution, or who is unable to complete his contribution due to *force majeure*, cannot oppose the use of that part of his contribution already created for the completion of the audiovisual work. He retains authorship in such contribution and the corresponding rights.

A specific regime similar to the one established in the French Code is implemented in Belgium[176] and Spain.[177] But other copyright Acts appear to implement more straightforward limitations on the exercise of moral rights.

In Germany, article 14 of the Copyright Act grants to authors the right to prohibit any distortion of their work that could harm their just and reasonable personal interests in the work. However, article 93 restricts the right of film authors and of authors of pre-existing works solely to the right to object to gross distortions or other gross injuries to their work.[178]

[174] Paris Court of Appeal, 2 December 1963, *Revue Dalloz*, 1964, p. 229, note Lyon-Caen.
[175] See para. 308. But this applies only to authors who have agreed to the final version. Accordingly, film producer should obtain the agreement of all co-author, instead of the agreement of the sole director.
[176] Arts. 15 and 16 of the Copyright Act. The completed version is the result of an agreement between the film director and the producer.
[177] Arts. 91, 92 and 93 of the Copyright Act. Under Spanish copyright, the completed version is determined according to the provisions in the contract between the film director and the film producer.
[178] There is a similar condition in Dutch law.

It is also specified that in the exercise of their moral rights they must take into account the legitimate interests of other authors and of the producer. Legal commentators consider that cuts for advertisements could amount to a gross distortion of a work.[179] A German court, however, held that the act of changing the end of a book in its screen version was a gross distortion but was not an infringement of the right of integrity of the author, because the interest of the film producer prevailed.[180] The German Copyright Act further excludes for cinematographic works the right to revoke a transfer of a right if it is not exercised and the right to withdraw the work by reason of a change of opinion.[181]

In Italy, the limitation applies during production of the film: the producer has the right to alter pre-existing works and other contributions to the extent necessary for their adaptation in the film.[182] Disputes arising between co-authors and the production company as to this question of adaptation are settled by a special commission appointed by the government, whose decisions are final.[183]

In the Netherlands, contributors to a film work are deemed, unless otherwise agreed in writing, to have waived their rights to object to modifications of the work made by the producer or on his behalf.[184] This limitation would not appear to extend to gross distortions or mutilations.

291.   Absence of further exemptions similar to copyright exemptions

As a general rule there are no further exceptions to moral rights similar to those applicable to economic rights, concerning for example private use, news reporting, libraries, official use, incidental inclusion, etc. Courts may, however, view uses such as parodies with leniency.[185]

292.   General limitations

The exercise of moral rights is not discretionary. In most authors' rights countries, general theories can help to prevent an author abusing his moral right.[186] In France, for example, it has been consistently held that an author cannot use a moral right as a pretext for a claim which is in essence a monetary claim. Also a claim raised with the sole motive of

---

[179] G. Schricker, *Urheberrecht Kommentar*, Munich, 1987 (who also cites product placements); see also F.-K. Beier, H. Götting, M. Lehmann and R. Moufarg, *Urhebervertragsrecht: Festgabe für Gerhard Schricker zum 60 Geburstag*, Munich, 1995 pp. 399–400.
[180] OLG Munich, ZUM, 1986, p. 467, GRUR, 1986, p. 260.
[181] Copyright Act, art. 90.   [182] Copyright Act, art. 47.   [183] *Ibid.*
[184] Art. 45f of the Copyright Act.   [185] See para. 222.   [186] See para. 216.

harming the film producer would be held to be an abuse of right. In a language which is more favourable to producers, article 39 of the German Act allows alterations of a work and its title which the author 'cannot reasonably refuse'.

293.   Case law on the right of integrity

The discussion below, unless otherwise specified, concentrates on the case law developed in France. It should be remembered, however, that French law provides a high level of protection for moral rights and that French courts are very protective of the interests of authors. These solutions may not be applicable under other *droit d'auteur* systems.

294.   Colourisation

In France, in the famous *Huston* case,[187] the heirs of John Huston successfully relied on the moral right of integrity of the US film director to object to the colourisation of the film 'Asphalt Jungle' and to its broadcasting on French television. On remand from the Supreme Court, the Court of Appeal of Versailles stated:

the 'colourisation' of a film without the authorisation and control of the authors or of their heirs damages the creative activity of the directors even if it satisfies, for obvious commercial reasons, a certain public demand; the implementation of this process without the agreement [of the heirs] infringes the moral right of the authors, as mandatorily protected by French law ... the broadcasting also constitutes a direct and certain infringement of the moral right.

There is little doubt that in several continental countries the colourisation of a black-and-white film would be held to be an infringement of the moral right of integrity.

295.   Directions and artistic control

Instructions given by the film producer or the commissioner to a film's authors during production are unlikely to constitute a case of moral rights infringement if they do not imply the modification of an already existing work. This was held by the French Supreme Court in an interesting case involving claims by the authors of a promotional documentary on Gabon, who later objected to the final work which resulted

---

[187] *Turner Entertainment* v. *Huston* (*Asphalt Jungle*), Paris Court of Appeal, 6 July 1989, Court of Cassation, 28 May 1991, noted in (1991) 4 *Entertainment Law Review* E-55. Versailles Court of Appeal, 19 December 1994, RIDA, April 1995, p. 389, note Kerever.

326   Film copyright in the European Union

from the instructions of the commissioner. The court rejected their moral rights claims on the ground that moral rights do not exist before the work is completed.[188]

296.   Editing and modifications of the film

Post-production editing usually amounts to an infringement of the moral rights in a film.[189] In France, the motive for the editing or the importance of the cut are in most cases irrelevant: respect for the integrity of the film implies that it is released in an unabridged form.

In one French case, a film created by a salaried director was edited by his employer, who considered the film unusable as it stood. The court held that, even if the contract authorised the assignee of the copyright to modify the title and to edit the film, the author retains his moral rights for this purpose. Accordingly, the author can claim moral rights infringement when the public was not informed of the fact that the film presented was in fact an abridged version of the much longer film created by the director.[190]

In a case in the Tribunal of First Instance of Paris,[191] the German version of a French film was reduced in duration by the German distributor from 131 minutes to 119 minutes without the consent of the French film director. The director, who retained a contractual right to final cut, sued the French producer and the German distributor for breach of contract and infringement of moral rights. The Tribunal held that the French and German distributors were jointly liable for moral rights infringement, and that the producer could not base his defence on an alleged 'abuse' by the director of his moral right. The French and German film producers were enjoined (i) not to release the modified version without the authorisation of the author, (ii) to provide the film director with a list of distributors and sub-distributors of the film, and (iii) to inform the distributors and sub-distributors of the injunction.[192]

The insertion of a warning during the credits of a documentary on the Vietnam War made in 1967, aimed at explaining the documentary's context, was also held to be an infringement of the right of integrity of its author.[193] A change in the duration of a television series by the merging of

---

[188] Court of Cassation, 9 April 1987, *Revue Dalloz*, 1988, p. 97.

[189] Tribunal of First Instance of Seine, 6–7 April 1949, *La Semaine Juridique*, 1950, II, No. 5462 (*Blanchard et Zimmer v. Gaumont*, and *Prévert et Carné v. Pathé*).

[190] Court of Cassation, 17 January 1995, *Colet Sté Téléproductions Bartoli v. Michel Blaise*.

[191] 23 March 1994, RIDA, 1994, p. 401.

[192] The decision on moral rights would certainly have been the same in the absence of a contractual right to final cut.

[193] Court of Cassation, 4 April 1991, *Ivens v. Argos Films, Images Juridiques*, No. 82, 15 May 1991.

some episodes,[194] and the broadcasting of a theatrical film on television in two distinct parts[195] were also held to be an infringements of moral rights. Further cases concerned the substitution or addition of musical backgrounds, which are consistently held to be an infringement of moral rights in the film.[196]

297. Advertising breaks

Courts on the continent have shown in the past different attitudes towards the question of advertising cuts. French courts have always decided against the broadcaster,[197] whereas some Italian decisions have taken into account the circumstances of the cuts to validate or invalidate them.[198] Although the matter of advertising cuts is now regulated in domestic broadcasting laws, such administrative regulations are without prejudice to the exercise of the moral rights of authors.[199]

298. Derogatory association

In a case in the Court of Appeal of Paris, a film director objected to the showing of his film as part of a longer television programme consisting of an introduction to the film, the broadcasting of the film itself, and

---

[194] Tribunal of First Instance of Paris, 14 March 1990, RIDA, October 1990, para. 146.320, confirmed by Paris Court of Appeal, 4 March 1991. The same solution was reached for the reduction of the duration of a short documentary from thirteen minutes to ten minutes (Tribunal of First Instance of Paris, 29 March 1990, *Atmosphere Communication* v. *La Cinq SA* (damages of FFr30,000 awarded to each author)).

[195] Paris Court of Appeal, 26 November 1990, *Images Juridiques*, No. 74, 15 January 1991, p. 2 (damages awarded to the authors of FFr100,000).

[196] In Switzerland, a substitution of background music in the film 'The Gold Rush' by Charlie Chaplin held an infringement of the moral right of integrity (Federal Tribunal, ATF 96, II, p. 421, noted in English in (1971) IIC 315 at 323). For a similar case in France, see Paris Court of Appeal, 29 April 1959, *Revue Dalloz*, 1959, p. 402. In Germany, see the 'Christopher Columbus' case, Court of Appeal of Munich, 26 September 1991, ZUM, 1992, p. 307, GRUR Int., 1993, p. 332 (action by the composer of the original music against a substitution of music in a film).

[197] Tribunal of First Instance of Paris, 29 May 1989, RIDA, January 1990, p. 353; Tribunal of First Instance of Paris, 25 October 1989, *La Semaine Juridique*, 1990, I, No. 3478.

[198] Frequent interruptions have been held an infringement of moral rights, but for example a decision of the *Praetor Roma* of 30 July 1985 (Giur. It., 1986, 1, 2, p. 81, note Garutti) rejected the claim of the director, Frederico Fellini, against the insertion of advertising cuts during the broadcast of one of his films. According to the Rome Court of Appeal, 16 November 1989, *Germi* v. *Reteitalia and Rissoli Film*, RIDA, 1990, No. 144, p. 184, courts must take into consideration the quality of the film, the duration of the film, and the number and duration of the advertising cuts.

[199] In France, see Tribunal of First Instance of Paris, 29 May 1989, RIDA, January 1990, p. 353; Paris Court of Appeal, 26 November 1990, *Images Juridiques*, 15 January 1991, p. 2; Tribunal of First Instance of Paris, 25 October 1990, *La Semaine Juridique*, 1990, I, No. 3478.

then a debate on a certain theme in connection with the film. The film was on the life of a saint, Sainte Thérèse de Lisieu, and the theme of the debate following the film was on religious experience. The film director sought a preliminary injunction restraining the broadcasting of the film, claiming that his work was not a religious work, and that the inclusion of his film within the longer programme was untrue to its spirit. The Court of Appeal, after noting that the film was to be performed without cuts or alterations, held that the plaintiff did not produce sufficient evidence as to a possible infringement of his moral rights by the mere association of his film with the theme of the debate.

But certain forms of association can be an infringement of moral rights. This was decided in several cases involving the inclusion of music in advertising.[200] In a recent case, the unauthorised reproduction of part of the decor of a silent film on the walls of a restaurant in Paris was held to be an infringement of both the economic and the moral rights of the author of the old film.[201]

299.   Display of a broadcaster's logo during a telecast

The display of a broadcaster's logo during a telecast was, at least twice, held by French courts to be an infringement of the right of integrity.[202]

300.   Parody

Parody is usually considered an exception to moral rights under the same conditions as described for economic rights.[203]

301.   Use of musical works

The synchronisation of musical works in film soundtracks, especially in promotional or advertising programmes, appears to cause a great deal of litigation on moral rights, with sometimes unwelcome results for film

---

[200] See e.g. Tribunal of First Instance of Paris, 15 May 1991, *La Semaine Juridique*, 1992, II, No. 21919, note Daverat; Paris Court of Appeal, 7 April 1994, *Revue Dalloz*, 1995, Sommaire, p. 56 (films for an erotic telephone dating service).

[201] Tribunal of First Instance of Paris, 13 January 1999, *Fontaine* v. *Sté Planet Hollywood International*, *Juris-Data*, No. 042220, *Communication Commerce Electronique*, October 1999, p. 13, note Caron (the film was Melies' 'A Trip to the Moon').

[202] Tribunal of First Instance of Paris, 29 June 1988, RIDA, October 1988, para. 138, p. 328; *La Semaine Juridique*, 1989, I, No. 3376; confirmed by Paris Court of Appeal, 25 October 1989, *Revue Dalloz*, 1990, Sommaire, p. 54 (damages of FFr50,000 awarded). Tribunal of First Instance of Paris, 13 September 1989, *Youri* v. *M6*, unreported (damages of FFr40,000 awarded).

[203] See para. 222.

producers and broadcasters. It was held, for example, that the inclusion of a song within advertising material infringes the moral rights of the author of the song, even if this synchronisation was licensed by a collecting society.[204]

The French case *Clegg and EMI* v. *TF1*[205] involved the use of excerpts from a song in a short trailer for a television programme on the football world cup, without any indication of the author. It was held to be an infringement of the moral rights of integrity and of paternity of the author-performer. This solution was endorsed by the Court of Appeal of Paris in a case concerning the inclusion of music in a promotional programme (trailers for future programmes).[206] The song was mixed with voices of children and dialogue. The Court of Appeal granted an injunction, including the broadcasting of public apologies on prime-time television (twenty-eight runs of this message!).

302.   Excerpts

In a case tried by the Tribunal of First Instance of Paris, an excerpt from a film was broadcast, without the consent of the authors, within a larger documentary programme. The film director's claim was successful on copyright infringement grounds, but failed on moral rights grounds: the court held that the film director had not demonstrated that the broadcasting of an excerpt from his film, which he did not authorise, amounted to a distortion of his film.[207]

In contrast, the Court of Appeal of Paris held that the inclusion of an audiovisual work within a larger work necessarily implied a distortion of the original work.[208]

303.   Non-exploitation of the work

The refusal to release a film mainly affects the moral right of divulgation (the right to decide upon first publication or release), which is discussed below.[209] But could this also constitute a derogatory treatment prejudicial to the reputation of the film-maker (such reputation being harmed by the

---

[204] Paris Court of Appeal, April 1994, RIDA, 1995, No. 164.
[205] Tribunal of First Instance of Nanterre, *Clegg and EMI* v. *TF1*, 5 November 1997, unreported.
[206] Paris Court of Appeal, 24 September 1997, *Banglater* v. *SNP France 2*, unreported (appeal from interlocutory judgment).
[207] Tribunal of First Instance of Paris, 14 September 1994, RIDA, 1995, No. 164.
[208] Paris Court of Appeal, 12 December 1995, *Legipresse*, December 1996, No. 137, p. 155.
[209] See para. 308.

absence of release)? In the French case of *Dewever* v. *EMI France*,[210] a film director sued the co-producers of his films for the non-exploitation of his films. His claims on copyright and contractual grounds were rejected for procedural reasons. The French Supreme Court held that the loss of fame resulting from the non-exploitation of the film did not amount to an infringement of the film director's right of integrity.

304.   Re-exploitation of the film

Could a new exploitation or release of a film be objected to by its author(s) on pure moral rights grounds? The question was addressed in France by the Tribunal of First Instance of Paris, in the *Terrangle et al.* v. *Canal J* case.[211] The plaintiff was co-author and performer of a TV show for children. Within the context of a larger claim for copyright infringement, he claimed that the new release of the old show, which was more than ten years old, constituted an infringement of his moral right. The court held that the rebroadcast to the public of a work, more than ten years after its first broadcast, constituted an infringement of the moral right of an author or of a co-author who does not wish to have his participation in such work brought to the attention of the public or, more generally, who fears that his participation appears dated or unfashionable.[212]

Similar decisions in France have involved performers who in their early days played in pornographic or erotic movies and who, having since become famous, sought injunctions preventing the exploitation of these films.[213]

The right of paternity

305.   The right of paternity

In most continental copyright Acts the right of paternity is stated in terms generally similar to those of article 6*bis* of the Berne Convention, and no specification is made concerning the modalities of its application. In

---

[210] Court of Cassation, 10 May 1995, RIDA, October 1995, p. 285.

[211] 28 June 1996, unreported.

[212] Damages were awarded but the restraining injunction was refused on the ground that the author did not join his co-authors in the suit.

[213] On the grounds of the 'rights of personality'. See Tribunal of First Instance of Paris, 7 March 1986, *Ringer, Revue Dalloz*, 1987, Sommaire, p. 367, note Hassler; and Court of Cassation, 3 March 1982, *Beccarie*, Bull. Civ., I, No. 99. However, this protection cannot be wider than a statutory moral right. For example, it was held that the mere fact of giving a secondary exploitation to a performance, neither authorised nor remunerated, cannot in itself constitute a violation of a right of personality. Paris Court of Appeal, 30 November 1974, RIDA, 1975, No. 84.

relation to films, however, the Italian, Dutch and Portuguese copyright Acts specify the right for film authors to be credited on the film. In the other continental countries, this right is considered as an aspect of the general right of paternity.

306.   Limitations on the right of paternity

Member States of the *droit d'auteur* tradition do not provide for specific limitations on the right of paternity in relation to films. The reason for this is that its exercise is thought to be less disruptive of the film production and distribution processes. Also, in contrast to the general rules on waivers, 'anonymity clauses' are usually upheld by courts to some extent.[214]

307.   Case law on the right of paternity

French case law leaves no doubt that authors must have their names mentioned in the credits of a film.[215] But the attribution must also be displayed on secondary exploitation copies, such as videotapes. In France, it was held, for example, that the absence of the name of the film director on the cover of a videotape of his film infringed his moral right. The fact that the contract did not mention a credit on this type of material did not affect his right to claim a credit on this and other materials or media.[216]

There is no exemption to this rule concerning excerpts or extracts from a work.[217] The Court of Appeal of Paris also held that the absence of identification of the author of a song used in an advertisement is an infringement of his right of paternity, if no consent for such use was obtained.[218] Film authors can also rely on their right of paternity to claim against wrong or incomplete identifications in credits.[219] In addition, the name of the author must be stated in such a way as to permit identification of the author and of his work.[220]

---

[214] See para. 311.
[215] Paris Court of Appeal, 17 January 1995, *System IV* v. *Verrecchia*.
[216] Injunction granted and FFr30,000 damages for moral rights infringement awarded. Tribunal of First Instance of Nanterre, 27 April 1994, RIDA, 1995, No. 163, p. 235.
[217] Tribunal of First Instance of Nanterre, *Clegg and EMI* v. *TF1*, 5 November 1997, unreported.
[218] Paris Court of Appeal, 6 March 1991, *SA Film 13* v. *Pascal di Fusco*, *Revue Dalloz*, 1992, Sommaire, p. 75.
[219] Held that the accreditation of the author on the credits as a mere technician, i.e. the author of the images from the audiovisual work, when he was in fact the author of the film, infringed his moral right of attribution (Court of Cassation, 17 January 1995, *Colet Sté Téléproductions Bartoli* v. *Michel Blaise*).
[220] Paris Court of Appeal, 26 June 1996, *Stock* v. *Dudognon*, RIDA, No. 174, October 1997, p. 250 (concerning reproductions of photographs in a book).

There does not appear to be any case law on the question of 'possessory credit', and it is not clear whether a film director, otherwise mentioned on the credits of a film, could rely on his right of paternity to claim a possessory credit in the form of 'a film by X' or 'X's [title]'. Such a claim could create conflicts with the other co-authors of the film, if any, who would have a similar right to such a credit under most copyright Acts.

Other moral rights

308.   The rights of divulgation and of reconsideration

Most continental countries implement two other moral rights: (i) a 'right of divulgation' (also called the 'right of dissemination' or the 'right of publication') (i.e. the right to decide when and how a work should be made public, including the right not to make it public); and (ii) the right to revoke a grant of right or to withdraw a work from commercial exploitation (the 'right of reconsideration' or 'right of revocation'). The right of reconsideration, however, does not exist in Belgium, nor apparently in the Netherlands nor in Scandinavian countries.

The *right of divulgation* is usually defined in broad terms, and its exercise is not subject to conditions.[221] Although it would seem logical to consider that this right can only be exercised once, some legal commentators are of the opinion that the author should retain the right to make his work public through secondary modes of exploitation. This view was accepted by courts in France, but apparently in situations in which the exploitation in question was neither contemplated nor intended by the author at the time of the initial release.[222]

As mentioned above, several continental copyright Acts provide that courts may authorise publication of a joint work in case of conflict between joint authors,[223] or, alternatively, that a joint author cannot unreasonably refuse his consent to the publication, alteration or modification of the joint work.[224] In addition, we saw that the French Intellectual Property Code provides that, when an author refuses to complete or cannot complete his contribution to the audiovisual work, he cannot object to

---

[221] E.g. the French Intellectual Property Code laconically provides that 'the author has the sole right to divulgate his work'. Art. 12 of the German Act provides that the author 'shall have the right to decide whether and how his work is to be published'.

[222] See e.g. Tribunal of First Instance of Paris, 20 November 1991, RIDA, July 1992, p. 340, note Kerever (publication of lectures). Paris Court of Appeal, 23 June 2000, *Propriétés Intellectualles* 2001, p. 60.

[223] See para. 285. The French Intellectual Property Code, art. L.113-3(3); Belgian Act, art. 4; Spanish Copyright Act, art. 7.

[224] German Act, art. 8(2); Italian Act, art. 10.

the use, for the completion of the audiovisual work, of that part of his contribution which is already made.[225] This provision is repeated in other Member States.[226]

In France, and probably in other *droit d'auteur* countries as well, the acceptance of the final cut by film authors implies the exercise of their right of divulgation.[227]

The various copyright Acts do not provide for an indemnification where a commissioner suffers a prejudice resulting from the decision by an author not to divulgate a work. However, it appears that, in such a case, a commissioner could rely on contractual or extra-contractual doctrines to obtain an indemnification or a reimbursement of his costs (especially if he has paid the author or if he has incurred substantial costs in the production).

The *right of reconsideration* is potentially a powerful tool in the hands of authors. However, it is very rarely exercised, mainly due to the obligation of prior indemnification of the assignee implemented in all copyright Acts. In addition, in relation to films (as opposed to underlying works), it appears that in most Member States the exercise of the right of reconsideration would involve an agreement by all co-authors. In practice, refusals to divulgate are usually associated with a claim against derogatory treatment of some sort.

In France, the right of reconsideration is called the 'right to reconsider or of withdrawal' (*droit de repentir ou de retrait*).[228] It can be exercised notwithstanding assignment of the right of exploitation, before or after publication of the work. However, the author may only exercise this right if he indemnifies the assignee beforehand for any prejudice the withdrawal may cause him. Also, if the author decides to have his work published after having exercised his right to reconsider or to withdraw, he must first offer his rights to the original assignee, under the conditions originally determined. There is no condition regarding the motive of withdrawal.

In contrast, in some countries, withdrawal is possible only in certain circumstances, for example where the exploitation may prejudice the legitimate interests of the author or in case of change of opinion.

Under the German Copyright Act, the right to revoke a transfer of a right if it is not exercised and the right to withdraw the work by reason of a change of opinion are not applicable to cinematographic works.[229] In Italy, the right of reconsideration is only exercisable when 'serious

---

[225] See para. 285.
[226] E.g. Belgium, Copyright Act, art. 15; Spain, Copyright Act, art. 91 (only in the case of 'unjustified refusal' or *force majeure*).
[227] See para. 290.   [228] Art. L.121-4.   [229] Copyright Act, art. 90.

moral reasons' arise.[230] It is also subject to the indemnification of the assignee.

309.   Case law on the right of divulgation

The right of divulgation must be considered in both its positive and negative aspects. In its positive aspect, the right of divulgation is the right for the author of the film to have his film released. Therefore, a refusal by the film producer to release a film could infringe the moral rights of its co-authors.[231] A French court has even decided that the ability of an assignee of exploitation rights in a film to prevent the sale of the film to a broadcaster constituted an infringement of the right of divulgation of the author.[232] However, a minimal release would probably not be held to infringe the right of divulgation. Also, a refusal to exploit the film on a certain media (for example, in video) would probably not be an infringement of this right.[233]

Other case law in France on the positive right of divulgation concerns the question of access by authors or their heirs to the copies of the film owned or archived by the film producer, in order to enable their release or exploitation. The French Intellectual Property Code provides in such a case for a right of access.[234]

In its negative aspect, the right of divulgation is the right not to divulgate the film. We saw that this right cannot be exercised before the film is completed. It could, in theory, be exercised after completion of the film, but this appears purely theoretical: first, it would involve a reimbursement or an indemnification of the film producer(s);[235] secondly, the right of non-divulgation would conflict with the co-authors' right of divulgation.

310.   Other rights

As already stated, moral rights ought not to be confused with those rights which grant an economic protection to authors, such as the resale royalty

---

[230] Copyright Act, art. 142.

[231] Note that the refusal by a film producer to release a film could also constitute a violation of his mandatory duty to produce the film. See para. 165. The main difference is the possibility for the author to rescind the contract for breach.

[232] Tribunal of First Instance of Paris, 10 October 1988, *Cahiers du Droit d'Auteur*, February 1989, p. 11.

[233] Although some legal commentators consider that this right is not 'exhausted' by a first release.

[234] Art. L.113-3. For an application to films, see e.g. Paris Court of Appeal, 29 September 1995, RIDA, April 1996, p. 293:.

[235] See para. 308.

right (the French *droit de suite*, which is not applicable to films), the compulsory royalty right and the rules intended to prevent assignments of future works or long-term contracts, which are studied elsewhere. Provisions in the copyright Acts providing for a retention of adaptation rights or dubbing rights by authors may also permit an author to control potential derogatory uses of their works.

In addition to these rights, several copyright Acts contain specific provisions intended to ensure the archiving of a copy of the film. This is the case in Belgium, France, Portugal and Spain. For example, the French Intellectual Property Code prohibits any destruction of the master copy of the film and implies a clause in the production contract providing for a list of elements to be preserved and the modalities of their conservation;[236] in practice, theatrical film prints (a positive and the negative of the film) are deposited in the national film library (the *Cinémathèque Française*).

Common questions

311. Waivers and consents

As a matter of principle, moral rights in continental countries are inalienable and cannot be waived. However, the prohibition of waivers is applied with different emphasis by Member States. The principle of prohibition of waivers appears to be strictly enforced in Germany, but it may be possible to waive the right of paternity to a certain extent (at least temporarily).[237] The situation appears similar in Italy[238] and in Spain.

Several jurisdictions appear more ready to accept waivers drafted in specific terms and directed to clearly identified uses. In France, as a general rule, waivers of the right of integrity are considered null and void.[239] However, clauses in production contracts drafted in specific terms and authorising in advance well-defined and foreseeable uses of a work may be considered enforceable by French courts under certain circumstances. For example, in a recent decision, the Court of Appeal of Paris validated a clause in a copyright assignment contract by which the co-authors of a song agreed that their song may be modified for use in an advertisement.[240] The clause granted the assignee the right to add or

---

[236] Art. L.132-24.
[237] A. Dietz, in M. B. Nimmer and D. Geller (eds.), *International Copyright Law and Practice*, Matthew Bender, looseleaf, para. 7[b] *in fine*.
[238] Subject to the possibility of consent; see below.
[239] But it would not, however, invalidate the entire agreement.
[240] Paris Court of Appeal, 28 June 2000, *Barbelivien et Montagné* v. *Sté Agence Business, Communication Commerce Electronique*, November 2000, p. 15, note Caron.

to cause third parties to add new words to the music for exploitation in advertising soundtracks. The court considered that, in the context of the case, such a wording did not amount to an alienation in advance of moral rights, but rather constituted the exercise, in full knowledge, of these moral rights. Note, however, that such a solution may not be applicable outside the field of advertising. In contrast to waivers of the right of integrity, 'anonymity clauses' in publishing contracts are considered valid, as long as they are temporary and the author has the right to reclaim paternity of the work at any time.[241]

In Belgium, a waiver drafted as a specific authorisation allowing certain exploitations (as opposed to a general waiver of moral right) would appear to be enforceable against the author.[242] The situation appears similar in Greece[243] and in Sweden.[244] In contrast to pure 'waivers', clauses of film production agreements imposing artistic requirements are certainly enforceable to a certain extent. Also, it is always open to an author to consent to uses of his work which could otherwise be held derogatory. But consents given in advance are likely to be considered as waivers of moral rights, in which case they will follow their regime.[245]

312.   Transfer and exercise of moral rights

Moral rights are not transferable but are transmissible *mortis causa*, under various schemes, to individual, legal persons and even sometimes to the State. In most countries, the author may, during his life, entrust a collecting society or a third party (which may well be a legal person) with the exercise of his or one of his moral rights.

313.   The duration of moral rights in films

In France, Italy and Spain, the rights of paternity and integrity are perpetual.[246] In Belgium, Germany, the Netherlands, Portugal and Sweden,

---

[241] Court of Cassation, 5 May 1993, *Gérard de Villiers* v. *Brigitte Soton* (appeal from Paris, 18 December 1990).
[242] See A. Strowel, in M. B. Nimmer and D. Geller (eds.), *International Copyright Law and Practice*, Matthew Bender, looseleaf, para. 7[4].
[243] See Copyright Act, arts. 14 and 16. G. Koumantos, in M. B. Nimmer and D. Geller (eds.), *International Copyright Law and Practice*, Matthew Bender, looseleaf, para. 7[4].
[244] Copyright Act, art. 3.
[245] But this is not always the case. For example, in Italy, art. 22 of the Copyright Act provides that the author cannot prevent the performance of his work or demand its suppression if he was aware of and has accepted the modifications to which he later objects.
[246] Other moral rights may endure for the life of the author or for the duration of copyright protection.

the rights of paternity and integrity subsist for the duration of the copyright. Note that, in those countries where moral rights are perpetual, it is generally acknowledged that moral rights have a different function after the death of the author (their function becomes only 'preservative') and in fact will lapse with the passage of time.[247]

314.   Remedies and offences for infringement of moral rights

Sanctions and remedies for infringement of moral rights are the same as those regarding infringement of copyright. These generally include an award of damages and injunctions. In addition, in most authors' rights countries infringement of moral rights is a criminal offence carrying the same penalties as infringement of economic rights. However, civil actions are almost always preferred.

315.   Preservation of other causes of action

In the presence of strong statutory moral rights, authors in continental Europe have little or no interest in relying on contract law or on general principles of civil liability to object to derogatory treatments of their works. However, in some limited cases, these doctrines may assist in the absence of certain moral rights such as the rights of divulgation and of reconsideration, and thus allow an author to retain control over the exploitation of his work.[248]

---

[247] In a recent case tried by the tribunal of first instance of Paris, a descendant of Victor Hugo sued the publisher of a sequel to *Les Misérables* for infringement of the moral right of the author. The tribunal dismissed the claim on the grounds that the plaintiff did not provide evidence that he was the holder of the moral right of Victor Hugo under the law of succession. The tribunal also insisted on the fact that Victor Hugo denied to his heirs the right to exercise his moral rights. Tribunal of first instance of Paris, 12 September 2001, *La Semaine Juridique* 2001, II, 10636, note Caron.

[248] The protection granted to performers by the French courts through the personality rights before the implementation of the statutory neighbouring rights is a perfect example of their use as a possible 'substitute' for moral rights. See e.g. the case law in para. 304 *in fine*.

9   Performers' rights

316.   Introduction

The protection of performances is an area in which the law and practice in the European Union has undergone major changes in the last
twenty years. This evolution led to a situation in which performers are
granted a level of protection which, in most countries, is close to the
protection granted to authors (subject to a shorter term, to different
rules on transfers and remuneration and to the absence of moral rights
in some jurisdictions). The economic and practical significance of these
changes is enormous. In most European Union Member States not only
has contractual practice had to be adjusted to take into account the new
rights, but the entire rights clearance system had to be changed under the
influence of emerging collecting societies or of performers' unions with
increased bargaining powers. In order to understand fully this change, it is
necessary to describe briefly the evolution of protection before European
harmonisation in this field took place.

317.   The situation in the European Union
before harmonisation

The development of mechanical reproduction of sounds and of cinematography at the beginning of twentieth century prompted the introduction in several European countries of legislation to counter the
unauthorised fixation of performances. In the UK, the Dramatic and
Musical Performers' Protection Act 1925 established criminal sanctions
to prevent the act of bootlegging, i.e. recording without authorisation the
live performances of artists, and subsequent acts of dealing with such
illicit recordings. In Austria, the Law of 9 April 1936 granted to performers a right of mechanical fixation, a right of mechanical reproduction and a right to authorise the communication to the public or the
broadcasting of their live performances.[1] In addition, performers were

---

[1] Arts. 55 et seq.

granted moral rights in these performances.[2] A protection akin to copyright was also instituted in Italy in articles 80 *et seq.* of the Law of 22 April 1941.

In the other European countries, the protection of performances was more uncertain. Certain jurisdictions protected performers as 'adapters', i.e. as authors of derivative works. This theory was instituted in Germany in the Act of 22 May 1910 amending the 1901 Copyright Act.[3] It was apparently followed in Denmark, Finland and Switzerland.[4] This idea was proposed at the Rome Conference of the Berne Union in 1928 but was eventually rejected.

In other countries, in the absence of a statutory scheme for protection, performers were either denied civil rights of action with respect to their performances, or were protected indirectly through contract and tort law, as was the case in France. In this respect, we may observe that in the parliamentary *travaux préparatoires* to the French 1957 Act, no mention was made of performers. It appears that authors and producers feared a possible reduction of their remuneration and also conflicts between the rights of performers and authors.[5] This idea was commonplace in Europe at that time. In subsequent years, French courts granted performers the right to oppose the unauthorised fixation and exploitation of their performances.[6]

Most domestic laws were later amended in order to implement the minimum level of protection set out in the Rome Convention of 1961. However, the provisions of the Convention did not oblige Member States to implement exclusive property rights for performers, and protection could be granted only through criminal provisions. Accordingly, the UK and Ireland continued to treat certain unauthorised acts relating to performances as criminal offences and conferred no civil rights of action on performers. However, following the introduction of a neighbouring right for performers in the German Act of 1965, performers' rights were implemented throughout Europe in the 1980s in the context of the modernisation of copyright laws. But the protection afforded varied to a large extent from one Member State to another.

---

[2] Art. 68.

[3] German Act of 1901, as amended in 1910, art. 2; *Kammergericht* of Berlin, 17 June 1925, Copyright Act 1926, p. 18.

[4] G. Lyon-Caen and P. Lavigne, *Traité théorique et pratique du droit du cinema français et comparé*, LGDJ, 1957, p. 375.

[5] See R. Plaisant in *Copyright Bulletin*, 1984, VIII, No. 4, p. 6.

[6] Paris Court of Appeal, 13 February 1957, *Fürtwaengler, La Semaine Juridique*, 1957, II, No. 9838; Court of Cassation, 4 January 1964, *Revue Dalloz*, 1964, p. 322.

In the UK, after several unsuccessful attempts,[7] performers were eventually entitled to bring a civil action for breach of the statutory duties under the Performers Protection Acts in *Rickless* v. *United Artists Corp.*[8] Following the recommendations of the Whitford Committee, the CDPA 1988 repealed the previous Performers Protection Acts and introduced two separate rights in performances into UK law by granting 'performers' rights' to performers (and thus the long awaited civil remedies), and 'recording rights' to the persons who have exclusive recording contracts with them. However, performers were only granted rights against the fixation or broadcasting of their live performances. Other countries implemented full property rights akin to copyright. This was the case in France with the Law of 3 July 1985, and in Spain with the Copyright Act of 1987. But the scope and duration of these 'neighbouring rights' varied. Subject to the minimum protection afforded under the Rome Convention, performers had no statutory rights in Belgium, Greece or the Netherlands.

318.   European harmonisation

These disparities created distortions in the European internal market, as evidenced in several cases submitted to the European Court of Justice in the field of neighbouring rights.[9] In order to limit these impediments to the internal market, the European Commission, in its 1988 Green Paper on Copyright and the Challenge of Technology,[10] proposed a harmonisation of protection at the European level, in the form of a Community-wide protection for performers. The harmonisation process in this field led to the provisions of the Rental Directive of 19 November 1992, and was completed by specific provisions in the Satellite and Cable Retransmission Directive of 27 September 1993, in the Term Directive of

---

[7] The first one was made in *Musical Performers Protection Association Ltd* v. *British International Picture* (1930) 46 TLR 485, known as the 'Blackmail case'. Despite some successes, such as *Island Records Ltd* v. *Corkindale; sub nom. ex parte Island Records Ltd* [1978] Ch 122; [1978] 3 WLR 23; [1978] 3 All ER 824, CA, the Court of Appeal in *RCA Corp. and RCA Ltd* v. *Pollard* [1983] Ch 135; [1982] 3 WLR 1007; [1982] 3 All ER 771, CA, refused the possibility of a civil right of action for performers.

[8] [1988] QB 40; [1987] 2 WLR 945; [1987] 1 All ER 679. In this case, the famous actor's estate objected to the use in the film 'The Trail of the Pink Panther' of out-takes and clips from previous 'Pink Panther' films.

[9] See e.g. Case 78/70, *Deutsche Grammophon Gesellschaft GmbH* v. *Metro SB Grossmarkte GmbH & Co. KG* [1971] ECR 487; [1971] CMLR 631, ECJ; and Case 341/87, *EMI Electrola GmbH* v. *Patricia Im- und Export Verwaltungsgesellschaft mbH* [1989] ECR 79; [1989] 2 CMLR 413; [1989] 1 FSR 544, ECJ.

[10] COM (88) 172 final, OJ 1988 No. C71/89.

29 October 1993 and in the Directive on Copyright and Related Rights
in the Information Society of 22 May 2001.

**319.   The Rental Directive and the extension
        of the related right of performers**

The Directive of 19 November 1992 on rental rights and lending rights
and on certain rights related to copyright in the field of intellectual property harmonised the level of protection granted by Member States to
performers to a high level. Although the Directive does not contain a
definition of performers, its provisions clearly cover both musical and
non-musical (stage, audiovisual, etc.) performances. Under the Directive,
Member States are required to implement four basic sets of rights for
performers:

1. the right to authorise or prohibit the fixation of their performance
   (fixation right);[11]
2. the right to authorise or prohibit the direct or indirect reproduction of
   fixations of their performances;[12]
3. the exclusive right to authorise or prohibit the broadcasting by wireless
   means and the communication to the public of their performances;[13]
   an exception to this exclusive right is made where the performance is
   itself already a broadcast performance or is made from a fixation;[14]
   also, the Directive institutes a compulsory licence for the broadcasting or communication to the public of commercially published phonograms;[15] and
4. a distribution right in respect of fixations of their performances,[16]
   defined as 'the exclusive right to make available these objects, including copies thereof, to the public by sale or otherwise', and subject to
   Community exhaustion.[17]

This distribution right includes the rental right granted to performers in
respect of fixations of their performances under Chapter I of the Directive.
As with authors, Member States may derogate from the exclusive lending
right with respect to public lending, but those who chose not to implement the public lending right are not required to pay a 'remuneration' to
performers.[18]

The Directive allows Member States to provide for limitations on the
economic rights of performers in respect of private use, the use of short
excerpts in connection with the reporting of current events, ephemeral
fixations by a broadcasting organisation by means of its own facilities and

---

[11] Art. 6.   [12] Art. 7.   [13] Art. 8.   [14] Art. 8.
[15] Art. 8.2.   [16] Art. 9.   [17] Art. 9.2.   [18] Art. 5.

for its own broadcasts, and use solely for the purposes of teaching or scientific research.[19] In addition, Member States may provide for the same kinds of limitation as they provide for in connection with the protection of copyright in literary and artistic works.[20] However, compulsory licences are allowed only to the extent to which they are compatible with the Rome Convention.

320.   The special regime of film production contracts and the right of equitable remuneration

A special case is made for films in article 2(5) and (7) of the Directive. The Directive provides that the rental right can be transferred to the film producer either by a presumption of assignment, subject to any clause to the contrary (article 2(5)),[21] or by an automatic assignment or *cessio legis* (article 2(7)).[22] In any case, this transfer is always subject to an equitable right to remuneration similar to that of film authors.[23]

For the other rights mentioned in Chapter II of the Directive (fixation, reproduction, communication to the public and distribution) Member States have the possibility of providing for an automatic assignment of rights under article 2(7). A simple presumption of transfer, subject to agreement to the contrary, is probably admissible as well.

It seems to follow from the last phrase of article 2(7) that the automatic transfer of these other rights would have to be subject to a right of equitable remuneration similar to the one granted in consideration of the rental right.

321.   The Satellite and Cable Directive

The Satellite and Cable Retransmission Directive of 27 September 1993 extends the protection granted to performers under the Rental Directive to acts of communication to the public by satellite and to cable retransmissions of their performances.[24] Concerning the exercise of the cable retransmission right, the Directive provides, as with authors, that the

---

[19] Art. 10(1).   [20] Art. 10(2).

[21] 'Without prejudice to paragraph 7, when a contract concerning film production is concluded, individually or collectively, by performers with a film producer, the performer covered by this contract shall be presumed, subject to contractual clauses to the contrary, to have transferred his rental right, subject to Article 4.'

[22] 'Member States may provide that the signing of a contract concluded between a performer and a film producer concerning the production of a film has the effect of authorising rental, provided that such contract provides for an equitable remuneration within the meaning of Article 4. Member States may also provide that this paragraph shall apply *mutatis mutandis* to the rights included in Chapter II.'

[23] Art. 4.   [24] See para. 189.

rights of performers to grant or refuse authorisation to a cable operator for a cable retransmission may be exercised only through a collecting society, under a similar regime.[25]

322.   The Term Directive

The Term Directive of 29 October 1993 harmonises the term of performers' rights. Article 3 of the Directive provides that the rights of performers shall expire fifty years from 1 January of the year following the date of the performance. However, if a fixation of the performance is lawfully published or lawfully communicated to the public within this period, the rights shall expire fifty years from 1 January of the year following the date of the first such publication or the first such communication to the public, whichever is the earlier.[26]

Transitional provisions are similar to those described in relation to authors.[27]

323.   The Directive on Copyright and Related Rights in the Information Society

The Directive on Copyright and Related Rights in the Information Society of 22 May 2001 further harmonises the following aspects of the protection of performers:

1. the right of communication to the public;
2. the right of distribution;
3. the applicable exemptions to performers' rights; and
4. technological measures and rights-management information.

These provisions have been described in the preceding chapters.[28] Note, however, that recital 20 of the Directive makes clear that the Directive does not, unless otherwise provided, affect the basic principles and rules under the other copyright directives.[29] Accordingly, the new definition of the exclusive rights (in particular, the right of communication to the public) do not affect the limitations contained in the Rental Directive.[30]

---

[25] Art. 9.   [26] Arts. 3(1) and 8.   [27] Art. 10. See para. 103.

[28] See Chapters 6 and 7 above.

[29] 'This Directive is based on principles and rules already laid down in the Directives currently in force in this area, in particular Directives 91/250/EEC, 92/100/EEC, 93/83/EEC, 93/98/EEC and 96/9/EC, and it develops those principles and rules and places them in the context of the information society. The provisions of this Directive should be without prejudice to the provisions of those Directives, unless otherwise provided in this Directive.'

[30] See para. 319.

344 Film copyright in the European Union

324.   Other international instruments

The level of protection afforded under the three directives discussed above exceeds the protection established under most international and regional agreements in this field. A notable exception is the WIPO Performances and Phonograms Treaty of 1996, which provides for moral rights for performers. However, these agreements remain of importance for those European States outside the European Union. We will briefly address their main provisions.

325.   The Rome Convention of 1961

Article 7 of the International Convention for the Protection of Performers, Producers of Phonograms and Broadcasting Organisations of 1961 grants performers the right to prevent the aural or audiovisual fixation, without their consent, of their unfixed live performances.[31] It also grants performers the right to prevent the reproduction of a fixation of their performance,[32] but only if: (i) the original fixation itself was made without their consent; or (ii) the reproduction is made for purposes different from those for which the performers gave their consent; or (iii) the original fixation was made in accordance with the provisions of article 15 (exceptions and limitations), and the reproduction is made for purposes different from those referred to in those provisions.

The Convention leaves it for the domestic law of the contracting States where protection is claimed to regulate the protection against rebroadcasting, fixation for broadcasting purposes and the reproduction of a fixation made for broadcasting purposes,[33] and to determine the terms and conditions governing the use by broadcasting organisations of fixations made for broadcasting purposes.[34]

Article 12 provides for a single equitable remuneration for performers, which only covers certain uses of phonograms. In addition to article 15, which provides for certain limitations on the exclusive rights (for private use, reporting of current events, ephemeral fixation by a broadcasting organisation, teaching or scientific research), article 19 contains an important limitation on the right to prevent the reproduction of audiovisual fixations of performances (the so-called 'cut-off' provision): it provides that 'once a performer has consented to the incorporation of his performance in a visual or audiovisual fixation, article 7 shall have no further application'. Accordingly, article 19 in effect removes all protection in audiovisual fixations which are made with the consent of the performer.

---

[31] Art. 7.1(b).   [32] Art. 7.1(c).   [33] Art. 7.2(1).   [34] Art. 7.2(2).

As of 15 October 2001, all EU Member States, with the exception of Portugal, were party to this Convention.[35]

326.   The TRIPs Agreement of 1994

Article 14(1) of this Agreement provides only for rights limited to phonograms, including the right to prevent unauthorised fixations of live performances on phonograms and rights in such fixations.

327.   The WIPO Performances and Phonograms Treaty of 1996

The WIPO Performances and Phonograms Treaty of 1996 is primarily concerned with performances fixed on phonograms. However, several of its provisions are applicable to audiovisual performances and to the exploitation of performances fixed on audiovisual media. The Treaty grants performers both economic and moral rights.

For the purpose of the Treaty, performers are defined as 'actors, singers, musicians, dancers, and other persons who act, sing, deliver, declaim, play in, interpret, or otherwise perform literary or artistic works or expressions of folklore'.[36] Accordingly, this definition covers dramatic and audiovisual performances as well as aural and musical performances.

Article 6 of the Treaty grants performers exclusive economic rights in their unfixed (live) performances, defined as the right to authorise:

1. the broadcasting and communication to the public of their unfixed performances except where the performance is already a broadcast performance; and
2. the fixation of their unfixed performances.

The right granted under point 1 covers both aural and audiovisual performances. In contrast, the 'fixation' referred to in point 2 is defined as 'the embodiment of sounds, or the representations thereof, from which they can be perceived, reproduced or communicated through a device'.[37] Accordingly, this right is limited to the fixation of sounds, from aural or audiovisual performances, and is not applicable to the fixation of purely visual performances, or to the mere fixation of images (without sounds) taken from an audiovisual performance. But note that the fixation, thus

---

[35] Subject to declarations under certain articles: Austria (from 9 June 1973); Belgium (2 October 1999); Denmark (23 September 1965); Finland (21 October 1983); France (3 July 1987); Germany (21 October 1966); Greece (6 January 1993); Ireland (19 September 1979); Italy (8 April 1975); Luxembourg (25 February 1976); Netherlands (7 October 1993); Spain (14 November 1991); Sweden (18 May 1964), and the UK (18 May 1964).
[36] Art. 2(a).   [37] Art. 2(c).

defined, can be in the form of a fixation on a film or other audiovisual device.

Articles 7–10 and 15 grant performers various economic rights in their fixed performances, but these rights are limited to performances fixed in phonograms only.[38]

The definition of 'phonogram' in article 2 excludes 'a fixation incorporated in a cinematographic or other audiovisual work'. This certainly excludes direct fixations on films or videotapes, and probably phonograms directly derived from these master audiovisual recordings. But the definition could apply to sound recordings created independently of the film, and later recorded in the film.[39] In this respect, one should note that the Treaty excludes 'a fixation incorporated' in a film, and not a 'fixation to be incorporated' or 'created in order to be incorporated' in a film. This construction is also confirmed by the agreed statements concerning article 2(b), which provides:

It is understood that the definition of phonogram provided in article 2(b) does not suggest that rights in the phonogram are in any way affected through their incorporation into a cinematographic or other audiovisual work.

Article 5 of the Treaty is the only provision at the international level which deals with moral rights for performers. It grants performers moral rights in their live aural performances or performances fixed in phonograms, defined as:

The right to claim to be identified as the performer of his performances, except where omission is dictated by the manner of the use of the performances, and to object to any distortion, mutilation or other modification of his performances that would be prejudicial to his reputation.

The term of protection granted to performers under the Treaty must last, at least, until the end of a period of fifty years from the end of the year in which the performance was fixed in a phonogram.[40] The WIPO Performances and Phonograms Treaty was signed by the European Community and by all fifteen Member States, but was not ratified by these signatories and has not yet entered into force.[41]

---

[38] Rights of reproduction (art. 7), of distribution (art. 8), of rental (art. 9), a right of making available their performance to the public (art. 10), and the right to a 'single equitable remuneration' for the direct and indirect use of phonograms published for commercial purposes for broadcasting or for any communication to the public (art. 15).

[39] Which is important, as film soundtrack music is usually made in this way.

[40] Art. 17(1).

[41] Under art. 29, the Treaty will enter into force three months after thirty instruments of ratification or accession by States have been deposited with the Director-General of WIPO.

328.   A new instrument on audiovisual performances?

In spite of the efforts of most delegations during the diplomatic conference which led to the adoption of the WIPO Performances and Phonograms Treaty, the Treaty does not cover the rights of performers in the
audiovisual fixations of their performances.[42] In December 2000, WIPO
organised in Geneva a diplomatic conference on the protection of audiovisual performances. Despite intensive negotiations, a treaty on audiovisual performances could not be concluded. Agreement was reached on
nineteen articles covering important issues such as national treatment,
economic rights (right of reproduction, distribution, rental, broadcasting
and communication to the public) and even moral rights (audiovisual
performers would have been granted a right of integrity). However, an
agreement proved impossible on the question of the law applicable to
transfers of economic rights from performers to film producers. The
US insisted on the application of the law of the country where the film
is produced, whether other countries, including Member States of the
European Union, sought the preservation of mandatory rules in the country where protection is claimed. The conference recommended that a new
conference be reconvened by the Assemblies of WIPO Member States.[43]

329.   Implementation of the EC directives

The provisions of the Rental, Satellite and Term Directives have been
implemented in almost all Member States.

   In Member States of the copyright tradition, the protection of performers was profoundly modified in this process. In the UK, the Copyright
and Related Rights Regulations 1996 introduced, in addition to the already existing statutory rights, new 'property rights', transmissible as
personal or moveable property, consisting in reproduction, distribution,
rental and lending rights.[44] It excepted from the lending right lending by
educational establishments and certain libraries and archives, and enables
compulsory licensing of this right.[45] It made provision for the transfer of
and dealing with the new property right,[46] and introduced a presumption
of assignment of the rental right to the film producer.[47] It also granted
performers two rights to equitable remuneration: the first for public performance or inclusion of a commercially published sound recording in
a broadcast or cable programme service;[48] the second for the rental of
the recording of the performance, when the rental right is transferred

---

[42] Except to the limited extent described in para. 327.
[43] Which could meet in 2002.   [44] Reg. 20, new s. 191A.
[45] Reg. 20(3).   [46] Reg. 21.   [47] Reg. 21.   [48] Reg. 20, new s. 182D.

to the sound recording or film producer, as the case may be.[49] It also made provision for licensing schemes and licensing bodies in respect of performers' property rights similar to those implemented in relation to copyright.[50]

In Ireland, the protection of performers was restated in the Copyright and Related Rights Act 2000. Although the provisions of the Act were inspired by the provisions of the UK CDPA 1988, as amended, a major difference lies in the introduction of moral rights for performers in Part IV of the Irish Act. The scope of performers' property rights is also wider.[51]

Among *droit d'auteur* Member States, Belgium, Greece and the Netherlands had to introduce neighbouring rights for performers.[52] Other Member States adapted their duration provisions and implemented the specific schemes of the rental, satellite and cable retransmission rights.

330.   Structure

We will distinguish between performer's economic rights (discussed in Section I below) and performers' moral rights (discussed in Section II below).

SECTION I

Performers' economic rights

331.   Introduction

The European harmonisation of performers' economic rights is one of the most complete harmonisation processes undertaken in Europe in the area of copyright and neighbouring rights. However, even if the domestic implementation is done correctly (which may not be the case), there will remain disparities between EU Member States, due to several gaps in the directives.

A first disparity concerns the persons entitled to protection, in the absence of a definition of performers in the directives. Some Member States have adopted a broad definition encompassing all performers, including ancillary performers or extras, while other Member States exclude the latter category. In both cases, there remain difficulties for specific

---

[49] Reg. 21, new s. 191G.   [50] Reg. 22.   [51] See para. 333.

[52] In Belgium, in the Copyright Act 1994; in Greece, in the Copyright Act 1993; in the Netherlands, with the Act of 18 March 1993.

performers, such as session musicians and chorus or orchestra members. There may also be difficulties regarding fringe activities: sportsmen, for example, do not appear to be covered by the definition of performers in any Member State.

A second disparity concerns the right of communication to the public. In some countries, performers' exclusive rights are extended beyond the minimum requirements of the directives, and cover the communication to the public of performances fixed on phonograms and/or audiovisual media.

The third disparity concerns the presumption of assignment of economic rights to the film producer. As mentioned above, the Rental Directive provides for a presumption of assignment of the rental right of the performer to the film producer when a film production contract is concluded, subject to contractual clauses to the contrary.[53] As an alternative, Member States may implement a mandatory assignment of this right to the film producer, subject to equitable remuneration.[54] In addition, Member States may also extend this mandatory assignment to the exclusive rights of fixation, of reproduction, of communication to the public and of distribution provided for in Chapter II of the Directive. As a result, the scope and nature of the presumptions implemented may vary from one Member State to another.

A fourth disparity concerns the definition of the statutory right to equitable remuneration granted to performers. However, in this respect the disparities should be less important than those in relation to the right of equitable remuneration of authors. In most Member States of the *droit d'auteur* tradition, performers are not granted a statutory royalty right, but rather a right to equitable remuneration, which may take the form of an additional lump sum.

332.   The protected performances

In the UK,[55] for the purpose of Part II of the 1988 Act, the term 'performance' means:

(a) a dramatic performance (which includes dance and mime);
(b) a musical performance;
(c) a reading or recitation of a literary work; or
(d) a performance of a variety act or any similar presentation.[56]

---

[53] Art. 2(5).   [54] Art. 2(7).
[55] See R. Arnold, *Performers' Rights*, 2nd edn, Sweet & Maxwell, 1997.
[56] Section 180(2).

Most performances in a theatrical motion picture are dramatic or musical performances.[57] In television programmes, they are likely to be of all kinds, depending on the type of audiovisual work. From the above list, we can infer that sporting performances are not protected in the UK (subject to the case of artistic sports such as ice-dancing). This is probably also true of interviews.[58]

Concerning improvisations, the different nature of the right granted invites us to treat separately Part I (copyright) and Part II of the Act, and to consider that a performance under Part II does not have to be a performance of a work protected under Part I. Thus, improvisations could be protected as performances (except under subparagraph (c) above, which refers to recitation or reading, and thus suggests a pre-existing work).

The statutory definition of performance is similar in Ireland.[59] In both countries there is no exclusion for ancillary or supporting performers.

Under French law, the performer (*artiste-interprète ou exécutant*) is 'the person who renders, sings, plays, recites, declaims or performs in any other way a literary or artistic work, a variety, circus or puppet show'.[60] The director of a play is excluded from this protection, but is likely to have a copyright on his stage-setting. The musical arranger is also excluded from this protection. The reference to a 'literary or artistic work' would appear to exclude sportsmen or persons giving a non-artistic performance.[61] However, performers would be protected for their improvisations.

In France, the Intellectual Property Code expressly excludes from protection 'ancillary performers, so considered by the practice of the profession'.[62] The distinction between a performer and an 'ancillary' performer is an uneasy one, and in this respect the reference to the uses of the profession is of little help. Some courts have considered that a performer is not an ancillary performer if his role is 'essential'.[63] Other decisions refer to the 'duration' or 'importance' of the contribution. In one case, the French Supreme Court referred to the 'originality of the contribution' to overturn a decision denying protection to a performer in an advertising film.[64] However, originality is not a requirement for protection of the

[57] But the film also embodies musical performances, and both can subsist in for example an opera singer.
[58] It is submitted that the mention of reading or recitation of a literary work excludes improvised speeches.
[59] Copyright and Related Rights Act 2000, s. 202.
[60] Art. L.212-1 of the Intellectual Property Code.
[61] It should nevertheless be recalled that, under French law, individuals have a right over their image (more or less equivalent to a right of publicity).
[62] Art. L.212-1.
[63] Paris Court of Appeal, 26 November 1986, *Juris-Data*, No. 028705, cited by C. Caron, *Communication Commerce Electronique*, December 1999, p. 21.
[64] Court of Cassation, 6 July 1999, *Téléma* v. *Leclaire*, *Communication Commerce Electronique*, December 1999, p. 21.

performance, and the Court did not indicate the criteria to be used to distinguish between 'non-original' performances.

The Belgian Act contains no definition of performers. However, article 35 of the Act provides that ancillary performers shall not be considered performers. As in France, ancillary performers are those who are considered as such by the practice of the profession. The Act also specifies that variety and circus artists are considered performers.

In Spain, under the Intellectual Property Law of 12 April 1996, a performer is defined as 'the person who presents, sings, reads, recites, interprets or executes a work in any form'.[65] There is no exclusion for ancillary performers.

In Germany, the Copyright Act 1965, as amended by the Law of 19 July 1996, defines the performer as 'a person who recites or performs a work or participates artistically in the recitation or performance of a work'.[66] This wide definition is generally thought to include supporting performers. It is also interesting to note the extension to persons who participate artistically in the performance, which may include certain technicians such as the stage or musical director, the lightning director or make-up artists in certain circumstances.[67]

The Italian law on performer's right was modified by a Decree of 16 November 1994, implementing the provisions of the Rental Directive. Under article 80 of the Act, performers' rights are granted to actors, singers, musicians, dancers and any other persons who play, sing, recite or perform, in whatever manner, intellectual works, whether protected or in the public domain. The definition is further specified in article 82. Of interest for our purpose is the inclusion of persons who, in the performance of any dramatic, literary or musical work or composition, play 'a significant artistic part, even if in a supporting role', which resembles the German definition.

333.   Exclusive rights

A distinction must be made here between copyright and *droit d'auteur* Member States. In the UK, the implementation of the provisions of the copyright directives on the exclusive rights of performers resulted in what has been characterised as an 'extraordinarily impenetrable amalgam of

---

[65] Art. 105. The Act adds that directors, stage performances and orchestral conductors are granted the rights conferred on performers.

[66] Art. 73.

[67] See A. Dietz, in M. B. Nimmer and D. Geller (eds.), *International Copyright Law and Practice*, Matthew Bender, looseleaf, para. 9[1][a], who reports, however, a decision from the Federal Court of Justice that a film director cannot claim protection as a performer, if the creation of the film and the artistic participation constitute an inseparable accomplishment (BGH, 24 November 1983, noted in (1985) IIC 119).

provisions'.[68] Exclusive rights of performers are organised under two series of rights: performers' property and non-property rights.

Performers' non-property rights correspond to the rights granted under
the CDPA 1988, as enacted. They consist in:

1. a right to consent to the recording of their live performance;[69]
2. a right to consent to the broadcasting live or inclusion live in a cable
   programme service of their performance;[70]
3. a right to consent to the recording of their performance directly from a
   broadcast of, or cable programme including, their live performance;[71]
4. a right to consent to the showing or playing in public of their performance or to the broadcasting or inclusion in a cable programme of
   the same by means of a recording of the performance made without
   consent;[72] and
5. a right against unauthorised importing, possession of or dealing with
   illicit recordings (secondary infringement).[73]

In contrast to performers' property rights, these non-property rights cannot be assigned *inter vivos*, but they may be licensed and transmitted on
death.

Performers' property rights consist in: (a) a reproduction right;[74] (b) a
right to issue copies to the public (subject to EEA-wide exhaustion);[75] and
(c) rental and lending rights.[76] Performers are not granted a right of communication to the public of any performance recorded with their consent.

In Ireland, performers' non-property rights consist in the exclusive
rights to authorise or prohibit: (a) the recording of their live performance;
(b) the broadcasting live, or inclusion live in a cable programme service, of
their live performance; and (c) the recording of a broadcast or cable
programme including their live performance.[77] As in the UK, these non-
property rights are non-assignable or transmissible except *mortis causa*.[78]

Performers' property rights consist in: (a) a reproduction right;[79] and
(b) a right of making available to the public copies of recordings of their
performance.[80] The latter right is defined in broad terms and includes
the following:

---

[68] W. R. Cornish, *Intellectual Property*, 4th edn, Sweet & Maxwell, 1999, para. 13-90.
[69] Section 182(1)(a). A performer's right are not infringed by the making of any such
recording by a person for his private and domestic use (s. 182(2)).
[70] Section 182(1)(b).
[71] Section 182(1)(c). A performer's right are not infringed by the making of any such
recording by a person for his private and domestic use (s. 182(2)).
[72] Section 183.   [73] Section 184.   [74] Section 182A.   [75] Section 182B.
[76] Section 182C.   [77] Section 213.   [78] Section 300.
[79] Section 204. The reproduction right is not infringed by the making of a copy for his or
her private domestic use (s. 204(4)).
[80] Section 205.

(1) making available to the public copies of a recording, by wire or wireless means, in such a way that members of the public may access the recording from a place and at a time individually chosen by them, including the making available of copies through the Internet,

(2) showing or playing a copy of the recording in public,

(3) broadcasting a copy of the recording,

(4) including a copy of the recording in a cable programme service,

(5) issuing copies of the recording to the public [subject to EEA-wide exhaustion under section 206],

(6) renting copies of the recording, or

(7) lending copies of the recording without the payment of remuneration to the rights owner.

Accordingly, performers rights in Ireland are more extended than the rights granted to performers under the UK Act, since they cover acts of communication to the public of their performance.

This (cumbersome) dichotomy between property and non-property rights is not repeated in *droit d'auteur* countries. In France, the exclusive rights granted to performers cover the right of fixation of their performance, of reproduction of these fixations, and of communication to the public of the same. These rights are repeated in relation to audiovisual works by article L.212-3 of the Intellectual Property Code, which provides that the performer must authorise in writing the fixation of his performance, its reproduction and its communication to the public, together with the separate use of the sound and image of the performance, when the latter is fixed for both sound and image.

The Court of Appeal of Paris held that, when a performer has given consent for the recording and broadcasting of his performance for a cinematographic film, a new consent is necessary for the broadcasting of a serialised television version of the film.[81] In this case, the television version was longer than the cinematographic version, and was held to constitute a new work for which a separate consent must be given.

Performers have no right of distribution under French law.

In Germany, performers' economic rights include: (a) a right of public communication of the performance via a screen, a loudspeaker or a similar technical device;[82] (b) a fixation, reproduction and distribution right;[83] and (c) a broadcasting right.[84] However, performances lawfully fixed on published audio or video recordings may be broadcast without

---

[81] Paris Court of Appeal, 18 December 1989, *Revue Dalloz*, 1990, Sommaire, p. 353, note Hassler.

[82] Art. 74. But the article refers to communications by these means 'in a place other than that in which [the performance] takes place'.

[83] Art. 75.   [84] Art. 76.

the consent of the performer, provided equitable remuneration is paid.[85] An equitable remuneration must be paid to performers when their performances are publicly communicated by video or audio recordings or are broadcast.[86]

However, this compulsory licence for the broadcast of audiovisual performances does not appear to be repeated in other Member States. In Belgium,[87] Italy,[88] Spain,[89] Sweden[90] and other Member States, performers' economic rights appear to correspond to the rights and limitations provided in the copyright directives.

334.   Limitations and exemptions

In the UK, the list of permitted acts in relation to rights in performances is included in Schedule 2 to the 1988 Act.[91] The Copyright and Related Rights Regulations 1996 introduced into Schedule 2 exceptions from the lending right in favour of educational establishments and certain libraries and archives, and a provision allowing the Secretary of State to make orders to the effect that the lending of copies of films or sound recordings is to be treated as licensed subject to the payment of a reasonable royalty.[92] The Irish Act also includes a long list of permitted acts in relation to performances.[93]

---

[85] Art. 76.   [86] Art. 77.   [87] Art. 35.   [88] Art. 80(2).

[89] Art. 106 (fixation); art. 107 (reproduction); art. 108 (broadcast, communication to the public, including the compulsory licence and equitable remuneration); and art. 109 (distribution including provisions for rental and equitable remuneration).

[90] Art. 45.

[91] They concern: fair dealing for criticism, review and news reporting (s. 2); the incidental inclusion of performances or recordings (s. 3); acts done for the purposes of instruction or examination (s. 4); the playing or showing of sound recordings, films, broadcasts or cable programmes at educational establishments (s. 5); the recording of broadcasts and cable programmes by educational establishments (s. 6); copy of the work required to be made as a condition of export (s. 7); parliamentary and judicial proceedings (s. 8); royal commissions and statutory inquiries (s. 9); public records (s. 10); acts done under statutory authority (s. 11); the transfer of copies of works in electronic form (s. 12): the use of recordings of spoken works in certain cases (s. 13); recordings of folksongs (s. 14); the playing of sound recordings for the purposes of club, societies, etc. (s. 15); the incidental recording for the purposes of broadcasts or cable programmes (s. 16); recordings for the purposes of supervision and control of broadcasts and cable programmes (s. 17); the free public showing or playing of broadcasts or cable programmes (s. 18); the reception and retransmission of broadcasts in cable programme service (s. 19); the provision of subtitled copies of broadcasts or cable programmes (s. 20); and the recording of broadcasts or cable programmes for archival purpose (s. 21).

[92] Sched. 2, paras. 6A, 6B and 14A.

[93] Fair dealing for the purposes of criticism or review or reporting current events (s. 221); incidental use of performances (s. 222); the copying of a performance for the purpose of instruction (s. 223); acts by educational establishments (ss. 224 and 225); and lending by some educational establishment or establishment to which members of the public

In Member States of the *droit d'auteur* tradition, the copyright or neighbouring rights Acts generally either repeat the exceptions to authors' rights in relation to performers' rights,[94] or specify that the limitations on the exclusive rights of authors are applicable *mutatis mutandis* to the rights of performers.[95]

335.   Duration

All EU Member States have implemented the duration provisions of the Term Directive: rights in performances expire at the end of the period of fifty years from the end of the calendar year in which the performance takes place, or, if during that period a recording of the performance is lawfully made available to the public, fifty years from the end of the calendar year in which such recording is released.[96]

336.   Ownership and transfers of exclusive rights

As mentioned above, in the UK, a performer's non-property rights are non-assignable and are transmissible *mortis causa*.[97] The Copyright Tribunal is given power to override a performer's refusal of consent when he 'unreasonably withholds his consent' or when his 'identity or whereabouts cannot be ascertained by reasonable inquiry'.[98] In contrast, a performer's property rights are transmissible by assignment, by testamentary disposition or by operation of law, as personal or moveable property, and may be licensed.[99] These transfers can be partial, that is limited in scope and time. The 1988 Act further states that an assignment of a performer's property rights is not effective unless it is in writing signed by or on behalf

have access, as determined by the minister; these establishments are exempt from the payment of remuneration (s. 226); acts by certain libraries and archives (ss. 227–236); acts by the public administration or for public administration purposes (ss. 237–240); acts done under statutory authority (s. 241); certain acts regarding certain recordings in electronic forms, when the purchaser is allowed to make further recordings in relation to his or her use of the recording (s. 242); certain acts of use of recordings of spoken words (s. 243); transient and incidental copies (s. 244); recordings of works of folklore (s. 245); playing or showing sound recordings, broadcasts and cable programmes in certain premises (ss. 246 and 246); recording for the purposes of broadcasts or cable programmes (s. 248); recording for the purposes of supervision and control of broadcasts and cable programmes (s. 249); recording for the purpose of time-shifting (s. 250); reception and retransmission of broadcasts in cable programme services (s. 251); the provision of modified recordings (s. 252); and recording for archival purposes (s. 253).

[94] E.g. French Intellectual Property Code, art. L.211-3.
[95] E.g. German Copyright Act, art. 84.
[96] E.g. UK Act, s. 191; Irish Act, s. 291; French Intellectual Property Code, art. L.211-4; Spanish Act, art. 112; Italian Act, art. 85; German Act, art. 82; and Dutch Act, art. 12.
[97] Section 192A.   [98] Section 190.   [99] Section 191B.

of the assignor.[100] Licences do not have to be done in writing, unless they are exclusive licences.[101]

Of particular interest here are the provisions relating to the presumption of transfer of rental right in the case of a film production agreement. Section 191F of the 1988 Act provides that, where an agreement concerning film production is concluded between a performer and a film producer, the performer shall be presumed, unless the agreement provides to the contrary, to have transferred to the film producer any rental right in relation to the film arising from the inclusion of a recording of his performance in the film.[102] The right to equitable remuneration on the transfer of the rental right applies in such a case, and also applies in the case of an actual transfer of the rental right.[103]

This right may not be assigned by the performer, except to a collecting society for the purpose of enabling it to enforce the right on his behalf.[104] It is, however, transmissible by testamentary disposition or by operation of law as personal or moveable property; and it may be assigned or further transmitted by any person into whose hands it passes.[105]

The remuneration is payable by the person for the time being entitled to the rental right, that is, the person to whom the right was transferred or any successor in title of his.[106] The amount payable by way of equitable remuneration is as agreed by or on behalf of the persons by and to whom it is payable, subject to a possible reference of the amount to the Copyright Tribunal[107] The reference is subject to a similar regime as the one applicable to authors.[108] In particular, the Act provides that remuneration shall not be considered inequitable merely because it was paid by way of a single payment or at the time of the transfer of the rental right.[109]

An agreement is of no effect in so far as it purports to exclude or restrict the right to equitable remuneration under this section.[110] The equitable remuneration for a public performance and broadcast of a sound recording ought not to be applicable to films, as film soundtracks are now excluded from protection as sound recordings.[111] The Copyright Tribunal

---

[100] Section 191B(3).   [101] Section 191D.

[102] Where this provision applies, the absence of signature by or on behalf of the performer does not exclude the operation of s. 191C (effect of purported assignment of future rights). The section further provides that reference to an agreement concluded between a performer and a film producer includes any agreement having effect between those persons, whether made by them directly or through intermediaries.

[103] Section 191G.   [104] Section 191G(2).   [105] *Ibid.*

[106] Section 191G(3).   [107] Section 191G(4).   [108] Section 191H.

[109] Section 191H(4).   [110] Section 191G(5).

[111] However, it might apply when the film soundtrack includes a previously commercially published sound recording (which remains protected as a sound recording): in that case, the film (soundtrack) is a copy of the commercially published sound recording; thus, logically, the right should arise in relation to such copies. This construction is confirmed

has jurisdiction to hear and determine proceedings relating to the various equitable remuneration and licensing schemes established under the Act.[112] The Act contains provisions for licensing schemes and licensing bodies in respect of property rights similar to those in relation to copyright.[113]

The scheme established by the Irish Copyright and Related Rights Act 2000 is similar. In particular, the Act implements the presumption of transfer of rental right in the case of a film production agreement, save agreement to the contrary.[114] The right to equitable remuneration where the rental right has been transferred is defined in a manner similar to the same right for authors.[115]

In France, article L.762-1 of the French Labour Code establishes a presumption of paid employment (i.e. of there being an employment contract subject to labour law) in the case of contracts entered into by performing artists, which presumption may be rebutted only in limited cases. As a result, the regime covering performers' agreement is strongly influenced by labour law and collective agreements.

Under article L.212-3 of the Intellectual Property Code, the written authorisation of the performer is required for the fixation of his performance, its reproduction and communication to the public and for any separate use of the sounds or images of his performance where both sounds and images have been fixed. It would appear that this consent has to be given only once, which then amounts to an assignment. Accordingly, consent is not required for further reproductions by the film producer's assignee, provided the scope of the reproduction complies with the initial authorisation and does not amount to a separate use of the sounds or images of the performance under article L.212-3.

The Code provides for a broad presumption of consent to the film producer. Article L.212-4 provides that the signature of a contract between a performer and a producer for the making of an audiovisual work shall imply a consent to 'fix, reproduce and communicate to the public the performance of the performer'. In contrast to the presumption concerning authors' rights, the Code does not mention the possibility of a clause to the contrary.

The Code further specifies that a separate remuneration must be provided for each mode of exploitation of the work. Accordingly, it will be

---

by art. 8(2) of the Rental Directive on the equitable remuneration for broadcasting, which relates to 'a phonogram published for commercial purposes, *or a reproduction of such phonogram*'. This is also suggested by the new s. 182A(2) of the CDPA 1988 which provides that 'it is immaterial whether the copy [of the recording of the performance] is made directly or indirectly'.

[112] Section 205B.   [113] Section 205A and Sched. 2A.
[114] Section 297.   [115] Sections 298 and 299.

necessary to detail in the contract the modes of exploitation of the work and the corresponding remuneration. Nothing in the Code provides for a remuneration in the form of a royalty right. It is clear, however, that this remuneration should be distinct from any salary, and drafters should be careful in allocating the global remuneration negotiated with the performer. In addition, article L.212-5 provides that, when the individual contract or the collective agreement do not mention remuneration for one or several modes of exploitation, the remuneration must be determined by reference to the schedules established under the specific industrial agreement concluded in each sector of activity.

There are no further provisions on contracts in the Code, and it is not clear whether the regime of copyright contracts relating to authors (relating, for example, to assignment of future works, as-yet-unknown modes of exploitation, restrictive construction, etc.) could be extended in some cases to performers' contracts. It would be safer to assume that they do to a certain extent.

In Belgium, the Copyright Act includes numerous provisions on performers' agreements, similar to those relating to authors.[116] Article 36 of the Act provides that, save agreement to the contrary, the performer is deemed to have assigned to the producer of an audiovisual work the exclusive right of audiovisual exploitation of his performance, including the economic rights required for such exploitation such as the right to add subtitles or to dub the performance. The Act also provides that if a performer is unable or unwilling to complete his participation in the audiovisual work, he may not oppose the use of his participation to complete the work.[117] Except for performances carried out in the making of audiovisual productions in the non-cultural field or for advertising, performers are entitled to separate remuneration for each exploitation mode, which does not have to be proportional. A right of equitable remuneration is granted for rental and lending.

In Germany, performers' economic rights may be assigned under article 78 of the Copyright Act. Article 79 provides that, in the case of

---

[116] E.g. art. 35(2) provides that 'all contracts relating to performers shall require written form', and that such contracts shall be interpreted restrictively. Also, the assignee of performers' rights is required to carry out exploitation of the performance in accordance with fair practice in the profession. The Act further provides that the assignment of rights relating to as yet unknown forms of exploitation is null and void, and that the assignment of economic rights relating to future performances shall only be valid 'for a limited time and only if the types of performance concerned by the assignment are specified'. These provisions are not applicable when the performance is carried out in execution of an employment contract, under a service relationship or in execution of a commission in the non-cultural field or in advertising (art. 35(3)). But, in such cases, the assignment of rights must always be expressly provided.

[117] Art. 36.

employment or service contracts, and in the absence of a specific clause in the agreement, the scope of the transfer is to be determined by reference to the nature of the contract of employment or service.[118] Article 92 provides for a broad presumption of assignment of the performers' economic rights to the film producer.

In Italy, the presumption of assignment to the film producer is drafted in broad terms in article 84(1). Save provision to the contrary, performers are deemed to have assigned to the film producer under the film production contract their rights of fixation, reproduction, broadcasting (including communication to the public by satellite), distribution and also the right to authorise rental. Performers 'who play important acting parts' in the audiovisual work, even as supporting actors, are entitled to equitable remuneration for every use of the work.

In Spain, the Copyright Act provides rules on employment or commission contracts. Article 110 provides that, where the performance is given under an employment or commission contract, unless otherwise specified, the employer or commissioning party acquires the exclusive rights to authorise the reproduction and communication to the public of the performance. The rental right is also transferred, subject to agreement to the contrary, and subject to the payment of an equitable remuneration for rental.

In other countries, film producers benefit from broad presumptions of assignment, subject to applicable rights to remuneration.

337.   Recording rights and other forms of protection

Some countries have implemented additional forms of protection for those persons who have exclusive contracts with performers. In the UK, the CDPA 1988 grants 'recording rights' in relation to the performance to persons having an exclusive recording contract with the performer (recording meaning both film and sound recordings of the performance). Recording rights are not in principle assignable, nor transmissible,[119] but the recording contract can be assigned, and the assignee, if he is a qualifying person, is entitled to the recording rights.[120] It is an infringement of the recording rights:

(a) to make a recording of the whole or a substantial part of the performance, without the consent of the owner of the recording rights or the consent of the performer;[121]

---

[118] WIPO translation.   [119] Section 192B.
[120] Section 185(2)(b).   [121] Section 186.

(b) to show or play in public, broadcast or include in a cable programme service the whole or a substantial part of the performance by using a recording made without the consent of the owner of the recording rights or the consent of the performer;[122] and

(c) to import, possess or deal with illicit recordings.[123]

The duration of protection follows that of performances. The Irish Copyright and Related Rights Act 2000 established a similar protection.[124]

In Germany, 'organisers of performances' are granted a specific neighbouring right under article 81. This article provides that, if a performance is organised by an enterprise, the consent of the owner (in addition to the consent of the performer) of the enterprise shall be required for the communication to the public by screen or loudspeaker, or for the fixation, reproduction or broadcasting of a performance. This right lasts for twenty-five years from the performance or from the publication of a recording of the performance, as the case may be.[125]

SECTION II

Performers' moral rights

338. Introduction

Performers are not granted statutory moral rights in the UK. This contrasts with the situation in Ireland, where the Copyright and Related Rights Act 2000 introduced such a protection for performers, similar to that of authors. As a result of the recent amendments to domestic copyright Acts, performers are granted moral rights in most Member States of the authors' rights tradition. However, performers' moral rights are generally more limited than the rights granted to authors. For example, as a general rule performers are not entitled to specific moral rights such as the right to divulgate (or not to divulgate) their performances and are not granted a right of reconsideration. But the extent to which the rights of paternity and of integrity are protected also varies. In France, Belgium and Sweden, the rights of paternity and integrity are stated in a language similar to those of authors. In Greece, Portugal and Spain, these rights are defined in a more restrictive language. In Germany the Copyright Act grants only one moral right of integrity to performers, and no right of paternity. The duration of performers' moral rights also varies.

---

[122] Section 187.   [123] Section 188.   [124] Chapter 3, ss. 215 *et seq.*   [125] Art. 82.

339. Performers' moral rights in Ireland

In Ireland, under the Copyright and Related Rights Act 2000, performers are granted moral rights in the form of a right to be identified as performer, a right to object to derogatory treatments of a performance and a right against false attribution of a performance. The right to be identified as the performer of his or her performance[126] is not infringed in case of incidental uses of the performance,[127] copying for the purpose of an examination,[128] parliamentary or judicial proceedings[129] and statutory inquiries.[130] The right does not apply in relation to a performance or a recording of a performance made for the purpose of reporting current events.[131]

The right to object to derogatory treatment is defined as the right for a performer to object 'to any distortion, mutilation or other modification of, or other derogatory treatment action in relation to, his or her performance or a recording thereof, which would prejudice his or her reputation'.[132] This right is subject to exemptions. First, it does not apply in relation to a performance or a recording of a performance made for the purpose of reporting current events.[133] Secondly, the right is not infringed by anything done for the purpose of

1. avoiding any contravention of civil or criminal law;
2. complying with a duty imposed by or under an enactment; or
3. in the case of authorised broadcasters or authorised cable programme service providers, avoiding the inclusion in a programme which is broadcast or included in a cable programme service by those broadcasters or providers, of anything which offends public morality or which is likely to encourage or incite crime or to lead to public disorder.[134]

However, this limitation is not applicable unless the performer is identified at the time of the act concerned or has previously been identified in or on a recording of the performance which has been lawfully made available to the public and there is a sufficient disclaimer.[135] A 'sufficient disclaimer' is defined as 'a clear and reasonably prominent indication given at the time of the act, or, where the performer is then identified, appearing along with the identification, that the recording has been subjected to an action to which the performer has not consented'.[136]

Various acts of possessing or dealing with recording of a performance subject to derogatory action under section 311 are secondary infringement

---

[126] Section 309.   [127] Sections 310(1) and 222.   [128] Sections 310(1) and 223(2).
[129] Sections 310(1) and 237.   [130] Sections 310(1) and 238.
[131] Section 310(2).   [132] Section 311(1).   [133] Section 312(1).
[134] Section 312(2).   [135] Section 312(3).   [136] Section 312(4).

of the integrity right.[137] Performers are also granted a right to object to the false attribution of performances.[138] Performers' moral rights are not assignable or alienable,[139] but are transmissible on death.[140]

Moral rights may be waived under section 316 of the Act. The waiver must be in writing and signed by the person waiving the right, but the act expressly reserves the operation of general contract law or estoppel in relation to informal waivers. In addition, the person entitled to the right may consent to acts which would otherwise constitute infringements of moral rights.[141] Infringement of moral rights is actionable as a breach of statutory duty.[142]

The moral rights thus granted expire with the economic rights.[143]

340.   Performers' moral rights in continental Europe

All Member States of the *droit d'auteur* tradition grant moral rights to performers. These rights usually consist of a right of integrity and a right of paternity (except in Germany, where performers are not granted a statutory right of paternity). As a general rule, performers are not granted a right of divulgation or a right of reconsideration. The content, regime and limitations of these moral rights are usually similar to those of authors.[144]

Several acts implement specific provisions for films. For example, in Germany, the right of integrity of performers, like that of authors, is the right to object to 'gross distortions or other gross mutilations' of their contributions to the audiovisual work.[145] In Italy, the right of performers to have their name indicated on the film or other published edition or diffusion of their performances is limited to the 'main performers'.[146] The Spanish Act also requires the consent of the performer for the post-synchronisation of his performance in his own language.[147]

The duration of performers' moral rights varies from one Member State to another. For example, such rights would appear to be perpetual in France. In Belgium, moral rights of performers endure for fifty years after performance or publication of the performance.[148] In Spain, these

---

[137] Section 313.   [138] Section 314.   [139] Section 317.
[140] Section 318.   [141] Section 316(5).   [142] Section 319(1).
[143] That is, fifty years from the end of the calendar year in which the performance takes place, or where within that period a recording of the performance is lawfully made available to the public, that recording is first so lawfully made available to the public (s. 315).
[144] In Greece, however, the moral right of integrity granted to performers would appear to be more limited than the right granted to authors, as the law only grants performers the right to 'prevent any *transformation* of their performance' (art. 50 of the Law of 1993).
[145] Art. 95.   [146] Art. 83.
[147] Art. 113. It is not clear whether this right is an economic or a moral right (as art. 113 concerns 'other rights' and includes the moral rights of integrity and paternity).
[148] Copyright Act, art. 34.

rights endure for the life of the artist and twenty years thereafter.[149] In Germany the right of integrity expires on the death of the performer or fifty years after the performance, whichever is later. In the Netherlands, moral rights last as long as economic rights.

341.   Conflicts between moral rights of performers and moral rights of authors

In the same way as described above in relation to co-authors, moral rights of performers could conflict with the interests of film authors, especially when an injunction restraining the public performance, broadcasting or distribution of the film is sought. In general, copyright Acts do not provide rules to solve these conflicts. However, the French Intellectual Property Code contains a general declaration of the superiority of authors' rights:[150]

Neighbouring rights do not prejudice the rights of authors. As a consequence, no provision in this title shall be construed so as to limit the exercise of the author's right by its owner.

A similar clause is included in several continental Acts. Such clauses implement the declarations contained in article 1 of the Rome Convention of 26 October 1961 and in article 14 of the Rental Directive of 19 November 1992. Although such a clause does not prevent conflicts and remains silent on the means to be used to solve them, it might provide some guidance as to the type of remedy to use in such cases.

This was illustrated in France in the *Rostropovitch* case,[151] which involved a claim from the famous cellist against the use of his performance in a film soundtrack. Rostropovitch conducted and performed the music included in the soundtrack of the film 'Boris Godunov', based on the opera of the same name. In the final version of the film, the director had modified its volume level and had added some sounds to the soundtrack over the music. Among these sounds were, for example, spitting by a priest, the sound of someone urinating and the gaspings of a woman. Rostropovitch invoked his moral right of integrity to object to these derogatory treatments. The Tribunal of First Instance of Paris held that Rostropovitch, as a performer entitled to neighbouring rights, could not prejudice the right of the film director by asking for a modification of the latter's work. It was held, however, that the performer nevertheless had the right to object to derogatory treatments of his performance; the Tribunal found that, even if some technical and creative requirements of

---

[149] Art. 113.   [150] Intellectual Property Code, art. L.211-1.
[151] Tribunal of First Instance of Paris, 10 January 1990.

film production can justify changes in the volume level of the soundtrack music, nevertheless some additions of sounds can harm the right of the performer, especially if he is famous and has made an important contribution to the film. In consequence, the Tribunal ordered insertion, after the title, of a disclaimer.

Another illustration of a conflict between authors' rights and a performer's moral rights is given by a case tried by the Court of Appeal of Paris, in which a performer objected to the cutting by the film director and the producer of scenes he performed in a film. These scenes had been cut because of their graphic violence. The performer claimed that this deletion infringed his moral rights as performer. The Court of Appeal rejected his claim on the ground that he did not provide evidence that the director and the producer, by cutting his scenes, had abused their right to modify the film.[152] This requirement of an 'abuse of the author's right' in the case of a conflict between the performer's right and the author's right is a serious limitation on the exercise of performers' moral rights.

---

[152] Paris Court of Appeal, 21 September 1999, *Adam de Villiers* v. *TF1*, *Communication Commerce Electronique*, December 1999, p. 21.

10   Protection of foreign film works

342.   Introduction

This work would not be complete without an overview of the treatment of foreign film works within the European Union. The matter is simplified to a certain extent by the fact that all Member States have ratified the Berne Convention (Paris Act) and the other relevant international agreements in this field.[1] Currently, as far as copyright protection is concerned, only a few countries remain outside these agreements, and none of the latter has a significant film industry. Accordingly, the determination of the protection of foreign film works within the European Union will in most cases imply an examination of the main international copyright agreements and of their implementation in domestic law.

There are, however, numerous gaps in these agreements, for example with respect to issues such as authorship and ownership of copyright, contracts, copyright exemptions and moral rights.[2] And national legislators or courts may place different constructions on certain of their provisions. Also, the international protection of related rights is notoriously imperfect, in particular when it comes to audiovisual performances and videograms.

It is also worth noting that, although the existing bilateral agreements entered into by EU Member States are superseded by their adherence to the existing multilateral conventions, these bilateral agreements may convey rights not assured under the conventions, such as extended terms of protection.[3]

As a consequence, a complete study of the subject would involve an account, in each jurisdiction, of three sets of rules: first, the basic private

---

[1] As of 14 March 2001, however, Ireland had not ratified the Paris Act of the Berne Convention, and Portugal had still not ratified the Rome Convention. Ireland, Greece and Belgium have not ratified the 1971 revision of the Universal Copyright Convention.

[2] See J. C. Ginsburg, 'The Role of Natural Copyright in an Era of International Copyright Norms', in ALAI, *The Role of National Legislation in Copyright Law*, Berlin Congress, 16–19 June 1999, pp. 219 *et seq.*

[3] See para. 354.

international law rules applicable to copyright and related rights (the status of foreign authors and the conflict of laws); secondly, the relevant provisions of existing bilateral agreements, if any; thirdly, the application and construction of the relevant multilateral agreements in domestic law. In addition, consideration would need to be given to transitional provisions, in order to determine the status of old films.

This task goes well beyond the scope of this book.[4] What we propose to do in this chapter is to give a short presentation of the main provisions relevant to the protection of foreign film works, and of the possible problem areas. We will be concerned only with the protection of foreign film works (audiovisual works, underlying works, broadcasts, cable programmes and audiovisual performances) within the European Union. The question of the law applicable to copyright agreements is addressed in Chapter 5 above.[5] We will not address the question of the law applicable to infringements.[6]

Due to their practical importance, we will address the basic rules derived from international agreements before domestic rules. The scope of these agreements imposes a distinction between 'classic' copyright works (literary, dramatic, artistic and musical works), on the one hand, and works protected by one of the related rights described in Chapters 3 and 9 of this book (performers' rights, rights of phonogram and videogram producers, rights of broadcasting organisations), on the other hand, irrespective of whether the latter are characterised as copyright works in domestic law.[7]

343.   Multilateral conventions in the field of copyright

As mentioned above, all European Union Member States are members of the Berne Convention[8] and contracting parties to the TRIPs Agreement. Accordingly, all Member States are required to provide protection for literary, dramatic, musical and artistic works and cinematographic films (including analogous audiovisual works) originating from other WTO

---

[4] See S. Ricketson, *The Berne Convention on the Protection of Literary and Artistic Works*, Kluwer, 1987; W. Nordemann, K. Vinck and P. W. Hertin, *International Copyright and Neighbouring Rights Law* (trans. G. Meyer), VCH, 1990. For a detailed account in English of domestic law of EU Member States, see M. B. Nimmer and D. Geller (eds.), *International Copyright Law and Practice*, Matthew Bender, looseleaf.

[5] See para. 168.

[6] See e.g. André Lucas, in 'Private International Law Aspects of the Protection of Works and Objects of Related Rights Transmitter Through Digital Networks', WIPO Report (GCPIC/1), 25 November 1998.

[7] As is the case in the UK and Ireland for broadcasts, phonograms and videograms.

[8] Paris Act, with the exception of Ireland (see Appendix 4 below).

members on the basis of national treatment, as required by article 5(1) of the Berne Convention and by articles 3 and 9(1) of the TRIPs Agreement.

We will not address here the provisions of the Universal Copyright Convention (UCC) of 1952, to which all European Union Member States are also party.[9] The UCC is also based on a principle of national treatment but its geographical scope is defined in a somewhat narrower way.[10] Also, its provisions are becoming less relevant since the US, Russia and China have joined the Berne Union. In this respect, it should be remembered that under an appendix declaration to its article XVII, the UCC is not applicable to relationships between countries of the Berne Union in so far as it relates to the protection of works having as their country of origin, within the meaning of the Berne Convention, a country of the Berne Union.

344.   National treatment under the Berne Convention and TRIPs Agreement

We will concentrate here on the 'principle of national treatment', which is one of the basic principles of the Berne Convention (together with the principles of automatic protection[11] and independence of protection[12]). The principle requires that works originating in a Union country must be given protection in each of the Union countries equivalent to that granted to works of their own nationals. Under article 3(1) of the Berne Convention, national treatment under the Convention applies to:

(a) authors who are nationals of one of the countries of the Union, for their works, whether published or not; and

(b) authors who are not nationals of one of the countries of the Union, for their works first published in one of those countries, or simultaneously in a country outside the Union and in a country of the Union.

In addition, authors who are not nationals of one of the countries of the Union but who have their habitual residence in one of them are assimilated to nationals of that country for the purposes of the Convention.[13] A work is considered as having been published simultaneously in several

---

[9] However, Ireland, Greece and Belgium have not ratified the 1971 revision.
[10] In contrast to art. 3(3) of the Berne Convention, the criteria of habitual residence is not assimilated to that of nationality in the UCC, and signatory States may only substitute, by domestic legislation, the criteria of domicile with that of nationality (art. II(3)). Also, there is no specific provision on cinematographic works similar to that of art. 4 of the Berne Convention.
[11] Under which the enjoyment and the exercise of the rights under the Convention shall not be subject to any formality.
[12] Under which, rights under the Treaty shall be enjoyed and exercised independently of the existence of protection in the country of origin of the work.
[13] Art. 3(2).

countries if it has been published in two or more countries within thirty days of its first publication.[14]

Article 4 of the Convention provides specific criteria for eligibility for cinematographic works, works of architecture and certain artistic works. In relation to cinematographic works, it provides that the protection of the Convention applies, even if the conditions of article 3 are not fulfilled, to authors of cinematographic works the maker of which has his headquarters or habitual residence in one of the countries of the Union.

Article 1(3) of the TRIPs Agreement incorporates these criteria for eligibility by reference.

The Berne Convention permits certain exemptions from the national treatment principle, which are preserved by article 3(1) of the TRIPs Agreement. These include the well-known 'shorter term' rule of article 7(8), which provides that, unless the legislation of the country where protection is claimed otherwise provides, the term of protection shall not exceed the term fixed in the country of origin of the work. Its application within the European Union is discussed below.[15]

Also, article 6 of the Convention allows the restriction of protection by a Union country in respect of certain works of nationals of certain countries outside the Union (who are not habitually resident in one of the countries of the Union), where any such country fails to protect in an adequate manner the works of authors who are nationals of the Union country.[16] To date, no use of article 6 has been notified under the Berne Convention.

The Convention includes its own transitional provisions. Article 18 of the Convention regulates its application to works existing on its entry into force or in the case of new accessions.[17] Its contains three basic principles:

1. Article 18(1) provides that the Convention shall apply to all works which, at the moment of its coming into force, have not yet fallen into the public domain in the country of origin through the expiry of the term of protection.

2. Article 18(2) provides that if, through the expiry of the term of protection which was previously granted, a work has fallen into the public domain of the country where protection is claimed, that work shall not be protected anew.

[14] Art. 3(3). For the meaning of publication in relation to film works, see para. 343.
[15] See para. 355.
[16] In such a case, the other countries of the Union are not required to grant to works thus subjected to special treatment a wider protection than that granted to them in the country of first publication. However, the exercise of the right granted under art. 6 is subject to a notice to the Director-General of WIPO.
[17] And to cases in which protection is extended by the application of art. 7 or by the abandonment of reservations.

3. Article 18(3) provides that the application of these principles shall be subject to any provisions contained in special conventions to that effect existing or to be concluded between countries of the Union. In the absence of such provisions, the respective countries shall determine, each in so far as it is concerned, the conditions of application of this principle.

345.   Difficulties in relation to film works

As mentioned above, there are significant gaps in the system organised by the Berne Convention. In addition, the interpretation of certain of its provisions may differ among Union countries. We will mention here three difficulties under the Convention's regime which may affect the protection of foreign film works. The first difficulty relates to the law applicable to the definition of the author. The second difficulty relates to the law governing the definition of the owner of copyright. The third difficulty relates to the definition of 'publication'.

346.   The law applicable to the definition of 'author'

Authorship is an important connecting factor under the Berne Convention. We saw, however, that there is no definition of the term 'author' in the Convention, and that its conventional meaning is still the subject of controversy.[18] Since the EC copyright directives give no definition of this term,[19] the definition of the author of the film varies, not only among Union countries, but also within the European Union. Accordingly, in an international context, the determination of the law applicable to the definition of the author may have consequences for the question of entitlement to copyright or moral rights. It is therefore necessary to determine which law will govern the definition of the author.

The Berne Convention does not address this question, but contains a specific provision for 'ownership' of cinematographic works in article 14*bis*(2):

Ownership of copyright in a cinematographic work shall be a matter for legislation in the country where protection is claimed.

This provision is of little help, as it does not address the issue of 'authorship', as opposed to 'ownership'. This distinction between authorship and ownership is important, as we saw that within the European Union the author of the film is not necessarily the first owner of the

[18] See para. 108.   [19] See para. 111.

copyright in it, and *vice versa*.[20] Accordingly, the legislation in the country where protection is claimed under the Convention would not necessarily determine the definition of the author, as opposed to the initial owner of copyright.

In any case, concerning other classes of works under the Convention, the general understanding is that no general rule can be implied from article 14*bis*(2), which should be regarded as a *sui generis* provision. It is then left to Member States to apply their private international law principles. In this respect, the solutions may vary from one Member State to another. The following two examples are illustrative.

In the UK, the 1988 Act contains no clear answer to that question. It uses authorship as a connecting factor for the application of the Act,[21] but does not specify which law applies for the determination of the author. Unless it can be inferred from its provisions that the definition is necessarily the one given by the Act, the solution must be found in common law. What can be said is that, under common law, private international law principles on authorship and initial ownership are rather uncertain.[22] Several elements seem to suggest, however, that the applicable law in this respect should be the law under which the work is created.[23]

In France, private international law principles would appear to designate the law of origin of the work (the law of first publication). The question was addressed by the Court of Appeal of Paris in the *Huston* case,[24] which confirmed this view. The decision of the Court of Appeal was overturned by the Court of Cassation, but on the ground that the author for the purposes of *moral rights* entitlement was to be determined by French law as the law of international public order (*loi de police*).[25] Accordingly, the Supreme Court did not reject the conflict of law analysis by the Court of Appeal, which should therefore remain applicable to *economic rights*. Therefore, the law applicable to the definition of the author appears to be, for economic rights, the law of origin and, for moral rights, French law as the law of international public order. To complicate the matter further, article L.311-7 of the Intellectual Property Code grants the remuneration for private copying of phonograms and videograms to authors '*within the meaning of French law*'.

---

[20] See Chapter 4 above.   [21] See para. 353.

[22] See G. Austin', Private International Law and Intellectual Property Rights, A Common Law Overview', WIPO Doc. WIPO/PIL/01/5, 15 January 2001, pp. 36 *et seq.*

[23] *Ibid.* In the US case of *Itar-Tass Russian* v. *Russian Kurier*, 153 F. 3d 82 (2nd Cir. 1998), the Federal Court of Appeals for the 2nd Circuit, in a suit for an alleged infringement of a work of Russian origin in the US, applied Russian law to determine the ownership of the copyrights alleged to have been infringed, as the law of the State with the most significant relationship with the work and the parties.

[24] Paris Court of Appeal, 6 July 1989, RIDA, 1990, p. 329, note Françon.

[25] See para. 287.

In several other Member States, the private international law rule appears to designate the local law (as *lex loci protectionis*) as the law applicable to the definition of the author, for both economic and moral rights. This appears to be the case under Italian, German and Spanish law.

In general, and following the French example in the *Huston* case, it is to be expected that, at least in those countries with strong moral rights principles, the determination of the author for moral rights purposes is considered a matter of international public order.

347.   The law applicable to the definition of the owner of copyright

As noted above, the Berne Convention addresses this question in relation to the cinematographic works in its article 14*bis*(2)(a):

Ownership of copyright in a cinematographic work shall be a matter for legislation in the country where protection is claimed.

This means that a country in which protection for a film is claimed will apply its own law to determine who is the owner of the copyright in the film. This may give rise to different solutions as to film ownership among members of the Union, especially when initial ownership is at stake. However, this unworkable solution is tempered by the fact that, if there is a contract between the film producer and the film authors conveying the copyright in the film, the provisions of the contract should be applied by the law in which protection is sought (according to the *lex contractus*). This should, in principle, lead to a single solution as to ownership (provided that the contract addresses the question of ownership in detail, so that very few uncertainties may remain, and that local rules on film ownership accept such clauses).

In addition, where the *lex loci protectionis* does not consider the film producer as the owner of the copyright in the film, the latter may benefit from the presumption of legitimation under article 14*bis*(2)(b), which provides:

However, in the countries of the Union which, by legislation, include among the owners of copyright in a cinematographic work authors who have brought contributions to the making of the work, such authors, if they have undertaken to bring such contributions, may not, in the absence of any contrary or special stipulation, object to the reproduction, distribution, public performance, communication to the public by wire, broadcasting or any other communication to the public, or to the subtitling or dubbing of texts, of the work.

This presumption is, however, limited in several ways. It is limited first in article 14*bis*(3), which excludes or allows the exclusion of the main (if not all in certain legal systems) co-authors of film works from its scope:

Unless the national legislation provides to the contrary, the provisions of paragraph (2)(b) above shall not be applicable to authors of scenarios, dialogues and musical works created for the making of the cinematographic work, or to the principal director thereof. However, those countries of the Union whose legislation does not contain rules providing for the application of the said paragraph (2)(b) to such director shall notify the Director General by means of a written declaration, which will be immediately communicated by him to all the other countries of the Union.

Secondly, article 14*bis*(2d)(c) sets specific conditions for the proof by the producer that the film author has undertaken to bring a contribution to the making of the film under paragraph (b):

The question whether or not the form of the undertaking referred to above should, for the application of the preceding subparagraph (b), be in a written agreement or a written act of the same effect shall be a matter for the legislation of the country where the maker of the cinematographic work has his headquarters or habitual residence. However, it shall be a matter for the legislation of the country of the Union where protection is claimed to provide that the said undertaking shall be in a written agreement or a written act of the same effect. The countries whose legislation so provides shall notify the Director General by means of a written declaration, which will be immediately communicated by him to all the other countries of the Union.[26]

Thirdly, the presumption is subject to 'contrary or special stipulation' in paragraph (b).[27]

The question of the law applicable to the definition of the owner of *underlying rights* is not addressed by the Convention, and is left to the conflict rules of Member States.[28] There appears, however, to be a tendency to apply the law of origin.[29] Again, where there is a written agreement, it is likely that the provisions of the agreement will be enforced, provided they comply with the *lex contractus*.

Note that pure ownership provisions will in most cases not be considered an element of international public order. In European Union Member States this question may arise, for example, in relation to mandatory rights such as the mandatory royalty right of film authors. To take the example of French law, it is very unlikely that such provision would be considered as a rule of international public order (like moral rights in the

---

[26] Portugal made a declaration on 5 November 1986 to the effect that the undertaking by authors to bring contributions to the making of a cinematographic work must be in a written agreement.

[27] Under para. (d), 'contrary or special stipulation' means 'any restrictive condition which is relevant to the aforesaid undertaking'.

[28] Although it has been suggested that the application of the law of the country of origin could be deducted *a contrario* from art. 14*bis*(2).

[29] See para. 346. See also e.g. art. 67 of the Greek Law of 1993.

Huston case). The reason for this is that the Intellectual Property Code contains numerous exemptions to that rule, and expressly allows, in the case of publishing contracts, that a lump sum remuneration may be paid for the assignment of rights by or to a person or enterprise established abroad.[30] This is a very different situation from that of moral rights, to which there are almost no exceptions.

348. The definition of 'publication' under the Berne Convention

Another difficult question relates to the Convention's definition of 'publication', and to its application to film works. For a long time, films were mainly 'published' by way of theatrical exhibition and copies were not made available to the public. Even with the spread of videotechnology, the first act of publication of the film remains theatrical exhibition. But does theatrical exhibition constitute a valid publication under the Convention? And what is 'publication' in relation to a film?

The answer to this question is important not only with regard to the criterion of eligibility of article 3(1)(b), but also with regard to the extent of protection under the Convention. This is because publication is used in the definition of the 'country of origin' in article 5(4), which may have implications for the protection granted under the Convention. Thus, under article 5(1), authors are required to enjoy, for their works protected under the Convention, national treatment and the rights under the Convention in countries of the Union other than the country of origin. Publication is also relevant in the application of the 'rule of shorter term'[31] and in the protection of works in existence on the Convention's entry into force.[32]

In the Brussels Act of the Convention, under article 4(4), 'published works' were defined as works, copies of which have been issued and made available in sufficient quantities to the public, whatever may be the means of manufacture of the copies. The article further added that the presentation of a dramatic, dramatico-musical or cinematographic work, the public recitation of a literary work, the transmission or the radiodiffusion of a literary or artistic work do not constitute 'publication'.

Such a definition created difficulties for films, which were not 'made available in sufficient quantities to the public', *stricto sensu*. The definition was relaxed in article 3(3) of the Paris Act, and the expression 'published

---

[30] Art. L.132-6.   [31] Art. 7(8); see para. 350.

[32] Art. 18(1): 'This Convention shall apply to all works which, at the moment of its coming into force, have not yet fallen into the public domain in the country of origin through the expiry of the term of protection.'

works' now means 'works published with the consent of their authors, whatever may be the means of manufacture of the copies, provided that the availability of such copies has been such as to satisfy the reasonable requirements of the public, having regard to the nature of the work'.[33] Accordingly, it is now clear that the theatrical distribution of a film, without actual distribution of copies to the public, is sufficient publication under the Convention. However, it must be noted that the terms of article 3(3) leave some questions unanswered, *inter alia*: how many copies must be distributed to constitute publication?[34] Is it necessary that the exhibition has started? When does publication start? etc. These questions may be answered differently by national courts.

349.   General rules applicable to related rights (national treatment)

Since all EU Member States are WTO members, they are required under article 3 of the TRIPs Agreement to provide protection on the basis of national treatment with respect to all related or neighbouring rights originating from other WTO members.[35] These neighbouring rights include the rights of performers, producers of sound recordings and broadcasting organisations (which may be characterised as copyright in certain countries). The TRIPs Agreement includes references to the Rome Convention of 1961, to which all EU Member States are also parties (with the notable exception of Portugal).[36]

Videograms and videogram producers are excluded from the protection under the Rome Convention.[37] The definition of phonograms under the Convention is restricted to any exclusively aural fixation of sounds, and thus excludes film soundtracks.[38] Accordingly, we will limit our description to the protection of performances and broadcasting organisations.

In relation to *performances*, article 4 of the Rome Convention provides that national treatment under the Convention applies to:

(a) performances taking place in another Contracting State;
(b) performances incorporated in a phonogram which is protected under article 5 of this Convention; and

---

[33] The Paris Act further provides that the 'performance of a dramatic, dramatico-musical, cinematographic or musical work, the public recitation of a literary work, the communication by wire or the broadcasting of literary or artistic works, the exhibition of a work of art and the construction of a work of architecture shall not constitute publication'.
[34] Arguably, the mere showing in a film festival does not constitute publication.
[35] See n. 34 above.   [36] Art. 1(3).   [37] Art. 3(b) and (c).   [38] Art. 3(b).

(c) to performances, not being fixed on a phonogram, carried by a broadcast which is protected by article 6 of this Convention.

The definition of 'performers' in article 3 is broad, and includes actors, singers, musicians, dancers, and other persons who act, sing, deliver, declaim, play in, or otherwise perform literary or artistic works. In addition, under article 9, any contracting State may, by its domestic laws and regulations, extend the protection provided for in the Convention to artists who do not perform literary or artistic works.

Concerning *broadcasts*, article 6 provides for national treatment of broadcasting organisations if either of the following conditions is met:

(a) the headquarters of the broadcasting organisation is situated in another Contracting State;
(b) the broadcast was transmitted from a transmitter situated in another Contracting State.

However, a contracting State may declare, by means of a notification to the Secretary-General of the United Nations, that it will protect broadcasts only if both conditions are met. Under article 3(f), 'broadcasting' means the transmission by wireless means for public reception of sounds or of images and sounds, and therefore excludes cable transmissions.

The Rome Convention allows limited exemptions from the national treatment principle, which exemptions are preserved by article 3(1) of the TRIPs Agreement.[39] These concern equitable remuneration for secondary uses of phonograms and the right of communication to the public of broadcasts (if such publication is made in places accessible to the public against payment of an entrance fee).[40]

The TRIPs Agreement provides that the provisions of article 18 of the Berne Convention (1971 text) on retroactive protection shall also apply, *mutatis mutandis*, to the rights of performers and producers of phonograms in phonograms, but that this provision is not extended to the rights of broadcasting organisations.

The adoption of the EC Directive on Copyright and Related Rights in the Information Society opened the way for ratifications of the WIPO Performances and Phonograms Treaty of 1996. Protection under the WIPO Treaty will be granted to performers and producers of phonograms who are nationals of contracting parties.[41] Those nationals shall be understood to be those performers or producers of phonograms who would meet the criteria for eligibility for protection provided under the Rome Convention.

[39] See the text above.   [40] Art. 16.   [41] Art. 3.

The Treaty includes a definition of the phonogram producer which is slightly different from that of the Rome Convention[42] and specifies the definitions of 'phonogram',[43] 'fixation',[44] 'publication'[45] and 'broadcasting'[46] in order to encompass new technological means of exploitation. The rights granted under the Treaty have been defined elsewhere.[47] Protection is not extended to videogram producers or to fixations of sounds incorporated into audiovisual works.[48] Accordingly, to date audiovisual performances, cable transmissions, videograms and film soundtracks are partly outside the international protection of neighbouring rights.

350.   National treatment under the EC Treaty

The principle of national treatment is fully applicable between European Union Member States in relation to nationals from other Member States. This principle covers all types of intellectual property, including moral rights. This principle derives from the judgment of the European Court of Justice (ECJ) of 20 October 1993 in the *Phil Collins* case,[49] in which the Court held that copyright and related rights fall within the scope of application of the EC Treaty, and more particularly within the meaning of the first paragraph of article 12 of the Treaty (formerly article 7) which lays down a general principle of non-discrimination on the grounds of nationality.[50]

351.   Most-favoured-nation treatment under the TRIPs Agreement

Finally, it is worth noting that article 4 of the TRIPs Agreement, providing for a most-favoured-nation treatment of foreign nationals, is also applicable to all categories of intellectual property covered by the Agreement:

With regard to the protection of intellectual property, any advantage, favour, privilege or immunity granted by a Member to the nationals of any other country shall be accorded immediately and unconditionally to the nationals of all other Members.

---

[42] Art. 2(d): 'producer of a phonogram' means the person, or the legal entity, who or which takes the initiative and has the responsibility for the first fixation of the sounds of a performance or other sounds, or the representations of sounds.
[43] Art. 2(b).   [44] Art. 2(c).   [45] Art. 2(e).   [46] Art. 2(f).
[47] See paras. 179, 188, 194, 200, 209 and 332.
[48] Art. 2(b) and (c).
[49] Joined Cases C-92/92 and C-326/92, *Collins* v. *Imtrat Handelsgesellschaft mbH* [1993] ECR I-5145; [1993] 3 CMLR 773; [1994] EMLR 108; [1994] FSR 166, ECJ.
[50] 'Within the scope of application of this Treaty, and without prejudice to any special provisions contained therein, any discrimination on grounds of nationality shall be prohibited.'

Such a provision could be of interest where a national law grants to a foreign national under a bilateral agreement more favourable rights than those granted under the multilateral conventions. However, the same article exempts from this obligation 'any advantage, favour, privilege or immunity accorded by a Member':

(a) deriving from international agreements on judicial assistance or law enforcement of a general nature and not particularly confined to the protection of intellectual property;

(b) granted in accordance with the provisions of the Berne Convention (1971 text) or the Rome Convention authorising that the treatment accorded be a function not of national treatment but of the treatment accorded in another country;

(c) in respect of the rights of performers, producers of phonograms and broadcasting organisations not provided under this Agreement;

(d) deriving from international agreements related to the protection of intellectual property which entered into force prior to the entry into force of the WTO Agreement, provided that such agreements are notified to the Council for TRIPs and do not constitute an arbitrary or unjustifiable discrimination against nationals of other Members.

Although the construction of what constitutes 'an arbitrary or unjustifiable discrimination' under point (d) may raise some difficulties, article 4(d) certainly excludes from the scope of the principle existing bilateral agreements, on the condition that they are notified to the WTO. Several European Union Member States have notified their pre-existing agreements under article 4(d).[51] It is difficult to say, however, if all relevant agreements have been notified.

352.   The protection of foreign film works in domestic laws

An illustration of the way foreign film works are protected in domestic laws is given below. Most copyright Acts contain specific provisions to protect foreign films. Sometimes, however, protection outside multilateral or bilateral conventions is left to case law, whereupon general doctrines of private international law apply.

353.   The protection of foreign film works in the UK

The UK is a party to the major international agreements in the copyright field. Treaties, however, are not self-executing in the UK, and their provisions need to be implemented through statutes. When it comes to the protection of foreign works, the CDPA 1988 distinguishes between an

---

[51] Notifications made under art. 4(d) can be viewed on the WTO website, under the reference IP/N/4/*.

'extension' and an 'application' of the Act. Under section 157 of the Act, the protection under the Part I (copyright and moral rights) of the Act can be 'extended' (subject to exemptions and modifications), by Order-in-Council, to 'any of the Channel Islands, the Isle of Man, or any colony'. No such orders have been made under the 1988 Act, but equivalent orders under the 1956 Act remain in effect. Under section 159 of the Act, the protection of Part I of the Act can be 'applied' (subject to exemptions and modifications), by Order-in-Council, to a country to which the Act does not extend. Reciprocity applies, except in the case of a country which is a party to a convention relating to copyright to which the UK is also a party, or in the case of another EU Member State. Orders made under section 208 of the Act designate countries whose performers enjoy protection in respect of their performances. Several orders under sections 159 and 208 implemented the UK's obligations under the various applicable international copyright or neighbouring rights conventions.[52]

The qualification for copyright protection is defined under sections 153–156 of the Act. Section 153 provides for three possible connecting factors to qualify for copyright protection by UK copyright: authorship,[53] country of first publication[54] or, in the case of a broadcast or cable programme, the place of transmission.[55]

Authorship

Under section 154, a work qualifies for copyright protection if the author was at the 'material time' a qualifying person, that is:

(a) a British citizen, a British Dependent Territories citizen, a British National (Overseas), a British Overseas citizen, a British subject or a British protected person within the meaning of the British Nationality Act 1981, or
(b) an individual domiciled or resident in, or a body incorporated under the law of, the United Kingdom or another country to which the relevant provisions of this Part extend,

---

[52] Copyright (International Conventions) Order 1979 (SI 1979 No. 1715); Copyright (International Conventions) (Amendment) Order 1989 (SI 1989 No. 157); Copyright (International Conventions) (Amendment No. 3) Order 1988 (SI 1988 No. 1855); Copyright (Application to Other Countries) Order 1993 (SI 1993 No. 942) (amended); Copyright (Application to Other Countries) (Amendment) Order 1995 (SI 1995 No. 2987). The UK complied with its obligations under the TRIPs Agreement by the Copyright (Application to Other Countries) (Amendment) Order 1995 (SI 1995 No. 2987) and the Performances (Reciprocal Protection) (Convention Countries) Order 1995 (SI 1995 No. 2990), with effect from 1 January 1996. The Performances (Reciprocal Protection) (Convention Countries) Order 1995 was replaced by the Performances (Reciprocal Protection) (Convention Countries) Order 1999 (SI 1999 No. 1752).
[53] CDPA 1988, s. 154.   [54] *Ibid.*, s. 155.   [55] *Ibid.*, s. 156.

(c) a citizen or subject of, an individual domiciled or resident in, or a body incorporated under the law of, a country to which the Act applies by Order under section 159.[56]

The meaning of 'material time' is defined by section 154(4) and (5). Specific provisions for works of joint authorship are made under section 154(3). Under section 154(3), a work of joint authorship qualifies for copyright protection if at the material time any of the authors satisfies the requirements of section 154(1) or (2). However, where a work qualifies for copyright protection only under this section, only those authors who satisfy those requirements shall be taken into account for the purposes of first ownership of copyright, and the entitlement of the author or the author's employer,[57] the duration of copyright[58] and the rules on anonymous or pseudonymous works.[59]

Country of first publication

Under section 155, a literary, dramatic, musical or artistic work, a sound recording or film, or the typographical arrangement of a published edition, will qualify for copyright protection, irrespective of authorship, if it is first published (a) in the UK, or (b) in another country to which the relevant provisions of Part I extend or apply. Publication in one country shall not be regarded as other than the first publication by reason of simultaneous publication elsewhere; and for this purpose publication elsewhere is defined as publication within the previous thirty days.[60]

Place of transmission

Under section 156, a broadcast qualifies for copyright protection if it is made from, and a cable programme qualifies for copyright protection if it is sent from, a place (a) in the UK, or (b) in another country to which the relevant provisions of Part I extend or apply.

Transitional provisions

Under paragraph 5(1) of Schedule 1 to the 1988 Act, copyright subsists in an existing work after the date of commencement of the Act only

---

[56] *Ibid.*, s. 154(2).   [57] *Ibid.*, s. 11(1) and (2).

[58] *Ibid.*, ss. 12 and 9(4) (meaning of 'unknown authorship') so far as it applies for the purposes of s. 12.

[59] *Ibid.*, s. 57 (anonymous or pseudonymous works: acts permitted on assumptions as to expiry of copyright or death of author).

[60] *Ibid.*, s. 155(3).

if copyright subsisted in the work immediately before commencement. In order to determine whether protection for a foreign film work was afforded under the 1956 Act, it is necessary to examine the provisions of the orders made under that Act.[61]

However, section 5(2) specifies that section 5(1) does not prevent an existing work qualifying for copyright protection after commencement under section 155 of the Act (qualification by reference to country of first publication) or by virtue of an order under section 159 of the Act. Orders made under the 1956 and 1988 Acts may contain specific transitional provisions designed to preserve acts done at the time the work was not protected and became later protected by operation of the order.[62]

Performers

Under section 181 of the 1988 Act, a performance qualifies for protection under the provisions of the Act relating to performers' rights if the performance is given by a 'qualifying individual' or takes place in a 'qualifying country'. Under section 206, 'qualifying individual' means a citizen or subject of, or an individual resident in, a qualifying country; 'qualifying country' means the UK, another Member State of the European Union, or a country designated by Order-in-Council under section 208 as enjoying reciprocal protection. The current order is the Performances (Reciprocal Protection) (Convention Countries) Order 1999.[63]

354.   The law in droit d'auteur countries

In most continental countries, the provisions of an international agreement, once ratified, are directly incorporated into national legislation, without further formal requirement.[64] However, an express reference to these international agreements is often found in the copyright Acts.[65] As mentioned above, at present all EU Member States have ratified the Berne Convention (Paris Act), the Rome Convention and the TRIPs

---

[61] Copyright (International Conventions) Order 1979 (SI 1979 No. 1715) as amended by the Copyright (International Conventions) (Amendment) Order 1989 (SI 1989 No. 1570).

[62] See e.g. art. 7 of the Copyright (Application to Other Countries) (No. 2) Order 1989 (SI 1989 No. 1293). A similar provision can be found in the Copyright (International Conventions) (Amendment) Order 1989 (SI 1989 No. 1570), art. 3.

[63] SI 1999 No. 1752.

[64] See e.g. art. 55 of the French Constitution.

[65] See, e.g. arts. 121(4) and 125(5) of the German Act; and art. 79(1) of the Belgian Act.

Agreement.[66] Thus, it can be said that national treatment is afforded under these agreements to foreign works or performances.

When the provisions of the international treaties do not apply, domestic copyright Acts generally provide for a reciprocity principle,[67] but their provisions can be complex. However, the protection of moral rights is sometimes granted to foreign authors irrespective of their nationality and without conditions. Examples of French, German and Italian laws are discussed below. The discussion, however, does not deal with transitional provisions.

In France, the basic provision on copyright and moral rights is article L.111-4 of the Intellectual Property Code, which codified the provisions of a Law of 8 July 1964.[68] This article provides for a limited reciprocity principle, subject to the provisions of international conventions:

Subject to the international conventions to which France is party, in the event that it is ascertained, after consultation with the Minister for Foreign Affairs, that a State does not afford to works disclosed for the first time in France, in any form whatsoever, protection that is adequate and effective, works disclosed for the first time on the territory of such State shall not enjoy the copyright protection afforded by French legislation. However, neither the integrity nor the authorship of such works may be impaired.[69]

The caveat of international conventions includes all multilateral and bilateral agreements and EC law. The exclusion of the moral rights of integrity and paternity from reciprocity means that all foreign authors benefit from these rights in France.[70] It is not clear whether other aspects of moral rights (such as the right of divulgation) would fall under the general rule of the article, or whether they would benefit from the same regime as the right of integrity. This may prove important, as far as the right of divulgation is concerned. This latter right would be covered by the Community-wide national treatment principle, but not by the Berne Convention.

Bilateral agreements in the field of copyright are of little relevance in France, as they provide for a lesser protection that multilateral conventions.

---

[66] See Appendix 4 below.

[67] See art. 79(3) of the Belgian Act, and art. 96.1 of the Austrian Act; but there my be bilateral agreement.

[68] Note also art. L.311-2 of the Intellectual Property Code which sets an indirect form of reciprocity by subjecting remuneration for private copy for phonograms and videograms and the remuneration of performers and phonogram producers for the broadcasting of sound recordings to the condition that the phonogram or videogram be 'fixed for the first time in France'. See para. 228.

[69] WIPO translation.

[70] See para. 346 on the *Huston* case and the notion of 'author' for private international law purposes.

The provision of article L.111-4 is not repeated in relation to neighbouring rights, and the Intellectual Property Code contains no provision
on foreign performances. Outside the scope of the relevant international
conventions, it appears that French courts would apply national treatment
and French law as the *lex loci delicti* to claims by foreign performers.[71] The
solutions regarding moral rights of authors can certainly be extended to
performers.

In Germany, the provisions of the Copyright Act 1965 are more complex and detailed. In relation to copyright, a distinction should be made
between moral rights and economic rights. Regarding moral rights, under
section 121(6) of the 1965 Act, foreign nationals enjoy protection of the
rights of divulgation, integrity and paternity under articles 12–14 with
respect to all of their works, irrespective of any further condition.

Under article 121(4), foreign nationals further enjoy copyright protection as provided by the applicable international treaties. In this respect,
in addition to the multilateral treaties described above, bilateral agreements may be of particular importance in relation to certain works. For
example, it has been said that the Agreement for the Mutual Protection of
Copyright between the United States and Germany of 15 January 1892
could be successfully relied upon by US authors to avoid the 'shorter
term rule' under the Berne Convention.[72]

Outside the scope of these treaties, protection is in general subject
to reciprocity. There are, however, cases in which the protection under
the Act applies to foreign works without reference to reciprocity or treaty
provisions. These include works by German nationals and nationals of EU
and EEA Member States, whether or not such works have been published
and regardless of the place of publication,[73] works of foreign nationals
published first in Germany or at least within thirty days of its publication
abroad,[74] or works by stateless persons or foreign refugees resident in
Germany.[75]

Foreign nationals may benefit from related rights in Germany in accordance to the international treaties. Outside the scope of these treaties, the
following rules apply. The foreign performer's moral right of integrity is
protected irrespective of any precondition.[76] Performers of German and

[71] See A. Lucas, in M. B. Nimmer and D. Geller (eds.), *International Copyright Law and Practice*, Matthew Bender, looseleaf, para. 6[1][b][ii].
[72] See A. Dietz, in M. B. Nimmer and D. Geller (eds.), *International Copyright Law and Practice*, Matthew Bender, looseleaf, paras. 6[4][a] and 3[3][c][i].
[73] Art. 120. In the case of a work created by joint authors, it is sufficient if one of the joint authors is a German national.
[74] Art. 121(1).   [75] Arts. 122 and 123.   [76] Art. 125(6).

EU or EEA nationality enjoy the protection for all their performances, irrespective of where the performance takes place.[77] Under article 125(2) foreign nationals enjoy protection with respect to all of their performances which take place in Germany. If performances by foreign nationals are lawfully fixed on video or audio recordings, and if such recordings have been published, the foreign nationals enjoy the exclusive right to reproduce and distribute them, the right of equitable remuneration for broadcasting and public communication if they have been published in Germany, unless such recordings have been published outside Germany more than thirty days before their publication within that territory.[78] If performances of foreign nationals have been lawfully broadcast, the foreign nationals shall enjoy protection against the video or audio recording of the broadcast,[79] against the rebroadcasting of the broadcast[80] and the equitable remuneration for public communication if the broadcast was transmitted from Germany.[81]

The exclusive rights to object to transmission by screen or loudspeaker, or to the recording of a performance on a video or audio medium are enjoyed by foreign nationals with respect to all of their performances, even if the conditions contained in articles 125(2) to (5) are not fulfilled. The same applies to the right to consent to broadcasts under article 76(1) where a direct broadcast of the performance is concerned.[82]

Concerning broadcasting organisations, article 127(1) provides that broadcasting organisations which have their headquarters in Germany or in an EU or EEA Member State enjoy protection under the Act with respect to all of their broadcasts, irrespective of where they are broadcast. Broadcasting organisations which do not have their headquarters in Germany enjoy protection for all of their broadcasts which are broadcast from Germany. However, in such a case, protection expires at the latest on expiry of the term of protection in the State in which the broadcasting organisation has its headquarters, without exceeding the term of protection under the Act.[83]

Concerning film producers, article 128 provides that German nationals, nationals of EU or EEA Member States and German enterprises which have their headquarters in Germany or in an EU or EEA Member State enjoy the protection afforded by articles 94 and 95 with respect to their video or video and audio recordings, irrespective of whether and where they have been published. Foreign nationals or foreign enterprises which do not have their headquarters in Germany enjoy protection for

---

[77] Art.125(1).   [78] Art.125(3).   [79] Of art. 75(1).   [80] Of art. 76(1).
[81] Art. 125(4).   [82] Art. 125(6).   [83] Art. 127(2)

their video recordings or 'moving pictures' published in that territory unless the work was published outside Germany more than thirty days before it was published in that territory. Protection expires, however, at the latest on expiry of the term of protection in the State of which the producer possesses the nationality or in which the enterprise has its headquarters, without exceeding the term of protection under the German Act.

In Italy, outside the scope of the international conventions and bilateral agreements,[84] article 185 of the Copyright Act sets out the general principle that protection under the Copyright Act applies to all works of Italian authors, wherever first published, and to works of a foreign author domiciled in Italy which are first published in Italy. However, these rules apply to cinematographic works, phonograms and similar recordings, to photographs and to the right of performers only if such works or performances are created in Italy or can be considered as national works under Italian law.[85] Law No. 1213 of 4 November 1965 deems films produced or co-produced by a person of Italian nationality or domiciled in Italy to be of Italian nationality.[86]

The protection of works of foreign authors not domiciled in Italy or which are not first published in Italy is subject to a reciprocity principle.[87]

355.   The rule of shorter term

In relation to copyright, article 7(8) of the Berne Convention provides that, unless the legislation of that country otherwise provides, the term of protection shall not exceed the term fixed in the country of origin of the work. In the European Union, due to the ruling of the ECJ in the *Phil Collins* case,[88] this 'shorter term' rule is not applicable to works of nationals of other EU Member States. However, in all other cases, the rule is made mandatory by the EC Term Directive. Its recital 22 provides that, for works whose country of origin within the meaning of the Berne Convention is a third country and whose author is not a Community national, a comparison of the terms of protection should be applied, provided that the term accorded in the Community does not exceed the term laid down in the Term Directive.

The Directive's regime is detailed in article 7, entitled 'Protection *vis-à-vis* third countries'. Article 7(1) provides that, where the country

---

[84] Referred to in art. 186 of the Act.   [85] Art. 189.

[86] M. Fabiani, in M. B. Nimmer and D. Geller (eds.), *International Copyright Law and Practice*, Matthew Bender, looseleaf, para. 6[1].

[87] Art. 187, under Legislative Decree No. 82 of 23 August 1946.

[88] Joined Cases C-92/92 and C-326/92, *Collins v. Imtrat Handelsgesellschaft mbH* [1993] ECR I-5145; [1993] 3 CMLR 773; [1994] EMLR 108; [1994] FSR 166, ECJ.

of origin of a work within the meaning of the Berne Convention is a third country, and the author of the work is not a Community national, the term of protection granted by the Member States shall expire on the date of expiry of the protection granted in the country of origin of the work, but may not exceed the term laid down in article 1 of the Directive.

Under article 7(2), the terms of protection laid down in article 3 of the Directive shall also apply in the case of rightholders who are not Community nationals, provided Member States grant them protection. However, without prejudice to the international obligations of the Member States, the term of protection granted by Member States shall expire no later than the date of expiry of the protection granted in the country of which the rightholder is a national and may not exceed the term laid down in article 3.

Article 7(3), however, allows the survival of more favourable bilateral agreements. It provides that Member States which, at the date of adoption of the Directive, pursuant to their international obligations, granted a longer term of protection than that which would result from article 7(1) and (2) may maintain this longer term of protection until the conclusion of international agreements on the term of protection by copyright or related rights.

Concerning performers, phonogram producers and broadcasting organisations, the Rome Convention and the TRIPs Agreement do not provide for a 'comparison of terms' or for a rule of 'shorter term'. Accordingly, although national provisions of EU Member States outside the scope of the international conventions may provide for rules to that effect,[89] such rules are overruled by their international obligations.[90]

---

[89] E.g. in Germany, see ss. 125(7) and s. 126(2), second sentence, of the Copyright Act.
[90] E.g. in Germany, see s. 125(5) and 123(3) of the Copyright Act.

Appendix 1: A basic guide to the European Union

The following is intended to assist readers unaware of the institutional system of the European Union and of Community law. It provides the minimum necessary to understand the various expressions used and references made in this book. Further information can be found in textbooks on EC law or on the website of the European Union at www.europa.eu.int.

THE EUROPEAN UNION, THE EUROPEAN COMMUNITY AND THE EUROPEAN ECONOMIC AREA

The *Treaty of the European Economic Community* (also known as the 'EEC Treaty', or the 'Treaty of Rome') was signed on 25 March 1957 and came into force on 1 January 1958. The EEC is one of the three existing European Communities, along with the European Coal and Steel Community (ECSC) (1951) and the European Atomic Energy Community (EAEC, or 'Euratom') (1957).

From November 1993 (the date of entry into force of the Treaty on European Union (see below)), the EEC Treaty is referred to as the *EC Treaty*, and the European Economic Community is called the *European Community*. The letters 'EC' replace the letters 'EEC' in all acts adopted after this date. This change of name reflects the enlargement of the scope of the Treaty beyond mere economic questions.

The European Community has fifteen Member States. The six founding countries were Belgium, France, Germany, Italy, Luxembourg and the Netherlands. Denmark, Ireland and the UK joined in 1973; Greece in 1981; Spain and Portugal in 1986; and Austria, Finland and Sweden in 1995.

The EC Treaty provides for:

1. the creation of a customs union, including a prohibition, as between Member States, of quantitative restrictions and other measures having equivalent effect;

2. an internal market,[1] characterised by the abolition, as between Member States, of obstacles to the free movement of goods, persons, services and capital, and by measures concerning the entry and movement of persons;
3. a monetary union;
4. a common commercial policy;
5. common policies in the sphere of agriculture, fisheries and transport;
6. a competition law system ensuring that competition in the internal market is not distorted;
7. the approximation of the laws of Member States to the extent required for the functioning of the common market; and
8. various policies or coordination programmes relating to employment, to the environment, to the competitiveness of Community industry and to the promotion of research and technological development, health protection, education and training, culture, consumer protection, energy, civil protection and tourism.

The harmonisation of intellectual property rights is undertaken in the context of the strengthening of the internal market.

The *Treaty on European Union* (or the 'Maastricht Treaty'), was signed in Maastricht on 7 February 1992, and came into force on 1 November 1993. The Treaty creates a *European Union*, which does not replace the European Communities but places them under the same 'umbrella' with two new policies and forms of cooperation. Therefore, it is generally said that the Union is based on three 'pillars':

1. The first (main) pillar consists of the above-mentioned European Communities.
2. The second (new) pillar consists of a common foreign and security policy laid down in the Treaty on European Union.
3. The third (new) pillar consists of cooperation in the fields of justice and home affairs, also laid down in the Treaty on European Union.

Unlike the European Community, the European Union is not a legal entity. EC Member States are also EU Member States, and *vice versa*.

The *Agreement creating the European Economic Area* (EEA) was signed in May 1992 between the EC and member countries of the EFTA (European Free Trade Association). The Agreement entered into force on 1 January 1994. It now comprises the fifteen EU Member States and Norway, Iceland and Liechtenstein (Switzerland decided after a referendum not to participate in the EEA). The EEA Agreement is mainly

---

[1] The expressions 'common market', 'internal market' and 'single market' are often used synonymously (in particular by the ECJ). Legal commentators, however, disagree on their respective scope. In this book, we will not distinguish between them.

concerned with the four freedoms of movement established by the EC Treaty (freedom of movement of goods, of persons, of services and of capital). Subject to limited exemptions, all EC legislation in these areas is extended to EEA countries. This includes the directives in the field of copyright.

INSTITUTIONAL STRUCTURE

The European Union has the same institutional structure as the European Community, consisting of the European Council, the European Parliament, the Council, the Commission, the Court of Justice and the Court of Auditors.

The *European Council* is composed of the heads of State or government of the fifteen Member States and of the President of the European Commission. It should not be confused with the Council of Europe (an international organisation distinct from the EU (see below)) or with the Council of the European Union (referred to as 'the Council'). It provides the Union with the necessary impetus for its development and defines its general political guidelines. In contrast to the other institutions described below, the European Council is not legally an institution of the European Community. It has, however, an important influence on the Council of the European Union, which is composed of representatives from Member States at ministerial level.

The *European Parliament* is elected every five years by European citizens by direct universal suffrage. It shares with the Council, under various modalities, the power to adopt directives, regulations and decisions. It adopts the budget of the EU and supervises the Commission.

The *Council of the European Union* (or 'the Council') is the embodiment of the Member States. It is composed of fifteen members (one minister from each government), but this composition varies according to the subject under consideration. It is the legislative body of the Union. However, for a wide range of issues, it exercises its legislative power with the European Parliament, under a so-called cooperation or a co-decision procedure (as the case may be).

The *Commission* is the executive body of the Union (and of the Communities). It embodies and upholds the general interest of the Union, and acts as guardian of the Treaties. Its president and members are appointed by the Member States after they have been approved by the European Parliament. The Commission has the power to initiate legislation, and presents legislative proposals to the Parliament and the Council. It also represents the Union on the international scene, and negotiates (solely or in cooperation with Member States, as the case may be) international agreements.

The *Court of Justice* (ECJ) ensures that Community law is uniformly interpreted and effectively applied. It has an important role in defining Community law. For example, in its judgment of 5 February 1963 in *Van Gend and Loos*,[2] it laid down the principle of direct effect of Community law in Member States. In its judgment of 15 July 1964 in *Costa* v. *ENEL*,[3] it laid down the principle of primacy of Community law over national law.

The courts of Member States have jurisdiction to review the implementation of Community law and to uphold the rights directly conferred on their nationals. The EC Treaty provides, however, for a system of preliminary rulings in case of doubt as to the interpretation or validity of Community law. The referring court must then apply the law, as interpreted by the ECJ. This interpretation also serves as a guide for other national courts dealing with a similar issue.

SOURCES OF COMMUNITY LAW

The sources of Community law consist mainly of the following:
1. primary legislation, i.e. the Treaties and the general principles of law laid down by the ECJ;
2. the EC's international agreements;
3. secondary legislation (in the form of regulations, directives and decisions); and
4. conventions between Member States.

Regulations have general application. They are binding in all their provisions and directly applicable in all Member States, which means that individuals may cite their provisions against the Member State or State agencies, but also, as the case may be, against other individuals.

Directives are binding, as to the result to be achieved, upon each Member State to which they are addressed, but leave to the national authorities the choice of form and method of implementation. Accordingly, Member States have some discretion in transposing directives into domestic law. In contrast to regulations, directives are not directly applicable in principle. However, the ECJ has held that the provisions of a directive may have direct effect despite the absence of an act of transposition when: (1) at the expiry of the period for transposition, the Directive has not been transposed or has been transposed inadequately; (2) its provisions are clear, imperative and unconditional; and (3) the Directive confers rights on individuals. Non-compliance with the provisions of a

[2] [1963] ECR 3.   [3] [1964] ECR 1141.

directive is a violation of the Treaty. In some exceptional cases, an individual citizen is entitled to claim compensation from a Member State which has not transposed a directive or has done so inadequately.

Decisions are binding in their entirety upon those to whom they are addressed.

Competent institutions may only use these instruments if they are empowered to do so by a provision of the Treaty. The adoption procedure may vary according to the field of the instrument. The co-decision procedure may allow the Parliament to block the legislative process. In the field of copyright, the approximation of the laws of Member States takes the form of EC directives.

COUNCIL OF EUROPE

The Council of Europe, which has met in Strasbourg since 1949, is an intergovernmental organisation. Its main purpose is to draft conventions in areas such as the protection of human rights, culture and education. It is entirely distinct from the European Union and has its own institutional structure. The Council of Europe has forty-one member countries (including Russia and Turkey). All fifteen EU members are members of the Council of Europe.

One of the main international treaties adopted within the framework of the Council of Europe is the European Convention on Human Rights, which came into force in 1953, and which sets its own enforcement machinery, through the European Court of Human Rights established in Strasbourg.

Several treaties in the field of copyright have been adopted within the Council of Europe.

Appendix 2: Principal national copyright legislation

The table below includes only references to the basic copyright Acts which are currently in force in the fifteen EU Member States. Note that in several Member States, specific aspects of copyright protection (e.g. copyright agreements, collecting societies. etc.) are dealt with in separate Acts or regulatory instruments, which are not mentioned here. Also, important provisions may remain uncodified in various amendment Acts, in particular in those transposing the EC copyright directives. In addition, provisions of previous Acts may be preserved in relation to old films through transitional arrangements made in the current Acts.

Austria	Federal Law Concerning Copyright in Works of Literature, Art and Neighbouring Rights of 9 April 1936 (No. 111/1936), as amended.
Belgium	Law of 30 June 1994 on Copyright and Neighbouring Rights, as amended.
Denmark	Law of 14 June 1995 (No. 395) on Copyright in Literary and Artistic Works and Neighbouring Rights, as amended.
Finland	Copyright Act of 8 July 1961, as amended.
France	Intellectual Property Code (Law No. 92-597 of 1 July 1992), as amended. Part I of the Code codifies the Law of 11 March 1957 on Literary and Artistic Property, the Law on Authors' Rights and the Law of 3 July 1985 on the Rights of Performers, Producers of Phonograms and Videograms and Audiovisual Communication Enterprises.
Germany	Copyright Law of 9 September 1965, as amended.
Greece	Law 2121/1993, on Copyright, Related Rights and Cultural Matters, as amended.
Ireland	Copyright and Related Rights Act 2000.
Italy	Law No. 633 of 22 April 1941 for the Protection of Copyright and Other Rights Connected with the Exercise Thereof (Copyright Statute), as amended.
Luxembourg	Law on Copyright, Neighbouring Rights and Databases of 18 April 2001.
Portugal	Code of Copyright and Neighbouring Rights (Law No. 45/85 of 17 September 1985), as amended.

(cont.)

Spain	Law on Intellectual Property (Royal Legislative Decree 1/1996, of 12 April 1996), as amended.
Sweden	Act on Copyright in Literary and Artistic Works (1960:729), as amended.
The Netherlands	Copyright Act 1912, as amended.
	Law of 18 March 1993 containing rules on the Protection of Performers, Phonogram Producers and Broadcasting Organisations.
United Kingdom	Copyright, Designs and Patents Act 1988, as amended.
	Duration of Copyright and Rights in Performances Regulations 1995 (SI 1995 No. 3297).
	Copyright and Related Rights Regulations 1996 (SI 1996 No. 2967).

Appendix 3: EC copyright directives

Council Directive 91/250/EEC of 14 May 1991 on the legal protection of computer programs, OJ L 122, 17 May 1991, p. 42

Council Directive 92/100/EEC of 19 November 1992 on rental right and lending right and on certain rights related to copyright in the field of intellectual property, OJ L 346, 27 November 1992, p. 61

Council Directive 93/83/EEC of 27 September 1993 on the coordination of certain rules concerning copyright and rights related to copyright applicable to satellite broadcasting and cable retransmission, OJ L 248, 6 October 1993, p. 15

Council Directive 93/98/EEC of 29 October 1993 harmonising the term of protection of copyright and certain related rights, OJ L 290, 24 November 1993, p. 9

Directive 96/9/EC of the European Parliament and of the Council of 11 March 1996 on the legal protection of databases, OJ L 77, 27 March 1996, p. 20

Directive 2001/29/EC of the European Parliament and of the Council of 22 May 2001 on the harmonisation of certain aspects of copyright and related rights in the information society, OJ L 167, 22 June 2001, p. 10

Directive 2001/84/EC of the European Parliament and of the Council of 27 September 2001 on the resale right for the benefit of the author of an original work of art, OJ L 272, 13 October 2001, p. 32

Appendix 4: Status of the adherence of EU Member States to international copyright conventions

BERNE CONVENTION

Berne Convention for the Protection of Literary and Artistic Works (1886), completed at Paris (1896), revised at Berlin (1908), completed at Berne (1914), revised at Rome (1928), Brussels (1948), Stockholm (1967) and Paris (1971), and amended in 1979. Status of adherence of EU Member States as of 14 March 2001.

State	Date on which State became party to the Convention	Latest Act of the Convention to which State is party	Date on which State became party to that Act
Austria	1 October 1920	Paris	21 August 1982
Belgium	5 December 1887	Paris	29 September 1999
Denmark	1 July 1903	Paris	30 June 1979
Finland	1 April 1928	Paris	1 November 1986
France	5 December 1887	Paris	Articles 1–21: 10 October 1974
		Paris	Articles 22–38: 15 December 1972
Germany	5 December 1887	Paris	Articles 1–21: 10 October 1974[a]
		Paris	Articles 22–38: 22 January 1974
Greece	9 November 1920	Paris	8 March 1976
Ireland	5 October 1927	Brussels	5 July 1959
		Stockholm	Articles 22–38: 21 December 1970
Italy	5 December 1887	Paris	14 November 1979
Luxembourg	20 June 1888	Paris	20 April 1975
Netherlands	1 November 1912	Paris	Articles 1–21: 30 January 1986
		Paris	Articles 22–38: 10 January 1975
Portugal	29 March 1911	Paris	12 January 1979[b]

(*cont.*)

State	Date on which State became party to the Convention	Latest Act of the Convention to which State is party	Date on which State became party to that Act
Spain	5 December 1887	Paris	Articles 1–21: 10 October 1974
		Paris	Articles 22–38: 19 February 1974
Sweden	1 August 1904	Paris	Articles 1–21: 10 October 1974
		Paris	Articles 22–38: 20 September 1973
United Kingdom	5 December 1887	Paris	2 January 1990[c]

Source: WIPO. The list is regularly updated on the WIPO website, www.wipo.org.
Notes:
[a] WIPO note: 'This State has declared that it admits the application of the Appendix of the Paris Act to works of which it is the State of origin by States which have made a declaration under article VI(1)(i) of the Appendix or a notification under article I of the Appendix. The declarations took effect on October 18, 1973.'
[b] WIPO note: 'Pursuant to the provisions of article 14*bis*(2)(c) of the Paris Act, this State has made a declaration to the effect that the undertaking by authors to bring contributions to the making of a cinematographic work must be in a written agreement. This declaration was received on 5 November 1986.'
[c] WIPO note: 'This State has declared that it admits the application of the Appendix of the Paris Act to works of which it is the State of origin by States which have made a declaration under article VI(1)(i) of the Appendix or a notification under article I of the Appendix. The declarations took effect on September 27, 1971.'

UNIVERSAL COPYRIGHT CONVENTION

Universal Copyright Convention adopted at Geneva in 1952, revised at Paris in 1971. Status of adherence of EU Member States as of 1 January 2000.

State	Geneva text and its three protocols	Paris text and its two protocols
Austria	2 April 1957	14 May 1982
Belgium	31 May 1960	
Denmark	9 November 1961	11 April 1979
Finland	16 January 1963	1 August 1986 (not to 1st and 2nd protocols)
France	14 October 1955	1 September 1972
Germany	3 June 1955	18 October 1973
Greece	24 May 1963	

(*cont.*)

State	Geneva text and its three protocols	Paris text and its two protocols
Ireland	20 October 1958	
Italy	24 October 1956 (19 December 1966 for the 1st protocol)	25 October 1979[a]
Luxembourg	15 July 1955	
Netherlands	22 March 1967	30 August 1985
Portugal	25 September 1956	30 April 1981
Spain	27 October 1954 (not to 1st and 3rd protocols)	10 April 1974[b]
Sweden	1 April 1961	27 June 1973
United Kingdom	27 June 1957	15 May 1972

Source: UNESCO

Notes:

[a] Declaration with reference to article IV, paragraph 4.

[b] Declaration on the second protocol.

ROME CONVENTION

International Convention for the Protection of Performers, Producers of Phonograms and Broadcasting Organisations of 26 October 1961. Status of adherence of EU Member States as of 15 January 2001.

State	Date on which State became party to the Convention	Declarations made under the articles mentioned hereafter[a]
Austria	9 June 1973	Article 16(1)(a)(iii) and (iv) and 1(b) [1973, p. 67]
Belgium	2 October 1999	Articles 5(3) (concerning articles 5(1)(c)), 6(2) and 16(1)(a)(iii) and (iv) [1999, p. 119]
Denmark	23 September 1965	Articles 6(2), 16(1)(a)(ii) and (iv) and 17 [1965, p. 214]
Finland	21 October 1983	Articles 16(1)(a)(i), (ii) and (iv) and 17 [1983, p. 287 and 1994, p. 152]
France	3 July 1987	Articles 5(3) (concerning articles 5(1)(c)) and 16(1)(a)(iii) and (iv) [1987, p. 184]
Germany	21 October 1966	Articles 5(3) (concerning articles 5(1)(b)) and 16(1)(a)(iv) [1966, p. 237]

(cont.)

State	Date on which State became party to the Convention	Declarations made under the articles mentioned hereafter[a]
Greece	6 January 1993	
Ireland	19 September 1979	Articles 5(3) (concerning articles 5(1)(b)), 6(2) and 16(1)(a)(ii) [1979, p. 218]
Italy	8 April 1975	Articles 6(2), 16(1)(a)(ii), (iii) and (iv), 16(1)(b) and 17 [1975, p. 44]
Luxembourg	25 February 1976	
Netherlands	7 October 1993	Article 16(1)(a)(iii) and (iv) [1993, p. 253]
Portugal		
Spain	14 November 1991	Articles 5(3) (concerning articles 5(1)(c)), 6(2) and 16(1)(a)(iii) and (iv) [1991, p. 221]
Sweden	18 May 1964	Article 16(1)(a)(iv) [1962, p. 211; 1986, p. 382]
United Kingdom	18 May 1964	Articles 5(3) (concerning articles 5(1)(b)), 6(2) and 16(1)(a)(ii), (iii) and (iv) [1963, p. 244]

Source: WIPO. The list is regularly updated on the WIPO website, at www.wipo.org.
Note: Reference are to publication in *Le Droit d'auteur* (Copyright) for the years 1962 to 1964, in *Copyright* for the years 1965 to 1994, in *Industrial Property and Copyright* until May 1998 and, in *Intellectual Property Laws and Treaties* since June 1998.

GENEVA CONVENTION ON PHONOGRAMS

Convention for the Protection of Producers of Phonograms Against Unauthorised Duplication of Their Phonograms of 29 October 1971. Status of adherence of EU Member States as of 2 March 2001.

State	Date on which State became party to the Convention
Austria	9 June 1973
Belgium	
Denmark	24 March 1977
Finland[a]	18 April 1973
France	18 April 1973
Germany	18 May 1974
Greece	9 February 1994
Ireland	

(*cont.*)

State	Date on which State became party to the Convention
Italy[b]	24 March 1977
Luxembourg	8 March 1976
Netherlands	12 October 1993
Portugal	
Spain	24 August 1974
Sweden	18 April 1973
United Kingdom	18 April 1973

Source: WIPO. The list is regularly updated on the WIPO site, at www.wipo.org.

Notes:

[a] WIPO note: 'This State has declared, in accordance with article 7(4) of the Convention, that it will apply the criterion according to which it affords protection to producers of phonograms solely on the basis of the place of first fixation instead of the criterion of the nationality of the producer.'

[b] WIPO note: 'This State has declared, in accordance with article 7(4) of the Convention, that it will apply the criterion according to which it affords protection to producers of phonograms solely on the basis of the place of first fixation instead of the criterion of the nationality of the producer.'

BRUSSELS CONVENTION

Convention Relating to the Distribution of Programme-Carrying Signals Transmitted by Satellite, Brussels, 21 May 1974. Status of adherence of EU Member States as of 15 January 2001.

State	Date on which State became party to the Convention
Austria	6 August 1982
Belgium	
Denmark	
Finland	
France	
Germany[a]	25 August 1979

(*cont.*)

State	Date on which State became party to the Convention
Greece	22 October 1991
Ireland	
Italy[b]	7 July 1981
Luxembourg	
Netherlands	
Portugal	11 March 1996
Spain	
Sweden	
United Kingdom	

Source: WIPO. The list is regularly updated on the WIPO website, www.wipo.org.

Notes:

[a] WIPO note: 'With a declaration, pursuant to article 2(2) of the Convention, that the protection accorded under article 2(1) is restricted in its territory to a period of twenty-five years after the expiry of the calendar year in which the transmission by satellite has occurred.'

[b] WIPO note: 'With a declaration, pursuant to article 2(2) of the Convention, that the protection accorded under article 2(1) is restricted in its territory to a period of twenty-five years after the expiry of the calendar year in which the transmission by satellite has occurred.'

TRIPs AGREEMENT

All Member States of the EU became members of the World Trade Organisation on 1 January 1995, and consequently became parties to the TRIPs Agreement on the same date.

WIPO COPYRIGHT TREATY 1996

As at 29 March 2001, this treaty was not yet in force.

WIPO PERFORMANCES AND PHONOGRAMS TREATY 1996

As at 29 March 2001, this treaty was not yet in force.

Appendix 5: US copyright relations with EU Member States

AUSTRIA

Bilateral agreement of 20 September 1907
Berne Convention (Paris)
Universal Copyright Convention (Geneva + Paris)
Brussels Convention
Geneva Convention on Phonograms
WTO

BELGIUM

Bilateral agreement of 1 July 1891
Berne Convention (Paris)
Universal Copyright Convention (Geneva)
WTO

DENMARK

Bilateral agreement of 8 May 1893
Berne Convention (Paris)
Universal Copyright Convention (Geneva + Paris)
Geneva Convention on Phonograms
WTO

FINLAND

Bilateral agreement of 1 January 1929
Berne Convention (Paris)
Universal Copyright Convention (Geneva + Paris)
Geneva Convention on Phonograms
WTO

FRANCE

Bilateral agreement of 1 July 1891
Berne Convention (Paris)

Universal Copyright Convention (Geneva + Paris)
Geneva Convention on Phonograms
WTO

GERMANY

Bilateral agreement of 15 April 1892
Berne Convention (Paris)
Universal Copyright Convention (Geneva + Paris)
Brussels Convention
Geneva Convention on Phonograms
WTO

GREECE

Bilateral agreement of 1 March 1932
Berne Convention (Paris)
Universal Copyright Convention (Geneva)
Brussels Convention
Geneva Convention on Phonograms
WTO

IRELAND

Bilateral agreement of 1 October 1929
Berne Convention (Brussels)
Universal Copyright Convention (Geneva)
Geneva Convention on Phonograms
WTO

ITALY

Bilateral agreement of 31 October 1892
Berne Convention (Paris)
Universal Copyright Convention (Geneva + Paris)
Brussels Convention
Geneva Convention on Phonograms
WTO

LUXEMBOURG

Bilateral agreement of 20 June 1888
Berne Convention (Paris)
Universal Copyright Convention (Geneva)

Geneva Convention on Phonograms
WTO

NETHERLANDS

Bilateral agreement of 20 November 1899
Berne Convention (Paris)
Universal Copyright Convention (Geneva + Paris)
Geneva Convention on Phonograms
WTO

PORTUGAL

Bilateral agreement of 20 July 1893
Berne Convention (Paris)
Universal Copyright Convention (Geneva + Paris)
Brussels Convention
WTO

SPAIN

Bilateral agreement of 10 July 1895
Berne Convention (Paris)
Universal Copyright Convention (Geneva + Paris)
Geneva Convention on Phonograms
WTO

SWEDEN

Bilateral agreement of 1 June 1911
Berne Convention (Paris)
Universal Copyright Convention (Geneva + Paris)
Geneva Convention on Phonograms
WTO

UNITED KINGDOM

Bilateral agreement of 1 July 1891
Buenos Aires Convention of 1910
Berne Convention (Paris)
Universal Copyright Convention (Geneva + Paris)
Geneva Convention on Phonograms
WTO

Source: United States Copyright Office, 'International Copyright Relations of the USA' (Circular 38a, May 1999)

Index

abuse of dominant position, 265, 266
abuse of right, 268–9, 325, 326
adaptations
  audiovisual works, 218, 220–3
  author's rights tradition, 223–6
  authorship, 41, 42, 43, 135, 158
  Berne Convention, 217, 218, 240
  cinematographic films, 219–20
  contracts, 180–1
  copyright infringement, 16, 17, 31, 37,
    219, 220–3
  copyright protection, 13, 16, 17, 20, 31,
    37, 41, 43, 218–19
  copyright transfer, 48
  dramatic works, 13, 37
  economic rights, 49, 211
  exclusive rights, 24, 211, 217–26
  exploitation rights, 47
  France, 223–6
  Ireland, 211, 218, 219, 220
  literary works, 13, 16, 17, 20
  moral rights, 319
  presumption of assignment, 218
  rental rights, 242
  reproduction rights, 211
  uncontemplated uses, 190
  underlying work, 218
  United Kingdom, 211, 218, 219–23
  videograms, 218
advertising
  contracts, 176
  European Union (EU), 305
  musical works, 328–9, 331, 335–6
  remuneration, 205
  television, 304–5
  videos, 295
advertising cuts, 4, 289, 304–5, 315, 327
artistic directors, 150, 160
artistic works
  Berne Convention, 228
  cinematographic works, 19, 21
  co-authorship, 150

copyright infringement, 221
costumes, 102, 167, 222
decor, 102, 167
destruction, 303
distribution rights, 240
drawings, 102
initial ownership, 170
limitations, 88, 111
moral rights, 295
paternity, 309
photographs, 17
public display, 210
rental rights, 170, 200
story-boards, 103
term of protection, 121
titles, 107
assignment
  contributory works, 28, 37, 133
  director authorship, 27
  distribution rights, 88
  dramatic works, 27
  future works, 48, 134, 189–90, 285
  legal *see cessio legis*
  modes of exploitation, 29, 188
  musical works, 44
  neighbouring rights, 101
  presumption *see* presumption of
    assignment
  producers, 27, 37, 44, 47, 131, 133,
    134, 161, 162, 165, 170
  production companies, 27, 28
  property rights, 355–6
  re-assignment, 178
  remuneration, 42, 134
  rental rights, 88, 165, 169, 200
  reversion, 179, 191, 194
  term of protection, 179–80
  videograms, 101
  writing, 180–1
audiovisual industry, 1, 2
audiovisual works
  accessory nature, 80

audiovisual works (*cont.*)
  adaptations, 218, 220–3
  animation, 75, 76
  borderline works, 79–84
  cumulation of copyright, 86
  definitions, 44, 75–7
  direct/indirect protection, 65
  double protection, 63–5, 85–7, 100, 123
  dramatic works, 34, 36–7, 65, 67–74, 97, 137, 141–53, 220–3
  fixation, 44, 60, 74, 120, 123, 344–7
  moral rights, 43, 291–2, 293–4
  moving images, 76
  neighbouring rights, 39, 44, 59–60, 77
  originality, 35, 96–7
  photographs, 34
  presentation, 84–8
  public performance, 2
  recordings, 84–8
  remuneration, 44
  reversionary rights, 28
  screen displays, 79
  subject-matter of protection, 66–7
  term of protection, 37, 55, 64, 120–9
  videogames *see* videogames
Australia, 31, 32, 132, 234
Austria
  cessio legis, 162, 166, 186
  co-authorship, 318
  copyright protection, 18, 49–50
  copyright transfer, 177, 186
  economic rights, 155
  equitable remuneration, 195
  initial ownership, 162
  moral rights, 318, 320, 338–9
  performers, 338–9
  photographs, 18, 49, 50
  private copying, 280
  public lending rights, 247
  subject-matter of protection, 76, 102, 109
  term of protection, 50
  unfair competition, 84
authorial rights
  economic rights, 39
  exploitation, 133
  meaning, 174
  remuneration *see* equitable remuneration
  residual rights, 133
author's rights tradition
  adaptations, 223–6
  authorship, 153–61, 165–6
  broadcasting, 117–18
  commissioned works, 172
  communication to the public, 238–9

construction of grants, 48, 187–9, 223
contracts, 173–4
copyright tradition compared, 21, 60–1, 132–5
creativity, 4, 21, 38, 61, 132, 153–5, 161
distribution rights, 245–7
employment, 38–9, 171–2, 174
entrepreneurial copyright, 61
European Union (EU), 5, 57
evolution, 38–58
fixation, 78–9
foreign film works, 380–4
France *see* France
historical development, 153–5
integrity, 321–30
licensing, 7
moral rights, 21, 38, 284–6, 316–37
neighbouring rights, 3, 37, 39, 59, 101, 117, 161
originality, 78, 87
overview, 38–9
paternity, 330–2
producer authorship, 21, 133, 153–5, 161
producers, 21, 38, 39, 133, 153–5
protected uses, 7
reproduction rights, 216–17, 245
romantic vision, 21, 156
subject-matter of protection, 60, 75–9
television formats, 82–3
titles, 105
underlying work, 170–2, 319
videograms, 100–2, 218
authorship
  'film' (absent producer), 140
  adaptations, 41, 42, 43, 135, 158
  author's rights tradition, 153–61, 165–6
  authorship entitlement, 142–3
  Berne Convention, 131–2
  cinematographic works, 40–1, 46, 168
  co-authors *see* co-authorship
  collective bargaining, 168, 174
  contract for services, 164
  contract of service, 40, 153, 164
  creative *see* creativity
  decor, 168, 184
  definition, 139, 369–71
  derivative works, 86
  determination, 143–4
  dialogue, 41, 42, 55, 121, 122, 135, 146–7, 158, 170
  directors *see* director authorship
  dramatic works, 13, 27–9, 32, 141–53
  European Commission, 135–6
  European Union (EU), 135–7

foreign *see* foreign authors
France, 153–4, 370
harmonisation, 135–6
identification *see* paternity
initial ownership, 142–3, 170
Ireland, 141, 165
joint authors *see* joint authorship
legal persons, 27, 38, 41, 154
Luxembourg, 52, 153, 160–1, 318
material time, 378–9
moral rights *see* moral rights
multiple claims, 32, 138
musical works, 41, 43, 46, 55, 121, 122,
     135, 148–9, 158, 167, 170
natural persons, 41, 136, 153, 154
Netherlands, 50, 155, 156, 158, 318
photographs, 26–7
post-1994 films, 140–1, 164
pre-1994 films, 138–9, 164
pre-existing works, 41, 43, 158, 184
producers *see* producer authorship
production companies, 20, 154
publishers, 41
remuneration, 21, 39, 42, 43, 134
rental rights, 5, 54, 64, 136–7, 165, 170,
     241, 242
satellite broadcasting, 5
scenarios, 28, 41, 42, 46, 160
screenplays, 55, 121, 122, 170
screenwriters, 142, 167
scripts, 28, 135, 146–7, 152, 158, 168
term of protection, 29, 64, 121, 122, 142
United Kingdom, 137–53, 164–5, 370,
     378–9

Belgium
co-authorship, 43, 134, 160, 318
collecting societies, 207
copyright protection, 17, 43, 45, 100
copyright transfer, 181, 189, 192
distribution rights, 246–7
economic rights, 211
employment, 172, 190
equitable remuneration, 195, 205, 358
exemptions, 256, 272, 274, 278
future works, 189
integrity, 321, 322, 323, 360
moral rights, 318, 320, 335, 336, 360,
     362
neighbouring rights, 348
performers, 340, 348, 351, 354, 358,
     360, 362
photographs, 17
presumption of assignment, 166, 176,
     184

private copying, 280, 281–2
public lending rights, 247
reproduction rights, 217
subject-matter of protection, 76, 100,
     101, 109, 118
term of protection, 124, 125, 126, 127,
     128
transmissibility, 177
uncontemplated uses, 190
unfair competition, 84
Berne Convention
adaptations, 217, 218, 240
artistic works, 228
authorship, 131–2
Berlin conference (1908), 10, 18–21
broadcasting, 107, 108, 195, 228
cinematographic works, 18–21, 50, 228,
     240
communication to the public, 227–9
compromise, 134
contributory works, 168, 182
distribution rights, 240
documentaries, 40
dramatic works, 19, 1240
equitable remuneration, 195
exemptions, 256–8
foreign film works, 365–9, 371–4,
     380–2, 384–5
formalities, 20–1, 40
France, 16, 18, 40
initial ownership, 168, 182
international tensions, 3
licensing, 228, 229, 257
literary works, 228, 240
moral rights, 286–8, 289, 292, 297,
     321
national treatment, 367–9
Netherlands, 50
newsreels, 40
ownership, 132, 162–4, 369–70, 371–2
Paris Act, 120, 213
paternity, 330
photographs, 19, 20, 40, 50, 228
presumption of assignment, 162–4, 182
publication defined, 373–4
related rights, 228
reproduction rights, 212–13, 257
Rome conference (1928), 107, 339
rule of shorter term, 384–5
Russia, 367
Stockholm Act, 162
subject-matter of protection, 61, 63
term of protection, 20, 120, 121
United Kingdom, 22, 23, 33, 89, 218
United States, 367

broadcasting
see also television
author's rights tradition, 117–18
Berne Convention, 107, 108, 195, 228
broadcasting organisations, 117, 118
cable *see* cable television
copyright infringement, 35
copyright protection, 32, 33
Council of Europe, 109–10
definitions, 112, 227, 234
digital *see* digital broadcasting
distribution rights, 111
entrepreneurial copyright, 85
fixation, 30, 40, 88, 108, 111, 344
harmonisation, 107
interactivity, 111, 117, 118
lawful receipt, 112, 113
licensing, 111, 195, 227, 228, 229,
    231, 234, 257, 341
moral rights, 296
most-favoured-nation, 108
national treatment, 107
neighbouring rights, 3, 39, 117
new technologies, 6, 30–1, 208
originality, 35
Part II copyright, 32
performing rights, 208, 226–7
place of transmission, 379
public *see* communication to the public
public performance, 30
radio, 107
rental rights, 110, 111–12, 118
reproduction rights, 111
Rome Convention (1961), 107–8,
    111, 385
satellite *see* satellite broadcasting
subject-matter of protection, 107–18
sui generis works, 33
term of protection, 108, 110, 112
TRIPs Agreement, 108
wireless telegraphy, 112–13, 114, 227
Brussels Convention (1974), 109

cable retransmission
collecting societies, 112, 197, 198,
    231
communication to the public, 229,
    230–1, 232, 237, 239
contracts, 111–12, 188
encryption, 234, 238
equitable remuneration, 55, 197, 198
European Union (EU), 5, 55, 111–12,
    229, 230–1, 342–3
France, 188
licensing, 230, 231, 232

must-carry duty, 234, 237–8
passive distribution, 227
performers, 342–3
United Kingdom, 234
cable television
cable programme service, 113, 115, 237
copyright infringement, 35, 113
copyright protection, 32
definition, 113, 117
deregulation, 1
entrepreneurial copyright, 85
European Union (EU), 5, 110, 111,
    118, 175
exceptions, 113
Internet services, 115, 116, 117, 227
moral rights, 296
neighbouring rights, 3, 39
originality, 35
ownership, 55
related rights, 112
rental rights, 111–12
retransmission rights *see* cable
    retransmission
websites, 116, 117
cameramen, 149
Canada, 31, 32, 72, 73–4
cartoons, 103, 104
causative contribution/intent, 98
CD-ROMs, 79, 80, 92, 271
cessio legis
Austria, 162, 166, 186
European Union (EU), 163, 169, 342
exploitation, 174, 186
initial ownership, 162
Italy, 162, 166, 186
joint authorship, 182
Luxembourg, 166, 187
rental rights, 342
characters
cartoons, 103, 104, 277
merchandising, 104
names, 104
spin-offs, 222
unfair competition, 104, 277
cinematograph production, terminology,
    22, 24–5
Cinématographe, 9, 10
cinematographer, 149, 150
cinematographic films
see also underlying work
adaptations, 219–20
copyright infringement, 35
definition, 66, 88–91
dramatic works, 22, 23, 34
entrepreneurial copyright, 85

fixation, 99
Ireland, 37–8, 99–100, 141
literary works, 22
moral rights, 41–2, 284–337
moving images, 89–92
musical works, 22
Part II copyright, 32
recording technology, 91
recordings, 89, 91, 92, 218
scenarios *see* scenarios
soundtracks, 34, 95
special effects, 167
subject-matter of protection, 88–99
term of protection, 34, 95
terminology, 10
cinematographic works
artistic works, 19, 21
as photographs *see* photographs
authorship, 40–1, 46, 168
Berne Convention, 18–21, 50, 228, 240
fixation, 35, 49, 123
France, 15, 17, 40, 75
literary works, 19, 40
originality, 50
term of protection, 40
terminology, 10
United Kingdom, 11, 22–3
co-authorship
see also authorship
artistic directors, 150, 160
artistic works, 150
Austria, 318
Belgium, 43, 134, 160, 318
collaboration, 28, 42, 135, 143–4, 147
collective works *see* collective works
composite works, 32, 135, 148, 154
contributions *see* contributory works
creativity, 134
Denmark, 156, 157, 318
determination, 134–5
directors *see* director authorship
directors of photography, 149–50, 152, 318
editors, 149, 152
European Union (EU), 54, 55, 121, 136, 137
evaluation of claims, 144
Finland, 156, 157, 318
France, 41, 42–3, 134, 135, 158–60, 318
Germany, 48, 49, 135, 156, 157, 318
Greece, 318
independent contractors, 165
Ireland, 38, 52
Italy, 46–7, 135, 160, 318

joint authors *see* joint authorship
lists
disparities, 206
France, 42–3, 135, 158–60, 318
no list, 50, 156–8
rental rights, 136–7
Luxembourg, 52, 318
moral rights, 47, 296, 317–18, 319
musical works, 148–9, 158, 160
Netherlands, 50, 156, 158, 318
originality, 143
ownership, 29
performers, 151–2
Portugal, 160, 318
presumption, 135, 136, 146, 154, 158–9, 160
producer authorship, 145–6, 164, 170
Scandinavia, 51
screenwriters, 146–7
Spain, 160, 318
Sweden, 156, 157, 318
technicians, 152, 156
television, 145, 150, 152
theatrical films, 149, 150, 152
tracing, 29
United Kingdom, 28, 29, 37, 38, 52, 135, 137, 140–1, 143–53, 164, 170
United States, 134, 145
collecting societies
authorisations, 218
Belgium, 207
cable retransmission, 112, 197, 198, 231
competition law, 206–7
digital rights, 199
equitable remuneration, 196, 197–9, 280
European Union (EU), 54, 175, 196, 206–7, 230, 231
foreign authors, 283
France, 44, 149, 180, 184, 197, 203–4, 246, 281
Germany, 157
licensing, 87, 184, 198, 199, 206–7
musical works, 148–9, 167
private copying, 198, 280, 281, 283
proportional remuneration, 203
public performance, 198
rental rights, 198, 200, 356
reproduction rights, 204
satellite broadcasting, 230, 231
television, 198
collective works
see also co-authorship; contributory works

collective works (*cont.*)
  Finland, 51
  France, 41, 80, 154, 158
  initial ownership, 171
  Netherlands, 50, 155
  organised collective activity, 48
  producers, 41, 48, 154, 155
colourisation
  derivative works, 98
  moral rights, 4, 289, 303, 315, 318, 325
  subject-matter of protection, 80–1, 98
Commission of the European
      Communities *see* European
      Commission
commissioned works
  assignment *see* presumption of
      assignment
  author's rights tradition, 172
  copyright infringement, 212
  musical works, 121, 122, 148–9, 158,
      167, 170
  performers, 359
  photographs, 47
communication to the public
  agreements, 188
  author's rights tradition, 238–9
  Berne Convention, 227–9
  cable retransmission, 229, 230–1, 232,
      237, 239
  copyright infringement, 231
  digital networks, 227, 228, 234–7, 239
  dramatico-musical works, 228
  European Union (EU), 88, 100, 111,
      169, 208, 229–33, 349
  exclusive rights, 210, 226–39
  exhaustion, 232, 264
  France, 188, 238
  Germany, 238
  hotel rooms, 231, 234, 236
  Information Society Directive, 231–2
  Ireland, 237–8
  Italy, 239
  making available, 237
  Netherlands, 239
  on-demand transmissions, 228, 232, 239
  performers, 229, 349
  phonograms, 229, 230, 232, 349
  principal rights, 211
  rental rights, 111, 229
  rights management information, 248–9
  satellite broadcasting, 229–30, 237
  Spain, 238
  United Kingdom, 233–4
  video-on-demand, 235, 236, 237
  videograms, 101–2

competition law
  see also unfair competition
  abuse of dominant position, 265, 266
  collecting societies, 206–7
  concerted practices, 265
  limitations, 264–6
computer programs
  European Union (EU), 78, 215, 241,
      242, 248
  exemptions, 258
  games *see* videogames
  integrity, 299
  moving images, 90–1
  originality, 78
  paternity, 310
  pre-programmed animation, 92
  private copying, 270
  remuneration, 242
  rental rights, 241, 242, 243
  technological measures, 249
computers
  computer imagery, 5–6
  memory (RAM), 214, 216
Conditional Access Directive, 251–2
consents
  exploitation, 218
  moral rights, 311–12, 335–6, 362
  performers, 352, 353
contract for services, 164
contract of service/employment
  see also employment
  authorship, 40, 153, 164
  ownership, 27, 37, 142, 143, 172
contracts
  adaptations, 180–1
  advertising, 176
  author's rights tradition, 173–4
  bargaining power, 168, 174
  cable retransmission, 111–12, 188
  contributory works, 27, 40, 142
  copyright transfer, 43, 173, 175–6
  duration, 134
  duty to produce/distribute, 191–2
  European Union (EU), 173, 174
  film rights, 42
  freedom of contract, 173, 288, 289
  freelance workers, 164
  general law, 173, 174
  implied terms, 142–3
  independent contractors, 164, 165, 170
  lex contractus, 193, 372
  licences *see* licensing
  mandatory rules, 194–5
  modes of exploitation, 188
  performance, 176, 180

production *see* production contracts
publishing *see* publishing contracts
remuneration, 199, 202
rescission, 179, 193, 201, 317
Rome Convention (1980), 193–5
strict performance, 179
talent agents, 180
television formats, 81
theatrical films, 181–2
uncontemplated uses, 190
contributory works
    see also co-authorship; collective works
    assignment, 28, 37, 133
    atomisation of inputs, 130
    Berne Convention, 168, 182
    collective works *see* collective works
    compilations, 50, 155
    complexity, 130
    composite works, 32, 135, 148, 154
    contracts, 27, 40, 142
    creativity, 146
    derivative works, 98
    director authorship, 155–6
    dramatic works, 71
    employment, 131, 153, 164, 165
    independent contractors, 170
    independent exploitation, 130, 157
    moral rights, 49, 50, 291–2, 320
    organisation, 48
    performers, 35, 151–2
    presumption of assignment, 182
    separate/separable contributions, 130,
        134, 144, 146, 148, 157
    subject-matter of protection, 102–7
    term of protection, 95, 121, 123
    underlying work, 102–3, 167, 168
copyright infringement
    adaptations, 16, 17, 31, 37, 219, 220–3
    artistic works, 221
    broadcasting, 35
    cable television, 35, 113
    cinematographic films, 35
    commissioned works, 212
    communication to the public, 231
    decor, 222
    double protection, 87
    dramatic incidents, 31, 221, 222
    dramatic works, 17, 31, 220–3
    exclusive rights, 177, 209, 211–12
    fair use, 269
    film frames, 93
    France, 223–6
    freedom of expression, 267–8
    images lifted, 31
    infringing acts, 209

issue of copies to the public, 235
joint ownership, 153
jump cutting, 70
literary works, 224–5
musical works, 221, 222–3
originality, 222
parody, 277
photographs, 31, 216
plots, 31, 221, 222
pre-existing works, 10
private copying, 270
public performance, 31
secondary infringement, 235, 253
substantiality, 97, 215, 216, 221, 222
unauthorised copying, 31
underlying work, 85, 212, 298
unlicensed theatres, 10
copyright protection
    adaptations, 13, 16, 17, 20, 31, 37, 41,
        43, 218–19
    broadcasting, 32, 33
    computer imagery, 5–6
    deposit, 16, 17
    dramatic works, 12–14, 17, 23–4, 34
    early national legislation, 11–18
    early stages (1896-1908), 10–21
    GATT, 2
    modern period (1908-1992), 21–58
    musical works, 36, 85
    photographs, 12, 15–18, 20, 23, 24, 34
    scripts, 12–13, 25, 36, 218
    sound recordings, 36, 85
    subject matter *see* subject-matter of
        protection
copyright tradition
    authorship, 4
    authorship' rights compared, 21, 60–1,
        132–5
    Ireland *see* Ireland
    UK *see* United Kingdom
    USA *see* United States
copyright transfer
    adaptations, 48
    applicable law, 193–5
    assignment *see* assignment
    Austria, 177, 186
    Belgium, 181, 189, 192
    construction of grants, 48, 187–9, 223
    contracts, 43, 173, 175–6
    Denmark, 192
    divisibility, 179
    duty to produce/distribute, 191–2
    Finland, 192
    formalities, 180–1
    France, 178, 180–2, 187–93

copyright transfer (*cont.*)
  future works, 48, 134, 189–90
  Germany, 48, 177, 181, 189–90
  Greece, 181
  harmonisation, 174, 175
  introduction, 172, 174–5
  Italy, 182, 186, 189
  mortis causa, 175, 177
  Netherlands, 181
  performing rights, 43
  Portugal, 189, 192
  presumption *see* presumption of
    assignment
  producers, 191–3
  registration/priority, 181–2
  regulation, 21
  reversion, 179, 191, 194
  Spain, 181, 182, 189, 190, 192
  Sweden, 192
  Switzerland, 177–8
  third parties, 178–9
  transmissibility, 176–8
  uncontemplated uses, 190–1
  United Kingdom, 176, 182–3, 187
Copyright Tribunal, 126, 200, 356–7
costumes, 102, 167, 222
Council of Europe, 109–10
counterfeiting, 57, 58
creativity
  see also originality
  author's rights tradition, 4, 21, 38, 61,
    132, 153–5, 161
  co-authorship, 134
  contributory works, 146
  creative artists, 27
  creative authorship, 4, 21, 27, 28, 50,
    60, 61, 132, 141–55, 161
  director authorship, 146
  historical development, 153–5
  producer authorship, 144–6
  subject-matter of protection, 60
  videogames, 79

databases
  European Union (EU), 118–19, 251,
    259
  exemptions, 259
  multimedia, 119
decor
  artistic works, 102, 167
  authorship, 168, 184
  copyright infringement, 222
  reproduction rights, 188
defamation, 277, 290, 304
Denmark

  see also Scandinavia
  co-authorship, 156, 157, 318
  copyright protection, 51
  copyright transfer, 192
  distribution rights, 245
  equitable remuneration, 205
  exemptions, 272
  moral rights, 318
  performers, 339
  presumption of assignment, 166, 186
  private copying, 280, 282
  producer authorship, 155
  re-assignment, 178
  subject-matter of protection, 102,
    109, 118
  term of protection, 120
  transmissibility, 177
deregulation, 1
derivative works
  authorship, 86
  colourisation, 98
  dramatic works, 73, 80
  enhancement, 80
  exploitation, 218
  fixation, 99
  formats, 80, 98, 99
  free use of original, 218
  originality, 97–9
  performers, 48, 170, 339
  pre-existing works, 86, 147, 218–19
  prequels, 218
  producers, 85
  remakes, 184, 218
  rental rights, 242
  scripts, 86, 147
  sequels, 184, 218
  soundtracks, 94
  spin-offs, 218, 222
dialogue
  see also scripts
  authorship, 41, 42, 55, 121, 122,
    135, 146–7, 158, 170
  dramatic works, 147
  moral rights, 297–8, 303–4
  translations, 297–8, 303–4
dictionaries, 154
digital copying, 215
digital enhancement, 98, 99
digital networks
  bulletin boards, 115, 235, 236
  communication to the public, 227,
    228, 234–7, 239
  downloading, 235, 236
  interactivity, 228
  Internet, 115, 116, 117, 227, 232

servers, 235, 236
subject-matter of protection, 111,
    114
technological development, 2
transmissions, 116
United Kingdom, 234–7
digital rights, 199
digitisation
    meaning, 6
    modes of exploitation, 209
    multimedia, 7
    private copying, 270, 271
    reproduction rights, 215
director authorship
    assignment, 27
    contributory works, 155–6
    creativity, 146
    dramatic works, 146
    European Union (EU), 54, 55, 56, 121,
        122, 136
    France, 41, 43, 155–6, 158
    Greece, 160
    Italy, 46
    musical works, 148
    ownership, 38
    rental rights, 5, 54, 165, 200, 242
    United Kingdom, 27, 28, 38, 56,
        140–1, 164
directors
    co-directors, 295–6
    directing actors, 151
    director's cut, 80, 98
    dramatic works, 36
    equitable remuneration, 199
    independent contractors, 165
    integrity, 294
    moral rights, 36, 155, 292, 294–5,
        308–9
    paternity, 294, 308, 309
directors of photography, 149–50, 152,
    318
distribution
    duty to produce/distribute, 191–2
    MMDS, 113, 116
    passive, 227
distribution rights
    artistic works, 240
    assignment, 88
    author's rights tradition, 245–7
    Belgium, 246–7
    Berne Convention, 240
    broadcasting, 111
    Denmark, 245
    European Union (EU), 169, 241–3
    exclusive rights, 240–7

exhaustion, 87, 244, 245, 264
France, 211, 353
Germany, 245
Greece, 245
harmonisation, 241–3
Information Society Directive, 242–3
Ireland, 245
Italy, 245
literary works, 240
neighbouring rights, 241
Netherlands, 245
performers, 341
Portugal, 245
principal rights, 210
producers, 87
rental rights, 241–2, 341
Spain, 245
Sweden, 245
TRIPs Agreement, 240–1
United Kingdom, 243–5
divulgation, 285, 319, 323, 329, 332–4,
    337, 362
documentaries
    Berne Convention, 40
    copyright protection, 49
    directors of photography, 150
    dramatic works, 72
    integrity, 325–6
    neighbouring rights, 46, 49
    originality, 78, 150
    photographs, 46, 48, 49
    subject-matter of protection, 72, 77
dramatic works
    see also theatrical films
    action/movement, 69
    adaptations, 13, 37
    assignment, 27
    audiovisual works, 34, 36–7, 65, 67–74,
        97, 137, 141–53, 220–3
    authorship, 13, 27–9, 32, 141–53
    Berne Convention, 19, 240
    cinematographic films, 22, 23, 34
    copyright infringement, 17, 31, 220–3
    copyright protection, 12–14, 17, 23–4,
        34
    definition, 24, 67–8
    derivative works, 73, 80
    dialogue, 147
    director authorship, 146
    directors, 36
    director's cut, 80
    documentaries, 72, 75
    dramatic entertainment, 68
    dramatic incidents, 31, 221, 222
    fixation, 12, 13, 25, 26

dramatic works (*cont.*)
  initial ownership, 170
  licensing, 37
  live play filmed, 23
  make-up, 222
  moral rights, 37, 143, 295–6
  multimedia, 79
  originality, 22, 23, 24, 73, 97
  ownership, 27, 28, 29
  performance, 68
  performing rights, 13, 14
  play-right, 13, 14
  plots, 31, 221, 222
  pop videos, 72
  producer's cut, 80
  rental rights, 170, 199
  scenarios, 34
  scènes-à-faire, 222
  scenic effects, 221, 222
  scripts, 25, 36, 69, 71, 102, 165, 167
  sketches, 34
  subject-matter of protection, 22–3,
      24–6, 65, 67–74
  television, 73
  television formats, 81
  term of protection, 14, 24, 29, 123
  videogames, 79
drawings, 102, 103
droit d'auteur see author's rights tradition
droit de suite, 210, 285, 335
dubbing, 47, 298, 303–4
duration *see* term of protection
DVD, 6, 119, 240

economic rights
  adaptations, 49, 211
  Austria, 155
  authors, 39
  Belgium, 211
  employment, 171
  equitable remuneration, 39
  foreign authors, 296, 370, 371
  France, 211, 353, 370
  Germany, 211, 353–4, 358–9
  illustrative lists, 211
  international obligations, 164
  Italy, 155
  moral rights, 285, 317
  Netherlands, 171, 211
  performers, 44, 50, 169, 345, 346,
      348–60
  Portugal, 211
  presumption of assignment, 133, 166,
      169, 349
  producers, 44, 49, 155
  remuneration *see* remuneration

Spain, 211
subject-matter of protection, 4, 210
Switzerland, 211
WIPO, 345, 346
Edison, Thomas Alva, 9
editors, 149, 152
education
  educational use, 198, 279
  teaching/research, 88, 111, 262–3
electronic commerce, 253–5, 260
employment
  assignment, 37
  author's rights tradition, 38–9, 171–2,
      174
  contracts *see* contract of
      service/employment
  contributory works, 131, 153, 164,
      165
  economic rights, 171
  France, 172, 357
  Germany, 172, 358–9
  moral rights, 171, 300
  paternity, 310
  producer authorship, 153
  producer ownership, 131, 161, 165,
      170, 183
entrepreneurial copyright
  author's rights tradition, 61
  broadcasting, 85
  cable television, 85
  cinematographic films, 85
  multiple authorship, 32, 138
  originality, 32
  producers, 84
  subject-matter of protection, 66
ephemeral fixation, 88, 111, 258, 260
ephemeral reproduction, 216, 217
equitable remuneration
  see also remuneration
  additional remuneration, 195
  Austria, 195
  authorial rights, 195–207
  Belgium, 195, 205, 358
  Berne Convention, 195
  bestseller clause, 195, 205
  collecting societies, 196, 197–9, 280
  Denmark, 205
  directors, 199
  economic rights, 39
  European Commission, 196
  European Union (EU), 5, 54, 55, 56,
      57, 169, 173, 175, 195–7
  exemptions, 260
  forms, 197–9
  France, 42, 127, 134, 195, 200–4
  Germany, 127, 195, 205, 282, 354

Greece, 195, 205
Ireland, 199, 200, 357
Italy, 47, 195, 205, 359
lump sums, 196, 202, 205, 349
merchandising, 204
Netherlands, 195, 205
performers, 342, 344, 347, 349, 356–7
photographs, 47
Portugal, 205
presumption of assignment, 134, 169
rental rights, 5, 54, 57, 169, 173, 175,
    183, 196, 199–200, 242, 342, 349,
    356–7
screenwriters, 199
Spain, 195, 204, 359
statutory royalty right, 195, 201, 202,
    285, 349
Sweden, 205
United Kingdom, 56, 183, 199–200,
    347, 356–7
European Commission
authorship, 135–6
collective management, 57, 207
cultural policy, 53
digitisation, 6
enforcement, 57–8
equitable remuneration, 196
Green Paper (1988), 53, 340
Green Paper (1995), 6, 58, 232, 287
Green Paper (1996), 55, 58, 207, 214,
    233, 287
moral rights, 58, 287
term of protection, 120–1
European Union (EU)
advertising, 305
author's rights tradition, 5, 57
authorship, 135–7
blank videotapes, 198
cable television, 5, 110, 111, 118, 175,
    228
cessio legis, 163, 169, 342
co-authorship, 54, 55, 121, 136
collecting societies, 54, 175, 196, 206–7,
    230, 231
communication to the public, 88, 100,
    111, 169, 208, 229–33, 349
computer programs, 78, 215, 241, 242,
    248
contracts, 173, 174
databases, 118–19, 251, 259
directives, 2, 5
director authorship, 54, 55, 56, 121,
    122, 136, 137
distribution rights, 169, 241–3
double protection, 63–5, 85–7, 100, 123
duration see term of protection

equitable remuneration, 5, 54, 55, 56,
    57, 169, 173, 175, 195–7
European Parliament, 121, 136
exemptions, 256, 258–66
exhaustion, 232, 244, 263–4
foreign film works, 365–6, 380–5
free movement of goods, 53, 78, 193,
    263–4
harmonisation see harmonisation
information society see Information
    Society Directive
intermediaries, 253–5, 260
Ireland, 5, 56
moral rights, 287–8
national treatment, 375, 376
ownership, 163–4
performers, 338–43, 347–8
presumption of assignment, 169, 175
public lending right, 87–8, 196, 241,
    341
rental rights see rental rights
reproduction rights, 169, 197, 214–15,
    260
rights management information, 248,
    249, 251
satellites see satellite broadcasting
subject-matter of protection, 62, 63–5
technological measures, 248, 249–51
United Kingdom, 5
exclusive rights
adaptation see adaptations
commercial designations, 106
communication see communication to
    the public
copyright infringement, 177, 209,
    211–12
definitions, 3, 209–12
distribution see distribution rights
exploitation, 177
France, 353
Germany, 210
Greece, 210
Information Society Directive, 88
Ireland, 209, 211
Italy, 210
media-specific rights, 209–10
performers, 341, 345, 351–4
photographs, 77
principal rights, 210
producers, 44, 49, 87, 88, 101, 102
reproduction see reproduction rights
right to use, 177
satellite broadcasting, 5, 118
structure, 212
United Kingdom, 209, 210–11, 351–3
videograms, 101, 102

exemptions
  Belgium, 256, 272, 274, 278
  Berne Convention, 256–8
  computer programs, 258
  criticism/review, 275, 276
  databases, 259
  definition, 4
  Denmark, 272
  equitable remuneration, 260
  European Union (EU), 256, 258–66
  fair compensation, 261–2, 281
  film works, 269–80
  Finland, 272
  France, 256, 272, 273–4, 275, 276–7,
    278, 279, 280, 373
  Germany, 272, 274, 275, 276, 278–9
  Greece, 272
  harmonisation, 258–9
  incidental inclusion, 278–9
  Ireland, 256, 269, 271, 273, 275, 280,
    361
  Italy, 274, 276
  library privileges, 256, 279–80
  Luxembourg, 272
  Netherlands, 272, 274, 276, 279
  news reporting, 257, 258, 275–6
  parody/satire, 276–8
  performance in restricted circles, 272–4
  Portugal, 272
  private copying, 253, 258, 270–2
  quotations, 275, 276
  rental rights, 258–9
  Spain, 272, 274, 276, 278, 280
  Sweden, 274, 276
  Switzerland, 278
  TRIPs Agreement, 257
  United Kingdom, 256, 269–71, 273,
    275, 278, 279
exhaustion
  communication to the public, 232, 264
  distribution rights, 87, 244, 245, 264
  European Union (EU), 232, 244, 263–4
  free movement of goods, 263–4
  public lending rights, 244
  TRIPs Agreement, 240
exhibition
  public exhibition, 16
  right of exhibition, 12
  theatrical exhibition, 197–8
exploitation
  adaptations, 47
  authorial rights, 133
  cessio legis, 174, 186
  consents, 218
  contributory works, 130, 157

costs, licensing, 87
derivative works, 218
dubbing rights, 47
exclusive rights, 177
joint ownership, 153
modes see modes of exploitation
multimedia, 87
non-exploitation, 329–30
pre-1995 exploitation, 125, 126
producers, 161
re-exploitation, 330
under-exploitation, 305

false attribution
  see also moral rights
  colourisation, 303
  Ireland, 308
  misrepresentation, 307
  mutilation, 307–8
  United Kingdom, 290, 303, 307–8
fees, 3, 6
film frames
  copyright infringement, 93
  merchandising, 92
  photographs, 23, 92–3, 96, 99
  reproduction rights, 216, 217
  subject-matter of protection, 92–4, 96,
    99
final cut, 323, 326, 333
Finland
  see also Scandinavia
  co-authorship, 156, 157, 318
  collective works, 51
  copyright protection, 51
  copyright transfer, 192
  exemptions, 272
  integrity, 322
  moral rights, 318
  performers, 339
  presumption of assignment, 166, 186
  private copying, 280, 282
  producer authorship, 155
  transmissibility, 177
fixation
  audiovisual works, 44, 60, 74, 120, 123,
    344–7
  author's rights tradition, 78–9
  broadcasting, 30, 40, 88, 108, 111, 344
  cinematographic films, 99
  cinematographic works, 35, 49, 123
  derivative works, 99
  dramatic works, 12, 13, 25, 26
  ephemeral, 88, 111, 258, 260
  photographs, 26
  rental rights, 54, 64, 65, 99, 241, 341

television, 40
videograms, 101
foreign authors
  applicable law, 369–71
  author defined, 369–71
  collecting societies, 283
  economic rights, 296, 370, 371
  France, 370, 371, 372–3, 381–2
  moral rights, 296, 317, 321, 370
  private copying, 282–3
  United Kingdom, 370, 378–9
foreign film works
  see also national treatment
  applicable law, 369–73
  author's rights tradition, 380–4
  Berne Convention, 365–9, 371–4,
    380–2, 384–5
  European Union (EU), 365–6, 380–5
  Germany, 382–4
  Italy, 384
  most-favoured-nation, 108, 376–7
  ownership, 369–70, 371–3
  performers, 380
  publication defined, 373–4
  related rights, 374–6
  rule of shorter term, 384–5
  TRIPs Agreement, 366–8, 374–7, 385
  United Kingdom, 377–80
formalities
  Berne Convention, 20–1, 40
  copyright transfer, 180–1
  deposit, 16, 17
fortuitous films, 96, 97
France
  1791/1793 laws, 15, 16, 39, 211
  1957 law, 42–3, 176
  1985 law, 44, 85, 176
  1986 Law, 117
  abuse of right, 269, 326
  adaptations, 223–6
  audiovisual communication enterprise,
    117, 118
  auteur theory, 156
  authorship, 153–4, 370
  Berne Convention, 16, 18, 40
  Cinémathèque Française, 335
  cinematographic works, 15, 17, 40, 75
  Civil Code, 83, 84, 180, 289
  co-authorship, 41, 42–3, 134, 135,
    158–60, 318
  Code of Cinematography, 181
  collecting societies, 44, 149, 180, 184,
    197, 203–4, 246, 281
  communication to the public, 188, 238
  copyright infringement, 223–6

copyright transfer, 178, 180–2, 187–93
deposit, 16, 17
director authorship, 41, 43, 155–6, 158
distribution rights, 211, 353
divulgation, 332–3
droit de destination, 211, 246, 247
duty to produce/distribute, 191–2
early protection, 14–16, 211
economic parasitism, 84
economic rights, 211, 353, 370
employment, 172, 357
equitable remuneration, 42, 127, 134,
  195, 200–4
evolution of protection, 39–42
exclusive rights, 353
exemptions, 256, 271–2, 273–4, 275,
  276–7, 278, 279, 280, 373
foreign authors, 370, 371, 372–3, 381–2
future works, 189
integrity, 44, 322–30, 335, 360
Intellectual Property Code, 44, 75,
  100–1, 118, 124, 153, 154, 158–9,
  172, 176, 178, 179, 180, 183,
  187–9, 191, 193, 201–2, 223, 238,
  245, 271, 273, 275, 276, 278, 281,
  282, 322–3, 332, 335, 350, 353,
  357–8, 363, 373
Labour Code, 357
loi de police, 370
moral rights, 318, 320, 322–3, 324–5,
  328–9, 335–6, 360, 362, 363–4,
  370
National Centre of Cinematography,
  182, 201
paternity, 44, 331, 360
performers, 339, 340, 350–1, 353,
  357–8, 360, 362, 363–4
performing rights, 211
photographs, 15, 16
pre-emption rights, 179
presumption of assignment, 44, 134,
  166, 183–4
private copying, 280, 281, 282
producer authorship, 16, 40–1, 153–4
production contracts, 176, 179, 181,
  201, 203–4, 335
programmes, 117
public lending rights, 247
publishing contracts, 176, 178, 179,
  180, 336, 373
re-assignment, 178
reproduction rights, 211, 216, 217,
  223, 245–6
subject-matter of protection, 15, 75,
  77, 105, 109, 117

France (*cont.*)
  telediffusion, 238
  term of protection, 16, 40, 101, 124,
    125, 126, 127, 128, 180
  theatrical commercial exploitation,
    203–204
  trademarks, 105
  transmissibility, 177
  uncontemplated uses, 190
  unfair competition, 83–4
  winding up, 179
free movement of goods, 53, 78, 193,
  263–4
free speech, 266–8
future works assignment, 48, 134, 189–90,
  285

General Agreement on Tariffs and Trade
  (GATT), 2, 284
Germany
  Bildfolgen, 76, 77
  co-authorship, 48, 49, 135, 156, 157,
    318
  commercial designations, 106
  communication to the public, 238
  copyright protection, 17–18, 47–9
  copyright transfer, 48, 177, 181, 189–90
  distribution rights, 245
  economic rights, 211, 353–4, 358–9
  employment, 172, 358–9
  equitable remuneration, 127, 195, 205,
    282, 354
  exclusive rights, 210
  exemptions, 272, 274, 275, 276, 278–9
  Filmwerke, 76
  foreign film works, 382–4
  future works, 48, 189–90
  integrity, 49, 295, 320, 321–2, 323–4,
    325, 360, 362, 363
  licensing, 48, 354
  monistic theory, 177
  moral rights, 49, 318, 320, 333, 335,
    336, 360, 362, 363
  neighbouring rights, 360
  performers, 339, 351, 353–4, 358–9,
    360, 363, 363
  photographs, 17–18, 47, 48
  presumption of assignment, 166, 171,
    185, 359
  private copying, 280, 282, 283
  public lending rights, 247
  reproduction rights, 216, 217
  right to use, 177
  subject-matter of protection, 76–7, 78,
    85, 101, 102, 106, 109, 117, 118

  term of protection, 18, 48, 49, 59, 120,
    126, 127, 129
  uncontemplated uses, 190
  unfair competition, 84
Greece
  co-authorship, 318
  copyright protection, 52
  copyright transfer, 181
  director authorship, 160
  distribution rights, 245
  equitable remuneration, 195, 205
  exclusive rights, 210
  exemptions, 272
  future works, 189
  integrity, 322, 360
  moral rights, 332, 336, 360
  neighbouring rights, 348
  performers, 340, 348, 360
  presumption of assignment, 166, 171,
    186
  private copying, 280, 282
  re-assignment, 178
  reproduction rights, 217
  subject-matter of protection, 76, 102,
    109, 117, 118
  term of protection, 180
  transmissibility, 177

harmonisation
  authorship, 135–6
  broadcasting, 107
  copyright transfer, 174, 175
  distribution rights, 241–3
  EU measures, 4–5, 53–8, 78, 85, 175,
    214, 34–1
  exemptions, 258–9
  internal market, 4–5
  national implementation, 56–7
  performers, 340–1
  reproduction rights, 214
  technological measures, 249
  term of protection, 121–2
  WIPO, 2, 56, 214
high-density recording media, 6
human rights
  European Convention, 267
  free speech, 267–8
  moral rights, 287
  Universal Declaration, 287

Iceland, 280
independent contractors, 164, 165, 170,
  172
India, 31, 32, 132
Information Society Directive

broadcasting, 110, 111, 112, 118
communication to the public, 231–2
distribution rights, 242–3
exclusive rights, 88, 209
exemptions, 256, 259–63
Green Paper (1995), 6, 58, 232
harmonisation, 55–6, 100, 242–3, 249
performers, 343
presumption of assignment, 169
private copying, 197, 281
reproduction rights, 197, 214–15, 260
rights management information, 249
scope, 56
technological measures, 249–51
videograms, 102
information technology convergence, 1–2
initial ownership
    see also ownership
    artistic works, 170
    Austria, 162
    authorship, 142–3, 170
    Berne Convention, 168, 182
    cessio legis, 162
    collective works, 171
    dramatic works, 170
    introduction, 161
    Italy, 162
    legal persons, 80
    literary works, 170
    musical works, 170
    producers, 133, 141, 161, 166–8
    production companies, 145
    scripts, 165
    underlying work, 166–8
integrity
    see also moral rights
    artistic/creative requirements, 300–1,
        306
    author's rights tradition, 321–30
    Belgium, 321, 322, 323, 360
    broadcaster's logo, 304, 328
    case law, 325
    censorship, 299, 300
    characterisation, 301–2
    co-authorship, 47, 291
    colourisation, 303, 325
    computer programs, 299
    definitions, 297, 321–2
    derogatory association, 327–8
    derogatory treatment, 297, 298, 300,
        302, 303, 304, 305, 306, 315, 337,
        361
    destruction, 303
    direction/artistic control, 325–6
    directors, 294

documentaries, 325–6
editing/modification, 326–7
exceptions/qualifications, 299, 300
excerpts, 329
final cut, 323, 326
Finland, 322
France, 44, 322–30, 335, 360
Germany, 49, 295, 320, 321–2,
    323–4, 325, 360, 362, 363
Greece, 322, 360
inappropriate context, 304
infringement, 298
Ireland, 306–7
Italy, 47, 324
meaning, 285
modes of exploitation, 323
modification of duration, 305
mutilation/distortion, 297, 304–5, 329
Netherlands, 321, 322, 324
objectionable treatments, 297–8
panning/scanning, 305–6
parody, 306, 328
performers, 44, 47, 287, 360, 362,
    363
Portugal, 321, 322, 360
producers, 49, 295, 320
product placements, 306
soundtracks, 302
Spain, 322, 323, 360
statutory adaptations, 322–4
Sweden, 321, 360
theatrical films, 305, 327
underlying work, 298
United Kingdom, 290, 291, 294,
    297–307, 315
WIPO, 287
interactivity
    broadcasting, 111, 117, 118
    digital networks, 228
    on-demand services, 250
    pre-programmed animation, 92
    two-way services, 115
    videogames, 80, 116
intermediaries
    agents, 183
    European Union (EU), 253–5, 260
    liabilities, 252–5
    meaning, 252
international tensions, 3–4
Internet, 115, 116, 117, 227, 232
investment
    producers, 101
    value, 1
Ireland
    adaptations, 211, 218, 219, 220

Ireland (*cont.*)
  audiovisual works, 37
  authorship, 141, 165
  cinematographic films, 37–8, 99–100,
    141
  communication to the public, 237–8
  distribution rights, 245
  equitable remuneration, 199, 200, 357
  European Union (EU), 5, 56
  exclusive rights, 209, 211
  exemptions, 256, 269, 271, 273, 275,
    278, 280, 361
  false attribution, 308
  integrity, 306–7
  licensing, 180
  moral rights, 291, 292, 293, 296, 348,
    360, 361–2
  paternity, 311
  performers, 348, 350, 352–3, 357,
    360, 361–2
  photographs, 99–100
  presumption of assignment, 176, 182,
    183
  private copying, 280
  production contracts, 357
  property rights, 348, 352–3
  reproduction rights, 216, 352
  subject-matter of protection, 61, 65,
    74, 99–100, 116–17
  term of protection, 38, 59, 120
  transmissibility, 177
  UK influence, 31, 132
Italy
  1941 law, 46–7, 155, 160
  cessio legis, 162, 166, 186
  co-authorship, 46–7, 135, 160, 318
  communication to the public, 239
  copyright protection, 17, 45–7, 100
  copyright transfer, 182, 186, 189
  distribution rights, 245
  economic rights, 155
  employment, 172
  equitable remuneration, 47, 195, 205,
    359
  exclusive rights, 210
  exemptions, 274, 276
  foreign film works, 384
  future works, 189
  initial ownership, 162
  integrity, 47, 324
  moral rights, 318, 320, 333–4, 335,
    336, 362
  paternity, 47, 331
  performers, 339, 351, 354, 359, 362
  photographs, 17, 47, 77, 217

  presumption of assignment, 359
  private copying, 280, 282
  public lending rights, 247
  reconsideration, 333–4
  reproduction rights, 217
  subject-matter of protection, 76, 77,
    102, 106, 109, 117, 118
  term of protection, 46, 47, 77, 124, 125,
    126, 128, 129
  transmissibility, 177

joint authorship
  see also co-authorship
  cessio legis, 182
  determination, 135, 157
  France, 154, 158–9
  Germany, 48
  moral rights, 294–5, 318, 332
  not separable, 143, 151
  originality, 143
  pre-1957 works, 28
  presumption, 158
  production companies, 145
  screenwriters, 146–7
  United Kingdom, 28, 143, 145–7,
    151–3, 294–5

Kinetograph, 9, 23
Kinetoscope, 9

legal persons, 27, 38, 41, 80, 154
licensing
  author's rights tradition, 7
  Berne Convention, 228, 229, 257
  broadcasting, 111, 195, 227, 228, 229,
    231, 234, 257, 341
  cable retransmission, 230, 231, 232
  collecting societies, 87, 184, 198, 199,
    206–7
  collective licensing, 206–7
  dramatic works, 37
  equitable licences, 180
  exploitation costs, 87
  Germany, 48, 354
  implied licences, 134, 187
  Ireland, 180
  musical works, 94, 257
  new technologies, 6–7
  phonograms, 258–9
  producers, 27, 165, 170, 180
  property rights, 348, 355–7
  rental rights, 88, 243, 341, 342
  revived copyright, 126
  Rome Convention (1961), 342
  satellite broadcasting, 229

sound recordings, 234
termination, 193
uncontemplated uses, 190
United Kingdom, 7, 180, 187, 190, 348,
    354, 355–7
literary works
adaptations, 13, 16, 17, 20
Berne Convention, 228, 240
cinematographic films, 22
cinematographic works, 19, 40
copyright infringement, 224–5
distribution rights, 240
dramatic works distinguished, 68
initial ownership, 170
limitations, 88, 111
moral rights, 295
multimedia, 90
paternity, 308
pre-existing works, 167
rental rights, 170, 199
scripts, 102
term of protection, 121
titles, 105, 107
Lumiére, Louis and Auguste, 9, 10
Luxembourg
authorship, 52, 153, 160–1, 318
cessio legis, 166, 187
co-authorship, 52, 318
copyright protection, 52
exemptions, 272
moral rights, 161, 318, 320
presumption of assignment, 166, 171,
    187
private copying, 280
producer authorship, 160–1
subject-matter of protection, 76, 101
transmissibility, 177

merchandising, 92, 184, 204
microwave transmissions, 113, 114, 116
misappropriation, 81, 83–4, 104
mise-en-scène, 130, 156
modes of exploitation
assignment, 29, 188
contracts, 188
digital technology, 209
integrity, 323
receipts, 193
remuneration, 44, 134, 205
unforeseen, 29, 42, 43, 190–1
moral rights
adaptations, 319
advertising cuts, 4, 289, 304–5, 315,
    327
archival copies, 335

artistic works, 295
audiovisual works, 43, 291–2, 293–4
Austria, 318, 320, 338–9
author's rights tradition, 21, 38, 284–6,
    316–37
basic problems, 291–2
Belgium, 318, 320, 335, 336, 360, 362
Berne Convention, 286–8, 289, 292,
    297, 321
broadcasting, 296
cable television, 296
causes of action, 316, 337
cinematographic films, 41–2, 284–337
co-authorship, 47, 296, 317–18
colourisation, 4, 289, 303, 315, 318, 325
computer imagery, 6
conflict of interest, 292, 319–20, 363–4
consents, 311–12, 335–6, 362
contributory works, 49, 50, 291–2, 320
copyright doctrine, 288–91
defamation, 277, 290, 304
Denmark, 318
dialogue, 297–8, 303–4
directors, 36, 155, 292, 294–5, 308–9
disclaimer, 314, 317, 361, 364
dissemination, 285
divulgation, 285, 319, 323, 329, 332–4,
    337, 360
doctrine, 284–6
dramatic works, 37, 143, 295–6
economic rights, 285, 317
employment, 171, 300
entitlement, 293–6, 317–21
European Commission, 58, 287
European Union (EU), 287–8
expiry, 291
false attribution *see* false attribution
Finland, 318
foreign authors, 296, 317, 321, 370, 371
France, 318, 320, 322–3, 324–5, 328–9,
    335–6, 360, 362, 363–4, 370
GATT, 284
general limitations, 324–5
general rules, 317
Germany, 49, 318, 320, 333, 335, 336,
    360, 362, 363
Greece, 332, 336, 360
human rights, 287
identification *see* paternity
infringement, 298, 313–14, 337
injurious falsehood, 290
integrity *see* integrity
Ireland, 291, 292, 293, 296, 348, 360,
    361–2
Italy, 318, 320, 333–4, 335, 336, 362

moral rights (*cont.*)
  joint authorship, 294–5, 318, 332
  literary works, 295
  Luxembourg, 161, 318, 320
  musical works, 328–9, 336
  Netherlands, 318, 336, 363
  offences, 337
  parody, 277, 306, 328
  performers, 38, 39, 44, 50, 287, 344, 360–4
  Portugal, 318, 335, 336, 360
  pre-existing works, 295
  preservation, 337
  privacy, 290
  producers, 38, 49–50, 102, 293, 295, 320
  reconsideration, 285, 333–4, 337, 360, 362
  remedies, 313–14, 337
  revocation of grant, 285
  screenwriters, 297–8, 303–4, 306
  Spain, 318, 320, 335, 336, 360, 362
  statutory adaptations, 322–4
  structure, 292
  Sweden, 318, 321, 336, 360
  term of protection, 291, 313, 336–7, 360, 362–3
  torts, 289, 290, 320
  transitional provisions, 303, 314–16
  transmissibility, 286, 291, 336, 362
  underlying work, 294, 295–6, 319
  United Kingdom, 288, 289–91, 292–316
  United States, 288, 295
  vesting, 51
  videograms, 102
  waiver, 194–5, 291, 295, 310–13, 335–6
  WIPO, 286, 287, 344, 345, 346
most-favoured-nation, 108, 376–7
motion pictures, invention, 9
moving images
  animation, 75, 76, 92
  audiovisual works, 76
  cinematographic films, 89–92
  computer programs, 90–1
  multimedia, 92
  videogames, 90
multimedia
  databases, 119
  digitisation, 7, 90, 91
  dramatic works, 79
  exploitation costs, 87
  literary works, 90
  moving images, 92
  scenarios, 79
  scripts, 79

subject-matter of protection, 79–80, 90, 92
  technology convergence, 2
multiplex cinemas, 1
Multipoint Microwave Distribution System (MMDS), 113, 116
musical works
  advertising, 328–9, 331, 335–6
  assignment, 44
  authorship, 41, 43, 46, 55, 121, 122, 135, 148–9, 158, 167, 170
  cinematographic films, 22
  co-authorship, 148–9, 158, 160
  composers, 121, 122, 135, 148–9, 160, 167, 168
  copyright infringement, 221, 222–3
  copyright protection, 36, 85
  director authorship, 148
  dramatico-musical works, 134, 148, 153, 223, 228
  initial ownership, 170
  licensing, 94, 257
  moral rights, 328–9, 336
  paternity, 308–9
  performance, 167
  performing rights, 13, 148–9
  pre-existing works, 167
  rental rights, 170, 200, 242
  rights societies, 148–9, 167
  soundtracks, 96, 242, 302, 328–9, 336
  specially commissioned, 121, 122, 148–9, 158, 167, 170
  synchronisation, 328–9
mutilation
  false attribution, 307–8, 324
  integrity, 297, 304–5, 324

National Film Archive, 303
national treatment
  Berne Convention, 367–9
  European Union (EU), 375, 376
  performance, 374–5
  Rome Convention (1961), 107, 374–6
  TRIPs Agreement, 280, 282, 367, 368, 374, 375
neighbouring rights
  assignment, 101
  audiovisual works, 39, 44, 59–60, 77
  author's rights tradition, 3, 37, 39, 59, 101, 117, 161
  Belgium, 348
  broadcasting, 3, 39, 117
  cable television, 3, 39
  common elements, 39
  distribution rights, 241

documentaries, 46, 49
economic rights *see* economic rights
Germany, 360
Greece, 348
moral rights *see* moral rights
Netherlands, 348
newsreels, 46
originality, 39, 77
performers, 39, 47, 50, 101, 340, 348,
 360
photographs, 46, 77, 87–8, 217
producers, 49, 59–60, 85, 120, 123
sound recordings, 39, 85, 120
term of protection, 59–60, 88, 120, 123
titles, 106
videograms, 88, 100, 101, 102
Netherlands
authorship, 50, 155, 156, 158, 318
Berne Convention, 50
co-authorship, 50, 156, 158, 318
communication to the public, 239
copyright protection, 50, 76, 84, 100
copyright transfer, 181
distribution rights, 245
economic rights, 171, 211
equitable remuneration, 195, 205
exemptions, 272, 274, 276, 279
future works, 189
integrity, 321, 322, 324
moral rights, 318, 336, 363
neighbouring rights, 348
paternity, 331
performers, 340, 348, 363
presumption of assignment, 166, 176,
 186
private copying, 280
producer authorship, 50, 155
public lending rights, 247
reproduction rights, 217
subject-matter of protection, 76, 100,
 101, 117, 118
term of protection, 50
transmissibility, 177
unfair competition, 84
work-made-for-hire doctrine, 170–1
new technologies
see also video-on-demand
broadcasting, 6, 30–1, 208
convergence, 1–2, 5–7
impact, 5–7
licensing, 6–7
on-line *see* on-line delivery
one-to-one transmission, 114, 115, 236
point-to-point services, 114, 115, 227,
 236

related rights, 55–6
subject-matter of protection, 112,
 114–16
two-way services, 115
New Zealand, 31, 132
news reporting, 257, 258, 275–6, 299
newsreels
Berne Convention, 40
copyright protection, 49
neighbouring rights, 46
originality, 78, 96
photographs, 46, 48, 77
producers, 100
subject-matter of protection, 71, 75, 77,
 96–7

on-demand transmissions
communication to the public, 228, 232,
 239
interactivity, 250
videos *see* video-on-demand
on-line delivery
compression techniques, 6
conditional access, 252
expansion, 2
subject-matter of protection, 116, 209
originality
see also creativity
audiovisual works, 35, 96–7
author's rights tradition, 78, 87
broadcasting, 35
cable television, 35
cinematographic works, 50, 369
co-authorship, 143
computer programs, 78
copyright infringement, 222
definition, 77, 78
derivative works, 97–9
documentaries, 78, 150
dramatic works, 22, 23, 24, 73, 97
entrepreneurial copyright, 32
neighbouring rights, 39, 77
newsreels, 78, 96
performers, 151–2
photographs, 20, 23, 77, 78
sound recordings, 85
subject-matter of protection, 59, 60, 61,
 63, 77–8
television, 71–2, 77, 152
titles, 105, 106
ownership
Berne Convention, 132, 162–4, 369–70,
 371–2
cable television, 55
contract of service, 27, 37, 142, 172

ownership (*cont.*)
  determination, 143–4
  director authorship, 38
  dramatic works, 27, 28, 29
  European Union (EU), 163–4
  extended rights, 128–9
  foreign film works, 369–70, 371–3
  initial *see* initial ownership
  joint ownership, 153
  joint tenants, 153
  photographs, 26–7
  producers, 27, 131
  production companies, 27, 28
  revived copyright, 125–6
  satellite broadcasting, 55
  tenants in common, 153

parody
  copyright infringement, 277
  exemptions, 276–8
  moral rights, 277, 306, 328
passing off
  characters, 103–4
  false attribution, 307, 308
  misrepresentation, 307
  moral rights, 290, 297, 307, 308
  television formats, 83
paternity
  see also moral rights
  anonymity clauses, 331, 336
  artistic works, 309
  assertion, 291, 293, 311
  author's rights tradition, 330–2
  Berne Convention, 330
  case law, 331–2
  co-authorship, 47
  computer programs, 310
  directors, 294, 308, 309
  employment, 310
  exceptions/qualifications, 310
  form of identification, 309–10
  France, 44, 331, 360
  Ireland, 311
  Italy, 47, 331
  limitations, 331
  literary works, 308
  meaning, 285
  musical works, 308–9
  Netherlands, 331
  performers, 44, 47, 287, 360
  Portugal, 331, 360
  possessory credit, 332
  pre-1957 films, 315
  pseudonym, 310
  United Kingdom, 290, 291, 294,
    308–11, 315

videos, 331
WIPO, 287
performance
  actors, 161, 167
  contracts, 176, 180
  definition, 233, 349–50
  downloading, 236
  dramatic works, 68
  improvisations, 350
  musical works, 167
  national treatment, 374–5
  restricted circles, 272–4
  television formats, 82
performers
  ancillary performers, 350, 351
  Austria, 338–9
  Belgium, 340, 348, 351, 354, 358, 360,
    362
  bootlegging, 338
  cable retransmission, 342–3
  co-authorship, 151–2
  commissioned works, 359
  communication to the public, 229, 349
  consents, 352, 353
  contributory works, 35, 151–2
  copyright, 35, 42
  Denmark, 339
  derivative works, 48, 170, 339
  distribution rights, 341
  economic rights, 44, 50, 169, 345, 346,
    348–60
  equitable remuneration, 342, 344, 347,
    349, 356–7
  European Union (EU), 338–43, 347–8
  exclusive rights, 341, 345, 351–4
  exemptions/limitations, 354–5
  Finland, 339
  foreign film works, 380
  France, 339, 340, 350–1, 353, 357–8,
    360, 362, 363–4
  Germany, 339, 351, 353–4, 358–9, 360,
    362, 363
  Greece, 340, 348, 360
  harmonisation, 340–1
  Information Society Directive, 343
  integrity, 44, 47, 287, 360, 362, 363
  Ireland, 348, 350, 352–3, 357, 360,
    361–2
  Italy, 339, 351, 354, 359, 363
  main performers, 151–2
  moral rights, 38, 39, 44, 50, 287, 344,
    360–4
  neighbouring rights, 39, 47, 50, 101,
    340, 348, 360
  Netherlands, 340, 348, 363
  non-property rights, 352, 355

originality, 151–2
paternity, 44, 47, 287, 360
Portugal, 335, 336, 360
pre-existing works, 151–2
presumption of assignment, 342, 347, 349
property *see* property rights
recording rights, 340, 359–60
remuneration, 47, 56, 167–8, 169
rental rights, 64, 169, 170, 341–2, 347–8
Rome Convention (1961), 339, 340, 342, 344–5, 375
satellite broadcasting, 342
Spain, 340, 351, 354, 359, 360, 362
sporting events, 349, 350
Sweden, 354, 360
Switzerland, 339
term of protection, 343, 355, 362–3
United Kingdom, 338, 340, 347–52, 355–7, 359–60, 380
peforming rights
actors, 151
broadcasting, 208, 226–7
copyright, 22
copyright transfer, 43
dramatic works, 13, 14
France, 211
musical works, 13, 148–9
phonograms, 227, 344
photographs, 12
principal rights, 210, 211
rental rights, 87
performing rights societies, 206
personal representatives, revived copyright, 125–6
personality rights, 286
phonograms
communication to the public, 229, 230, 232, 349
definition, 374, 376
licensing, 258–9
performers, 227, 344
public lending rights, 242
remuneration, 242, 281, 282, 344
rental rights, 241, 242
reproduction rights, 213–14, 246
TRIPs Agreement, 345
WIPO, 345–6, 375–6
photo-plays, 10, 12
photographs
artistic works, 17
audiovisual works, 34
Austria, 18, 49, 50
authorship, 26–7
Belgium, 17

Berne Convention, 19, 20, 40, 50, 228
copyright infringement, 31, 216
copyright protection, 12, 15–18, 20, 23, 24, 34
definition, 271
deposit, 16, 17
documentaries, 46, 48, 49
exclusive rights, 77
film frames, 23, 92–3, 96, 99
fixation, 26
France, 15, 16
Germany, 17–18, 47, 48
imitations, 31
Ireland, 99–100
Italy, 17, 47, 77, 217
neighbouring rights, 46, 77, 217
newsreels, 46, 48, 77
non-dramatic films, 24, 40
originality, 20, 23, 77, 78
ownership, 26–7
registration, 12, 18
right of exhibition, 12
Scandinavia, 18
Spain, 17
Switzerland, 18
term of protection, 16, 17, 18, 24, 78, 95
United Kingdom, 12, 23
videotechnology, 30
piracy, 57, 58
play-right, dramatic works, 13, 14
plots, copyright infringement, 31, 221, 222
point-to-point services, 114, 115, 227
Portugal
co-authorship, 160, 318
copyright protection, 45
copyright transfer, 189, 192
distribution rights, 245
economic rights, 211
employment, 172
equitable remuneration, 205
exemptions, 272
future works, 189
integrity, 321, 322, 360
moral rights, 318, 335, 336, 360
paternity, 331, 360
performers, 335, 336, 360
presumption of assignment, 166, 186
private copying, 280
production contracts, 176
Rome Convention (1961), 345
subject-matter of protection, 76, 101, 102, 109, 117
term of protection, 180
transmissibility, 177

pre-existing works
  see also adaptations
  authorship, 41, 43, 158, 184
  copyright infringement, 10
  derivative works, 86, 147, 218–19
  literary works, 167
  moral rights, 295
  musical works, 167
  performers, 151–2
  presumption of assignment, 186
  public performance, 41
  scripts, 147
  sound recordings, 167
presumption of assignment
  see also assignment
  adaptations, 218
  Belgium, 166, 176, 184
  Berne Convention, 162–4, 182
  contributory works, 182
  Denmark, 166, 186
  economic rights, 133, 166, 169, 349
  European Union (EU), 169, 175
  Finland, 166, 186
  France, 44, 134, 166, 183–4
  Germany, 166, 171, 185, 359
  graphic rights, 184
  Greece, 166, 171, 186
  initial ownership, 171
  Ireland, 176, 182, 183
  Italy, 359
  limited scope, 133, 161, 163, 168, 184
  Luxembourg, 166, 171, 187
  merchandising, 184
  Netherlands, 166, 176, 186
  ownership granted, 131, 161, 174
  performers, 342, 347, 349
  Portugal, 166, 186
  pre-existing works, 186
  production contracts, 176, 342
  remakes, 184
  remuneration, 44, 134, 168, 169
  rental rights, 169, 170, 175, 176, 183,
    347, 349
  sequels, 184
  Spain, 166, 171, 176, 185–6
  Sweden, 166, 176, 186
  theatrical rights, 184
  TRIPs Agreement, 182
  underlying work, 185
  United Kingdom, 176, 182–3, 347
private copying
  Austria, 280
  Belgium, 280, 281–2
  collecting societies, 198, 280, 281, 283
  computer programs, 270
  copyright infringement, 270

definition, 3
Denmark, 280, 282
digitisation, 270, 271
exemptions, 253, 268, 270–2
Finland, 280, 282
foreign authors, 282–3
France, 280, 281, 282
Germany, 280, 282, 283
Greece, 280, 282
Iceland, 280
Ireland, 280
Italy, 280, 282
Luxembourg, 280
Netherlands, 280
Portugal, 280
private use, 88, 111, 258, 260, 261
remuneration, 44, 49, 88, 198, 280–3
Spain, 280
Sweden, 280
Switzerland, 280
technological measures, 250
time-shifting, 208, 270–1
United Kingdom, 280
producer authorship
  author's rights tradition, 21, 133, 153–5,
    161
  co-authorship, 145–6, 164, 170
  creativity, 144–6
  deemed authorship, 27, 131
  Denmark, 155
  Finland, 155
  France, 16, 40–1, 153–4
  Ireland, 38
  Luxembourg, 160–1
  Netherlands, 50, 155
  subject-matter of protection, 4
  United Kingdom, 4, 27, 29, 32, 35, 132,
    140–1, 162, 164, 170, 183
  United States, 162
  work-made-for-hire doctrine, 4, 29, 132,
    170–1
producers
  assignment, 27, 37, 44, 47, 131, 133,
    134, 161, 162, 165, 170
  author's rights tradition, 21, 38, 39, 133,
    153–5
  authorship *see* producer authorship
  collective agreements, 167
  collective works, 41, 48, 154, 155
  copyright transfer, 191–3
  definition, 101, 139–41
  derivative works, 85, 170
  distribution rights, 87
  economic rights, 44, 49, 155
  employers *see* employment
  entrepreneurial copyright, 84

exclusive rights, 44, 49, 87, 88, 101, 102
executive producers, 144, 145
exploitation, 161
initial ownership, 133, 141, 166–8
integrity, 49, 295, 320
investment, 101
licensing, 27, 165, 170, 180
moral rights, 38, 49–50, 102, 293,
    295, 320
neighbouring rights, 49, 59–60, 85,
    87–8, 120, 123
newsreels, 100
non-release, 305
ownership, 27, 131, 161
producer's cut, 80
related rights, 123
rental rights, 54, 64, 65, 85, 87–8,
    165, 176, 200, 242
reproduction rights, 87
television, 145, 152
television formats, 145
term of protection, 123
videograms, 65, 101
production companies
    assignment, 27, 28
    authorship, 20, 154
    executive producers, 144, 145
    functions, 144
    initial ownership, 145
    ownership, 27, 28
    production process, 130–1
    production supervisors, 144
production contracts
    audiovisual production contracts, 176,
        179, 180, 201
    co-productions, 203–4
    formalities, 180
    France, 176, 179, 181, 201, 203–4,
        335
    Ireland, 357
    Portugal, 176
    presumption of assignment, 176, 342
    regulation, 44
    rental rights, 54, 342, 356, 357
    rescission, 317
    specific regimes, 174, 175–6
    termination, 179
    theatrical films, 201
    United Kingdom, 176, 180, 356
property rights
    assignment, 355–6
    Ireland, 348, 352–3
    licensing, 348, 355–7
    United Kingdom, 56, 347, 348, 352–3
protection
    copyright see copyright protection

duration see term of protection
history, 9–58
subject matter see subject-matter of
    protection
public domain, 126–8, 252
public exhibition, 16
public lending rights
    Austria, 247
    Belgium, 247
    derogations, 341
    European Union (EU), 87–8, 196, 241,
        341
    exhaustion, 244
    France, 247
    Germany, 247
    Italy, 247
    lending defined, 244
    Netherlands, 247
    phonograms, 242
    remuneration, 242, 247, 354
    Spain, 247
    United Kingdom, 243, 244, 347, 354
    videograms, 242
public performance
    see also communication to the public
    audiovisual works, 2
    broadcasting, 30
    case law, 233–4
    collecting societies, 198
    copyright infringement, 31
    pre-existing works, 41
    public exhibition, 16
publication
    country of first publication, 379
    definition, 373–4
publishers, authorship, 41
publishing contracts
    anonymity clauses, 336
    formalities, 180
    France, 176, 178, 179, 180–1, 336, 373
    regulation, 44, 47
    specific regimes, 174, 176
    term of protection, 180

recording rights, 340, 359–60
related rights
    Berne Convention, 228
    cable television, 112
    foreign film works, 374–6
    information society see Information
        Society Directive
    new technologies, 55–6
    producers, 123
    rental rights, 54, 64, 169
    term of protection, 64, 121, 123
    treatment, 21

remastered films, 80–1
remuneration
  assignment, 42, 134
  audiovisual works, 44
  authorship, 21, 39, 42, 43, 134
  computer programs, 242
  contracts, 199, 202
  equitable *see* equitable remuneration
  levies/taxes, 198, 280
  modes of exploitation, 44, 134, 205
  performers, 47, 56, 167–8, 169
  phonograms, 242, 281, 282, 344
  private copying, 44, 49, 88, 198, 280–3
  proportional, 39, 43, 44, 134, 201, 202, 203, 204
  public lending rights, 242, 247, 354
  revived copyright, 126, 127
  satellite broadcasting, 55, 57
  screenwriters, 167–8
  societies *see* collecting societies
  videograms, 281, 282
rental rights
  adaptations, 242
  artistic works, 170, 200
  assignment, 88, 165, 169, 200
  authorship, 5, 54, 64, 136–7, 165, 170, 241, 242
  broadcasting, 110, 111–12, 118
  cable television, 111–12
  cessio legis, 342
  collecting societies, 198, 200, 356
  communication to the public, 111, 229
  computer programs, 241, 242, 243
  definition, 241
  derivative works, 242
  director authorship, 5, 54, 165, 200, 242
  distribution rights, 241–2, 341
  dramatic works, 170, 199
  equitable remuneration, 5, 54, 57, 169, 173, 175, 183, 196, 199–200, 242, 342, 349, 356–7
  European Union (EU), 5, 21, 54, 56, 62, 64, 65, 85, 87–8, 99, 100, 110, 111–12, 118, 136–7, 169, 175, 196, 241–2, 342
  exemptions, 258–9
  fixation, 54, 64, 65, 99, 241, 341
  licensing, 88, 243, 341, 342
  limitations, 88, 111
  literary works, 170, 199
  musical works, 170, 200, 242
  performers, 64, 169, 170, 341–2, 347–8
  performing rights, 87
  phonograms, 241, 242
  presumption of assignment, 169, 170, 175, 176, 183, 347, 349

producers, 54, 64, 65, 85, 87–8, 165, 176, 200, 242
production contracts, 54, 342, 356, 357
related rights, 54, 64, 169
remote presentation, 235
rental defined, 241–2, 243, 244
satellite broadcasting, 230
sound recordings, 243
subject-matter of protection, 62, 64
successors in title, 200
videos, 198, 242
reproduction rights
  adaptations, 211
  author's rights tradition, 216–17, 245
  Belgium, 217
  Berne Convention, 212–13, 257
  broadcasting, 111
  collecting societies, 204
  copying, 215–16
  decor, 188
  definition, 214–15, 216
  electronic storage, 215–16
  European Union (EU), 169, 197, 214–15, 260
  fair compensation, 197
  film frames, 216, 217
  France, 211, 216, 217, 223, 245–6
  Germany, 216, 217
  Greece, 217
  harmonisation, 214
  Information Society Directive, 197, 214–15, 260
  Ireland, 216, 352
  Italy, 217
  magnetic tapes, 188
  Netherlands, 217
  phonograms, 213–14, 246
  principal rights, 210, 211
  producers, 87
  publishing right, 211
  Spain, 217
  Sweden, 217
  three steps test, 257
  transient/ephemeral reproduction, 216, 217
  United Kingdom, 215–16
  videos, 198, 204
  WIPO, 213–14
rescission of contract, 179, 193, 201, 317
restraint of trade, 313
reversionary rights
  audiovisual works, 28
  copyright transfer, 179, 191, 194
  moral rights, 288
right of exhibition, photographs, 12

rights management information
    communication to the public, 248–9
    definition, 248, 251
    European Union (EU), 248, 249, 251
    WIPO, 248–9
Rome Convention (1961)
    broadcasting, 107–8, 111, 385
    licensing, 342
    national treatment, 107, 374–6
    performers, 339, 340, 342, 344–5, 375
    Portugal, 345
    reproduction rights, 213
Rome Convention (1980), contracts,
        193–5
royalty rights, 195, 201, 202, 285, 334–5,
        349, 354, 372
Russia, 367

satellite broadcasting
    applicable law, 227, 229–30
    authorship, 5
    Brussels Convention (1974), 109
    collecting societies, 230, 231
    communication to the public, 229–30,
        237
    deregulation, 1
    European Union (EU), 5, 55, 110, 111,
        112, 113, 118, 175, 227, 229–30,
        234
    exclusive rights, 5, 118
    hotel rooms, 231
    licensing, 229
    ownership, 55
    performers, 342
    remuneration, 55, 57
    rental rights, 230
    up-leg/down-leg, 227, 229
Scandinavia
    copyright protection, 18, 51–2
    Denmark see Denmark
    Finland see Finland
    photographs, 18
    subject-matter of protection, 76
    Sweden see Sweden
scenarios
    authorship, 28, 41, 42, 46, 160
    dramatic works, 34
    multimedia, 79
screenplays, 55, 121, 122, 170
screenwriters
    authorship, 142, 167
    co-authorship, 146–7
    dialogue see dialogue
    equitable remuneration, 199
    moral rights, 297–8, 303–4, 306
    remuneration, 167–8

scripts see scripts
    translations, 297–8, 303–4
scripts
    see also dialogue
    authorship, 28, 135, 146–7, 152, 158,
        168
    copyright protection, 12–13, 25, 36, 218
    derivative works, 86, 147
    dramatic works, 25, 36, 69, 71, 102,
        165, 167
    initial ownership, 165
    literary works, 102
    multimedia, 79
    pre-existing works, 147
    television, 152
    theatrical films, 36
    videogames, 79
security cameras, 78, 96, 97
sketches, dramatic works, 34
Societé Civile des Auteurs Multimedia
        (SCAM), 184, 203, 204
Societé des Auteurs Belges-Belgische
        Auteurs Maatschappij (SABAM),
        207
Societé des Auteurs et Compositeurs
        Dramatiques (SACD), 149, 184,
        197, 203, 204
Societé des Auteurs et Compositeurs
        Editeurs de Musique (SACEM),
        184, 197, 203, 246
software see computer programs
sound films, introduction, 29–30, 155, 190
sound recordings
    copyright protection, 36, 85
    definition, 95
    digital enhancement, 98
    double protection, 86
    licensing, 234
    neighbouring rights, 39, 85, 120
    originality, 85
    pre-existing works, 167
    rental rights, 243
    soundtracks, 30, 34, 100, 122
    term of protection, 120, 122
soundtracks
    cinematographic films, 34, 95
    derivative works, 94
    integrity, 302
    musical works, 96, 242, 302, 328–9, 336
    sound recordings, 30, 34, 100, 122
    subject-matter of protection, 94–6, 100
    term of protection, 95, 122
Spain
    co-authorship, 160, 318
    communication to the public, 238
    copyright protection, 17, 45

Spain (*cont.*)
  copyright transfer, 181, 182, 189, 190, 192
  distribution rights, 245
  economic rights, 211
  employment, 359
  equitable remuneration, 195, 204, 359
  exemptions, 272, 274, 276, 278, 280
  future works, 189
  integrity, 322, 323, 360
  moral rights, 318, 320, 335, 336, 360, 362
  performers, 340, 351, 354, 359, 360, 362
  photographs, 17
  presumption of assignment, 166, 171, 176, 185–6
  private copying, 280
  public lending rights, 247
  reproduction rights, 217
  subject-matter of protection, 76, 101, 105, 109, 117, 118
  term of protection, 17, 45, 59, 120, 179–80
  transmissibility, 177
  uncontemplated uses, 190–1
  unfair competition, 84
sporting events, 73–4, 349, 350
Stationers' Hall, 12
subject-matter of protection
  audiovisual works, 66–7
  Austria, 76, 102, 109
  author's rights tradition, 60, 75–9
  Belgium, 76, 100, 101, 109, 118
  Berne Convention, 61, 63
  borderline works, 79–84
  broadcasting, 107–18
  Canada, 72, 73–4
  characters, 103–4
  cinematographic films, 88–99
  colourisation, 80–1, 98
  contributory works, 102–7
  creativity, 60
  Denmark, 102, 109, 118
  determination, 60–1
  documentaries, 72, 75, 77
  dramatic works, 22–3, 24–6, 65, 67–74
  economic rights, 4, 210
  entrepreneurial copyright, 66
  European Union (EU), 62, 63–5
  film frames, 92–4, 96, 99
  France, 15, 75, 77, 105, 109, 117
  Germany, 76–7, 78, 85, 101, 102, 106, 109, 117, 118

Greece, 76, 102, 109, 117, 118
  international/regional protection, 61–2
  Ireland, 61, 65, 74, 99–100, 116–17
  Italy, 76, 77, 102, 106, 109, 117, 118
  Luxembourg, 76, 101
  multimedia, 79–80, 90, 92
  Netherlands, 76, 100, 101, 117, 118
  new technologies, 112, 114–16
  newsreels, 71, 75, 77, 96–7
  originality, 59, 60, 61, 63, 77–8
  Portugal, 76, 101, 102, 109, 117
  protected works, 60
  recordings, 35, 218
  rental rights, 62, 64
  Scandinavia, 76
  soundtracks, 94–6, 100
  Spain, 76, 101, 105, 109, 117, 118
  Sweden, 101, 107, 109, 118
  Switzerland, 109
  titles, 105–7, 222
  TRIPs Agreement, 61
  United Kingdom, 3–4, 22–6, 32–5, 59–61, 65–74, 85, 88–91, 109, 112–16, 218
  United States, 3, 60, 107, 108
  Universal Copyright Convention, 61
  video-on-demand, 115–16, 209, 271
subsistence of copyright
  duration *see* term of protection
  introduction, 59–60
  subject matter *see* subject-matter of protection
subtitles, 298, 303–4
sui generis works, 33, 130
Sweden
  see also Scandinavia
  co-authorship, 156, 157, 318
  copyright protection, 51–2
  copyright transfer, 192
  distribution rights, 245
  equitable remuneration, 205
  exemptions, 274, 276
  future works, 189
  integrity, 321, 360
  moral rights, 318, 321, 336, 336, 360
  performers, 354, 360
  presumption of assignment, 166, 176, 186
  private copying, 280
  re-assignment, 178
  reproduction rights, 217
  subject-matter of protection, 101, 107, 109, 118
  transmissibility, 177
  unfair competition, 84

Switzerland
  copyright transfer, 177–8
  economic rights, 211
  exemptions, 278
  performers, 339
  photographs, 18
  private copying, 280
  subject-matter of protection, 109
  term of protection, 18, 52

teaching/research, 88, 111, 262–3
technicians, 152, 156
technological measures
  computer programs, 249
  definition, 250
  European Union (EU), 248, 249–51
  harmonisation, 249
  private copying, 250
  WIPO, 248, 249
telecommunications *see* digital networks
television
  see also broadcasting
  advertising, 304–5
  cable *see* cable television
  camera operators, 150
  co-authorship, 145, 150, 152
  collecting societies, 198
  dramatic works, 73
  fixation, 40
  game shows, 81, 83
  individual producers, 145, 152
  listing guides, 265–6
  originality, 71–2, 77, 152
  panning/scanning, 305–6
  pay-per-view, 114, 115, 237, 240, 252,
    271
  proportional remuneration, 204
  scripts, 152
  sporting events, 73–4
  television pictures, 30
  television producers, 145, 152
television formats
  author's rights tradition, 82–3
  contracts, 81
  dramatic works, 81
  misappropriation, 81, 83–4
  passing off, 83
  performance, 82
  producers, 145
  unfair competition, 81, 83–4
term of protection
  artistic works, 121
  assignment, 179–80
  audiovisual works, 37, 55, 64, 120–9
  Austria, 50

authorship, 29, 64, 121, 142
Belgium, 124, 125, 126, 127, 128
Berne Convention, 20, 120, 121
broadcasting, 108, 110, 112
cinematographic films, 34, 95
cinematographic works, 40
contributory works, 95, 121, 123
definition, 4
Denmark, 120
dramatic works, 14, 24, 29, 123
European Union (EU), 5, 17, 21, 55,
    56, 57, 59, 64, 78, 88, 99, 101, 112,
    120–6, 136, 137, 343
extended duration, 120–2
extended rights, 124–5, 128–9
foreign film works, 384–5
France, 16, 40, 101, 124, 125, 126, 127,
    128, 180
Germany, 18, 48, 49, 59, 120, 126, 127,
    129
Greece, 180
harmonisation, 121–2
Ireland, 38, 59, 120
Italy, 46, 47, 77, 124, 125, 126, 128, 129
literary works, 121
moral rights, 291, 313, 336–7, 360,
    362–3
neighbouring rights, 59–60, 88, 120, 123
Netherlands, 50
performers, 343, 355, 362–3
photographs, 16, 17, 18, 24, 78, 95
Portugal, 180
pre-1995 exploitation, 125, 126
producers, 123
publishing contracts, 180
related rights, 64, 121, 123
revival, 5, 14, 17, 125–8
rule of shorter term, 384–5
sound recordings, 120, 122
soundtracks, 95, 122
Spain, 17, 45, 59, 120, 179–80
Switzerland, 18, 52
United Kingdom, 14, 24, 29, 34, 37, 56,
    59, 95, 120, 122–4, 126–7, 128
United States, 122
videograms, 101
war extensions, 124–5
theatrical exhibition, 197–8
theatrical films
  co-authorship, 149, 150, 152
  contracts, 181–2
  direct-to-video release, 305
  directors of photography, 150, 152
  editors, 149, 152
  feature films, 150

theatrical films (*cont.*)
  integrity, 305, 327
  modification of duration, 305
  production contracts, 201
  scripts, 36
titles
  artistic works, 107
  author's rights tradition, 105
  literary works, 105, 107
  neighbouring rights, 106
  originality, 105, 106
  subject-matter of protection, 105–7, 222
  unfair competition, 106–7
torts, 289, 290, 320
trademarks, 105, 264, 277, 295
transmissibility
  copyright transfer, 176–8
  moral rights, 286, 291, 336, 362
  non-property rights, 352, 355
  property rights, 355–6
TRIPs Agreement
  assignment, 163
  broadcasting, 108
  distribution rights, 240–1
  exemptions, 257
  exhaustion, 240
  foreign film works, 366–8, 374–7, 385
  most-favoured-nation, 108, 376–7
  national treatment, 280, 282, 367, 368
  negotiations, 3, 4
  phonograms, 345
  presumption of assignment, 182
  subject-matter of protection, 61

underlying work
  adaptations, 218
  author's rights tradition, 170–2, 319
  contributory works, 102–3, 167, 168
  copyright, 34, 85, 164, 165, 212
  copyright infringement, 85, 212, 298
  initial ownership, 166–8
  integrity, 298
  moral rights, 294, 295–6, 319
  presumption of assignment, 185
undue influence, 313
unfair competition
  see also competition law
  characters, 104, 277
  television formats, 81, 83–4
  titles, 106–7
Union Syndicale de la Production
  Audiovisuelle (USPA), 204
United Kingdom
  adaptations, 211, 218, 219–23
  authorship, 137–53, 164–5, 370,
    378–9

Berne Convention, 22, 23, 33, 89, 218
Cable and Broadcasting Act (1984), 32,
  234
cable retransmission, 234
cinematographic works, 11, 22–3
co-authorship, 28, 29, 37, 38, 52, 135,
  137, 140–1, 143–53, 164, 170
communication to the public, 233–4
Copyright, Designs and Patent Act
  (1988), 35–7, 67, 68, 70, 89, 92,
  93, 132, 137, 138, 152, 164, 170,
  183, 233, 243, 270–1, 273, 278,
  290, 293–316, 340, 352, 378–9
Copyright Act (1842), 12, 13, 25, 68
Copyright Act (1911), 14, 22–32, 67,
  85, 92, 94, 96–7, 141–2, 152, 315
Copyright Act (1956), 32–5, 37, 67, 85,
  88–9, 95, 96, 132, 138, 141, 270,
  290, 303
copyright specifics, 137
copyright transfer, 176, 182–3, 187
digital networks, 234–7
director authorship, 27, 28, 38, 56,
  140–1, 164
distribution rights, 243–5
Dramatic Copyright Act (1833), 12, 25,
  68
early copyright protection, 11–14
equitable remuneration, 56, 183,
  199–200, 347, 356–7
European Union (EU), 5
exclusive rights, 209, 210–11, 351–3
exemptions, 256, 269–71, 273, 275,
  276, 278, 279
fair dealing, 269, 275
false attribution, 290, 303, 307–8
Fine Arts Copyright Act (1862), 11, 12,
  303
foreign authors, 370, 378–9
foreign film works, 377–80
Gorell Committee (1909), 22, 23
Gregory Committee (1952), 32–3, 139,
  153
integrity, 290, 291, 294, 297–307, 315
joint authorship, 28, 143, 145–7, 151–3,
  294–5
licensing, 7, 180, 187, 190, 348, 354,
  355–7
moral rights, 288, 289–91, 292–316
new technologies, 29–31
paternity, 290, 291, 294, 308–11, 315
performers, 338, 340, 347–52, 355–7,
  359–60, 380
photographs, 12, 23
presumption of assignment, 176, 182–3,
  347

private copying, 280
producer authorship, 4, 27, 29, 32, 35,
    132, 140–1, 162, 164, 170, 183
production contracts, 176, 180, 356
property rights, 56, 347, 348, 352–3
public lending rights, 243, 244, 347, 354
reproduction rights, 215–16
subject-matter of protection, 3–4, 22–6,
    32–5, 59–61, 65–74, 85, 88–91,
    109, 112–16, 218
term of protection, 14, 24, 29, 34, 37,
    56, 59, 95, 120, 122–4, 126–7, 128
transitional provisions, 379–80
transmissibility, 177
Whitford Committee (1977), 290, 340
United States
    audiovisual industry, 2
    Berne Convention, 367
    co-authorship, 134, 145
    Coyright Act (1909), 69
    fair use, 269
    moral rights, 288, 295
    subject-matter of protection, 3, 60, 107,
        108
    term of protection, 122
    work-made-for-hire doctrine, 4, 29, 132,
        170
Universal Copyright Convention, 61, 367
Uruguay Round, 3

video-on-demand
    communication to the public, 235, 236,
        237
    conditional access, 252
    downloading, 236
    expansion, 2
    point-to-point services, 114, 115, 236
    subject-matter of protection, 115–16,
        209, 271
videogames
    creativity, 79
    dramatic works, 79
    interactivity, 80, 116
    moving images, 90
    scripts, 79
    technology convergence, 2
videograms
    adaptations, 218
    assignment, 101
    author's rights tradition, 100–2, 218
    communication to the public, 101–2
    definition, 101
    exclusive rights, 101, 102
    fixation, 101

moral rights, 102
neighbouring rights, 88, 100, 102
performers rights, 101
producers, 65, 101
public lending rights, 242
remuneration, 281, 282
term of protection, 101
videos
    advertising, 295
    amateur videos, 78, 96
    lending, 198
    paternity, 331
    pop videos, 72
    private libraries, 270–1
    rental rights, 198, 242
    reproduction rights, 198, 204
    sales, 198, 204
    security cameras, 78, 96, 97
videotechnology
    sequences of images, 101
    series of photographs, 30
    technological development, 6

wireless telegraphy, 112–13, 114
work-made-for-hire doctrine, 4, 29, 132,
    170–1
World Intellectual Property Organisation
    (WIPO)
    audiovisual works
        performance protection, 2
        registration, 61
    communication to the public, 228,
        231, 237, 248–9
    digitisation, 6
    distribution rights, 240–1
    Draft Model Provisions, 61
    economic rights, 345, 346
    exemptions, 257–8
    harmonisation, 2, 56, 214
    intermediaries, 253
    moral rights, 286, 287, 344, 345, 346
    phonograms, 345–6, 375–6
    presumption of assignment, 182
    rental rights, 241
    reproduction rights, 213–14
    rights management information, 248–9
    subject-matter of protection, 61
    technological measures, 248, 249
    Treaties (1996), 2, 6, 56, 61, 163, 182,
        213, 214, 228, 231, 237, 240–1,
        253, 257–8, 286, 287, 344, 345–6,
        375–6
World Trade Organisation (WTO), 283,
    374, 377

Cambridge Studies in Intellectual Property Rights

Books in the series

Brad Sherman and Lionel Bently
The Making of Modern Intellectual Property Law
0 521 56363 1

Huw Beverley-Smith
The Commercial Appropriation of Personality
0 521 80014 5

Irini A. Stamatoudi
Copyright and Multimedia Works
0 521 80819 7

Pascal Kamina
Film Copyright in the European Union
0 521 77053 X